Class Declaration Summary

```java
import java.awt.*;

import javabook.*;

class SampleDialog extends JavaBookDialog implements ActionListener
{

    private    TextField    editBox;
    private    Button       button;
    private    Frame        myOwner;

    public SampleDialog(Frame owner)
    {
        //set the properties of the dialog
        super(owner);
        setTitle("Sample Dialog");
        setResizable(false);
        setLayout(null);
        myOwner = owner;

        //create and add GUI objects to the dialog
        editBox = new TextField("");
        button = new Button("CLEAR");
        add(editBox);
        add(okButton);

        //set the dialog as an action listener
        okButton.addActionListener( this );
    }

    protected void adjustSize()
    {
        addNotify();

        Insets inset = getInsets();

        setSize(inset.left + inset.right + 150,
                inset.top + inset.bottom + 100);

        editBox.setBounds (inset.left + 30, inset.top +  25, 150, 20);
        button.setBounds(inset.left + 75, inset.top + 155,  50, 25);
    }

    public void actionPerformed( ActionEvent event )
    {
        //tell the owner frame the value entered by the user
        myOwner.valueEntered(editBox.getText() );

        editBox.setText("");        //clears the entry
    }

}
```

An Introduction to Object-Oriented Programming with Java™

C. Thomas Wu

Naval Postgraduate School

Boston   Burr Ridge, IL   Dubuque, IA   Madison, WI   New York   San Francisco
St. Louis   Bangkok   Bogotá   Caracas   Lisbon   London   Madrid
Mexico City   Milan   New Delhi   Seoul   Singapore   Sydney   Taipei   Toronto

WCB/McGraw-Hill

A Division of The McGraw-Hill Companies

AN INTRODUCTION TO OBJECT-ORIENTED PROGRAMMING WITH JAVA

Copyright © 1999 by The McGraw-Hill Companies, Inc. All rights reserved. Printed in the United States of America. Except as permitted under the United States Copyright Act of 1976, no part of this publication may be reproduced or distributed in any form or by any means, or stored in a data base or retrieval system, without the prior written permission of the publisher.

This book is printed on acid-free paper.

2 3 4 5 6 7 8 9 0 DOC/DOC 9 3 2 1 0 9

ISBN 0-256-25462-1

Vice president/Editor-in-Chief: *Kevin T. Kane*
Publisher: *Thomas Casson*
Executive editor: *Elizabeth A. Jones*
Developmental editor: *Bradley K. Kosirog*
Marketing manager: *John T. Wannemacher*
Project manager: *Kari Geltemeyer*
Production supervisor: *Michael R. McCormick*
Designer: *Kiera Cunningham*
Supplement coordinator: *Rose M. Range*
Typeface: *10/12 Times Roman*
Printer: *R. R. Donnelley & Sons Company*

Library of Congress Cataloging-in-Publication Data

Wu, C. Thomas
     An introduction to object-oriented programming with Java / C.
  Thomas Wu. -- 1st ed.
        p.   cm.
     Includes index.
     ISBN 0-256-25462-1
     1. Object-oriented programming (Computer Science) 2. Java
  (Computer program language) I. Title.
  QA76.64.W78   1999
  005.13'3--dc21   98-45586

http://www.mhhe.com

To my family

Contents

Preface

This book is intended as an introductory text on object-oriented programming, suitable for use in a one-semester CS1 course. This book assumes no prior programming experience from the students. Those who already have experience in traditional process-oriented programming languages such as C, BASIC, and others can also use this book as an introduction to object-oriented programming, graphical user interface, and event-driven programming. The two main objectives of this book are to teach

· Object-oriented programming.
· The foundations of real-world programming.

Object orientation has become an important paradigm in all fields of computer science, and it is important to teach object-oriented programming from the first programming course. Teaching object-oriented programming is more than teaching the syntax and semantics of an object-oriented programming language. Mastering object-oriented programming means becoming conversant with the object-oriented concepts and being able to apply them effectively and systematically in developing programs. This book teaches object-oriented programming and students will learn how to develop true object-oriented programs.

The second objective of this book is to prepare students for real-world programming. Knowing object-oriented concepts is not enough. Students must be able to apply that knowledge to develop real-world programs. Sample programs in many introductory textbooks are too simplistic. Students rarely encounter sample programs in other textbooks that define more than three classes. But in real-world projects, programmers must use many classes from the libraries and define many classes of their own. In this book, we teach students how to use classes from the class libraries and how to define their own classes. For example, the sample program from Chapter 14 defines 10 classes and uses numerous classes from the existing class libraries.

Major Features

There are many pedagodical features that make this book unique among the introductory textbooks on object-oriented programming.We will describe the major features of this book.

Feature 1   ### Java

We chose Java for this book. Unlike C++, Java is a pure object-oriented language, and it is an ideal language to teach object-oriented programming because Java is logical and easy to program. Java's simplicity and clean design make it one of the most easy-to-program object-oriented languages. Java does not include any complex language features that could be a road block for beginners in learning object-oriented concepts. Although we use Java, we must emphasize that this book is not about Java programming. As this book is about object-oriented programming, we do not cover every aspect of Java. We do, however, cover enough language features of Java to make students competent Java programmers.

Feature 2   ### The javabook Package

We provide a class library (a *package* in Java terminology) called javabook that includes a number of classes we use throughout the book. We wrote a series of articles in 1993, in the *Journal of Object-Oriented Programming* (Vol. 6 nos. 1, 4, and 5), on how to teach object-oriented programming. The core pedagogic concept we described in the series is that one must become an object user before becoming an object designer. In other words, before being able to design one's own classes effectively, one must first learn how to use predefined classes. The use of javabook is based on this philosophy.

There are many advantages in using the javabook package:

1. *It shows students how real-world programs are developed.* We do not develop practical programs from scratch. Instead, we use predefined classes whenever possible. One of the major benefits of object-oriented programming is enhanced programmer productivity from reusing the existing classes. Students will get hands-on experience of code reuse by using classes from the javabook package.

2. *It minimizes the impact of programming language syntax and semantics.* The use of javabook classes lets students concentrate on learning concepts instead of the Java language features.We have seen many cases where novice programmers started out with a well-designed program, yet ended up with a very poorly constructed program. Often, because they do not understand the programming language fully, their design is not translated into a syntactically and semantically correct program. When they encounter an error while developing a program, instead of correcting the program code, they change their program design. Using predefined classes minimizes the impact of programming language because these predefined classes hide the complexity of the underlying programming language. Students will have a much easier time implementing their program design into a working program code using the javabook classes.

3. *It allows students to write useful programs from very early on, which helps to sustain the students' initial interest and motivation to learn.* Without using predefined classes, students must learn far too many details of programming language before they can start writing interesting and practical programs. But before they reach that point, many of them may lose interest in programming, drowning in the boring details of language syntax and semantics. Using the predefined classes from the standard Java libraries such as java.awt from the beginning, however, is not practical because these classes require programming sophistication that beginning students do not possess. Easy-to-use and intuitive predefined classes such as the javabook classes are more appropriate for beginning programmers.

4. *It provides the necessary foundation before students can start designing their own classes*. The ultimate goal of learning object-oriented programming is to master the skills necessary for designing effective classes. But before being able to design such classes, students must first learn how to use existing classes. Again, teaching how to use the standard Java classes to novice programmers from the beginning is not pedagogically sound because the majority of the classes from java.awt, java.io, and others are not easy

enough for beginning programmers to use. We designed the javabook classes with novice programmers in mind.

5. ***You can customize the* javabook *package to meet your needs*.** For example, there is a class called MainWindow in the package that serves as a top-level window of a program. You can easily extend this class to display your school's logo when this window appears on the screen. Or you can add a help menu that will list your T.A.'s office and phone numbers. You can extend other javabook classes as well. The javabook package can also be a training ground for your graduate or upper-division undergraduate students. By designing classes for the javabook package used by hundreds of beginning students, they will learn firsthand what it takes to make classes reliable and truly reusable.

One concern raised about the use of javabook is whether the students are able to write programs without using the javabook package. The answer is, of course, yes. The javabook package is not an end, but a means for students to learn the standard packages. It is a stepping stone, a kind of training wheel for the standard packages. In addition to the javabook classes, we cover many classes from the standard Java packages such as java.awt and java.io. By the time the students finish this book, they can program using the standard Java packages as comfortably as they program using the javabook package.

The source code of all javabook classes is provided, and students are encouraged to study them as they are practical examples of reusable classes. After finishing Chapter 12, students can understand almost all of the javabook classes. We say "almost" because some of the classes in javabook are implemented using the standard classes that are not explained in the book. If the students take time to look up these standard classes in a reference manual, then they should be able to understand the javabook classes 100 percent.

Feature 3   Full-Immersion Approach

We adopt a full-immersion approach in which students learn how to use objects from the first program. It is very important to ensure that the core concepts of object-oriented programming are emphasized from the beginning. Our first sample program from Chapter 1 is this:

```
/*
    Program FunTime

    The program will allow you to draw a picture by
    dragging a mouse (move the mouse while holding the left mouse
```

```
    button down; hold the button on Mac). To erase the picture and
    start over, click the right mouse button (command-click on Mac).
*/

import javabook.*;

class FunTime
{
    public static void main(String args[])
    {
        SketchPad       doodleBoard;
        doodleBoard = new SketchPad();
        doodleBoard.show();
    }
}
```

This program captures the most fundamental notion of object-oriented programming. That is, an object-oriented program uses objects. As obvious as it may sound, many introductory books do not really emphasize this fact. In the program, we use a SketchPad object called doodleBoard that allows the user to draw a picture. Almost all other introductory textbooks begin with a sample program such as

```
/*
    Hello World Program
*/

class HelloWorld
{
    public static void main(String args[])
    {
        System.out.println("Hello World");
    }
}
```

or

```
/*
    Hello World Applet
*/
import java.applet.*;
import java.awt.*;

public class HelloWorld extends Applet
{
    public void paint( Graphics g)
    {
        g.drawString("Hello World", 50, 50);
    }
}
```

Both programs have problems. They do not illustrate the key concept that object-oriented programs use objects. The first program does indeed use an object System.out, but the use of System.out does not illustrate the object declaration and creation. Beginners normally cannot differentiate classes and objects. So it is very important to emphasize the concept that you need to declare and create an object from a class before you can start using the object. Our first sample program does this.

Another problem with the System.out program is that no real window-based programs use it for output. Some textbooks not only use System.out in their first program, they rely on System.out almost exclusively for program output. This is not real-world programming. In this book, we use System.out only to output data for verification purposes while developing programs.

The second HelloWorld program is an applet, which, as its name suggests, is a mini-application with a very specific usage. Although applets are fun, teaching applets exclusively is a problem because students will learn only a very limited view of programming.We will discuss more on applications versus applets later in the preface.

Another major problem with these two programs is that they are not adaptable to real-world situations. In contrast, our first sample program can be a main program of a commercial application by replacing SketchPad with another class, say, WordProcessor. In fact, our second sample program from Chapter 2 is this (Note: This is the first program we actually explain line by line):

```
/*
    Program MyFirstApplication

    The first sample Java application.
*/

import javabook.*;

class MyFirstApplication
{
    public static void main(String args[])
    {
        MainWindow  mainWindow;
        mainWindow = new MainWindow();    //create and
        mainWindow.show();                //display a window
    }
}
```

The structure of this program is identical to the structure of the first sample program. Our second sample program reinforces the concept that we program by using objects, and by changing objects, we create a different program.

Feature 4   **Illustrations**

We believe a picture is worth a thousand words. Difficult concepts can be explained nicely with lucid illustrations. We use *object diagrams* to show the relationships among objects and classes. Diagrams are an important tool for designing and documenting programs, and no programmers will develop real-world software applications without using some form of diagramming tools. We use simple and informal diagrams, but the diagrams we use in this book are modeled after the industry standard object diagrams. After becoming comfortable with the object diagrams in this book, students are well prepared to study more formal object-oriented design methodology.

This book includes numerous illustrations that are used as a pedagogic tool to explain core concepts such as inheritance, difference between private and public methods, and so forth. Notations used in the object diagrams are used consistently in all types of illustrations. Figure 1 is one example from Chapter 2, and there are over 230 such illustrations and diagrams in this book. Other representative illustrations can be found in pages 90, 168, 250, 390, 398, 443, 651, and 711.

FIGURE 1   Correspondence between message sending as represented in the object diagram and in the actual Java statement.

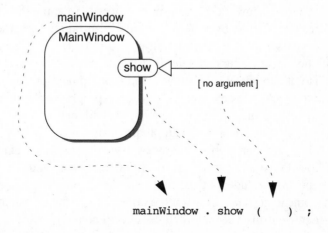

In addition to object diagrams, we use *method call sequence diagrams* that indicates the sequence of method calls such as the one shown in Figure 14.1 on page 697. The method call sequence diagrams are very useful in showing the flow of messages. We use method call sequence diagrams extensively in documenting an advanced sample program in Chapter 14.

Feature 5

Incremental Development

We teach object-oriented software engineering principles in this book. Instead of dedicating a separate chapter for the topic, we have interleaved program development principles and techniques with other topics. Every chapter from Chapter 2 to Chapter 13 includes at least one sample program to illustrate the topics covered in the chapter, and we develop the program using the same design methodology consistently. Chapter 14 is the case study chapter in which we develop a substantially large program for the CS 1 standard.

One major problem with many of the other introductory programming books on the market today is that they teach two-decade-old structured programing, which just does not work with object-oriented programs. This book really teaches a software design methodology that is conducive to object-oriented programming. All sample programs in this book are developed by using a technique we characterize as incremental development. The incremental development technique is based on the modern iterative approach (some call it a spiral approach), which is a preferred methodology of professional object-oriented programmers.

Beginning programmers tend to mix high-level design and low-level coding details, and their thought processes get all tangled up. Presenting the final program is not enough if we want to teach students how to develop programs. We must show the development process. An apprentice will not become a master builder just by looking at finished products, whether they are furniture or houses. Software construction is no different. It is often the case with other textbooks that a single chapter is dedicated to showing software development. This is not enough. We must show the development process more than just once. In this book, we develop every sample program incrementally to show students how to develop programs in a logical and methodical manner.

Source code of all sample programs at every step of development is available from our Web site. However, we do not encourage students to simply follow the development presented in the book and read the source code. We encourage students to actually build the sample programs following the development steps presented in the book. This is the surest and quickest way for students to truly master software development.

Feature 6

Design Guidelines, Helpful Reminders, and Quick Checks

Throughout the book, we include numerous design guidelines and helpful reminders. Almost every section of the chapters is concluded with a number of Quick Check questions to make sure that students have mastered the basic points of that section.

Design guidelines are indicated with a pencil icon like this:

Design a class that implements a single well-defined task. Do not overburden the class with multiple tasks.

Helpful reminders come in different styles. The first style is indicated with a thumbtack icon like this:

Watch out for the off-by-one error (OBOE).

The second style is Dr. Caffeine's monologue:

> **Dr. Caffeine**
>
> On occasions, programming can be very frustratiing because no amount of effort on your part would make the program run correctly. You are not alone. Professional programmers often have the same feeling, including this humble self. But, if you take time to think through the problem and don't lose your cool, you will find a solution. If you don't, well, it's just a program. Your good health is much more important than a running program and a good grade.

The third style is a dialogue between Dr. Caffeine and his honor students Ms. Latte or Mr. Espresso. Ms. Latte and Mr. Espresso appear in alternate chapters.

> **Dr. & Ms.**
>
> **Ms. Latte:**   I appear in the odd-numbered chapters and ask great questions.
>
> **Dr. Caffeine:**   That's right, and your questions are insightful and helpful to other students.

> **Dr. & Mr.**
>
> **Mr. Espresso:**   I appear in the even-numbered chapters and also ask questions.
>
> **Dr. Caffeine:**   Yes, and I like your questions, too.

Quick Check questions appear at the end of the sections with the following banner:

Quick Check

1. Who are the two honor students of Dr. Caffeine?
2. Name the purpose of the pencil and thumbtack icons.

Feature 7   **Graphical User Interface and Event-Driven Programming**

Since modern real-world programs are GUI-based and event-driven, we cannot skirt around them if we want to teach the foundation of real-world programming. Some may feel that GUI and event-driven programs are difficult topics for beginning students to master. Although they are not trivial, we believe they can be made approachable to beginning students by presenting the topics piecemeal. We cover in depth GUI and event-driven programming in Chapter 12. However, students will start writing GUI-based programs exclusively beginning in Chapter 2 using the javabook classes and will learn the rudiments of event handling in Chapter 5. By the time they reach Chapter 12, they are well prepared to absorb the topics. (For this reason, it is preferable to cover Chapter 5, but as we explain later, you may skip the chapter if you do not wish to cover applets.)

Feature 8   **Applications and Applets**

We teach both Java applications and applets, but we put emphasis on developing applications. Some introductory books rely heavily or exclusively on applets, but the use of applets is limited. We don't write applets exclusively in the real world, and an introductory programming book should not teach just applets. At the same time, we should not shy away from teaching applets. We should teach both. Although the use of applets is limited, writing applets is generally fun for students, and we can use applets as an effective pedagogic tool. In this book, we use applets to introduce the basics of event handling and GUI programming in Chapter 5.

Although we cover applets and recommend that instructors teach them, we organize the book so instructors can skip the coverage on applets without losing the continuity.

Supplement Materials

All supplement materials are available from our Web site at www.mhhe.com/ engcs. Materials available from our Web site include

1. **Source code for all sample programs and the** javabook **classes.** For all sample programs, source code at every development step is available. Both byte code and source code are available for the javabook classes. Documentation for the javabook package is also available.

2. **Additional topics and/or sample programs for selected chapters**. Many sample applets we did not include in the book are available from the Web site. Also, for some chapters, we have additional sample

programs. For example, the sample program in Chapter 6 involves the drawing of shapes. We have a simple sample program on the Web that illustrates the use of selection statements but that does not use the graphics. We will try our best to include additional sample programs for the majority of the chapters, so you will have an option of choosing a sample program that is appropriate to the group of students you teach. Additional sample programs will also give students more opportunity to study program development.

3. **Hand outs on how to use popular Java compilers**. We have step-by-step instructions on how to edit, compile, and run the programs using Symantec Cafe, Borland JBuilder, Microsoft J++, Supercede, and the plain JDK compiler.

4. **Solutions to the selected chapter exercises**. For small programming exercises, we provide a complete source code listing along with a brief description on the development steps. For large programming exercises, we only provide suggestions on the program design and development steps.

5. **More exercises for the chapters.** We have additional exercises on the Web to give you more flexibility in assigning homework. We will try to add new exercises periodically.

6. **Transparency masters.** This material is available to the instructors who adopt the textbook.

7. **Chapter notes and suggestions for teaching**. This material is available to the instructors who adopt the textbook.

We want our Web site to be a plaza for a world-wide community of instructors and students. We do not want our site to be a one-way provider of information. We call for your help to make this site everybody's site. If you have a nice sample program to share, may we make it available on our site or add a link to your site so other instructors and students can share it? The same goes for the reusable classes, programming exercises, and topics not covered in the book. For instance, if you have a great handout on layout managers or exception handling, allow us to make it available on our site or add a link to your site. Needless to say, we will properly credit you for your contribution. We welcome contributions from both instructors and students.

Book Organization

There are 16 chapters in this book, with more than enough topics for one semester. Basically the chapters should be covered in linear sequence. Chapter 0 can be skipped or assigned as outside reading if you want to jump right into programming. If you do not wish to cover applets, then you can skip Chapter 5 altogether. Section 3.8 on numerical representation and Section 7.10 on recursive methods are optional and can be skipped. Chapter 15 can be covered anytime after the array (Chapter 9) is covered. Chapter 15 covers basic searching and sorting algorithms and recursion. You can cover only searching and nonrecursive sorting algorithms or only recursion.

In the following, we will give a short description for each chapter:

- **Chapter 0** is an optional chapter. We provide background information on computers and programming languages. This chapter can be skipped or assigned as outside reading if you wish to start with object-oriented programming concepts.

- **Chapter 1** provides a conceptual foundation of object-oriented programming. We describe the key components of object-oriented programming and illustrate each concept with a diagrammatic notation. The first sample program we present in this chapter is a fun drawing program.

- **Chapter 2** covers the basics of Java programming and the processes of editing, compiling, and running a program. We introduce both applications and applets in this chapter. We also introduce two classes—MainWindow and MessageBox—from the javabook package. The last section of the chapter that covers an applet can be skipped if you do not cover applets.

- **Chapter 3** introduces variables, constants, and expressions for manipulating numerical data. We explain the standard Math class from java.lang and introduce and use two more classes—InputBox and OutputBox— from the javabook package. These classes handle the input and output of an application program. The optional section explains how the numerical values are represented in memory space.

- **Chapter 4** teaches how to define instantiable classes. The key topics covered in this chapter are constructors, visibility modifiers (public and private), local variables, parameter passing, and value-returning methods. By the end of Chapter 4, students will have a basic understanding of how to use classes from the packages and how to define their own (simple) classes.

- **Chapter 5** covers applets. We teach how to process input with applets. GUI objects Label, TextField, and Button from the java.awt package are introduced. This chapter provides a first glimpse of event handling that serves as a nice foundation for a fuller coverage of GUI objects and event-driven programming in Chapter 12. We recommend that instructors cover this chapter, but we understand some prefer not to cover applets. If that is the case, this chapter can be skipped without any loss of continuity.

- **Chapter 6** explains the selection statements if and switch. We cover boolean expressions and nested-if statements. To illustrate the use of selection statements, the ListBox class from the javabook package is introduced and used in the sample program.

- **Chapter 7** explains the repetition statements: while, do–while, and for. We introduce two more classes—ResponseBox and Format—from the javabook package and use them in the sample program. The optional last section of the chapter introduces recursion as another technique for repetition.

- **Chapter 8** covers nonnumerical data types: characters and strings. Both the String and StringBuffer classes are explained in the chapter. Using these objects, we explain the difference between primitive and reference data types. We also explain how the objects are passed as parameters to methods and how they are returned from the methods.

- **Chapter 9** teaches arrays. We cover arrays of primitive data types and of objects. Arrays are objects in Java, and we reiterate how objects are passed to methods using arrays as an example in this chapter. The self-referencing pointer this is introduced here. We describe how to process two-dimensional arrays and explain that a two-dimensional array is really an array of arrays in Java.

- **Chapter 10** explains the file I/O. Standard objects such as File and FileDialog objects from java.awt and java.io are explained. We cover all types of file I/O, from a low-level byte I/O to a high-level object I/O. This coverage of object I/O is unique among the introductory textbooks. As a part of file processing, we introduce exception handling in this chapter.

- **Chapter 11** explores reusable classes and describes package organization. In the chapter, we show how to classify objects into four categories as an aid to designing classes. As an illustration of how a class can be made reusable, we will convert the earlier sample classes into reusable classes.

- **Chapter 12** covers event-driven programming and GUI objects. The GUI objects we explain in this chapter are Button, Menu, Dialog, Frame, and Applet. GUI objects introduced in Chapter 5 are also used in this chapter. We will also teach the processing of mouse events.

- **Chapter 13** discusses inheritance and polymorphism and how to use them effectively in program design. The effect of inheritance an member accessibility and constructors is explained. We also explain the purpose of abstract classes and abstract methods.

- **Chapter 14** is a case study chapter. We will use the techniques learned in the book to develop a large program. The program uses objects from both the javabook and standard Java packages in addition to the 10 classes we design for the program. No other introductory textbooks include a sample program that is composed of as large a number of classes as this sample program.

- **Chapter 15** covers two traditional computer science topics. One is searching and sorting, and the other is recursion. You may skip the mathematical analysis of searching and sorting algorithms depending on the students' background. Because we want to show the examples where the use of recursion really shines, we did not include any recursive algorithm (other than those used for explanation purposes) that really should be written nonrecursively.

Acknowledgments

First, I would like to thank the following reviewers for their comments, suggestions, and encouragement.

Allen Brookes	Linfield College
Ann Ford	University of Michigan
Michael Hoffhines	Maui Community College
Lily Hou	Carnegie Mellon University
Chung Lee	California State Polytechnic University at Pomona

John Lowther	Michigan Technical University
John Phillips	Dodge City Community College
Bina Ramamurthy	SUNY at Buffalo
Nan C. Schaller	Rochester Institute of Technology
Zhong Shao	Yale University
Lou Steinberg	Rutgers University
Deborah Trytten	University of Oklahoma
Allen Tucker	Bowdoin College

After the first review, I was forced to make a major revision of the book based on the reviewers' suggestions. Although it took me longer to complete the book than I originally planned, I think the end result is a much better product. I thank Deborah Trytten especially for her insistence on "don't just give code, explain the design process." Her excellent suggestions were instrumental to improving the quality of the book. Thank you, Deborah.

Many students have gone through the earlier versions of the book and given me valuable feedback. They used my early drafts with no index and the java-book package with incomplete documentation. Despite these shortcomings, they responded enthusiastically to the notion of using the javabook classes. This gave me confidence that I am on the right track. I thank all of my former students for their patience and understanding.

I thank Chris Eagle for going over all sample code in the book, checking for consistency and correctness. He also helped me debug and improve the java-book package. I thank Jin Takamura for reading the chapters from the student's viewpoint. His comments gave me confidence that my full-immersion approach is working.

I thank my friends at McGraw-Hill. On the production side, I thank Beth Cigler, Kiera Cunningham, and Kari Geltemeyer. On the editorial side, I thank Emily Gray, Brad Kosirog, and Betsy Jones. I thank Emily for filling the position of Brad without a hitch when Brad moved on to take a new job. I thank Brad for his all-around help I received while working on the project. I thank Betsy for her unwavering confidence in me that the project will be a huge success. I thank all of you for helping me improve the book and waiting patiently until the completion.

Finally, I thank my family for their love and support.

Introduction to Computers and Programming Languages

OBJECTIVES

After you have read and studied this chapter, you should be able to

- State briefly a history of computers.
- Name and describe four major components of the computer.
- Convert binary numbers to decimal numbers and vice versa.
- State the difference between the low-level and high-level programming languages.

Introduction

Before we embark on our study of computer programming, we will present some background information on computers and programming languages in this optional chapter. We provide a brief history of computers from the early days to present and describe the components found in today's computers. We also present a brief history of programming languages from low-level machine languages to today's object-oriented languages.

0.1   A History of Computers

Mankind has evolved from a primitive to a highly advanced society by continually inventing tools. Stone tools, fire powder, wheels, and other inventions have changed the lives of humans dramatically. In recent history, the computer is arguably the most important invention. In today's highly advanced society, computers affect our lives 24 hours a day: your class schedules are formulated by computers, your student records are maintained by computers, your exams are graded by computers, your dorm security system is monitored by computers, and numerous other functions that affect you are controlled by computers.

Charles Babbage

Difference Engine

Although the first true computer was invented in the 1940s, the concept of a computer is actually more than 160 years old. Charles Babbage is credited with inventing a precursor to the modern computer. In 1823 he received a grant from the British government to build a mechanical device he called the *Difference Engine,* intended for computing and printing mathematical tables. The device was based on rotating wheels and was operated by a single crank. Unfortunately, the technology of the time was not advanced enough to build the device. He ran into difficulties and eventually abandoned the project.

Analytical Engine

But an even more grandiose scheme was already with him. In fact, one of the reasons he gave up on the Difference Engine may have been to work on his new concept for a better machine. He called his new device the *Analytical Engine*. This device was also never built. His second device was also ahead of its time; the technology did not exist to make the device a reality. Although never built, the Analytical Engine was a remarkable achievement because its design was essentially based on the same fundamental principles of the modern computer. One principle that stands out was its programmability. With the Difference Engine Babbage would have been able to compute only mathematical tables, but with the Analytical Engine he would have been able to compute any calculation by inputting instructions on punch cards. The method of inputting programs to computers on punch cards was actually adopted for real machines and was still in wide use as late as the 1970s.

The Analytical Engine was never built, but a demonstration program was written by Ada Lovelace, a daughter of the poet Lord Byron. The programming language Ada was named in honor of Lady Lovelace, the first computer programmer.

In the late 1930s John Atanasoff of Iowa State University, with his graduate student Clifford Berry, built the prototype of the first automatic electronic calculator. One innovation of their machine was the use of binary numbers. (We discuss binary numbers in the next section.) At around the same time, Howard Aiken of Harvard University was working on the *Automatic Sequence-Controlled Calculator,* known more commonly as MARK I, with support from IBM and the U.S. Navy. MARK I was very similar to the Analytical Engine in design and was described as "Babbage's dream come true."

MARK I was an electromechanical computer based on relays. Mechanical relays were not fast enough, and MARK I was quickly replaced by machines based on electronic vacuum tubes. The first completely electronic computer, ENIAC I (*Electronic Numerical Integrator and Calculator*), was built at the University of Pennsylvania under the supervision of John W. Mauchly and J. Presper Eckert. Their work was influenced by the work of John Atanasoff.

ENIAC I was programmed laboriously by plugging wires into a control panel that resembled an old telephone switchboard. Programming took an enormous amount of the engineers' time, and even making a simple change to a program was a time-consuming effort. While programming activities were going on, the expensive computer sat idle. To improve its productivity, John von Neumann of Princeton University proposed storing programs in the computer's memory. This *stored-program* scheme not only improved computation speed but also allowed far more flexible ways of writing programs. For example, because a program is stored in the memory, the computer can change the program instructions to alter the sequence of the execution, thereby making it possible to get different results from a single program.

We characterized these early computers with vacuum tubes as *first-generation computers. Second-generation computers,* with transistors replacing the vacuum tubes, started appearing in the late 1950s. Improvements in memory devices also increased processing speed further. In the early 1960s, transistors were replaced by integrated circuits and *third-generation computers* emerged. A single integrated circuit of this period incorporated hundreds of transistors and made the construction of minicomputers possible. Minicomputers are small enough to be placed on desktops in individual offices and labs. The early computers, on the other hand, were so huge, they easily occupied the whole basement of a large building.

Ada Lovelace

MARK I

ENIAC I

stored-program

generations of computers

Advancement of integrated circuits was phenomenal. Large-scale integrated circuits, commonly known as *computer chips* or *silicon chips*, packed the power equivalent to thousands of transistors and made the notion of a "computer on a single chip" a reality. With large-scale integrated circuits, *microcomputers* emerged in the mid 1970s. The machines we call *personal computers* today are descendants of the microcomputers of the 1970s. The computer chips used in today's personal computers pack the power equivalent to several millions of transistors. Personal computers are *fourth-generation computers*.

Early microcomputers were isolated, stand-alone machines. The word *personal* describes a machine as a personal device intended to be used by an individual. However it did not take long to realize there was a need to share computer resources. For example, early microcomputers required a dedicated printer. Wouldn't it make more sense to have many computers share a single printer? Wouldn't it also make sense to share data among computers, instead of duplicating the same data on individual machines? Wouldn't it be nice to send electronic messages between the computers? The notion of networked computers arose to meet these needs.

network

Computers of all kinds are connected into a *network*. A network that connects computers in a single building or in several nearby buildings is called a *local area network* (LAN). A network that connects geographically dispersed computers is called a *wide area network* (WAN). These individual networks can be connected further to form interconnected networks called *internets*. The most famous internet is simply called the *Internet*. The Internet makes the sharing of worldwide information possible and easy. The hottest tool for viewing information on the Internet is a *Web browser*. A Web browser allows you to view *multimedia information* consisting of text, audio, video, and other types of information. We will describe how Java is related to the Internet and Web browsers in the last section of the chapter.

Internet

Dr. Caffeine

If you want to learn more about the history of computing, there is a wealth of information available on the Web. You can start your exploration from http://www.yahoo.com/Computers_and_Internet/History. For a nice slide show on the evolution of computing machines, visit http://www.computer-museum.org. For more information on the pioneers of computers, visit http:www.comlab.ox.ac.uk/archive/other/museums/computing.html.

1. Who was the first computer programmer?
2. Who designed the Difference and Analytical Engines?
3. How many generations of computers are there?

0.2   Computer Architecture

A typical computer has four basic components: RAM, CPU, storage devices, and I/O (input/output) devices. Figure 0.1 illustrates these four components. Before we describe the components of a computer, we will first explain the binary numbering system used in a computer.

Binary Numbers

To understand the binary number system, let's first review the decimal number system in which we use 10 digits: 0, 1, 2, 3, 4, 5, 6, 7, 8, 9. To represent a number in the decimal system, we use a sequence of one or more of these digits. The value that each digit in the sequence represents depends on its position. For example, consider the numbers 234 and 324. The digit 2 in the first number represents 200, whereas the digit 2 in the second number represents 20. A position in a sequence has a value that is an integral power of 10. The following diagram illustrates how the values of positions are determined:

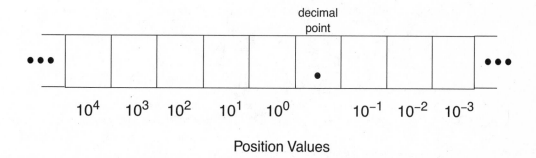

Position Values

FIGURE 0.1   A simplified view of an architecture for a typical computer.

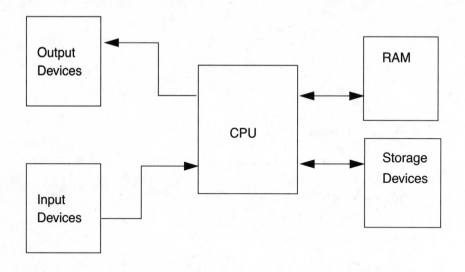

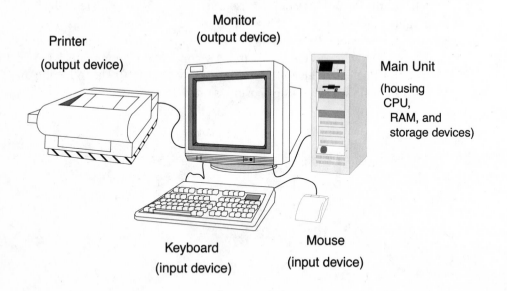

The value of a decimal number (represented as a sequence of digits) is the sum of the digits multiplied by their position values, as illustrated below:

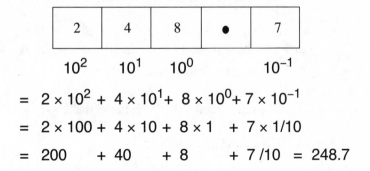

$$= 2 \times 10^2 + 4 \times 10^1 + 8 \times 10^0 + 7 \times 10^{-1}$$
$$= 2 \times 100 + 4 \times 10 + 8 \times 1 + 7 \times 1/10$$
$$= 200 \quad + 40 \quad + 8 \quad + 7/10 = 248.7$$

In the decimal number system, we have 10 symbols, and the position values are integral powers of 10. We say that 10 is the *base* or *radix* of the decimal number system. The binary number system works the same as the decimal number system but uses 2 as its base. The binary number system has two digits (0 and 1) called *bits*, and position values are integral powers of 2. The following diagram illustrates how the values of positions are determined in the binary system:

base-2 numbers

bits

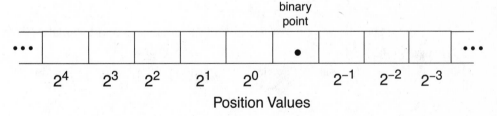

The value of a binary number (represented as a sequence of bits) is the sum of the bits multiplied by their position values, as illustrated below:

binary-to-decimal
conversion

$$= 1 \times 2^2 + 0 \times 2^1 + 1 \times 2^0 + 1 \times 2^{-1}$$
$$= 1 \times 4 \quad + 0 \times 2 \quad + 1 \times 1 + 1 \times 1/2$$
$$= 4 \quad + 0 \quad + 1 \quad + 1/2 \quad = 5.5$$

So the binary number 101.1 is numerically equivalent to the decimal number 5.5. This illustration shows how to convert a given binary number to the decimal equivalent. How about converting a given decimal number to its binary equivalent?

We will show you how to convert a decimal number (only the whole numbers) to the equivalent binary number. The basic idea goes something like this:

decimal-to-binary
conversion

1. Divide the number by 2.

2. The remainder is the bit value of the 2^0 position.

3. Divide the quotient by 2.

4. The remainder is the bit value of the 2^1 position.

5. Divide the quotient by 2.

6. The remainder is the bit value of the 2^2 position.

7. Repeat the procedure until you cannot divide any further; that is, the quotient becomes 0.

The following diagram illustrates the conversion of decimal number 25.

The binary system is more suitable for computers than the decimal system because it is far easier to design an electrical device that can distinguish two states (bits 0 and 1) than 10 states (digits 0 through 9). For example, you can represent 1 by turning the switch on and 0 by turning the switch off. In a real computer, 0 is represented by electrical voltage below a certain level and 1 by electrical voltage at or above this level.

RAM

byte

Random access memory (RAM) is a repository for both program instructions and data manipulated by the program during execution. RAM is divided into *cells* with each cell having a unique address. Typically, each cell consists of 4 *bytes*, and a single byte in turn consists of 8 *bits*. Each bit, which can be either on or off, represents a single binary digit. RAM is measured by the number of bytes it contains. For example, 16 megabytes (Mb) of RAM contains $16 \times 2^{20} =$ 16,777,216 bytes. We use the term *mega* (M), which is 10^6, to represent the value 2^{20}, because 1 kilo (K) $= 10^3 = 1000$ is a close approximation to $2^{10} = 1024$. And $10^6 = 10^3 \times 10^3 \approx 2^{10} \times 2^{10} = 2^{20}$. With 4 bytes to a cell, 16 Mb of RAM contains 4,194,304 cells. In 1998, a typical computer has anywhere from 32 Mb to 64 Mb of RAM. In contrast, the first Macintosh computer introduced in 1984 came with 128 kilobytes (Kb) of RAM ($128 \times 2^{10} = 131,072$ bytes).

CPU

clock speed

The *central processing unit* (CPU) is the brain of a computer. The CPU is the component that executes program instructions by fetching an instruction (stored in RAM), executing it, fetching the next instruction, executing it, and so on until it encounters an instruction to stop. The CPU contains a small number of *registers*, which are high-speed devices for storing data or instructions temporarily. The CPU also contains the *arithmetic-logic unit* (ALU), which performs arithmetic operations such as addition and subtraction and logical operations such as comparing two numbers.

CPUs are characterized by their clock speeds. For example, in the Intel Pentium 200, the Pentium-type CPU has a clock speed of 200 megahertz (MHz). A *hertz* is a unit of frequency equal to one cycle per second. A *cycle* is a period of time between two on states or off states. So 200 megahertz equals 200,000,000 cycles per second. The fastest CPU for commercially available personal computers was around 200 MHz in 1997. But by the beginning of 1998, many vendors started selling 300 MHz machines. And in a mere six months, by the middle of 1998, the top-of-the-line personal computers are 400 MHz machines. The increase of the CPU speed in the last 20 years is truly astonishing. The clock speed of the Intel 8080, the CPU introduced in 1974 that started the PC revolution, was a mere 2 MHz. In contrast, the clock speed of the Intel Pentium

Pro-200 introduced in 1995 was 200 MHz. Table 0.1 lists some of the Intel processors.

TABLE 0.1   A table of Intel processors. For some CPUs, more than one type with different clock speeds are possible. In such case, only the fastest clock speed is shown. For more information on Intel CPUs, visit http://www.intel.com/intel/museum.

	CPU	Date Introduced	Clock Speed (MHz)
1970s	4004	11/15/71	0.108
	8008	04/01/72	0.108
	8080	04/01/74	2
	8088	06/01/79	9
1980s	80286	02/01/82	12.5
	80386SX	06/16/88	33
	80486DX	04/10/89	50
1990s	Pentium	03/22/93	166
	Pentium Pro	11/01/95	200
	Pentium II	05/07/97	300
	Pentium Xeon	06/29/98	400

I/O Devices

Input/output (I/O) *devices* allow communication between the user and the CPU. Input devices such as keyboards and mice are used to enter data, programs, and commands in the CPU. Output devices such as monitors and printers are used to display or print information. Other I/O devices include barcode readers, magnetic strip readers, digital video cameras, and musical instrument digital interface (MIDI) devices.

Storage Devices

Storage devices such as disk and tape drives are used to store data and programs. Secondary storage devices are called *nonvolatile memory,* while RAM is called *volatile memory. Volatile* means the data stored in a device will be lost when the power to the device is turned off. Being nonvolatile and much cheaper than RAM, secondary storage is an ideal medium for permanent storage of large volumes of data. A secondary storage device cannot replace RAM, though, because secondary storage is far slower in data access (getting data out and writing data in) compared to RAM.

The most common storage device today for personal computers is a disk drive. There are two kinds of disks: hard and floppy (also known as diskettes). A typical personal computer has one hard disk drive and one floppy disk drive. Hard disks provide much faster performance and larger capacity, but are normally not removable; that is, a single hard disk is permanently attached to a disk drive. Floppy disks, on the other hand, are removable, but their performance is far slower and their capacity far smaller than hard disks. Hard disks can store a huge amount of data, typically ranging from 2.1 Gb (gigabyte; giga $= 10^9$) to 6.4 Gb for a standard desktop PC in 1998. Most of the floppy disks in use today can store approximately 1.44 Mb. Some new breeds of disk drives use removable disks, typically ranging in capacity from 100 Mb to 1 Gb, with performance that rivals nonremovable hard disks.

Compact discs (CDs) are also very popular today for storing massive amounts of data, approximately 660 Mb. Many software packages you buy today—computer games, word processors, and others—come with a single CD. Before the CD became a popular storage device for computers, some software came with more than 20 floppy diskettes. Because of its massive storage capacity, the current trend is for computer vendors to get rid of printed manuals altogether by putting the manuals on the CD.

Quick Check

1. Name four major components of a computer.
2. What is the difference between volatile and nonvolatile memory?
3. How many generations of computers are there?

0.3 Programming Languages

Programming languages are broadly classified into three levels: machine languages, assembly languages, and high-level languages. Machine language is the only programming language the CPU understands. Each type of CPU has its own machine language. For example, the Intel Pentium and Motorola PowerPC understand different machine languages. *Machine-language* instructions are binary coded and very low level—one machine instruction may transfer the contents of one memory location into a CPU register or add numbers in two

machine
language

registers. Thus we must provide many machine-language instructions to accomplish a simple task such as finding the average of 20 numbers. A program written in machine language might look like this:

machine code
```
10110011 00011001
01111010 11010001 10010100
10011111 00011001
01011100 11010001 10010000
10111011 11010001 10010110
```

assembly
language

One level above machine language is *assembly language*, which allows "higher level" symbolic programming. Instead of writing programs as a sequence of bits, assembly language allows programmers to write programs using symbolic operation codes. For example, instead of 10110011, we use MV to move the contents of a memory cell into a register. We can also use symbolic, or mnemonic, names for registers and memory cells. A program written in assembly language might look like this:

assembly code
```
MV      0,   SUM
MV      NUM, AC
ADD     SUM, AC
STO     SUM, TOT
```

assembler

Since programs written in assembly language are not recognized by the CPU, we use an *assembler* to translate programs written in assembly language into machine-language equivalents. Compared to writing programs in machine language, writing programs in assembly language is much faster, but not fast enough for writing complex programs.

high-level
languages

High-level languages were developed to enable programmers to write programs faster than when using assembly languages. For example, FORTRAN (FORmula TRANslator), a programming language intended for mathematical computation, allows programmers to express numerical equations directly as

high-level code
```
X = (Y + Z) / 2
```

COBOL (COmmon Business Oriented Language) is a programming language intended for business data processing applications. FORTRAN and COBOL were developed in the late 1950s and early 1960s and are still in use. BASIC (Beginners All-purpose Symbolic Instructional Code) was developed specifically as an easy language for students to learn and use. BASIC was the first high-level language available for microcomputers. Another famous high-level language is Pascal, which was designed as an academic language. Since programs written in a high-level language are not recognized by the CPU, we must use a *compiler* to translate them into machine-language equivalents.

compiler

The programming language C was developed in the early 1970s at AT&T Bell Labs. The C++ programming language was developed as a successor of C in the early 1980s to add support for object-oriented programming. Object-oriented programming is a style of programming gaining wider acceptance today. Although the concept of object-oriented programming is old (the first object-oriented programming language, Simula, was developed in the late 1960s), its significance wasn't realized until the early 1980s. Smalltalk, developed at Xerox PARC, is another well-known object-oriented programming language. The programming language we use in this book is Java, the newest object-oriented programming language, developed at Sun Microsystems. We describe Java in the next section.

0.4 Java

Java is a new object-oriented language that is receiving wide attention from both industry and academia. Java was developed by James Gosling and his team at the Sun Microsystems in California. The language was based on C and C++ and was originally intended for writing programs that control consumer appliances such as toasters, microwave ovens, and others. The language was first called Oak, named after the oak tree outside of Gosling's office, but the name was already taken, so the team renamed it Java.

applet

Java is often described as a *Web programming language* because of its use in writing programs called *applets* that run within a Web browser. That is, you need a Web browser to execute Java applets. Java is receiving phenomenal attention today because of applets, a feature unique to Java. Applets allow more dynamic and flexible dissemination of information on the Internet, and this feature alone makes Java an attractive language to learn. However, we are not limited to writing applets in Java. We can write Java applications also. A Java *application* is a complete stand-alone program that does not require a Web browser. A Java application is analogous to a program we write in other programming languages. Although we cover both applets and applications in this book, we place more emphasis on Java applications because our objective is to teach the fundamentals of object-oriented programming that are applicable to all object-oriented programming languages.

application

We chose Java for this textbook not only for its relevance to the Internet but also for its clean design. The language designers of Java took a minimalist approach; they included only features that are indispensable and eliminated features that they considered excessive or redundant. This minimalist approach makes Java a much easier language to learn than other object-oriented programming languages. Java is an ideal vehicle for teaching the fundamentals of object-oriented programming.

0.5   Exercises

1. Visit your school's computer lab or a computer store and identify the different components of the computers you see. Do you notice any unique input or output devices?

2. Visit your school's computer lab and find out the CPU speed, RAM size, and hard disk capacity of its computers.

3. Convert the following binary numbers to decimal numbers:
    a. 1010
    b. 110011
    c. 110.01
    d. 111111

4. Convert the following decimal numbers to binary numbers:
    a. 35
    b. 125
    c. 567
    d. 98

5. What is the maximum decimal number you can represent in 4 bits? 16 bits? N bits?

6. If a computer has 48 Mb of RAM, how may bytes are there?

Introduction to Object-Oriented Programming and Software Development

---

OBJECTIVES

After you have read and studied this chapter, you should be able to

- Name the basic components of object-oriented programming.
- Differentiate classes and objects.
- Differentiate class and instance methods.
- Differentiate class and instance data values.
- Draw object diagrams using icons for classes, objects, and other components of object-oriented programming.
- Describe the significance of inheritance in object-oriented programs.
- Name and explain the stages of the software life cycle.

Introduction

Before we begin to write actual programs, we need to introduce a few basic concepts of *object-oriented programming*, the style of programming you will learn in this book. The purpose of this chapter is to give you a feel for object-oriented programming and to introduce a conceptual foundation of object-oriented programming. You may want to refer back to this chapter as you progress through the book.

> **Dr. Caffeine**
>
> Those of you who have some experience in programming, whether object-oriented or non-object-oriented, will probably find many similarities between Java and the programming languages you already know. This similarity may accelerate your learning process, but in many cases what seems to be similar at first may turn out to be quite different. So please do not jump to any conclusions about similarity prematurely.

Another purpose of this chapter is to introduce the software development process. To be able to write programs, knowing the components of object-oriented programs is not enough. You must learn the process of developing programs. We will provide a brief description of the software development process in this chapter.

1.1   Classes and Objects

object

The two most important concepts in object-oriented programing are the class and the object. In the broadest term, an *object* is a thing, both tangible and intangible, which we can imagine. A program written in object-oriented style will consist of interacting objects. For a program to maintain bank accounts for a bank, we may have many Account, Customer, Transaction, and ATM objects. An object is comprised of data and operations that manipulate these data. For example, an Account object may consist of data such as account number, owner, date opened, initial balance, and current balance and operations such as deposit, transfer, and withdrawal. We will use the diagram shown in Figure 1.1 throughout the book to represent an object.

Almost all nontrivial programs will have many objects of the same type. For example, in the bank program we expect to see many Account, Customer, and other objects. Figure 1.2 shows two Customer objects with the names Jack and Jill and one Account object with the name SV129.

FIGURE 1.1 A graphical representation of an object.

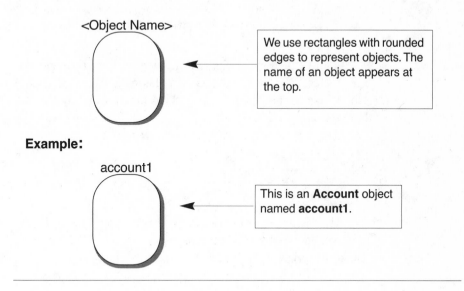

Example:

FIGURE 1.2 Two **Customer** objects with the names **Jack** and **Jill** and one **Account** object with the name **SV129**.

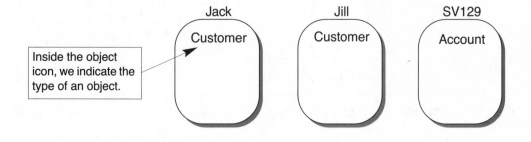

class

instance

Inside a program we write instructions to create objects. For the computer to be able to create an object, we must provide a definition, called a *class*. A class is a kind of mold or template that the computer uses to create objects. An object is called an *instance* of a class. An object is an instance of exactly one class. An instance of a class *belongs to* the class. The two Customer objects Jack and Jill are instances of the Customer class. Once a class is defined, we can create as many objects of the class as a program requires.

> A class must be defined before you can create an
> instance (object) of the class.

Figure 1.3 shows a diagram that we will use throughout the book to represent a class. Figure 1.4 shows two classes and five objects. Notice that we include the class names of the objects to identify clearly the classes to which they belong.

Quick Check

1. Draw an object diagram for a Person class and two Person objects Ms. Latte and Mr. Espresso.
2. What must be defined before you can create an object?

FIGURE 1.3   A graphical representation of a class.

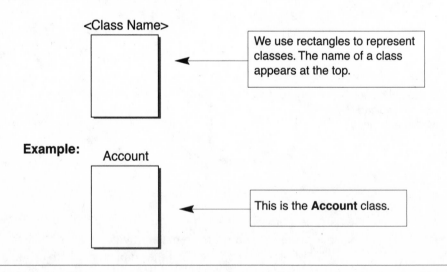

FIGURE 1.4   Two classes, **Account** and **Customer**, with two **Account** objects and three **Customer** objects.

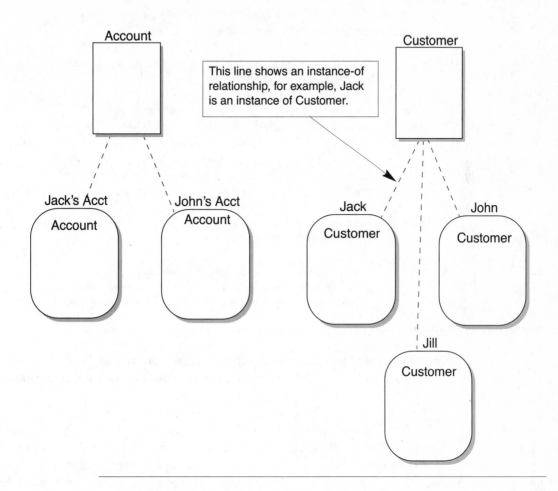

1.2   Messages and Methods

In writing object-oriented programs we first define classes, and while the program is running, we create objects from these classes to accomplish tasks. A task can range from adding two numbers to computing an interest payment for your college loan to calculating the reentry angle of a space shuttle. To instruct a class or an object to perform a task, we send a *message* to it. For example, we

message

Dr. & Ms.

Ms. Latte:	Dr. Caffeine, the difference between the class and the object is unclear to me. Could you explain the difference?
Dr. Caffeine:	Sure thing. Have you ever seen a print made from a woodcut by Hiroshige, the 19th-century Japanese artist?
Ms. Latte:	Yes, as a matter of fact, I think I have. The one I saw is a print from the series titled *Fifty-Three Stations of Tokaido*.
Dr. Caffeine:	Very good. For those of you who haven't, you can visit the Tokaido Hiroshige Art Museum home page at **http://www.across.or.jp/ podhome/e_hiros1.html**. Anyway, an object is like a print, and a class is like a woodcut. Once you have a woodcut, you can make as many prints as you wish. Just like a woodcut and its many prints, there's one class, but many objects from that class.
Ms. Latte:	Just as a print cannot exist without a woodcut, an object cannot exist without a class from which it is created?
Dr. Caffeine:	Yes, precisely. And just as people appreciate prints more than they appreciate the woodcut itself, objects are more predominant in programs, but classes are as indispensable as woodcuts are.

send a message **new** to the **Account** class to create an instance (an **Account** object), and then we may send a message **deposit** to this **Account** object to deposit $100.

For a class or an object to process the message it must be programmed accordingly. You cannot just send a message to any class or object. You can send a message only to the classes and objects that understand the message you send to them. For a class or an object to process the message it receives, it must possess a matching *method*, which is a sequence of instructions a class or an object follows to perform a task. A method defined for a class is called a *class method,* and a method defined for an object is an *instance method*.

method

class and instance method

Let's look at an example of an instance method first. Suppose a method called **deposit** is defined for an **Account** object and instructs the object to deposit a given amount to the account. With this method defined, we can send the message **deposit** to an **Account** object, along with the amount to be deposited. A value we pass to an object is called an *argument* of a message. Notice that the name

argument

Dr. Caffeine

Have you ever left a message on the wrong person's answering machine by mistake? When the machine said, "Hi, I cannot come to the phone right now, but if you leave your message...," You answered, "Hi. It's me. Please come to SP105 right now." Of course, nothing happens, because the receiver of your message does not recognize it.

Similarly, you cannot send a message to a class or an object unless it is programmed to handle the message; that is, it must contain a matching method. Sending a message to a class or an object is the way to execute the matching method, and if there's no matching method, nothing happens (actually, an error will occur).

of the message we send to an object or a class must be the same as the method's name. In Figure 1.5 we represent the sending of a message.

The diagram shown in Figure 1.5 illustrates one-way communication; that is, an object carries out the requested operation (it deposits the given amount) but does not respond to the message sender. In many situations we need two-way communication, in which an object responds by returning a value to the message sender. For example, suppose we want to know the monthly fee charged for an account. We can define a method getMonthlyFee that returns the monthly fee. The diagram in Figure 1.6 shows a method that returns a value to the message sender. Instead of returning a numerical value, a method can report back the status of the requested operation. For example, we can define a method deduct to return the status fail if subtracting the passed amount would result in a negative balance.

Now let's look at two examples of class methods. The first is the indispensable class method new, which creates an instance of the class. Figure 1.7 illustrates how the message new is sent to the Account class and the newly created instance is returned to the message sender. The second example is a class method getAverageBalance that returns the average balance of all Account objects. A method such as getAverageBalance that deals with collective information about the class instances is usually defined as a class method. So you define an instance method for a task that pertains to an individual instance and a class method for a task that pertains to multiple instances.

Notice how we use different icons for representing class methods (rectangles) and instance methods (rectangles with rounded corners). Since the class definition is the place we define the methods its instances possess, we need to attach both class and instance methods to the class icon. Dotted lines represent instance methods; the dotted lines indicate that you cannot send instance mes-

FIGURE 1.5   Sending the message **deposit** to an **Account** object.

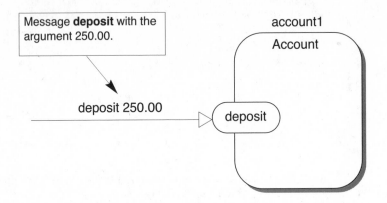

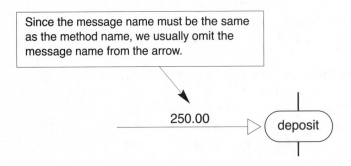

sages to the class itself. Figure 1.8 summarizes the drawings used for representing a class, an instance, and their methods.

Quick Check

1. Draw an object diagram of an Account object with instance methods deposit and withdraw.
2. Which message do you send to a class to create an instance of the class?

FIGURE 1.6   The result **monthly fee** is returned to the sender of the message.

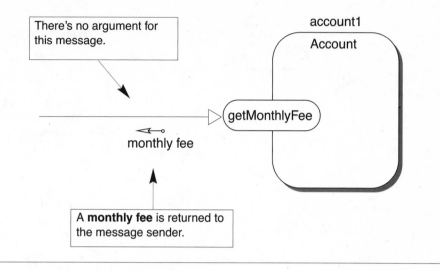

FIGURE 1.7   The newly created **Account** object is returned to the sender of a message.

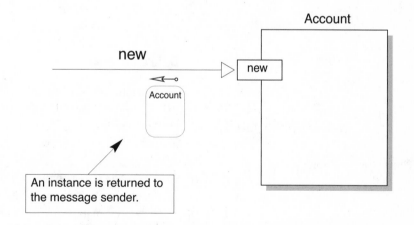

FIGURE 1.8   Graphical representation for classes, instances, and their methods.

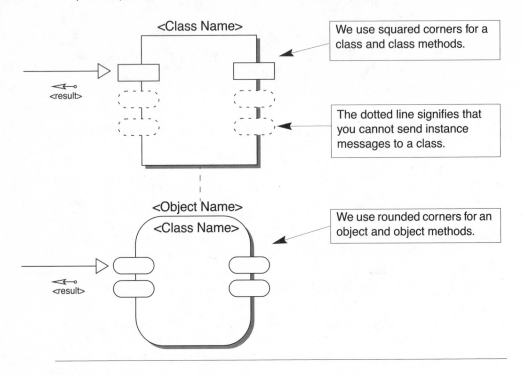

1.3   Class and Instance Data Values

The method deposit of an Account object instructs the object to deposit a given amount to the current balance. But where does the object keep the current balance? Remember that an object is comprised of data values and methods. Analogous to defining class and instance methods, we need to define class and instance data values. For example, we define an *instance data value* current balance for Account objects to record the current balance. Figure 1.9 shows three Account objects with their data values current balance. Notice that they all have the same data value current balance. All instances of the same class will possess the same set of data values. The actual dollar amounts for current balance, as the diagram illustrates, differ from one instance to another. Items such as opening balance and account number are other possible instance data values for Account objects.

instance data value

FIGURE 1.9   Three **Account** objects possess the same data value **current balance**, but the actual dollar amounts differ.

class data value

A *class data value* is used to represent information shared by all instances or to represent collective information about the instances. For example, if every account must maintain a minimum balance, say $100, we can define a class data value minimum balance. An instance can access the class data values of the class to which it belongs, so every Account object can access the class data value minimum balance. Figure 1.10 shows how we represent a class data value.

To appreciate the significance of a class data value, let's see what happens if we represent minimum balance as an instance data value. Figure 1.11 shows three Account objects having different dollar amounts for the current balance but the same dollar amount for the minimum balance. Obviously, this duplication of minimum balance is redundant and wastes space. Consider, for example, what happens if the bank raises the minimum balance to $200. If there are 100 Account objects, then all 100 copies of minimum balance must be updated. We can avoid this by defining minimum balance as a class data value.

variable and constant data values

There are two types of data values: those that can change over time and those that cannot. A data value that can change is called a *variable* and one that cannot change is a *constant*. Figure 1.12 illustrates how we represent and distinguish between variables and constants. We use a lock icon for constants to indicate that they cannot change. Notice that we now have four kinds of data values: class variables, class constants, instance variables, and instance constants.

Quick Check

1. What is the difference between a constant and a variable?
2. Draw an object diagram of a Person object with three instance variables name, age, and gender.

FIGURE 1.10   Three **Account** objects sharing information (**minimum balance** = $100) stored as a class data value.

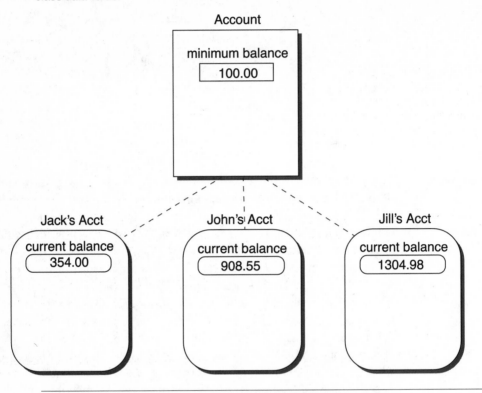

FIGURE 1.11   Three **Account** objects duplicating information (**minimum balance** = $100) in instance data values.

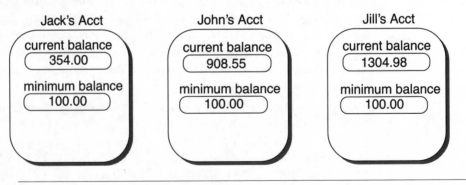

FIGURE 1.12   Graphical representations for four types of data values: class variable, class constant, instance variable, and instance constant.

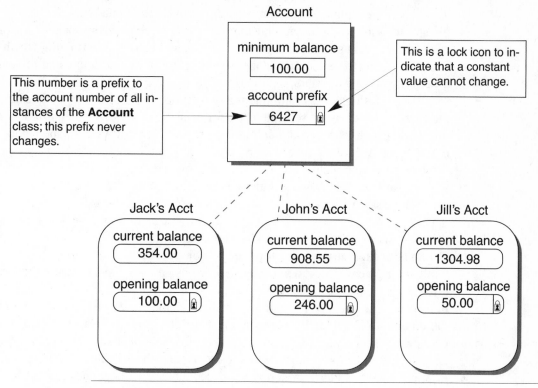

1.4   Inheritance

When we used the Account class and its instances to illustrate object-oriented concepts, some of you were probably thinking about checking accounts, while others may have been thinking about savings accounts. We did not distinguish between the two in the examples. When you look at the problem a little more carefully, you will realize that in fact these two types of accounts are different, even though they share many features.

In general, using only a single class to model two or more entities that are similar but different is not good design. Let's study why this is the case using the Account class. Suppose the bank requires you to maintain different minimum balances for savings and checking accounts. How could we model this situation using only a single class? We could choose one of the two possible solutions: (1) make minimum balance an instance variable or (2) set up two class variables minimum savings balance and minimum checking balance. Both solutions have major drawbacks. Solution 1 duplicates the same value, which we already mentioned is a very poor programming technique. Solution 2 complicates the processing of withdrawals because we need to determine the type of account and then use the corresponding minimum balance. Determining whether a given object is either a savings or a checking account requires additional processing and a data value.

If using a single class for modeling two or more entities is not good design, then should we design a separate class for each distinct type of entity? For the preceding example, we would define two classes: Savings Account and Checking Account. This alternative design is not a good one either, because we would end up duplicating methods. For example, if the way we deduct the amount of a withdrawal from a savings account and the check amount from a checking account is the same, then we will have to define identical methods for both classes, duplicating the same code. Thus the problem we identified with data value duplication may also occur with method duplication.

So both alternatives have problems. In object-oriented programming, we actually use a mechanism called *inheritance* to design two or more entities that are different but share many common features. First we define a class that contains the common features of the entities. Then we define classes as an extension of the common class inheriting everything from the common class. We call the common class the *superclass* and all classes that inherit from it *subclasses*. We also call the superclass an *ancestor* and the subclass a *descendant*. For the bank example, we can define a superclass Account and then define Savings and Checking as subclasses of Account. We represent the superclass and its subclasses as shown in Figure 1.13. Notice that we draw arrows from each subclass to its superclass because a subclass can refer to items defined in its superclass, but not vice versa.

A subclass will inherit everything from its superclass. We cannot say we want a subclass to inherit 50 percent of its superclass. However, it is possible for a subclass to override inherited components. For example, the Account class defines a class variable minimum balance of $100.00, but the Savings class overrides this value with the amount $250.00. Other inherited components can also be overridden. For example, the Checking class may override the inherited method deduct by adding instructions applicable to instances of the class (e.g., charge $1.00 for every withdrawal after more than 10 checks are drawn in any given month). Also, a subclass can add methods and data values to those inherited from its superclass. The Checking class may add a new instance variable to keep track of the number of checks issued in a month.

inheritance

superclass and
subclass

FIGURE 1.13   A superclass **Account** and its subclasses **Savings** and **Checking**.

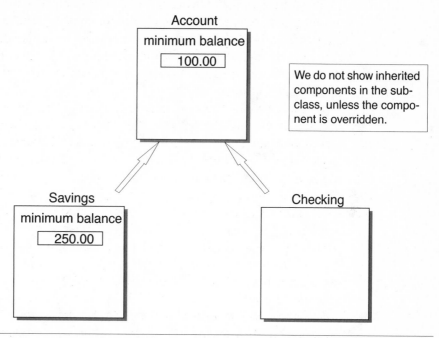

Inheritance is not limited to one level. A subclass can be a superclass of other classes, forming an inheritance hierarchy. Consider the example shown in Figure 1.14. Inheritance is very powerful, and if used properly, we can develop complex programs very efficiently and elegantly. The flip side of using a very powerful tool is that if you are not careful, you can misuse it and end up in a far worse situation than if you did not use it. We will discuss inheritance and how to use it properly throughout this book.

Quick Check

1. If Class A inherits from Class B, which is a superclass? Which is a subclass?

2. Draw an object diagram that shows Class A is inheriting from Class B.

FIGURE 1.14   An example of inheritance hierarchy among different types of accounts.

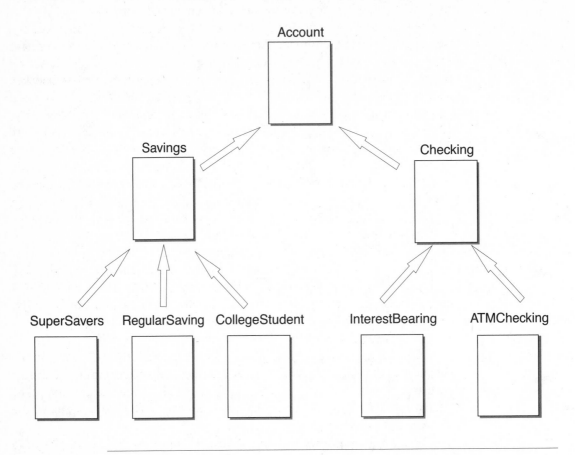

1.5   Software Engineering and Software Life Cycle

When we say *computer programming*, we are referring not only to writing Java commands, but to a whole process of software development. Knowing a programming language alone is not enough to become a proficient software developer. You must know how to design a program. This book will teach you how to design programs in an object-oriented manner.

We construct a house in well-defined stages and apply the engineering principles in all stages. Similarly, we build a program in stages and apply disciplined methodology in all stages of program development. The sequence of

software life cycle

software
engineering

stages from conception to operation of a program is called *software life cycle*. And *software engineering* is the application of a systematic and disciplined approach to the development, testing, and maintenance of a program.

There are five major phases in software life cycle: analysis, design, coding, testing, and operation. Software starts its life from the needs of a customer. A

analysis

person wants an online address book, for example. In the *analysis* phase, we perform a feasibility study. We analyze the problem and determine whether a solution is possible. Provided that a solution is possible, the result of this phase is a *requirements specification* which describes the features of a program. The features must be stated in a manner that are testable. One of the features for the address book program may be the capability to search for a person by giving his/her first name. We can test this feature by running the program and actually searching for a person. We verify that the program behaves as specified when the first name of a person in the address book and the first name of a person not in the address book are entered as a search condition. We do this testing in the testing phase, which we will explain shortly.

design

In the *design* phase, we turn a requirements specification into a detailed design of the program. For an object-oriented design, the output from this phase will be a set of classes/objects that fulfill the requirements. The classes/objects must be fully defined, showing how they behave and how they communicate among themselves. For the address book program, we may design objects such as Person, Phone, and others.

coding

In the *coding* phase, we implement the design into an actual program, in our case, a Java program. Once we have a well-constructed design, implementing it into actual code is really not that difficult. The difficult part is the creation of the design, and in this book, we place more emphasis on the design aspect of the software construction.

testing

When the implementation is completed, we move to the *testing* phase. In this phase, we run the program using different sets of data to verify that the program runs according to the specification. Two types of testing are possible for object-oriented programs: *unit testing* and *integration testing*. With unit testing, we test classes individually. With integration testing, we test that the classes work together correctly. Activity to eliminate programming error is called *de-*

debugging

bugging. An error could be a result of faulty implementation or design. When there's an error, we need to backtrack to earlier phases to eliminate the error.

operation

Finally, after the testing is successfully concluded, we enter the *operation* phase in which the program will be put into actual use. The most important and time-consuming activity during the operation phase is *software maintenance*.

software
maintenance

After the software is put to use, we almost always have to make changes to it. For example, the customer may request additional features or previously undetected errors may be found. Software maintenance means making changes to software. It is estimated that close to 70 percent of the cost of software is related to software maintenance. So naturally, when we develop software, we should aim for software that is easy to maintain. We must not develop a piece of software hastily to reduce the software development cost. We should take time and care to design and code software correctly even if it takes longer and costs more to develop initially. In the long run, carefully crafted software will have a lower total cost because of the reduced maintenance cost. Here's an important point to remember:

> **Well-designed and constructed software is easy to maintain.**

In this book, we will focus on the design, coding, and testing phases. We will present a requirements specification in the form of a problem statement for the sample programs we will develop in this book. You will see the first sample program developed by following the design, coding, and testing phases in Chapter 3. We will come back to the discussion of software engineering and software life cycle throughout the book and provide more details.

Quick Check

1. Name the stages of the software life cycle.
2. How does the quality of design affect the software maintenance cost?
3. What is debugging?

1.6   Having Fun with Java

Before we get into the details of computer programming, let's have some fun with Java. The following Java application allows you to draw a picture by dragging the mouse (i.e., moving the mouse while holding down the left mouse button). You can erase the drawing by clicking the right mouse button. (Note to Mac users: Please click the mouse button when the text refers to the left mouse button and command-click the mouse button when the text refers to the right mouse button.) You can also erase the drawing by minimizing the window and opening it again. You don't have to understand the details of the program yet;

just run the program and have fun.[1] We will explain the program code in the next chapter. Here we describe only the general ideas and classes used in the program.

```
/*
    Program FunTime

    The program will allow you to draw a picture by
    dragging a mouse (move the mouse while holding the left mouse
    button down; hold the button on Mac). To erase the picture and
    start over, click the right mouse button (command-click on Mac).
*/

import javabook.*;

class FunTime
{

    public static void main(String args[])
    {
        SketchPad    doodleBoard;
        doodleBoard = new SketchPad();
        doodleBoard.show();
    }

}
```

> This statement creates a new **SketchPad** object **doodleBoard**.

> This statement makes **doodleBoard** appear on the screen.

When the program is executed, the window shown in Figure 1.15 appears on the screen. Figure 1.16 is the same window after a picture is drawn on it. The program consists of two classes: FunTime and SketchPad. The FunTime class is defined in the above program. The SketchPad class is predefined outside of this program (in a place called the javabook package). This program opens a Sketch-Pad window named doodleBoard and makes it appear on the screen by sending the message show to it. An *object diagram* identifies the classes and objects used in a program, and the object diagram for this program is shown in Figure 1.17.

object diagram

---

1. For instructions on running the program, please consult your instructor or visit our Web site. We will discuss the general steps you take to run a Java program in the next chapter, but you will need instructions specific to the computers and software you will be using to write your own Java programs.

FIGURE 1.15   The window that appears on the screen when the program starts running.

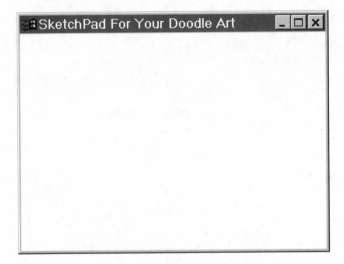

FIGURE 1.16   The same window after a picture is drawn.

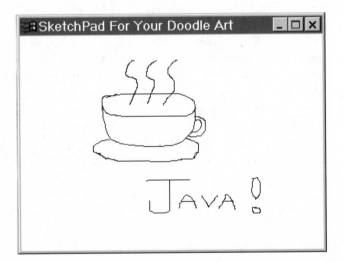

FIGURE 1.17   The object diagram for the **FunTime** program.

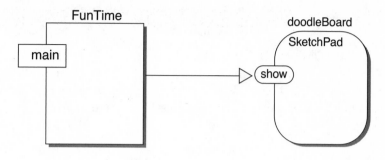

1.7   Exercises

1. Draw an object diagram of a Vehicle class and three Vehicle objects named car1, car2, and car3.

2. Identify all errors in the following object diagram:

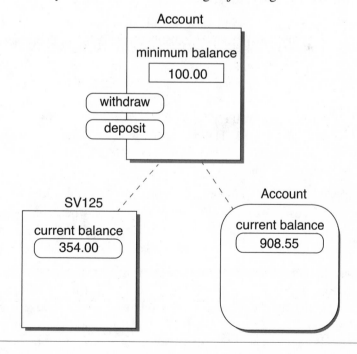

3. Draw an object diagram of a Person class with the following components:
    - Instance variables name, age, and gender.
    - Instance methods setName, getName, and getAge.
    - Class methods new and getAverageAge.

4. Design a CD class where a CD object represents a single music CD. What kinds of information (artist, genre, total playing time, etc.) do you want to know about a CD? Among the information about which you are interested, which are instance variables? Are there any class variables or class constants?

5. Suppose the Vehicle class in exercise 1 is used in a program that keeps track of vehicle registration for the Department of Motor Vehicles. What kinds of instance variables would you define for such Vehicle objects? Can you think of any useful class variables for the Vehicle class?

6. Suppose the following formulas are used to compute the annual vehicle registration fee for the vehicle registration program of exercise 5:
    - For cars, the annual fee is 2 percent of the value of the car.
    - For trucks, the annual fee is 5 percent of the loading capacity (in lbs) of the truck.

    Define two new classes Car and Truck as subclasses of Vehicle. Hint: Associate class and instance variables common to both Car and Truck to Vehicle.

7. Consider a student registration program used by the registrar's office. The program keeps track of students who are registered for a given semester. For each student registered, the program maintains the student's name, address, phone number, the number of classes in which the student is enrolled, and total credit hours. The program also keeps track of the total number of registered students. Define instance and class variables of a Student class that is suitable for this program.

8. Suppose the minimum and maximum number of courses for which a student can register is different depending on whether the student is a graduate, undergraduate, or work/study student. Redo exercise 7 by defining classes for different types of students. Relate the classes using inheritance.

9. Imagine you are given a task of designing an airline reservation system that keeps track of flights for a commuter airline. List the classes you think would be necessary for designing such a system. Describe the data values and methods you would associate with each class you identify. Note: For this and the next four exercises, we are not expecting you to design the sys-

tem in complete detail. The objective of these exercises is to give a taste of thinking about a program at a very high level. Try to identify about a half dozen or so classes, and for each class, describe several methods and data values.

10. Repeat exercise 9 designing a university course scheduling system. The system keeps track of classes offered in a given quarter, the number of sections offered, and the number of students enrolled in each section.

11. Repeat exercise 9 designing the state Department of Motor Vehicles registration system. The system keeps track of all licensed vehicles and drivers. How would you design objects representing different types of vehicles (e.g., motorcycles, trucks) and drivers (e.g., class A for commercial licenses, class B for towing vehicles)?

12. Repeat exercise 9 designing a sales tracking system for a fast-food restaurant. The system keeps track of all menu items offered by the restaurant and the number of daily sales per menu item.

13. When you write a term paper, you have to consult many references: books, journal articles, newspaper articles, and so forth. Repeat exercise 9 designing a bibliography organizer that keeps track of all references you used in writing a term paper.

14. Consider the inheritance hierarchy given in Figure 1.13. List the features common to all classes and the features unique to individual classes. Propose a new inheritance hierarchy based on the types of accounts your bank offers.

15. Consider a program that maintains an address book. Design an inheritance hierarchy for the classes such as Person, ProfessionalContact, Friend, and Student, that can be used in implementing such program.

16. Do you think the design phase is more important than the coding phase? Why or why not?

17. How does the quality of design affect the total cost of developing and maintaining software?

Java Programming Basics

OBJECTIVES

After you have read and studied this chapter, you should be able to

- Identify the basic components of Java programs.

- Distinguish two types of Java programs—applications and applets.

- Write simple Java applications and applets.

- Describe the difference between object declaration and object creation.

- Describe the process of creating and running Java programs.

- Use MainWindow and MessageBox classes from the javabook package to write Java applications.

- Use the Graphics class from the standard Java package.

Introduction

We will introduce both Java applications and applets in this chapter and describe the basic structure of simple Java programs. We will also describe the steps you follow to run programs. We expect you to actually run these sample programs to verify that your computer[1] is set up properly to run the sample programs presented in the book. It is important to verify now. Otherwise, if you encounter a problem later, you won't be able to determine whether the problem is the result of a bad program or a bad setup.

We will develop a sample application program in Section 2.4 following the design, coding, and testing phases of the software life cycle. We will develop all of our sample programs in this manner. We stress here again that our objective in this book is to teach object-oriented programming and how to apply object-oriented thinking in program development. Java language is merely a means to implement a design into an executable program. We chose Java for this book, because Java is a much easier language than other object-oriented programming languages to translate a design into an actual code. Beginning students often get lost in the language details and forget the main objective of learning how to design, but the use of Java should minimize this happening.

To help you concentrate on program design and programming fundamentals instead of language details, we provide predefined classes for you to use in writing Java programs. We will introduce two of these predefined classes in this chapter. As nice and logical as Java can be, beginners must still learn quite a few details before becoming proficient in Java language. We provide these predefined classes so that you can start writing meaningful programs immediately without knowing too much about Java language specifics. Please read the Preface for more reasons for using predefined classes in this book.

2.1   The First Java Application

Our first Java application program displays a window on the screen, as shown in Figure 2.1. The size of the window is slightly smaller than the screen, and the window is positioned at the center of the screen. Also, the window has a title Sample Java Application. Although this program is very simple, it still illustrates the fundamental structure of an object-oriented program, which is

An object-oriented program uses objects.

---

1. Either your own computer or the one at your computer lab.

It may sound too obvious, but let's begin our study of object-oriented programming with this obvious notion. Here's the program code:

```
/*
    Program MyFirstApplication

    This program displays a window on the screen. The window is
    positioned at the center of the screen, and the size of the
    window is almost as big as the screen.
*/

import javabook.*;

class MyFirstApplication
{
    public static void main(String args[])
    {
        MainWindow  mainWindow;
        mainWindow = new MainWindow();
        mainWindow.show();
    }
}
```

FIGURE 2.1   Result of running the **MyFirstApplication** program. The window has a default title **Sample Java Application**. (We'll show you how to change the default title later.)

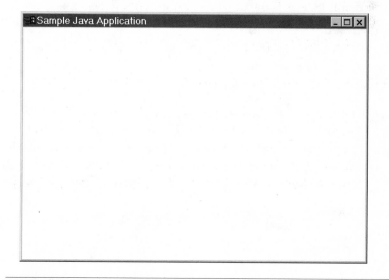

The object diagram of the sample program is shown in Figure 2.2.

FIGURE 2.2   The object diagram for the **MyFirstApplication** program.

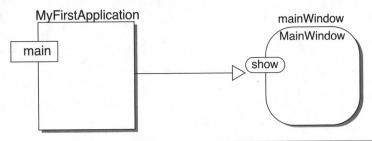

In the remainder of this section, we will explain the following three lines of code:

```
MainWindow    mainWindow;
mainWindow = new MainWindow();
mainWindow.show();
```

We will explain the rest of the program in the next section. Here's the rule to remember in using objects:

> To use an object in a program, we first declare and create an object, and then we send messages to it.

Object Declaration

Every object we use in a program must be declared. An object declaration designates the name of an object and the class to which the object belongs. Its syntax is

object declaration
syntax

```
<class name>  <object names>  ;
```

where <object names> is a sequence of object names separated by commas and <class name> is the name of a class to which these objects belong. Here's how the general syntax is matched to the object declaration of the program:

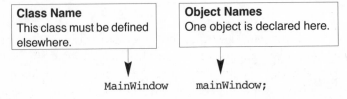

Class Name	Object Names
This class must be defined elsewhere.	One object is declared here.

```
MainWindow    mainWindow;
```

Here are more examples:

```
Account    checking;
Customer   john, jack, jill;
```

The first declaration declares an Account object named checking, and the second declaration declares three Customer objects.

To declare an object as an instance of some class, the class must be defined already. We will first study how to use objects from predefined classes. Later in the book, we will show you how to define your own classes, from which you can create instances.

identifier

When we declare an object we must give it a name. Any valid identifier that is not reserved for other uses can be used as an object name. An *identifier* is a sequence of letters, digits, underscores, and dollar signs with the first one being a letter. We use an identifier to name a class, object, method, and others. The following words are all valid identifiers:

```
MyFirstApplication
FunTime
ComputeArea
```

Upper- and lowercase letters are distinguished, so the following four identifiers are distinct:

```
mainwindow        mAinWindow
MAINWindow        mainWINDOW
```

No spaces are allowed in an identifier, and therefore, the following three lines

```
Sample Program
My First Application
Program FunTime
```

are all invalid identifiers.

naming convention

Since upper- and lowercase letters are distinguished, you can use mainWindow as the name for an object of the class MainWindow. We name objects in this manner whenever possible in this book so we can easily tell to which class the object belongs. We follow the Java naming convention of using an uppercase letter for the first letter of the class names and a lowercase letter for the first letter of the object names in this book. It is important to follow the standard naming convention so others who read your program can easily distinguish the purposes of identifiers. Programs that follow the standard naming convention are easier to read than those that do not follow the standard. And remember that software maintenance is easier with easy-to-understand programs.

When an identifier consists of multiple words, the first letter from every word, except the first word, will be capitalized, e.g., myMainWindow, not mymainwindow.

> Follow the standard naming convention in writing your
> Java programs to make them easier to read.

Object Creation

No objects are actually created by the declaration. An object declaration simply declares the name (identifier), which we use to refer to an object. For example, the declaration

```
Account     account;
```

designates that the name account is used to refer to an Account object, but the actual Account object is not yet created. We create an object by invoking the new command. The syntax for new is

object creation
syntax

```
<object name> = new <class name> ( <arguments> ) ;
```

where <object name> is the name of a declared object, <class name> is the name of the class to which the object belongs, and <arguments> is a sequence of values passed to the method. Let's match the syntax to the actual statement in the sample program:

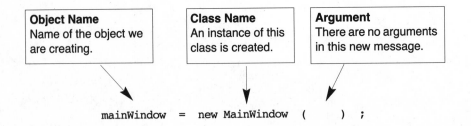

We can pass an argument in the new command to specify the title of the window. For example, if we replace the preceding line with

```
mainWindow = new MainWindow( "This is my first window" );
```

and run the program, the window shown in Figure 2.3 will appear on the screen. Notice the change in the window title. The double quotes (") are used to specify a string data value. If you don't use double quotes, then the system will treat

FIGURE 2.3   Result of running the program **MyFirstApplication** when the argument to the **new** command is the string argument **"This is my first window"**.

them as five identifiers, and this will result in an error.

Figure 2.4 shows the distinction between object declaration and creation. The object diagram notation we introduced in Chapter 1 is a simplified version of the state of memory diagram, as shown in Figure 2.5.

Now, consider the following object declaration and two statements of object creation:

FIGURE 2.4   Distinction between object declaration and object creation.

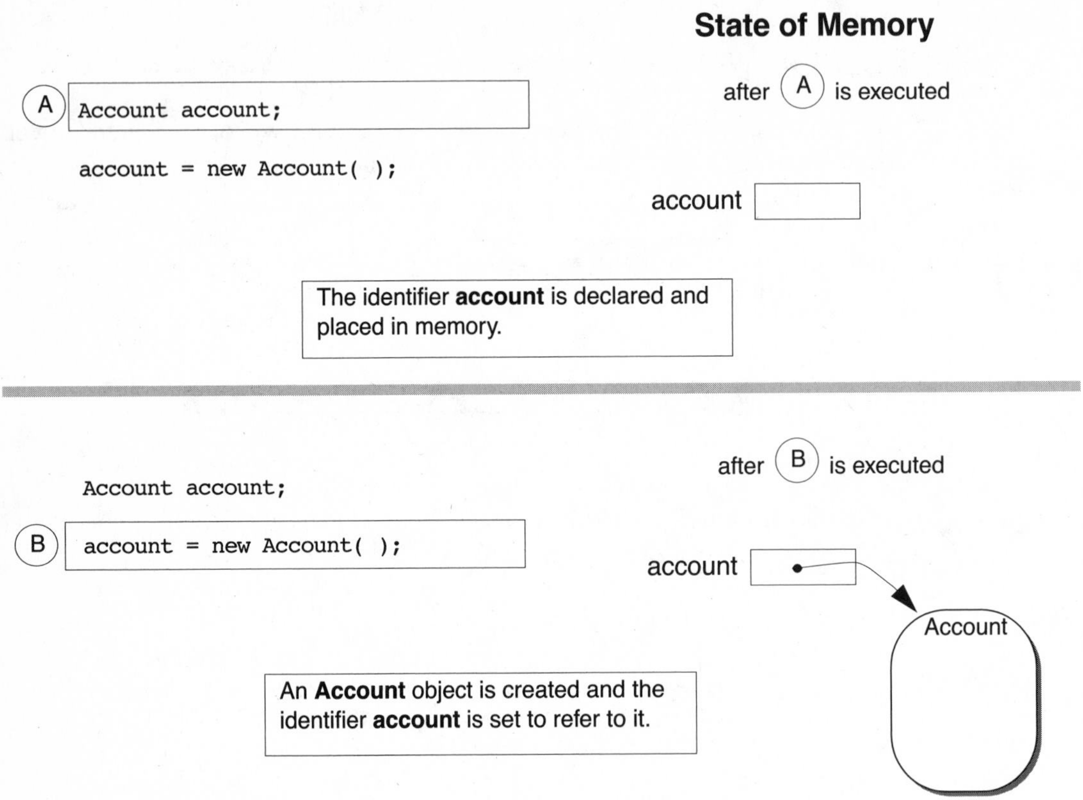

State of Memory

(A)
```
Account account;
```

```
account = new Account( );
```

after (A) is executed

account [   ]

> The identifier **account** is declared and placed in memory.

---

after (B) is executed

```
Account account;
```

(B)
```
account = new Account( );
```

account [•———→]

      Account

> An **Account** object is created and the identifier **account** is set to refer to it.

```
Customer    customer;
customer = new Customer( );
customer = new Customer( );
```

What do you think will happen? An error? No. It is possible to use the same name to refer to different objects of the same class. Figure 2.6 shows the state of memory after the second new is executed. Since there is no reference to the first Customer object anymore, it will eventually be erased and returned to the system. Remember that when an object is created, a certain amount of memory space is allocated for storing this object. If this allocated but unused space is not returned to the system for other uses, the space gets wasted. This returning of

FIGURE 2.5   Relationship between the state-of-memory diagram and the object diagram notation.

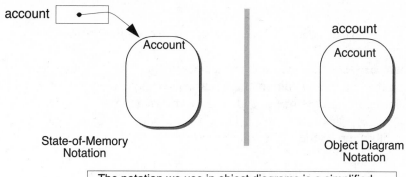

State-of-Memory
Notation

Object Diagram
Notation

The notation we use in object diagrams is a simplified
version of the one used in state-of-memory diagrams.

space to the system is called *deallocation*, and the mechanism to deallocate unused space is called *garbage collection*.

FIGURE 2.6   The state after two **new** commands are executed.

```
Customer customer;
customer = new Customer();
customer = new Customer();
```

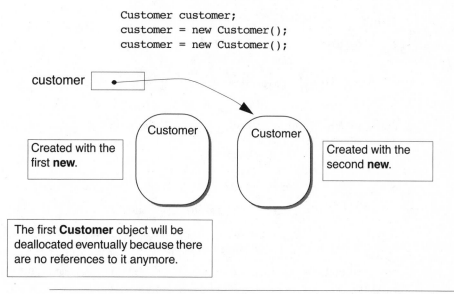

Created with the
first **new**.

Created with the
second **new**.

The first **Customer** object will be
deallocated eventually because there
are no references to it anymore.

Message Sending

After the object is created, we can start sending messages to it. The syntax for sending a message to an object is

message sending
syntax

```
<object name> . <method name> ( <arguments> ) ;
```

where <object name> is an object name, <method name> is the name of a method of the object, and <arguments> is a sequence of values passed to the method. In the sample program, we send the show message to the mainWindow object to make it appear on the screen. Once again, let's match the components in the general syntax to the actual statement:

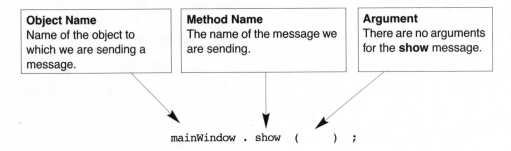

Figure 2.7 shows the correspondence between message sending as represented in the object diagram and the Java statement.

Quick Check

1. Which of the following are invalid identifiers?

   a. one
   b. my Window
   c. 1234
   d. acct122

   e. hello
   f. JAVA
   g. hello,there
   h. DecafeLattePlease

2. What's wrong with the following code?

   ```
   MainWindow mainWindow();
   mainWindow.show();
   ```

3. Is there anything wrong with the following declarations?

   ```
   mainWindow              MainWindow;
   Account, Customer       account, customer;
   ```

FIGURE 2.7 Correspondence between message sending as represented in the object diagram and in the actual Java statement.

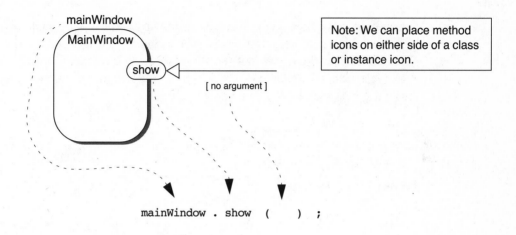

2.2 Program Components

Now that we have covered the crux of the first sample program, let's examine the rest of the program. The first sample application program MyFirstApplication is composed of three parts: comment, import statement, and class declaration. These three parts are included universally in Java programs.

> A Java program is composed of comments, import statements, and class declarations.

You can write a Java program that includes only a single class declaration, but that is not a norm. In any nontrivial program, you will see these three components. We will explain the three components and their subparts in this section.

Comments

In addition to the instructions for computers to follow, programs contain comments in which we state the purpose of the program, explain the meaning of code, and provide any other descriptions to help programmers understand the program. Here's the comment in the sample MyFirstApplication program:

```
/*

    Program MyFirstApplication

    This program displays a window on the screen. The window is
    positioned at the center of the screen, and the size of the
    window is almost as big as the screen.
*/

import javabook.*;

class MyFirstApplication
{
    public static void main(String args[])
    {
        MainWindow   mainWindow;
        mainWindow = new MainWindow();
        mainWindow.show();
    }
}
```

Comment

comment markers   A comment is any sequence of text that begins with the marker /* and terminates with another marker */. The beginning and ending markers are matched in pairs; that is, every beginning marker must have a matching ending marker. A beginning marker is matched with the next ending marker that appears. Any beginning markers that appear between the beginning marker and its matching ending marker are treated as part of the comment. In other words, you cannot put a comment inside another comment. The examples in Figure 2.8 illustrate how the matching is done.

single-line comment marker   Another marker for a comment is double slashes //. This marker is used for a single-line comment. Any text between the double-slash marker and the end of a line is a comment. The following example shows the difference between multiline and single-line comments:

```
/*
    This is a comment with
    three lines of
    text.
*/

// This is a comment
// This is another comment
// This is a third comment
```

FIGURE 2.8   How the beginning and ending comment markers are matched.

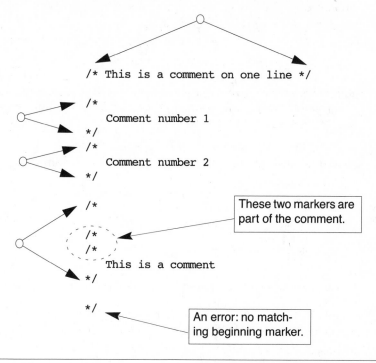

Although not required to run the program, comments are indispensable in writing easy-to-understand code.

Comments are intended for the programmers only and are ignored by the computer. Therefore, comments are really not necessary in making a program executable, but they are an important aspect of documenting the program. It is not enough to write a program that executes correctly. We need to document the program, and commenting the program is an important part of program documentation. Other parts of program documentation include object diagrams, programmers' work log, design documents, and user manuals. If you can write a program once and use it forever without ever modifying it, then writing a program with no comments may be tolerable. However, in the real world, using programs without ever making any changes almost never happens. For example, you may decide to add new features and capabilities or modify the way the user interacts with the program. Even if you don't improve the program, you still have to modify the program when you detect some errors in it. Also, for commercial programs, those who change the programs are most often not the ones who developed them. When the time comes for a programmer to modify his or someone else's program, he must first understand the program, and program documentation is an indispensable aid to understanding the program.

header comment

There are several different uses of comments. The first is the header comment. At the beginning of a program, we place a comment to describe the program. We characterize such a comment as a *header comment*. We may also include header comments at the beginning of methods to describe their purposes. Depending on the length and complexity of programs, the description may range from short and simple to long and very detailed. A typical header comment for a beginning programming class may look something like this:

typical header comment for a beginning programming class

```
/***********************************************

   Program:       TextEditor

   Author:        C. Thomas Wu
                  ctwu@cs.nps.navy.mil

   Written:       January 1, 1998

   Course:        Comp Sci 101
                  Spring 98
                  Program Assignment No. 7

   Compiler:      JDK 1.1.5
   Platform:      Windows 95

   Description:
     This is a simple text editor. The editor allows the user to
     save text to a file and read text from a file. The editor dis-
     plays text using Courier font only and does not allow format-
     ting (e.g., bold, italic, etc.). The editor supports standard
     editing functions Cut, Copy, and Paste, but does not support
     Undo. For more details, please refer to the TxEditReadme
     file.

***********************************************/
```

For your own programs, you should write header comments following the guideline provided by your instructor. For listing the sample programs in the book, we will include only the program name and a short description in the header comment, mainly for reference purposes. The header comment in the actual programs, available from our Web site, includes additional information such as compiler used, any discrepancies in running the program with different versions of Java compilers, copyright notices, and so forth.

Another use of comments is to explain code whose purpose may not be obvious. Your aim is always to write easily understandable, self-explanatory program code. But there are times this is not possible, and you should attach comment to code that is not so easy to understand. There are also times when the original code may not work as intended, and as a temporary measure, you modify the code slightly so the program will continue to work. You should clearly mark such modification with a comment, so you remember what you have done. If you did not put in appropriate comments and later read your code without remembering about the modification, you would have no idea why you wrote such code. If you cannot understand your own code, imagine the frustration of other programmers (or your T.A. or instructor) trying to understand your modified code.

Yet another use of comments is to identify or summarize a block of code. Suppose a program is divided into three major parts: getting input values from the user, performing computation using the input values, and displaying the computation results. You can place comments at the top of each part to delineate the three major parts clearly.

Remember that adding comments to a poorly designed program will not make it a better program. Your foremost goal is to develop a well-designed program that runs efficiently and is easy to understand. Commenting a program is only a means toward that goal, not a goal itself. In fact, excessive use of comments makes it harder to follow and understand a program.

Dr. Caffeine

Comment markers are useful in disabling a portion of a program. Let's say you find a portion that may be causing the program to crash and you want to try out different code for the problem portion. Instead of replacing the whole problem portion with new code, you can leave the questionable code in the program by converting it into a "comment" with comment markers. You can remove the comment markers if you need this code later.

Import Statement

We develop object-oriented programs by using predefined classes whenever possible and defining our own classes when no suitable predefined classes are

package

javabook

available. In Java, classes are grouped into *packages*. The Java compiler comes with many packages, and we supply one package called javabook with this text-book. We will explain the motivation behind using the javabook package in the next section. You can also put your own classes into a package so they can be used in other programs. Here's the import statement in the same MyFirstApplication program:

```
/*
     Program MyFirstApplication

     This program displays a window on the screen. The window is
     positioned at the center of the screen, and the size of the
     window is almost as big as the screen.
     .
     .
*/
import javabook.*;

class MyFirstApplication
{
     public static void main(String args[])
     {
          MainWindow        mainWindow;
          mainWindow = new MainWindow();
          mainWindow.show();
     }
}
```

Import Statement
The **import** statement allows the program to use classes (and their instances) defined in the designated package.

To use a class from a package, you may refer to the class in your program using the following format:

```
<package name> . <class name> ;
```

For example, to use the MainWindow class in the javabook package, we refer to it as

```
javabook.MainWindow;
```

dot notation

which we read as "javabook dot MainWindow." This notation is called *dot notation*. Notice that the import statement is terminated by a semicolon.

A package can include subpackages, forming a hierarchy of packages. In referring to a class in a deeply nested package, we use multiple dots. For example, we write

```
java.awt.image.ColorModel;
```

to refer to the class ColorModel in the java.awt.image package; that is, the image package is inside the awt package, which in turn is inside the java package. Dot notation with the names of all packages to which a class belongs is called the class's *fully qualified name*. Using the fully qualified name of a class is frequently too cumbersome, especially when you have to refer to the same class many times in a program. You can use the import statement to avoid this problem.

fully qualified name

An import statement at the beginning of your program eliminates the need for fully qualified names. Instead of using the expression java.awt.image.Color-Model to refer to the class, you can refer to it simply as

```
ColorModel
```

by including the import statement

```
import java.awt.image.ColorModel;
```

at the beginning of the program. If you need to import more than one class from the same package, then instead of using an import statement for every class, you can import them all using asterisk notation:

```
<package name> . * ;
```

For example, if we state

```
import java.awt.image.*;
```

then we are importing all classes from the java.awt.image package. We use this asterisk notation in our sample program, although we use only one of the many classes available in the javabook package. We could have used

```
import javabook.MainWindow;
```

but it is more conventional to use asterisk notation.

Notice that the package names are all in lowercase letters. This is another standard Java naming convention. When you create your own packages, which you will in Chapter 11, make sure to follow this naming convention.

Class Declaration

A Java program is composed of one or more classes, some of them are pre-defined classes, while others are defined by ourselves. In this sample program, there are two classes—MainWindow and MyFirstApplication. The MainWindow class is from the javabook package and the MyFirstApplication class is the class we define ourselves. To define a new class, we must *declare* it in the program. The syntax for declaring the class is

```
class <class name>
{

    <class member declarations>

}
```

where <class name> is the name of the class and <class member declarations> is a sequence of class member declarations. A class member is either a data value or a method. We can use any valid identifier to name the class. Here's the class declaration in the sample MyFirstApplication program:

```
/*
    Program MyFirstApplication

    This program displays a window on the screen. The window is
    positioned at the center of the screen, and the size of the
    window is almost as big as the screen.
    .
*/

import javabook.*;

class MyFirstApplication
{
    public static void main(String args[])
    {
        MainWindow      mainWindow;
        mainWindow = new MainWindow();
        mainWindow.show();
    }
}
```

Class Declaration
Every program must include at least one class.

reserved word
        The word class is a reserved word. A *reserved word* is an identifier that is used for a specific purpose and cannot be used for any other purpose such as using it for the name of an object. The reserved word class is used to mark the beginning of a class declaration.

main class

One of the classes in a program must be designated as the *main class*. The main class of the sample program is MyFirstApplication. Exactly how you designate a class as the main class of the program depends on which Java program development tool you use. We will use the name of a main class to refer to a whole application. For example, we say the MyFirstApplication class when we refer to the class itself and say the MyFirstApplication application when we refer to the whole application.

If we designate a class as the main class, then we must define a method called main, because when a Java program is executed, the main method of a main class is executed first. We will explain how to define a method in the next section.

Method Declaration

The syntax for method declaration is

```
<modifiers> <return type> <method name> ( <parameters> )
{
    <method body>
}
```

where <modifiers> is a sequence of terms designating different kinds of methods, <return type> is the type of data value returned by a method, <method name> is the name of a method, <parameters> is a sequence of values passed to a method, and <method body> is a sequence of instructions. Here's the method declaration for the main method:

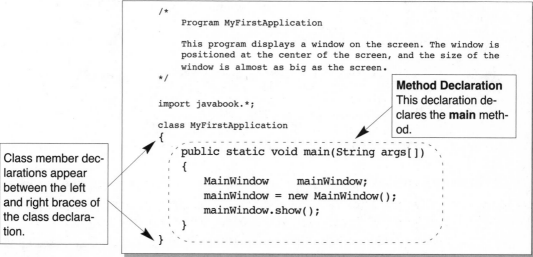

```
/*
    Program MyFirstApplication

    This program displays a window on the screen. The window is
    positioned at the center of the screen, and the size of the
    window is almost as big as the screen.
*/

import javabook.*;

class MyFirstApplication
{
    public static void main(String args[])
    {
        MainWindow    mainWindow;
        mainWindow = new MainWindow();
        mainWindow.show();
    }
}
```

Method Declaration
This declaration declares the **main** method.

Class member declarations appear between the left and right braces of the class declaration.

Let's match these components to the actual method declaration of the sample program.

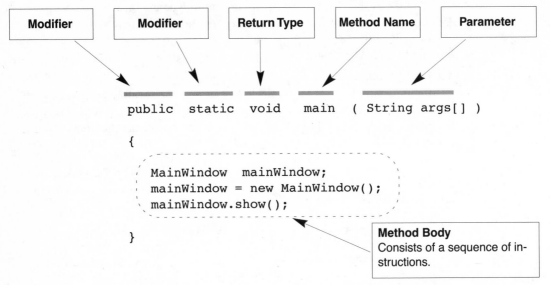

```
public   static   void   main   ( String args[] )

{

    MainWindow  mainWindow;
    mainWindow = new MainWindow();
    mainWindow.show();

}
```

Method Body
Consists of a sequence of instructions.

We will not explain the meanings of modifiers, return types, and parameters here. We will explain them in detail gradually as we progress through the book. For now, we ask you to follow a program template that we will present next.

A Program Template for Simple Java Applications

The diagram in Figure 2.9 shows a program template for simple Java applications. You can follow this program template to write very simple Java applications. The structure of the sample program MyFirstApplication follows this template.

Quick Check

1. Name three components of a Java program.
2. Locate three program components in the FunTime program from Chapter 1.
3. Compare FunTime and MyFirstApplication and list the similarities and differences.

FIGURE 2.9   A program template for simple Java applications.

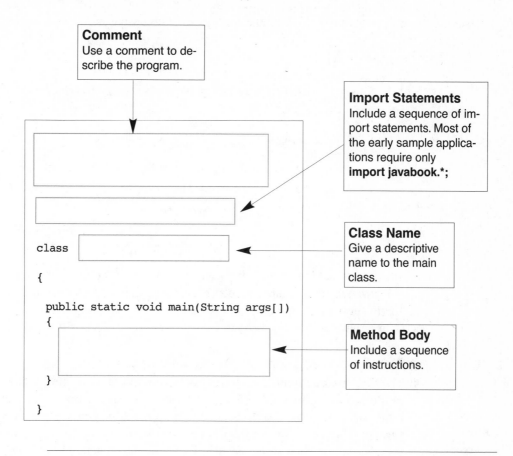

2.3   Edit–Compile–Run Cycle

We will walk through the steps involved in executing the first sample program. What we outline here are the overall steps common to any Java development tool you use. You need to get detailed instructions on how to use your chosen development tool to actually run programs. The steps we present in this section should serve as a guideline for more detailed instruction specific to your program development tool.

Step 1

Type in the program using an editor and save the program to a file. Use the name of the main class and the suffix .java for the filename. This file, in which the program is in a human-readable form, is called a *source file*.

source file

MyFirstApplication.java

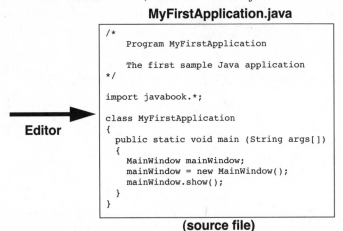

(source file)

It is critical that you configure the development tool properly so the compiler knows where to locate the javabook package. Each development tool requires you to set the configuration differently, so please consult the relevant materials for more information.

Step 2

project file

Compile the source file. Many compilers require you to create a *project file* and then place the source file in the project file in order to compile the source file. When the compilation is successful, the compiled version of the source file is created. This compiled version is called *bytecode*, and the file that contains bytecode is called a *bytecode file*. The compiler-generated bytecode file will have the same name as the source file with the suffix .class.

bytecode
bytecode file

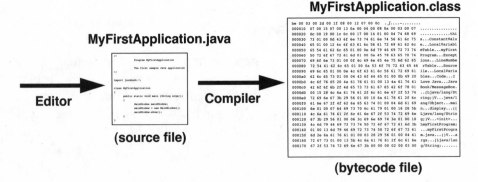

When any error occurs in a program, an error message will be displayed. If the sample program contains no errors in syntax, then instead of an error message, you will get a message stating something like "Compiled successfully." To see what kind of error messages are displayed, try compiling the following program. We purposely introduced three errors—can you find them? Make sure to compile the correct MyFirstApplication again before proceeding to the next step.

```
class MyFirstApplication //BAD version
{
    public static main(String args[])
    {
        mainWindow = new MainWindow();
        mainWindow.show()
    }
}
```

compilation error

Errors detected by the compiler are called *compilation errors*. Compilation errors are actually the easiest type of errors to correct. Most compilation errors are due to the violation of syntax rules.

Step 3

Execute the bytecode file. An interpreter will go through the bytecode file and execute the instructions in it. If your program is error free, a window will appear on the screen.

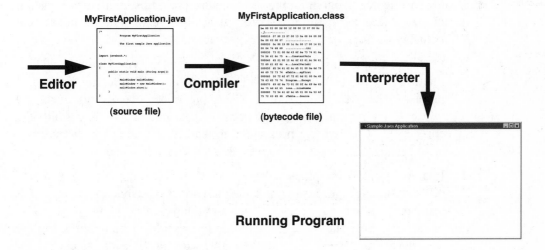

execution error

If an error occurs while running the program, the interpreter will catch it and stop its execution. Errors detected by the interpreter are called *execution errors*. If you did not see the expected results, go back to the previous steps and verify that your program is entered correctly. If you still do not see the expected results, then most likely your development environment is not set up correctly. Please refer to other sources of information for further help.

2.4   The javabook **Package**

We have used the MainWindow and SketchPad classes from the javabook package in our sample programs. There are many useful classes in the javabook package, and in the next section, we will show you the third class from the package. We decided to provide the javabook package with this book because

> To become a good object-oriented programmer, one must first learn how to use predefined classes.

Eventually, you must learn how to define your own classes, the classes you will reuse in writing programs. But before you can become adept in defining your own classes, you must first learn how to use existing classes. For this purpose, we provide the javabook classes in this book. Learning first to use the predefined javabook classes has the following advantages:

1. It gives you a taste of how real-world programs are developed. In real-world object-oriented programming, you develop programs by reusing existing classes whenever possible. You will get hands-on experience of code reuse by using classes from the javabook package.

2. It minimizes the impact of programming language syntax and semantics. The use of javabook classes lets students concentrate on learning concepts instead of Java language features. Using predefined classes minimizes the impact of programming language because these predefined classes hide the complexity of underlying programming language. Remember that our objective is to teach object-oriented thinking, not Java language.

3. It allows you to write practical programs without learning too many details of the Java language. Java comes with a number of standard packages, but using the standard classes such as java.awt from the beginning is not practical because these classes require programming sophistication that beginning students do not possess. Easy-to-use classes such as the javabook classes are most appropriate for beginning programmers.

4. It serves as a good example of how to design classes. When the time comes for you to design your own classes, intuitive and easy-to-use classes from javabook should serve as your model.

Although we begin teaching object-oriented programming by using the javabook classes, you will not be dependent on them. You will become an object-oriented programmer, not a javabook programmer. We use javabook because it is pedagogically sound to do so. Complete documentation of the javabook classes are provided in Appendix A.

Mr. Espresso: If I learn programming using **javabook** classes, will I be able to program only by using **javabook** classes? Will I still be able to program without using them?

Dr. Caffeine: Keep in mind that **javabook** classes are not the only predefined classes we use in this book. You will learn many classes from the standard Java packages such as **java.awt** and **java.io**. By the time you finish Chapter 12, you can program with or without the **javabook** package.

Mr. Espresso: Another concern I have is what happens after I complete your course? Can I continue to use **javabook**?

Dr. Caffeine: Yes, you are free to use the **javabook** classes. There are no restrictions on using them. You may use the **javabook** classes as is, or better yet, you can modify the classes to suit your needs. You can take **javabook** as the starting point of your own package. Source code for all the classes in the **javabook** package is available to you.

Dr. & Mr.

2.5 Sample Program: Displaying Messages

Now that you have acquired a basic understanding of Java application programs, let's write a new application. We will go through the design, coding, and testing phases of the software life cycle to illustrate the development process. Since the program we develop here is very simple, we can write it without really going through the phases. However, it is extremely important for you to get into a habit of developing a program following the software life cycle stages. Small programs can be developed in a haphazard manner, but not large programs. We will teach you the development process with small programs first, so you will be ready to use it to develop large programs later.

Problem Statement

We start our development from a problem statement. The problem statement for our sample programs will be short, ranging from a sentence to a paragraph, but the problem statement for complex and advanced applications may contain many pages. Here's the problem statement for this sample program:

Write an application that displays the message I Love Java.

Design

In the design stage, we translate the given problem statement into a design document that can be implemented. For object-oriented programs, a design document will include a list of classes. The classes in the design document are either predefined or custom-made. For each class in the list, we identify its purpose, the methods and data values that will be defined, assumptions made in its use, and so forth. We will begin with a very simplistic design document and gradually build more detailed design documents as our sample programs become more complex later in the book.

The problem states that the program is to display a message. It does not specify how, so in the design stage, we will decide how to do this. From what we know so far, we can do this by setting the title of the MainWindow object like this:

Alternative ◁
Design

```
MainWindow   mainWindow;
mainWindow = new MainWindow("I Love Java");
mainWindow.show();
```

Is this a good design? This is the best we could do from our limited knowledge, but most likely, this is not what the user wants. When the design does not meet the user's needs, we go back to the drawing board and redesign.

The first thing we do in redesign is to search for a class or classes that will perform the task we want to implement. We may start searching from the standard Java classes. If we can find suitable classes, we will use them. We may have to build a new class from these existing classes. If no suitable classes are found or building one from the existing classes seems too difficult, we will search other packages. We could search for free packages available on the Internet or packages supplied by your school's computer center. Some software companies may sell a package that contains the classes we want. If the package is within our budget, we may buy it. If no such package can be found, then we will develop the necessary classes ourselves.

In our case, we will search the javabook package first. As you become more proficient in Java language, you may want to search the Java standard libraries first. If you go through the package documentation in Appendix A, you will notice a class called **MessageBox**. This is the class we are looking for.

We will describe **MessageBox** very briefly here. More information on **MessageBox** will be given later as we use more of its features. A **MessageBox** object is used to display a single line of text. Figure 2.10 shows the **MessageBox** object with the message I Love Java. When you click the OK button, the object disappears from the screen. The sequence of declaring, creating, and sending the message is

Alternative Design 2

```
MessageBox messageBox;
messageBox = new MessageBox( mainWindow );
messageBox.show("I Love Java");
```

dialog box

A **MessageBox** object is a special kind of window called a *dialog box*, or more simply, *dialog*. Every dialog box requires another kind of window called a

FIGURE 2.10   Result of running the **DisplayMessage** program.

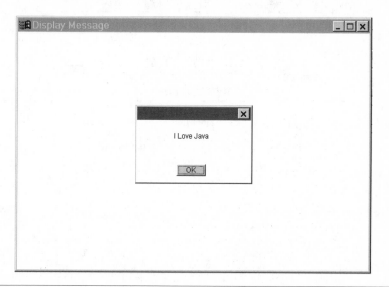

frame

frame as its *owner*. MainWindow is a frame window. We will elaborate on their differences later. For now, it suffices to know that a frame is a general-purpose window and a dialog is a limited-purpose window used primarily for displaying simple information such as error messages or getting a simple response such as yes or no.

subordinate

We call a dialog box a *subordinate* of the owner frame. One characteristic of this relationship is that a subordinate dialog always appears in front of its owner frame. The owner–subordinate relationship is established when a dialog box is created by passing the owner frame window as an argument in new, as in

```
messageBox = new MessageBox( mainWindow );
```

And we display the text by passing it as an argument in the show message to a Messagebox object:

```
messageBox.show( "I Love Java" );
```

The object diagram of the program is shown in Figure 2.11 and here's the design document of the program:

Design Document:	DisplayMessage
Class	**Purpose**
DisplayMessage	The main class of the program.
MainWindow	The main frame window of the program. The title is set to Display Message. This class is from javabook.
MessageBox	The dialog for displaying the required message. This class is from javabook.

Coding

After the design is completed, we translate it into an actual code. We will implement this program using the program template of Figure 2.9.

Here's the source code for the program DisplayMessage:

```
/*
    Program DisplayMessage

    The program displays the text "I Love Java". The program uses a MessageBox
    object from the javabook package to display the text.
*/
```

FIGURE 2.11   The object diagram for the **DisplayMessage** program.

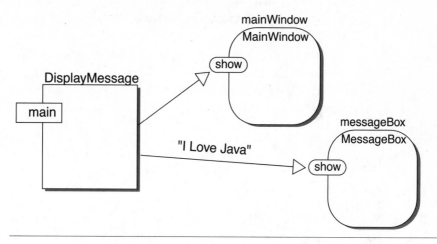

```
import javabook.*;

class DisplayMessage
{
    public static void main(String args[])
    {
        //declare two objects
        MainWindow mainWindow;
        MessageBox messageBox;

        //create two objects
        mainWindow = new MainWindow("Display Message");
        messageBox = new MessageBox(mainWindow);

        //display two objects: first the frame and then the dialog
        mainWindow.show();
        messageBox.show("I Love Java");
    }
}
```

Testing

After the program is written, we test the program to verify that the program runs as intended. Since this program is very simple, there's not much testing strategy we can employ here. We just run the program and make sure that the main window and the dialog appear on the screen as shown in Figure 2.10. For subsequent sample programs, the testing strategy will be more involved.

2.6   The First Java Applet

Now let's move on to the second type of Java program—an applet. Here's a Java applet that displays the message I Love Java and draws a rectangle around the text:

```
/*
    Program MyFirstApplet

    An applet that displays the text "I Love Java"
    and a rectangle around the text.
*/

import java.applet.*;
import java.awt.*;

public class MyFirstApplet extends Applet
{
    public void paint( Graphics graphic)
    {
        graphic.drawString("I Love Java",70,70);
        graphic.drawRect(50,50,100,30);
    }

}
```

Notice a resemblance in the program structure between this applet and the applications we wrote earlier. Applications and applets are both programs, and, therefore, they share the same program structure, composed of three parts: a comment, an import statement, and a class declaration. Figure 2.12 identifies the three components in the applet. We include the header comment to describe the applet and two import statements to import the required java.applet and java.awt packages. The classes Applet and Graphics used in the applet are defined in java.applet and java.awt. The object diagram of MyFirstApplet is shown in Figure 2.13.

Notice that MyFirstApplet does not have a main method, because the Applet-Viewer class is the main class of the program. For applications, we define our own main class, but for applets, we use the predefined main class AppletViewer. For applets, we define a subclass of Applet that the AppletViewer uses when executed. A subclass of Applet is declared as

applet declaration
syntax

```
public class <applet subclass> extends Applet
{
    <class member declarations>
}
```

FIGURE 2.12   The applet **MyFirstApplet** with the three program components identified.

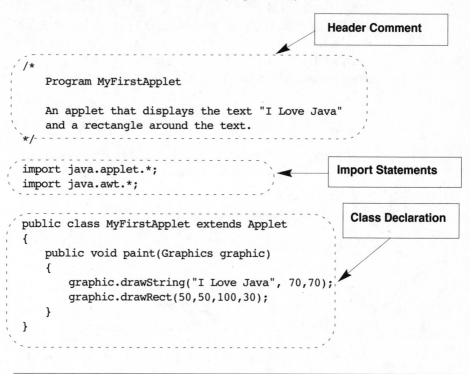

Header Comment

```
/*
    Program MyFirstApplet

    An applet that displays the text "I Love Java"
    and a rectangle around the text.
*/

import java.applet.*;
import java.awt.*;

public class MyFirstApplet extends Applet
{
    public void paint(Graphics graphic)
    {
        graphic.drawString("I Love Java", 70,70);
        graphic.drawRect(50,50,100,30);
    }
}
```

Import Statements

Class Declaration

FIGURE 2.13   The object diagram for the **MyFirstApplet** program.

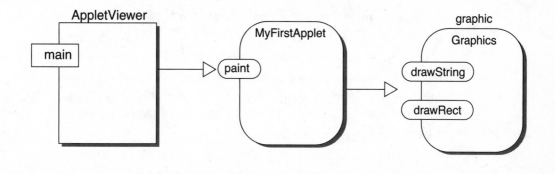

public class

Notice the modifier public before class, which designates the class as a *public class*. We will discuss the significance of this modifier in Chapter 11. For now, just remember that an applet viewer requires classes to be declared as public. The Java interpreter that runs application programs does not impose this requirement, and therefore, we do not use this modifier in declaring the main class

extends

of an application (although it won't hurt if we do). The reserved word extends designates an inheritance (superclass/subclass) relationship. So by declaring

```
public class MyFirstApplet extends Applet
```

we are using inheritance and establishing MyFirstApplet as a subclass of Applet. In diagram we represent the relationship as

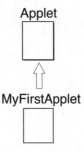

We declared one method in the MyFirstApplet class:

paint method

```
public void paint(Graphics graphic)
{
    graphic.drawString("I Love Java", 70, 70);
    graphic.drawRect(50, 50, 100, 30);
}
```

The AppletViewer class automatically sends the paint message with a Graphics object as an argument to an applet. We use Graphics objects to display text, lines, and other graphics. In the sample applet, we send two messages to the object graphic. The first message

```
graphic.drawString("I Love Java", 70, 70);
```

displays the text I Love Java at the specified position (70, 70). The position is determined in the manner illustrated in Figure 2.14.

FIGURE 2.14   The diagram illustrates how the position of text is determined by the **drawString** method.

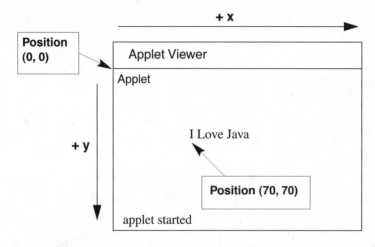

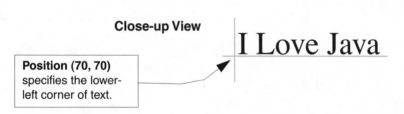

The second message

```
graphic.drawRect(50, 50, 100, 30);
```

displays a rectangle 100 pixels wide and 30 pixels high at the specified position (50, 50). The position is determined as illustrated in Figure 2.15.

A program template for simple Java applets is shown in Figure 2.16.

FIGURE 2.15 The diagram illustrates how the position of a rectangle is determined by the **drawRect** method.

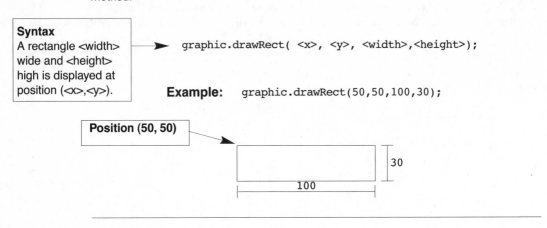

Syntax
A rectangle <width> wide and <height> high is displayed at position (<x>,<y>).

```
graphic.drawRect( <x>, <y>, <width>,<height>);
```

Example: `graphic.drawRect(50,50,100,30);`

Position (50, 50)

30

100

FIGURE 2.16 A program template for simple Java applets.

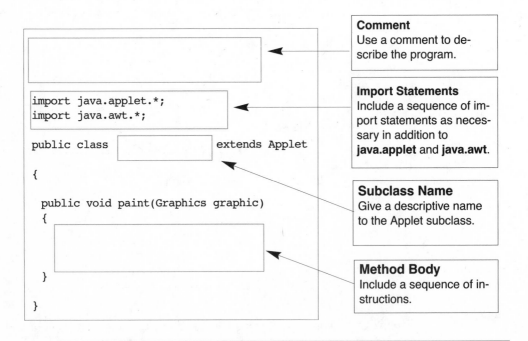

```
import java.applet.*;
import java.awt.*;

public class                    extends Applet

{

  public void paint(Graphics graphic)
  {



  }

}
```

Comment
Use a comment to describe the program.

Import Statements
Include a sequence of import statements as necessary in addition to **java.applet** and **java.awt**.

Subclass Name
Give a descriptive name to the Applet subclass.

Method Body
Include a sequence of instructions.

Table 2.1 lists some of the available graphic-drawing methods.

TABLE 2.1   A partial list of drawing methods defined for the **Graphics** class.

Method	Meaning
`drawLine(x1,y1,x2,y2)`	Draws a line between (x1,y1) and (x1,y2).
`drawRect(x,y,w,h)`	Draws a rectangle with width w and height h at (x,y).
`drawRoundRect(x,y,w,h,aw,ah)`	Draws a rounded-corner rectangle with width w and height h at (x,y). Parameters aw and ah determine the angle for the rounded corners.
`drawOval(x,y,w,h)`	Draws an oval with width w and height h at (x,y).
`drawString("text",x,y)`	Draws the string text at (x,y).

The steps you take to run the applet are essentially the same as those you take to run the application. The only difference is the creation of an html file and the use of an applet viewer (or a Web browser) to run the applet. The next diagram illustrates the steps you take to run the applet:

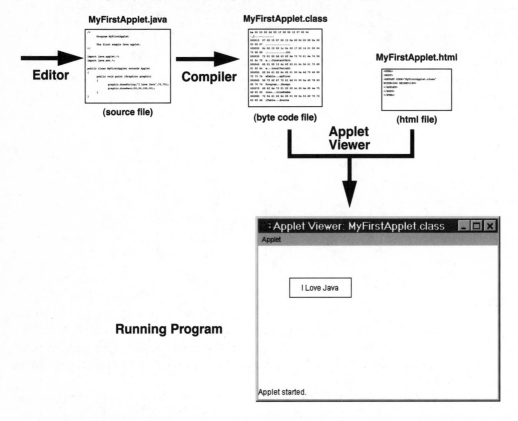

applet viewer

Executing the applet MyFirstApplet displays a window called an *applet viewer* on the screen, as shown in Figure 2.17. The AppletViewer class is responsible for displaying an applet viewer window and running the applet within the applet viewer window. The applet viewer provides a quick and easy way to run and test applets without using any Web browser. When you use a Web browser to run applets, the browser assumes the role of the main class.

We mentioned that an applet is a mini-application that is intended to be executed within a Web browser. A Web browser reads a formatted document called a *Web document* or *Web page*. A Web document written in *HyperText Markup Language* (HTML) is called an *HTML document*, and a file that contains an

HTML

FIGURE 2.17   Result of running the applet **MyFirstApplet**.

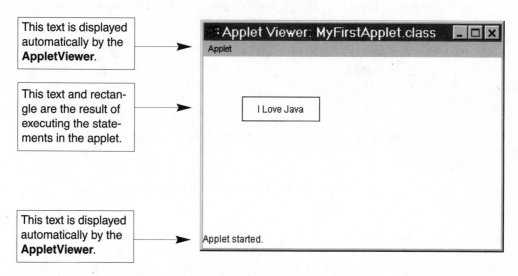

This text is displayed automatically by the **AppletViewer**.

This text and rectangle are the result of executing the statements in the applet.

This text is displayed automatically by the **AppletViewer**.

markup
elements

HTML document is an *HTML file*. We use the suffix .html to name an HTML file. HTML is the standard language used for writing Web documents and consists of text and formatting tags called *markup elements* that specify the format for headers, paragraphs, hyperlinks, and other components of a document. One of the markup elements specifies the execution of an applet, giving the name of an applet to be executed, the area in the browser in which the applet is executed, and so forth.

We need an HTML file that refers to an applet's bytecode file to run the applet. We use the HTML file MyFirstApplet.html to run the MyFirstApplet applet.

MyFirstApplet.html

```
<HTML>
<BODY>
<APPLET CODE="MyFirstApplet.class" WIDTH=300 HEIGHT=190>
</APPLET>
</BODY>
</HTML>
```

The details of HTML are beyond the scope of this book However, we will describe the portion necessary to run our sample applets. You can use this HTML file as a template to use with other applets by changing the APPLET tag (the third line in the MyFirstApplet.html file). This tag indicates the applet's bytecode filename and the size of the rectangular area reserved for the applet:

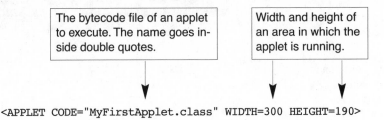

```
<APPLET CODE="MyFirstApplet.class" WIDTH=300 HEIGHT=190>
```

For example, to run MyFirstApplet in a smaller area, we can change the tag to

```
<APPLET CODE="MyFirstApplet.class" WIDTH=200 HEIGHT=100>
```

Although the AppletViewer class can read any Web page, it processes only the APPLET tag and ignores other tags. So if you want to run an applet in a Web page that processes all tags, you need to use a Java-aware Web browser.[2] Figure 2.18 shows MyFirstApplet executed in a popular Web browser, Netscape Navigator (version 3.0). Notice that Navigator is running on the Macintosh. The applet was written on the Windows 95 platform but executed in a browser on a different platform. We use the HTML file javabook.html containing more tags (such as specifying the title Intro to Programming with Java and the background spiral notebook image).

Quick Check

1.   How are an applet viewer and a Web browser different?
2.   Which class is the main class of an applet?
3.   Which method of the Graphics class do you use to draw a rectangle?
4.   What is the purpose of the APPLET tag in an HTML file?

---

2. Some Web browsers do not understand the APPLET tag. You need Java-aware Web browsers, such as Netscape Navigator 4.0 or later and MS Internet Explorer 3.0 or later that understand the APPLET tag to run Java applets.

FIGURE 2.18   Result of running the applet **MyFirstApplet** in Netscape Navigator.

MyFirstApplet is set to run in this boxed area.

2.7   Exercises

1. Identify all errors in the following program:

```
/*
    Program Exercise1

    A program with many errors.
//
import javabook.mainwindow;

class Exercise 1
{
    public void Main()
    {
        MainWindow mainWindow;
        mainWindow.show()
    }
}
```

2. Identify all errors in the following program:

```
//
    Program Exercise2

    A program with many errors.
//

import     JavaBook.*;

class TWO
{
    public static void main method()
    {
        mainWindow      mainWindow;
        MessageBox      mybox1, mybox2;

        mainWindow = new MainWindow();
        messageBox.show();
        mybox2 = new MessageBox();
        mybox2.show;
    }
}
```

3. Identify all of the errors in the following program:

```
/*
    Program Exercise12

    A program with many errors.
//
import java.applet;

class Exercise1 extends applet
{
    static public void paint()
    {
        graphic.drawString("Internet fun and useful"));
    }
}
```

4. Describe the purpose of comments. Name the types of comments available. Can you include comment markers inside a comment?

5. What is the purpose of the import statement? Does a Java program always have to include an import statement?

6. Show the syntax for importing one class and all classes in a package.

7. Describe the class that must be included in any Java application.

8. What is a reserved word? List all the Java reserved words mentioned in this chapter.

9. Which of the following are invalid identifiers?

a. R2D2	g. 3CPO
b. Whatchamacallit	h. This is okay.
c. HowAboutThis?	i. thisIsReallyOkay
d. Java	j. aPPlet
e. GoodChoice	k. Bad-Choice
f. 12345	l. A12345

10. Describe the steps you take to run a Java application and the tools you use in each step. What are source files and bytecode files? What different types of errors are detected at each step?

11. Describe the difference between object declaration and object creation. Use a state-of-memory diagram to illustrate the difference.

12. Show a state of memory diagram after each of the following statements is executed:

```
MainWindow      window1;
MessageBox      mbox1, mbox2;

window1    = new MainWindow();
mbox1      = new MessageBox();
mbox2      = new MessageBox();
window1    = new MainWindow();
```

13. Show a state-of-memory diagram after each of the following statements is executed:

```
Person          person1, person2;

person1    = new Person();
person2    = new Person();
person2    = new Person();
```

14. Which of the following identifiers violate the naming convention for class names?

a.	r2D2	e.	CPO
b.	whatchamacallit	f.	ThisIsReallyOkay
c.	Java	g.	java
d.	GoodName	h.	aPPlet

15. Which of the following identifiers violate the naming convention for object names?

a.	R2D2	e.	3CPO
b.	isthisokay?	f.	ThisIsReallyOkay
c.	Java	g.	java
d.	goodName	h.	anotherbadone

16. How are Java applets different from Java applications?

17. What is a Web page? What tag is required to run an applet in a Web browser?

18. Write a Java application that displays a MainWindow window 300 pixels wide and 200 pixels high with the title This is My first application.

19. Write a Java application that displays two separate messages I Can Design and And I Can Program.

20. Write a Java application that displays a very long message. Try a message that is wider than the display of your computer screen and see what happens.

21. Write a Java applet that displays the text Hello in an applet viewer as illustrated below:

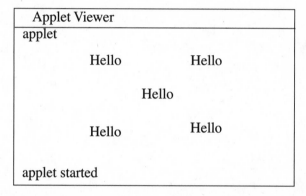

22. Write a Java applet that draws a house in an applet viewer. You might want to draw a house that is much more interesting than the one shown here. Use the methods listed in Table 2.1 as needed.

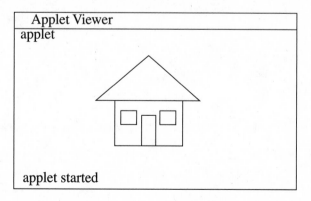

23. Add the moon and a tree to the house you drew in exercise 22.

24. If you know how to open an HTML file from a Web browser, run the Java applets from exercises 21 through 23 in a Web browser.

3

Numerical Data

OBJECTIVES

After you have read and studied this chapter, you should be able to

- Select proper types for numerical data.
- Write arithmetic expressions in Java.
- Evaluate arithmetic expressions using the precedence rules.
- Describe how the memory allocation works for objects and primitive data values.
- Write mathematical expressions using methods in the Math class.
- Write programs that input and output data using the InputBox and OutputBox classes from the javabook package.
- Apply the incremental development technique in writing programs.
- (Optional) Describe how the integers and real numbers are represented in memory.

Introduction

In writing computer programs, it is helpful for beginners to visualize three tasks: input, computation, and output. We view computer programs as getting input, performing computation on the input data, and outputting the results of the computations. For example, consider a metric converter program that accepts measurements in U.S. units (input), converts the measurements (computation), and displays their metric equivalents (output). The three tasks are not limited to numerical values, though. An input could be a mouse movement. A drawing program may accept mouse dragging (input), remember the points of mouse positions (computation), and draw lines connecting the points (output). Selecting a menu item is yet another form of input. For beginners, however, it is easiest to start writing programs that read numerical values as input and display the result of numerical computation as output.

In this chapter, we will study how to manipulate numerical data in computer programs. We will also introduce two classes—InputBox and OutputBox—from the javabook package. We use an InputBox object to get input data from the user and an OutputBox object to output data. Lastly, we will present a technique for writing programs called *incremental development*. With this technique we implement programs in small incremental steps, an approach indispensable in developing large programs. We will implement a sample program using the incremental development technique.

incremental development

3.1   Variables

Suppose we want to compute the sum and difference of two numbers. Let's call the two numbers x and y. In mathematics, we say

$$x + y$$

and

$$x - y$$

To compute the sum and difference of x and y in a program, we must first declare what kind of data will be assigned to them. After we assign values to them, we can finally compute their sum and difference.

Let's say x and y are integers. To declare that the type of data assigned to them is an integer, we write

```
int    x, y;
```

variable

When this declaration is made, memory locations to store data values for x and y are allocated. These memory locations are called *variables*, and x and y are the names we associate with the memory locations. Any valid identifier can be used as a variable name. After the declaration is made, we can assign only integers to x and y. We cannot, for example, assign real numbers to them.

A variable has three properties: a memory location to store the value, the type of data stored in the memory location, and the name used to refer to the memory location.

Although we must say "x and y are variable names" to be precise, we will use abbreviated forms "x and y are variables" or "x and y are integer variables" whenever appropriate.

The general syntax for declaring variables is

variable declaration
syntax

```
<data type> <variables> ;
```

where <variables> is a sequence of identifiers separated by commas. Every variable you use in a program must be declared. We may have as many declarations as we wish. For example, we can declare x and y separately as

```
int    x;
int    y;
```

However, you cannot declare the same variable more than once; therefore, the second declaration below is invalid because y is declared twice:

```
int    x, y, z;
int    y;
```

six numerical
data types

There are six numerical data types in Java: byte, short, int, long, float, and double. The data types byte, short, int, and long are for integers, and the data types float and double are for real numbers. The data type names byte, short, and others are all reserved words. The difference among these six numerical data types is in the range of values they can represent, as shown in Table 3.1.

TABLE 3.1   Java numerical data types and their precisions.

Data Type	Content	Default Value	Minimum Value	Maximum Value
byte	Integer	0	−128	127
short	Integer	0	−32768	32767
int	Integer	0	−2147483648	2147483647
long	Integer	0	−9223372036854775808	9223372036854775807
float	Real	0.0	−3.40282347E+38[†]	3.40282347E+38
double	Real	0.0	−1.79769313486231570E+308	1.79769313486231570E+308

† The character E indicates a number is expressed in scientific notation. This notation is explained on page 99.

A data type with a larger range of values is said to have a *higher precision*. For example, the data type double has a higher precision than the data type float. The trade-off for higher precision is memory space—to store a number with higher precision, you need more space. A variable of type short requires 2 bytes and a variable of type int requires 4 bytes, for example. If your program does not use many integers, then whether you declare them as short or int is really not that critical. The difference in memory usage is very small and not a deciding factor in the program design. The storage difference becomes significant only when your program uses thousands of integers. Therefore, we will almost always use the data type int for integers. We use long when we need to process very large integers that are outside the range of values int can represent. The same argument holds for float and double. We almost always use float for real numbers, using double only when we need to process very large real numbers outside the range of values float can represent. We will describe how the numbers are stored in memory in Section 3.8.

Here is an example of declaring variables of different data types:

```
int        i, j, k;
float      numberOne, numberTwo;
long       bigInteger;
double     bigNumber;
```

At the time a variable is declared, it can also be initialized. For example, we may initialize the integer variables count and height to 10 and 34 as

```
int count = 10, height = 34;
```

Dr. Caffeine

In the same way that you can initialize variables at the time you declare them, you can declare and create an object at the same time. For example, the declaration

```
MainWindow mainWindow = new MainWindow();
```

is equivalent to

```
MainWindow mainWindow;
mainWindow = new MainWindow();
```

assignment statement

We assign a value to a variable using an *assignment statement*. To assign the value 234 to the variable named firstNumber, for example, we write

```
firstNumber = 234;
```

Be careful not to confuse mathematical equality and assignment. For example, the following are not valid Java code:

```
4 + 5 = x;
x + y = y + x;
```

The syntax for the assignment statement is

assignment statement syntax

```
<variable> = <expression> ;
```

where <expression> is an arithmetic expression, and the value of <expression> is assigned to the <variable>. The following are sample assignment statements:

```
sum       = firstNumber + secondNumber;
solution  = x * x - 2 * x + 1;
average   = (x + y + z) / 3.0;
```

We will present a detailed discussion of arithmetic expressions in Section 3.2. One key point you need to remember about variables is

Before using a variable, you must first declare and assign a value to it.

The diagram in Figure 3.1 illustrates the effect of variable declaration and assignment. Notice the similarity with this and memory allocation for object

---

FIGURE 3.1   A diagram showing how two memory locations (variables) with names **firstNumber** and **secondNumber** are declared, and values are assigned to them.

State of Memory

after (A) is executed

(A)   `int firstNumber, secondNumber;`

```
firstNumber    = 234;
secondNumber   = 87;
```

firstNumber [   ]

secondNumber [   ]

The variables **firstNumber** and **secondNumber** are declared and set in memory.

---

after (B) is executed

`int firstNumber, secondNumber;`

(B)
```
firstNumber    = 234;
secondNumber   = 87;
```

firstNumber [234   ]

secondNumber [87   ]

Values are assigned to the variables **firstNumber** and **secondNumber**.

---

declaration and creation illustrated in Figure 2.4 on page 46. Figure 3.2 compares the two. What we have been calling object names are really variables. The only difference between a variable for numbers and a variable for objects is the contents in the memory locations. For numbers, a variable contains the numerical value itself, and for objects, a variable contains an address where the object is stored. We use an arrow in the diagram to indicate that the content is an address, not the value itself.

Figure 3.3 contrasts the effect of assigning the content of one variable to another variable for numerical data values and for objects. Because the content of

FIGURE 3.2   A difference between object declaration and numerical data declaration.

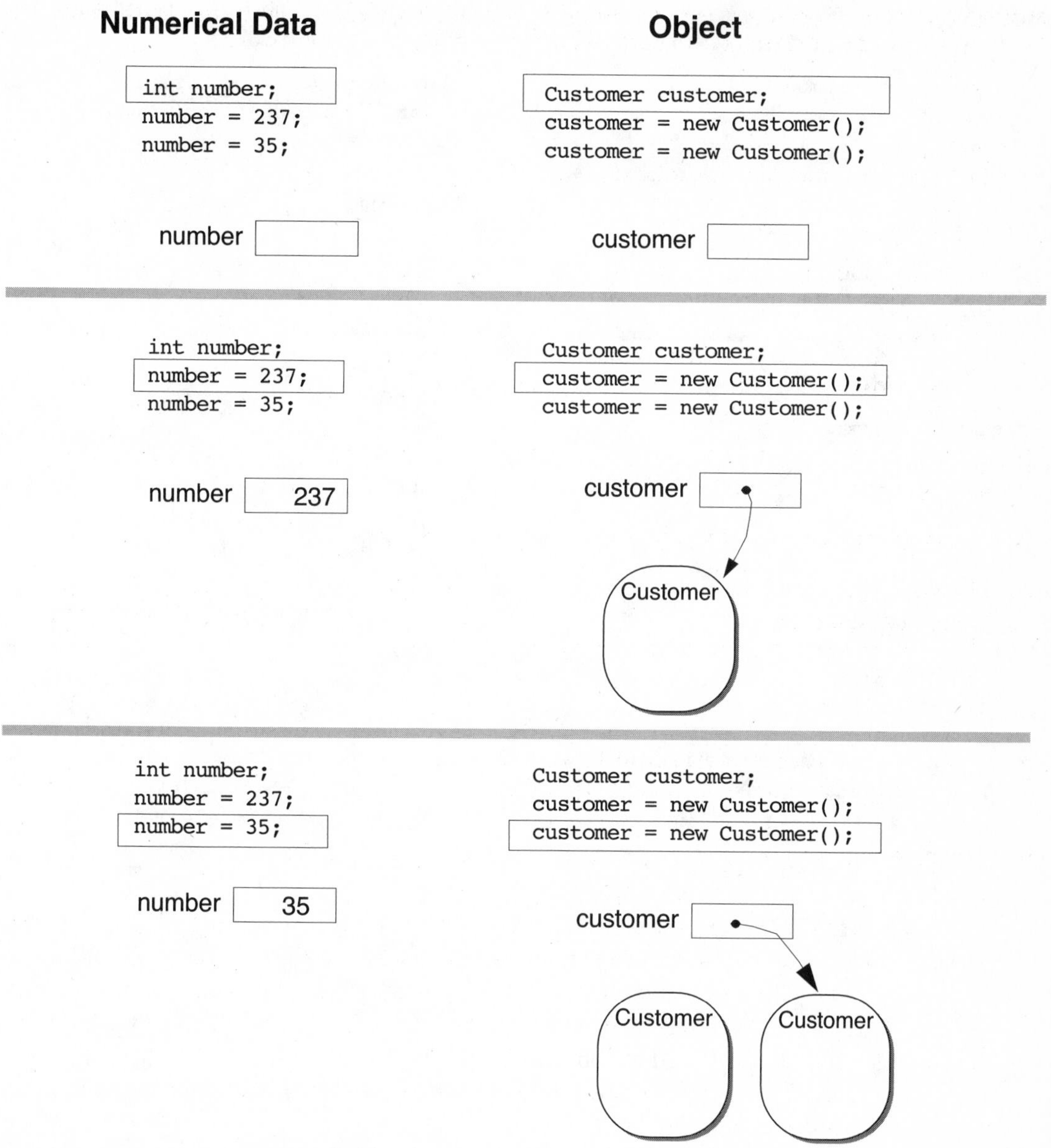

Numerical Data	Object

```
int number;
number = 237;
number = 35;
```

```
Customer customer;
customer = new Customer();
customer = new Customer();
```

number [   ]

customer [   ]

```
int number;
number = 237;
number = 35;
```

```
Customer customer;
customer = new Customer();
customer = new Customer();
```

number [237   ]

customer [•   ]

Customer

```
int number;
number = 237;
number = 35;
```

```
Customer customer;
customer = new Customer();
customer = new Customer();
```

number [35   ]

customer [•   ]

Customer   Customer

FIGURE 3.3   An effect of assigning the content of one variable to another.

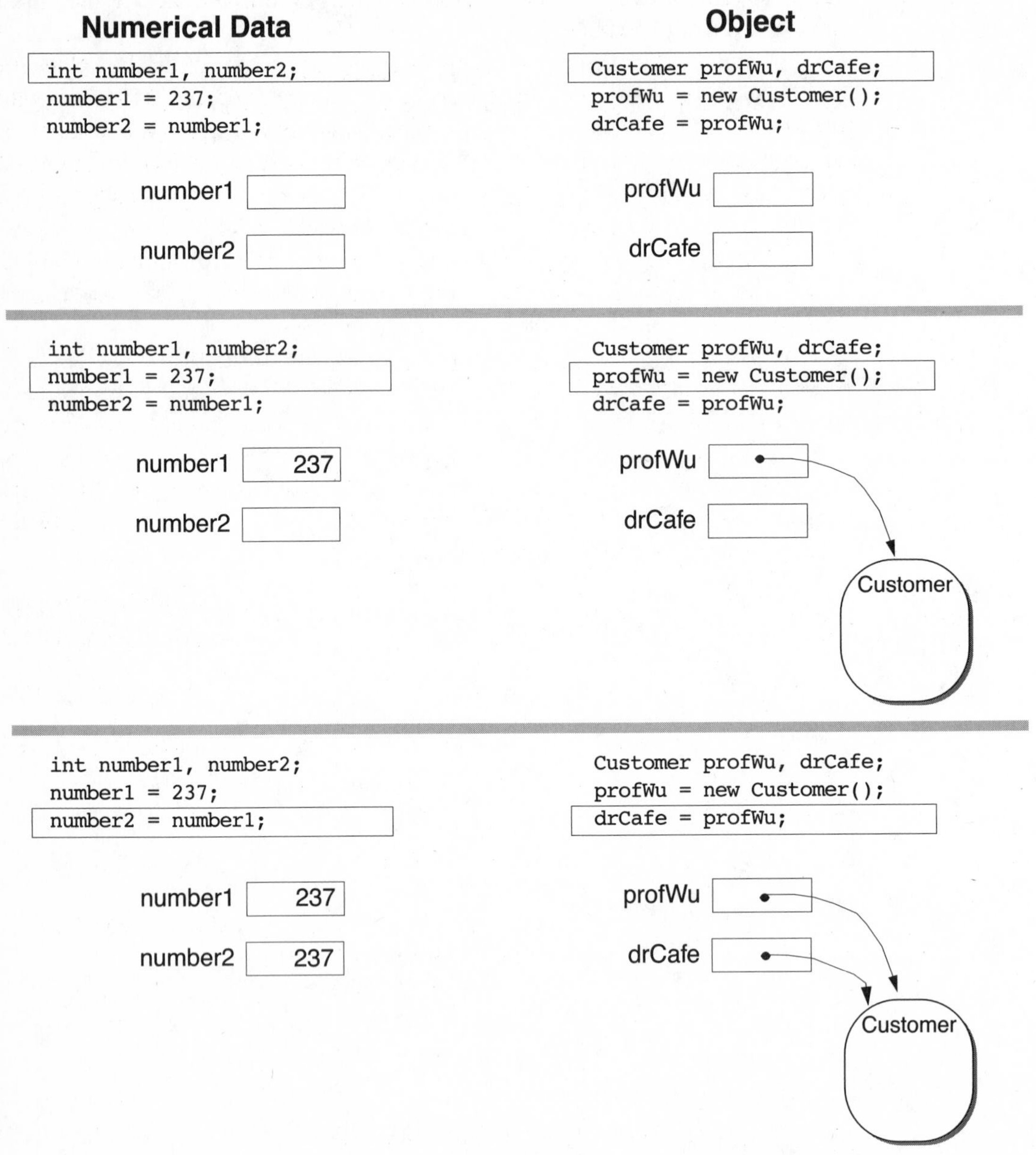

Numerical Data

```
int number1, number2;
number1 = 237;
number2 = number1;
```

number1 [   ]

number2 [   ]

Object

```
Customer profWu, drCafe;
profWu = new Customer();
drCafe = profWu;
```

profWu [   ]

drCafe [   ]

```
int number1, number2;
number1 = 237;
number2 = number1;
```

number1 [237   ]

number2 [   ]

```
Customer profWu, drCafe;
profWu = new Customer();
drCafe = profWu;
```

profWu [•   ]

drCafe [   ]

(Customer)

```
int number1, number2;
number1 = 237;
number2 = number1;
```

number1 [237   ]

number2 [237   ]

```
Customer profWu, drCafe;
profWu = new Customer();
drCafe = profWu;
```

profWu [•   ]

drCafe [•   ]

(Customer)

a variable for objects is an address, assigning the content of a variable to another makes two variables that refer to the same object. Assignment does not create a new object. Without executing the new command, no new object is created. You can view the situation where two variables refer to the same object as the object having two distinct names.

For numbers, the amount of memory space required is fixed. The values for data type int require 4 bytes, for example, and this won't change. However, with objects, the amount of memory space required is not constant. One instance of the Account class may require 120 bytes, while another instance of the same class may require 140 bytes, for example. The difference in space usage for the account objects would occur if we have to keep track of checks written against the accounts. If one account has 15 checks written and the second account has 25 checks written, then we need more memory space for the second account than the first account.

We use the new command to actually create an object. Remember that declaring an object only allocates the variable whose content will be an address. On the other hand, we don't "create" an integer because the space to store the value is already allocated at the time the integer variable is declared. Because the contents are addresses that refer to memory locations where the objects are actually stored, objects are called *reference data types*. In contrast, numerical data types are called *primitive data types*.

reference vs.
primitive
data types

Quick Check

1. Why are the following declarations all invalid?

    ```
    int        a, b, a;
    float      x, int;
    float      w, int x;
    bigNumber  double;
    ```

2. Assuming the following declarations are executed in sequence, why are the second and third declarations invalid?

    ```
    int        a, b;
    int        a;
    float      b;
    ```

3. Name six data types for numerical values.

4. Which of the following are valid assignment statements (assuming the variables are properly declared)?

```
x     =   12;
12    =   x;
y + y =   x;
y     =   x + 12;
```

5. Draw the state-of-memory diagram for the following code:

```
Account latteAcct, expressoAcct;

latteAcct     = new Account();
expressoAcct  = new Account();
latteAcct     = expressoAcct;
```

3.2   Arithmetic Expressions

An expression involving numerical values such as

```
23 + 45
```

operator

is called an *arithmetic expression*, because it consists of arithmetic operators and operands. An *arithmetic operator*, such as + in the example, designates numerical computation. Table 3.2 summarizes the arithmetic operators available in Java.

TABLE 3.2   Arithmetic operators.

Operation	Java Operator	Example	Value (x=10, y=7, z =2.5)
Addition	+	x + y	17
Subtraction	-	x - y	3
Multiplication	*	x * y	70
Division	/	x / y	1
		x / z	4.0
Modulo division (remainder)	%	x % y	3

Notice how the division operator works in Java. When both numbers are integers, the result is an integer quotient. That is, any fractional part is truncated. Division between two integers is called *integer division*. When either or both number are float or double, the result is a real number. Here are some division examples:

integer division

Division Operation	Result
23 / 5	4
23 / 5.0	4.6
25.0 / 5.0	5.0

The modulo operator returns the remainder of a division. Here are some examples:

Modulo Operation	Result
23 % 5	3
23 % 25	23
15.5 % 4	3.5

operand

An *operand* in arithmetic expressions can be a constant, a variable, a method call, or another arithmetic expression, possibly surrounded by parentheses. Let's look at examples. In the expression

```
x + 4
```

binary operator

we have one addition operator and two operands, a variable x and a constant 4. The addition operator is called a *binary operator* because it operates on two operands. All other arithmetic operators, except the minus, are also binary. The minus and plus operators can be both binary and unary. A unary operator operates on one operand as in

```
- x
```

In the expression

```
x + 3 * y
```

subexpression

the addition operator acts on operands x and 3 * y. The right operand for the addition operator is itself an expression. Often a nested expression is called a *subexpression*. The subexpression 3 * y has operands 3 and y. The following diagram illustrates this relationship.

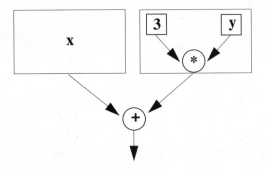

precedence
rules

When two or more operators are present in an expression, we determine the order of evaluation by following the *precedence rules*. For example, multiplication has a higher precedence than addition. Therefore, in the expression x + 3 * y, the multiplication operation is evaluated first, and the addition operation is evaluated next. Table 3.3 summarizes the precedence rules for arithmetic operators.

TABLE 3.3   Precedence rules for arithmetic operators and parentheses.

Order	Group	Operator	Rule
High	subexpression	( )	Subexpressions are evaluated first. If parentheses are nested, the innermost subexpression is evaluated first. If two or more pairs of parentheses are on the same level, then they are evaluated from left to right.
	unary operator	-, +	Unary minuses and pluses are evaluated second.
	multiplicative operator	*, /, %	Multiplicative operators are evaluated third. If two or more multiplicative operators are in an expression, then they are evaluated from left to right.
Low	additive operator	+, -	Additive operators are evaluated last. If two or more additive operators are in an expression, then they are evaluated from left to right.

The following example illustrates the precedence rules applied to a complex arithmetic expression:

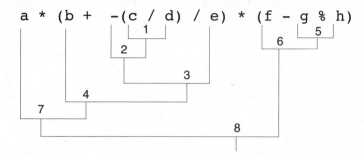

When an arithmetic expression consists of variables and constants of the same data type, then the result of the expression will be that data type also. For example, if the data type of a and b is int, then the result of the expression

```
a * b + 23
```

is also an int. When the data types of variables and constants in an arithmetic expression are of different data types, then a casting conversion will take place. A *casting conversion*, or *type casting*, is a process that converts a value of one data type to another data type. Two types of casting conversions in Java are *implicit* and *explicit*. An implicit conversion called *numeric promotion* is applied to the operands of an arithmetic operator. The promotion is based on the rules stated in Table 3.4. This conversion is called promotion because the operand is converted from a lower to a higher precision.

type casting

numeric promotion

TABLE 3.4   Rules for arithmetic promotion.

Operator Type	Promotion Rule
Unary	1. If the operand is of type byte or short, then it is converted to int.
	2. Otherwise, the operand remains the same type.
Binary	1. If either operand is of type double, then the other operand is converted to double.
	2. Otherwise, if either operand is of type float, then the other operand is converted to float.
	3. Otherwise, if either operand is of type long, then the other operand is converted to long.
	4. Otherwise, both operands are converted to int.

Instead of relying on implicit conversion, we can use explicit conversion to convert an operand from one data type to another. Explicit conversion is applied to an operand by using a *type cast operator*. For example, to convert the int variable x in the expression

type cast
operator

```
x / 3
```

to float so the result will not be truncated, we apply the type cast operator (float) as

```
(float) x / 3
```

The syntax is

type casting
syntax

```
( <data type> ) <expression>
```

The type cast operator is a unary operator and has a precedence higher than any binary operator. You must use parentheses to type cast a subexpression; for example, the expression

```
a + (double) (x + y * z)
```

will result in the subexpression x + y * z type casted to double.

Assuming the variable x is an int, then the assignment statement

```
x = 2 * (14343 / 2344);
```

will assign the integer result of the expression to the variable x. However, if the data type of x is other than int, then an implicit conversion will occur so the data type of the expression becomes the same as the data type of the variable. An *assignment conversion* is another implicit conversion that occurs when the variable and the value of an expression in an assignment statement are not of the same data type. An assignment conversion occurs only if the data type of the variable has a higher precision than the data type of the expression's value. For example,

assignment
conversion

```
double number;
number = 25;
```

is valid, but

```
int number;
number = 234.56;
```

is not.

If we wish to assign a value to multiple variables, we can cascade the assignment operations as

```
x = y = 1;
```

which is equivalent to saying

```
y = 1;
x = 1;
```

The assignment symbol = is actually an operator and its precedence order is lower than any other operators. Assignment operators are evaluated right to left.

Dr. Caffeine

Quick Check

1. Evaluate the following expressions:

   a. 3 + 5 / 7
   b. 3 * 3 + 3 % 2
   c. 3 + 2 / 5 + -2 * 4
   d. 2 * (1 + -(3/4) / 2) * (2 - 6 % 3)

2. What is the data type of the result of the following expressions?

   a. (3 + 5) / 7
   b. (3 + 5) / (float) 7
   c. (float) ((3 + 2) / 7)

3.3   Constants

constant

While running a program, different values may be assigned to a variable at different times (thus the name *variable*, since the values it contains can *vary*), but in some cases we do not want this to happen. In other words, we want to "lock" the assigned value so that no changes can take place. If we want a value to remain fixed, then we use a *constant*. A constant is declared in a manner similar to a variable but with the additional reserved word final. A constant must be initialized at the time of declaration. Here's an example declaring four constants:

```
final double  PI = 3.1416;
final short   FARADAY_CONSTANT = 23060; // unit is cal/volt
final double  CM_PER_INCH = 2.34;
final int     MONTHS_IN_YEAR = 12;
```

We use the standard Java convention to name a constant using only capital letters and underscores. Judicious use of constants makes programs more readable. You will be seeing many uses of constants later in the book, beginning with the sample program in this chapter.

named constant

literal constant

The constant PI is called a *named* or *symbolic constant*. We refer to symbolic constants with identifiers such as PI and FARADAY_CONSTANT. The second type of constant is called a *literal constant*, and we refer to it using an actual value. For example, the following statements contain three literal constants:

```
final double  PI     = 3.1415  ;
float area;
area = 2 * PI * 345.79 ;
```

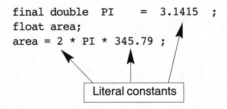

Literal constants

When we use the literal constant 2, the data type of the constant is set to int by default. Then how can we specify a literal constant of type long?[1] We append the constant with an l (a lowercase letter *L*) or L as

---

1. In most cases, it is not significant to distinguish the two because of automatic type conversion; see Section 3.2.

```
2L * PI * 345.79
```

How about the literal constant 345.79? Since the literal constant contains a decimal point, its data type can only be float or double. But which one? The answer is double. If a literal constant contains a decimal point, then it is of type double by default. To designate a literal constant of type float, we must append the letter f or F. For example:

```
2 * PI * 345.79F
```

To represent a double literal constant, we may optionally append a d or D. So, the following two constants are equivalent:

```
2 * PI * 345.79
```
is equivalent to   `2 * PI * 345.79D`

We can also express float and double literal constants in scientific notation

$$number \times 10^{exponent}$$

which in Java is expressed as

exponential
notation in Java   `<number> E <exponent>`

where <number> is a literal constant that may or may not contain a decimal point and <exponent> is a signed or unsigned integer. Lowercase e may be substituted for the exponent symbol E. The whole expression may be suffixed by f, F, d, or D. The <number> itself cannot be suffixed with symbols f, F, d, or D. Here are some examples:

```
12.40e+209
23E33
29.0098e-102
234e+5D
4.45e2
```

Here are some additional examples of constant declarations:

```
final double SPEED_OF_LIGHT = 3.0E+10D; // unit is cm/sec
final short  MAX_WGT_ALLOWED = 400;
```

3.4   The Math Class

Using only the arithmetic operators to express numerical computations is very limiting. Many computations require the use of mathematical functions. For example, to express the mathematical formula

$$\frac{1}{2}\sin\left(x - \frac{\pi}{\sqrt{y}}\right)$$

we need the trigonometric sine and square root functions. The Math class in the java.lang package contains class methods for commonly used mathematical functions. Table 3.5 is a partial list of class methods available in the Math class. The class also has two class constants PI and E for π and the natural number e. Using the Math class constant and methods, we can express the preceding formula as

```
(1.0 /2.0) * Math.sin( x - Math.PI / Math.sqrt(y) )
```

Notice how the class methods and class constants are referred to in the expression. The syntax is

```
<class name> . <method name>
```

or

```
<class name> . <class constant>
```

TABLE 3.5   **Math** class methods for commonly used mathematical functions.

Class Method	Argument Type	Result Type	Description	Example
abs(a)	int	int	Returns the absolute int value of **a.**	abs(10) → 10 abs(-5) → 5
	long	long	Returns the absolute long value of **a.**	
	float	float	Returns the absolute float value of **a.**	

TABLE 3.5   **Math** class methods for commonly used mathematical functions. (Continued)

Class Method	Argument Type	Result Type	Description	Example
acos(a)[†]	double	double	Returns the arc cosine of **a**.	acos(-1) → 3.14159
asin(a)[†]	double	double	Returns the arc sine of **a**.	asin(1) → 1.57079
atan(a)[†]	double	double	Returns the arc tangent of **a**.	atan(1) → 0.785398
ceil(a)	double	double	Returns the smallest whole number greater than or equal to **a**.	ceil(5.6) → 6.0 ceil(5.0) → 5.0 ceil(-5.6) → -5.0
cos(a)[†]	double	double	Returns the trigonometric cosine of **a**.	cos(π/2) →0.0
exp(a)	double	double	Returns the natural number e (2.718...) raised to the power of **a**.	exp(2) → 7.389056099
floor(a)	double	double	Returns the largest whole number less than or equal to **a**.	floor(5.6) → 5.0 floor(5.0) → 5.0 floor(-5.6)→ -6.0
log(a)	double	double	Returns the natural logarithm (base e) of **a**.	log(100) → 2.0
max(a, b)	int	int	Returns the larger of **a** and **b**.	max(10, 20) → 20
	long	long	Same as above.	
	float	float	Same as above.	
min(a, b)	int	int	Returns the smaller of **a** and **b**.	min(10, 20) → 10
	long	long	Same as above.	
	float	float	Same as above.	
pow(a, b)	double	double	Returns the number **a** raised to the power of **b**.	pow(2.0, 3.0) → 8.0
random( )	<no argu­ment>	double	Generates a random number greater than or equal to 0.0 and less than 1.0	Examples given in Chapter 6.

TABLE 3.5   **Math** class methods for commonly used mathematical functions. (Continued)

Class Method	Argument Type	Result Type	Description	Example
round(a)	float	int	Returns the int value of **a** rounded to the nearest whole number.	round(5.6) → 6 round(5.4) → 5 round(−5.6) → −6
	double	long	Returns the float value of **a** rounded to the nearest whole number.	
sin(a)†	double	double	Returns the trigonometric sine of **a**.	sin(π/2) → 1.0
sqrt(a)	double	double	Returns the square root of **a**.	sqrt(9.0) → 3.0
tan(a)†	double	double	Returns the trigonometric tangent of **a**.	tan(π/4) → 1.0

† All trigonometric functions are computed in radians.

Quick Check

1. What's wrong with the following?

    a. y = (1/2) * Math.sqrt(X) ;

    b. y = sqrt(38.0);

    c. y = Math.exp(2, 3);

    d. y = math.sqrt(b*b - 4*a*c) / (2 * a);

2. If another programmer writes the following statements, do you suspect any misunderstanding on the part of this programmer? What will be the value of y?

    a. y = Math.sin(360) ;

    b. y = Math.cos(45);

3.5   InputBox

We mentioned at the beginning of the chapter that computer programs include the three tasks of input, computation, and output. We explained how to implement numerical computation in Java using arithmetic expressions and assignment statements. We will now introduce two new dialog classes from the javabook package in this chapter: InputBox, which is used for input in this section, and OutputBox, which is used for output in the next section.

Like MessageBox, an InputBox object is a dialog, which means we must specify an owner frame when we create the object. As before, we will use Main-Window as its owner. Here's how we declare and create an InputBox object:

InputBox
declaration and
creation

```
InputBox inputBox;
inputBox = new InputBox(mainWindow);
```

getInteger

To input an integer, we send the getInteger message to an InputBox object as

```
inputBox.getInteger();
```

Executing the getInteger method will display the input dialog box shown in Figure 3.4.

FIGURE 3.4   The **InputBox** dialog after its method **getInteger** is executed.

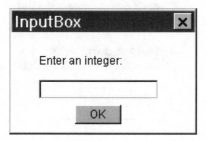

The getInteger method will only accept an integer. When the user enters a value other than an integer (e.g., a number with a decimal point or nondigit

characters), an error message is displayed, as shown in Figure 3.5. Also, the input dialog box cannot be closed until a valid integer is entered.

FIGURE 3.5   The **InputBox** dialog after a noninteger value is entered by the user.

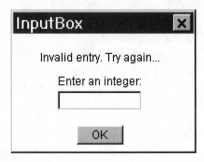

A better interface would include a meaningful prompt to inform the user what is expected. We can optionally pass text as a prompt. For example, executing the message

```
inputBox.getInteger("Enter your age:");
```

will result in the InputBox shown in Figure 3.6.

FIGURE 3.6   An **InputBox** object with a programmer-specified prompt.

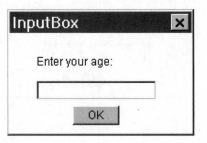

getFloat

To input real numbers, we use the getFloat method. This method works just like getInteger. If we call the getFloat method, then the InputBox object will not close until the user enters a valid real number (a number with or without a decimal point).

To use an input value in a program, we will save it to a variable first as in

```
int    birthYear;
birthYear = inputBox.getInteger("You were born in (eg 1980):");
```

The following code inputs the width and length of a rectangle and computes the area:

```
float  width, length, area;
width  = inputBox.getFloat("Enter the width of a rectangle");
length = inputBox.getFloat("Enter the length of a rectangle");
area   = width * length;
```

Table 3.6 is a partial list of available InputBox methods.

TABLE 3.6   A partial list of **InputBox** methods.

CLASS:	InputBox	
Method	**Argument**	**Description**
getFloat	\<none\> or text	Allows the user to enter a real number, a number with or without a decimal point. The InputBox dialog object will not close until the user enters a valid real number. If there is no argument, then the default prompt Enter a Float is displayed in the dialog. If a text value is passed as the argument, then it is used as a prompt in the dialog.
getInteger	\<none\> or text	Allows the user to enter an integer, a number without a decimal point. The InputBox dialog object will not close until the user enters a valid integer. If there is no argument, then the default prompt Enter an Integer is displayed in the dialog. If a text value is passed as the argument, then it is used as a prompt in the dialog.

Quick Check

1. What is the difference between the code in (a) and (b)?

    ```
    a.  int age = 10;
        messageBox.show( age );
    ```

    ```
    b.  messageBox.show( "age" );
    ```

2. Will the following code work?

    ```
    messageBox.show( 345 );
    messageBox.show( 12.33 );
    ```

3.6   OutputBox

In this section, we will explain the third dialog class from the javabook package called OutputBox. We already know one dialog class that is used for output. To output a value, we can use a MessageBox object. We used a MessageBox object to display a text as in

```
messageBox.show("Java is fun");
```

We can use it to display an integer or real number also, as in

```
birthYear = inputBox.getInteger("You were born in (eg 1980):");
messageBox.show( birthYear );
```

However, the purpose of MessageBox is to display a short message, such as an error or warning message. It is never intended to display the whole output of a program. For example, a single MessageBox is not capable of displaying more than one line of text, such as

```
You are born in 1980.
In year 2000, you will be 20 years old.
```

> In object-oriented programming, efficient and effective program development hinges on the appropriate use of classes. You must use a class for its intended purpose just as you use the most appropriate tool for a given task. When you want to build a deck, you would use a circular saw for cutting, but when you want to build a birdhouse, you would probably use a more precision-cutting jigsaw. A key to successful object-oriented programming is to learn how to select the most appropriate class for a given task. Later, you will learn how to design a new class if no suitable class is available.

Dr. Caffeine

An OutputBox object is intended for displaying such output that contains textual data (i.e., no drawings). Like the other dialogs MessageBox and Input-Box, we must specify the owner frame at the time we create an instance of Out-putBox. Here's how we declare and create an OutputBox object whose owner is a MainWindow object:

OutputBox declaration and creation

```
OutputBox  outputBox;
outputBox = new OutputBox(mainWindow);
```

For the following examples, we assume the objects mainWindow, inputBox, and outputBox are properly created. We also assume that both mainWindow and outputBox are made visible by executing

```
mainWindow.show();
outputBox.show();
```

The method print displays an argument in an OutputBox object. For example, executing the code

```
outputBox.print("Hello, Dr. Caffeine.");
```

will result in the OutputBox object shown in Figure 3.7.

The print method will continue printing from the end of the currently displayed output. Executing the following statements after the preceding print message will result in the OutputBox object shown in Figure 3.8.

FIGURE 3.7   Result of executing **outputBox.print("Hello, Dr. Caffeine.")**.

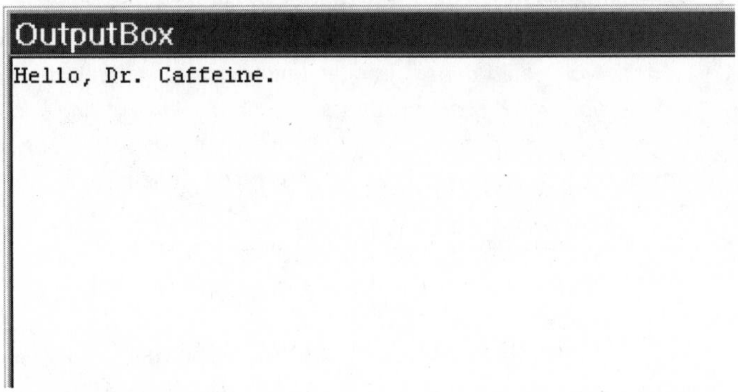

```
OutputBox
Hello, Dr. Caffeine.
```

FIGURE 3.8   Result of sending five **print** messages to **outputBox** of Figure 3.7.

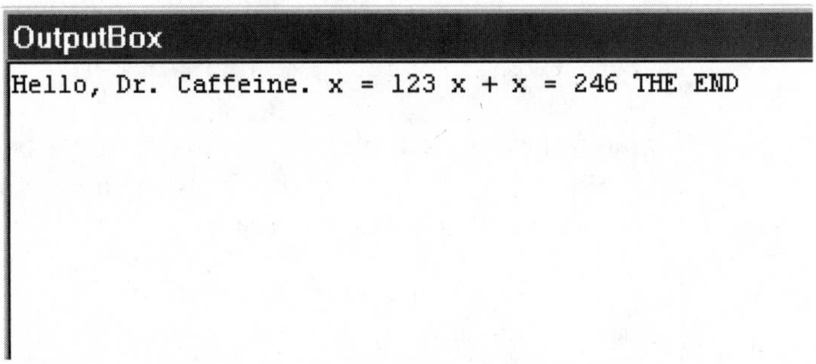

```
OutputBox
Hello, Dr. Caffeine. x = 123 x + x = 246 THE END
```

```
int x, y;
x = 123;
y = x + x;
outputBox.print(" x = ");
outputBox.print( x );
outputBox.print(" x + x = ");
outputBox.print( y );
outputBox.print(" THE END");
```

Notice that we have a space here so there will be a blank space between the equal sign and the number in the output.

We can print an argument and skip to the next line so that subsequent output will start on the next line by sending printLine instead of print. The OutputBox object of Figure 3.9 will result if we use printLine instead of print in the preceding example, that is

```
int x, y;
x = 123;
y = x + x;
outputBox.printLine("Hello, Dr. Caffeine.");
outputBox.print(" x = ");
outputBox.printLine( x );
outputBox.print(" x + x = ");
outputBox.printLine( y );
outputBox.printLine(" THE END");
```

print here,
not printLine.

FIGURE 3.9   Result of sending four **printLine** messages to **outputBox**.

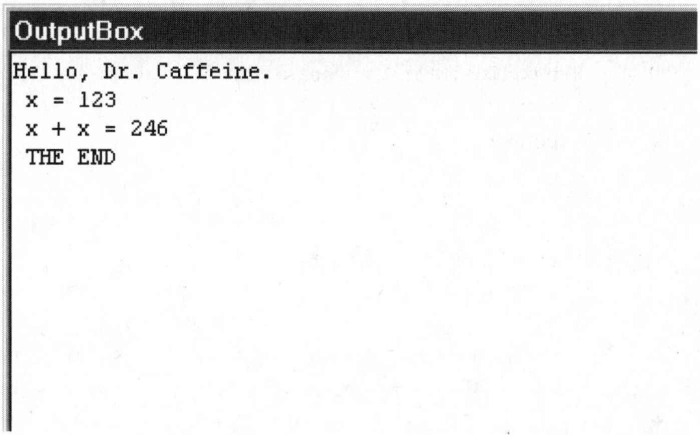

```
OutputBox
Hello, Dr. Caffeine.
 x = 123
 x + x = 246
 THE END
```

You can also print a specified number of blank lines with the skipLine message. For example:

```
outputBox.printLine("one");
outputBox.skipLine(2);
outputBox.printLine("two");
```

will leave two blank lines between the output lines displaying one and two. Notice that if you execute

```
outputBox.print("one");
outputBox.skipLine(2);
outputBox.printLine("two");
```

there will be only one blank line in the output.

Now suppose we want to let the user enter his/her age and display

```
You are <age> years old.
```

where <age> is replaced by the actual value entered by the user. Instead of executing

```
int age;
age = inputBox.getInteger();
outputBox.print("You are ");
outputBox.print( age );
outputBox.print(" years old.");
```

we can execute

```
int age;
age = inputBox.getInteger();
outputBox.print("You are " + age + " years old.");
```

In Java and many other programming languages, the same symbols are sometimes used for different purposes. The two plus symbols that appear in the show message are not arithmetic additions, but concatenation of values. The variable age contains an integer and this integer value is concatenated with the text "You are " and " years old" to its left and right. Notice the blank spaces after *are* and before *years*. If you don't put in these blank spaces, you would see an output like

```
You are20years old.
```

instead of

```
You are 20 years old.
```

The plus symbol in Java can signify either an arithmetic addition or a concatenation of values. A symbol that is used to represent more than one operation is called an *overloaded operator*. When the Java compiler encounters an overloaded operator, how does it know which operation the symbol represents? The Java compiler determines the meaning of a symbol by its context. If the left and the right operand of the plus symbol are numerical values, then the compiler will treat the symbol as addition. Otherwise, it will treat the symbol as concatenation. The plus symbol operator is evaluated from left to right, and the result of concatenation is a text, so the code

```
x = 1;
y = 2;
outputBox.print( "test" + x + y );
```

will result in the output

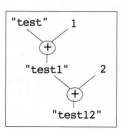

```
test12
```

while the code

```
outputBox.print( x + y + "test" );
```

will result in the output

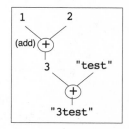

```
3test
```

You can store the text displayed in an OutputBox object to a file by specifying the filename as an argument to the saveToFile message. For example, to save the contents to a file called prog1out.txt, you execute

```
outputBox.saveToFile( "prog1out.txt" );
```

You can pass any valid filename, surrounded by double quotes, as an argument to the method. If the designated file already exists, then its current contents will be erased with the contents of outputBox. If you want to keep the current contents of the file and add the contents of outputBox to the end of the file, you use the appendToFile method

```
outputBox.appendToFile( "prog1out.txt" );
```

Once the text data are stored in the file, you can open the file using any text editor and print them. This is one way for you to get a hardcopy of the program output so you can submit it as a part of the program assignment. The second way to get a hardcopy is by taking a screen capture. (Note: Please consult our Web site or your instructor for more information on how to take a screen capture.)

Table 3.7 is a partial list of OutputBox methods.

TABLE 3.7   A partial list of **OutputBox** methods.

CLASS:	OutputBox	
Method	**Argument**	**Description**
print	number or text	Prints out the number or text passed as an argument in the dialog. Printing will continue from the end of currently displayed output.
printLine	number or text	Same as the print method, but the line is skipped after the output so the next output will continue from the next line.
skipLine	integer	Skips N lines where N is an integer passed as an argument.
saveToFile	filename	Saves the contents of an OutputBox to a file whose name is passed as an argument. If the designated file already exists, then the current contents of the file are erased and replaced by the contents of the OutputBox.
appendToFile	filename	Appends the contents of an OutputBox to a file whose name is passed as an argument. If the designated file does not exist, then this method works like the saveToFile method.

1. What's wrong with the following?

    a. ```
        int age = 10;
        outputBox.show(age);
        ```

    b.  ```
        int age = 20;
        outputBox.print( "Your age is age" );
        ```

2. Will the following code work?

    ```
    age = 20;
    messageBox.show( "Your age is " + age );
    ```

3. Write a code (not a full program) to input the year of birth and output

    ```
    You are born in 1980.
    In year 2000, you will be 20 years old.
    ```

3.7 Sample Program: Loan Calculator

In this section, we will develop a simple loan calculator program. We will develop this program using an incremental development technique, which will develop the program in small incremental steps. We start out with a barebone program and gradually build up the program by adding more and more code to it. At each incremental step, we design, code, and test the program before moving on to the next step. This methodical development of a program allows us to focus our attention on a single task at each step, and this reduces the chance of introducing errors into the program.

Problem Statement

Next time you buy a new TV or a stereo, watch out for those "0% down, 0% interest till next July" deals. Read the fine print, and you'll notice that if you don't make the full payment by the end of a certain date, a hefty interest will start accruing. You may be better off to get an ordinary loan from the beginning with a cheaper interest rate. What matters most is the total payment (loan amount + total interest) you'll have to make. To compare different loan deals, let's develop a loan calculator. Here's the problem statement:

Write a loan calculator program that computes both monthly and total payments for a given loan amount, annual interest rate, and loan period.

Overall Plan

Our first task is to map out the overall plan for development. We will identify classes necessary for the program and the steps we will follow to implement the program. We begin with the outline of program logic. For a simple program such as this one, it is kind of obvious, but to practice the incremental development, let's put down the outline of program flow explicitly. We can express the program flow as having three tasks:

*program
tasks*

1.   Get three input values: loanPayment, interestRate, and loanPeriod.
2.   Compute the monthly and total payments.
3.   Output the results.

Having identified the three major tasks of the program, we will now identify the classes we can use to implement the three tasks. First, we need an object to handle the input of three values. At this point, we have only learned about the InputBox class, so we will use it here. Second, we need an object to display the monthly and total payments. We can use either MessageBox or OutputBox. Since a MessageBox object is capable of only displaying one line of text, we will use an OutputBox object, so we can display both results along with the input values for a better output. Finally, we need to consider how we are going to compute the monthly and total payments. There are no objects in standard packages or javabook that will do the computation, so we have to write our own code to do the computation.

The formula for computing the monthly payment can be found in any mathematics book that covers geometric sequences. Its formula is

$$\text{Monthly Payment} = \frac{L \times R}{\left[1 - \left(\frac{1}{1+R}\right)^{N}\right]}$$

where L is the loan amount, R is the monthly interest rate, and N is the number of payments. The monthly rate R is expressed in a fractional value, e.g., 0.01 for

1 percent monthly rate. Once the monthly payment is derived, the total payment can be determined by multiplying the monthly payment and the number of months the payment is made. Since the formula includes exponentiation, we will have to use the pow method of the Math class.

Finally, we need a top-level window for the application, so we will use the only top-level window we have learned so far—a MainWindow object. We will use these objects from the main class, which we will call LoanCalculator. Let's summarize these in a design document:

program
classes

Design Document:	LoanCalculator
Class	**Purpose**
LoanCalculator	The main class of the program.
MainWindow	The main frame window of the program. The title is set to Loan Calculator. This class is from javabook.
InputBox	An InputBox object is used to get three input values: loan amount, annual interest rate, and loan period. This class is from javabook.
OutputBox	An OutputBox object is used to display the input values and two computed results: monthly payment and total payment. This class is from javabook.
Math	The pow method is used to evaluate exponentiation in the formula for computing the monthly payment. This class is from java.lang. Note: You don't have to import java.lang. The classes in java.lang are available to a program without importing.

The object diagram of the program based on the classes listed in the design document is shown in Figure 3.10. Keep in mind that this is only a preliminary design. Although we are not going to see any changes made to this design document because this sample application is very simple, changes to the design document are expected as the programs we develop become larger and more complex. The preliminary document is really a working document that we will modify and expand as we progress through the development steps.

Before we can actually start our development, we must sketch the steps we will follow to implement the program. There are more than one possible sequence of steps to implement a program, and the number of possible sequences will increase as the program becomes more complex. For this program, we will implement the program in the following four steps:

FIGURE 3.10   The object diagram for the program **LoanCalculator**.

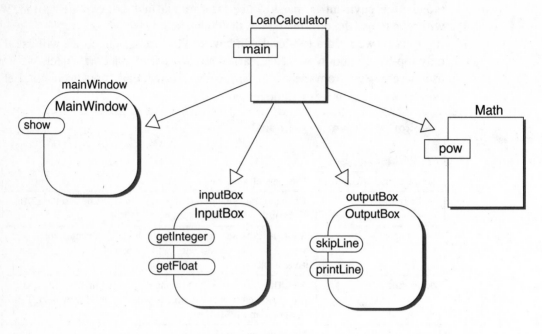

1. Start with a program skeleton. In this step, we write a program skeleton that includes only object/variable declaration and object creation.

2. Add code to accept three input values.

3. Add code to output the results.

4. Add code to compute the monthly and total payments.

Notice how the four steps are defined. The first step is used to verify that the objects we need to use in the program are declared and created properly. The remaining three steps deals with the input, output, and computation aspects of the program.

The first step is almost the same for all programs. For the last three steps, any order is feasible. So why did we choose this particular order? The main reason is our desire to defer the most difficult task till the end. It's possible, but if we implement the computation part in the second incremental step, then we need to code some temporary output routines to verify that the computation is done correctly. However, if we implement the real output routines before implementing the computation routines, then there is no need for us to worry about temporary output routines. As for Step 2 and Step 3, their relative order does not matter much. We simply chose to implement the input routine before the output routine because input comes before output in the program.

Step 1 Development: Program Skeleton

Step 1 Design   The design aspect of Step 1 is almost always trivial, especially for the sample programs from early chapters. All we need to do is to design the skeleton for the main class of the program.

Step 1 Code   We begin with a program skeleton. Here's the skeleton:

```
/*
    Program LoanCalculator (Step 1)

    A program to compute the monthly and total payments for a given loan
    amount, annual interest rate, and number of years.

    Input:      loan amount (float)
                annual interest rate (float)
                loan period - number of years (int)

    Compute:    monthly payment (float)
                total payment (float)
*/

import javabook.*;

class LoanCalculator
{
    public static void main (String args[])
    {
        MainWindow   mainWindow   = new MainWindow("Program LoanCalculator");
        InputBox     inputBox     = new InputBox(mainWindow);
        OutputBox    outputBox    = new OutputBox(mainWindow);
        mainWindow.show();
        outputBox.show();
    }
}
```

> No **import** statement is necessary for the **java.lang** package. It is available to every program by default.

Step 1 Test   The skeleton program may seem so trivial and not so useful, but it does serve a very useful purpose. Successful execution of this skeleton verifies that the program setup is okay, the necessary packages are imported, and the objects are declared correctly. After the Step 1 program is compiled and executed correctly, we move on to Step 2.

Step 2 Development: Accept Input Values

Step 2 Design   The next task is to determine how we will accept the input values. We will use the InputBox class we learned in this chapter. A single InputBox object is used to accept three input values: loan amount, annual interest rate, and loan period. The problem statement does not specify the exact format of input, so we will decide that now. Based on how people normally refer to loans, the input values will be accepted in the following format:

Input	Format	Data Type
Loan amount	In dollars and cents (e.g., 15000.00)	float
Annual interest rate	In percent (e.g., 12.5)	float
Loan period	In years (e.g., 30)	int

Notice that we need to convert the annual interest rate to the monthly interest rate and the input value loan period to the number of monthly payments to use the given formula. In this case, the conversion is very simple, but even if the conversion routines were more complicated, we must do the conversion. It is not acceptable to ask users to enter an input value that is unnatural to them. For example, people do not think of interest rates in fractional values such as 0.07. They think of interest in terms of percentage such as 7%. Computer programs work for humans, not the other way around. Programs we develop should not support an interface that is difficult and awkward for humans to use.

When the user inputs an invalid value, for example, a negative loan amount, the program should respond accordingly, such as by printing an error message. We do not possess enough skills to implement such a robust program yet, so we will make the following assumptions: (1) the input values are nonnegative and (2) the loan period is a whole number.

One important objective of this step is to verify that the input values are read in correctly by the program. To verify this, we will use an OutputBox to print out the values accepted by the InputBox object. This method of printing out
echo printing   the values just entered is called *echo printing*. Since we are going to use an OutputBox in the final program, we will use it for echo printing in this step. In the next chapter, we will explain another technique for echo printing that uses an object from a standard Java package.

Step 2 Code   Here's our Step 2 program with the added portion surrounded by a rectangle:

```
/*
    Program LoanCalculator (Step 2)
```

```
    A program to compute the monthly and total payments for a given loan
    amount, annual interest rate, and number of years.

    Input:      loan amount (float)
                annual interest rate (float)
                loan period - number of years (int)

    Compute:    monthly payment (float)
                total payment (float)
*/

import javabook.*;

class LoanCalculator
{
    public static void main (String args[])
    {
        MainWindow mainWindow    = new MainWindow("Program LoanCalculator");
        InputBox   inputBox      = new InputBox(mainWindow);
        OutputBox  outputBox     = new OutputBox(mainWindow);
        mainWindow.show();
        outputBox.show();
```

```
        float loanAmount, annualInterestRate;
        int   loanPeriod;

        //get input
        loanAmount          = inputBox.getFloat("Loan Amount (Dollars&Cents):");
        annualInterestRate  = inputBox.getFloat("Annual Interest Rate (eg 9.5):");
        loanPeriod          = inputBox.getInteger("Loan Period - # of years:");

        //echo print the input values
        outputBox.printLine("Loan Amount:          $" + loanAmount);
        outputBox.printLine("Annual Interest Rate: " + annualInterestRate + "%");
        outputBox.printLine("Loan Period (years):   " + loanPeriod);
```

```
    }
}
```

Step 2 Test   To verify the input routine is working correctly, we run the program multiple times and enter different sets of data. We enter invalid data and make sure the InputBox object accepts only the values of correct data type. We make sure the values are displayed in outputBox as entered.

Step 3 Development: Output Values

Step 3 Design   The third step is to add code to display the output values. We will use the OutputBox class we learned in this chapter for displaying output values. We need to display the result in a layout that is meaningful and easy to read. Just displaying numbers such as the following is totally unacceptable.

```
132.151  15858.1
```

We must label the output values so the user can tell what the numbers represent. In addition, we must display the input values with the computed result so it will not be meaningless. Imagine the user did many different loan calculations and saved the results. When he refers back to the loan figures some time later, which one of the two shown in Figure 3.11 do you think is more meaningful to him?

FIGURE 3.11   Two different display formats: one with input values displayed and the other with only the computed values displayed.

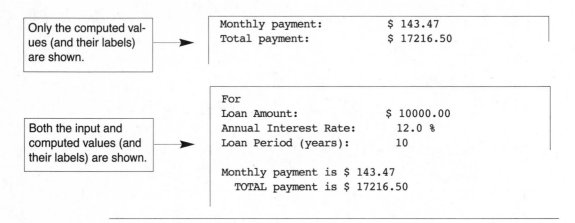

The output format of this program will be

```
For
Loan Amount:              $ <amount>
Annual Interest Rate:        <annual interest rate> %
Loan Period (years):         <year>

Monthly payment is $ <monthly payment>
   TOTAL payment is $ <total payment>
```

with <amount>, <annual interest rate>, and others replaced by the actual figures.

Since the computations for the monthly and total payments are not yet implemented, we will use the following dummy assignment statements:

```
monthlyPayment    = 135.15;
totalPayment      = 15858.10;
```

We will replace these statements with the real ones in the next step.

Step 3 Code   Here's our Step 3 program:

```
/*
    Program LoanCalculator (Step 3)

    A program to compute the monthly and total payments for a given loan
    amount, annual interest rate, and number of years.

    Input:    loan amount (float)
              annual interest rate (float)
              loan period - number of years (int)

    Compute:  monthly payment (float)
              total payment (float)
*/

import javabook.*;

class ComputeMonthlyPayment
{
    public static void main (String args[])
    {
        MainWindow mainWindow      = new MainWindow("Program LoanCalculator");
        InputBox   inputBox        = new InputBox(mainWindow);
        OutputBox  outputBox       = new OutputBox(mainWindow);
        mainWindow.show();
        outputBox.show();

        float   loanAmount, annualInterestRate;
        int     loanPeriod;

        double monthlyPayment,
               totalPayment;

        //describe the program
        outputBox.printLine("This program computes the monthly and total");
        outputBox.printLine("payments for a given loan amount, annual ");
        outputBox.printLine("interest rate, and loan period.");
        outputBox.printLine("Loan Amount in dollars and cents, e.g. 12350.50");
        outputBox.printLine("Annual interest rate in percentage, e.g. 12.75");
        outputBox.printLine("Loan period in number of years, e.g. 15");
        outputBox.skipLine(2);
```

```
            //get input
            loanAmount         = inputBox.getFloat("Loan Amount (Dollars&Cents):");
            annualInterestRate = inputBox.getFloat("Annual Interest Rate (eg 9.5):");
            loanPeriod         = inputBox.getInteger("Loan Period - # of years:");
```

```
            //compute the monthly payment
            monthlyPayment   = 132.15;        //Temporary code
            totalPayment     = 15858.10 ;     //Temporary code

            //display the result
            outputBox.printLine("For");
            outputBox.printLine("Loan Amount:           $" + loanAmount);
            outputBox.printLine("Annual Interest Rate: " + annualInterestRate + "%");
            outputBox.printLine("Loan Period (years):   " + loanPeriod);
            outputBox.skipLine(1);

            outputBox.printLine("Monthly payment is $ " + monthlyPayment);
            outputBox.printLine("  TOTAL payment is $ "  + totalPayment);
```

```
       }
   }
```

Step 3 Test   To verify the output routine is working correctly, we run the program and verify
                   the layout. Most likely, we have to run the program several times to fine-tune the
                   arguments for the printLine methods until we get the layout that looks clean and
                   nice on the screen.

Step 4 Development: Compute Loan Amount

Step 4 Design   To verify the input routine is working correctly, we run the program multiple
                   times and enter different sets of data. We enter invalid data and make sure the In-
                   putBox object accepts only the values of correct data type. We make sure the
                   values are displayed in outputBox as entered. We are now ready to complete the
                   program by implementing the formula derived in the design phase. The formula
                   requires the monthly interest rate and the number of monthly payments. The in-
                   put values to the program, however, are the annual interest rate and the loan pe-
                   riod in number of years. So we need to convert the annual interest rate to a
                   monthly interest rate and the loan period to the number of monthly payments.
                   The two input values are converted as

```
            monthlyInterestRate = annualInterestRate / 100.0f / MONTHS_IN_YEAR;
            numberOfPayments    = loanPeriod          * MONTHS_IN_YEAR;
```

where MONTHS_IN_YEAR is a symbolic constant with value 12. Notice that we need to divide the input annual interest rate by 100 first because the formula for loan computation requires that the interest rate is a fractional value, for example, 0.01, but the input annual interest rate is entered as a percentage point, for example, 12.0. The formula for computing the monthly and total payments can be expressed as

```
monthlyPayment =  (loanAmount * monthlyInterestRate)
                  /
                  (1 - Math.pow( 1/(1 + monthlyInterestRate),
                                       numberOfPayments) );


totalPayment = monthlyPayment * numberOfPayments;
```

Let's put in the necessary code for the computations and complete the program. Here's our final program:

Step 4 Code

```
/*
    Program LoanCalculator

    A program to compute the monthly and total payments for a given loan
    amount, annual interest rate, and number of years.

    Input:      loan amount (float)
                annual interest rate (float)
                loan period - number of years (int)

    Compute:    monthly payment (float)
                total payment (float)
*/

import javabook.*;

class LoanCalculator
{

    public static void main (String args[])
    {

        final int MONTHS_IN_YEAR = 12;


        MainWindow mainWindow    = new MainWindow("Program LoanCalculator");
        InputBox   inputBox      = new InputBox(mainWindow);
        OutputBox  outputBox     = new OutputBox(mainWindow);
        mainWindow.show();
        outputBox.show();
```

```
float   loanAmount, annualInterestRate, monthlyInterestRate;

int     loanPeriod, numberOfPayments;
```

```
double monthlyPayment,
       totalPayment;

//describe the program
outputBox.printLine("This program computes the monthly and total");
outputBox.printLine("payments for a given loan amount, annual ");
outputBox.printLine("interest rate, and loan period.");
outputBox.printLine("Loan Amount in dollars and cents, e.g. 12350.50");
outputBox.printLine("Annual interest rate in percentage, e.g. 12.75");
outputBox.printLine("Loan period in number of years, e.g. 15");
outputBox.skipLine(2);

//get input
loanAmount          = inputBox.getFloat("Loan Amount (Dollars&Cents):");
annualInterestRate = inputBox.getFloat("Annual Interest Rate (eg 9.5):");
loanPeriod          = inputBox.getInteger("Loan Period - # of years:");

//compute the monthly payment
```

```
monthlyInterestRate = annualInterestRate / 100.0f / MONTHS_IN_YEAR;
numberOfPayments    = loanPeriod         * MONTHS_IN_YEAR;

monthlyPayment = (loanAmount * monthlyInterestRate)
                        /
                 (1 - Math.pow(1/(1 + monthlyInterestRate),
                               numberOfPayments ) );

totalPayment   =  monthlyPayment * numberOfPayments;
```

```
//display the result
outputBox.printLine("For");
outputBox.printLine("Loan Amount:             $" + loanAmount);
outputBox.printLine("Annual Interest Rate: " + annualInterestRate + "%");
outputBox.printLine("Loan Period (years):  " + loanPeriod);
outputBox.skipLine(1);

outputBox.printLine("Monthly payment is $ " + monthlyPayment);
outputBox.printLine("  TOTAL payment is $ "  + totalPayment);

      }
   }
```

Step 4 Test   After the program is coded, we need to run the program through a number of tests. Since we made the assumption that the input values must be valid, we will only test the program for valid input values. If we don't make that assumption, then we need to test that the program will respond correctly when the invalid values are entered. We will perform such testing beginning in Chapter 6.

To check that this program produces correct results, you can run the program with the following input values. The right two columns show the correct results. Try other input values as well.

Input			Output	
Loan Amount	Annual Interest Rate	Loan Period (in years)	Monthly Payment	Total Payment
10000	10	10	132.151	15858.1
15000	7	15	134.824	24268.4
10000	12	10	143.471	17216.5

Dr. & Ms.

Ms. Latte: I don't like the output of the program **LoanCalculator**. The output values have varying numbers of decimal places. I want to show only two decimal places for the monthly and total payments. Isn't there a way to do that?

Dr. Caffeine: Yes, of course. You can format a **float** value X to two decimal places by the expression

```
Math.round(X * 100) / 100f
```

Can you tell how it works? By the way, this solution is not perfect. It will display two decimal places only if the second decimal place (i.e., the digit at the 1/100th position) is nonzero. You will learn more about output formatting in Chapter 7.

3.8 Numerical Representation (Optional)

In this section we explain how integers and real numbers are stored in memory. Although computer manufacturers have used various formats for storing numerical values, today's standard is to use the *twos-complement* format for storing integers and the *floating-point* format for real numbers. We describe these formats in this section.

twos-complement

An integer can occupy 1, 2, 4, or 8 bytes depending on which data type (i.e., byte, short, int, or long) is declared. To make the examples easy to follow, we will use 1 byte (= 8 bits) to explain twos-complement form. The same principle applies to 2, 4, and 8 bytes. (They just utilize more bits.)

The following table shows the first five and the last four of the 256 positive binary numbers using 8 bits. The right column lists their decimal equivalents.

8-Bit Binary Number	Decimal Equivalent
00000000	0
00000001	1
00000010	2
00000011	3
00000100	4
...	
11111100	252
11111101	253
11111110	254
11111111	255

sign bit

Using 8 bits, we can represent positive integers from 0 to 255. Now let's see the possible range of negative and positive numbers that we can represent using 8 bits. We can designate the leftmost bit as a *sign bit*: 0 means positive and 1 means negative. Using this scheme, we can represent integers from −127 to +127 as shown in the following table:

8-Bit Binary Number (with a sign bit)	Decimal Equivalent
0 0000000	+0
0 0000001	+1
0 0000010	+2
...	
0 1111111	+127
1 0000000	−0
1 0000001	−1
...	
1 1111110	−126
1 1111111	−127

Notice that zero has two distinct representations (+0 = 00000000 and −0 = 10000000), which adds complexity in hardware design. Twos-complement format avoids this problem of duplicate representations for zero. In twos-complement format all positive numbers have zero in their left-most bit. The representation of a negative number is derived by first inverting all the bits (changing 1s to 0s and 0s to 1s) in the representation of the positive number and then adding 1. The following diagram illustrates the process:

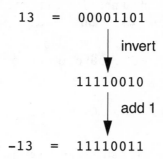

$$13 \quad = \quad 00001101$$

invert

$$11110010$$

add 1

$$-13 \quad = \quad 11110011$$

The following table shows the decimal equivalents of 8-bit binary numbers using twos-complement representation. Notice that zero has only one representation.

8-Bit Binary Number (twos-complement)	Decimal Equivalent
00000000	+0
00000001	+1
00000010	+2
•••	
01111111	+127
10000000	−128
10000001	−127
•••	
11111110	−2
11111111	−1

Now let's see how real numbers are stored in memory in floating-point format. We will present only the basic ideas of storing real numbers in computer memory here. We will omit the precise details of the IEEE (Institute of Electronics and Electrical Engineers) Standard 754 that Java uses to store real numbers.

Real numbers are represented in the computer using scientific notation. In base 10 scientific notation, a real number is expressed as

$$A \times 10^N$$

where A is a real number and N an integral exponent. For example, the mass of a hydrogen atom (in grams) is expressed in decimal scientific notation as 1.67339×10^{-24}, which is equal to 0.00000000000000000000000167339.

We use base 2 scientific notation to store real numbers in computer memory. Base 2 scientific notation represents a real number as

$$A \times 2^N$$

The float and double data types use 32 bits and 64 bits, respectively, with the number A and exponent N stored as

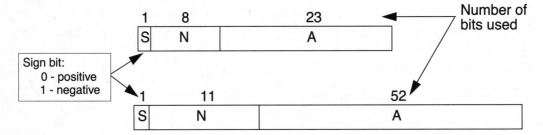

normalized
fraction

The value A is a *normalized fraction*, where the fraction begins with a binary point, followed by a 1 bit, and the rest of the fraction. (Note: A decimal number has a decimal point; a binary number has a binary point.) The following numbers are sample normalized and unnormalized binary fractions:

Normalized	Unnormalized
.1010100	1.100111
.100011	.0000000001
.101110011	.0001010110

Since a normalized number always start with a 1, this bit does not have to be actually stored. The following diagram illustrates how the A value is stored.

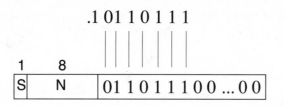

The sign bit S indicates the sign of a number, so A is stored in memory as an unsigned number. The integral exponent N can be negative or positive. Instead of using twos-complement for storing N, we use a format called *excess format*. The 8-bit exponent uses the excess-127 format, and the 11-bit exponent uses the excess-1023 format. We will explain the excess-127 format here. The excess-1023 works similarly. With the excess-127 format, the actual exponent is computed as

excess format

$$N - 127$$

Therefore, the number 127 represents an exponent of zero. Numbers less than 127 represent negative exponents, and numbers greater than 127 represent positive exponents. The following diagram illustrates that the number 125 in the exponent field represents $2^{125-127} = 2^{-2}$.

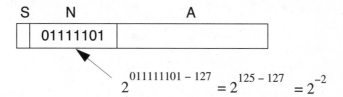

3.9   Exercises

1.   Suppose we have the following declarations:

```
int i = 3, j = 4, k = 5;
float x = 34.5f, y = 12.25f;
```

Determine the value for each of the following expressions or explain why it is not a valid expression.

```
a. (x + 1.5) / (250.0 * (i/j))      f. Math.exp(3, 2)
b. x + 1.5 / 250.0 * i / j          g. y % x
c. -x*-y * (i + j) / k              h. Math.pow(3, 2)
d. (i / 5) * y                      i. (int)y % k
e.  Math.min(i, Math.min(j,k))      j. i / 5 * y
```

2.   Suppose we have the following declarations:

```
int m, n, i = 3, j = 4, k = 5;
float v, w, x = 34.5f, y = 12.25f;
```

Determine the value assigned to the variable in each of the following assignment statements or explain why it is not a valid assignment.

```
a. w = Math.pow(3,Math.pow(i,j));   f. m = n = i * j;
b. v = x / i;                       g. n = k / (j * i) * x + y;
c. w = Math.ceil(y) % k;            h. i = i + 1;
d. n = (int) x / y * i / 2;         i. w = float(x + i);
e. x = Math.sqrt(i*i - 4*j*k);      j. x = x / i / y / j;
```

3.   Suppose we have the following declarations:

```
int     i, j;
float   x, y;
double  u, v;
```

Which of the following assignments are valid?

```
a. i = x;
b. x = u + y;
c. x = 23.4 + j * y;
d. v = (int) x;
e. y = j / i * x;
```

4.   Write Java expressions to compute the following:

a. The square root of $B^2 + 4AC$ (A and C are distinct variables).

b. The square root of $X + 4Y^3$.

c. The cube root of the product of X and Y.

d. The area πR^2 of a circle.

e. a sin C / sin A.

5.   Determine the output of the following program without running it:

```
/*
    Program TestOutputBox

*/

import javabook.*;

class TestOutputBox
{
    public static void main (String args[])
    {
        MainWindow mainWindow;
        OutputBox outputBox;

        mainWindow = new MainWindow("Program TestOutputBox");
        outputBox = new OutputBox(mainWindow);
        mainWindow.show();
        outputBox.show();

        outputBox.printLine("One");
        outputBox.print("Two");
        outputBox.skipLine(1);
        outputBox.print("Three");
        outputBox.printLine("Four");
        outputBox.skipLine(1);
        outputBox.print("Five");
        outputBox.printLine("Six");
    }
}
```

6.   Determine the output of the following code:

```
int x, y;
x = 1;
y = 2;
```

```
messageBox.show("The output is " + x + y );
messageBox.show("The output is " + (x + y) );
```

7.   Write an application that displays the following pattern in an **OutputBox** dialog:

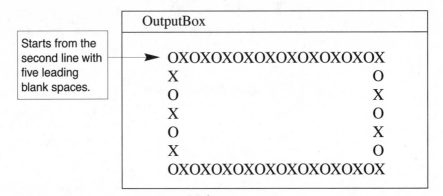

Note: The **OutputBox** is not drawn to scale.

8.   Write an application to convert centimeters (input) to feet and inches (output). Use **InputBox** for input and **OutputBox** for output. 1 inch = 2.54 centimeters.

9.   Write an application that inputs temperature in Celsius and prints out the temperature in Fahrenheit. Use **InputBox** for input and **OutputBox** for output. The formula to convert Celsius to the equivalent Fahrenheit is

$$fahrenheit = 1.8 \times celsius + 32$$

10.   Write an application that accepts a person's weight and displays the number of calories the person needs in one day. A person needs 19 calories per pound of body weight, so the formula expressed in Java would be

```
calories = bodyWeight * 19;
```

Use an **OutputBox** dialog for display. Draw the object diagram of the program. (Note: We are not distinguishing between genders.)

11. A quantity known as *Body Mass Index* (BMI) is used to calculate the risk of weight-related health problems. BMI is computed by the formula

$$\text{BMI} = \frac{w}{h^2}$$

where w is weight in kilogram and h is height in meters. A BMI of about 20 to 25 is considered "normal." Write an application that accepts weight and height (both integers) and outputs the BMI.

12. Your weight is actually the amount of gravitational attraction exerted on you by the earth. Since the moon's gravity is only 1/6 of the earth's gravity, on the moon you would weigh only 1/6 of what you weigh on the earth. Write an application that inputs the user's earth weight and outputs his/her weight on Mercury, Venus, Jupiter, and Saturn. Use the values in the table below:

Planet	Multiply the Earth Weight by
Mercury	0.4
Venus	0.9
Jupiter	2.5
Saturn	1.1

13. When you say you are 18 years old, you are really saying that the earth has circled the sun eighteen times. Since other planets take less or more days than the earth to travel around the sun, your age would be different on other planets. You can compute how old you are on other planets by the formula

$$y = \frac{x \times 365}{d}$$

where x is the age on the earth, y is the age on planet Y, and d is the number of earth days the planet Y takes to travel around the sun. Write an application that inputs the user's earth age and prints out his/her age on

Mercury, Venus, Jupiter, and Saturn. The values for d are listed in the table below:

Planet	d = Approximate Number of Earth Days for This Planet to Travel around the Sun
Mercury	88
Venus	225
Jupiter	4380
Saturn	10767

14.   Write an application to solve quadratic equations of the form

$$Ax^2 + Bx + C = 0$$

where the coefficients A, B, and C are real numbers. The two real number solutions are derived by the formula

$$x = \frac{-B \pm \sqrt{B^2 - 4AC}}{2A}$$

For this exercise, you may assume that $A \neq 0$ and the relationship

$$B^2 \geq 4AC$$

holds, so there will be real-number solutions for x.

15.   Write an application that reads a purchase price and an amount tendered and then displays the change in dollars, quarters, dimes, nickels, and pennies. Two input values are entered in cents, for example, 3540 for $34.50

and 70 for $0.70. Use InputBox for input and OutputBox for output. Display the output in the following format:

```
Purchase Price:   $ 34.50
Amount Tendered:  $ 40.00

Your change is:   $ 5.50

                    5 one-dollar bill(s)
                    2 quarter(s)

Thank you for your business. Come back soon.
```

Notice the input values are to be entered in cents (int data type), but the echo printed values must be displayed with decimal points (float data type).

16.   Write an application that accepts the unit weight of a bag of coffee in pounds and the number of bags sold and displays the total price of the sale, computed as

```
totalPrice        = unitWeight * numberOfUnits * 5.99f;
totalPriceWithTax = totalPrice + totalPrice * 0.0725f;
```

where 5.99 is the cost per pound and 0.0725 the sales tax. The letter f after 5.99 and 0.0725 designates that these two numbers are of type float. Display the result in the following manner:

```
Number of bags sold:  32
    Weight per bag:  5 lbs
    Price per pound:  $5.99
        Sales tax:  7.25%

    Total price: $ 1027.884
```

Draw the object diagram of the program.

17. If you invest P dollars at R% interest rate compounded annually, in N years, your investment will grow to

$$\frac{P\left(1-\left(\frac{R}{100}\right)^{N+1}\right)}{1-\left(\frac{R}{100}\right)}$$

dollars. Write an application that accepts P, R, and N and computes the amount of money earned after the N years.

18. Leonardo Fibonacci of Pisa was one of the greatest mathematicians of the Middle Ages. He is perhaps most famous for the Fibonacci sequence that can be applied to many diverse problems. One amusing application of the Fibonacci sequence is finding the growth rate of rabbits. Suppose a pair of rabbits matures in two months and is capable of reproducing another pair every month after maturity. If every new pair has the same capability, how many pairs will there be after one year? (We assume here that no pairs die.) The table below shows the sequence for the first seven months. Notice that at the end of the second month, the first pair matures and bears its first offspring in the third month, making the total two pairs.

Month #	# of pairs
1	1
2	1
3	2
4	3
5	5
6	8
7	13

The Nth Fibonacci number in the sequence can be evaluated with the formula

$$F_N = \frac{1}{\sqrt{5}}\left[\left(\frac{1+\sqrt{5}}{2}\right)^N - \left(\frac{1-\sqrt{5}}{2}\right)^N\right]$$

Write an application that accepts N and displays F_N. Note that the result of computation using the Math class is double. You need to display it as an integer.

19. Java^2 Coffee Outlet runs a catalog business. It sells only one type of coffee beans harvested exclusively in the remote area of Irian Jaya. The company sells the coffee in 2-lb bags only, and the price of a single 2-lb bag is $5.50. When a customer places an order, the company ships the order in boxes. The boxes come in three sizes: the large box holds 20 2-lb bags, the medium 10 bags, and the small 5 bags. The cost of a large box is $2.00, a medium box $1.00, and a small box $0.50. The order is shipped using the least number of boxes with the cheapest cost. For example, the order of 25 bags will be shipped in two boxes, one large and one small. Write an application that computes the total cost of an order. Use Input-Box to accept the number of bags for an order and OutputBox to display the total cost including the cost of boxes. Display the output in the following format:

```
Number of Bags Ordered:   52 - $ 286.00

            Boxes Used:
                          2 Large   - $4.00
                          1 Medium - $1.00
                          1 Small   - $0.50

      Your total cost is:    $ 241.50
```

Remember that you can format a float value X to two decimal places by the expression
```
Math.round( X * 100) / 100f
```

20. According to Newton's universal law of gravitation, the force F between two bodies with masses M_1 and M_2 is computed as

$$F = k\left(\frac{M_1 M_2}{d^2}\right)$$

where d is the distance between the two bodies and k is a positive real number call the *gravitational constant*. The gravitational constant k is approximately equal to 6.67E-8 dyne cm^2/gm^2. Write an application that accepts the mass for two bodies in grams and the distance between the two bodies in centimeters and compute the force F. Use the appropriate format for the output. For your information, the force between the earth and the moon is 1.984E25 dynes. The mass of the earth is 5.983E27 grams, the mass of the moon is 7.347E25 grams, and the distance between the two is 3.844E10 centimeters.

21.   Dr. Caffeine's Law of Program Readability states that the degree of program readability R (whose unit is *mocha*) is determined as

$$R = k \cdot \frac{CT^2}{V^3}$$

where k is Ms. Latte's constant, C is the number of lines in the program that contain comments, T is the time spent (in minutes) by the programmer developing the program, and V is the number of lines in the program that contain nondescriptive variable names. Write an application to compute the program readability R. Ms. Latte's constant is 2.5E2 mocha lines^2/min^2. (Note: This is just for fun. Develop your own law using various functions from the Math class.)

22.   If the population of a country grows according to the formula

$$y = ce^{kx}$$

where y is the population after x years from the reference year, then we can determine the population of a country for a given year from two census figures. For example, given that a country with a population of 1,000,000 in 1970 grows to 2,000,000 by 1990, we can predict the country's population in year 2000. Here's how we do the computation. Letting x be the number of years after 1970, we obtain the constant c is 1,000,000 because

$$1,000,000 = ce^{k0} = c$$

Then we determine the value of k as

$$y = 1,000,000 \, e^{kx}$$

$$\frac{2,000,000}{1,000,000} = e^{20k}$$

$$k = \frac{1}{20} \ln\left(\frac{2,000,000}{1,000,000}\right) \approx 0.03466$$

Finally we can predict the population in the year 2000 by substituting 0.03466 for k and 30 for x (2000 - 1970 = 30). Thus, we predict

$$y = 1,000,000 \, e^{0.03466(30)} \approx 2,828,651$$

as the population of the country for year 2000. Write an application that accepts five input values—year A, population in year A, year B, population in year B, and year C—and predict the population for year C.

4

Defining Instantiable Classes

OBJECTIVES

After you have read and studied this chapter, you should be able to

- Define an instantiable class with multiple methods and a constructor.

- Differentiate the local and instance variables.

- Define and use value-returning methods.

- Distinguish private and public methods.

- Distinguish private and public data members.

- Describe how the arguments are passed to the parameters in method definitions.

- Use System.out for temporary output to verify the program code.

Introduction

The sample application programs we have written so far included only one class, the main class of the program. And the main class contained only one method, the main method. From this main method, we used only predefined classes from javabook and other standard packages such as java.lang. For small programs, this arrangement may be acceptable. But for large programs, it is not. We cannot develop large application programs in a similar manner for the following two reasons:

1. Placing all programming code for a large application in a single method main makes the method very huge and impossible to manage.

2. Predefined classes alone cannot satisfy all of our programming needs in writing a large application.

Even for the simple LoanCalculator program in the previous chapter the size of its main method is approaching the limit that can be considered acceptable. We don't write a program whose main method is 10 pages long. A large program that is properly built will include many classes—some predefined and others we defined—and each of these classes will include many methods.

instantiable class

Learning how to define instantiable classes is the first step toward mastering the skills necessary in building large programs. A class is *instantiable* if we can create instances of the class. The MainWindow, InputBox, and OutputBox classes are all instantiable classes while the Math class is not. In this chapter you will learn how to define instantiable classes and different types of methods included in the instantiable classes.

4.1   Defining Instantiable Classes

Suppose we want to write a program that converts Japanese yen to U.S. dollars and vice versa. What kinds of objects do you think are necessary? Well, we can do a simple input and output with InputBox and OutputBox. But what about the conversion process? Is there any class in javabook or standard Java packages that does currency conversion? No, so we will have to define one ourselves. As an illustration for defining instantiable classes, we will define a class called CurrencyConverter. Through this example, we will provide you the basics of defining instantiable classes. We will cover only the very basics in this section. We will provide in the remainder of the chapter a more detailed explanation of the basic features introduced here.

When we design our own class, we start with the specification for the class. We must decide how we want to interact with the class and its instances. We must decide what kinds of instance and class methods the class should support. We will design the class so that we can use it in a way that is natural and logical for us to use. Let's start with one possible design. After we design the class, we will discuss an alternative way to design the class.

How should a CurrencyConverter object behave? What would be a natural and logical way for us to interact with it? Since we want the object to be able to do the conversion between a foreign currency and the U.S. dollar, let's define two methods, one for converting U.S. dollars to the equivalent amount in the foreign currency and another for the reverse transaction. Let's call these methods fromDollar and toDollar. To convert $200 U.S. to Japanese yen, for example, we will have to write something like this:

```
CurrencyConverter      yenConverter;
float                  amountInYen, amountInDollar;

yenConverter   = new CurrencyConverter();
...
amountInYen    = yenConverter.fromDollar( 200 ); //from dollar
                                                 //to yen
```

And to convert ¥15,000 to U.S. dollars, we will write

```
amountInDollar = yenConverter.toDollar( 15000 );//yen to dollar
```

Since the exchange rate fluctuates, we need a method, say, setExchangeRate, to set the exchange rate before doing the conversion. Assuming the exchange rate is ¥130.77 for $1.00 U.S., we will do the conversion as

```
CurrencyConverter      yenConverter;
float                  amountInYen, amountInDollar;

yenConverter   = new CurrencyConverter();
yenConverter.setExchangeRate(130.77f);

amountInYen    = yenConverter.fromDollar( 200 );
amountInDollar = yenConverter.toDollar( 15000 );
```

Once the class is defined, we can easily create additional CurrencyConverter objects for other currencies. For example, if we want to convert U.S. dollars into German marks and Japanese yen, then we can do the following:

```
CurrencyConverter       yenConverter, markConverter;
float                   amountInYen, amountInMark;

yenConverter        = new CurrencyConverter();
yenConverter.setExchangeRate(130.77f);

markConverter       =   new CurrencyConverter( );
markConverter.setExchangeRate(1.792f);

amountInYen    =   yenConverter.fromDollar( 200 );
amountInMark   =   markConverter.fromDollar( 200 );
```

Because any currency can be converted to a dollar equivalent and vice versa, we can do the conversion between two currencies other than the U.S. dollar, for example, between Japanese yen and German marks. For example, to convert ¥10,000 to the equivalent in German marks, we first convert the yen to dollars and then the dollars to marks as in

```
amountInDollar    = yenConverter.toDollar( 10000 );
amountInMark      = markConverter.fromDollar( amountInDollar );
```

Being able to do a conversion easily between any two currencies is a direct benefit of defining a separate class for currency conversion.

A CurrencyConverter object has three methods: setExchangeRate, toDollar, and fromDollar. Its object diagram (at this point) is

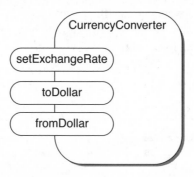

Alternative Design for CurrencyConverter

We gave one possible design for the CurrencyConverter class. Is there any alternative design? The way the class is implemented, we must create a new instance of each foreign currency for which we want to do a conversion. Another possibility is to design the class so that one instance of the class can handle conversions for more than one foreign currency. We won't get into any more detail here because we do not yet have the necessary programming skills to implement this alternative design.

Suppose we know how to implement the alternative design of CurrencyConverter. Which design alternative is better? When we design a class, we must always consider alternative designs to select the one most appropriate for a given program. Whether one design is better than the other depends on how the class is used in programs. Unlike the engineering disciplines, we do not have a formula to measure the effectiveness of a software. Instead of mathematical formulae, we have design guidelines we can follow in designing classes. One such guideline is keep the class simple. Whenever appropriate in the remainder of the book, we will mention the design alternatives for the classes used in the sample programs and discuss their pros and cons.

The CurrencyConverter Class

Let's implement the class using the first design. Figure 4.1 is a template for defining a class. In this class, we need to define three methods—setExchangeRate, toDollar, and fromDollar—and any data values used by these methods. We call the data values for the class *data members*, which include variables and constants. We will first identify the data members of the class and then define the three methods. We will explain the rules for defining the data members and methods along the way.

data members

What kind of data members does a CurrencyConverter object need in order for the object to carry out the conversion task? To do the conversion, the object must keep track of the exchange rate. This exchange rate is used by the two methods toDollar and fromDollar. What will be the data type for the exchange rate? The data type int is not acceptable because we expect the rate will include decimal places. So the data type should be either float or double. But which? Since the magnitude of the number is small, float is adequate, so we will use the data type float for the exchange rate. Here's the partial class declaration with the variable exchangeRate declared as data type float:

```
/*
    Class:          CurrencyConverter

    Description:
                    An object of this class is used to do the
                    currency conversion between a foreign
                    currency and the U.S. dollar.
```

```
                    */

               class CurrencyConverter
               {
                   private float exchangeRate; //how much $1.00 U.S. is worth
                                               //in the foreign currency

                   //method declarations come here

               }
```

The variable exchangeRate is declared within the class declaration, but outside of any method of the class. The variable exchangeRate is an *instance variable*, which is equivalent to the term *instance data value* we used in Chapter 1. Every object of the class will have its own copy of an instance variable.

instance
variable

FIGURE 4.1   A program template for a class definition.

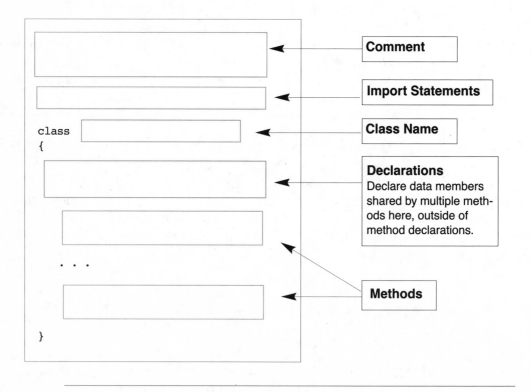

Figure 4.2 shows that two CurrencyConverter objects have their own copy of exchangeRate.

FIGURE 4.2   Every object of a class has its own copy of instance variables. **CurrencyConverter** objects have their own copy of **exhangeRate** instance variables.

```
CurrencyConverter        markConverter,
                         yenConverter;

markConverter = new CurrencyConverter();
markConverter.setExchangeRate(1.792f);

yenConverter   = new CurrencyConverter();
yenConverter.setExchangeRate(130.77f);
```

markConverter

yenConverter

Notice the use of the reserved word private in declaring exchangeRate. This modifier is called a *visibility modifier*, and it specifies the visibility, or accessibility, of the data members and methods. Another visibility modifier is public. The full explanation of the visibility modifier will require a whole section, so we will defer its discussion until the next section. For now, it suffices to know that the data type for exchangeRate is float.

Now let's study how the methods are defined. We will start with the setExchangeRate method. Its purpose is to set the instance variable exchangeRate to the value passed to the method. The method is declared as

```
public void setExchangeRate( float rate )
{
    exchangeRate = rate;
}
```

visibility
modifier

The syntax for defining a method, as given in Chapter 2, is

```
<modifiers> <return type> <method name> ( <parameters> )
{

    <statements>

}
```

The following diagram shows how the components in the general syntax correspond to the actual elements in the exchangeRate method:

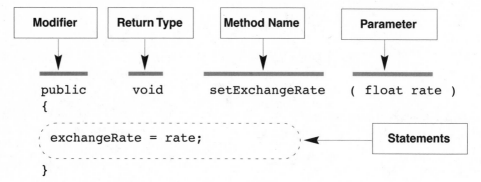

Since the method returns no value, it is declared as void. Notice that the method has no static modifier. If the method declaration includes the static modifier, then it is a class method. If the method declaration does not include the static modifier, then it is an instance method.

Instance methods are declared WITHOUT the static modifier. Class methods are declared WITH the static modifier.

We must declare the setExchangeRate method as an instance method because class methods cannot access instance variables, but this method needs to access the instance variable exchangeRate. Class methods can access only the class variables and constants, while the instance methods can also access them in addition to the instance variables.

Class methods can access class variables and constants, but not instance variables. Instance methods can access all of them.

When we define an instantiable class, we are in essence defining how the instances of the class will behave. So it makes sense that the methods we define for the class are instance methods. There are times when a class method is useful and necessary, but for the most part, when we define an instantiable class, we will define the instance methods almost exclusively. We will describe the use of class methods for the instantiable classes later in the book.

The visibility modifier public designates the setExchangeRate method as accessible from outside methods. If two methods belong to different classes, then they are *outside methods* relative to each other. If this method is declared private, then we will not be able to call the method from outside as in

outside method

```
class TestProgram
{
    public static void main (String args[] )
    {
        CurrencyConverter yenConverter;
        yenConverter = new CurrencyConverter();

        yenConverter.setExchangeRate( 130.77f );
        ...
    }
}
```

This call is valid if the method is declared **public** and invalid if the method is declared **private**.

Since all three methods are intended to be called from the outside methods, the three methods are all declared public.

method header comment

As a part of class documentation, we include a *method header comment* to every method to describe the method. A typical method header comment looks something like this:

```
/*
  Method:       setExchangeRate

  Purpose:      Sets the exchange rate to the value passed
                to this method

  Parameters:
                float rate
                    - the exchange rate

  Returns:      None
*/
```

In the method header comment, we record the name, purpose, list of parameters passed to the method, and the value returned from the method. Your instructor may require you to include other information for your program assignments. For the list of parameters, we attach a short description of each parameter, in addition to the parameter's name and data type. To save space, we will show the method comments only in the final listing of the class.

Now let's move on to the second method. The toDollar method accepts an amount in a foreign currency and returns the equivalent amount in U.S. dollars. The amount in the foreign currency, which is a float value, is passed to the method as an argument, so the corresponding parameter is declared as float. Since the method returns a float value, we must declare its return type as float. The method is therefore declared as

```
public float toDollar( float foreignMoney )
{
    //method body comes here
}
```

value-returning method

We call a method that returns a value a *value-returning method*, or *non*-void *method*. A value-returning method must include a return statement of the format

return statement syntax

```
return <expression> ;
```

The void method, on the other hand, must not include any return statement.

We can convert a given value foreignMoney into the equivalent dollar amount by the expression

```
foreignMoney / exchangeRate
```

so the complete method is defined as

```
public float toDollar( float foreignMoney )
{
    return (foreignMoney / exchangeRate) ;
}
```

We use the parentheses in the return statement to delineate the expression part of the statement clearly.

The method to convert a given amount in dollars to the equivalent amount in a foreign currency is similarly defined as

```
public float fromDollar( float dollar )
{
    return (dollar * exchangeRate) ;
}
```

We are now ready to provide the complete listing of the CurrencyConverter class. In listing the data members and methods of a class, we will use the following convention:

class listing convention

```
class <class name>
{
    // data members

    // public methods

    // private methods
}
```

We first list the data members, then the public methods in alphabetical order, and finally the private methods in alphabetical order. For the public and private method groups, we will include a block comment that provides a quick reference to the methods in the group. For example, we will include the following comment for the public method group of the CurrencyConverter class:

```
/*****************************
  Public Methods:

    float   fromDollar      (   float   )
    float   toDollar        (   float   )
    void    setExchangeRate (           )

*****************************/
```

Java compiler does not care how we order the methods and data members in the class declaration. We adopt the listing convention to make the class declaration easier for us to follow.

Here's the class declaration:

```
/*
    Class:         CurrencyConverter

    Description:
                   An object of this class is used to do the
                   currency conversion between a foreign
                   currency and the U.S. dollar.
*/

class CurrencyConverter
{

/**********************
    Data Members
**********************/

    private float exchangeRate; //how much $1.00 U.S. is worth
                                //in the foreign currency

/*****************************
    Public Methods:

        float      fromDollar        (   float      )
        float      toDollar          (   float      )
        void       setExchangeRate   (   float      )

*****************************/


    /* Method:       fromDollar

       Purpose:      Converts a given amount in dollars into
                     an equivalent amount in a foreign currency
       Parameters:
                     float dollar
                        -  amount in dollars

       Returns:      float foreignCurrency
                        -  amount in foreign currency equivalent
                           to the given dollar amount
    */
    public float fromDollar( float dollar )
    {
        return (dollar * exchangeRate) ;
    }


    /* Method:       toDollar

       Purpose:      Converts a given amount in a foreign currency
                     into an equivalent dollar amount.
       Parameters:
                     float foreignMoney
                        -  amount in foreign currency
```

```
     Returns:      float dollar
                       -   dollar amount equivalent to the given
                           foreign currency amount
*/
public float toDollar( float foreignMoney )
{
    return (foreignMoney / exchangeRate) ;
}


/*  Method:       setExchangeRate

    Purpose:      Sets the exchange rate to the value passed
                  to this method
    Parameters:
                  float rate
                      -   the exchange rate

    Returns:      None
*/
public void setExchangeRate( float rate )
{
    exchangeRate = rate;
}

}
```

Quick Check

1. The following is invalid.Why?

    ```
    public void myMethod( int one )
    {
        return  (one + one) ;
    }
    ```

2. Which of the following methods are class methods?

    ```
    public  static void    one( ) { ... }
    private        int     two( ) { ... }
    private static int     three( ) { ... }
    public         float   four( ) { ... }
    ```

4.2   Instantiable Classes and Constructors

When we design a class, we try to make the class as robust as we can. We do not want the class to be so fragile that a simple misstep by the programmer will cause the class to stop working properly. Consider the following sequence of statements that use a CurrencyConverter object to convert $200 to the equivalent in yen:

```
CurrencyConverter     yenConverter;
float                 amountInYen;

yenConverter     = new CurrencyConverter();
amountInYen      = yenConverter.fromDollar( 200 );
```

Does the code work? No, it does not, because the method setExchangeRate is not called to set the exchange rate. The programmer must call the setExchange-Rate method before calling the fromDollar method in order to perform the currency conversion correctly.

The way the class is currently defined, the correct value for exchangeRate is not set when an instance of the CurrencyConverter class is created. This means that we must rely on the programmer to call the setExchangeRate method before calling the fromDollar method. But there's no way for us to ensure that the programmer will call the setExchangeRate method. When we design a class, we must define the class as robust as it can be so the class will not "break" easily under the programmer's misuse of the class. One possible solution is to define a special method called a constructor so that an instance of the Currency-Converter class cannot be created without setting the value for exchangeRate.

constructor   A *constructor* is a special method that is executed when the new message is sent to the class; that is, when a new instance of the class is created. The name of a constructor must be the same as the name of the class.[1] For the Currency-Converter class, we can define its constructor as

```
public CurrencyConverter( float rate )
{
    exchangeRate = rate;
}
```

---

1. The rule that the message name and the method name must be the same does not apply to the constructor. If the rule were enforced for all methods, then the constructor would be named new.

To call this constructor, we create a new CurrencyConverter object

```
CurrencyConverter     moneyChanger;
moneyChanger = new CurrencyConverter( 130.45f );
```

The syntax of a constructor is

```
public <class name> ( <parameters> )
{
    <statements>
}
```

where <class name> is the name of the class to which this constructor belongs. The following diagram shows how the components in the general syntax correspond to the actual elements in the constructor of the CurrencyConverter class:

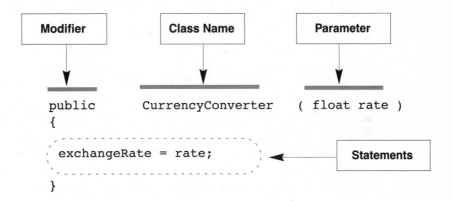

Notice that a constructor does not have a return type. Although there is no static modifier in the declaration, the constructor is a class method. The modifier of a constructor does not have to be public, but non-public constructors are rarely used, so we will not discuss non-public constructors.

If no constructor is defined for a class, then the Java compiler will include a default constructor. Since we did not define any constructor for the Currency-Converter class before, the default constructor

```
public CurrencyConverter()
{
}
```

was added to the class by the compiler. A default constructor has no parameters. Once we define our own constructor, no default constructor is added. This means once the constructor

```
public CurrencyConverter( float  rate )
{
    exchangeRate = rate;
}
```

is defined, we will not be allowed to create a CurrencyConverter object as

```
CurrencyConverter      moneyChanger;
moneyChanger  =  new CurrencyConverter( );
```

because no matching constructor is defined for the class. However, it is possible to define multiple constructors for a class, so the programmer can create a new instance of the class in different ways. For example, if we want the programmers to create a new instance either as

```
moneyChanger = new CurrencyConverter( );
```

or

```
moneyChanger = new CurrencyConverter( 142.00f );
```

we simply define two constructors for the class.

There will be no problems defining multiple constructors as long as the constructors defined for a class have either

1. A different number of parameters.

2. Different data types for the parameters if the number of parameters is the same.

For example, the following three constructors

```
public ClassA( int X )
{
    ...
}
```

```
public ClassA(       ) //different number of parameters
{
    ...
}

public Class( float X )   //same number of parameters as the
{                         //first one, but a different data type
    ...
}
```

are valid, but the following two constructors

```
public ClassB( int X , float Y )
{
    ...
}

public ClassB( int A, float B  )
{                         //invalid: same number and same data types
    ...
}
```

are not. Notice that parameter names are irrelevant in deciding whether the constructor is valid or not. Only the number of parameters and their data types are relevant.

The purpose of the constructor is to initialize an object to a valid state. For example, when the CurrencyConverter class has the default constructor only, then a newly created CurrencyConverter object is not in a valid state since the object does not have a valid exchange rate at the time of its creation. Whenever an object is created we must ensure that it is created in a valid state by properly initializing all data members in a constructor. We can guarantee this by always defining a constructor to a class and initializing data members in the constructor's method body.

Always define a constructor and initialize data members fully in the constructor so an object will be created in a valid state.

Remember that even after we add constructors to the CurrencyConverter class, the setExchangeRate method is still necessary for the class because we want the programmer to be able to change the exchange rate to different rates after the object is created.

Quick Check

1. Which of the following constructors are invalid?

    ```
    public int ClassA( int one )
    {
        ...
    }

    public ClassB( int one, int two )
    {
        ...
    }

    void ClassC( )
    {
        ...
    }
    ```

2. Are there any conflicts in the following three constructors for ClassX to be valid?

    ```
    public ClassX( int X )
    {
        ...
    }

    public ClassX( float X )
    {
        ...
    }

    public ClassX( int Y )
    {
        ...
    }
    ```

4.3   **Visibility Modifiers:** public **and** private

The modifiers public and private designate the accessibility of data members and methods. Although valid in Java, we do not recommend that programmers, especially beginners, leave out the visibility modifier in declaring data members and methods. From the object-oriented design standpoint, we recommend you always designate the data members and methods as private or public. We will explain how to use these modifiers in this section.

The instance variable exchangeRate of CurrencyConverter is declared private. No outside methods—the methods that belong to classes other than CurrencyConverter—can therefore directly access exchangeRate. To explain why we declare the instance variable private, let's see what happens if we declare exchangeRate as public. Suppose we change the declaration to

```
class CurrencyConverter
{
    public float exchangeRate;
    ...
}
```

If a data member is declared public, then any outside method can access it using dot notation. For example, we can set the exchange rate without using the setExchangeRate method as

```
CurrencyConverter yenConverter;
yenConverter = new CurrencyConverter( );

yenConverter.exchangeRate = 130.77f;
```

Direct access to the public instance variable using dot notation.

You can read the value of exchangeRate just as well by using dot notation as in the following code:

```
float yenRate = yenConverter.exchangeRate;
outputBox.printLine("One U.S. dollar is worth "
                    + yenRate + " yen." );
```

On the surface, it seems better to declare the data members public. Why bother hiding exchangeRate by declaring it private and defining the method setExchangeRate to set the value if you can read and write the value of exchangeRate directly by declaring it public? To explain why declaring data members public is considered a bad design, let's modify the class so that a fee is automatically charged and deducted from the converted amount. Let's say the rate of charge is 5 percent of the exchange rate. We add the second instance variable feeRate to store this fee rate. We will declare feeRate as public to illustrate the point. The fee rate is based on the exchange rate, so we will set it inside the setExchangeRate method as

```
public void setExchangeRate( float rate )
{
    exchangeRate = rate;
    feeRate = rate * 0.05f;
}
```

The conversion routines are now defined as

```
public float toDollar( float foreignMoney )
{
    return (foreignMoney / exchangeRate)
              - (foreignMoney / feeRate) ;
}
```

```
public float fromDollar( float dollar )
{
    return (dollar * exchangeRate)
              - (dollar * feeRate) ;
}
```

Because the instance variable feeRate is public, we cannot prevent programmers from writing code such as

```
CurrencyConverter     yenConverter;
yenConverter  =   new CurrencyConverter( );
yenConverter.setExchangeRate( 130.77 );

yenConverter.feeRate = 0.0f;
...
```

thereby breaking the CurrencyConverter class. If the instance variable feeRate is private, then programmers using the CurrencyConverter class cannot modify its value directly. They can modify the value only through the setExchangeRate method. So by declaring the data members private, we can maintain the integrity of the class and enforce the rule, because the values of the data members are changed only via the methods we define. The programmers cannot access or modify the data member values through the back door.

Declaring the data members private **ensures the integrity of the class.**

Consider another scenario. Imagine what would happen had we designed the CurrencyConverter class without the setExchangeRate method. We declare the instance variable exchangeRate as public and let the programmers modify its value directly. Now, suppose we need to modify the class to keep track of two exchange rates that automatically include charge, one for converting a dollar amount to the equivalent amount in a foreign currency and another for converting an amount in a foreign currency to the equivalent dollar amount. We will call these rates fromDollarRate and toDollarRate, respectively. The methods for conversion become something like

```
public float toDollar( float foreignMoney )
{
    return ( foreignMoney / toDollarRate );
}

public float fromDollar( float dollar )
{
    return ( dollar * fromDollarRate );
}
```

When the public instance variable exchangeRate is replaced by two rates fromDollarRate and toDollarRate, then all statements in the programmer's code that refers to exchangeRate, such as

```
yenConverter.exchangeRate = 130.77f;
```

must be replaced by something like

```
yenConverter.toDollarRate = 130.77f * 1.05f;
yenConverter.fromDollarRate = 130.77f * 0.95f;
```

assuming the rate of charge is 5 percent of the exchange rate. Forcing the programmers to make such changes is not good. We can avoid changing the programmer's code if the exchangeRate is declared private and we define the method setExchangeRate. We only need to replace the private instance variable exchangeRate by two private instance variables toDollarRate and fromDollarRate. They are set in the new setExchangeRate method as

```
public void setExchangeRate( float rate )
{
    exchangeRate    = rate;
    toDollarRate    = rate * 1.05f;
    fromDollarRate = rate * 0.95f;
}
```

The programmer's code that includes the statement

```
yenConverter.setExchangeRate( 130.77f );
```

will continue to work without modification.

When we design an instantiable class, we are designing the behavior of the instances. Behavior of the instances is determined by the set of public methods we define for the class. We use data members to keep track of data values necessary to support the public methods. We consider the data members as an internal detail of the class. As such, we should declare them private. Similarly, we may need to define a set of methods that are used only by the methods of the same class. Since the methods are used internally, we should declare these methods private also. Any components that are only for internal use should be declared private.

The only data member we may want to declare as public is the class constants. Since a class constant is "read only" by its nature, it won't have a negative impact if we declare it as public. For example, we may include a class constant FEE_RATE, which is declared as

```
public static float FEE_RATE = 0.05f; //fee rate is 5%;
```

and define the setExchangeRate method as

```
public void setExchangeRate( float rate )
{
```

```
    exchangeRate    = rate;
    toDollarRate    = rate * (1.00f + FEE_RATE);
    fromDollarRate = rate * (1.00f - FEE_RATE);
}
```

With this modification in place, the programmer can write code such as

```
float dollarAmount;

yenConverter.setExchangeRate( 130.77f );

dollarAmount = yenConverter.toDollar( 15000.0f );

outputBox.printLine("Y15,000.00 is equal to");
outputBox.printLine("$ " + dollarAmount);
outputBox.printLine("with the fee rate: "
                           + CurrencyConverter.FEE_RATE);
```

Notice that the class data members and class methods are accessed by the syntax

```
<class name> . <class data members | class methods>
```

where the vertical bar (|) represents *or*. This is how we used the methods and constants from the Math class. Keep in mind that a class constant may or may not be public. That depends on its usage.

Here are some guidelines for you to follow.

Guidelines in determining the visibility of data members and methods:

1. Declare the class and instance variables private.

2. Declare the class and instance methods private if they are used only by the other methods in the same class.

3. Declare the class constants public if you want to make their values directly readable by outside methods. If the class constants are used for internal purposes only, then declare them private.

Quick Check

1. If the data member feeRate is private, is the following statement valid?

   ```
   feeCharge = currencyChanger.feeRate;
   ```

2. Suppose you wrote down important information such as your bank account number, student registration ID, and so forth, on a single sheet of paper. Will this sheet be declared private, and kept in your desk drawer, or public, and placed next to the dorm's public telephone?

4.4   Local Variables, Return Values, and Parameter Passing

We will provide more detailed coverage on methods in this section. Specifically, we will discuss how local variables are declared, how values are returned from a method, and how arguments are passed to a method.

local variable

We begin with local variables. A variable declared within the method declaration is called a *local variable*. Local variables are used for temporary purposes, such as storing intermediate results of a computation. For example, we can rewrite the method

```
public float fromDollar( float dollar )
{
    return (dollar * exchangeRate)
                 - (dollar * feeRate) ;
}
```

using local variables as

```
public float fromDollar( float dollar )
{
    float amount, fee;

    amount = dollar * exchangeRate;
    fee    = dollar * feeRate;

    return (amount - fee);
}
```

These are
local variables.

While instance variables are accessible from all methods of the class, local variables are accessible only from the method in which they are declared and they are available only while the method is being executed. Memory space for local variables is allocated at the beginning of the method and erased upon exit from the method. Figure 4.3 shows how memory space is allocated and deallocated for local variables when the modified fromDollar method is executed.

FIGURE 4.3   How memory space for a local variable is allocated and deallocated.

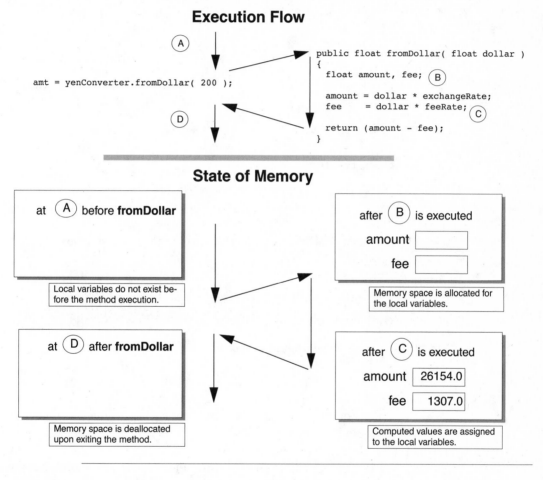

Local variables are erased when the execution of a method is completed.

Now let's study how values are returned from methods. Consider the following toDollar method:

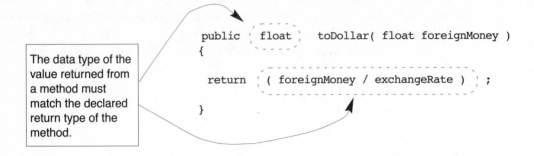

The data type of the value returned from a method must match the declared return type of the method.

```
public  float   toDollar( float foreignMoney )
{

    return  ( foreignMoney / exchangeRate )  ;

}
```

Because a value is returned from the method, we can place the call to the method anywhere an expression can appear. For example, the following statement is valid:

```
float totalAmount;

totalAmount = yenConverter.toDollar( 100 )
                    + yenConverter.toDollar( 50 ) ;
```

Similarly, we can pass the returned value as an argument to another method call, such as

```
int yenAmount;

yenAmount
    = yenConverter.fromDollar( markConverter.toDollar(100) ) ;
```

to convert 100 German marks to the equivalent yen. Note: Fees are charged twice here because there are two conversions. See exercise 12 on page 191.

Let's move on to the last topic of the section, the mapping of arguments to the corresponding parameters. When a method is called, the value of the argument is passed to the matching parameter, and separate memory space is allocated to store this value. This way of passing the value of arguments is called a *pass-by-value scheme*. Since separate memory space is allocated for each parameter during the execution of the method, the parameter is local to the meth-

pass-by-value

od, and therefore, changes made to the parameter will not affect the value of the corresponding argument.

Consider the following myMethod method of the Tester class. The method does not do anything meaningful. We use it here to illustrate how the pass-by-value scheme works.

```
class Tester
{
    public void myMethod( int one, float two )
    {
        one = 25;
        two = 35.4f;
    }
}
```

What will be the output from the following code?

```
Tester tester;
int    x, y;

tester = new Tester();
x = 10;
y = 20;

tester.myMethod( x, y );

outputBox.printLine( x + "    " + y );
```

The output will be

```
10    20
```

because with the pass-by-value scheme, the values of arguments are passed to the parameters, but changes made to the parameters are not passed back to the arguments. Figure 4.4 shows how the pass-by-value scheme works.

Notice that the arguments are matched against the parameters in the left-to-right order; that is, the value of the leftmost argument is passed to the leftmost parameter, the value of the second leftmost argument is passed to the second

FIGURE 4.4   How memory space for the parameters is allocated and deallocated.

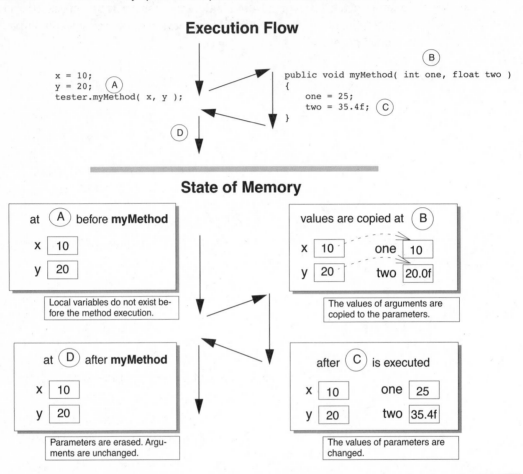

leftmost parameter, and so forth. The number of arguments in the method call must match the number of parameters in the method definition. For example, the following calls to myMethod of the Tester class are all invalid because the number of arguments and parameters does not match.

```
tester.myMethod( 12 );
tester.myMethod( x, y, 24.5);
```

Since we are assigning the value of an argument to the matching parameter, the data type of an argument must be assignment compatible with the data type of matching parameter. For example, we can pass an integer argument to a float parameter, but not vice versa. In the following, the first call is valid, but the second one is invalid:

```
tester.myMethod( 12, 25 );
tester.myMethod( 23.0, 34.5 );
```

The name of the parameter and the argument can be the same. Keep in mind, however, that the values of arguments are still passed to a method by the pass-by-value scheme; that is, local copies are made whether the argument and the parameter share the same name or not.

The key points to remember about arguments and parameters:

1. Arguments are passed to a method using the pass-by-value scheme.

2. Arguments are matched to the parameters from left to right. The data type of an argument must be assignment compatible to the data type of the matching parameter.

3. The number of arguments in the method call must match the number of parameters in the method definition.

4. Parameters and arguments do not have to have the same name.

5. Local copies, which are distinct from arguments, are created even if the parameters and arguments share the same name.

6. Parameters are input to a method, and they are local to the method. Changes made to the parameters will not affect the value of corresponding arguments.

4.5   Loan Calculator Program with an Instantiable Class

In the previous chapter, we wrote a loan calculator program that computes the monthly and total payments for a given loan amount, loan period, and interest rate. We wrote the program using the simplified program structure where we had one main class with one method (main). We will implement the program again, but this time we will use an instantiable class called LoanCalculator. The problem statement is given on page 114. We will go through the incremental development process to derive the instantiable LoanCalculator class. We will also introduce the syntax for calling a method from another method that belongs to the same class.

Problem Statement

The problem statement is the same as before from Chapter 3. We will repeat the statement to refresh your memory:

> *Write a loan calculator program that computes both monthly and total payments for a given loan amount, annual interest rate, and loan period.*

Overall Plan

The tasks we identified in the previous chapter for the program are still the same. They are

program tasks

1. Get three input values: loanPayment, interestRate, and loanPeriod.
2. Compute the monthly and total payments.
3. Output the results.

The main difference in this implementation is the use of an instantiable LoanCalculator class. Instead of building the program using only the main class and performing all the tasks in one big main method, we will define an instantiable class LoanCalculator. An instance of the LoanCalculator class will manage other objects such as MainWindow, InputBox, and OutputBox. The LoanCalculator class is organized logically with multiple methods. Figure 4.5 shows the structural difference between the two programs.

An instance of the LoanCalculator class acts like a top-level agent that manages all other objects in the program. The purpose of the main class is to create a LoanCalculator object and give it a command to carry out the loan calculation.

FIGURE 4.5   The object diagrams for the Chapter 3 **LoanCalculator** program and the one we are designing here. Not all methods are shown here to simplify the diagrams.

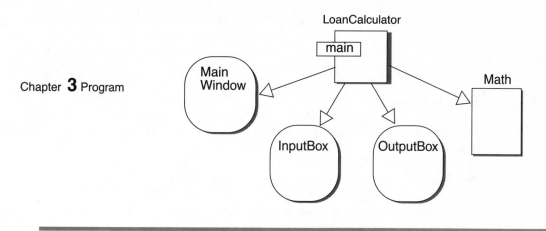

Chapter **3** Program

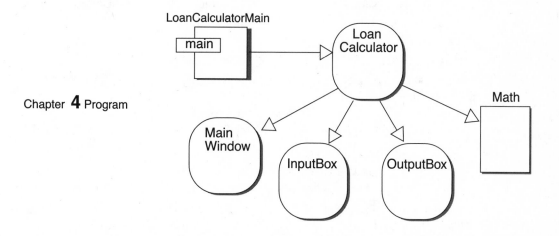

Chapter **4** Program

The LoanCalculator object is built from a number of methods with each method doing a single function. What kinds of methods will the object need?

Since the LoanCalculator object is the top-level agent of the program that manages other objects, we need a method to create these objects. We will do this in the constructor. We will define separate methods for input, computation, and output to organize the class more logically. Designing a set of single-task methods is more manageable and easier to understand than having one method that performs all three tasks of input, computation, and output. We will call the methods getInput, computePayment, and displayOutput. We will also include one method called describeProgram that describes the purpose of the program to the user.

> **Dr. Caffeine**
>
> One of our goals in developing programs is to design them so that they are easy to understand, which is critical in program maintenance. Program maintenance includes correcting errors undetected during development, making minor adjustments, and performing other tasks related to the upkeep of the program. Those who maintain programs are not normally the people who developed them, and maintenance personnel must understand the programs they maintain. A class with a number of cleanly written short methods is more understandable than a class with one gigantic method even if it is cleanly written. Even if the developers themselves perform maintenance, the same argument applies. You may not easily understand code you wrote a week earlier.

We need the main class for the program, and we need to define its main method. In this main method, we have to create an instance of the LoanCalculator class. How should the main method interact with the LoanCalculator object?

Alternative Design

One possibility is to call the methods getInput, computePayment, and so forth, individually as in

```
public static void main ( String args[ ] )
{
    LoanCalculator loanCalculator;
    loanCalculator = new LoanCalculator( );

    loanCalculator.describeProgram();
    loanCalculator.getInputs();
    loanCalculator.computePayment();
    loanCalculator.displayOutput();
}
```

The methods are all public methods and are called individually from the main method. The object diagram for this design is shown in Figure 4.6.

Notice that these four methods must be called in the correct sequence. For example, the program will not work if the main method calls displayOutput before calling computePayment. Except for the describeProgram method, these methods are not independent of each other. They must be called in the right sequence. The reason we divide the class into several methods is to make the class understandable for those who will implement and maintain the class.

FIGURE 4.6   The object diagram for Alternative Design 1. **MainWindow**, **OutputBox**, and **InputBox** objects are not shown.

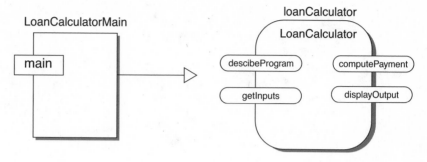

We should provide a lot simpler interface to the user of the LoanCalculator class. Since an instance of the class is the top-level agent, much like a general contractor, we will provide one method the programmer can call to initiate the whole task. We will name the method start. All other methods will be private and called from the start method. The object diagram for this design is shown in Figure 4.7. We will adopt this design for our implementation.

Alternative Design 2

FIGURE 4.7   The object diagram for Alternative Design 2. **MainWindow**, **OutputBox**, and **InputBox** objects are not shown.

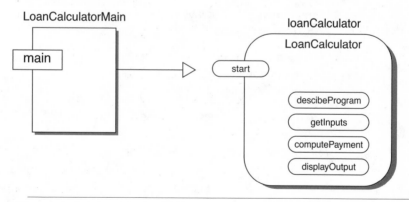

Let's summarize Alternative Design 2 for the LoanCalculator class:

Design Document: The LoanCalculator Class		
Method	**Visibility**	**Purpose**
start	public	Starts the loan calculation by calling the other private methods.
computePayment	private	Given three parameters—loan amount, loan period, and interest rate—it computes monthly and total payments.
describeProgram	private	Displays a short description of the program in Output-Box.
displayOutput	private	Displays the result—monthly and total payments—in OutputBox.
getInputs	private	Uses InputBox to get three input values—loan amount, loan period, and interest rate.

We will implement the program in five steps:

development
steps

1.   Start with the main class and a skeleton of the LoanCalculator class. The skeleton LoanCalculator class will include only object/variable declaration and a constructor to create objects.

2.   Implement the getInput method of LoanCalculator to accept three input values.

3.   Implement the displayOutput method of LoanCalculator to display the results.

4.   Implement the computePayment method of LoanCalculator to compute the monthly and total payments.

5.   Implement the describeProgram method of LoanCalculator to display a brief description of the program.

Step 1 Development: Program Skeleton

Step 1 Design
There are two classes we have to define for the program: LoanCalculatorMain and LoanCalculator. The main class is now called LoanCalculatorMain. Its main method will declare and create an instance of LoanCalculator and send a message start to it to carry out the loan computation. So the method body of the main method will look like this:

```
LoanCalculator    loanCalculator;
```

```
loanCalculator = new LoanCalculator();
loanCalculator.start();
```

This is all we have to design for the main class because the real workhorse of this program is a LoanCalculator object. For the LoanCalculator class, we will begin with the skeleton and develop it incrementally. The purpose of the skeleton LoanCalculator class is to declare and create all the necessary data members. Since these data members will be shared among the methods, we will declare them as instance variables. We will include one class constant MONTHS_IN_YEAR. Their declaration will be as follows:

```
class LoanCalculator
{
    private final int       MONTHS_IN_YEAR = 12;

    private MainWindow      mainWindow;
    private InputBox        inputBox;
    private OutputBox       outputBox;

    private float           loanAmount,
                            annualInterestRate,
                            monthlyInterestRate;

    private double          monthlyPayment,
                            totalPayment;

    private int             loanPeriod,    //loan period in years
                            numberOfPayments;
    ...
}
```

We will not repeat the design for the data members here because their role is the same as in the Chapter 3 program. Some of these data members have to be initialized correctly when a new LoanCalculator object is created, so we will define a constructor to do the necessary initialization. The constructor will be defined as

```
public LoanCalculator()
{
    mainWindow  = new MainWindow("L O A N   C A L C U L A T O R");
    inputBox    = new InputBox(mainWindow);
    outputBox   = new OutputBox(mainWindow);
}
```

Since the main method calls the start method of LoanCalculator, we need to implement this method before we can compile the program. The start method will call the other private methods. It is written as

```
public void start ( )
{
    mainWindow.show();
    outputBox.show();

    describeProgram();
    getInputs();
    computePayment();
    displayOutput();
}
```

No dot notation is used here.

Notice that dot notation is not used in calling the four private methods. When a call is made from a method to another method that belongs to the same class, dot notation is not used. This rule applies equally to both data members and methods. Figure 4.8 illustrates the difference between calling another method of the same class and a method of a different class.

Dot notation is not necessary when you call a method from another method if these two methods belong to the same class.

We will define the four private methods with only a temporary output statement inside their method body to verify that the methods are called correctly. A method that has no "real" statements inside the method body is called a *stub*. The four methods are defined as

stub

```
private void describeProgram()
{
    outputBox.printLine("inside describeProgram"); //TEMP
}

private void getInput()
{
    outputBox.printLine("inside describeProgram"); //TEMP
}

private void computePayment()
```

```
        {
            outputBox.printLine("inside computePayment");   //TEMP
        }

        private void displayOutput()
        {
            outputBox.printLine("inside displayOutput");   //TEMP
        }
```

FIGURE 4.8   The difference between calling a method belonging to the same class and a method belonging to a different class.

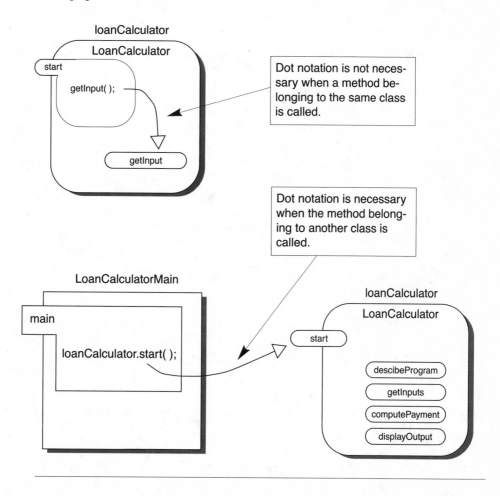

Notice the comment marker //TEMP after the output statements. It is our convention to attach this comment marker so we can easily and quickly locate temporary statements.

For the temporary output statements, we use an OutputBox object because we will be using an OutputBox object in the class anyway. However, we can use a system object to do this type of temporary output for code verification purposes. This system object is available in the System class, and we refer to the output object as System.out. We can use this object just like an OutputBox object, with the only difference being the method name println instead of the more meaningful printLine. For example, you can include the statement

System.out

```
System.out.println("inside setup");
```

instead of

```
outputBox.printLine("inside setup");
```

When you call the println method of System.out, the text is displayed in the default standard output window. The exact appearance of this output window depends on the system you are using. You may want to experiment with System.out and see how it works on your system.

Step 1 Code   Let's put our design in an actual code. The class declaration for the main class is as follows:

```
/*
    Class LoanCalculatorMain

    A program to compute the monthly and total payments for a given loan
    amount, annual interest rate, and number of years.

    Input:      loan amount (float)
                annual interest rate (float)
                loan period - number of years (int)

    Compute:    monthly payment (float)
                total payment (float)
*/


class LoanCalculatorMain
{
    public static void main (String args[])
    {
        LoanCalculator loanCalculator;
        loanCalculator = new LoanCalculator( );
```

```
        loanCalculator.start();
    }
}
```

And the skeleton LoanCalculator class is defined as follows:

```
/*
    Class LoanCalculator (Step 1)

    A class to handle the actual input, computation, and output of loan
    calculation.
*/

import javabook.*;

class LoanCalculator
{

/****************************
    Data Members
****************************/
    private final int     MONTHS_IN_YEAR = 12;

    private MainWindow    mainWindow;
    private InputBox      inputBox;
    private OutputBox     outputBox;

    private float         loanAmount,
                          annualInterestRate,
                          monthlyInterestRate;

    private double        monthlyPayment,
                          totalPayment;

    private int           loanPeriod,            //loan period in years
                          numberOfPayments;

/****************************
    Constructors
****************************/

    public LoanCalculator()
    {
        mainWindow = new MainWindow("L O A N   C A L C U L A T O R");
        inputBox   = new InputBox(mainWindow);
        outputBox  = new OutputBox(mainWindow);
    }


/****************************
    Public Methods

        void    start    (        )

****************************/
```

```
/*   Method:       start

     Purpose:      Top-level method that calls other private methods
                   to compute the monthly and total loan payments.

     Parameters:   None

     Returns:      None
*/
public void start ( )
{
    mainWindow.show();
    outputBox.show();

    describeProgram();     //tell what the program does
    getInput();            //get three input values
    computePayment();      //compute the monthly payment and total
    displayOutput();       //display the results
}


/***************************
    Private Methods

        void    computePayment    (            )
        void    describeProgram    (            )
        void    displayOutput      (            )
        void    getInput           (            )

***************************/

/*   Method:       computePayment

     Purpose:      Compute the monthly and total loan payments.

     Parameters:   None

     Returns:      None
*/
private void computePayment()
{
    outputBox.printLine("inside computePayment");      //TEMP
}


/*   Method:       describeProgram

     Purpose:      Provide a brief explanation of the program to the user.

     Parameters:   None

     Returns:      None
*/
private void describeProgram()
{
    outputBox.printLine("inside describeProgram");      //TEMP
}
```

```
/* Method:          displayOutput

    Purpose:        Display the input values and monthly and total payments.

    Parameters:     None

    Returns:        None
*/
private void displayOutput()
{
    outputBox.printLine("inside displayOutput");        //TEMP
}


/* Method:          getInput

    Purpose:        Get three input values--loan amount, interest rate, and
                    loan period--using an InputBox object.

    Parameters:     None

    Returns:        None
*/
private void getInput()
{
    outputBox.printLine("inside getInput");             //TEMP
}

}
```

Step 1 Test   We run the Step 1 program and verify that both mainWindow and outputBox appear on the screen and the following text appears in outputBox:

```
inside describeProgram
inside getInput
inside computePayment
inside displayOutput
```

After the Step 1 program is compiled and executed correctly, we move on to Step 2.

Step 2 Development: Accept Input Values

Step 2 Design   In the second step of coding, we implement the getInput method. We will reuse the design of using inputBox for input and echo printing for program verification that we derived in Chapter 3.

Step 2 Code   Here's the method:

```
private void getInput()
{
    loanAmount
        = inputBox.getFloat("Loan Amount (Dollars&Cents):");
    annualInterestRate
        = inputBox.getFloat("Annual Interest Rate(eg 9.5):");
    loanPeriod
        = inputBox.getInteger("Loan Period - # of years:");

    //TEMP
    outputBox.printLine("Loan Amount: $" + loanAmount);
    outputBox.printLine("Annual Interest Rate:"
                            + annualInterestRate + "%");
    outputBox.printLine("Loan Period (years):" + loanPeriod);
    //TEMP
}
```

Step 2 Test As before, to verify the input routine is working correctly, we run the program multiple times. For each run, we enter a different set of data to verify that the InputBox object will not accept any invalid input. We also make sure the values entered are displayed correctly in outputBox.

Step 3 Development: Output Values

Step 3 Design In the third step of development, we implement the displayOutput method. We use outputBox to display the three input values and monthly and total payments. We will again reuse the design of output layout from Chapter 3. Since the computePayment method is not yet implemented, we will include the temporary assignment statements for monthly and total payments in the computePayment method. The real computePayment will be implemented in the next step.

Step 3 Code   Here are the two methods:

```
private void displayOutput()
{
    outputBox.printLine("For");
    outputBox.printLine("Loan Amount: " + loanAmount);
    outputBox.printLine("Annual Interest Rate: "
                                + annualInterestRate + "%");
    outputBox.printLine("Loan Period (years): " + loanPeriod);
    outputBox.skipLine(1);

    outputBox.printLine("Monthly payment is $ "+ monthlyPayment);
    outputBox.printLine("  TOTAL payment is $ "   + totalPayment);
}
```

```
private void computePayment()
{
    monthlyPayment   = 132.15;        //TEMP
    totalPayment     = 15858.10 ;     //TEMP
}
```

Step 3 Test

To verify the output routine is working correctly, we run the program multiple times and verify the layout looks okay for different values. It is common for a programmer to run the program several times before the layout looks clean on the screen.

Step 4 Development: Compute Loan Amount

Step 4 Design

In the fourth step of development, we replace the temporary computePayment method with the final one. We have already used the necessary formula in Chapter 3. We will reuse the formula here.

Step 4 Code

Here's the method:

```
private void computePayment()
{
    monthlyInterestRate
            = annualInterestRate / 100.f / MONTHS_IN_YEAR;

    numberOfPayments
            = loanPeriod  *  MONTHS_IN_YEAR;

    monthlyPayment
            =   (loanAmount * monthlyInterestRate)
                /
                (1 - Math.pow( 1 / (1 + monthlyInterestRate),
                                numberOfPayments ) );

    totalPayment  =  monthlyPayment * numberOfPayments;

}
```

Step 4 Test

After the method is added to the class, we need to run the program through a number of test data. As in Chapter 3, we made the assumption that the input values must be valid, so we will only test the program for valid input values. For sample test data, we repeat the table from Chapter 3. The right two columns show the correct results. Remember that these three values are only suggestions, not a complete list of test data. You must try other input values as well.

Input			Output	
Loan Amount	Annual Interest Rate	Loan Period (in years)	Monthly Payment	Total Payment
10000	10	10	132.151	15858.1
15000	7	15	134.824	24268.4
10000	12	10	143.471	17216.5

Step 5 Development: Finalize

Step 5 Design

Now in the last step of development, we finalize the class declaration by completing the describeProgram method, the only method still undefined. We may give a very long description or a very terse one. An ideal program will let the user decide. We do not know how to write such code yet, so we will display a short description of the program to outputBox.

Step 5 Code

Here's the method.

```
private void describeProgram()
{
    outputBox.printLine
            ("This program computes the monthly and total");
    outputBox.printLine
            ("payments for a given loan amount, annual ");
    outputBox.printLine
            ("interest rate, and loan period (# of years).");
    outputBox.skipLine(2);
}
```

Step 5 Test

You may feel that there's not much testing we can do in this step. After all, we add only a single method that carries out a simple output routine. However, many things can go wrong between Step 4 and Step 5. You may have deleted some lines of code inadvertently. You may have deleted a necessary file by mistake. Anything could happen. The point is to test after every step of development to make sure everything is in order.

4.6   Exercises

1. Consider the following instantiable class.

```
class QuestionOne
{
    public    final int    A = 345;
    public    int          b;
    private   float        c;

    private void methodOne( int a)
    {
        b = a;
    }

    public float methodTwo( )
    {
        return 23;
    }
}
```

Identify invalid statements in the following main class. For each invalid statement, state why it is invalid.

```
class Q1Main
{
    public static void main( String args[] )
    {
        QuestionOne q1;
        q1 = new QuestionOne( );

        q1.A = 12;
        q1.b = 12;
        q1.c = 12;

        q1.methodOne( 12 );
        q1.methodOne( );
        System.out.println( q1.methodTwo( 12 ) );
        q1.c = q1.methodTwo( );
    }
}
```

2. What will be the output from the following code?

```
class Q2Main
{
```

```
        public static void main( String args[] )
        {
            QuestionTwo q2;
            q2 = new QuestionTwo( );
            q2.init();

            q2.increment();
            q2.increment();

            System.out.println( q2.getCount() );
        }
    }

    class QuestionTwo
    {
        private  int   count;

        public void init( )
        {
            count = 1;
        }

        public void increment( )
        {
            count = count + 1;
        }

        public int getCount( )
        {
            return count;
        }
    }
```

3. What will be the output from the following code? Q3Main and Question-Three classes are the slightly modified versions of Q2Main and QuestionTwo.

```
    class Q3Main
    {
        public static void main( String args[] )
        {
            QuestionThree q3;
            q3 = new QuestionThree( );
            q3.init();

            q3.count = q3.increment() + q3.increment();
```

```
                      System.out.println( q3.increment() );
                  }
              }

              class QuestionThree
              {
                  public  int    count;

                  public void init( )
                  {
                      count = 1;
                  }

                  public int increment( )
                  {
                      count = count + 1;
                      return count;
                  }
              }
```

4. Determine the output of the following program.

```
/*
    Program Question4

*/
class Question4
{
    private int x, y, z;
    private MainWindow mainWindow;
    private OutputBox outputBox;

    public void start ( )
    {
        int    x, y;

        setup();

        x = y = 10;
        modify(x, y);

        printout();
    }


    private void setup( )
    {
        mainWindow = new MainWindow( );
        outputBox = new OutputBox(mainWindow);
        x = 100;
        y = 200;
        z = 300;
    }
```

```
    private void modify( int x, int y)
    {
        z = x + y;
        x = z;
        y = 2 * z;
    }

    private void printout( )
    {
        outputBox.printLine("x = " + x);
        outputBox.printLine("y = " + y);
        outputBox.printLine("x = " + z);
    }

}
```

```
/* Main Class */
class Q4Main
{
    public static void main( String args[ ] )
    {
        Question4 q4;
        q4 = new Question( );
        q4.start( );
    }
}
```

5. Improve the following program Question5 by converting the class into two classes: the main Q5Main class and the instantiable Question5 class. Avoid duplicating the same code for computing the circumference of two circles. Define a private method in Question5 that accepts the radius of a circle as its parameter and returns the circumference of the circle.

```
/*
    Program Question5

*/
class Question5
{

    public static void main (String args[] )
    {
        int            radius ;
        float          circumference;
        MainWindow     mainWindow;
        OutputBox      outputBox;
        InputBox       inputBox;
        int            smallRadius, largeRadius;
        float          smallCircum, largeCircum;

        mainWindow     = new MainWindow( );
```

```
outputBox      = new OutputBox(mainWindow);
inputBox       = new InputBox(mainWindow);

//compute circumference of a smaller circle
smallRadius = inputBox.getInteger("Radius of smaller circle:");
radius = smallRadius;
smallCircum = (float) (2 * Math.PI * radius);

//compute circumference of a larger circle
largeRadius = inputBox.getInteger("Radius of larger circle:");
radius = largeRadius;
largeCircum = (float) (2 * Math.PI * radius);

//Display the difference
outputBox.printLine("Difference in circumference of two circles");
outputBox.printLine("Circumference of smaller circle: " + smallCircum);
outputBox.skipLine(2);
outputBox.printLine("Circumference of larger circle: " + largeCircum);
ouputBox.skipLine(2);
outputBox.printLine("Differnce: " + (largeCircum - smallCircum));
    }

}
```

6. Write an application that converts centimeters (input) to feet and inches (output). Use InputBox for input and OutputBox for output. 1 inch = 2.54 centimeters. Implement this application by defining and using an instantiable class whose instance is capable of converting metric measurements to U.S. units and vice versa. Some of the possible public methods are

```
public float toFeet      ( float centimeter ) { ... }
public float toInches    ( float centimeter ) { ... }
public float toCentimeter( int    feet,
                           int    inches   ) { ... }
public float toCentimeter( float yard      ) { ... }
```

7. Write an application that displays the recommended weight given the user's age and height. The formula for calculating the recommended weight is

```
recommendedWeight = (height - 100 + age % 10) * 0.90
```

8. Write an application that computes the total ticket sales of a concert. There are three types of seatings: A, B, and C. The program accepts the number of tickets sold and the price of a ticket for each of the three types of seats. The total sales are computed as

```
totalSales =   numberOfA_Seats * pricePerA_Seat +
```

```
numberOfB_Seats * pricePerB_Seat +
numberOfC_Seats * pricePerC_Seat;
```

Write this application using only one class, the main class of the program.

9. Redo exercise 8 by using an instantiable SeatType class. An instance of the SeatType class keeps track of the ticket price for a given type of seat (A, B, or C).

10. Write an application that accepts the unit weight of a bag of coffee in pounds and the number of bags sold and displays the total price of the sale, computed as

```
totalPrice        = unitWeight * numberOfUnits * 5.99f;
totalPriceWithTax = totalPrice + totalPrice * 0.0725f;
```

where 5.99 is the cost per pound and 0.0725 the sales tax. Display the result in the following manner:

```
Number of bags sold:   32
    Weight per bag:   5 lbs
   Price per pound:   $5.99
        Sales tax:   7.25%

      Total price: $ 1027.884
```
You don't have to worry about formatting.

11. Write an application that computes the area of a circular region (the shaded area in the diagram) given the radius of the inner and outer circles r_i and r_o.

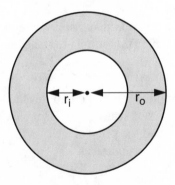

We compute the area of the circular region by subtracting the area of the inner circle from the area of the outer circle. Define an instantiable Circle class that has methods to compute the area and circumference. You set the circle's radius with the setRadius method.

12. In Section 4.3, we modified the conversion methods of the CurrencyConverter class to include the fee deduction. With the modified methods, the sequence of calls such as

```
yenAmount
    = yenConverter.fromDollar( markConverter.toDollar(100) ) ;
```

will result in charging the fee twice. Modify the class to eliminate this double-charging problem.

13. Write an instantiable WeightConverter class. An instance of this class is created by passing the gravity of an object relative to the earth's gravity (see exercise 12 on page 133). For example, the moon's gravity is approximately 0.167 of the earth's gravity, so we create a WeightConverter instance for the moon as

```
WeightConverter   moonWeight;
moonWeight = new WeightConverter( 0.167f );
```

To compute how much you weigh on the moon, you pass your weight on earth to the convert method as

```
yourMoonWeight = moonWeight.convert( 160 );
```

Define the WeightConverter class. Use this class and redo exercise 12 on page 133.

14. Write an application that teaches children how to read a clock. Use two InputBox objects to enter the hour and minute. The application program draws a clock that looks something like

To draw a clock hand, you use the drawLine method of the Graphics class. The endpoints of the line are determined as

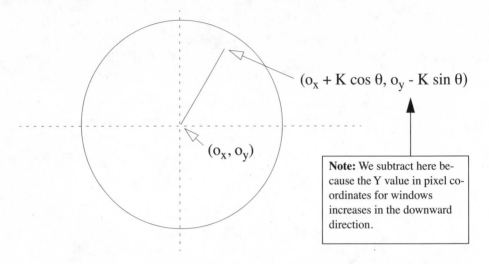

$(o_x + K \cos \theta, o_y - K \sin \theta)$

(o_x, o_y)

Note: We subtract here because the Y value in pixel coordinates for windows increases in the downward direction.

The value for constant K determines the length of the clock hand. Make the K larger for the minute hand than for the hour hand. The angle θ is expressed in radians. The angle θ_{min} of the minute hand is computed as

$$(90 - Minute \times 6.0)\frac{\pi}{180}$$

and the angle θ_{hr} of the hour hand is computed as

$$\left(90 - \left(Hour + \frac{Minute}{60.0}\right) \times 30.0\right)\frac{\pi}{180}$$

where Hour and Minute are input values. The values 6.0 and 30.0 designate the degrees for one minute and one hour (i.e., the minute hand moves 6 degrees in one minute and the hour hand moves 30.0 degrees in one hour). The factor $\frac{\pi}{180}$ converts a degree into the radian equivalent.

You can draw the clock on the main window by getting the window's Graphic object as

```
MainWindow mainWindow = new MainWindow();
mainWindow.show();
Graphics graphic = mainWindow.getGraphics();
        //make sure mainWindow is visible on the screen
        //before calling its getGraphics method
...
graphic.drawOval(100, 100, 200, 200);
...
```

15. Extend the application in exercise 14 by drawing a more realistic, better-looking clock. For example,

Visit Dr. Caffeine's homepage at http://www.cs.nps.navy.mil/~ctwu and see the applet version of the clock.

5

Processing Input with Applets

Introduction

In this chapter, we will teach you how to write applets that can process input data. To write an input-processing applet, you need to know how to define a class with multiple methods, the topic you learned in the previous chapter, because an input-processing applet will necessarily require multiple methods. To understand how an applet processes input data, you must learn what events are and how events are handled in Java programs. We will cover the basics of events and event handling in this chapter.

event

Actions such as moving a mouse, selecting a menu item, entering data, and pressing the ENTER key are all events. When the user makes one of these actions, we say an *event is generated*. We program applets so that a designated method will be executed in response to the generated events. We will cover only a rudimentary event-handling technique in this chapter and defer a more detailed discussion on event handling until Chapter 12.

5.1   Placing GUI Objects on Applets

To write an applet that is capable of processing input data, you must first master a number of new concepts. Not to overwhelm you with too many new concepts, we will keep the number of new concepts introduced in this chapter to a bare minimum, just enough for you to be able to write simple input-processing applets. To explain and illustrate the new concepts introduced here, we will build a sample applet called GreetingApplet. This applet accepts a name entered by the user and replies back with a personalized greeting. For example, when the user enters her name Mireille and presses the ENTER key (the RETURN key on the Mac), the applet displays the greeting Nice to meet you, Mireille. Figure 5.1 shows the applet viewer window when the applet starts.

Figure 5.2 shows the same applet viewer window after the user enters her name and presses the ENTER key.

We will develop this applet in two steps. In this section, we describe how to place objects—one for displaying text and another for accepting the user input—on the applet. In the next section, we will show you how to add code that will be executed when the ENTER key is pressed.

We begin with a new template for an applet. This new template, shown in Figure 5.3, is a more general version of the one we introduced in Chapter 2. Using this template our GreetingApplet is declared as

```
/*

   Program GreetingApplet
```

FIGURE 5.1   The applet viewer window when the applet **GreetingApplet** is started.

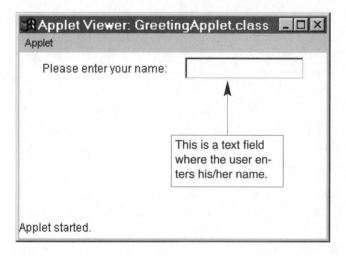

FIGURE 5.2   The applet viewer window after the user enters her name and presses the ENTER key.

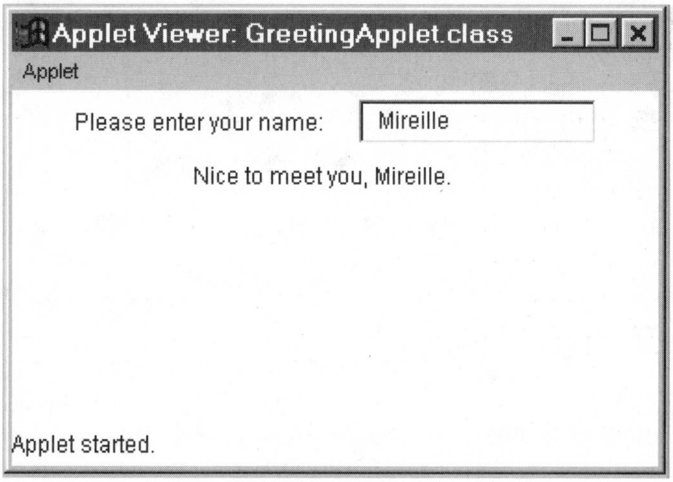

```
        An applet that reads the user's name and
        displays a personalized greeting.
*/

import java.applet.*;
import java.awt.*;

public class GreetingApplet extends Applet
{
    //Object declarations come here

    //Method declaration come here
}
```

Now, let's identify the objects we need for this applet. To process the user input and display a message on an applet, we will use objects from the standard Java class library. Specifically, we use a Label object to display a text and a Text-Field object to accept the user input. The Label and TextField classes are from the standard java.awt package. Objects from these classes are called *GUI* (graphical user interface) objects because they are used for the graphical, win-

Label and
TextField

GUI

FIGURE 5.3   A template for an applet that is more general than the one we introduced in Chapter 2.

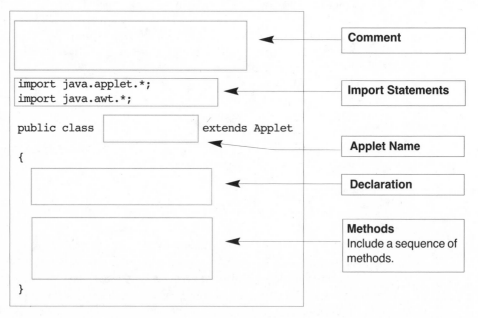

dows-based user interface. The word awt in the java.awt stands for *abstract windowing toolkit*, and the java.awt package contains classes for supporting GUI.

For this applet, we use two Label objects, which we will name prompt and greeting, and one TextField object, which we will name inputLine. These three objects are data members of the class that are shared by multiple methods. As such we will declare them within the class declaration but outside of any method. We declare them as

```
public class GreetingApplet extends Applet
{
    private Label        prompt;
    private Label        greeting;
    private TextField    inputLine;

    //Method declaration come here
}
```

Now that the declaration is done, we need a place to create them. Following the guideline of always declaring a constructor and creating data members in it, we will define a constructor to create them.

To create a Label object, we either pass the text that will be displayed on an applet, as in

```
prompt = new Label("Please enter your name:");
```

or pass no argument, as in

```
greeting = new Label( );
```

To create a TextField object, we specify its size by providing the number of characters visible. For example, the statement

```
inputLine = new TextField( 15 );
```

creates a TextField object wide enough to show 15 characters. Notice that this is the maximum number of characters that are visible, not the number of characters you can enter. If you enter more than 15 characters, you will see the text is scrolled to the left as you enter more characters, always showing the maximum of 15 characters.

The constructor for the GreetingApplet is declared as

```
        public GreetingApplet( )
        {
            prompt    = new Label("Please enter your name:");
            greeting  = new Label( );
            inputLine = new TextField( 15 );
        }
```

To make these three GUI objects visible on the applet, creating them inside the constructor is not enough. We are required to associate these objects with the applet by "adding" them to the applet as in

```
        add( prompt   );
        add( greeting  );
        add( inputLine );
```

in order to make these objects visible. Note: Since we did not assign any text to greeting, it won't be visible yet. We will introduce the code later to assign the greeting message to greeting.

The add method is inherited from its superclass Applet, and, therefore, no dot notation is necessary. We will put these three statements inside the constructor. Here's the full definition of the Step 1 GreetingApplet class:

```
/*
    Program GreetingApplet (Step 1)

    An applet that reads the user's name and
    displays a personalized greeting.
*/

import java.applet.*;
import java.awt.*;

public class GreetingApplet extends Applet
{
/************************
    Data Members
************************/
    private Label       prompt;    //to prompt user for input
    private Label       greeting;  //to display the personalized greeting
    private TextField   inputLine; //to accept user input


/************************
    Constructor
************************/
    public GreetingApplet( )
    {
        //create the data members
        prompt    = new Label("Please enter your name:");
```

```
        greeting   = new Label( );
        inputLine  = new TextField( 15 );

        //now attach them to an applet, so they become
        //visible on the applet.
        add( prompt    );
        add( greeting  );
        add( inputLine );
    }
}
```

Executing the class (with a corresponding HTML file) will produce the applet viewer window shown in Figure 5.1.

You might want to comment out three add statements in the constructor and verify that no GUI objects will be visible. Also, change the order of the three add statements and see what happens.

The order of adding GUI objects is actually significant. If you switch the order of the add statements in the constructor to

```
    add( inputLine );
    add( prompt    );
    add( greeting  );
```

then the applet viewer window shown in Figure 5.4 will appear on the screen. The placement of GUI objects on an applet is dictated by the layout manager associated with the applet. A *layout manager* is an object that controls the placement and size of GUI objects laid out on a container. A *container* object is an object that can contain other GUI objects; for example, frame windows, dialogs, and applets are all containers. There are several layout manager classes in the java.awt package. Three of the more common ones are FlowLayout, CardLayout, and GridLayout. The default layout manager for an applet is a FlowLayout object. With this layout manager, the GUI objects are placed in the left-to-right, top-to-bottom order. If the next GUI object to be placed does not fit in the current row, then it will be placed on the next row. For example, if we change the text of label to Would you kindly enter your name?, the applet viewer window shown in Figure 5.5 will appear on the screen. The second object inputLine does not fit on the first row, so it is placed on the second row. Notice that the GUI objects on each row are center aligned.

Although layout managers are interesting and useful in writing more advanced programs, learning different ones is not essential to understanding the fundamentals of object-oriented programming. We also would like to keep our discussion of input-processing applets simple, so we will not cover the layout

layout manager

container

FIGURE 5.4   The applet viewer window with the order of the **add** statements switched.

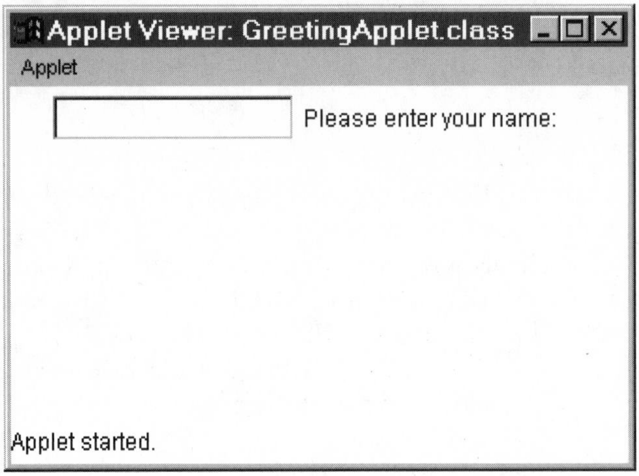

FIGURE 5.5   The applet viewer window with a longer message for the label. Notice that objects in a single row are center-aligned. Alignment becomes more evident if there's only one object in a single row.

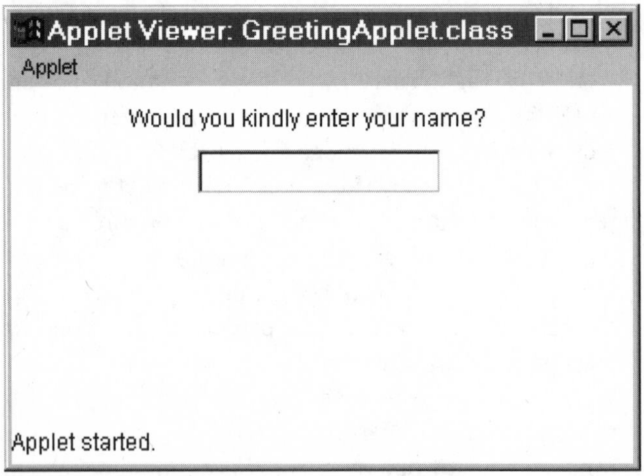

managers any further. However, we do cover in Section 5.3 a technique called *absolute positioning* to place GUI objects without using a layout manager.

Quick Check

1. What is a layout manager?
2. Which method of an applet do you use to make GUI objects visible on the applet?
3. What is the purpose of the numerical argument in the following statement?

```
myTextField = new TextField( 20 );
```

Ms. Latte:	Instead of using **Label** and **TextField**, why can't we simply use an **InputBox** for input?
Dr. Caffeine:	Because **InputBox** and other dialog windows we used in sample applications require a **Frame** object as their owner. An **Applet** object cannot be an owner of dialog windows. Even though it is possible to use dialog boxes in applets, it is strongly recommended that you don't mix the two.
Ms. Latte:	Why?
Dr. Caffeine:	Because applets and dialog boxes are not compatible. Remember that an applet is intended to be executed within a browser. Imagine a situation where an applet opens a dialog box, but instead of interacting with this dialog box, the user moves on to a next Web page. This dialog box remains on the screen, but the applet itself is gone from the screen because the browser is now showing a different page.

Dr. & Ms.

5.2   Adding an Action Listener to an Event Source

When you run the Step 1 GreetingApplet program, you will notice that you can enter text into the TextField object inputLine. You can press the backspace key to delete a character, highlight the text, and perform other editing functions. The functionality that allows the user to enter and edit text is coded in the TextField class, so we don't have to do anything about it. However, when you press the ENTER key, nothing happens. We will now add code to process the pressing of the ENTER key. We will refer to the pressing of the ENTER key as the ENTER *key event*.

event source and event listener

To process an event, we need two types of objects: event source and event listener objects. An *event source* is an object that generates an event, and an *event listener* is an object that listens to the generated events. An event listener must register itself to an event source in order to "listen" to the events generated by the event source. When an event source generates an event, it calls a certain method of the registered event listeners.

Many GUI objects such as text fields, buttons, scroll bars, and others are primary event sources. A single event source can generate different types of events. For example, when a TextField object is active and the ENTER key is pressed, the object generates an *action event*. Not all GUI objects generate action events. In fact, among the GUI objects discussed in this chapter, only Text-Field and Button generate action events.

action event

TextField objects (and **Button** objects covered in Section 5.4) generate action events. **Label** objects do not generate action events.

mouse movement event

You know a TextField object is *active* when the vertical line is blinking in it. When the mouse cursor is moved over the TextField object, it generates a *mouse movement event* (even if it is not active). A TextField object can generate other types of events. Here we will discuss the action events only. We will cover other types of events in Chapter 12.

mouse motion and action event listeners

Any object can be an event listener. A type of event listener that listens to mouse movement events is called a *mouse motion event listener*. A type of event listener that listens to action events is called an *action event listener*. To process an action event generated by a TextField object, we need an action event listener. For the GreetingApplet program, we will set the applet to be an action event listener to the action events that inputLine generates.

To set a GreetingApplet object to be an action event listener, we must do four things:

1. Import the Java event-handling classes with

   ```
   import java.awt.event.*;
   ```

2. Modify the class declaration to include the clause implements Action-listener

   ```
   public class GreetingApplet extends Applet
                           implements ActionListener
   {
       ...
   }
   ```

3. Add the actionPerformed method to the GreetingApplet class declaration.

4. Register the GreetingApplet object to the event source inputLine as its action event listener.

interface

abstract
method

ActionListener is called an *interface*. Although technically they are different, we can view an interface as a special kind of a class that includes only a set of constants and a set of abstract methods. An *abstract method* is a method that has no method body. We say a class *implements* the interface if the class provides the method body for the abstract methods defined in the interface.

Dr. Caffeine

The purpose of interfaces in Java is to dictate common behavior among objects from diverse classes. Suppose we want objects from different classes such as **Truck**, **BankAccount**, **Appliance**, **Stock**, and so on to share one common behavior of computing their market value. We can define an interface, say, **Asset**, with one abstract method **computeCurrentWorth**. We will make all these classes implement the **Asset** interface by providing the method body for the **computeCurrentWorth** method. Notice that they share the common behavior of evaluating their worth, but the individual implementation, the formulas they use to evaluate the market value, will be very different. A similar effect can be achieved if the language allows a class to inherit from more than one superclass, but Java does not allow it. Instead, Java provides interfaces. We will not get into any more details here. You will see more examples of interfaces in Chapters 12 and later.

The ActionListener interface includes one abstract method called actionPerformed, and for the GreetingApplet to implement the ActionListener interface, its class declaration must include the definition for the actionPerformed method.

This actionPerformed method is the method the event source object calls when it generates an action event. Inside the method body, we place the code we want to be executed in response to the generated event. The outline of the Greet-ingApplet class looks like this:

```
public class GreetingApplet extends Applet
                               implements ActionListener
{
    //data member declaration

    public GreetingApplet( )
    {
        ...
    }

    public void actionPerformed( ActionEvent event )
    {
        //response code comes here
    }

}
```

This applet follows the template for input-processing applets. This template, shown in Figure 5.6, is an extension of the one shown earlier in Figure 5.3.

The actionPerformed method takes one parameter of type ActionEvent. For each type of event, Java defines a separate class. Other event classes include WindowEvent, MouseEvent, and TextEvent. These event objects contain infor-mation relevant to the generated event, which is useful in the method that pro-cesses the event.

We will add the code to register the applet to the event source as its action event listener in the constructor. The event source is inputLine, and to add an ac-tion listener to it, we call its addActionListener method with the action listener object as the argument, as in

```
inputLine.addActionListener( <action listener> );
```

with <action listener> replaced by the reference to the actual listener. We will make this call inside the constructor of the GreetingApplet, and to refer to an ob-

FIGURE 5.6   A template for an input-processing applet. This template is an extension of the one shown in Figure 5.3.

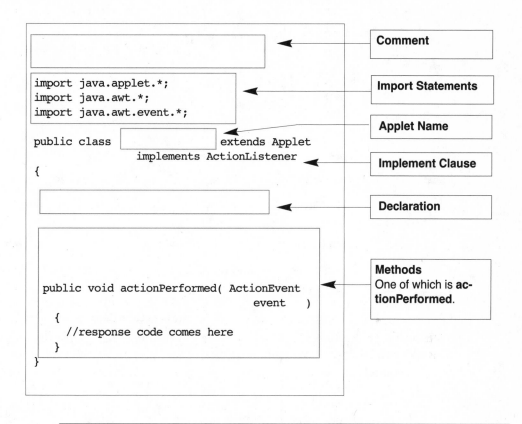

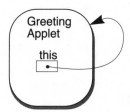

reserved word
this
ject itself within the method of the object, we use the reserved word this. In object diagram, we can represent the reserved word this as

Here's the modified constructor:

```
public GreetingApplet( )
{
    //create GUI objects
    prompt    = new Label("Please enter your name:");
    greeting  = new Label( );
    inputLine = new TextField( );

    //add GUI objects to the applet
    add( prompt    );
    add( greeting );
    add( inputLine );

    //add this applet as an action listener
    inputLine.addActionListener( this );
}
```

Inside the actionPerformed method, we include the code to process the EN-TER key event. Inside the method body, we

1. Fetch the name entered in inputLine by calling its getText method.

2. Concatenate the name returned by the getText method with the message Nice to meet you and the period as

    ```
    "Nice to meet you, " + inputLine.getText() + "."
    ```

3. Assign the resulting string from Step 2 to the Label object greeting by calling its setText method.

4. Call the add method to place greeting and call the doLayout method.

We call the add method again because a new text was assigned to greeting and this could change its dimension. Since the dimension of greeting has possibly changed, we ask the layout manager to adjust the placement of GUI objects based on their new sizes by calling the doLayout method. The actionPerformed method is defined as follows:

```
public void actionPerformed( ActionEvent event )
{
    greeting.setText( "Nice to meet you,"
                        + inputLine.getText( ) + "." );
    add( greeting );
    doLayout();
}
```

Notice that the ActionEvent parameter is not used in the method.

Here's the final, complete listing of GreetingApplet. Its object diagram is shown in Figure 5.7.

```
/*
    Class GreetingApplet

    This applet accepts the user's name via a TextField object. When the user
    presses the ENTER key, the applet displays a personalized greeting.

    Input: the user's name (String)

    Output: the personalized greeting
            "Nice to meet you, <user name>." with <user name> replaced by the
            actual name entered by the user.
*/

import java.awt.*;
import java.applet.*;
import java.awt.event.*;
```

> ActionListener and ActionEvent are defined in this package.

```
public class GreetingApplet extends Applet implements ActionListener
{
/***************************
    Data Members
***************************/

private     Label       prompt;     //to prompt user for input
private     Label       greeting;   //to display the personalized greeting
private     TextField   inputLine;  //to accept user input


/***************************
    Constructor
***************************/
    public GreetingApplet( )
    {
        //create GUI objects
        prompt    = new Label("Please enter your name:");
        greeting  = new Label( );
        inputLine = new TextField( );

        //add GUI objects to the applet
        add( prompt   );
        add( greeting );
        add( inputLine );

        //add this applet as an action listener
        inputLine.addActionListener( this );
    }


/***************************
    Public Methods
        void    actionPerformed    (           )
```

```
***************************/

    /*  Method:        actionPerformned

        Purpose:       Implements the abstract method defined in the interface
                       ActionListener. The method retrieves the text from the
                       TextField object inputLine and displays the personalized
                       greeting using the Label object greeting.

        Parameters:    None

        Returns:       None
    */
    public void actionPerformed( ActionEvent event )
    {
        greeting.setText( "Nice to meet you,"
                      + inputLine.getText( ) + "." );
        add( greeting );
        doLayout();
    }
}
```

FIGURE 5.7   The object diagram for the **GreetingApplet** program.

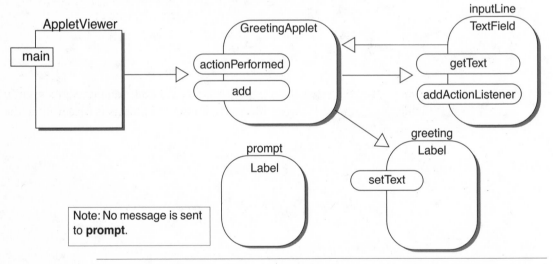

Quick Check

1.   What is the purpose of the addActionListener method?

2. In the GreetingApplet program, which object can be an event source and which object is an action event listener?

3. When does the class need to implement the actionPerformed method?

5.3   Absolute Positioning of GUI Objects

absolute
positioning

reserved word
null

We used the default FlowLayout manager in the previous section. It is also possible to place GUI objects without any layout manager by using the technique called *absolute positioning*. With this technique, we specify the size and the location of GUI objects to place on an applet. To use absolute positioning, we need to set the layout manager of an applet to null by passing the argument null to the setLayout method as in

setLayout
method

```
setLayout( null );
```

The reserved word null means nothing or no object. Thus, assigning null to a layout manager means the applet has no layout manager.

setBounds
method

We designate the location and size of GUI objects placed in the applet by calling the GUI objects' setBounds method. Its general syntax is

```
<object name> . setBounds( <x> , <y> , <width> ,  <height> );
```

where <x> and <y> specify the top, left corner and <width> and <height> specify the dimension of the object. The order of adding GUI objects is irrelevant in the case of absolute positioning.

If we change the constructor of the GreetingApplet to

```
public GreetingApplet()
{
    prompt    = new Label("Please enter your name:");
    inputLine = new TextField( ); //no argument here

    setLayout( null );    //no layout manager

    add( label    );    //attach the GUI
    add( inputLine );    //objects to this applet

    //set the position and size of GUI objects
        prompt.setBounds( 65, 20, 150, 25 );
    inputLine.setBounds( 65, 55, 150, 25 );
}
```

The applet will have no layout manager.

Set the position and size of GUI objects. Make sure the size of the **Label** object is big enough to make all of its text visible.

then you will see the applet viewer window shown in Figure 5.8. Figure 5.9 shows how the setBounds method works.

FIGURE 5.8   The applet with no layout manager and with absolute positioning of GUI objects.

If an applet is using the default FlowLayout manager, then the GUI objects in the applet will move when you resize the applet viewer window. However, with no layout manager and absolute positioning, the GUI objects on the applet will not move when you resize the applet viewer window. This is one effect of setting the layout manager to null and using absolute positioning. Remember that you can use absolute positioning only when you set the layout manger to null.

If you want to use the absolute positioning approach to place GUI objects on an applet, then you must set the layout manager to **null**.

5.4   The Button **Class**

In the GreetingApplet program, the user informs the program that she has finished entering her name by pressing the ENTER key, and the applet is programmed to respond to this ENTER key event. Let's modify the applet by

FIGURE 5.9   The **setBounds** method takes four arguments: x, y, width, and height in pixel values .

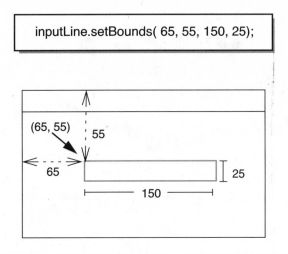

adding another GUI object. Instead of the user pressing the ENTER key, she will now click a button.

A type of button called a *pushbutton* is one of the most common GUI objects used in today's windows-based programs. Figure 5.10 shows a modified GreetingApplet named GreetingAppletWithButton, which now includes a button.

To add a pushbutton to an applet, we create an instance of the Button class from the java.awt package. The way we interact with a Button object is very similar to the way we interact with other GUI objects. To create a Button object, we pass the label of a button (the text that appears inside a button). For example, the button in GreetingAppletWithButton is declared and created as

```
Button      helloButton;

helloButton = new Button( "Say Hello" );
```

A button is another kind of GUI object that generates action events. A button generates an action event when we click on it. So, if we want to process the button click event, then we add an action listener to a button. For the GreetingAppletWithButton, we add the applet as its action event listener in the constructor as

FIGURE 5.10   An applet viewer window running **GreetingAppletWithButton** after the user clicked on the button. This applet uses absolute positioning for laying out the GUI objects.

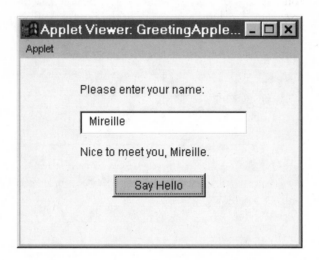

```
public GreetingAppletWithButton( )
{
    //code for creating GUI objects and
    //adding them to the applet

    helloButton.addActionListener( this );
}
```

The applet is the action event listener of **helloButton**.

When helloButton generates an action event, it calls the action listener's **actionPerformed** method. This **actionPerformed** method is the same as in **GreetingApplet** because the response the applet makes is still the same.

It is possible to register different action listeners to a single event source and to register a single action listener to different event sources. For example, we can register the applet as an action listener to both inputLine and helloButton. This means that the user can either click on a button or press the ENTER key (when inputLine is active) when she's done entering her name. To register the applet to both inputLine and helloButton, we simply include the following two statements in the constructor:

```
inputLine.addActionListener( this );

helloButton.addActionListener( this );
```

Both inputLine and helloButton will call the actionPerformed method of GreetingAppletWithButton when they generate an action event.

> You can register multiple event listeners to a single event source and register a single event listener to multiple event sources.

5.5   Converting Text to a Numerical Value

Suppose we want to write an applet that accepts the user's year of birth and print out the message You will be <N> years old in year 2000, with <N> replaced with the actual age of the user. This applet will be very similar to GreetingApplet of the previous section. We need to learn only one new concept to write this applet, namely, the data conversion from text to a numerical value.

A TextField object we use to input data from the user will accept data as text value. To perform a numerical computation on this input text data, we must first convert it to a number. Let's see how we can perform the data conversion. First, string   text data in Java is called a *string*, and we can use a variable of type String. We will only show a very simple use of String variables in this section. A full discussion of string manipulation will be presented in Chapter 8.

Using String variables, we can rewrite the actionPerformed method of GreetingApplet as

```
public void actionPerformed( ActionEvent event )
{
    String name, message;

    name       = inputLine.getText();
    message    = "Nice to meet you, " + name + ".";

    greeting.setText( message );
}
```

Because the getText method of TextField returns a String value, it is not valid to write

```
int age;
age = inputLine.getText();
```

because the data type does not match. We were able to do something like

```
int age;
InputBox inputBox = new InputBox(...);

age = inputBox.getInteger( );
```

because the getInteger method does the conversion for us. The InputBox class also uses a TextField object to get the user input, but the text input data are converted to an appropriate data type (int for getInteger, float for getFloat, and so forth) before returning the value to the caller.

Since we are using TextField objects directly in our applets, we must do our own data conversion. To convert string data to a float or int value, we can use a **Float** object. Do not confuse this Float with the numerical data type float. An instance of the Float class is an object that contains a float value as its value. The following diagram illustrates a Float object containing a float value 23.5f.

To convert a string to a float, we first create a Float object with the string as its argument. For example,

```
Float  floatObject;
floatObject = new Float( "234.5" );
```

An error will result if the passed string cannot be converted to a float value, for example, "12ABC". Once the Float object is created, we can get a float value by calling the object's floatValue method

```
float x;
x = floatObject.floatValue();
```

The float variable x will hold the numerical value 234.5f. It is also possible to get an int value from floatObject. If we execute

```
int i;
i = floatObject.intValue();
```

then the int variable i will hold the integer value 235. Notice the value is rounded.

We can convert a float value to a string value using a Float object also. The following code converts the float value 45.88f to the string value "45.88":

```
Float floatObject;
String str;

floatObject = new Float( 45.88f ); //pass a float value
str = floatObject.toString();
```

Notice that we pass a float value as an argument in creating a new Float object. We can create a Float object by passing either a string or a float value.

wrapper

The Float class is called a *wrapper* class because it "wraps" a float value with a set of methods useful in manipulating it. Other wrapper classes whose instances contain a numerical value are Integer, Long, and Double. Their respective conversion methods are intValue, longValue, doubleValue, and toString.

We will use these data conversion routines in the next section's sample program.

 Quick Check

1. What will be the state of memory after the following code is executed? Draw the state-of-memory diagram.

    ```
    Float      myFloatObj;
    myFloatObj = new Float( "12.345" );
    ```

2. What is the value of x?

    ```
    Float      myFloatObj1, myFloatObj2;
    float      x;

    myFloatObj1 = new Float( "12.0" );
    myFloatObj2 = new Float( "12.6" );

    x = myFloatObj1.floatValue()
            + myFloatObj2.intValue();
    ```

3.   What is the output?

```
Float      myFloatObj;

myFloatObj = new Float( "22.66" );

outputBox.printLine(
     (int) Math.round( myFloatObj.floatValue()) );
```

5.6   Sample Program: Finding Body Mass Index (BMI)

As a summary of the topics covered in this chapter, we will develop an applet that computes your body mass index. A *body mass index* (BMI) is defined by the formula

$$BMI = \frac{w}{h^2}$$

where w is weight in kilograms and h is height in meters. A person with a BMI of 20 to 26 is generally considered healthy, although there's no agreed-upon BMI at which health risks become significant. But most experts agree that you need to be concerned if your BMI is 27 or above. If you are interested in BMI and healthy living in general, you can start exploring the Web from http://www.healthyweight.com.

Problem Statement

Write an applet that displays a BMI of a person given his or her weight (in kilograms) and height (in meters).

Overall Plan

As always, our initial task is to map out the overall plan for development. Let's begin with the visual appearance of the applet and identify GUI objects necessary for the program. First, we need two TextField objects to input height and weight. For these two TextField objects, we need to attach labels so the user knows which is for weight and which is for height. We will use two Label objects for this purpose. We also need a third Label object to display the user's BMI.

Now, how should the user let the program know she's done entering the weight and height? We can let both TextField objects be an event source so the user can press the ENTER key when either one of the TextField objects is active. This approach will work but does not support a good user interface, because it's not obvious to the user just by looking at the applet that she must press the ENTER key to tell the applet to compute the BMI. It is a much better user interface if we use a pushbutton. When the user sees a pushbutton on an applet, it immediately becomes obvious that she needs to click on the button to initiate some action. Let's add a Button to the applet. Figure 5.10 is our draft design of the applet's visual appearance. And here's our initial design document:

program classes

Design Document:	BMIApplet Program
Class	**Purpose**
BMIApplet	The main applet class. The applet viewer will create an instance of this class.
TextField	Two TextField objects are used: one for inputting weight and another for inputting height.
Label	Three Label objects are used: two for labeling the TextField objects and the third one for displaying the BMI.
Button	One Button object with label compute BMI is used. When this button is clicked, the applet displays the computed BMI.

Figure 5.11 is the object diagram for the applet at this point. Notice the arrow from computeButton to the BMIApplet because computeButton is the one calling the applet's actionPerformed method.

We will develop the applet in the following four steps:

development steps

1. Start with a skeleton BMIApplet class. The skeleton class will include data member declarations and a partially defined constructor that creates and places GUI objects.

2. Add code to the constructor to create and place all GUI objects on the applet.

3. Define the actionPerformed method to process the button click action event. We will include a dummy output statement to verify the button click event is properly detected.

4. Add code to compute and display the BMI and finalize the code.

FIGURE 5.11   The object diagram for the program **BMIApplet**.

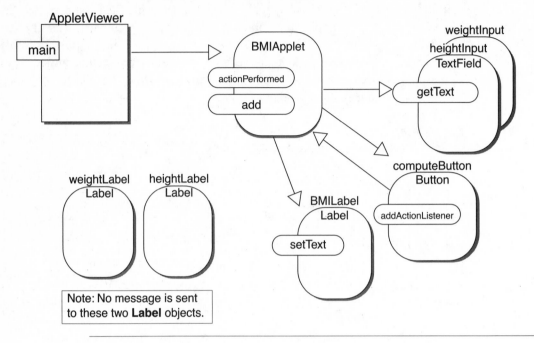

Step 1 Development: Applet Skeleton

Step 1 Design We will start with a skeleton for the BMIApplet. The structure we learned in this chapter is to make an applet an action event listener, so the class declaration will look like this:

```
public class BMIApplet extends Applet implements ActionListener
{
    ...
}
```

We have identified seven GUI objects in the overall planning stage, and these GUI objects will be the data members of the class. Their declaration will be as follows:

```
private    Label      heightLabel,
                      weightLabel,
                      BMILabel;
```

```
private    TextField  heightInput,
                      weightInput;


private    Button     computeButton;
```

Since the applet implements the ActionListener interface, we must include the actionPerformed method. We also need a constructor to create and place GUI objects on the applet. The class design document at this point is therefore as follows:

Design Document: The BMIApplet Class		
Method	**Visibility**	**Purpose**
`<Constructor>`	`public`	Create and place GUI objects on the applet.
`actionPerformed`	`public`	Includes response code for the button click action event. The method computes and displays the BMI for a given height and weight.

Step 1 Code

Let's put our design in an actual code. We will begin with a shell constructor that includes only a code to create and place a button. The actionPerformed method will include no statements in the method body. We will complete the method in Step 3. The class declaration for the Step 1 applet is as follows:

```
/*
    Program BMIApplet

    An applet that accepts the user's height and weight
    and displays his/her body mass index (BMI) according to the formula

            BMI = weight / (height * height)

    Input:    height (in meters, e.g., 1.82)
              weight (in kilograms, e.g., 75.3)

    Output:   Message "Your BMI is <NN>" with <NN> replaced by the
              actual number.
*/

import java.awt.*;
import java.applet.*;
import java.awt.event.*;

public class BMIApplet extends Applet implements ActionListener
{
/***************************
    Data Members
***************************/
```

```
private      Label        heightLabel,   //label for heightInput
                          weightLabel,   //label for weightInput
                          BMILabel;      //label for displaying a BMI

private      TextField    heightInput,   //to accept the user's height
                          weightInput;   //to accept the user's weight

private      Button       computeButton;//the user clicks this button
                                         //to compute the BMI

/***************************
   Constructor
***************************/
public BMIApplet( )
{
    //TEMP: Just add a button
    computeButton = new Button("Compute BMI");

    add( computeButton );

}


/***************************
   Public Methods
      void   actionPerformed   (           )

***************************/

   /* Method:        actionPerformned

      Purpose:       The method retrieves data from nameInput and heightInput
                     and displays the BMI.

      Parameters:    None

      Returns:       None
   */
   public void actionPerformed( ActionEvent event )
   {
       //code comes here
   }
}
```

Since this is an applet, we need an HTML file to run it. We will use our default HTML file whose content is shown below. The file is saved as **BMIApplet.html**.

```
<HTML>
<BODY>
<APPLET CODE="BMIApplet.class" WIDTH=300 HEIGHT=190></APPLET>
</BODY>
</HTML>
```

Step 1 Test

We run the Step 1 applet and verify that an applet appears with a button labeled compute BMI on it. After the Step 1 program is compiled and executed correctly, we move on to Step 2.

Step 2 Development: Layout of GUI Objects

Step 2 Design

In this step, we will complete the constructor by creating all GUI objects and placing them on the applet. We have two choices: use the default layout manager FlowLayout or set the layout manager to null and use absolute positioning.

Alternative Design 1

If we use the default layout manager, then we have to place the GUI objects in the right order. To realize the layout we designed in the overall planning stage, we must execute the following statements in order:

```
add( heightLabel );
add( heightInput );

add( weightLabel );
add( weightInput );

add( computeButton );

add( BMILabel );
```

Using the FlowLayout manager, the actual appearance is also affected by the length of the text assigned to the labels and the values assigned to WIDTH and HEIGHT in the BMIApplet.html. We have to try out different combinations before settling on the one that looks best.

Alternative Design 2

If we use absolute positioning, then we must set the layout manager to null and call the setBounds method for all GUI objects to set their position and size. If we call the setBounds method, then the order of adding the GUI objects is irrelevant. The sequence of calls may look something like this:

```
    heightLabel.setBounds( 60,  20, 150, 25 );
    heightInput.setBounds( 70,  50, 180, 25 );
    weightLabel.setBounds( 60,  80, 150, 25 );
    weightInput.setBounds( 70, 110, 180, 25 );
  computeButton.setBounds( 70, 140, 120, 25 );
       BMILabel.setBounds( 60, 170, 150, 25 );
```

We will adopt the first alternative design and leave the second alternative as an exercise.

Step 2 Code

Here's the code to create and place the GUI objects on the applet:

```
                 public BMIApplet( )
                 {
                     //create the GUI objects
                     heightLabel
                            = new Label("Your height (in meters, e.g. 1.88):");
                     heightInput = new TextField( 15 );

                     weightLabel
                         = new Label("Your weight (in kilograms, e.g., 180.5):");
                     weightInput   = new TextField( 15 );

                     computeButton = new Button("    Compute BMI    ");

                     BMILabel      = new Label( "This is your BMI Computer." );


                     //place the GUI objects on the applet
                     //order of adding is significant
                     add( heightLabel );
                     add( heightInput );

                     add( weightLabel );
                     add( weightInput );

                     add( computeButton );

                     add( BMILabel );

                 }
```

Step 2 Test   We run the Step 2 program and experiment with different combinations of the text for labels and the values for the WIDTH and HEIGHT attributes in BMI-Applet.html. After we get the right combinations that make the applet's visual appearance to our liking, we move on to Step 3.

Step 3 Development: Process the Button Click Event

Step 3 Design   In this step, we implement the actionPerformed method. The task of the action-Performed method is to accept two input values and compute the BMI. The input values are retrieved from the two TextField objects. Since the values returned by the getText method are string data, we need to convert them to numerical values. We discussed the conversion from string to numerical value in Section 5.5. Since the input values will include a decimal point, the numerical values will be of type float. Once we have two numerical values, we use the given formula to compute the BMI. Given float values for height and weight, the resulting BMI will also be float. If we use the float data type for the result, then we can get a number such as 24.6345. Since it is more common among health experts to use a whole number for BMI, we will round off the result to get an integer, that is, 25 instead of 24.6345.

Here's the outline of the actionPerformed method:

```
Task 1. Get input from heightInput and weightInput

Task 2. Convert textual input values to equivalent numerical
        values.

Task 3. Compute BMI from the given two numbers. Round off the
        result to integer.

Task 4. Display the result.
```

In order to make computeButton call the actionPerformed method of the applet, we must add the statement to register this applet as an action event listener to computeButton in the constructor as

```
computeButton.addActionListener( this );
```

Step 3 Code

We are now ready to put our design into an actual code. The actionPerformed method is defined as

```java
public void actionPerformed( )
{
    String heightString, weightString, result;
    float  height, weight;
    int    BMI;

    //Get input values
    heightString = heightInput.getText( );
    weightString = weightInput.getText( );

    //Convert input to numbers
    height = convertToFloat( heightString );
    weight = convertToFloat( weightString );

    //Compute the BMI
    BMI = computeBMI( height, weight );
```

```
            //Display the result
            result = "Your BMI is " + BMI;
            BMILabel.setText( result );
        }
```

Notice the use of the two methods convertToFloat and computeBMI. We use these two private methods to keep the actionPerformed method concise and, therefore, easy to comprehend. For the two private methods, we use the temporary method body, defined as

```
        private float convertToFloat( String str )
        {
            return 123.5f; //TEMP
        }

        private int computeBMI( float height, float weight )
        {
            return 24; //TEMP
        }
```

We modify the constructor to include the statement to add the applet as an action listener:

```
        public BMIApplet
        {
            //same as before

            computeButton.addActionListener( this );
        }
```

Step 3 Test   Run the Step 3 applet and verify that the message

```
        Your BMI is 24.
```

appears on the applet when you click the button.

Step 4 Development: Compute the BMI

Step 4 Design   The design document for the BMIApplet class now includes two private methods, which were defined in Step 3. Here's the design document:

Design Document: The BMIApplet Class		
Method	**Visibility**	**Purpose**
. . .	. . .	. . .
computeBMI	private	The method computes the BMI for given height and weight passed as parameters. The method returns the BMI as int.
convertToFloat	private	The method converts a given String value to a float value.

The final task is to complete these two private methods. The computeBMI method implements the formula that computes the BMI given values for height and weight in float. The statement will be

```
BMI = weight / (height * height);
```

Be careful not to express the formula erroneously as

```
BMI = weight / height * height;
```

This statement is wrong because it is equivalent to the mathematical expression

$$\frac{w}{h} \times h$$

Remember that the precedence rule causes the division to be evaluated before the multiplication.

We decided in the previous step that the value of BMI will be represented as an integer so we need to round off the value to the nearest integer value and typecast the result to type int. So the final form will be

```
BMI = (int) Math.round( weight / (height * height) );
```

The conversion of input text to a float value is done by using the technique explained in Section 5.5. We use a Float object and its floatValue method as

```
Float floatObj = new Float( str );   //str is a String value
float number   = floatObj.floatValue();
```

For this routine to work correctly, we must assume that the input values are valid. If the user enters an input that contains a character other than 0 through 9 or a decimal point, the conversion will not work. We have to make this assumption because we do not know yet how to test for the validity of input. We will learn this in the next chapter.

Step 4 Code   The computeBMI method is defined as

```
private int computeBMI( float height, float weight )
{
    int BMI;

    BMI = (int) Math.round( weight / (height * height) );

    return BMI;
}
```

The convertToFloat method is defined as

```
private float convertToFloat( String str )
{
    Float floatObj = new Float( str );
    return floatObj.floatValue();
}
```

Step 4 Test   Now we are ready to input different values and verify that the applet produces the correct results. Run the applet by entering many different input values. Here are some of the possible input values:

Input		Output
height	weight	BMI
1.82	70	21
1.82	90	27
1.65	55	20
1.79	80	25
1.70	65	22

5.7   Running an Applet as an Application

We used an applet viewer to run applets. To run simple applets like the ones we developed in this chapter, we actually do not need an applet viewer. We can use any frame window to run applets. The MainWindow class in javabook is one such frame window. Just as we place GUI objects on an applet, we can place an applet on a frame window because a frame window is a container and an applet is itself a GUI component.

We will show you how to run the GreetingApplet as an application. It is actually very simple. Assuming the GreetingApplet class is already defined, we just have to define the main class. In the main method, we create an instance of MainWindow and place a GreetingApplet object on this MainWindow object. Here's the main class:

```
/*
    Program GreetingApplication

    Run GreetingApplet as an application
*/

import javabook.*;

class GreetingApplication
{
    public static void main( String args[] )
    {
        MainWindow        mainWindow;
        GreetingApplet    greetingApplet;

        mainWindow        = new MainWindow("My Applet Runner");
        greetingApplet    = new GreetingApplet();

        greetingApplet.init(); //make sure you initialize it

        //add greetingApplet to mainWindow and show the window
        mainWindow.add( greetingApplet );
        mainWindow.show( );
    }
}
```

That's it. Now you can run any applet as an application. Remember we mentioned earlier that an applet viewer is the main class of the applet programs. We are simply defining our own main class, just as we do with any other application programs. Notice that when we run an applet as an application, an HTML file is no longer necessary. Being able to run an applet as an application gives programmers a lot of opportunities and flexibility. Using this technique, we can develop one applet and run the same applet as a regular applet on a browser or as a standalone application.

Since a MainWindow object by default is almost as big as the screen size, you may want to resize and position the window. You can do it by calling the window's setSize and move methods. You can put the following two statements before you show the window:

```
mainWindow.setSize( 400, 300 ); //pass the width and height

mainWindow.move( 250, 200 );    //set the top left corner to
                                // (x, y) == (250, 200)
```

5.8   Exercises

1. Identify the problems with the following constructor of an applet. Assume the GUI objects are all properly declared in the data member declaration section.

    ```
    public MyApplet( )
    {
        //create objects
        textField = new TextField( );
        label     = new Label( );

        label.addActionListener( this );
    }
    ```

2. What is the difference between Float and float?

3. If an applet is declared as

    ```
    public class MyApplet extends Applet implements ActionListener
    {
        ...
    }
    ```

    which public method must be added to this applet?

4. Identify which of the following statements are invalid:

```
Float       floatObj1  = new Float("123");
Integer     intObj     = new Integer("123.0");
Float       floatObj2  = new Float(12.3);
int sum = floatObj.floatValue( ) + floatObj.intValue();
```

5. (Challenge) Consider the last statement of the constructor from the Greet-ingApplet program in Section 5.2 page 204:

```
public GreetingApplet( )
{
    ...

    //add this applet as an action listener
    inputLine.addActionListener( this );
}
```

What will be the problem if we rewrite the constructor to

```
public GreetingApplet( )
{
    ...

    //add a GreetingApplet object as an action listener
    inputLine.addActionListener( new GreetingApplet() );
}
```

Note: The code does not have any syntax error.

6. Identify all errors in the following applet.

```
/*
    Class QuestionApplet

*/

import java.awt.*;
import java.applet.*;

private class QuestionApplet extends Applet
{

private    Button     button;
private    Label      greeting;
```

```
public Applet( )
{
    greeting    = new Label("Hello, how are you?");
    button      = new Button("Good Bye" );

    add( greeting );
    add( button );

}

public void actionPerformed( Event event )
{
    greeting.setText( "Well, good-bye.");
}
}
```

7. Write an applet that converts a given Celsius temperature to the equivalent Fahrenheit temperature. The formula for conversion is

```
fahrenheit = (9.0f/5.0f) * celsius + 32.0f;
```

8. Rewrite the LoanCalculator application in Chapter 4 as an applet. Use three TextField objects for getting the loan amount, interest rate, and loan period. Every time the user presses the ENTER key, the applet displays the monthly and total payments. Include appropriate labels for input and output.

9. Write an applet that converts centimeters (input) to feet and inches (output). Use TextField for input and two Label objects for output. 1 inch = 2.54 centimeters.

10. Write an applet that converts feet and inches (input) to centimeters.

11. Modify the BMIApplet so the applet computes the BMI when the user clicks on the button or presses the ENTER key. The ENTER key event is valid only when the weightInput object is active. The ENTER key event acts like a shortcut for clicking on the button, where the user enters her height, presses the TAB key to move to weightInput, enters her weight, and then presses the ENTER key. This sequence works faster than the user removing her hand from the keyboard and clicking on the button with a mouse after entering two values.

12. Modify the BMIApplet so the user can enter his/her weight in pounds (float) and height in feet (int) and inches (int). Use absolute position for the layout of the GUI objects as shown below:

13. Write an applet called RecommendedWeightApplet that computes the user's recommended weight given his/her height. For this applet use the following formula for calculating the recommended weight:

```
recommendedWeight = (height - 100 + age % 10) * 0.90;
```

The height is entered in centimeters.

14. Modify the RecommendedWeightApplet of exercise 13 so the user can enter his or her height in feet and inches. Use separate TextField objects for feet and inches input.

15. Write an applet that acts like an adding machine. The user enters numbers one number at a time. When the user presses the ENTER key or clicks on the Add button after each entry, the applet adds the number to the running sum. Display the running sum using a Label object.

16. Rewrite the clock application from Chapter 4, exercise 14 on page 191 as an applet. Use two TextField objects to enter the hour and minute. Define a private method drawClock that draws a clock given the hour and minute. The actionPerformed method gets the two values from TextField objects, converts them to float, and passes them as arguments to the drawClock method. The drawClock method should call other private methods such as drawFace, drawHourHand, and drawMinuteHand.

17. An earned run average (ERA) of a baseball pitcher is computed by multiplying the total earned runs by 9 and dividing the result by the total number of innings pitched. Write an applet that computes the ERA.

18. A slugging percentage of a baseball player is computed by dividing the total bases of all hits by the total times at bat (single = 1 base, double = 2 bases, triple = 3 bases, and home run = 4 bases). Write an applet that computes the slugging percentage. The applet accepts five input values: number of singles, number of doubles, number of triples, number of home runs, and number of times at bat.

19. Select one applet from the earlier exercises and run it without using an applet viewer or browser by defining your own main class.

Selection Statements

6

OBJECTIVES

After you have read and studied this chapter, you should be able to

1. Implement selection control in a program using if statements.

2. Implement selection control in a program using switch statements.

3. Write boolean expressions using relational and boolean operators.

4. Evaluate given boolean expressions correctly.

5. Nest an if statement inside another if statement's then or else part correctly.

6. Choose the appropriate selection control statement for a given task.

7. Write applications using the ListBox class from javabook and the Color class from the standard java.awt package.

Introduction

Decisions, decisions, decisions. From the moment we are awake until the time we go to sleep, we are making decisions. Should I eat cereal or toast? What should I wear to school today? Should I eat at the cafeteria today? And so forth. We make many of these decisions by evaluating some criteria. If the number of students in line for registration seems long, then come back tomorrow for another try. If today is Monday, Wednesday, or Friday, then eat lunch at the cafeteria.

sequential execution

control statement

Computer programs are no different. Any practical computer program contains many statements that make decisions. Often a course of action is determined by evaluating some kind of a test (e.g., Is the input value negative?). Statements in programs are executed in sequence, which is called *sequential execution* or *sequential control flow*. However, we can add decision-making statements to a program to alter this control flow. For example, we can add a statement that causes a portion of a program to be skipped if an input value is greater than 100. The statement that alters the control flow is called a *control statement*. In this chapter we describe some important control statements, called *selection statements*. In the next chapter we will describe other control statements, called *repetition statements*.

6.1   The if **Statement**

Suppose we wish to enter a student's test score and print out the message You did not pass if the score is less than 70 and You did pass if the score is 70 or higher. Here's how we express this logic in Java:

```
//Assume messageBox and inputBox are declared and created
testScore = inputBox.getInteger("Enter test score:");

if (testScore < 70)

    messageBox.show("You did not pass");

else

    messageBox.show("You did pass");
```

> This statement is executed if the **testScore** is less than 70.

> This statement is executed if the **testScore** is 70 or higher.

We use an if statement to specify which block of code to execute. A block of code may contain zero or more statements. Which block is executed depends on the result of evaluating a test condition called a *boolean expression*. The if statement in the program follows this general format:

if statement
syntax

```
if ( <boolean expression> )
    <then block>

else
    <else block>
```

Figure 6.1 illustrates the correspondence between the if statement we wrote and the general format.

FIGURE 6.1   Mapping of the sample **if** statement to the general format.

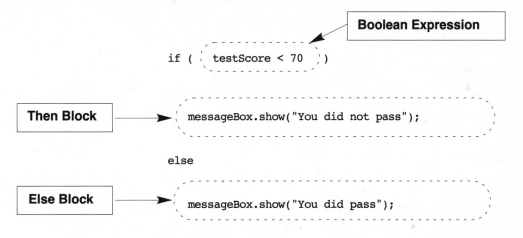

The <boolean expression> is a conditional expression that is evaluated to either true or false. For example, the following three expressions are all conditional:

```
testScore < 80
testScore * 2 > 350
30 < w / (h * h)
```

relational
operators

The six *relational operators* we can use in conditional expressions are

```
<           // less than
<=          // less than or equal to
==          // equal to
!=          // not equal
>           // greater than
>=          // greater than or equal to
```

Here are some more examples:

```
a * a <= c      //true if a * a is less than or equal to c
x + y != z      //true if x + y is not equal to z
a == b          //true if a is equal to b
```

If the boolean expression evaluates to true, then the statements in the <then block> are executed. Otherwise, the statements in the <else block> are executed. We will cover more complex boolean expressions in the next section. Notice that we can reverse the relational operator and switch the then and else blocks to derive the equivalent code, e.g.,

```
if (testScore >= 70)
    messageBox.show("You did pass");

else
    messageBox.show("You did not pass");
```

Notice that the reverse of < is >=, not >.

selection
statement

The if statement is called a *selection* or *branching statement* because it selects (or branches to) one of the alternative blocks for execution. In our example, either

```
messageBox.show("You did not pass");
```

or

```
messageBox.show("You did pass");
```

is executed depending on the value of the boolean expression. We can illustrate a branching path of execution with a diagram shown in Figure 6.2.

In the preceding if statement, both blocks contain only one statement. The then or else block can contain more than one statement. The general format for both the <then block> and the <else block> is either a

```
<single statement>
```

or a

FIGURE 6.2   The diagram showing the control flow of the sample **if** statement.

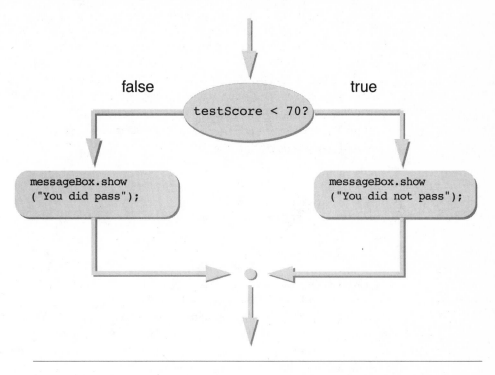

<compound statement>

where <single statement> is a Java statement and <compound statement> is a sequence of Java statements surrounded by braces as shown below with $n \geq 0$ statements:

```
{
    <statement 1>
    <statement 2>
    ...
    <statement n>
}
```

If multiple statements are needed in the <then block> or the <else block>, they must be surrounded by braces { and }. For example, suppose we want to print out additional messages for each case. Let's say we also want to print Keep up the good work when the student passes and print Try harder next time when the student fails. Here's how:

```
if (testScore < 70)
{
    messageBox.show("You did not pass");
    messageBox.show("Try harder next time");
}
else
{
    messageBox.show("You did pass");
    messageBox.show("Keep up the good work");
}
```

Compound Statement

The braces are necessary to delineate the statements inside the block. Without the braces, the compiler will not be able to tell whether a statement is a part of the block or the statement that follows the if statement.

Notice the absence of semicolons after the right braces. A semicolon is never necessary immediately after a right brace. A compound statement may contain zero or more statements, so it is perfectly valid for a compound statement to include only one statement. Indeed, we can write the sample if statement as

```
if (testScore < 70)
{
    messageBox.show("You did not pass");
}
else
{
    messageBox.show("You did pass");
}
```

Although not required, many programmers prefer to use the syntax for the compound statement even if the then or else block includes only one statement. In this textbook, we will use the syntax for the compound statement regardless of the number of statements inside the then and else blocks. Following this policy is beneficial for a number of reasons. One of them is the ease of adding temporary output statements inside the blocks. Frequently, we want to include a temporary output statement to verify the boolean expression is written correctly. Suppose we add output statements such as

```
if (testScore < 70)
{
    System.out.println("inside then: " + testScore);
    messageBox.show("You did not pass");
}
else
{
    System.out.println("inside else: " + testScore);
    messageBox.show("You did pass");
}
```

If we always use the syntax for the compound statement, we just add and delete the temporary output statements. However, if we use the syntax of the single statement, then we have to remember to add the braces when we want to include a temporary output statement. Another reason for using the compound statement syntax exclusively is to avoid the dangling else problem. We will discuss this problem in Section 6.3.

The placement of left and right braces does not matter to the compiler. The compiler will not complain if you write the preceding if statement as

```
if (testScore < 70)
{   messageBox.show("You did not pass");
    messageBox.show("Try harder next time"); } else {
    messageBox.show("You did pass");
    messageBox.show("Keep up the good work");
}
```

However, to keep your code readable and easy to follow, you should format your if statements using one of the two most common styles:

Style 1

```
if ( <boolean expression> ) {
    ...
}
else {
    ...
}
```

Style 2

```
if ( <boolean expression> )
{
    ...
}
else
{
    ...
}
```

In this book, we will use Style 1, mainly because this style is more common among programmers. If you prefer Style 2, then go ahead and use it. Whichever style you choose, be consistent, because consistent look and feel is very important to make your code readable. Let's summarize the key points to remember:

Rules for writing the then and else blocks:

1. Left and right braces are necessary to surround the statements if the then or else block contains multiple statements.

2. Braces are not necessary if the then or else clause contains only one statement.

3. A semicolon is not necessary after a right brace.

Now let's study a second version of if statement. Suppose we want to print out the message You are an honor student if the test score is 95 or above and print out nothing otherwise. For this type of testing, we use the second version of the if statement, whose general format is

if-then statement syntax

```
if ( <boolean expression> )
    <then block>
```

The second version contains only the <then block>. Using this version and the compound statement syntax, we express the selection control as

```
if (testScore >= 95) {
    messageBox.show("You are an honor student");
}
```

Figure 6.3 shows the diagram that illustrates the control flow for this if statement. To distinguish the two, we call the first version *if–then–else* and the second version *if–then*.

FIGURE 6.3   The diagram showing the control flow of the second version of the **if** statement.

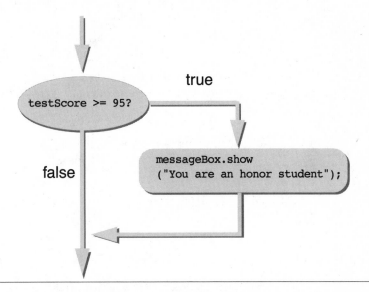

Notice that the if–then statement is not necessary, because we can write any if–then statement using if–then–else by including no statement in the else block. For instance, the sample if–then statement can be written as

```
if (testScore >= 95) {
    messageBox.show("You are an honor student");
}
else { }
```

In this book, we use if–then statements whenever appropriate.

Quick Check

1. Identify the invalid if statements:

    a.   if (a < b) then
                    x = y;

```
        else
            x = z;
```

b.   `if ( a < b ) else x = y;`

c.
```
        if ( a < b ) {
            x = y; } else
            x = z;
```

d.
```
        if ( a < b )
            x = y;
        else {
            x = z;
        };
```

2. Express the following if–then statements using if–then–else.

a.   `if ( a < b ) x = y;`

b.   `if ( a < b ) { }`

c.   `if ( a < b ) x = y;`
        `if ( a >= b) x = z;`

6.2   Boolean Expressions and Variables

boolean
operator

In addition to the arithmetic operators introduced in Chapter 4 and relational operators introduced in the previous section, boolean expressions can contain conditional and boolean operators. A *boolean operator*, also called *logical operator*, takes boolean values as its operands and returns a boolean value. Three boolean operators are *AND*, *OR*, and *NOT*. In Java, symbols &&, ||, and ! represent the AND, OR, and NOT operators. Table 6.1 explains how these operators work.

TABLE 6.1   Boolean operators and their meanings.

A	B	A && B	A ‖ B	!A
false	false	false	false	true
false	true	false	true	true
true	false	false	true	false
true	true	true	true	false

The AND operation results in true only if both A and B are true. The OR operation results in true if either A or B is true. The NOT operation is true if A is false and false if A is true. Combining boolean operators with relational and arithmetic operators, we can come up with a long boolean expression such as

```
(x + 150) == y || x < y && !(y < z && z < x)
```

Now consider the following expression:

```
x / y > z || y == 0
```

arithmetic exception

What will be the result if y is equal to 0? Easy, the result is true, many of you might say. Actually a runtime error called *arithmetic exception* will result, because the expression

```
x / y
```

divide-by-zero error

causes a problem known as a *divide-by-zero* error. Remember that you cannot divide a number by zero.

However, if we reverse the order to

```
y == 0 || x / y > z
```

then no arithmetic exception will occur because the test x / y > z will not be evaluated. For the OR operator ||, if the left operand is evaluated to true, then the right operand will not be evaluated, because the whole expression is true, whether the value of the right operand is true or false. We call such evaluation **short-circuit evaluation** method a *short-circuit evaluation*. For the AND operator &&, the right operand need not be evaluated if the left operand is evaluated to false, because the result will then be false whether the value of the right operand is true or false.

Just as the operator precedence rules are necessary to evaluate arithmetic expressions unambiguously, they are required for evaluating boolean expressions. Table 6.2 expands Table 3.3 by including all operators introduced so far.

In mathematics, we specify the range of values for a variable as

$$80 \leq x < 90$$

In Java, to test that the value for x is within the specified lower and upper bounds, we express it in Java as

```
80 <= x && x < 90
```

You cannot specify it as

```
80 <= x < 90          ◄──── [ WRONG ]
```

which is a syntax error because the relational operators (<, <=, etc.) are binary operators whose operands must be numerical values. Notice that the result of the subexpression

```
80 <= x
```

is a boolean value, which cannot be compared to the numerical value 90. Their data types are not compatible.

TABLE 6.2   Operator precedence rules. Groups are listed in descending order of precedence. An operator with a higher precedence will be evaluated first. If two operators have the same precedence, then their associativity rule is applied.

Group	Operator	Precedence	Associativity
subexpression	( )	9 (If parentheses are nested, then innermost subexpression is evaluated first.)	left to right
unary operators	– !	8	right to left
multiplicative operators	* / %	7	left to right
additive operators	+ –	6	left to right
comparison operators	< <= > >=	5	left to right
equality operators	== !=	4	left to right
boolean AND	&&	3	left to right
boolean OR	||	2	left to right
assignment	=	1	right to left

The result of a boolean expression is either true or false, which are the two values of data type boolean. As is the case with other data types, a value of a data type can be assigned to a variable of the same data type. In other words, we can declare a variable of data type boolean and assign a boolean value to it. Here are examples:

```
boolean pass, done;

pass = 70 < x;
done = true;
```

One possible usage of boolean variables is to keep track of the program settings or user preferences. A variable (of any data type, not only boolean) used for this purpose is called a *flag*. Suppose we want to allow the user to display either short or long messages. Many people, when using a new program, prefer to see long messages such as Enter a person's age and press the Enter key to continue. But once they are familiar with the program, many users prefer to see short messages such as Enter age. We can use a boolean flag to remember the user's preference. We can set the flag longMessageFormat at the beginning of the program to true or false depending on the user's choice. Once this boolean flag is set, we can refer to the flag at different points in the program as

boolean flag

```
if (longMessageFormat) {

    //display the message in long format
}
else {
    //display the message in short format
}
```

Dr. Caffeine

One very common error in writing programs is mixing up the assignment and equality operators. We frequently make a mistake of writing

```
if (x = 5) ...
```

when we actually wanted to say

```
if (x == 5) ...
```

Mr. Espresso: Dr. Caffeine, I realized, after executing the program, that my **if** statement was wrong. I wrote it as

```
if ( 70 <= x & x < 90 )
```

but it compiled and ran correctly. I thought the boolean AND is a double ampersand.

Dr. Caffeine: The single ampersand is also a boolean operator for AND. Unlike the double ampersand, the single ampersand will not do a short-circuit evaluation. It will evaluate both left and right operands. We also have a single vertical bar OR.

Mr. Espresso: Well then, which one should I use?

Dr. Caffeine: Use a double ampersand for AND and a double vertical bar for OR. You most likely will never encounter a situation where you cannot use the double ampersand or double vertical bar.

Dr. & Mr.

Quick Check

1. Evaluate the following boolean expressions. Assume x, y, and z have some numerical values.

   a.   `4 < 5 || 6 == 6`
   b.   `2 < 4 && (false || 5 <= 4)`
   c.   `x <= y && !(z != z) || x > y`
   d.   `x < y || z < y && y <= z`

2. Identify errors in the following boolean expressions and assignments.

   a.
   ```
   boolean done;
   done = x = y;
   ```

   b.
   ```
   2 < 4 && (3 < 5) + 1 == 3
   ```

   c.
   ```
   boolean quit;
   quit = true;
   quit == ( 34 == 20) && quit;
   ```

6.3   Nested-if Statements

nested-if
statement

The then and else clauses of an if statement can contain any statement including another if statement. An if statement that contains another if statement either in its then or else block is called a *nested-if* statement. Let's look at an example. In the earlier example, we printed out the messages You did pass or You did not pass depending on the test score. Let's modify the code to print out three possible messages. If the test score is lower than 70, then we print You did not pass as before. If the test score is 70 or higher, then we will check the student's age. If the age is less than 10, we will print You did a great job. Otherwise, we will print You did pass as before. Figure 6.4 is a diagram showing the logic of this nested test. The code is written as follows:

```
if (testScore >= 70) {
    if (studentAge < 10) {
        messageBox.show("You did a great job");
    }
    else {
        messageBox.show("You did pass"); //test score >= 70
    }                                    //and age >= 10
}
else { //test score < 70

    messageBox.show("You did not pass");
}
```

Since the then clause of the outer if contains another if statement, the outer if is called a nested-if statement. It is possible to write if tests in different ways to achieve the same result. For example, the preceding code can also be expressed as

```
if (testScore >= 70 && studentAge < 10) {

    messageBox.show("You did a great job");
}
else {
    //either testScore < 70 OR studentAge >= 10
    if (testScore >= 70) {
        messageBox.show("You did pass");
    }
    else {
        messageBox.show("You did not pass");
    }
}
```

Several other variations can also achieve the same result. As a general rule, we strive to select the one that is most readable (i.e., most easily understood) and most efficient. Often no one variation stands out, and the one you choose depends on your preferred style of programming.

Here's an example in which one variation is clearly a better choice. Suppose we input three integers and determine how many of them are negative. Here's

FIGURE 6.4   A diagram showing the control flow of the example nested-if statement.

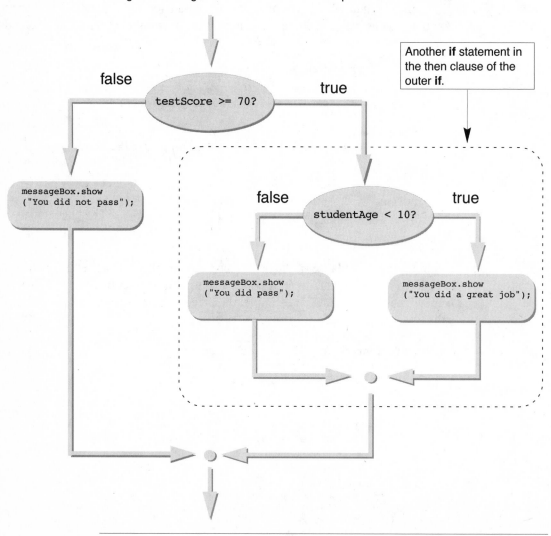

the first variation. To show the structure more clearly, we purposely do not use the braces in the then and else blocks.

```
if (num1 < 0)
    if (num2 < 0)
        if (num3 < 0)
            negativeCount = 3; //all three are negative
        else
            negativeCount = 2; //num1 and num2 are negative
    else
        if (num3 < 0)
            negativeCount = 2; //num1 and num3 are negative
        else
            negativeCount = 1; //num1 is negative
else
    if (num2 < 0)
        if (num3 < 0)
            negativeCount = 2; //num2 and num3 are negative
        else
            negativeCount = 1; //num2 is negative
    else
        if (num3 < 0)
            negativeCount = 1; //num3 is negative
        else
            negativeCount = 0; //no negative numbers
```

It certainly did the job. But elegantly? Here's the second variation:

```
negativeCount = 0;
if (num1 < 0)
        negativeCount++;
if (num2 < 0)
        negativeCount++;
if (num3 < 0)
        negativeCount++;
```

The statement

```
negativeCount++;
```

increments the variable by one and, therefore, is equivalent to

```
        negativeCount = negativeCount + 1;
```

increment and decrement operators

The double plus operator (++) is called the *increment operator*, and the double minus operator (--) is the *decrement operator* (which decrements the variable by one).

Which version do you like better? The second variation is the only reasonable way to go. The first variation is not even an option because it is very inefficient and very difficult to read. You apply the nested-if structure if you have to test conditions in some required order. In this example these three tests are independent of each other, so they can be executed in any order. In other words, it doesn't matter whether you test num1 first or last.

Dr. & Mr.

Mr. Espresso: Dr. Caffeine, in finding the count of negative integers, I can see the second variation is much better than the first one. But for the first example, it's not clear to me which one is better. How do you tell?

Dr. Caffeine: Well, it takes blood, sweat, and tears. When you become an accomplished programmer, you can instinctively tell which style is better.

Mr. Espresso: I don't mind bloodletting, sweating, and crying, but there must be some kind of guideline I can use before I can tell the difference "instinctively."

Dr. Caffeine: **Rule 1:** Minimize the number of nestings. **Rule 2:** Avoid complex boolean expressions. Make them as simple as possible. Don't include many ANDs and ORs. **Rule 3:** Eliminate any unnecessary comparisons. **Rule 4:** Don't be satisfied with the first correct statement. Always look for improvement. **Rule 5:** Read your code again. Can you follow the statement easily? If not, try to improve it.

Notice that we indent the then and else clauses to show the nested structure clearly. Indentation is used as a visual guide for the readers. It makes no difference to a Java compiler. For example, we make our intent clear by writing the statement as

```
    if (x < y)
        if (z != w)
            a = b + 1;
```

```
        else
            a = c + 1;
    else
        a = b * c;
```

But to the Java compiler, it does not matter if we write the same code as

```
if (x < y)if (z != w)a = b + 1;else a = c + 1; else a = b * c;
```

Although indentation is not required to run the program, using proper indentation is an important aspect of good programming style. Since the goal is to make your code readable, not to follow any one style of indentation, you are free to choose your own style. We recommend Style 1 or Style 2 shown on pages 241 and 242.

The next example shows a style of indentation accepted as standard for a nested-if statement in which nesting occurs only in the else clause. Instead of determining whether a student passes or not, we will now display a letter grade based on the following formula:

Test Score	Grade
$90 \le$ score	A
$80 \le$ score < 90	B
$70 \le$ score < 80	C
$60 \le$ score < 70	D
score < 60	F

The statement can be written as

```
if (score >= 90)
    messageBox.show("Your grade is A");
else
    if (score >= 80)
        messageBox.show("Your grade is B");
    else
        if (score >= 70)
            messageBox.show("Your grade is C");
        else
            if (score >= 60)
                messageBox.show("Your grade is D");
            else
```

```
                              messageBox.show("Your grade is F");
```

However, the standard way to indent the statement is

```
if (score >= 90)
    messageBox.show("Your grade is A");

else if (score >= 80)
    messageBox.show("Your grade is B");

else if (score >= 70)
    messageBox.show("Your grade is C");

else if (score >= 60)
    messageBox.show("Your grade is D");

else
    messageBox.show("Your grade is F");
```

We mentioned that indentation is meant for human eyes only. For example, we can clearly see the intent of a programmer just by looking at the indentation when we read

```
if (x < y)
    if (x < z)
        messageBox.show("Hello");
else
    messageBox.show("Good bye");
```

Indentation style A

A Java compiler, however, will interpret the above as

```
if (x < y)
    if (x < z)
        messageBox.show("Hello");
    else
        messageBox.show("Good bye");
```

Indentation style B

dangling else problem

This example has a *dangling else problem*. The Java compiler matches an else with the previous unmatched if, so the compiler will interpret the statement by matching the else with the inner if (if (x < z)), whether you use indentation style A or B. If you want to express the logic of indentation style A, you have to express it as

```
if (x < y) {
    if (x < z)
        messageBox.show("Hello");
}
else
    messageBox.show("Good bye");
```

This dangling else problem is another reason why we recommend that beginners use the syntax for <compound statement> in the then and else blocks. In other words, always use the braces in the then and else blocks.

Quick Check

1. Rewrite the following nested-if statements without using any nesting:

   a.
   ```
   if ( a < c)
       if ( b < c)
           x = y;
       else
           x = z;
   else
       x = z;
   ```

   c.
   ```
   if ( a < b  )
       if ( a >= b )
           x = z;
       else
           x = y;
   else
       x = z;
   ```

   b.
   ```
   if ( a == b )
       x = y;
   else
       if ( a > b )
           x = y;
       else
           x = z;
   ```

2. Format the following if statements with indentation.

   a.
   ```
   if ( a < b  ) if ( c > d ) x = y;
   else x = z;
   ```

   b.
   ```
   if ( a < b  ) { if ( c > d ) x = y; }
   else x = z;
   ```

   c.
   ```
   if ( a < b ) x = y; if ( a < c) x = z;
   else if (c < d) z = y;
   ```

6.4   ListBox

In many situations we want to give users an option of selecting one out of many choices. For example, in a drawing program we may provide users with a choice of colors. We can use the InputBox class to let users enter the name of the color, but they might misspell the color. For example, one user may enter "Maganta" instead of "Magenta." Therefore, we need to verify that the entry is a valid color. By providing a list of choices, we force users to make a valid choice, and we can simplify input processing.

It is considered a better interface to allow the user to enter only values that are valid instead of detecting errors after the user has entered an invalid value.

A ListBox object in the javabook package provides a list of items the user can select. Here's an example that lists the names of five colors. A ListBox object is a dialog and requires an owner frame window. We create a ListBox instance as in

```
MainWindow mainWindow = new MainWindow();
ListBox colorList = new ListBox(mainWindow);
```

The default ListBox is modal. (Note: A modal dialog box disables all other windows of the program once it appears on the screen.) We will discuss how to use a modal ListBox in this chapter and how to use a modeless ListBox later in the book. The default ListBox has the title Select One. If you wish to specify your own title, pass the title as the second argument when you create an object, as in

```
colorList = new ListBox(mainWindow, "Select Color");
```

We add the names of the colors using the addItem message

```
colorList.addItem("Magenta");
colorList.addItem("Cyan");
colorList.addItem("Red");
colorList.addItem("Blue");
colorList.addItem("Green");
```

and execute

```
selection = colorList.getSelectedIndex();
```

to make the colorList appear on the screen as shown in Figure 6.5.

FIGURE 6.5   The **ListBox** object **colorList**. The figure on the right shows the index values of the items in the list.

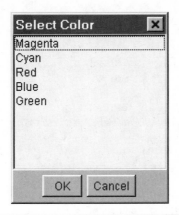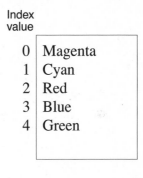

The variable selection is an int. When the user makes a selection by clicking on the choice and then clicking on the OK button, the getSelectedIndex method returns the index value of the selected choice. The choice at the top has the index value 0, the second from the top is 1, and so forth. Notice that the index of the first item in the list is zero, not one. Assigning zero to the first position is called *zero-based indexing*, which is used very frequently in computer programming.

zero-based indexing

> Zero-based indexing assigns the value of zero to the first item in a list of items.

The getSelectedIndex method returns NO_SELECTION if the user clicks the OK button without selecting a choice, and it returns CANCEL if the user clicks the Cancel button or the close box. After the value is returned by the get-SelectedIndex method, the ListBox disappears from the screen. NO_SELECTION and CANCEL are public class constants of type int, and we refer to them as

```
ListBox.NO_SELECTION
```

and

```
ListBox.CANCEL
```

The following code displays the name of the selected color:

```
selection = colorList.getSelectedIndex();

if (selection = ListBox.NO_SELECTION)
    messageBox.show("You made no selection");

else if (selection = ListBox.CANCEL)
    messageBox.show("You canceled the ListBox");

else if (selection == 0)
    messageBox.show("You selected Magenta");

else if (selection == 1)
    messageBox.show("You selected Cyan");

else if (selection == 2)
    messageBox.show("You selected Red");

else if (selection == 3)
    messageBox.show("You selected Blue");

else if (selection == 4)
    messageBox.show("You selected Green");
```

The value of NO_SELECTION is set to –1 and CANCEL to –2, so we could write the above code as

```
selection = colorList.getSelectedIndex();

if (selection == -1)
    messageBox.show("You made no selection");

else if (selection == -2)
    messageBox.show("You canceled the ListBox");
    . . .
```

but doing so would defeat the purpose of having public class constants defined in ListBox. Why? Because the use of a symbolic constant makes the code more readable and its modification easier. Suppose we wish to modify the ListBox to return distinct values for different events. By having a symbolic constant defined for each event, the code would look something like

```
selection = colorList.getSelectedIndex();

if (selection == ListBox.NO_SELECTION)
   . . .

else if (selection == ListBox.CANCEL)
   . . .
```

instead of the more cryptic

```
selection = colorList.getSelectedIndex();

if (selection == -1)
   . . .

else if (selection == -2)
   . . .
```

Also, without the use of a symbolic constant, modifying the code is more difficult. Suppose the value −1 becomes necessary for a different purpose. If a class constant is used, all we have to do is assign a different value to this constant and compile the class again. Code such as

```
if (selection == ListBox.NO_SELECTION)
```

would continue to work. However, code such as

```
if (selection == -1)
```

would have to be modified. If hundreds of programs used ListBox, you would have to modify all of them in this fashion. With the use of a constant, none of these programs would require modification. Every program would continue to work.

Table 6.3 is a partial list of ListBox methods and class constants.

TABLE 6.3   A partial list of **ListBox** methods.

CLASS:	ListBox	
Method	**Argument**	**Description**
`<constructor>`	`MainWindow`	Creates a ListBox object.
`addItem`	`String`	Adds the argument String value to the list. Items added to the list from top to bottom. The topmost item has the index value of zero, the next item's value is one, and so forth.
`getSelectedIndex`	`<none>`	Returns the index value of the selected item in the list. See the explanation of class constants.
Class Constant		**Description**
`NO_SELECTION`		This value is returned by getSelectedIndex method when the user clicks the OK button without selecting a choice.
`CANCEL`		This value is returned by the getSelectedIndex method when the user clicks the CANCEL button or the dialog's close box.

6.5   The switch **Statement**

Another Java statement that implements a selection control flow is the switch statement. Suppose we want to direct the students to the designated location for them to register for classes. The location where they register is determined by their grade level. The user enters 1 for freshman, 2 for sophomore, 3 for junior, and 4 for senior. Using the switch statement, we can write the code as

```
int gradeLevel;

gradeLevel
   = inputBox.getInteger("Grade (Frosh-1,Soph-2,...):" );

switch (gradeLevel) {

   case 1: outputBox.printLine("Go to the Gymnasium");
           break;

   case 2: outputBox.printLine("Go to the Science Auditorium");
```

```
                          break;

        case 3: outputBox.printLine("Go to Harris Hall Rm A3");
                break;

        case 4: outputBox.printLine("Go to Bolt Hall Rm 101");
                break;
    }
```

The syntax for the switch statement is

switch statement
syntax

```
switch ( <arithmetic expression> ) {

    <case label 1> : <case body 1>
    ...
    <case label n> : <case body n>
}
```

Figure 6.6 illustrates the correspondence between the switch statement we wrote and the general format.

The <case label i> has the form

default
reserved word

```
case <constant>        or        default
```

and <case body i> is a sequence of zero or more statements. Notice that <case body i> is not surrounded by left and right braces. The <constant> can be either a named or literal constant.

The data type of <arithmetic expression> must be char, byte, short, or int. (Note: We will cover the data type char in Chapter 8.) The value of <arithmetic expression> is compared against the constant value i of <case label i>. If there is a matching case, then its case body is executed. If there is no matching case, then the execution continues to the statement that follows the switch statement. No two cases are allowed to have the same value for <constant>, and the cases can be listed in any order.

Notice that each case in the sample switch statement is terminated with the break statement. The break statement causes execution to continue from the statement following this switch statement, skipping the remaining portion of the switch statement. The following example illustrates how the break statement works:

```
OutputBox outputBox = new OutputBox(mainWindow);
```

FIGURE 6.6   Mapping of the sample **switch** statement to the general format.

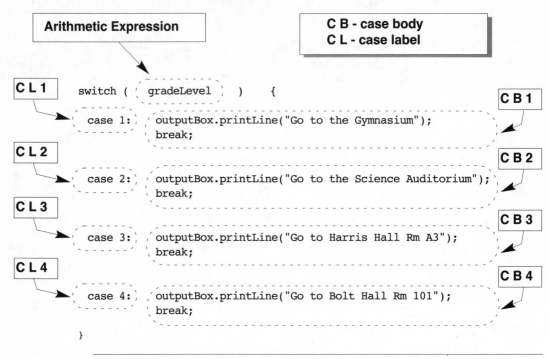

```
selection = 1;

switch (selection) {
    case 0: outputBox.printLine(0);
    case 1: outputBox.printLine(1);
    case 2: outputBox.printLine(2);
    case 3: outputBox.printLine(3);
}
```

When this code is executed the following output is produced:

```
1
2
3
```

because after the statement in case 1 is executed, statements in the remaining cases will be executed also. To execute statements in one and only one case, we need to include the break statement at the end of each case, as we have done in the first example. Figure 6.7 shows the effect of the break statement.

FIGURE 6.7   A diagram showing the control flow of the **switch** statement with and without the break statements.

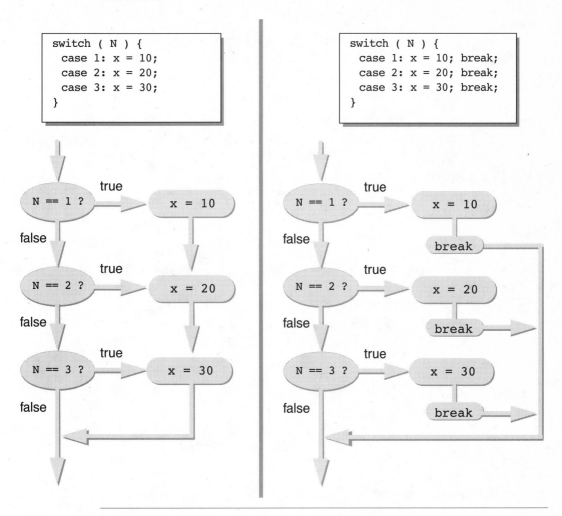

The break statement is not necessary in the last case, but for consistency we place it in every case. Also, by doing so we don't have to remember to include the break statement in the last case when we add more cases to the end of the switch statement.

Individual cases do not have to include a statement, so we can write something like

```
int ranking;
ranking = inputBox.getInteger();

switch (ranking) {
    case 10:
    case  9:
    case  8: messageBox.show("Master");
             break;

    case  7:
    case  6: messageBox.show("Journeyman");
             break;

    case  5:
    case  4: messageBox.show("Apprentice");
             break;
}
```

The code will print Master if the value of ranking is either 10, 9, or 8; Journeyman if the value of ranking is either 7 or 6; or Apprentice if the value of ranking is either 5 or 4.

We may include a default case that will always be executed if there is no matching case. For example, we can add a default case to print out an error message if any invalid value for ranking is entered.

```
switch (ranking) {

    case 10:
    case  9:
    case  8: messageBox.show("Master");
             break;

    case  7:
    case  6: messageBox.show("Journeyman");
             break;

    case  5:
    case  4: messageBox.show("Apprentice");
```

```
                    break;

        default: messageBox.show("Input error: Invalid Data");
                    break;
    }
```

There can be at most one default case. Since the execution continues to the next statement if there is no matching case (and no default case is specified), it is safer to always include a default case. By placing some kind of output statement in the default case, we can detect an unexpected switch value. Such style of programming is characterized as *defensive programming*. Although the default case does not have to be placed as the last case, we recommend you do so, in order to make the switch statement more readable.

defensive programming

Quick Check

1. What's wrong with the following switch statement?

```
switch ( N ) {
    case  0:
    case  1:   x = 11;
               break;
    default:   System.out.println("Switch Error");
               break;
    case  2:   x = 22;
               break;
    case  1:   x = 33;
               break;
}
```

2. What's wrong with the following switch statement?

```
switch ( ranking ) {
    case  >4.55:  pay = pay * 0.20;
                  break;

    case  =4.55:  pay = pay * 0.15;
                  break;

    default:      pay = pay * 0.05;
                  break;
}
```

6.6   Sample Program: Drawing Shapes

Let's write a program that will draw a geometric shape, such as a rectangle, in a size and color specified by the user. This program illustrates the use of ListBox and control statements. The program uses the class Color from the standard java.awt package for specifying the color of the drawing. As always, we will develop this program following incremental development steps.

Problem Statement

Write an application that will draw a geometric shape specified by the user. The user can specify the shape's position, size, and color. The program can draw lines, rectangles, and circles in the colors magenta, cyan, red, blue, or green.

Overall Plan

We will begin with our overall plan for the development. Let's begin with the outline of program logic. We want the user to select the shape, its position, and its color, and then draw the shape as specified.We express the program flow as having four tasks:

program
tasks

1.   Get the shape the user wants to draw.

2.   Get the color the user wants to use.

3.   Get the position and size of the selected shape.

4.   Draw the selected shape as specified.

Let's look at each task and determine an object that will be responsible for handling the task. For the first two tasks, we can use either an InputBox object or a ListBox object. Which one is the better one for this task? If we use an InputBox object, the user must remember the valid shapes and colors that can be entered. When the user enters an invalid shape, for example, the program needs to display an error message. Instead of doing it this way, we will use a ListBox object to list the selections of valid shapes. By using this ListBox object, the user cannot specify an invalid shape, he or she can only select one from the available shapes in the list. For the same reason, we will use a ListBox object to list the valid colors. Since we have to provide two separate lists—one for shapes and another for colors—we will use two separate ListBox objects.

We will use an InputBox for the third task. Since the user needs to enter three or four values depending on the shape selected, an InputBox object will be the simplest and most flexible to use for the purpose.

Finally, for the task of actually drawing the selected shape, we need to define our own class. The task is too specific to the program and there is no suitable object in the standard or javabook package that does the job. We will call the new class DrawingBoard. We will design the details of DrawingBoard in the later step.

In addition to the tasks identified, we need an object to display the program description. We will use an OutputBox for this purpose. This OutputBox will also be used for printing out temporary messages while developing the program.

We will define a top-level control object that manages all these objects. We will call this class DrawShape. Our main class will be DrawShapeMain, whose task is to create an instance of DrawShape and start the instance. Here's our working design document:

program classes

Design Document:	DrawShape
Class	**Purpose**
DrawShapeMain	The main class of the program.
DrawShape	The top-level control object that manages other objects in the program.
ListBox	One ListBox object is used for listing the available shapes: rectangle, circle, and line. Another ListBox object is used for listing the available colors: magenta, cyan, red, blue, and green. This class is from javabook.
InputBox	An InputBox object is used to get values for the position and size of the shape to be drawn. This class is from javabook.
OutputBox	An OutputBox object is used to display the program description. The object is used also for printing out temporary messages during the program development.
DrawingBoard	A core object that does the actual drawing.
MainWindow	The main window of the application.

Figure 6.8 is the object diagram for this program.

We will implement this program in the following six major steps:

development steps

1. Start with a program skeleton. Define the DrawShapeMain and DrawShape class.

2. Add code to allow the user to select a shape.

FIGURE 6.8   The object diagram for the **DrawShape** program.

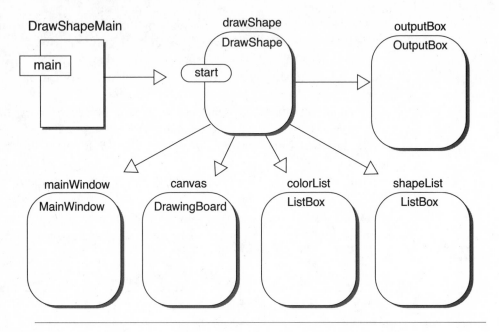

3. Add code to allow the user to select a color.

4. Add code to allow the user to specify the size and location of the selected shape.

5. Add code to draw the selected shape.

6. Finalize the code by tying up loose ends.

Notice that the steps we outline here follow the general pattern of implementing the input routines first, then the output routines, and finally the computation tasks. In this sample program, the drawing functionality includes the features of both output and computation tasks.

Step 1 Development: Program Skeleton

Step 1 Design

We begin the development with the main class and the skeleton DrawShape class. The purpose of the main class is to create an instance of DrawShape and let the object carry out the program tasks. So the code in the main method will look like

```
DrawShape drawShape = new DrawShape( );
drawShape.start( );
```

We will call the public method of the **DrawShape** class start. The purpose of this method is to carry out the program tasks, so we will declare it as

```
public void start( )
{
    describeProgram();    //tell what the program does
    selectShape();        //let the user select the shape
    selectColor();        //let the user select the color
    selectDimension();    //let the user set the position & size
    draw();               //draw the selected shape
}
```

By looking at this method, we can tell the responsibility assigned to a **Draw-Shape** object. The five methods called from the start method are all private, so the object diagram for the class at this point is

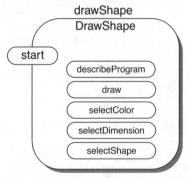

We will declare all these private methods in this step, but their method body does not contain any statement (except the temporary output statement). We will complete the method body in the subsequent development steps.

Since the **DrawShape** class is an instantiable class, we will define its constructor. Inside the constructor, we will create and initialize objects **DrawShape** manages. Since we are defining only a skeleton in this step, we will create and initialize only a **MainWindow** object and an **OutputBox** object inside the constructor. We use an **OutputBox** to display temporary messages to verify the methods we define here are called correctly. In the subsequent steps, we will add more code to create and initialize other objects.

Our working design document for the DrawShape class is as follows:

Design Document: The DrawShape Class		
Method	**Visibility**	**Purpose**
`<constructor>`	`public`	Creates and initializes the objects used by a DrawShape object.
`start`	`public`	Starts the shape drawing task by calling the other private methods.
`describeProgram`	`private`	Displays a short description of the program in an OutputBox.
`draw`	`private`	Draws the selected shape in the color and dimension set by the user.
`selectColor`	`private`	Lets the user select the color of the shape. Selection is made by using a ListBox object from javabook.
`selectDimension`	`private`	Lets the user specify the dimension of the shape to be drawn.
`selectShape`	`private`	Lets the user select the shape to draw. Selection is made by using a ListBox object from javabook. Possible choices are line, circle, and rectangle.

Step 1 Code

As mentioned already, we include temporary output statements in the five private methods to verify that they are called correctly in the right order. The main class DrawShapeMain will not change. The class given here is the final version. Here's the code:

```
/*
    Program DrawShape

    A program to draw the shape (rectangle, circle, or line) selected by the user
    in position, size, and color of the user's specification.

    Input:    shape
              color
              position
              size

    Output:   Display the shape drawn in the chosen color at the specified
              position and size.
*/

class DrawShapeMain
{
    public static void main (String args[])
    {
        DrawShape drawShape = new DrawShape( );
        drawShape.start();
    }
}
```

```
/*
    Class DrawShape (Step 1)

    The top level object for managing all other objects in the program.
*/

import javabook.*;

class DrawShape
{

/**************************
    Data Members
**************************/

    private MainWindow mainWindow;
    private OutputBox   outputBox;


/**************************
    Constructor
**************************/

    public DrawShape( )
    {
        mainWindow = new MainWindow("Drawing Shape");
        outputBox  = new OutputBox(mainWindow);

        mainWindow.show();
        outputBox.show();
    }


/*****************************
    Public Methods

        void start (        )

*****************************/

    public void start ( )
    {
        describeProgram();
        selectShape();
        selectColor();
        selectDimension();
        draw();
    }


/*****************************
    Private Methods

        void    describeProgram    (            )
        void    draw               (            )
        void    selectColor        (            )
        void    selectDimension    (            )
```

```
     void    selectShape          (          )
*****************************/


/*********************************************************
     Method:        describeProgram

     Purpose:       Describe what the program does.

     Parameters:    None

     Returns:       None
*/
private void describeProgram( )
{
    outputBox.printLine("Inside describeProgram");
}


/*********************************************************
     Method:        draw

     Purpose:       Draws the selected shape in a chosen color, position,
                    and size.

     Parameters:    None

     Returns:       None
*/
private void draw( )
{
    outputBox.printLine("Inside draw");
}


/*********************************************************
     Method:        selectColor

     Purpose:       Lets the user select the color from a ListBox.

     Parameters:    None

     Returns:       None
*/
private void selectColor( )
{
    outputBox.printLine("Inside selectColor");
}


/*********************************************************
     Method:        selectDimension

     Purpose:       Lets the user select the size and position using InputBox.

     Parameters:    None
```

```
       Returns:        None
    */
    private void selectDimension( )
    {
        outputBox.printLine("Inside selectDimension");
    }


    /**********************************************************
        Method:         selectShape

        Purpose:        Lets the user select the shape from a ListBox.

        Parameters:     None

        Returns:        None
    */
    private void selectShape( )
    {
        outputBox.printLine("Inside selectShape");
    }
}
```

Step 1 Test   We execute the main class and the skeleton DrawShape class to verify that the skeleton classes are coded correctly. When the mainWindow and outputBox appear on the screen, we know the constructor was executed properly. If the five private methods are coded correctly and called in the correct sequence, we will see the output

```
Inside describeProgram
Inside selectShape
Inside selectColor
Inside selectDimension
Inside draw
```

on an outputBox. After we verify the correct execution of the Step 1 program, we will proceed to implement the private methods of DrawShape.

Step 2 Development: Select a Shape

Step 2 Design   In the second development step, we add a routine that allows the user to select a shape. We decided in the overall planning step that we will use a ListBox object to list the available shapes. There are three choices: line, circle, and rectangle. We will define a symbolic constant for each of these shapes to make the program easier to read. We will create and initialize a ListBox object called shapeListBox in the constructor. The selection of a shape will be handled in the selectShape method. After the shape is selected by the user, the program will prompt the user for a color and dimension before drawing the selected shape.

This means that we have to remember which shape was selected in the select-Shape method. Since the getSelectedIndex method returns an integer, we will use an integer variable selectedShape to remember the selected shape.

Step 2 Code   The constants, a ListBox object, and an int variable are declared in the data member section of the DrawShape class as

```
/*************************
    Data Members
*************************/
private final int    LINE       = 0,
                     CIRLCE     = 1,
                     RECTANGLE  = 2;

private ListBox      shapeListBox;

private int          selectedShape;
```

The constructor will now include code to create and initialize shapeListBox:

```
public DrawShape( )
{
    ...

    shapeListBox = new ListBox(mainWindow, "Select Shape:");
    shapeListBox.addItem("Line");
    shapeListBox.addItem("Circle");
    shapeListBox.addItem("Rectangle");
}
```

Finally we implement the selectShape method as

```
private void selectShape( )
{
    outputBox.printLine("Inside selectShape"); //TEMP
    selectedShape = shapeListBox.getSelectedIndex();
    outputBox.printLine("Selected Shape: " + selectedShape);
                                                    //TEMP
}
```

Notice that we include a temporary output statement at the end of the method so we can verify the selection is made correctly.

Step 2 Test

Now we run the program several times, each time selecting a different shape, and verify the correct message shows up in outputBox. After we verify everything is okay, we proceed to the next step.

Step 3 Development: Select a Color

Step 3 Design

In the third development step, we add a routine that allows the user to select a color. This step is similar to Step 2. Instead of shape, we work with colors. So we will use another ListBox object to list the available colors. There are five choices: magenta, cyan, red, blue, and green. We will define a symbolic constant for each of these colors to make the program easier to read. We will create and initialize a ListBox object called colorListBox in the constructor. The selection of a color will be handled in the selectColor method. We will use an integer variable selectedColor to remember the selected color.

Step 3 Code

The constants, a ListBox object, and an int variable are declared in the data member section of the DrawShape class as

```
/*************************
    Data Members
*************************/
private final int     MAGENTA    = 0,
                      CYAN       = 1,
                      RED        = 2,
                      BLUE       = 3,
                      GREEN      = 4;

private ListBox       colorListBox;

private int           selectedColor;
```

The constructor will now include code to create and initialize colorListBox:

```
public DrawShape( )
{
    ...

    colorListBox = new ListBox(mainWindow, "Select Color:");
    colorListBox.addItem("Magenta");
    colorListBox.addItem("Cyan");
    colorListBox.addItem("Red");
    colorListBox.addItem("Blue");
    colorListBox.addItem("Green");
}
```

Finally we implement the selectColor method as

```
private void selectColor( )
{
    outputBox.printLine("Inside selectColor"); //TEMP
    selectedColor = colorListBox.getSelectedIndex();
    outputBox.printLine("Selected Color: " + selectedColor);
                                                //TEMP

}
```

Like the selectShape method, we place a temporary output statement at the end of the method so we can verify the color selection is made correctly.

Step 3 Test   Now we run the program several times, each time selecting a different color, and verify the correct message shows up in outputBox. After we verify everything is okay, we proceed to the next step.

Step 4 Development: Set the Shape Dimension

Step 4 Design In the fourth development step, we add a routine that allows the user to specify the dimension of the selected shape. The values the user must provide will be different for each of the three shapes. We will ask the user to specify a line by giving two end points. For a circle, we ask the user to enter the center point and the radius. We could have used a diameter, but we believe entering a radius is more natural. For a rectangle, we ask the user to enter the point for the top, left corner and the width and height of the rectangle.

Now, how shall we code the input routines for different shapes? Since each shape requires different input values, we will define a separate method for each type of shape: getCircleDimension, getLineDimension, and getRectangleDimension. The selectDimension method will call one of these methods based on the value of selectedShape. These individual methods will get input values appropriate for the shape and retain the values entered for later processing. We add the three new methods to our working design document of the DrawShape class.

Design Document: The DrawShape Class		
Method	**Visibility**	**Purpose**
...	...	...
getCircleDimension	private	Lets the user enter the circle's center point and radius.

Design Document: The DrawShape Class		
Method	**Visibility**	**Purpose**
getLineDimension	private	Lets the user enter the line's two end points.
getRectangleDi-mension	private	Lets the user enter the rectangle's point at the top, left corner and its width and height.

We will use an InputBox object for getting input values, the only object we know at this point for the data-inputting task. The actual drawing is done by another method, so the purpose of these methods is only to input required values and validate the input. We use the variables originX, originY, endX, endY, radius, width, and height for storing values. The variables originX and originY are used by all three methods. For a line, they represent one end point. For a circle, they represent the center point. And for a rectangle, they represent the top, left corner point. We will ask you to consider alternative ways of using only the local variables in the chapter exercise.

We consider any negative input value as invalid. When an invalid input value is entered, the get dimension method will display an error message. We will use a MessageBox object for displaying an error message. Since the drawing will not occur until the drawShape method is called, we need to keep the record of what has happened during the get dimension method, that is, whether there was any input error. If there is any error, the drawShape method will not draw any shape. Let's use a boolean variable canDraw for this purpose. The variable canDraw is set to false when there is an input error.

Step 4 Code   The objects and variables necessary for this step are declared in the data member section of the DrawShape class as

```
/**************************
    Data Members
 *************************/
private InputBox      inputBox;
private MessageBox    messageBox;

private boolean       canDraw; //false if there's an input error

private int           originX,
                      originY,
                      endX,
                      endY,
                      radius,
                      width,
                      height;
```

The constructor will now include code to create and initialize inputBox and messageBox:

```
public DrawShape( )
{
    ...

    inputBox   = new InputBox(mainWindow);
    messageBox = new MessageBox(mainWindow);


    ...

}
```

We implement the selectDimension method as

```
private void selectDimension( )
{
    switch (selectedShape) {

        case ListBox.CANCEL: //user canceled, so do nothing
                canDraw = false;
                break;
        case ListBox.NO_SELECTION: //no shape selected
                canDraw = false;
                break;
        case LINE:
                getLineDimension();
                break;

        case CIRCLE:
                getCircleDimension();
                break;

        case RECTANGLE:
                getRectangleDimension();
                break;
        default:
                messageBox.show("ListBox Error");
                canDraw = false;
                break;

    }
}
```

Notice how we add code for handling the cases in which no shape is selected. It is important for you to remember that whenever you use a selection control, you have to make sure that all possible cases are handled. Also, it is a good idea to include the default case to a switch statement.

When you write a selection control statement, make sure that all possible cases are covered.

Since the variable selectedShape is set to the value returned from a ListBox object, this default case should never be called. If it were ever called, then the List-Box class was not used correctly (e.g., adding items in the wrong order or adding incorrect items), so we display the message ListBox Error.

The three methods for getting dimensions are defined as follows:

```
private void getCircleDimension()
{
    originX     = inputBox.getInteger("X-coord of the center");
    originY     = inputBox.getInteger("Y-coord of the center");
    radius      = inputBox.getInteger("Radius of the circle");

    //make sure everything is positive
    if (originX < 0 || originY < 0 || radius < 0) {
        messageBox.show("Negative number is entered. " +
                            "Cannot draw a circle.");
        canDraw = false;
    }
    else { //input is okay
        canDraw = true;
        outputBox.printLine("circle dimensions okay"); //TEMP
    }
}


private void getLineDimension()
{
    originX = inputBox.getInteger("X-coord of starting point");
    originY = inputBox.getInteger("Y-coord of starting point");
    endX    = inputBox.getInteger("X-coord of ending point");
    endY    = inputBox.getInteger("Y-coord of ending point");

    //make sure everything is positive
    if (originX < 0 || originY < 0 || endX < 0 || endY < 0) {
        messageBox.show("Negative number is entered. " +
```

```
                                          "Cannot draw a line.");
                    canDraw = false;
                }
                else { //input is okay
                    canDraw = true;
                    outputBox.printLine("line dimensions okay"); //TEMP
                }
            }


            private void getRectangleDimension()
            {
                originX    = inputBox.getInteger("X-coord of origin");
                originY    = inputBox.getInteger("Y-coord of origin");
                width      = inputBox.getInteger("Rectangle width");
                height     = inputBox.getInteger("Rectangle height");

                //make sure everything is positive
                if (originX < 0 || originY < 0 || width < 0 || height < 0) {
                    messageBox.show("Negative number is entered. " +
                                    "Cannot draw a rectangle.");
                    canDraw = false;
                }
                else { //input is okay
                    canDraw = true;
                    outputBox.printLine("rectangle dimensions okay"); //TEMP
                }


            }
```

Step 4 Test   Now we run the program several times, each time selecting a different shape, and verify the correct get dimension method is called. We try both correct and incorrect input values and verify that the appropriate error message is displayed when invalid values are entered. After we verify the program, we move on to the most difficult step.

Step 5 Development: Draw the Shape

Step 5 Design   In the fifth development step, we add a routine that draws the selected shape in the color and dimension the user designated. The very first question we need to ask ourselves at this point is, "Who will do the drawing?" Which object should be the one responsible for taking care of drawing? Should it be DrawShape? We certainly can make a DrawShape object responsible for the drawing task by adding more methods to it. But will it be a good design? Adding code for the actual drawing operations to the DrawShape class would make it bloated. One design principle of object-oriented programming is to use many objects, with each object dedicated to a single well-defined task. It is not a good design to construct a single object that does everything. In other words, we want an object that is specialized in a single well-defined task, not a jack-of-all-trades, because single-task objects are much easier to mix and match in writing different programs. We call this design principle a *single-task object (STO) principle*.

The Single-Task Object (STO) Principle: Design an object that is specialized in a single well-defined task.

Remember that the responsibility of a DrawShape object is to manage other objects in the program. It controls two ListBox objects that allow the user to select the shape and color, for example. Objects such as InputBox, ListBox, and

interface objects   OutputBox are called *interface objects* because they handle the user interface

controller objects   component of the program. A DrawShape object is called a *controller object* because it controls and instructs other objects to perform the actual work. Following the STO principle will direct us to design our own class to handle the actual drawing operations. We will call this class DrawingBoard.

We will design the DrawingBoard class here, but we will defer the implementation until Chapter 11. There are two reasons for doing this. First, to implement this class fully and properly requires additional knowledge not yet covered. Trying to introduce all the necessary topics here will make this section too long. Second, and more importantly, it illustrates a real-world situation where a chief programmer or a system designer designs the class and leaves the

design vs.   implementation to another programmer. One of the major benefits of object-ori-

implementation   ented programming is the ease of delineating the roles of class designer and class implementor. The designer will determine how the object will interact with other objects in the program by defining the object's public methods. The class implementor will implement the class using whatever technique he decides is most appropriate. This division of labor allows the chief programmer to contract out the implementation of a class to multiple freelance programmers, for example, and choose the best implementation.

We will be a class designer of the DrawingBoard class here. We will be our own implementor for the class and implement it in Chapter 11. To complete this sample program, we will use the DrawingBoard class in the javabook package, which is implemented according to our design specification.

Now let's begin our design. What kind of public methods should a Drawing-Board object support? What would be a natural way for our DrawShape object to interact with a DrawingBoard object? Since the actual drawing is done by a DrawingBoard object, we will need three drawing methods, one for each shape:

drawLine, drawCircle, and drawRectangle. The arguments for these methods will be as follows:

Drawing Methods of DrawingBoard
`public void drawLine( int x1, int y1, int x2, int y2 )`
Draws a line from point (x1,y1) to (x2,y2)
`public void drawCircle( int centerX, int centerY, int radius)`
Draws a circle centered at (centerX,centerY) with radius radius.
`public void drawRectangle(int x, int y, int width, int height)`
Draws a rectangle whose top left corner is at (x,y) with width width and height height.

DrawingBoard Design Alternative 1

Where should this drawing take place? We need a window to draw a shape, so we will make DrawingBoard a window. The first alternative is to design the DrawingBoard class as a subclass of MainWindow using the inheritance we introduced in Chapter 2. This means a DrawingBoard object is a specialized MainWindow that has an added capability of drawing shapes, just like, say, a CheckingAccount object is a specialized Account that has additional rules for withdrawal. The SketchPad class we used in the sample program from Chapter 1 is also a subclass of MainWindow. If we make DrawingBoard a subclass of MainWindow, then the program will have only one window because an instance of DrawingBoard is also a main window.

DrawingBoard Design Alternative 2

The second alternative is to design the DrawingBoard class distinct from the MainWindow class. The DrawingBoard class will only have a drawing capability, and the program will need an instance of MainWindow for its main window. So if we take this alternative, the program will have two separate windows—one MainWindow and one DrawingBoard.

Which alternative is better? If a program supports a simple functionality, such as the FunTime program from Chapter 1 or a simple text editor that comes with a system (e.g., Notepad for the Windows or SimpleText for the Mac), then it is more appropriate to use only one window. Simple functionality requires a simple interface. It is also less threatening to novice users. If a program supports an advanced functionality, then a multiple window interface is more appropriate. For example, it is more of a standard to see one main window and multiple document windows in a high-end commercial software such as a word processing or illustration program.

The program we are developing here has a very simple functionality, so we will adopt the first alternative. Since the DrawingBoard class is a subclass of MainWindow, an instance of DrawingBoard will serve the role of main window.

This means the MainWindow class is not needed for the program anymore. We will therefore remove the class from the program and update the design document and the object diagram accordingly. Since the DrawingBoard object canvas is now the main window of the program, the statements to create various dialogs in the constructor are changed to

```
canvas      = new DrawingBoard( ); //subclass of MainWindow
outputBox = new OutputBox( canvas );

shapeListBox = new ListBox( canvas, "Select Shape:" );
colorListBox = new ListBox( canvas, "Select Color:" );

inputBox    = new InputBox( canvas );
messageBox = new MessageBox( canvas );
```

setColor
Design
Alternative 1

We now have one final design decision to make for the DrawingBoard class. Since we need to draw a shape in color, the DrawingBoard class must support a method we can use to designate the color. What would be a natural interface for such method? Since we are allowing the user to select one of the possible five colors, we define a method for each color, such as setColorToRed, setColorToCyan, and so forth. This approach is not acceptable because the class would be too limited in usage. What will happen if we want to draw in any one of 256 colors?

setColor
Design
Alternative 2

We can define a method by which we pass an integer. We can set an agreement that 1 means magenta, 2 means cyan, and so forth. With this approach, we will define a method like this:

```
public void setColor( int colorCode )
```
Sets the color to colorCode. All subsequent shapes will be drawn in the set color. Color coding is as follows: 1 for magenta, 2 for cyan, 3 for red, 4 for blue, and 5 for green.

This approach is also not acceptable. First, the class is not reusable. This class cannot be used for other programs that require 10 different colors, for example. If we want to support more colors in our DrawShape class, we will not be able to use this DrawingBoard class without modifying it. Second, the coding scheme as such is very limiting and restrictive. How can we extend this scheme to 256 colors?

java.awt.Color

To designate the color for drawing, we will use the Color class from the standard java.awt package. A Color object uses a coloring scheme called a *RGB scheme,* which specifies a color by combining three values, ranging from 0 to

255, for red, green, and blue. For example, the color black is expressed by setting red, green, and blue to zero, and the color white by setting all three values to 255. We create, for example, a Color object for the pink color by executing

```
Color pinkColor;
pinkColor = new Color(255,175,175);
```

Instead of dealing with the three numerical values, we can use the public class constants defined in the Color class. The class constants for common colors are

```
Color.black        Color.magenta
Color.blue         Color.orange
Color.cyan         Color.pink
Color.darkGray     Color.red
Color.gray         Color.white
Color.green        Color.yellow
Color.lightGray
```

setColor
Design
Alternative 3

Each of the above is a Color object with its RGB values correctly set up. We will pass a Color object as an argument to the setColor method.

setColor Method of DrawingBoard
`public void setColor( Color color)`
Sets the color to color. All subsequent shapes will be drawn in the color color.

We will call the setColor method of canvas to set its drawing color at the time the user selects the color, which is inside the selectColor method. The basic idea is something like this:

```
//let the user select the color
selectedColor = colorListBox.getSelectedIndex();

switch ( selectedColor ) {

    case MAGENTA: canvas.setColor( Color.magenta );
                        break;

    case CYAN:      canvas.setColor( Color.cyan );

    //and so forth
}
```

This code works fine as long as the user selects a color, but what if he clicks the Cancel button or the OK button without making a selection? Let's decide we will draw the selected shape in black if no color is selected. We will add the following case to the switch statement:

```
case ListBox.CANCEL:
case ListBox.NO_SELECTION:
        messageBox.show("No color selected. " +
                            "Will draw in black.");
        canvas.setColor( Color.black );
```

Finally, the actual drawing is done in the draw method. The boolean variable canDraw is set by one of the get dimension methods. If this variable is true, then we call a drawing method of canvas to draw the selected shape. The logic of the code can be expressed as

```
if (canDraw) {
    switch (selectedShape) {
        case LINE:
                //draw a line
                break;

        case CIRCLE:
                //draw a circle
                break;

        case RECTANGLE:
                //draw a rectangle;
                break;
    }
}
```

Step 5 Code   We are now ready to code. The Color class is from the java.awt package, so we need to add the import statement

```
import java.awt.*;
```

The declaration for mainWindow is removed and the one for canvas is added.

```
/*************************
    Data Members
*************************/

private DrawingBoard  canvas;
```

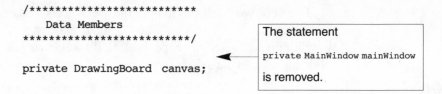

We modify the selectColor method to

```
private void selectColor( )
{
    selectedColor = colorListBox.getSelectedIndex( );

    switch (selectedColor) {

        case ListBox.CANCEL:
        case ListBox.NO_SELECTION:
                        messageBox.show("No color is selected. "
                                        + "Will draw in black.");
                        break;

        case MAGENTA:   canvas.setColor(Color.magenta);
                        break;

        case CYAN:      canvas.setColor(Color.cyan);
                        break;

        case RED:       canvas.setColor(Color.red);
                        break;

        case GREEN:     canvas.setColor(Color.blue);
                        break;

        case BLUE:      canvas.setColor(Color.green);
                        break;

        default:        messageBox.show("ListBox Error" );
                        break;
    }
}
```

The draw method will call a corresponding method of canvas to draw the selected shape, provided that the boolean flag canDraw is true:

```
private void draw( )
{
    if (canDraw) {
        switch (selectedShape) {
            case LINE:
                canvas.drawLine(originX, originY, endX, endY);
                break;

            case CIRCLE:
                canvas.drawCircle(originX, originY, radius);
                break;

            case RECTANGLE:
                canvas.drawRectangle(originX, originY,
                                            width, height);
                break;
        }
    }
}
```

Step 5 Test

Now we run the program multiple times and test that all three drawing methods work correctly. We try different colors and dimensions for each shape and verify that they are drawn correctly. When you run the program, most likely the first thing you will notice is that outputBox hides the shape drawn. And even after you moved or closed outputBox, you still do not see any shape is drawn. What happened? Is the drawing not working?

Let's say you drew a shape on a window. If you cover this shape by moving another window over it, then the shape will be erased. Similarly, if you attempt to draw a shape on a portion of a window that is hidden by another window, then the shape will not be drawn. (Note: There's a way to eliminate this problem, but that requires advanced techniques.) To test this, let's run the program again, but this time without showing an OutputBox object. To hide outputBox, we comment out the statement in the constructor:

```
public DrawShape( )
{
    ...
    //outputBox.show();   ◄─────   Comment this statement so
    ...                            outputBox won't be displayed
}                                  on the screen.
```

When you run the program again, you should see the shape is drawn correctly.

When you run the Step 5 program (the one that shows outputBox), you will notice that you cannot close outputBox until after you select a shape and color. But by that time it's too late to close it. What we need to do here is to allow the user to close outputBox before the selectShape method is executed. The Output-Box class has a method called waitUntilClose that will suspend the program execution until an OutputBox object is closed. We place a call to this method inside the describeProgram method as

waitUntilClose

```
private void describeProgram( )
{
    //printLine statements to describe the program
    //come here

    outputBox.printLine("Close this window to continue.");

    outputBox.waitUntilClose( );
}
```

Run the program with this describeProgram and verify that the program runs correctly.

Step 6 Development: Finalize

program
review

We finalize the program in the last step. We will perform a critical review of the program looking for any unfinished method, inconsistency or error in the methods, unclear or missing comments, and so forth. We should also not forget to improve the program for cleaner code and better readability.

The describeProgram method is incomplete, so we need to complete the method by adding code to describe the program. Please add whatever description you feel is appropriate. There are still temporary output statements we used for verification purposes. Either we delete them from the program or comment them out. We recommend you to leave them in the program by commenting them out so when the time comes for you to modify, debug, or update the program, you do not have to reenter them again.

6.7 Exercises

1. Indent the following if statements properly.

   a. `if (a == b) if (c == d) a = 1; else b = 1; else c = 1;`

   b. `if (a == b) a = 1; if (c == d) b = 1; else c = 1;`

   c. `if (a == b) {if (c == d) a = 1; b = 2; } else b = 1;`

   d. `if (a == b) {`
      `if (c == d) a = 1; b = 2; }`
      `else {b = 1; if (a == d) d = 3;`
      `else c = 1; }`

2. Which two of the following three if statements are equivalent?

   a. `if (a == b)`
      `if (c == d) a = 1;`
      `else b = 1;`

   b. `if (a == b) {`
      `if (c == d) a = 1; }`
      `else b = 1;`

   c. `if (a == b)`
      `if (c == d) a = 1;`
      `else b = 1;`

3. Evaluate the following boolean expressions. For each of the following expressions, assume x is 10, y is 20, and z is 30. Indicate which of the following boolean expressions are always true and which are always false, regardless of the values for x, y, or z.

   a. `x < 10 || x > 10`

   b. `x > y && y > x`

   c. `(x < y + z) & (x + 10 <= 20)`

   d. `z - y == x && Math.abs(y - z) == x`

   e. `x < 10 && x > 10`

   f. `x > y || y > x`

   g. `!(x < y + z) | !(x + 10 <= 20)`

   h. `!(x == y) && (x != y) && (x < y || y < x)`

4. Express the following switch statement using nested if statements.

```
switch (grade) {
    case 10:
    case  9: a = 1;
             b = 2;
             break;

    case  8: a = 3;
             b = 4;
             break;

    default: a = 5;
             break;
}
```

5. Write an if statement to find the smallest of three given integers without using the min method of the Math class.

6. Draw control flow diagrams for the following two switch statements.

```
switch (choice) {               switch (choice) {
    case 1:   a = 0;                case 1:   a = 0;
              break;
                                    case 2:   b = 1;
    case 2:   b = 1;
              break;                case 3:   c = 2;

    case 3:   c = 2;                default: d = 3;
              break;             }

    default: d = 3;
              break;
}
```

7. Write an if statement that prints out a message based on the following rules.

If the Total Points Are	Message to Print
≥ 100	You won a free cup of coffee.
≥ 200	You won a free cup of coffee and a regular-size doughnut.
≥ 300	You won a free cup of coffee and a regular-size doughnut and a 12 oz. orange juice.

If the Total Points Are	Message to Print
≥ 400	You won a free cup of coffee and a regular-size doughnut and a 12 oz. orange juice and a combo breakfast.
≥ 500	You won a free cup of coffee and a regular-size doughnut and a 12 oz. orange juice and a combo breakfast and a reserved table for one week.

8. Rewrite the following if statement using a switch statement.

```
selection = colorList.getSelectedIndex();

if (selection == ListBox.NO_SELECTION)
    messageBox.show("You made no selection");

else if (selection == ListBox.CANCEL)
    messageBox.show("You canceled the ListBox");

else if (selection == 0)
    messageBox.show("You selected Magenta");

else if (selection == 1)
    messageBox.show("You selected Cyan");

else if (selection == 2)
    messageBox.show("You selected Red");

else if (selection == 3)
    messageBox.show("You selected Blue");

else if (selection == 4)
    messageBox.show("You selected Green");
```

9. Describe how the following code runs without actually executing the code.

```
MainWindow mainWindow = new MainWindow();
OutputBox  outputBox  = new OutputBox( mainWindow );

outputBox.show();
outputBox.printLine("one");
outputBox.waitUntilClose( );
```

```
outputBox.show();
outputBox.printLine("two");
outputBox.waitUntilClose( );

outputBox.show();
outputBox.printLine("three");
outputBox.waitUntilClose( );

outputBox.show();
outputBox.printLine("four");
outputBox.waitUntilClose( );
```

10. At the end of movie credits you see the year movies are produced in Roman numerals, for example, MCMXCVII for 1997. To help the production staff determine the correct Roman numeral for the production year, write an applet or application that reads a year and displays the year in Roman numerals.

Roman Numeral	Number
I	1
V	5
X	10
L	50
C	100
D	500
M	1000

Remember that certain numbers are expressed using a "subtraction," for example, IV for 4, CD for 400, and so forth.

11. Write an applet or application that replies either Leap Year or Not a Leap Year given a year. It is a leap year if the year is divisible by 4 but not by 100 (e.g., 1796 is a leap year because it is divisible by 4 but not by 100). A year that is divisible by both 4 and 100 is a leap year if it is also divisible by 400 (e.g., 2000 is a leap year, but 1800 is not).

12. A million is 10^6 and a billion is 10^9. Write an applet that reads a power of 10 (6, 9, 12, etc.) and displays how big the number is (million, billion, etc.). Display an appropriate message for the input value that has no correspond-

ing word. The table below shows the correspondence between the power and the word for that number.

Power of 10	Number
6	Million
9	Billion
12	Trillion
18	Quintillion
21	Sextillion
30	Nonillion
100	Googol

13. Extend the TestScoreEvaluator program on page 236 to print out an appropriate message if the value entered is outside the range of possible test scores, that is, less than zero or greater than 100.

14. Write an applet RecommendedWeightAppletwithTest by extending the RecommendedWeightApplet (see exercise 13 on page 233 from Chapter 5). The extended applet will include the following test:

```
if (the height is between 140cm and 230cm)

    compute the recommended weight

else

    display an error message
```

15. Extend the RecommendedWeightAppletWithTest applet in exercise 14 by allowing the user to enter his/her weight and printing out the message You should exercise more if the weight is more than 10 pounds over the ideal weight and You need more nourishment if the weight is more than 20 pounds under the recommended weight.

16. After starting a successful coffee beans outlet business, Java^2 Coffee Outlet is now venturing into the fast-food business. The first decision the management makes is to eliminate the drive-through intercom. Java^2 Lo-Fat Burgers is the only fast-food establishment in town that provides a computer screen and mouse for its drive-through customers. You are hired as a freelance computer consultant. Write a program that lists items for three menu categories: entree, side dish, and drink. The following table lists the items

available for each entry and their prices. Use three ListBox objects for listing items from the three menu categories and an OutputBox object for displaying the total price of the order.

Entree		Side Dish		Drink	
Tofu Burger	$3.49	Rice Cracker	$0.79	Cafe Mocha	$1.99
Cajun Chicken	$4.59	No-Salt Fries	$0.69	Cafe Latte	$1.99
Buffalo Wings	$3.99	Zucchini	$1.09	Expresso	$2.49
Rainbow Fillet	$2.99	Brown Rice	$0.59	Oolong Tea	$0.99

17. Improve the clock program of exercise 14 page 191 from Chapter 4. Modify the program so you only accept numbers between 0 and 12 for hour and between 0 and 59 for minute. Print out an appropriate error message for an invalid input value.

18. Java^2 Coffee Outlet (see exercise 19 on page 137 from Chapter 3) decided to give discounts to volume buyers. The discount is based on the following table:

Order Volume	Discount
≥ 25 bags	5% of the total price
≥ 50 bags	10% of the total price
≥ 100 bags	15% of the total price
≥ 150 bags	20% of the total price
≥ 200 bags	25% of the total price
≥ 300 bags	30% of the total price

Each bag of beans costs $5.50. Write an application that accepts the number of bags ordered and prints out the total cost of the order in the following style using an OutputBox object.

```
Number of Bags Ordered:  173 - $ 951.50

              Discount:
                        20% - $ 190.30

  Your total charge is:  $ 761.20
```

19. Employees at Java^2 Lo-Fat Burgers earn the basic hourly wage of $7.25. They will receive time and a half of their basic rate for overtime hours. In addition to this, they will receive a commission on the sales they generate while tending the counter. The commission is based on the following formula:

Sales Volume	Commission
$1.00 to $99.99	5% of the total sales
$100.00 to $299.99	10% of the total sales
≥ $300.00	15% of the total sales

Write an application that inputs the number of hours worked and the total sales and computes the wage.

20. Combine exercise 18 and exercise 11 of Chapter 4 to compute the total charge including discount and shipping costs. The output should look like the following:

```
Number of Bags Ordered:  43 - $ 236.50

             Discount:
                       5% - $ 11.83

           Boxes Used:
                       1 Large - $3.00
                       2 Medium - $2.00

   Your total charge is:  $ 229.67
```

Note: The discount applies to the cost of beans only.

21. You are hired by Expressimo Delivery Service to develop an application that computes the delivery charge. The company allows two types of packaging, letter and box, and three types of service, Next Day Priority, Next

Day Standard, and 2-Day. The following table shows the formula for computing the charge:.

Package Type	Next Day Priority	Next Day Standard	2-Day
letter	$12.00, up to 8 oz.	$10.50, up to 8 oz.	Not available
box	$15.75 for the first lb. Add $1.25 for each additional lb over the first lb.	$13.75 for the first lb. Add $1.00 for each additional lb over the first lb.	$7.00 for the first lb. Add $0.50 for each additional lb over the first lb.

The program will input three values from the user: the type of package, the type of service, and the weight of the package.

22. Write an applet version of exercise 21. You can use TextField objects or Choice objects for input. If you use Choice objects, then you need to explore the class on your own. The Choice class from the standard java.awt package works very much like the ListBox class from the javabook package.

23. Ms. Latte's Mopeds 'R Us rents mopeds at Monterey Beach Boardwalk. To promote business during the slow weekdays, the store gives a huge discount. The rental charges are as follows:

Moped Type	Weekday Rental	Weekend Rental
50cc Mopette	$15.00 for the first three hours, $2.50 per hour after the first three hours.	$30.00 for the first three hours, $7.50 per hour after the first three hours.
250cc Mohawk	$25.00 for the first three hours, $3.50 per hour after the first three hours.	$35.00 for the first three hours, $8.50 per hour after the first three hours.

Write an application or an applet that computes the rental charge given the type of moped, when it is rented (either weekday or weekend), and the number of hours rented.

7

Repetition Statements

OBJECTIVES

After you have read and studied this chapter, you should be able to

1. Implement repetition control in a program using while statements.

2. Implement repetition control in a program using do–while statements.

3. Implement repetition control in a program using for statements.

4. Nest a loop repetition statement inside another repetition statement.

5. Choose the appropriate repetition control statement for a given task.

6. Prompt the user for a yes–no reply using the ResponseBox class from the javabook package.

7. Output formatted data using the Format class from the javabook package.

8. (Optional) Write simple recursive methods.

Introduction

The selection statements we covered in the previous chapter alter the control flow of a program. In this chapter we will cover another group of control statements called repetition statements. *Repetition statements* control a block of code to be executed for a fixed number of times or until a certain condition is met. We will describe Java's three repetition statements: while, do–while, and for. In addition to the repetition statements, we will introduce two classes for javabook: ResponseBox and Format. A ResponseBox object is used to get a yes or no response from the user, and it is a very convenient object to use in conjunction with a repetition statement. The Format class is helpful in displaying formatted output values. For example, we may want to output numerical values with their rightmost digit aligned to help the user see the magnitude of the numbers clearly and easily. Finally, in an optional section at the end of the chapter, we will describe recursive methods. A *recursive method* is a method that calls itself. Instead of using a repetition statement, a recursive method can be used to program the repetition control flow.

repetition statements

recursive method

7.1 The while Statement

Suppose we want to compute the sum of the first 100 positive integers 1, 2, . . . , 100. Here's how we compute the sum using a while statement:

```
int sum = 0, number = 1;

while (number <= 100) {
    sum    =  sum + number;
    number = number + 1;
}
```

Let's analyze the while statement. The statement follows the general format

while statement syntax

```
while ( <boolean expression> )

    <statement>
```

where <statement> is either a <single statement> or a <compound statement>. The <statement> of the sample while statement is a <compound statement> and therefore has the left and right braces. Repetition statements are also called *loop statements*, and we characterize the <statement> as the *loop body*. Figure 7.1 shows how this while statement corresponds to the general format. As long as

loop body

the <boolean expression> is true, the loop body is executed. Figure 7.2 is a diagram showing the control flow of the sample code.

FIGURE 7.1   Correspondence of the example **while** statement to the general format.

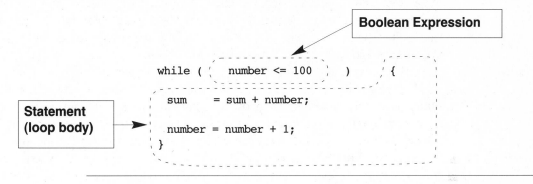

FIGURE 7.2   A diagram showing the control flow of a **while** statement.

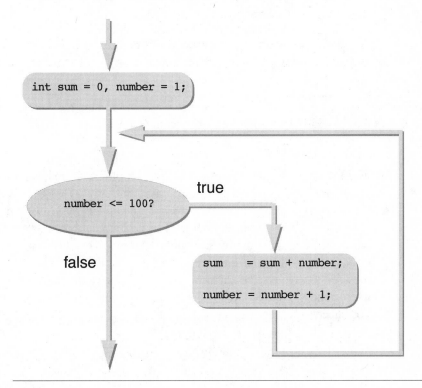

Let's modify the loop so this time we keep on adding the numbers 1, 2, 3, and so forth, until the sum becomes more than 1,000,000. Here's how we write the while statement:

```
int sum = 0, number = 1;

while ( sum <= 1000000 ) {
    sum     =  sum + number;
    number = number + 1;
}
```

Notice how the <boolean expression> is modified, and it is the only part of the while statement that is modified.

Let's try another example. This time, we compute the product of the first 20 odd integers. (Note: The ith odd integer is 2 * i – 1. For example, the fourth odd integer is 2 * 4–1 = 7.)

```
int product = 1, number = 1, count = 20, lastNumber;
lastNumber = 2 * count + 1;

while (number <= lastNumber) {
    product = product * number;
    number  = number + 2;
}
```

count-controlled loop

The first and the third sample while statements are called *count-controlled loops* because the loop body is executed for a fixed number of times (as if we were counting).

Now let's study how the repetition control in the program will improve the user interface of the program. In earlier sample programs, we assumed the input data were valid. The programs we have written may produce wrong results or simply stop running if the user enters an invalid value. Assuming that the input values are valid makes the writing of programs easier because we do not have to write code to handle the invalid values. Although easier for us to write such programs, it would be an inferior interface from the user's standpoint. Requiring the user to make no mistake in entering input values is too restrictive and not user-friendly. We need to develop programs that are more user-friendly. Imagine you successfully entered 19 values, but on the 20th input value, you mistyped. A user-hostile program would stop, and you would have to run the program again. A more user-friendly program would allow you to reenter a correct 20th value.

All we could have done using a selection statement was to print out an error message if the user enters an invalid value. To allow the user to reenter the value until the correct value is entered, we need a repetition control. Let's look at an example. Suppose we want to input a person's age, and the value must be between 0 and 130. We know the age cannot be negative, so the age input must be greater than or equal to 0. We set the upper bound to 130 to take into account the possibility of some long-living human beings in a remote hamlet in Timbuktu. (According to the *Guinness Book of Records,* 1997 edition, the oldest living person was 121 years old.) Let's say we will let the user enter the age until the valid age is entered. We can code this repetition control using a while statement:

```
age = inputBox.getInteger("Your Age (between 0 and 130):");

while (age < 0 || age > 130) {
    messageBox.show("An invalid age was entered. " +
                    "Please try again.");
    age = inputBox.getInteger("Your Age (between 0 and 130):");
}
```

Notice how we add the assignment

```
age = inputBox.getInteger("Your Age (between 0 and 130):");
```

to input the age *before* the while statement. Without this input statement, the variable age will not have a value when the boolean expression is evaluated for the very first time. This reading of a value before the testing is done is called a

priming read   *priming read*.

Our next example keeps reading in integers and computes their running sum until a negative number is entered.

```
int sum = 0, number;

number = inputBox.getInteger(); //priming read

while (number >= 0) {
    sum = sum + number;
    number = inputBox.getInteger();
}
```

The previous two sample statements are called sentinel-controlled loops.

sentinel-controlled
loop
With a *sentinel-controlled loop*, the loop body is executed repeatedly until any one of the designated values called a *sentinel* is encountered. The sentinel for

this example is any negative number and the sentinel for the one before is any valid age between 0 and 130.

1. Write a while statement to add numbers 11 through 20. Is this a count-controlled or sentinel-controlled loop?

2. Write a while statement to read in real numbers using InputBox and stop when a negative number is entered. Is this a count-controlled or sentinel-controlled loop?

7.2   Pitfalls in Writing Repetition Statements

infinite loop

No matter what you do with the while statement (and other repetition statements), make sure that the loop will eventually terminate. Watch out for an *infinite loop* such as this one:

```
int product = 0;

while (product < 500000)
    product = product * 5;
```

Do you know why this is an infinite loop? The variable product is multiplied by 5 in the loop body, so the value for product should eventually become larger than 500000, right? Wrong. The variable product is initialized to 0, so product remains 0. The boolean expression product < 500000 will never be false, and, therefore, this while statement is an infinite loop. You have to make sure the loop body contains a statement that eventually makes the boolean expression false.

Here's another example of an infinite loop.

```
int count = 1;

while (count != 10)
    count = count + 2;
```

Since the variable count is initialized to 1 and the increment is 2, count will never be equal to 10. Note: In theory, this while statement is an infinite loop, but in practice, this loop will eventually terminate because of an overflow error. An

overflow error will occur if you attempt to assign a value larger than the maximum value the variable can hold. For this example, the value inside the variable count will eventually become larger than the maximum integer we can store in an int variable. At that point, an overflow error will occur and the execution of the program will halt. Even though this loop may terminate because of an overflow error, the logic of the loop is still an infinite loop, and we must watch out for it. When you write a loop, you must make sure that the boolean expression of the loop will eventually become false.

overflow error

Another pitfall for which you have to watch out is using real numbers for testing and increment. Consider the following two loops:

imprecise
loop counter

```
//Loop 1
float count = 0.0f;

while (count != 1.0f)
    count = count + 0.3333333f; //there are seven 3s


//Loop 2
float count = 0.0f;

while (count != 1.0f)
    count = count + 0.33333333f; //there are eight 3s
```

The second while terminates correctly, but the first while is an infinite loop. Why the difference? Because only an approximation of real numbers can be stored in a computer. We know in mathematics that

$$\frac{1}{3} + \frac{1}{3} + \frac{1}{3}$$

is equal to 1. However, in a computer, an expression such as

```
1.0/3.0 + 1.0/3.0 + 1.0/3.0
```

may or may not get evaluated to 1.0 depending on how precise the approximation is. In general, you want to avoid using real numbers as counter variables because of this imprecision. However, at the same time, you should not shy away from writing a loop such as

```
float count = 0.0f;

while (count <= 1.0f) {
    ...
    count = count + 0.25f;
}
```

if it helps to express the logic more clearly.

off-by-one error

Another thing for which you have to watch out in writing a loop is the so-called *off-by-one error*. Suppose we want to execute the loop body 10 times. Does the following code work?

```
count = 1;
while (count < 10 ) {
    ...
    count++;
}
```

No, the loop body is executed nine times. How about the following code?

```
count = 0;
while (count <= 10 ) {
    ...
    count++;
}
```

No, this time the loop body is executed 11 times. The correct while loop is

```
count = 0;
while (count < 10 ) {
    ...
    count++;
}
```

or

```
count = 1;
```

```
while (count <= 10 ) {
   ...
   count++;
}
```

Yes, you can write the desired loop as

```
count = 1;
while (count != 10 ) {
   ...
   count++;
}
```

but this condition for stopping the count-controlled loop is dangerous. We already mentioned about the potential trap of an infinite loop. In summary,

Watch out for the off-by-one error (OBOE).

And here are the points for you to remember in writing a loop.

The checklist for the repetition control:

1. Make sure the loop body contains a statement that will eventually cause the loop to terminate.

2. Make sure the loop repeats exactly the number of times it should repeat.

3. If you want to execute the loop body N times, then initialize the counter to 0 and use the test condition counter < N or initialize the counter to 1 and use the test condition counter<=N.

The loop body in the sample repetition statements included statements such as

```
sum = sum + number;
```

shorthand
assignment
operator

This assignment statement can be expressed succinctly without repeating the same variable sum by using the *shorthand assignment operator* +=:

```
sum += number;
```

Table 7.1 lists shorthand assignment operators available in Java.

TABLE 7.1   Shorthand assignment operators.

Operator	Usage	Meaning
+=	a += b;	a = a + b;
-=	a -= b;	a = a - b;
*=	a *= b;	a = a * b;
/=	a /= b;	a = a / b;
%=	a %= b;	a = a % b;

These shorthand assignment operators have precedence lower than any other arithmetic operators, so for example, the statement

```
sum *= a + b;
```

is equivalent to

```
sum = sum * (a + b);
```

We will be using shorthand assignment operators from now on.

Quick Check

1.   Which of the following is an infinite loop?

    a.   ```
          int sum = 0, i = 0;
          while (i >= 0) {
              sum += i;
              i++;
          }
          ```

    b.    ```
          int sum = 0, i = 100;
          while ( i != 0 ) {
              sum += i;
              i--;
          }
          ```

2. For each of the following loop statements, determine the value of sum after the loop is executed.

a.
```
int count = 0, sum = 0;
while ( count < 10 ) {
    sum += count;
    count++;
}
```

b.
```
int count = 1, sum = 0;
while ( count <= 30 ) {
    sum    += count;
    count += 3;
}
```

c.
```
int count = 0, sum = 0;
while ( count < 20 ) {
    sum    += 3*count;
    count += 2;
}
```

7.3   The do–while **Statement**

pretest loop

The while statement is characterized as a *pretest loop* because the test is done before execution of the loop body. Because it is a pretest loop, the loop body may not be executed at all. The do–while is a repetition statement that is charac-

posttest loop

terized as a *posttest loop*. With a posttest loop statement, the loop body is executed at least once.

The general format for the do–while statement is

do–while syntax

```
do

    <statement>

while ( <boolean expression> ) ;
```

The <statement> is executed until the <boolean expression> becomes false. Remember that <statement> is either a <single statement> or a <compound statement>. We will adopt the same policy for the if statement; that is, we will use the syntax of <compound statement> even if there is only one statement in the loop body. In other words, we will use the left and right braces even if the loop body contains only one statement.

Let's look at a few examples. We begin with the third example from the previous section, which adds the whole numbers 1, 2, 3, . . . until the sum becomes larger than 1,000,000. Here's the equivalent code in a do–while statement:

```
int sum = 0, number = 1;
do {

    sum += number;
    number++;

} while ( sum <= 1000000 );
```

Figure 7.3 shows how this do–while statement corresponds to the general format and Figure 7.4 is a diagram showing the control flow of this do–while statement.

FIGURE 7.3   Correspondence of the example **do–while** statement to the general format.

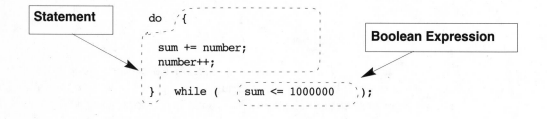

Let's rewrite the routine that inputs a person's age using the do–while statement. Here's our first attempt:

```
do {

    age = inputBox.getInteger("Your Age (between 0 and 130):");

} while (age < 0 || age > 130);
```

It works, but unlike the version using the while statement, the code does not display an error message. The user could be puzzled as to why the input is not accepted. Suppose the user tries to enter 130 but actually enters 139 unintentionally. Without an error message to inform the user that the input was invalid, he or she

FIGURE 7.4   A diagram showing the control flow of the **do–while** statement.

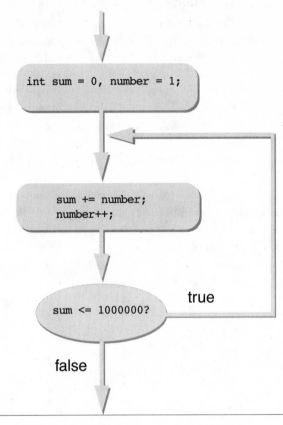

may wonder why the program is asking again for input. A program should not be confusing to the user. We must strive for a program with a user-friendly interface.

To display an error message, we rewrite the do–while statement as

```
do {

  age = inputBox.getInteger("Your Age (between 0 and 130):");

  if (age < 0 || age > 130) {
      messageBox.show("An invalid age was entered. "
                          "Please try again.");
  }

} while (age < 0 || age > 130);
```

This code is not as good as the version using the while statement. Do you know why? This do–while statement includes an if statement inside its loop body. Since the loop body is executed repeatedly, it is important not to include any extraneous statements. The if statement is repeating the same boolean expression of the do–while. Duplicating the testing conditions tends to make the loop statement harder to understand. For this example, we can avoid the extra test inside the loop body and implement the control flow a little more clearly by using a while statement. In general, the while statement is more frequently used than the do–while statement. However, the while statement is not universally better than the do–while statement. It depends on a given task, and our job as programmers is to use the most appropriate one. We choose the repetition statement that implements the control flow clearly, so the code is easy to understand.

boolean variable and loop

When you have multiple conditions to stop the loop and if you need to execute different responses to each of the multiple conditions, then the use of boolean variables often clarifies the meaning of the loop statement. Consider the following example. Suppose we need to compute the sum of odd integers entered by the user. We will stop the loop when the sentinel value 0 is entered, an even integer is entered, or the sum becomes larger than 1,000. Without using any boolean variables, we can write this loop as

```
sum = 0;
do {

    num = inputBox.getInteger();

    if (num % 2 == 0)    //invalid data
        messageBox.show("Error: even number was entered");

    else if (num == 0)    //sentinel
        messageBox.show("Sum = " + sum);

    else {
        sum += num;
        if (sum > 1000)  //pass the threshold
            messageBox.show("Sum became larger than 1000");
    }

} while ( !(num % 2 == 0 || num == 0 || sum > 1000) )
```

The ending condition is tricky. We need to stop the loop if any one of the three conditions num % 2 == 0, num == 0, or sum > 1000 is true. So we repeat the loop when none of the three conditions are true, which is expressed as

```
!(num % 2 == 0 || num == 0 || sum > 1000)
```

We can also state the condition as

> Note:
>
> !(a II b) is equal to (!a && !b)

```
do {

    ...

} while( num % 2 != 0 && num != 0 && sum <= 1000 )
```

which means "repeat the loop while num is odd and num is not 0 and sum is less than or equal to 1,000." Regardless of the method used, the test conditions are duplicated inside the loop body and in the boolean expression.

Now, using a boolean variable the loop becomes

> Be careful not to use the reserved word **continue** instead of **repeat**.

```
boolean repeat = true;

sum = 0;
do {

    num = inputBox.getInteger();

    if (num % 2 == 0)  {  //invalid data
        messageBox.show("Error: even number was entered");
        repeat = false;
    }
    else if (num == 0)  {  //sentinel
        messageBox.show("Sum = " + sum);
        repeat = false;
    }
    else {
        sum += num;
        if (sum > 1000) { //pass the threshold
            messageBox.show("Sum became larger than 1000");
            repeat = false;
        }
    }

} while ( repeat );
```

> Set the boolean variable to **false** so the loop terminates.

This loop eliminates duplicate tests. The use of boolean variables is helpful in making loop statements readable, especially when the loop has multiple stop conditions.

Quick Check

1. Write a do–while loop to compute the sum of first 30 positive odd integers.

2. Rewrite the following while loops as do–while loops.

   a.
```
int count = 0, sum = 0;
while ( count < 10 ) {
    sum += count;
    count++;
}
```

   b.
```
int count = 1, sum = 0;
while ( count <= 30 ) {
    sum    += count;
    count += 3;
}
```

7.4   ResponseBox

We will introduce another class from the javabook package that is used for getting a yes or no response from the user. Let's begin with a simple example. Executing the code

```
MainWindow mainWindow = new MainWindow();
ResponseBox yesNoBox = new ResponseBox(mainWindow);

yesNoBox.prompt("Do you love Java?");
```

will result in the window shown in Figure 7.5. The string argument you pass to the prompt method is displayed in the dialog. The dialog by default contains two buttons labeled Yes and No. When the user clicks on a button, a value identifying the clicked button is returned.

Let's see how the buttons are identified. Consider the following example:

```
int selection;

selection = yesNoBox.prompt("Click a button");
```

FIGURE 7.5   A **ResponseBox** dialog box with the prompt "Do you love Java?"

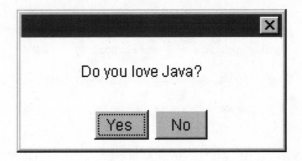

```
switch (selection) {

    case ResponseBox.YES:
        messageBox.show("Yes button was clicked");
        break;

    case ResponseBox.NO:
        messageBox.show("No button was clicked");
        break;
}
```

The yesNoBox object returns the value ResponseBox.YES when the user clicks the button labeled YES and ResponseBox.NO when the user clicks the button labeled NO. The YES and NO are the public class constants of the ResponseBox class.

All of the applications we have written so far performed a single task (e.g., calculated a monthly payment or drew a shape) and then stopped. A ResponseBox object can be used in conjunction with a control statement to provide a very convenient way of asking the user to repeat a task or not. Here's how we write such a program:

```
do {
    //code for one computation comes here

    choice = yesNoBox.prompt("Repeat again?");

} while (choice == ResponseBox.YES);
```

We could also use the while statement to prompt the user before doing any work. Such a prompt is useful if the task is long and the user cannot cancel it in the middle. Here's how:

```
choice = yesNoBox.prompt("Do you want to start the computation?");
while (choice == ResponseBox.YES) {

    //code for computation comes here

    yesNoBox.prompt("Repeat another computation?");
}
```

Notice that two statements, one before the while statement and another at the end of the loop body, prompt the user with different questions.

In some situations, instead of asking for a simple yes or no answer, we would like a user to select one of two options. For example, we can give the user a choice of Fahrenheit or Celsius for displaying the temperature of a given city. A ResponseBox object can be adapted for this purpose.

We can create an instance of the ResponseBox class with one, two, or three buttons by passing the number of buttons as the second argument in the new message. For example, to create a three-button ResponseBox, we say

```
ResponseBox threeButtonBox = new ResponseBox(mainWindow,3);
```

Buttons are identified from left to right by the class constants BUTTON1, BUTTON2, and BUTTON3. The labels for the buttons are set by the setLabel message. For example, to label the buttons left to right as OK, Cancel, and Help, we execute this code:

```
threeButtonBox.setLabel( ResponseBox.BUTTON1, "OK"     );
threeButtonBox.setLabel( ResponseBox.BUTTON2, "Cancel" );
threeButtonBox.setLabel( ResponseBox.BUTTON3, "Help"   );
```

The following code illustrates the creation of a two-button ResponseBox and how the response is tested:

```
int choice;
ResponseBox selectTemperature = new ResponseBox(mainWindow,2);
```

```
selectTemperature.setLabel(ResponseBox.BUTTON1, "Celsius");
selectTemperature.setLabel(ResponseBox.BUTTON2, "Fahrenheit");

choice = selectTemperature.prompt("Celsius or Fahrenheit?");

if (choice == ResponseBox.BUTTON1) {

    // display the temperature in Celsius
}
else {

    // display the temperature in Fahrenheit
}
```

Executing the code results in the ResponseBox object shown in Figure 7.6. Notice the size of a button is adjusted to the size of its label. If you prefer to have the same size for both buttons, pad the text of the shorter label with spaces so that both labels have the same number of characters (counting the spaces, of course), for example:

```
selectTemperature.setLabel(ResponseBox.BUTTON1, " Celsius ");
selectTemperature.setLabel(ResponseBox.BUTTON2, "Fahrenheit");
```

The yes–no ResponseBox is created by default if you don't pass a second argument to the new message. The labels Yes and No are assigned to the first and second buttons (from the left) automatically.

FIGURE 7.6   The **ResponseBox** object with user-specified button labels.

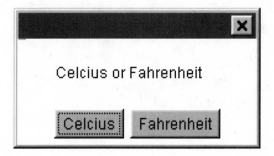

Table 7.2 is a list of ResponseBox methods and class constants.

TABLE 7.2   A list of **ResponseBox** methods.

CLASS:	ResponseBox	
Method	**Argument**	**Description**
<constructor>	MainWindow	Creates a ResponseBox object.
<constructor>	MainWindow, int	Creates a ResponseBox object with N (the second argument) buttons, 1 <= N <= 3. If an invalid N is passed, then the object will include one button.
prompt	String	Prompts the user with the text passed as an argument. Returns an integer that identifies the clicked button. See the explanation of the class constants.
setLabel	int, String	Sets the label of the designated button with the passed String. The first argument identifies the button. See the explanation of the class constants.

Class Constant	Description
YES	This value identifies the Yes button.
NO	This value identifies the No button.
BUTTON1	This value identifies the leftmost button. The value of BUTTON1 is equal to the value of YES.
BUTTON2	This value identifies the middle button. Note: the middle button becomes the rightmost button if there are only two buttons. The value of BUTTON2 is equal to the value of NO.
BUTTON3	This value identifies the rightmost button when the ResponseBox includes three buttons.

Quick Check

1. Write a code to create a ResponseBox with three buttons labeled ONE, TWO, and THREE.

2. Using the ResponseBox object created in question 1 above, write code that displays a message indicating which button was clicked.

7.5   The for **Statement**

The for statement is the third repetition control statement and is especially suitable for count-controlled loops. Let's begin with an example. The following code computes the sum of 20 integers entered by the user:

```
int i, sum = 0, number;
for (i = 0; i < 20; i++) {
    number = inputBox.getInteger();
    sum += number;
}
```

The general format of the for statement is

```
for ( <initialization>; <boolean expression>; <increment>  )

    <statement>
```

Figure 7.7 shows the correspondence of the sample code above to the general format. The diagram in Figure 7.8 shows how this statement is executed. The

control variable   variable i in the statement is called a *control variable*, and it keeps track of the number of repetitions. In the sample code, the control variable i is first initialized to 0, and immediately the boolean expression is evaluated. If the evaluation results in true, the loop body is executed. Otherwise, the execution of the for

FIGURE 7.7   Correspondence of the example **for** statement to the general format.

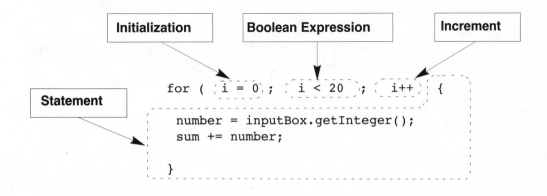

FIGURE 7.8   A diagram showing the control flow of the example for statement.

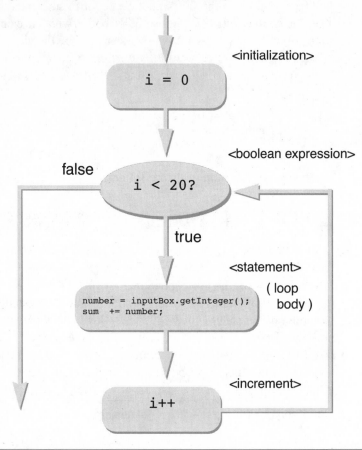

statement is terminated, and the control flows to the statement following this for statement. Every time the loop body is executed, the increment operator (i++) is executed and then the boolean expression is evaluated.

The <initialization> component can also include a declaration of the control variable. We can do something like this:

```
for (int i = 0; i < 10; i++)
```

instead of

```
int i;
for (i = 0; i < 10; i++)
```

The control variable may be initialized to any value, although it is almost always 0 or 1.

The <increment> expression in the example increments the control variable by 1. We can increment it with values other than one, including negative values; for example,

```
for (int i = 0; i < 100; i += 5) // i = 0, 5, 10, ...

for (int j = 2; j < 40; j *= 2)  // j = 2, 4, 8, 16, ...

for (int k = 100; k > 0; k--)    // k = 100, 99, 98, 97, ...
```

Notice that the control variable appears in all three components: <initialization>, <conditional expression>, and <increment>. A control variable does not have to appear in all three components, but this is the most common in the style. Many other variations are allowed for these three components, but for novices, it is safer to use this style exclusively.

Let's look at an example from physics. When an object is dropped from height H, the position P of the object at time t can be determined by the formula

$$P = -16t^2 + H$$

For example, if a watermelon is dropped from the roof of a 256-foot-high building, it will drop like this:

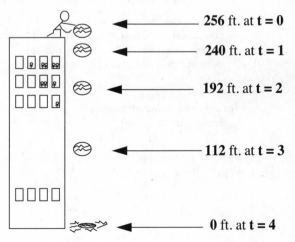

256 ft. at **t = 0**

240 ft. at **t = 1**

192 ft. at **t = 2**

112 ft. at **t = 3**

0 ft. at **t = 4**

We can use a for statement to compute the position P at time t. We will input the initial height and compute the position every second. We repeat this computation until the watermelon touches the ground. The time the watermelon touches the ground is derived by solving for t when $P = 0$.

$$0 = -16t^2 + H$$

$$t = \sqrt{\frac{H}{16}}$$

```
float           initialHeight,
                position,
                touchTime;

MainWindow      mainWindow = new MainWindow("Drop WaterMelon");
OutputBox       outputBox  = new OutputBox(mainWindow);
InputBox        inputBox   = new InputBox(mainWindow);

mainWindow.show();
outputBox.show();

initialHeight = inputBox.getFloat("Initial Height:");
touchTime     = (float) Math.sqrt(initialHeight / 16.0);

outputBox.printLine("   Time t     Position at Time t ");
outputBox.skipLine(1);

for (int time = 0; time < touchTime;  time++) {
    position = -16.0 * time*time + initialHeight;
    outputBox.print("    " + time);
    outputBox.printLine("             " + position);
}

//print the last second
outputBox.printLine("    " + touchTime + "         0.00");
```

Running the above code with the input value 500.0 for the initial height will result in the OutputBox shown in Figure 7.9.

FIGURE 7.9   The positions of a watermelon dropped from a height of 500 feet.

```
OutputBox
    Time t        Position at Time t

    0                 500.0
    1                 484.0
    2                 436.0
    3                 356.0
    4                 244.0
    5                 100.0
    5.59017             0.0
```

Quick Check

1. Write a for loop to compute

    a. the sum of $1, 2, \ldots, 100$.

    b. the sum of $2, 4, \ldots, 500$.

    c. the product of $5, 10, \ldots, 50$.

2. Rewrite the following while loops as for statements.

    a.
    ```
    int count = 0, sum = 0;
    while ( count < 10 ) {
        sum += count;
        count++;
    }
    ```

    b.
    ```
    int count = 1, sum = 0;
    while ( count <= 30 ) {
        sum    += count;
        count += 3;
    }
    ```

7.6   Nested for Statements

In many processing tasks, we need to place a for statement inside another for statement. In this section, we will introduce a simple nested for statement. We will be seeing more examples of nested for statements later in the book, especially in Chapter 12 on array processing.

Suppose we want to display a quick reference table for clerks at the Rugs-R-Us carpet store. The table Figure 7.10 lists the prices of carpets ranging in size from 11 × 5 feet to 20 × 25 feet. The width of a carpet ranges from 11 feet to 20 feet with an increment of 1 foot. The length of a carpet ranges from 5 feet to 25 feet with an increment of 5 feet. The unit price of a carpet is $19 per square foot.

FIGURE 7.10   The price table for carpets ranging in size from 11 × 5 feet to 20 × 25 feet whose unit price is $19 per square foot.

Length

Carpet Price Table					
	5	10	15	20	25
11	1045	2090	3135	4180	5225
12	1140	2280	3420	4560	5700
13	1235	2470	3705	4940	6175
14	1330	2660	3990	5320	6650
15	1425	2850	4275	5700	7125
16	1520	3040	4560	6080	7600
17	1615	3230	4845	6460	8075
18	1710	3420	5130	6840	8550
19	1805	3610	5415	7220	9025
20	1900	3800	5700	7600	9500

Width (labels the width column on the left: 11–20)

We use a nested for statement to print out the table. Let's concentrate first on printing out prices. We'll worry about printing out length and width values later. The following nested for statement will print out the prices:

```
int         price;
MainWindow  mainWindow   = new MainWindow();
OutputBox   outputBox    = new OutputBox(mainWindow);
```

```
mainWindow.show();
outputBox.setTitle("Carpet Price Table");
outputBox.show();

for (int width = 11; width <= 20; width++) {

    for (int length = 5; length <= 25; length += 5) {
        price = width * length * 19; //$19 per sq ft.
        outputBox.print("   " + price);
    }

    //finished one row; now move on to the next row
    outputBox.skipLine(1);
}
```

outer for

inner for

The outer for statement is set to range from the first row (width = 11) to the last row (width = 20). For each repetition of the outer for, the inner for statement is executed, which ranges from the first column (length = 5) to the fifth column (length = 25). The loop body of the inner for computes the price of a single carpet size and prints out this price. So the complete execution of the inner for, which causes its loop body to be executed five times, completes the output of one row. The following shows the sequence of values for the two control variables.

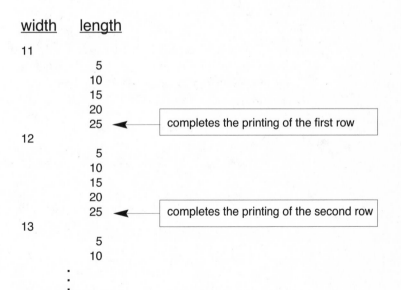

Now let's add the code to print out the row and column index values for width and length.

```
int             price;
MainWindow      mainWindow    = new MainWindow();
OutputBox       outputBox  = new OutputBox(mainWindow);
mainWindow.show();
outputBox.setTitle("Carpet Price Table");
outputBox.show();

outputBox.printLine("        5      10      15      20      25");
outputBox.skipLine(1);

for (int width = 11; width <= 20; width++) {

    outputBox.print(width + "    ");

    for (int length = 5; length <= 25; length += 5) {
        price = width * length * 19; //$19 per sq ft.
        outputBox.print("    " + price);
    }

    //finished one row; now move on to the next row
    ouputBox.skipLine(1);
}
```

Modified Parts

The next improvement is to include the labels Width and Length in the output. This enhancement is left as exercise 15 at the end of the chapter. Also, in the example, literal constants are used for the carpet sizes and the increment value on length (11, 20, 5, 25, and 5), but in a real program, named constants should be used.

Quick Check

1. What will be the value of sum after the following nested for loops are executed?

    ```
    a.  int sum = 0;
        for (int i = 0; i < 5; i++) {
            sum = sum + i;
            for (int j = 0; j < 5; j++) {
    ```

```
                            sum = sum + j;
                        }
                    }

      b)  int sum = 0;
          for (int i = 0; i < 5; i++) {
              sum = sum + i;
              for (int j = i; i < 5; j++) { //j is set to i
                  sum = sum + j;
              }
          }
```

2. What is wrong with the following nested for loop?

```
          int sum = 0;
          for (int i = 0; i < 5; i++) {
              sum = sum + i;
              for (int i = 5; i > 0; i--) {
                  sum = sum + j;
              }
          }
```

7.7 The Format Class

In the table shown in Figure 7.10, the values are aligned very nicely. We purposely selected the unit price and the ranges of width and length so that the table output would look good. Notice that the output values are all four digit numbers. Realistically, we cannot expect output values to be so uniform. Let's change the unit price to $15 and the range of widths to 5 through 14 and see what happens. The result is shown in Figure 7.11, which is not as neat as the previous output. What we need is a way to format the output so the values are printed out with the proper alignment.

Format class from javabook

In this section we introduce the Format class from the javabook package, which we use to format output values. Let's start with an example. When we execute the following code (assuming outputBox was properly created)

```
      int i = 12, j = 6789, k = 908766;
      double x = 123.4, y = 2.90899, z = 900.00;

      outputBox.printLine("i " + i);
      outputBox.printLine("j " + j);
      outputBox.printLine("k " + k);
```

FIGURE 7.11   The price table for carpets with $15 per square foot and width ranging from 5 through 14.

Carpet Price Table					
	5	10	15	20	25
5	375	750	1125	1500	1875
6	450	900	1350	1800	2250
7	525	1050	1575	2100	2625
8	600	1200	1800	2400	3000
9	675	1350	2025	2700	3375
10	750	1500	2250	3000	3750
11	825	1650	2475	3300	4125
12	900	1800	2700	3600	4500
13	975	1950	2925	3900	4875
14	1050	2100	3150	4200	5250

```
outputBox.skipLine(1);

outputBox.printLine("x " + x);
outputBox.printLine("y " + y);
outputBox.printLine("z " + z);
```

we will get the output shown in Figure 7.12. Values are printed using as many spaces as they require, no more and no less.

Now let's see how we can format these six values using the Format class. The basic idea of formatted output is to allocate the same amount of space for the output values and align the values within the allocated space. We call the

field   space occupied by an output value the *field* and the number of characters allocated to a field its *field width*.

Figure 7.13 shows the formatted output that is generated by executing the following code:

```
outputBox.printLine( "i " + Format.rightAlign(10, i) );
outputBox.printLine( "j " + Format.rightAlign(10, j) );
outputBox.printLine( "k " + Format.rightAlign(10, k) );
```

FIGURE 7.12   Unformatted output of integers and floats.

```
OutputBox
i 12
j 6789
k 908766
x 123.4
y 2.90899
z 900.0
```

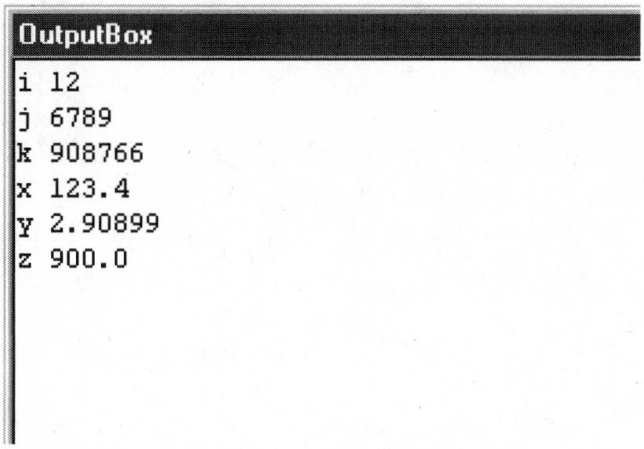

```
outputBox.skipLine(1);

outputBox.printLine( "x " + Format.rightAlign(10, 3, x) );
outputBox.printLine( "y " + Format.rightAlign(10, 3, y) );
outputBox.printLine( "z " + Format.rightAlign(10, 3, z) );
```

FIGURE 7.13   Formatted output of integers and floats.

```
OutputBox
i         12
j       6789
k     908766
x    123.400
y      2.909
z    900.000
```

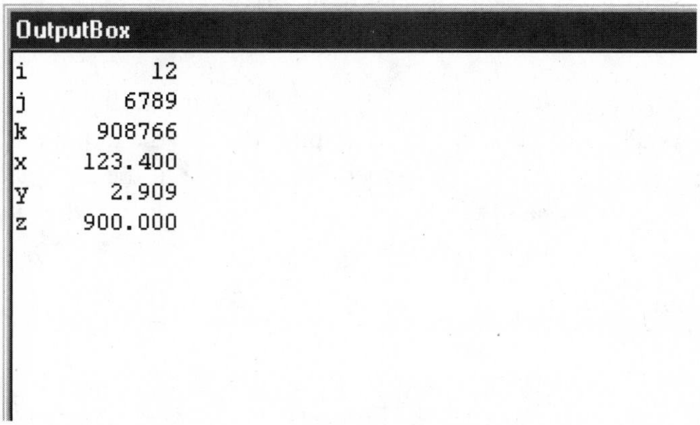

To format an integer, we use

formatting
integers

```
Format.leftAlign   ( <fieldWidth>, <int expression> );
Format.rightAlign  ( <fieldWidth>, <int expression> );
Format.centerAlign ( <fieldWidth>, <int expression> );
```

where <fieldWidth> designates the field width and <int expression> is an arithmetic expression whose value is int. The method names leftAlign, rightAlign, and centerAlign designate the alignment of an output value within a field. The following code will produce the output shown in Figure 7.14.

```
int i = 1234, j = 567, k = 89, l = 123456789;

outputBox.printLine( Format.leftAlign(6,i) + "I" );
outputBox.printLine( Format.leftAlign(6,j) + "Love" );
outputBox.printLine( Format.leftAlign(6,k) + "Java" );
outputBox.printLine( Format.leftAlign(6,l) + "Programming" );
outputBox.skipLine(1);

outputBox.printLine( Format.rightAlign(6,i) );
outputBox.printLine( Format.rightAlign(6,j) );
outputBox.printLine( Format.rightAlign(6,k) );
outputBox.printLine( Format.rightAlign(6,l) );
outputBox.skipLine(1);

outputBox.printLine( Format.centerAlign(6,i) + "Yes" );
outputBox.printLine( Format.centerAlign(6,j) + "Java" );
outputBox.printLine( Format.centerAlign(6,k) + "Is" );
outputBox.printLine( Format.centerAlign(6,l) + "Hot" );
```

When the integer to be displayed has more digits than designated in <fieldWidth>, then the number is displayed using the minimum number of spaces necessary to display the number. For example, if the designated field width is 3, but the integer has 5 digits, then the number is displayed using 5 spaces.

formatting
strings

The same format statements can be used for a string value. For example, the following code will produce the output shown in Figure 7.15.

```
for (int width = 10; width > 5; width-- )
    outputBox.printLine( Format.rightAlign(width, "Jakarta") );
```

FIGURE 7.14   Formatted output of integers, demonstrating various alignments.

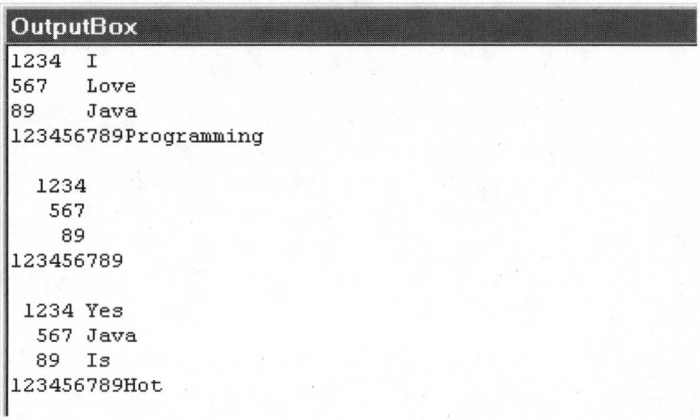

```
OutputBox
1234   I
567    Love
89     Java
123456789Programming

  1234
   567
    89
123456789

 1234 Yes
  567 Java
   89 Is
123456789Hot
```

FIGURE 7.15   Formatted output of the string "Jakarta".

```
OutputBox
   Jakarta
  Jakarta
 Jakarta
Jakarta
Jakarta
```

To format a real number (float or double), we need additional arguments to specify the decimal places:

formatting
real numbers

```
Format.leftAlign  (<fieldWidth>,<decimalPlaces>,<real expr>);
Format.rightAlign (<fieldWidth>,<decimalPlaces>,<real expr>);
Format.centerAlign(<fieldWidth>,<decimalPlaces>,<real expr>);
```

where <decimalPlaces> designates the number of digits shown to the right of the decimal point and <real expr> is an arithmetic expression whose value is either float or double. The value for <fieldWidth> must be at least as large as the value of <decimalPlaces> plus two. We add two because a decimal point and a minus sign will occupy one space each. When the real number to be displayed has more digits than designated in <fieldWidth>, the number is displayed using the minimum number of spaces necessary to display the number. Here's an example:

```
double x = -123.4, y = 5.67, z = 8.911, w = 12345.6789;

outputBox.printLine( Format.leftAlign(6,2,x) + "I" );
outputBox.printLine( Format.leftAlign(6,2,y) + "Love" );
outputBox.printLine( Format.leftAlign(6,2,z) + "Java" );
outputBox.printLine( Format.leftAlign(6,2,w) + "Programming" );
outputBox.skipLine(1);

outputBox.printLine( Format.rightAlign(6,3,x) );
outputBox.printLine( Format.rightAlign(6,3,y) );
outputBox.printLine( Format.rightAlign(6,3,z) );
outputBox.printLine( Format.rightAlign(6,3,w) );
outputBox.skipLine(1);

outputBox.printLine(Format.centerAlign(6,1,x) + "Yes");
outputBox.printLine(Format.centerAlign(6,1,y) + "Java");
outputBox.printLine(Format.centerAlign(6,1,z) + "Is");
outputBox.printLine(Format.centerAlign(6,1,w) + "Hot");
```

Figure 7.16 shows the results of executing the example code.

FIGURE 7.16   Formatted output of real numbers, demonstrating various alignments.

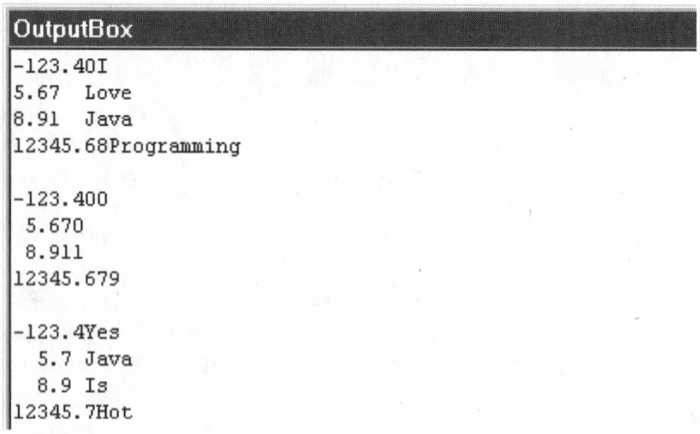

```
OutputBox
-123.40I
5.67  Love
8.91  Java
12345.68Programming

-123.400
 5.670
 8.911
12345.679

-123.4Yes
 5.7 Java
 8.9 Is
12345.7Hot
```

Table 7.3 is a list of Format methods.

TABLE 7.3   A list of **Format** methods.

CLASS:	Format	
Class Method	**Argument**	**Description**
leftAlign	int, long or int or String	The first argument designates the field width. The second argument is left aligned in the given field. The method return the formatted value as a String.
leftAlign	int, int, double or float	The first argument designates the field width. The second argument designates the decimal places. The third argument is left aligned in the given field. The method return the formatted value as a String.
centerAlign	int, long or int or String	Same as the first version of leftAlign, but with the center alignment.
centerAlign	int, int, double or float	Same as the second version of leftAlign, but with the center alignment.
rightAlign	int, long or int or String	Same as the first version of leftAlign, but with the right alignment.
rightAlign	int, int, double or float	Same as the second version of leftAlign, but with the right alignment.

Quick Check

1. Determine the output of the following code:

    ```
    outputBox.printLine(Format.leftAlign(8,2,10.23    + "X");
    outputBox.printLine(Format.centerAlign(8,2,12.094)+ "X");
    outputBox.printLine(Format.rightAlign(8,2,0.3333)  + "X");
    outputBox.printLine(Format.leftAlign(8,2,2.1)      + "X");
    ```

2. What's wrong with the following code?

    ```
    outputBox.printLine(Format.centerAlign(2,1033.23) + "Y");
    ```

```
outputBox.printLine(Format.leftAlign(12.94, 6, 2) + "Y");
outputBox.printLine(Format.rightAlign(6,2,"Hi")    + "Y");
```

7.8   Loan Tables

The LoanCalculator program computed the monthly and total payments for a given loan amount, annual interest rate, and loan period. To see the monthly payment for the same loan amount and loan period but with a different interest rate, we would need to repeat the calculation, entering the three values again. To illustrate the use of the concepts introduced in this chapter, let's design a program that generates a loan table (similar to the carpet price table) for a given loan amount so we can compare different monthly payments easily and quickly. The columns of the table are the loan periods in number of years (5, 10, 15, 20, 25, 30), and the rows are interest rates ranging from 6 percent to 10 percent in increments of 0.25.

In this section, we will provide a discussion of the relevant methods only. Let's begin with a design of the topmost start method of the modified LoanCalculator class, which we will call LoanTable. The start method can be expressed as

```
tell the user what the program does;
prompt the user "Do you want to generate a loan table?";
while (the user says YES) {

    input the loan amount;
    generate the loan table;

    prompt the user "Do you want another loan table?";
}
```

pseudocode   The start method is expressed in pseudocode. A *pseudocode* is an informal language we often use to express an algorithm. Pseudocode is useful in expressing an algorithm without being tied down to the rigid syntactic rules of a programming language. We can express a simple algorithm in the actual programming language statements, but for a more complex algorithm, especially those involving nonsequential control flow logic, pseudocode is very helpful in expressing the algorithm concisely and clearly. Whenever appropriate, we will be using pseudocode to express more complex algorithms in the remainder of the book.

Translating the pseudocode into Java code will result in

```
public void start ( )
{
    int response;

    describeProgram();
    response = yesNoBox.prompt("Do you want to run the program?");

    while (response == ResponseBox.YES) {

        loanAmount = getLoanAmount();          //get input
        generateLoanTable(loanAmount);         //generate one table

        response = yesNoBox.prompt("Do you want another loan table?");
    }
}
```

Notice how the use of objects yesNoBox and methods describeProgram and getLoanAmount makes the actual start method almost as easy to read as the pseudocode. By using objects and well-designed (sub)methods, we can express methods that are as easy to read as pseudocode.

The describeProgram method tells the user what the program does if the user requests it. The getLoanAmount method gets the loan amount from the user. The method will allow the user to enter the loan amount between 100.0 and 500,000.0. The generateLoanTable method generates the loan table, which we will explain in detail next.

We use a nested loop to generate the table. Both the inner and outer loops are count-controlled loops. The loop for columns (years) will range from 5 to 30 with an increment of 5 and the loop for rows (rates) will range from 6.0 to 10.0 with an increment of 0.25. So the nested loop will be as follows:

```
private static final int BEGIN_YEAR = 5;
private static final int END_YEAR   = 30;
private static final int YEAR_INCR  = 5;

private static final float START_RATE= 6.0f;
private static final float END_RATE = 10.0f;
private static final float RATE_INCR= 0.25f;

private int    year;
private float  rate;

...

for (rate = BEGIN_RATE; rate <= END_RATE; rate += RATE_INCR){
```

```
for (year = BEGIN_YEAR; year <= END_YEAR; year += YEAR_INCR){
...

    //compute and display the monthly loan payment
    //for a given year and rate
}
}
```

To compute the monthly loan payment, we define a method getMonthlyPayment that takes the arguments amount, monthlyRate, and numOfPayments for the loan amount, monthly interest rate, and the number of payments. The method is defined as follows:

```
private double getMonthlyPayment(    float   amount,
                                     float   monthlyRate,
                                     int     numOfPayments );
{
    double payment;

    payment = (amount * monthlyRate) /
            (1 - Math.pow(1 /(1 + monthlyRate), numOfPayments));

    return payment;
}
```

We use the field width of 10 and two decimal places for the monthly loan payments, so we display the loanAmount as

```
outputBox.print( Format.rightAlign(10, 2, loanAmount) );
```

To output the complete table with column and row labels, we write the nested loop as

```
//print the column labels
outputBox.print(Format.rightAlign(10," "));
for (year = BEGIN_YEAR; year <= END_YEAR; year += YEAR_INCR){
    outputBox.print( Format.centerAlign(10, year) );
}

outputBox.skipLine(1);

for (rate = BEGIN_RATE; rate <= END_RATE; rate += RATE_INCR){
```

```
                //print the row label
                outputBox.print( Format.centerAlign(10, 2, rate ) );

                //compute monthly rate
                monthlyRate = rate / MONTHS_IN_YEAR / 100.0f;

                for (year = BEGIN_YEAR; year <= END_YEAR; year+= YEAR_INCR){

                    payments = year * MONTHS_IN_YEAR; //total # of payments
                    loanPayment =
                            getMonthlyPayment(loanAmount, rate, payments);
                    outputBox.print( Format.rightAlign(10, 2, loanAmount) );
                }

                outputBox.skipLine(1);
        }
```

7.9   Sample Program: Hi-Lo Game

After the mundane task of dealing with mortgages, let's play a game. We will write a program that plays a Hi-Lo game. This program illustrates the use of repetition control, the random number generator, and the testing strategy. The objective of the game is to guess a secret number between 1 and 100. The program will respond with HI if the guess is higher than the secret number and LO if the guess is lower than the secret number. The maximum number of guesses allowed is six. If you allow up to seven, one can always guess the secret number. Do you know why?

Problem Statement

Write an application that will play Hi-Lo games with the user. The objective of the game is for the user to guess the computer-generated secret number in the least number of tries. The secret number is an integer between 1 and 100, inclusive. When the user makes a guess, the program replies with HI or LO depending on whether the guess is higher or lower than the secret number. The maximum number of tries allowed for each game is six. The user can play as many games as she wants.

Overall Plan

We will begin with our overall plan for the development. Let's identify the major tasks of the program. The first task is to generate a secret number every time the game is played, and the second task is to play the game itself. We also need to add a loop to repeat these two tasks every time the user wants to play the Hi-Lo game. We can express this program logic in pseudocode as

program
tasks

```
do {
     Task 1: generate a secret number;

     Task 2: play one game;

} while ( the user wants to play );
```

Let's look at the two tasks and determine objects that will be responsible for handling the tasks. For the first task, we will use the random method of the Math class. We will examine this method in detail later to determine whether it is the one we can use in the program. If this method does not meet our needs, then we will explore further and most likely have to derive our own random number generator.

For the second task of playing the game itself, we need an object to accept the user's guess and another object to respond to the user with a HI or LO. For input, we will use an InputBox object. For output, we will use a MessageBox object. If we want the game to be slightly easier, we could use an OutputBox and display the history of guesses along with the hints:

```
GUESS          HINT
 50             LO
 60             HI
 55             LO
```

We opt to use a MessageBox so the game player has to keep track of the guesses she made and the hints in her mind. At the end of one game, we use this MessageBox object to display either You guessed it in <N> tries or You lost. Secret number was <X> with <N> or <X> replaced with the actual value.

Finally, we will define a top-level control object that manages all other objects. We will call this class HiLo. Our main class will be HiLoMain, whose task is to create an instance of HiLo and start the instance. We also need a way for the user to tell the program whether to play another game or not. We will use a ResponseBox object for this purpose. Here's our working design document:

program
classes

Design Document:	DrawShape
Class	**Purpose**
HiLoMain	The main class of the program.
HiLo	The top-level control object that manages other objects in the program.
MessageBox	A MessageBox object is used to show the hint HI or LO after each guess. This class is from javabook.
InputBox	An InputBox object is used to get a guess from the player. This class is from javabook.
OutputBox	An OutputBox object is used to display the rules of the Hi-Lo game.
ResponseBox	A ResponseBox object is used to get the user's instruction to play another game or not.
MainWindow	The main window of the application.

Figure 7.17 is the object diagram for this program.

We will implement this program using the following four major steps:

development
steps

1. Start with a program skeleton. Define the HiLoMain and HiLo classes.

2. Add code to the HiLo class to play a game using a dummy secret number.

3. Add code to the HiLo class to generate a random number.

4. Finalize the code by removing temporary statements and tying up loose ends.

Step 1 Development: Program Skeleton

Step 1 Design

The structure of the HiLoMain class is the same as other main classes. All we need is to declare, create, and start a HiLo object. Instead of forcing the user to play at least one game, we will implement the program so the user has an option of not playing a game at all. In pseudocode we can express this logic as

```
describe the game rules;

prompt the user to play a game or not;

while ( answer is yes ) {

    generate the secret number;

    play one game;

    prompt the user to play another game or not;
}
```

Notice that we use a while loop here, so the user can quit the program without playing a game. If we use a do–while loop instead, then the user must play at least one game before stopping the program. We opt to use the while loop because the user may not want to play the game at all after reading the game rules.

We use a private method describeRules to display the game rules. To prompt the user to play a game or not, we will use a ResponseBox, and to generate a secret number, we define another private method called generateSecretNumber. Lastly, we define a third private method playGame to play one game.

FIGURE 7.17   The object diagram for the **HiLo** program.

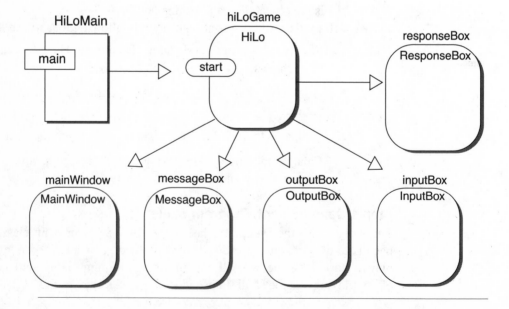

We declare these three methods private because these methods are for internal use. As always, we will use the constructor to perform necessary object creation and initialization. The object diagram for the HiLo class at this point is

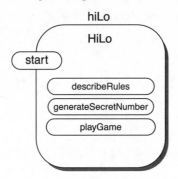

Our working design document for the HiLo class is as follows:

Design Document: The HiLo Class		
Method	**Visibility**	**Purpose**
`<constructor>`	`public`	Creates and initializes the objects used by a HiLo object.
`start`	`public`	Starts the Hi-Lo game playing. The user has an option of playing a game or not.
`describeRules`	`private`	Displays the game rules in OutputBox.
`generateSecret-Number`	`private`	Generates a secret number for the next Hi-Lo game.
`playGame`	`private`	Plays one Hi-Lo game.

Step 1 Code

For the skeleton program, we include temporary output statements in the private methods to verify that they are called correctly in the right order. Here's the skeleton:

```
/*
    Program HiLo

    A program to play Hi-Lo games. The objective of the game is to guess the
    secret number (any integer between 1 and 100) with the least number of tries.
    The maximum number of tries allowed is six.

    Input:     User guess

    Output:    Display the hint HI if the guess is higher than the secret number
               and LO if the guess is lower than the secret number. Display the
               message "You guessed it in <N> tries" or "You lost. Secret no.
```

```
                            was <X>" at the end of one game.
*/

class HiLoMain
{
    public static void main (String args[])
    {
        HiLo hiLo = new HiLo( );
        hiLo.start();
    }
}
```

```
/*
    Class HiLo (Step 1: Skeleton)

    The top-level object for managing all other objects in the program.
*/

import javabook.*;

class HiLo
{

/**************************
    Data Members
**************************/

    private MainWindow    mainWindow;
    private MessageBox    messageBox;
    private OutputBox     outputBox;
    private ResponseBox   responseBox;
    private InputBox      inputBox;

/**************************
    Constructor
**************************/
    public HiLo( )
    {
        mainWindow      = new MainWindow("Let's Play HiLo");
        outputBox       = new OutputBox    ( mainWindow );
        responseBox     = new ResponseBox  ( mainWindow );
        messageBox      = new MessageBox   ( mainWindow );
        inputBox        = new InputBox     ( mainWindow );

        mainWindow.show();
        outputBox.show();
    }


/*****************************
    Public Methods

        void start (       )

*****************************/
```

```
    public void start ( )
    {
        int answer;

        describeRules();

        answer = responseBox.prompt("Do you want to play a Hi-Lo game?);

        while ( answer = ResponseBox.YES ) {

            generateSecretNumber( );
            playGame();

            answer
                = responseBox.prompt("Do you want to play another Hi-Lo game?");
        }
    }
/*****************************
    Private Methods

    void    describeRules         (          )
    void    generateSecretNumber  (          )
    void    playGame              (          )

*****************************/

    /*********************************************************
        Method:        describeRules

        Purpose:       Describe what the program does.

        Parameters:    None

        Returns:       None
    */
    private void describeRules( )
    {
        outputBox.printLine("Inside describeRules");          //TEMP
    }


    /*********************************************************
        Method:        generateSecretNumber

        Purpose:       Generate a random number between 1 and 100.

        Parameters:    None

        Returns:       None
    */
    private void generateSecretNumber( )
    {
        outputBox.printLine("Inside generateSecretNumber");   //TEMP
    }
```

```
/**********************************************************
    Method:        playGame

    Purpose:       Play one Hi-Lo game.

    Parameters:    None

    Returns:       None
*/
private void playGame( )
{
    outputBox.printLine("Inside playGame");              //TEMP
}

}
```

Step 1 Test

The main class HiLoMain will not change. The class given here is the final version. We execute the main class and the skeleton HiLo class to verify that the classes are coded correctly. To verify the correct execution of Step 1 we attempt to play the game

1. Zero times.

2. One time.

3. One or more times.

For the first run, we select No to the prompt Do you want to play a Hi-Lo game? and make sure the program stops without playing a game. For the second run, we select Yes to the first prompt and verify that the messages Inside generateSecretNumber and Inside playGame are shown in outputBox. We select No to the prompt Do you want to play another Hi-Lo game? and make sure the program stops. For the third run, we make sure we can play more than one game. After we verify all the scenarios work correctly, we proceed to the next step.

Step 2 Development: Play a Game with a Dummy Secret Number

Step 2 Design

In the second development step, we add a routine that plays a Hi-Lo game. We decided in the overall planning step that we will use an InputBox object to accept the user guess and a MessageBox object to display a hint. Let's begin with the control flow of the playGame method.

There are two cases to end a Hi-Lo game: either the user guesses the number in less than six tries or uses up all six tries without guessing the number. So we need a counter to keep track of the number of guesses made. Let's call this counter guessCount. We stop the game when guessCount becomes larger than six or the user's guess is equal to the secret number. At the end of the game, we output an appropriate message. Expressing this in pseudocode, we have

```
//Method: playGame

set guessCount to 0;

do {
    get next guess;

    increment guessCount;

    if (guess < secretNumber) {
        print the hint LO;
    }
    else if (guess > secretNumber) {
        print the hint HI;
    }

} while (guessCount < number of guess allowed &&
            guess != secretNumber );

if (guess  == secretNumber) {

    print the winning message;
}
else {
    print the losing message;
}
```

All variables used in this method will be local except secretNumber, which will be an instance variable. The value for secretNumber is set inside the generate-SecretNumber method.

To support a better user interface, we will include an input error handling that allows the user to enter only values between 1 and 100. We will do this input-error-checking routine in a new private method getNextGuess because we do want to keep the playGame method clean and simple. If we include the code for input error handling directly inside the playGame method, the method would become too cluttered and lose the overall clarity of what the method is doing. Pseudocode for the getNextGuess method is

```
//Method: getNextGuess

get input value;
```

```
while ( input < 1 || input > 100 ) {
    print an error message;
    get input value;
}
```

The working design document of the class now includes this new private method:

Design Document: The HiLo Class		
Method	**Visibility**	**Purpose**
...	...	...
getNextGuess	private	Return the next guess from the user. Only accept a guess between 1 and 100. Print an appropriate error message when an invalid guess is entered.

Step 2 Code

In the Step 2 coding, we need to implement three methods. In addition to the playGame and getNextGuess methods, we need to define a temporary generateSecretNumber method so we can test the playGame method. The temporary generateSecretNumber method assigns a dummy secret number to the instance variable secretNumber. The temporary method is coded as

```
private void generateSecretNumber( )
{
    secretNumber = 45;          //TEMP
}
```

Any number will do; we simply picked the number 45. Knowing that the secret number is 45, we will be able to test whether the playGame method is implemented correctly or not.

We implement the playGame method as

```
private void playGame( )
{
    int guessCount = 0;
    int guess;

    do {
        //get the next guess
        guess = getNextGuess( );          ◄———  getNextGuess is a
                                                 new private method.
```

```
                     guessCount++;

                     //check the guess
                     if (guess < secretNumber) {
                         messageBox.show("Your guess is LO");
                     }
                     else if (guess > secretNumber) {
                         messageBox.show("Your guess is HI");
                     }
```

Repeat the loop if the number of tries is not used up and the correct guess is not yet made. ➤

```
                 } while ( guessCount < MAX_GUESS_ALLOWED &&
                           guess != secretNumber );
```

This is a class constant whose value is set to 6.

```
             //output appropriate message
             if ( guess == secretNumber ) {
                 messageBox.show("You guessed it in "
                                     + guessCount  + " tries.");
             }
             else {
                 messageBox.show("You lost. Secret No. was "
                                     + secretNumber);
             }
         }
```

The getNextGuess method will accept an integer between 1 and 100. The method uses a while loop to accomplish this:

```
         private int getNextGuess( )
         {
             int nextGuess;

             nextGuess
                 = inputBox.getInteger("Enter Guess between 1 and 100");

             while (nextGuess < 1 || nextGuess > 100) {
                 messageBox.show("Guess must be between 1 and 100");
                 nextGuess = inputBox.getInteger("Your Guess:");
             }

             System.out.println("Guess: " + nextGuess); //TEMP

             return nextGuess;
         }
```

The necessary constant and instance variable are declared in the data member section of the HiLo class as

```
/**************************
    Data Members
**************************/
private final int     MAX_GUESS_ALLOWED = 6;

private int           secretNumber;
```

Step 2 Test

We need to test two methods in this step. To verify the getNextGuess method, we input both invalid and valid guesses. Notice that we place a temporary output statement in the method to verify the input value. We verify the method by running the following tests:

1. Enter a number less than 1.

2. Enter a number greater 100.

3. Enter a number between 2 and 99.

4. Enter 1.

5. Enter 100.

test cases

The first two tests are called *error cases*, the third is called the *normal case*, and the last two are called *end cases*. One of the common errors beginners make is the loop statement that does not process the end cases correctly. When our code handles all three types of cases correctly, we will proceed to test the playGame method.

To verify the playGame method, we need to perform a more elaborate testing. Knowing that the dummy secret number is 45, we verify the playGame method by running the following tests:

1. Enter a number less than 45 and check that the correct hint LO is displayed.

2. Enter a number greater than 45 and check that the correct hint Hi is displayed.

3. Enter the correct guess and check that the game terminates after displaying the appropriate message.

4. Enter six wrong guesses and check that the game terminates after displaying the appropriate message.

When all four tests are successfully completed, we proceed to the next step.

Step 3 Development: Generate a Random Number

Step 3 Design

In the third development step, we add a routine that generates a random number between 1 and 100. We search for any existing class that will do the job, and luckily we found the method random from the Math package. If we were not successful in finding any existing class, then we would have to define our own random number generator consulting any relevant mathematics references (or searching the Internet).

pseudorandom number generator

The method random is called a *pseudorandom number generator* and returns a number (type double) that is greater than or equal to 0.0 but less than 1.0, that is, $0.0 \le X < 1.0$. The generated number is called a *pseudorandom number* because the number is not truly random. When we call this method repeatedly, eventually the numbers generated will repeat themselves. Therefore, theoretically the generated numbers are not random, but for all practical purposes, they are random enough. Since the number returned from the random method ranges from 0.0 up to but not including 1.0, we need to convert it to a number between 1 and 100. If an X is a number returned by random, then the following property holds:

$$0 \le X \times 100 < 100$$

Since the expression $X \times 100$ is a real number, we truncate it to get an integer value:

$$0 \le \lfloor X \times 100 \rfloor \le 99$$

Since we need a value between 1 and 100, the secret number is computed as

$$\text{secretNumber} = \lfloor X \times 100 \rfloor + 1$$

Step 3 Code

The generateSecretNumber method is defined as

```
private void generateSecretNumber( )
{
    double X = Math.random();

    secretNumber = (int) Math.floor( X * 100 ) + 1;

    System.out.println("Secret Number: " + secretNumber);//TEMP
}
```

The method includes a temporary statement to output the secret number so we can stop the game anytime we want by entering the correct guess.

Step 3 Test

To verify that the method generates correct random numbers, we will write a separate test program. If we don't use such a test program and instead include the method immediately in the HiLo class, we have to play the game, say, 100 times to verify that the first 100 generated numbers are valid. The test program generates N random numbers and stops whenever an invalid number is generated. We will set N to 1000. Here's the test program:

TestRandom
class for testing

```java
class TestRandom
{
    public static void main ( String args[] )
    {
        int     N = 1000, count = 0, number;
        double X;

        do {

            count++;

            X      = Math.random();
            number = (int) Math.floor( X * 100 ) + 1;

        } while ( count < N &&
                   1 <= number && number <= 100 );

        if ( number < 1 || number > 100 ) {
            System.out.println("Error: " + number);
        }
        else {
            System.out.println("Okay");
        }
    }
}
```

Keep in mind that successfully generating 1,000 valid random numbers does not guarantee that the 1,001st number is also valid. We did not make any formal mathematical proof that the routine for the random number generator works correctly. What we are doing here is making an assumption that no user wants to play more than 1,000 Hi-Lo games in one session, which we believe is a practical assumption. After the TestRandom class is executed correctly, we make the necessary changes to the HiLo class and run it. When we verify that the program runs as expected, we proceed to the final step.

Step 4 Development: Finalize

We finalize the program in the last step. We will perform a critical review of the program looking for any unfinished method, inconsistency, or error in the methods, unclear or missing comments, and so forth. We should also not forget to keep an eye on any improvement we can make to the existing code.

We still have a temporary code inside the describeRules method, so we will complete the method by adding code to describe the game rules. This method is left as an exercise. Use responseBox and display the game rules only if the user wants to see them.

There are still temporary output statements that we used for verification purposes. Either we can delete them from the program or comment them out. We will leave them in the program by commenting them out so when the time comes for us to modify, debug, or update the program, we do not have to reenter them.

7.10 (Optional) Recursive Methods

In addition to three repetition control statements we introduced in this chapter, there is a fourth way to control the repetition flow of a program by using recursive methods. A *recursive method* is a method that contains a statement (or statements) that makes a call to itself. We will explain recursive methods briefly in this section. Realistic examples of recursive methods will be given in Chapter 15.

So far, we have seen only methods that call other methods, something like

```
methodOne(...)
{
   ...
   methodTwo(...); //methodOne called methodTwo
   ...
}


methodTwo(...)
{
   ...
}
```

A recursive method calls itself, and it looks something like

```
methodOne(...)
{
  ...
  methodOne(...); //calls the method itself
  ...
}
```

At first glance, it seems like a recursive call will never end since the call is made to the same method. Indeed, if you do not follow the rules, you could end up with infinite recursive calls. In this section we will explain how to write recursive methods correctly.

Suppose we want to compute the factorial of N. The *factorial* of N is the product of the first N positive integers, denoted mathematically as

```
N! = N * (N-1) * (N-2) * ... * 2 * 1
```

We will write a recursive method to compute the factorial of N. Mathematically, we can define the factorial of N recursively as

$$
factorial(N) = \begin{cases} 1 & \text{if } N = 1 \\ N * factorial(N-1) & \text{otherwise} \end{cases}
$$

The definition states that if N is 1, then the function factorial(N) has the value 1. Otherwise, the function factorial(N) is the product of N and factorial(N–1). For example, the function factorial(4) is evaluated as

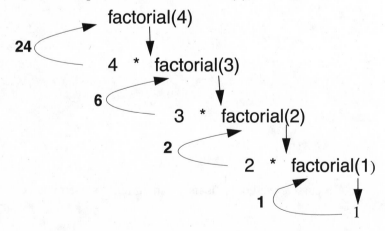

The recursive factorial method parallels the preceding mathematical definition. The method is defined as

```
public int factorial(int N)
{
    if (N == 1)

        return 1;

    else

        return N * factorial(N-1);
}
```

Test to stop or continue.

End case: recursion stops.

Recursive case: recursion continues with a recursive call.

The diagram in Figure 7.18 illustrates the sequence of calls for the recursive factorial method. Recursive methods will contain three necessary components.

The three necessary components in a recursive method are

1. **A test to stop or continue the recursion.**
2. **An end case that terminates the recursion.**
3. **A recursive call(s) that continues the recursion.**

To ensure that the recursion will stop eventually, we must pass arguments different from the incoming parameters. In the factorial method, the incoming parameter was N, while the argument passed in the recursive call was N–1. This difference of 1 between the incoming parameter and the argument will eventually make the argument in a recursive call be 1, and the recursion will stop.

Let's implement two more mathematical functions using recursion. The next method computes the sum of the first N positive integers $1, 2, \ldots, N$. Notice how this method includes the three necessary components of a recursive method.

```
public int sum ( int N )
{
    if (N == 1)
        return 1;
    else
        return N + sum( N-1 );
}
```

FIGURE 7.18   The sequence of calls for the recursive **factorial** method.

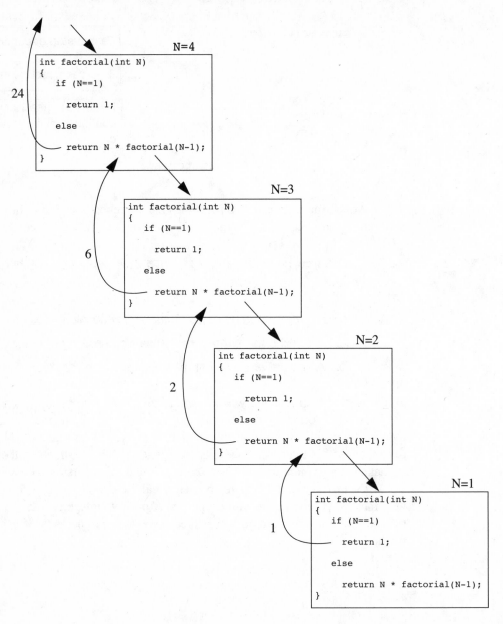

The last method computes the exponentiation A^N where A is a real number and N is a positive integer. This time, we have to pass two arguments: A and N. The value of A will not change in the calls, but the value of N is decremented after each recursive call.

```
public float exponent ( float A, int N )
{
    if (N == 1)
        return A;

    else
        return A * exponent( A, N-1 );
}
```

Although we use only mathematical functions to illustrate recursive methods, recursion is not limited to mathematical functions. More examples of recursive methods that implement nonnumerical operations appear in Chapter 15.

We used factorial, sum, and exponentiation as examples to introduce some of the basic concepts of recursion, but we should never write these methods using recursion. The methods can be written more efficiently with an iterative (i.e., nonrecursive) manner using a simple for loop. In practice, we use recursion if certain conditions are met.

Use recursion if

1. A recursive solution is natural and easy to understand.

2. A recursive solution does not result in excessive duplicate computation.

3. The equivalent iterative solution is too complex.

7.11 Exercises

1. Identify all errors in the following repetition statements. Some errors are syntactical while others are logical (e.g., infinite loops).

```
a. for (int i = 10; i > 0; i++) {
       x = y;
       a = b;
   }
```

```
b.  sum = 0;
    do {
        num = inputBox.getInteger();
        sum += num;
    } until (sum > 10000);

c.  while (x < 1 && x > 10) {
        a = b;
    }

d.  while (a == b) ;
    {
        a = b;
        x = y;
    }

e.  for (int i = 1.0; i <= 2.0; i += 0.1) {
        x = y;
        a = b;
    }
```

2. Write for, do–while, and while statements to compute the following sums and products.

a. $1 + 2 + 3 + \ldots + 100$

b. $5 + 10 + 15 + \ldots + 50$

c. $1 + 3 + 7 + 15 + 31 + \ldots + 2^{20} - 1$

d. $1 + \dfrac{1}{2} + \dfrac{1}{3} + \dfrac{1}{4} + \ldots + \dfrac{1}{15}$

e. $1 \times 2 \times 3 \times \ldots \times 20$

f. $1 \times 2 \times 4 \times 8 \times \ldots \times 2^{20}$

3. What will be the value of sum after each of the following nested loops is executed?

```
a.  sum = 0;
    for (int i = 0; i <= 10; i++)
        for (int j = 0; j <= 10; j++)
            sum += i ;

b.  sum = 0;
    j = 0;
    do {
```

```
            j++;
            for (int i = 5; i > j; i--)
                sum = sum + (i+j);
        } while (j < 11);

    c.  sum = 0;
        i = 0;
        while (i < 5) {
            j = 5;
            while (i != j) {
                sum += j;
                j--;
            }
            i++;
        }

    d.  sum = 0;
        for (int i = 0; i <= 10; i++)
            for (int j = 10; j > 2*i; j--)
                sum = sum + (j - i);
```

4. Determine the output from the following code.

```
num = 123;
for (int i = 0; i <= 5; i++) {
    display.printLine( Format.centerAlign(5 + 2*i, num) );
    display.skipLine( Math.ceil(i/2) );
}
for (int j = 0; j <= 6; j += 2) {
    display.printLine( Format.rightAlign(15-j,num) );
    display.skipLine( Math.ceil(i % 2) );
}
```

5. Rewrite the nested for statement using nested do–while and while statements.

```
    a.  sum = 0;
        number = 0;
        for (int i = 0; i <= 10; i++)
            for (int j = 10; j >= i; j--) {
                number++;
                sum = sum + (j - i);
            }

    b.  product = 1;
        number = 0;
        for (int i = 1; i < 5; i++)
```

```
        for (int j = 1; j < 5; j++) {
            number++;
            product *= number;
        }
```

6. Write an application to print out the numbers 10 through 49 in the following manner:

```
10 11 12 13 14 15 16 17 18 19
20 21 22 23 24 25 26 27 28 29
30 31 32 33 34 35 36 37 38 39
40 41 42 43 44 45 46 47 48 49
```

How would you do it? Here is an example of poorly written code:

```
MainWindow mainWindow = new MainWindow();
OutputBox outputBox = new OutputBox(mainWindow);

for (int i = 10; i < 50; i++)
    switch (i) {
        case 19:
        case 29:
        case 39: outputBox.printLine(" " + i); //move to the
                 break;                          //next line

        default: outputBox.print(" " + i);
    }
```

This code is not good because it works only for printing 10 through 49. Try to develop the code so that it can be extended easily to handle any range of values. You can do this coding in two ways: with a nested for statement or with modulo arithmetic. (If you divide a number by 10 and the remainder is 9 then the number is either 9, 19, 29, or 39, and so forth.)

7. A *prime number* is an integer greater than one and divisible only by itself and one. The first seven prime numbers are 2, 3, 5, 7, 11, 13, and 17. Write a method that returns true if its argument is a prime number. Write another method that prints out all factors of the argument.

8. A *perfect number* is a positive integer that is equal to the sum of its proper divisors. A proper divisor is a positive integer other than the number itself

that divides the number evenly (i.e., no remainder). For example, six is a perfect number because the sum of its proper divisors 1, 2, and 3 is equal to 6. Eight is not a perfect number, because $1 + 2 + 4 \neq 8$. Write an application that accepts a positive integer and determines whether the number is perfect. Also, display all proper divisors of the number. Try a number between 20 and 30 and another number between 490 and 500.

9. Write an application that lists all perfect numbers between six and N, an upper limit entered by the user. After verifying the program with a small number for N, gradually increase the value for N and see how long the program takes to generate the perfect numbers. Since there are only a few perfect numbers, you might want to display the numbers that are not perfect so you can easily tell that the program is still running.

10. Write a method that returns the number of digits in an integer argument; for example, 23,498 has five digits.

11. Your freelance work with Java^2 Lo-Fat Burgers was a success (see exercise 16 of Chapter 6). The management loved your new drive-through ordering system because the customer had to order an item from each of the three menu categories. As part of a public relations campaign, however, management decided to allow a customer to skip a menu category. Modify the program to handle this option. Before listing items from each category, use a ResponseBox object to ask the customer whether he or she wants to order an item from that category.

12. Extend the program in exercise 11 so that customers can order more than one item from each menu category. For example, the customer can buy two orders of Tofu Burgers and three orders of Buffalo Wings from the Entree menu category.

13. Complete the loan table application discussed in Section 7.8.

14. Implement the describeRules method of the HiLo class from Section 7.9. Use a ResponseBox object to ask the user whether or not to display the game rules.

15. The price table for carpet we printed out in Section 7.6 contains index values for width and length, but not labels to identify them. Write an application to generate the table below:

Carpet Price Table					
			LENGTH		
		5	10	15	20	25
	11	1045	2090	3135	4180	5225
	12	1140	2280	3420	4560	5700
	13	1235	2470	3705	4940	6175
	14	1330	2660	3990	5320	6650
WIDTH	15	1425	2850	4275	5700	7125
	16	1520	3040	4560	6080	7600
	17	1615	3230	4845	6460	8075
	18	1710	3420	5130	6840	8550
	19	1805	3610	5415	7220	9025
	20	1900	3800	5700	7600	9500

16. Using a DrawingBoard object, write an application that draws the following pattern of seven rectangles whose sides are 10, 20, 30, . . . , and 70 pixels wide.

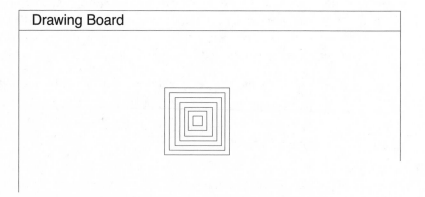

17. A formula to compute the *N*th Fibonacci number was given in exercise 18 in Chapter 3. The formula is useful in finding a number in the sequence, but a more efficient way to output a series of numbers in the sequence is to use

the recurrence relation $F_N = F_{N-1} + F_{N-2}$, with the first two numbers in the sequence F_1 and F_2 both defined as 1. Using this recurrence relation, we can compute the first 10 Fibonacci numbers as follows:

```
F1  = 1
F2  = 1
F3  = F2 + F1 =  1 +  1 =  2
F4  = F3 + F2 =  2 +  1 =  3
F5  = F4 + F3 =  3 +  2 =  5
F6  = F5 + F4 =  5 +  3 =  8
F7  = F6 + F5 =  8 +  5 = 13
F8  = F7 + F6 = 13 +  8 = 21
F9  = F8 + F7 = 21 + 13 = 34
F10 = F9 + F8 = 34 + 21 = 55
```

Write an application that accepts N, $N \geq 1$, from the user and displays the first N numbers in the Fibonacci sequence. Use OutputBox and Format for display.

18. Modify the application of exercise 17 to generate and display all numbers in the sequence until a number becomes larger than the value maxNumber entered by the user.

19. Extend the HiLo class to allow the user to designate the lower and upper bounds of the secret number. In the original HiLo class, the bounds are set to 1 and 100, respectively.

20. Improve the LoanCalculator class from Chapter 4 to accept only the valid input values for loan amount, interest rate, and loan period. The original LoanCalculator class assumed the input values are valid. For the exercise, let the loan amount between $100.00 and $1,000,000.00, the interest rate between 5% and 20%, and the loan period between 1 year and 30 years be valid.

21. The monthly payments for a given loan are divided into amounts that apply to the principal and to the interest. For example, if you make a monthly payment of $500, only a portion of the $500 goes to the principal and the remainder is the interest payment. The monthly interest is computed by multiplying the monthly interest rate and the unpaid balance. The monthly payment minus the monthly interest is the amount applied to the principal.

The following table is the sample loan payment schedule for a one-year loan of $5,000 with a 12 percent annual interest rate.

Payment #	Interest	Principal	Unpaid Balance	Total Interest to Date
1	50.00	394.24	4605.76	50.00
2	46.06	398.19	4207.57	96.06
3	42.08	402.17	3805.40	138.13
4	38.05	406.19	3399.21	176.19
5	33.99	410.25	2988.96	210.18
6	29.89	414.35	2574.61	240.07
7	25.75	418.50	2156.11	265.82
8	21.56	422.68	1733.42	287.38
9	17.33	426.91	1306.51	304.71
10	13.07	431.18	875.34	317.78
11	8.75	435.49	439.85	326.53
12	4.40	435.45	0.00	330.93

Write an application that accepts a loan amount, annual interest rate, and loan period (in number of years) and displays a table with five columns: payment number, the interest and principal paid for that month, the remaining balance after the payment, and the total interest paid to date. Note: The last payment is generally different from the monthly payment, and your application should print out the correct amount for the last payment. Use the Format class to align the output values neatly.

22. Instead of dropping a watermelon from a building, let's shoot it from a cannon and compute its projectile. The (x, y) coordinates of a watermelon at time t are

$$x = V \cdot \cos(\text{Alpha}) \cdot t$$

$$y = V \cdot \sin(\text{Alpha}) \cdot t - \frac{g \cdot t^2}{2}$$

where *g* is the acceleration of gravity, *V* is the initial velocity, and Alpha is the initial angle. The acceleration of gravity on earth is 9.8 m/sec^2.

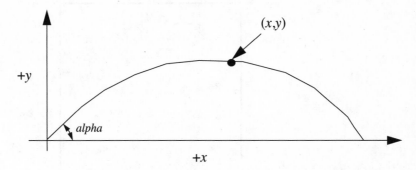

Write an application that inputs an initial velocity V (m/sec) and an initial angle alpha (in degrees) and computes the projectile of a watermelon cannon ball. The program should repeat the computation until the user wants to quit. The program outputs the (x,y) coordinate value for every second, that is, t = 0, 1, 2, and so forth. The program stops the output when the y value becomes zero or less. To use the cos and sin methods of the Math class, don't forget that you have to convert the input angle given in degrees to radians. You can convert using the following formula:

$$\text{Radian} = \frac{\text{Degree} \times \pi}{180}$$

Note: Air resistance is not considered in the formula. Also, we assumed the watermelon will not get smashed at firing.

23. Extend exercise 16 on page 233 by drawing a more realistic clock. Instead of drawing a clock like

draw a circle at five-minute intervals as

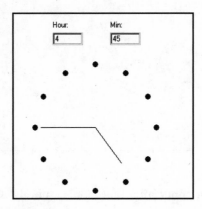

Use a for loop to draw 12 circles.

24. Write an applet that draws a multiplication table as shown below:

Applet Viewer									
applet									
	1	2	3	4	5	6	7	8	9
1	1	2	3	4	5	6	7	8	9
2	2	4	6	8	10	12	14	16	18
3	3	6	9	12	15	18	21	24	27
4	4	8	12	16	20	24	28	32	36
5	5	10	15	20	25	30	35	40	45
6	6	12	18	24	30	36	42	48	54
7	7	14	21	28	35	42	49	56	63
8	8	16	24	32	40	48	56	64	72
9	9	18	27	36	45	54	63	72	81
applet started									

Use the drawString and drawLine methods to draw the multiplication table.

25. Extend the applet from exercise 24 to allow the user to enter two single-digit numbers. When the user presses the ENTER key, draw a rectangle around the product of the two numbers. The applet should look something like this:

Applet Viewer									

applet   9   X   7

	1	2	3	4	5	6	7	8	9
1	1	2	3	4	5	6	7	8	9
2	2	4	6	8	10	12	14	16	18
3	3	6	9	12	15	18	21	24	27
4	4	8	12	16	20	24	28	32	36
5	5	10	15	20	25	30	35	40	45
6	6	12	18	24	30	36	42	48	54
7	7	14	21	28	35	42	49	56	63
8	8	16	24	32	40	48	56	64	72
9	9	18	27	36	45	54	63	72	81

applet started

Surround the product of two given numbers with a rectangle.

Use two TextField objects for entering single-digit numbers. Every time the user enters new numbers and presses the ENTER key, draw a new rectangle around the product. When you draw a new rectangle, you need to erase the previous rectangle. No erase method is available, but you can "erase" by drawing the same rectangle again in white (assuming that the background color is white). To change the color of a drawing to white, you send the message setColor to a Graphics object. The sequence for erasing the old rectangle and drawing a new rectangle is

```
graphic.setColor(Color.white);
graphic.drawRect(...);            //erase the old rectangle

graphic.setColor(Color.black);    //reset color to black or
                                  //any other color you prefer
graphic.drawRect(...);            //draw a new rectangle
```

Don't forget to resize the applet viewer in the HTML file to make the window wide enough for the entire multiplication table.

26. (Optional) Write a recursive method to compute the sum of the first *N* positive integers. Note: This is strictly for exercise. You should not write the real method recursively.

27. (Optional) Write a recursive method to compute the sum of the first *N* positive odd integers. Note: This is strictly for exercise. You should not write the real method recursively.

Characters and Strings

OBJECTIVES

After you have read and studied this chapter, you should be able to

- Declare and manipulate data of the char data type.

- Write string processing programs using String and StringBuffer objects.

- Differentiate the String and StringBuffer classes and use the correct class in solving a given task.

- Distinguish the primitive and reference data types and show how the memory allocation between the two is different.

- Tell the difference between equality and equivalence testings for String objects.

- Show, by using the state-of-memory diagrams, how objects are passed to methods and returned from methods.

Introduction

Early computers in the 1940s and 50s were more like gigantic calculators because they were used primarily for numerical computation. However, as computers have evolved to possess more computational power, our use of computers is no longer limited to numerical computation. Today we use computers for processing information of diverse types. In fact, most application software today such as word processors, database management systems, presentation software, and graphics design software is not specifically for number crunching. These programs still perform numerical computation, but their primary data are text, graphics, video, and other nonnumerical data. In this chapter you will learn about two nonnumerical data types in Java: char and String. The third nonnumerical data type boolean was already covered in Chapters 6 and 7.

8.1   Characters

In Java single characters are represented using the data type char. Character constants are written as symbols enclosed in single quotes, for example, 'a', 'X', and '5'. Just as we use different formats to represent integers and real numbers using 0s and 1s in computer memory, we use special codes of 0s and 1s to represent single characters. For example, we may assign 1 to represent 'A' and 2 to represent 'B'. We can assign codes similarly to lowercase letters, punctuation marks, digits, and other special symbols. In the early days of computing, different computers not only used different coding schemes but also different character sets. For example, one computer could represent the symbol π, while other computers could not. Individualized coding schemes did not allow computers to share information. Imagine sending electronic mail to your friend who uses a computer with a different coding scheme. You write, "Thank you for helping me with my programming assignment," and your friend reads, "τ✳✲σ ιο φυστ an εξαmple." To avoid this problem, U.S. computer manufacturers devised several

ASCII   coding schemes. One of the coding schemes widely used today is *ASCII* (American Standard Code for Information Interchange). We pronounce ASCII "askey." Table 8.1 shows the 128 standard ASCII codes.

Adding the row and column indexes gives you the ASCII code for a given character. For example, the value 87 is the ASCII code for the character 'W'. Not all characters in the table are printable. ASCII codes 0 through 31 and 127 are nonprintable control characters. For example, ASCII code 7 is the bell (the computer beeps when you send this character to output), and code 9 is the tab.

To represent all 128 ASCII codes, we need seven bits ranging from 000 0000 (0) to 111 1111 (127). Although seven bits are enough, ASCII codes occupy a byte (eight bits) because the byte is the smallest unit of memory you can access. Computer manufacturers use the extra bit for other nonstandard symbols (e.g., lines and boxes). Using 8 bits, we can represent 256 symbols in total, 128 standard ASCII codes and 128 nonstandard symbols.

TABLE 8.1   ASCII Codes.

	0	1	2	3	4	5	6	7	8	9
0	nul	soh	stx	etx	eot	enq	ack	bel	bs	ht
10	lf	vt	ff	cr	so	si	dle	dc1	dc2	dc3
20	cd4	nak	syn	etb	can	em	sub	esc	fs	gs
30	rs	us	sp	!	"	#	$	%	&	'
40	(	)	*	+	,	-	.	/	0	1
50	2	3	4	5	6	7	8	9	:	;
60	<	=	>	?	@	A	B	C	D	E
70	F	G	H	I	J	K	L	M	N	O
80	P	Q	R	S	T	U	V	W	X	Y
90	Z	[	\	]	^	_	`	a	b	c
100	d	e	f	g	h	i	j	k	l	m
110	n	o	p	q	r	s	t	u	v	w
120	x	y	z	{	}			~	del		

The standard ASCII codes work just fine as long as we are dealing with the English language because all letters and punctuation marks used in English are included in the ASCII codes. We cannot say the same for other languages. For languages such as French and German, the additional 128 codes may be used to represent character symbols not available in standard ASCII. But what about non-European languages? Chinese, Japanese, and Korean all use different coding schemes to represent Kanji (ideograph) characters. Eight bytes are not enough to represent thousands of ideographs. If you try to read Japanese characters using ASCII codes, you will see gibberish. See for yourself by visiting foreign Web sites, such as the home pages of foreign newspapers presented in their native languages.

Unicode

To accommodate the character symbols of non-English languages, the Unicode Consortium established the *Unicode Worldwide Character Standard*, commonly known simply as *Unicode*, to support the interchange, processing, and display of the written texts of diverse languages. The standard currently contains 34,168 distinct characters, which cover the major languages of the Americas, Europe, the Middle East, Africa, India, Asia, and Pacifica. To accommodate such a large number of distinct character symbols, Unicode characters occupy two bytes. Unicode codes for the character set shown in Table 8.1 are the same as ASCII codes.

Java, being a language for the Internet, uses the Unicode standard for representing char constants. Although Java uses the Unicode standard internally to store characters, many platforms cannot display non-ASCII characters. For example, you need a Japanese version of Windows 95 or special add-on software to read Japanese characters displayed on a computer screen. The same is true for the Chinese and Korean languages.

Characters are declared and used in a manner similar to data of other types. The declaration

```
char ch1, ch2 = 'X';
```

declares two char variables ch1 and ch2 with ch2 initialized to 'X'. We can display the ASCII code of a character by converting it to an integer. For example, we can execute

```
messageBox.show("ASCII code of character X is " + (int)'X' );
```

Conversely, we can see a character by converting its ASCII code to the char data type, for example,

```
message.show("Character with ASCII code 88 is " + (char) 88 );
```

Because the characters have numerical ASCII values, we can compare characters just as we compare integers and real numbers. For example, the comparison

```
'A' < 'c'
```

returns true because the ASCII value of 'A' is 65 while that of 'c' is 99.

Quick Check

1. Determine the output of the following statements:

    a.   `System.out.println( (char) 65 );`

    b.   `System.out.println( (int) 'C' );`

    c.   `System.out.println( 'Y' );`

    d.
    ```
    if ( 'A' < '?' )
        System.out.println( 'A' );
    else
        System.out.println( '?' );
    ```

2. How many distinct characters can you represent by using eight bits?

8.2   Strings

String class

A *string* is a sequence of characters that is treated as a single value. The String data type is used to represent strings in Java. We have been using strings all along. For example, the text with double quotes that we've been passing to a MessageBox object is a literal constant of type String. For example:

```
messageBox.show("Welcome to Bali");
```

Also, we used String variables to write code such as

```
String name, greeting;

name = inputLine.getText(); //inputLine is a TextField object
greeting = "Welcome to Bali, " + name;
```

In this section you will learn more about the String data type and how to manipulate strings. To input a string, we can send the getString message to an Input-Box object. The following code reads in a person's name and greets the user:

```
//assume inputBox and messageBox are declared
//and initialized correctly

String name;

name = inputBox.getString("What is your name?");
messageBox.show("Hello, " + name + ". Nice to meet you.");
```

Now let's see how we can manipulate strings. Let's say we want to input a person's name and determine the number of vowels the name contains. The basic idea is very simple:

```
for each character ch in the string {
    if (ch is a vowel) then {
        increment the counter
    }
}
```

There are two details we need to know before being able to translate the above into actual code. First, we need to know how to refer to an individual character in the string. Second, we need to know how to determine the size of the string, that is, the number of characters the string contains, so we can write the boolean expression to stop the loop correctly.

charAt

We access individual characters of a string by sending the message charAt to the String object. For example, to display the individual characters of the string Sumatra one at a time, we can say

```
String name = "Sumatra";
for (int i = 0; i < 7; i++) {
    messageBox.display( name.charAt(i) );
}
```

Each character in a string has an index we use to access the character. We use zero-based indexing; that is, the first character has index 0, the second character has index 1, the third character has index 2, and so forth. To refer to the first character of name, for example, we say

```
name.charAt(0)
```

FIGURE 8.1   An indexed expression is used to refer to individual characters in a string.

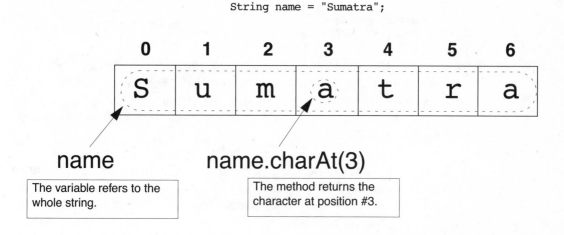

```
String name = "Sumatra";
```

Figure 8.1 illustrates how the charAt message works. Notice that we are sending a message to name; String is, in fact, a class in the java.lang package and name is an instance. Note: Strictly speaking, we must say "name is a variable of type String whose value is a reference to an instance of String." However, when the value of a variable X is a reference to an instance of class Y, we usually say "X is an instance of Y" or "X is a Y object." For example, we say canvas is a Drawing-Board object.

If the value of a variable X is a reference to an object of class Y, then we say "X is a Y object" or "X is an instance of Y."

Since String is a class, just like MainWindow, InputBox, and others, we need to create an instance of a class using the new method. The statements

```
String name1 = "Kona";

String name2;
name2 = "Espresso";
```

are actually shorthand for

```
String name1 = new String("Kona");
```
Equivalent to
```
String name1 = "Kona";
```

```
String name2;
name2 = new String("Espresso");
```
Equivalent to
```
name2 = "Espresso";
```

We will use shorthand notation in this book whenever appropriate. Remember that this shorthand works for the String class only. In the next section, we will discuss more about differences between objects such as String and the data types such as int, char, float, and others that are not objects (i.e., we cannot send messages to them).

In the sample code, we know exactly how many characters are in the string Sumatra, so there's no problem in expressing the condition to stop the execution of the for statement. But how can we write code that works on a string of any length? To find out the number of characters in any given string, we send the message length to the string. In order to print out individual characters of name, we would say

```
String name;
int numberOfCharacters;

name = inputBox.getString();
numberOfCharacters = name.length();

for (int i = 0; i < numberOfCharacters; i++) {
    messageBox.show( name.charAt(i) );
}
```

Notice that if the string's length is N, then the characters are indexed from 0 to N-1, so we could express the preceding for loop as

```
for (int i = 0; i <= numberOfCharacters - 1; i++)
```

We will use the first style almost exclusively to be consistent.

Now that we know how to determine the size of a given string and refer to individual characters of a string, we can implement the code for counting the number of vowels. Here is the code:

```
String      name;

int         numberOfCharacters,
            vowelCount = 0;

char        letter;

name = inputBox.getString("What is your name?");
numberOfCharacters = name.length();

for (int i = 0; i < numberOfCharacters; i++) {

    letter = name.charAt(i);

    if (   letter == 'a' || letter == 'A' ||
           letter == 'e' || letter == 'E' ||
           letter == 'i' || letter == 'I' ||
           letter == 'o' || letter == 'O' ||
           letter == 'u' || letter == 'U'    ) {

        vowelCount++;
    }
}

messageBox.show(name + ", your name has " +
                      vowelCount + " vowels");
```

We can shorten the boolean expression in the if statement by using the toUpperCase method of the String class. This method converts every character in a string to uppercase. Here's the rewritten code:

```
String      name, nameUpper;

int         numberOfCharacters,
            vowelCount = 0;

char        letter;

name = inputBox.getString("What is your name?");

numberOfCharacters = name.length();
nameUpper = name.toUpperCase();

for (int i = 0; i < numberOfCharacters; i++) {
```

```
            letter = nameUpper.charAt(i);

        if (    letter == 'A' ||
                letter == 'E' ||
                letter == 'I' ||
                letter == 'O' ||
                letter == 'U'    ) {

            vowelCount++;
        }
    }

    messageBox.show(name + ", your name has " +
                            vowelCount + " vowels");
```

Notice that the original string name is unchanged. A new, converted string is returned from the method and assigned to the second String variable nameUpper.

Let's try another example. This time we read in a string and count how many words the string contains. For this example we consider a word as a sequence of characters separated, or delimited, by blank spaces. We treat punctuation marks and other symbols as part of a word. Expressing the task in pseudocode, we have the following:

```
read in a sentence;

while (there are more characters in the sentence) {

    look for the beginning of the next word;

    now look for the end of this word;

    increment the word counter;

}
```

We use a while loop here instead of do–while to handle the case when the input sentence contains no characters, that is, it is an empty string. Let's implement the routine. Here's our first attempt:

```
//Attempt No. 1

int     index, wordCount, numberOfCharacters;
String sentence = inputBox.getString("Enter a sentence:");
```

```
numberOfCharacters    = sentence.length();
index                 = 0;
wordCount             = 0;

while (index < numberOfCharacters ) {

    //ignore blank spaces
    while (sentence.charAt(index) == ' ') {
        index++;
    }

    //now locate the end of the word
    while (sentence.charAt(index) != ' ') {
        index++;
    }

    //another word has been found, so increment the counter
    wordCount++;
}
```

Skip blank spaces until a character that is not a blank space is encountered. This is the beginning of a word.

Once the beginning of a word is detected, we skip nonblank characters until a blank space is encountered. This is the end of the word.

This implementation has a problem. The counter variable index is incremented inside the two while loops, and this index could become equal to numberOfCharacters, which is an error, because the position of the last character is numberOfCharacters – 1. We need to modify the two while loops so that index will not become larger than numberOfCharacters –1. Here's the modified code:

```
//Attempt No. 2

int    index, wordCount, numberOfCharacters;
String sentence = inputBox.getString();

numberOfCharacters    = sentence.length("Enter a sentence:");
index                 = 0;
wordCount             = 0;

while ( index < numberOfCharacters ) {

    //ignore blank spaces
    while (index < numberOfCharacters &&
           sentence.charAt(index) == ' ') {
        index++;
    }

    //now locate the end of the word
```

```
while (index < numberOfCharacters &&
       sentence.charAt(index) != ' ') {
    index++;
}

//another word is found, so increment the counter
wordCount++;

}
```

Notice that the order of comparisons in the boolean expression

```
index < numberOfCharacters && sentence.charAt(index) = ' '
```

is critical. If we switch the order to

```
sentence.charAt(index) = ' ' && index < numberOfCharacters
```

out-of-bound error

and if the last character in the string is a space, then an *out-of-bound error* will occur because the value of index is a position that does not exist in the string sentence. By putting the expression correctly as

```
index < numberOfCharacters && sentence.charAt(index) != ' '
```

we will not get an out-of-bound error because the boolean operator && is a short-circuit operator. If the relation index < numberOfCharacters is false, then the second half of the expression sentence.charAT(index) != ' ' will not get evaluated.

There is still a problem with the Attempt No. 2 code. If the sentence ends with one or more blank spaces, then the value for wordCount will be one more than the actual number of words in the sentence. It is left as an exercise to correct this bug (see exercise 17 on page 421).

Our third example counts the number of times the word Java occurs in the input. The repetition stops when the word STOP is read. Lowercase and uppercase letters are not distinguished when comparing an input word to Java, but the word STOP for terminating the loop must be in all uppercase letters. Here's the pseudocode:

```
javaCount  = 0;
repeat     = true;
```

```
while (repeat) {
    read in next word;

    if (word is "STOP") {
        repeat = false;
    }
    else if (word is "Java" ignoring cases) {
        javaCount++;
    }

}
```

And here's the actual code. Pay close attention to how the strings are compared.

```
int        javaCount  = 0;
boolean    repeat     = true;
String     word;

while ( repeat ) {

    word = inputBox.getString("Next word:");

    if ( word.equals("STOP") ) {
        repeat = false;
    }
    else if ( word.equalsIgnoreCase("Java") ) {
        javaCount++;
    }

}
```

compareTo

String comparison is done by two methods—equals and equalsIgnore-Case—whose meanings should be clear from the example. Another comparison method is compareTo. This method compares two String objects str1 and str2 as in

```
str1.compareTo( str2 );
```

and returns 0 if they are equal, a negative integer if str1 is less than str2, and a positive integer if str1 is greater than str2. The comparison is based on the lexicographical order of Unicode. For example, caffeine is less than latte. Also, the string jaVa is less than the string java because the Unicode value of V is smaller than the Unicode value of v. (See the ASCII table, Table 8.1)

Some of you may be wondering why we don't say

```
if ( word == "STOP" )
```

We can, in fact, use the equality comparison symbol == to compare two String objects, but the result is very different from the result of the method equals. We will explain the difference in the next section.

substring

Another useful string method is substring. This method returns a new string from a given string. If str is a String object, then the expression

```
str.substring ( beginIndex, endIndex )
```

returns a new string that is a substring of str from position beginIndex to endIndex – 1. The value of beginIndex must be between 0 and str.length() – 1 and the value of endIndex must be between 0 and str.length(). In addition, the value of beginIndex must be less than or equal to the value of endIndex. Passing invalid values for beginIndex or endIndex will result in a runtime error.

The following code creates a new string Javanist from Alpinist using the substring method.

```
String oldWord = "Alpinist";
String newWord = "Java" + oldWord.substring(4,8);
```

This method returns the substring of **old-word** from index **4** to **7**, that is, **"nist"**.

Our next example prints out the words from a given sentence using one line per word. For example, given an input sentence

```
I want to be a Java programmer
```

the code will print out

```
I
want
to
be
a
Java
programmer
```

This code is a modification of the previous sample code that counts the number of words in a given sentence. Instead of just counting the words, we need to extract the word from the sentence and print it out. Here's how we write the code:

```
int         index,      numberOfCharacters,
            beginIdx,   endIdx;

String      word,
            sentence = inputBox.getString();

numberOfCharacters = sentence.length();
index = 0;

while ( index < numberOfCharacters ) {

    //ignore leading blank spaces
    while (index < numberOfCharacters &&
            sentence.charAt(index) == ' ') {
        index++;
    }

    beginIdx = index;

    //now locate the end of the word
    while (index < numberOfCharacters &&
            sentence.charAt(index) != ' ') {
        index++;
    }

    endIdx = index;

    if (beginIdx != endIdx) {
        //another word is found, extract it from the sentence
        //and print it out
        word = sentence.substring( beginIdx, endIdx );
        outputBox.printLine( word );
    }

}
```

Can you tell the purpose of the test

```
if (beginIdx != endIdx)
```

in the code? For what kinds of input sentences will the variables beginIdx and endIdx be equal? We'll leave this as an exercise; see exercise 18 on page 421.

Quick Check

1. Determine the output of the following code:

    a.
    ```java
    String str = "Programming";
    for (int i = 0; i < 9; i+=2) {
        System.out.print( str.charAt( i ) );
    }
    ```

    b.
    ```java
    String str = "World Wide Web";
    for (int i = 0; i < 10; i ++ ) }
        if ( str.charAt(i) == 'W') {
            System.out.println( 'M' );
        }
        else {
            System.out.print( str.charAt(i) );
        }
    }
    ```

2. Write a loop that prints out a string in reverse. If the string is Hello, then the code outputs olleH. Use System.out.

3. Assume two String objects str1 and str2 are initialized as follows:

    ```java
    String str1 = "programming";
    String str2 = "language";
    ```

    Determine the value of each of the following expressions if they are valid. If they are not valid, state the reason why.

    a.   `str1.compareTo( str2 )`

    b.   `str2.compareTo( str2 )`

    c.   `str2.substring( 1, 1 )`

    d.   `str2.substring( 0, 7 );`

    e.   `str2.charAt( 11 );`

```
f.      str1.length( ) + str2.length( )
```

4. What is the difference between the two String methods equals and equalsIgnoreCase?

8.3   Primitive versus Reference Types

We discussed numerical data types in Chapter 5 and nonnumerical data types in this chapter. In addition, we have been using various javabook classes and their objects since Chapter 3. Let's study how these data types, classes, and objects are related. The taxonomy of data types is shown in Figure 8.2.

FIGURE 8.2   The taxonomy of data types.

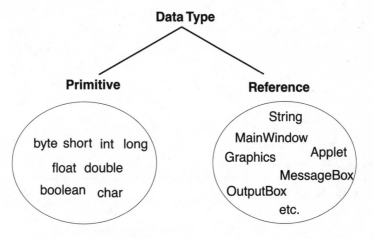

primitive vs. reference

Data types are classified into two groups: *primitive* and *reference*. Nonnumerical data types char and boolean and all of the numerical data types are primitive. All of the objects you have learned so far are reference data types.

Let's first review the use of the primitive data types. If w is a variable of the primitive data type X, then it means we can assign a value of type X to w; for example:

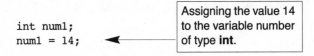

```
int num1;
num1 = 14;
```

Assigning the value 14 to the variable number of type **int**.

We stated in Chapter 3 that a variable has three attributes: name, data type, and value. A memory location is allocated to a variable where we can store a value of the declared data type and access the stored value using the given name. In Chapter 3, we explained the difference between object declaration and primitive (numerical) data declaration (see Figure 3.2 on page 89) and showed the effect of assigning the content of one variable to another (Figure 3.3 on page 90). Since knowing the difference between the primitive and the object data values clearly is very important, let's go over this topic again, this time using a String and an int. We will include here some new concepts not covered in Chapter 3.

By stating

```
int num1;
```

we are allocating a memory location to store a value of type int and naming this location num1. To store an integer value in this memory location, that is, to assign an integer value to the variable num1, we write

```
num1 = 14;
```

The diagram in Figure 8.3 illustrates the state of memory after this assignment is executed.

FIGURE 8.3   Effect of assigning an integer value to a variable.

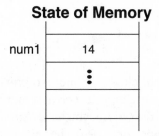

State of Memory

Now let's see what happens when we assign the value of a variable to another variable. Consider the following assignment statements using integers:

```
int num1, num2;
```

FIGURE 8.4   Effect of assigning values to integer variables.

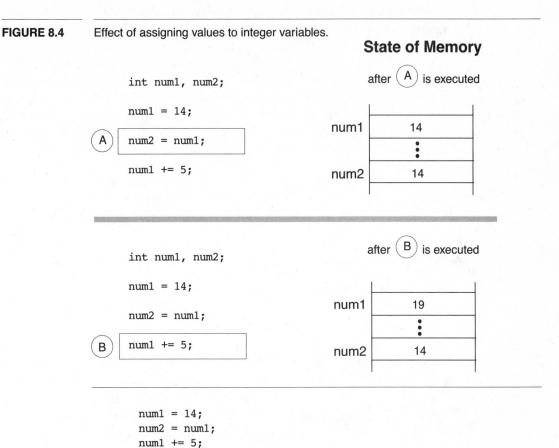

```
num1 = 14;
num2 = num1;
num1 += 5;
```

Figure 8.4 shows the effect of these assignment statements on memory. When two integer variables are declared, two memory locations are reserved to store integer values. For all primitive data types, the Java compiler knows exactly how many bytes of memory to allocate. An int variable, for instance, requires four bytes or 32 bits. The statements at points A and B in Figure 8.4 illustrate the effect of having two separate memory locations; that is, adding 5 to num1 affects only num1.

Let's study how memory allocation works when reference data types are used. Consider the following declaration:

```
String str;
str = "Jakarta";
```

FIGURE 8.5   Effect of assigning a **String** value to a variable.

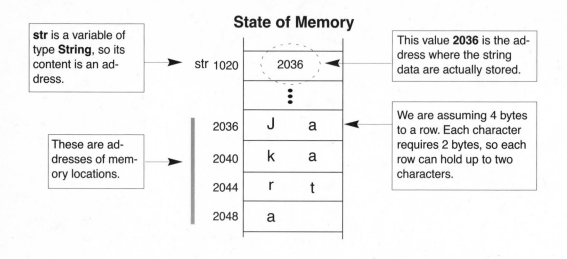

Figure 8.5 shows the state of memory after this assignment is executed. When a variable is of the reference data type, the memory location of the variable contains the address of another memory location where the data value is actually stored. Since the content of the variable is not a value but the address of another location where the data value is stored, this data type is called a reference data type. But why such a roundabout way of storing data? Why can't we just store the value in the manner shown in Figure 8.6?

With primitive data types, the number of bytes required to store a value is always the same. For example, once we allocate four bytes of memory for an int variable, we will always have enough space to store any integer of type int in this location because all integers require only four bytes. What about String data? What do you think would happen if we store the string values directly at the memory location 1020 and execute the following code?

```
String str;
str = "Jakarta";
...
str = "Irian Jaya";
```

FIGURE 8.6   Hypothetical memory management scheme for storing a **String** value.

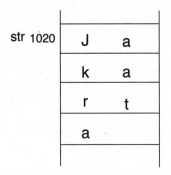

Assuming the memory location 1036 already contains an integer, the effect of executing the second assignment statement is shown in Figure 8.7. We ran out of space to store the last two characters. We cannot just store the last two characters in the next available memory locations beyond location 1040 because such noncontiguous allocation of memory for a single data value is cumbersome to manage and inefficient.

FIGURE 8.7   Memory shortage problem with the hypothetical memory management scheme.

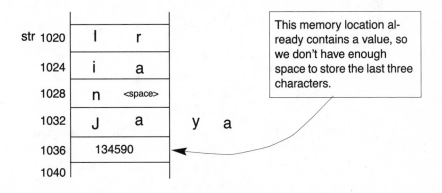

We see that a primitive data type requires a fixed amount of memory space, but a reference data type requires a varying amount of memory depending on the actual values assigned. In order to accommodate this varying size requirement, the memory location of a variable of reference data type will contain the address of another location where the actual value is stored. This allocation scheme is illustrated in Figure 8.5.

Because the values of reference data types are objects, we prefer the diagram in Figure 8.8 to the one shown in Figure 8.5. The arrow in Figure 8.8 clearly indicates that the content of variable str is an address and referring to another memory location. We will use this simplified diagram style in the rest of the chapter, whenever appropriate.

FIGURE 8.8   A preferred style of diagram for representing memory allocation for a reference data type.

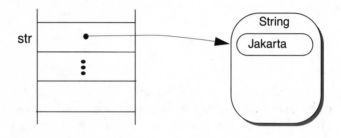

In object diagrams we simplify the diagram even further to

Figure 8.9 shows how memory allocation and assignment statements work with a reference data type. Because the contents of memory locations word1 and word2 are references, the assignment statement makes both variables refer to the same object. There's one object, and it makes no difference whether we access the object using word1 or word2. If you need to make word2 refer to another String object containing the string Java, then you must create another object as in

```
word2 = "Java" ; //or word2 = new String("Java");
```

FIGURE 8.9   Effect of assignment statements on reference data type **String**.

State of Memory

Both **word1** and **word2** are allocated
memory, but no actual objects are created yet, so both are **null**.

after (A) is executed

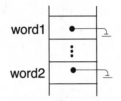

(A) `String word1, word2;`

`word1 = new String("Java");`

`word2 = word1;`

Both **word1** and
word2 are allocat-
ed memory, but
no actual objects
are created yet,
so both are **null**.

word1 ●⟶

word2 ●⟶

One **String** object is created and assigned to **word1**; that is, **word1** points
to the object.

after (B) is executed

`String word1, word2;`

(B) `word1 = new String("Java");`

`word2 = word1;`

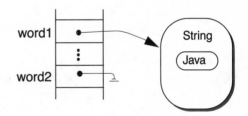

word1 ●⟶   String

Java

word2 ●⟶

Content of **word1** (which is a reference
to the **String** object) is assigned to
word2, making **word2** also point to the
same **String** object.

after (C) is executed

`String word1, word2;`

`word1 = new String("Java");`

(C) `word2 = word1;`

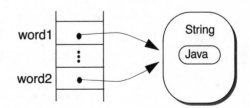

word1 ●⟶   String

Java

word2 ●⟶

which will result in the state of memory shown as case B in Figure 8.10.

Notice how declaration and object creation are different. No String objects are created by the declaration

```
String word1, word2;
```

Only the memory locations to store the addresses are allocated, as shown in the first diagram of Figure 8.9. We need to call the new method (either explicitly or implicitly) to create an object. We use the symbol ●————⟂ when the content of a variable is not referring to any address. We call such reference a *null reference* or *null pointer*. When a variable contains the address of a location where an object is stored, we say "a variable points to an object" or "a variable refers to an object." We can test whether a variable points to an object or not by using the reserved word null:

```
if ( word1 == null )
```

And we can reset a variable back to null as in

```
word1 = null;
```

As stated earlier, when the content of variable X is a reference to an instance of the class Y, the expression we commonly use is "X is a Y object" or "X is an instance of the Y class." For example, given the code

```
MessageBox display;
display = new MessageBox();
```

we commonly say "display is a MessageBox object" or "display is an instance of the MessageBox class" instead of saying "display is a variable that refers or points to a MessageBox object" or "display is a variable that refers or points to an instance of the MessageBox class."

We are now ready to explain the difference, which we mentioned at the end of Section 8.2, between the tests

```
if ( word1 == word2 ) ...
```

(margin notes)
null reference / null pointer

reserved word null

== vs. equals

and

```
if ( word1.equals(word2) ) ...
```

We can explain the difference very easily using Figure 8.10. The equality test == is true if the contents of memory locations allocated to variables are the same. For a primitive data type, the contents are values themselves, but for a reference data type, the contents are addresses. So for a reference data type, the equality test is true if both variables refer to the same object, because they both contain the same address. The equals method, on the other hand, is true if the String objects to which the two variables refer contain the same string value. To distinguish the two types of comparisons, we will use the term *equivalence test* for the equals method.

Quick Check

1. Show the state of memory after the following statements are executed:

```
String str1, str2, str3;
str1 = "Jasmine";
str2 = "Oolong";
str3 = str2;
str2 = str1;
```

8.4   StringBuffer

A String object is immutable, which means that once a String object is created, we cannot change it. In other words, we can read individual characters in a string, but we cannot add, delete, or modify characters of a String object. Remember that the methods of the String class, such as toUpperCase and substring, do not modify the original string; they return a new string. Java adopts this immutability restriction to implement an efficient memory allocation scheme for managing String objects.

Creating a new string from the old one will work for most cases, but sometimes manipulating the content of a string directly is more convenient. When we need to compose a long string from a number of words, for example, being able to manipulate the content of a string directly is much more convenient than cre-

FIGURE 8.10   The difference between the equality test and the equals method.

Case A: Referring to the same object.

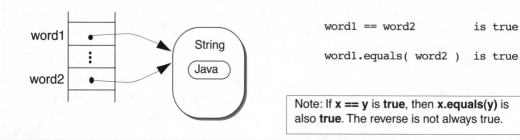

```
word1 == word2          is true

word1.equals( word2 )   is true
```

Note: If **x == y** is **true**, then **x.equals(y)** is also **true**. The reverse is not always true.

Case B: Referring to different objects having identical string values.

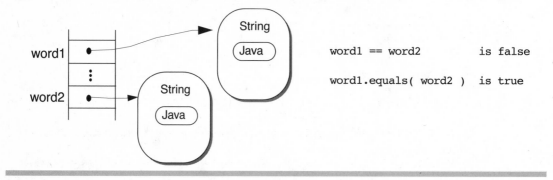

```
word1 == word2          is false

word1.equals( word2 )   is true
```

Case C: Referring to different objects having different string values.

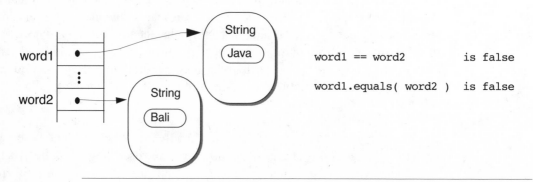

```
word1 == word2          is false

word1.equals( word2 )   is false
```

Mr. Espresso: I understand Figure 8.10, but what if one of the operands is a literal string constant, such as

```
word = inputBox.getString();
if (word == "STOP")
        repeat = false;
```

Dr. Caffeine: An unnamed **String** object is created automatically when a literal string constant appears in Java code. Executing your sample code will result in a situation like this:

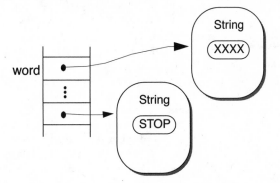

The equality testing and the **equals** method work just fine.

Mr. Espresso: But how can the Java interpreter access unnamed objects?

Dr. Caffeine: "Unnamed" simply means that no explicit name is given by the programmer. The Java interpreter keeps track of the memory location where the reference to this literal string constant is stored.

Dr. & Mr.

string
manipulation

ating a new copy of string. *Manipulation* here means operations such as replacing a character, appending a string with another string, deleting a portion of a string, and so forth. If we need to manipulate the content of a string directly, we must use the StringBuffer class. For example, the code

```
StringBuffer word = new StringBuffer( "Java" );
word.setCharAt(0, 'D');
word.setCharAt(1, 'i');
```

will modify the string Java to Diva. No new string is created, the original string Java is modified. Also, you must use the new method to create a StringBuffer object.

StringBuffer

Let's look at some examples using StringBuffer objects. The first example reads a sentence and replaces all vowels in the sentence with the character X.

```
StringBuffer   tempStringBuffer;
String         inSentence;
int            numberOfCharacters;
char           letter;

inSentence       = inputBox.getString("Enter a sentence:");
tempStringBuffer = new StringBuffer(inSentence);

numberOfCharacters = tempStringBuffer.length();
for (int index = 0; index < numberOfCharacters; index++) {

    letter = tempStringBuffer.charAt(index);

    if (    letter == 'a' || letter == 'A' ||
            letter == 'e' || letter == 'E' ||
            letter == 'i' || letter == 'I' ||
            letter == 'o' || letter == 'O' ||
            letter == 'u' || letter == 'U'    ) {

        tempStringBuffer.setCharAt(index,'X');
    }
}

messageBox.show( tempStringBuffer.toString() );
```

Create **tempStringBuffer** for string manipulation.

Notice the argument we passed to the show method of messageBox. You cannot input and output StringBuffer objects. You can only input and output String objects. For example, the following code is invalid:

```
StringBuffer strBuffer = new StringBuffer("Hello");
System.out.println( strBuffer );
```

We use the toString method of StringBuffer to convert it to a String object. To output a StringBuffer object, we do something like this:

```
StringBuffer strBuffer = new StringBuffer("Hello");
System.out.println( strBuffer.toString() );
```

You cannot input and output StringBuffer *objects. You can input and output* String *objects only.*

Our next example constructs a new sentence from input words that have an even number of letters. The program stops when the word STOP is read. Let's begin with the pseudocode:

```
set tempStringBuffer to empty string;

repeat = true;
while ( repeat ) {
    read in next word;

    if (word is "STOP")
        repeat = false;
    else if (word has even number of letters)
        append word to tempStringBuffer;

}
```

And here's the actual code:

> Create **StringBuffer** with the empty string for its value.

```
boolean    repeat = true;
String     word;

StringBuffer tempStringBuffer = new StringBuffer("");

while ( repeat ) {
    word = inputBox.getString("Next word:");

    if ( word.equals("STOP") )
        repeat = false;
    else if ( word.length() % 2 == 0 )
        tempStringBuffer.append(word + " ");

}
```

> Append word and a space to **temp-StringBuffer**.

We use the append method to append a String or a StringBuffer object to the end of a StringBuffer object. The method append can also take an argument of the primitive data type. For example, all the following statements are valid:

```
int     i   = 12;
float   x   = 12.4;
char    ch = 'W';

StringBuffer str = new StringBuffer("");

str.append(i);
str.append(x);
str.append(ch);
```

Any primitive data type argument is converted to a string before it is appended to a StringBuffer object.

Notice that we can write the second example using only String objects. Here's how:

```
boolean repeat = true;
String word, sentence, newSentence;

newSentence = ""; //empty string
while ( repeat ) {
    word = inputBox.getString("Next word:");

    if ( word.equals("STOP") )
        repeat = false;
    else if ( word.length() % 2 == 0 )
        newSentence = newSentence + word; //string concatenation

}
```

Although this code does not explicitly use any StringBuffer object, the Java compiler may use StringBuffer when compiling the string concatenation operator. For example, the expression

```
newSentence + word
```

can be compiled as if the expression were

```
new StringBuffer().append(word).toString()
```

Using the append method of StringBuffer is preferable to using the string concatenation operator + because we can avoid creating temporary string objects by using StringBuffer.

In addition to appending a string at the end of StringBuffer, we can insert a string at a specified position using the insert method. The syntax for this method is

```
<StringBuffer> . insert ( <insertIndex>, <value> ) ;
```

where the <insertIndex> must be greater than or equal to 0 and less than or equal to the length of <StringBuffer> and the <value> is an object or a value of the primitive data type. For example, to change the string

```
Java is great
```

to

```
Java is really great
```

we can execute the following code:

```
StringBuffer str = new StringBuffer("Java is great");
str.insert(8, "really ");
```

Quick Check

1. Determine the value of str after the following statements are executed:

   a.
   ```
   String str = "Caffeine";
   str.insert(0, "Dr. ");
   ```

   b.
   ```
   String      str   = "Caffeine";
   StringBuffer strl  =
            new StringBuffer( str.substring(1, 3) );
   strl.append('e');
   str = "De" + strl;
   ```

   c.
   ```
   String      str   = "Caffeine";
   StringBuffer strl  =
   ```

```
                               new StringBuffer( str.substring(4, 8) );
                   str1.insert(3,'f');
                   str = "De" + str1;
```

2. Assume a String object str is assigned as

```
    String str = inputBox.getString();
```

Write a code segment to replace all occurrences of lowercase vowels in a given string to letter C by using String and StringBuffer objects.

3. Find errors in the following code:

```
    String        str    = "Caffeine";
    StringBuffer  str1   = str.substring(1, 3);
    str1.append('e');
    System.out(str1);
    str1 = str1 + str;
```

8.5   Passing Objects as Parameters

pass-by-value

We explained in Section 4.4 that the value of the argument is passed to the matching parameter of a method, and separate memory space is allocated to store this value. This way of passing the value of arguments is called a *pass-by-value scheme*. We described how the pass-by-value scheme works using the primitive data type, specifically the numerical data type, in Section 4.4. We will go over the scheme in this section using the reference data type. We will use String and StringBuffer objects for examples.

Consider the following myMethod method of the Tester class. The method replaces the first character of strBuf with the character Y. The method is not doing anything useful. We use it here for illustration purposes only. To keep the example simple, we do not include any testing in the method to make sure that strBuf has one or more characters. Here's the class:

```
class Tester
{
    public void myMethod( StringBuffer strBuf)
    {
        strBuff.setCharAt(0, 'Y');
    }
}
```

What will be the output from the following code?

```
Tester        tester;
StringBuffer  word = new StringBuffer( "Java" );

tester = new Tester();
tester.myMethod( word );
outputBox.printLine( "Word is " + word );
```

The output is

```
Word is Yava
```

not

```
Word is Java
```

as some of you might have expected because the key rule of the pass-by-value scheme states

Changes made to the parameters will not affect the value of corresponding arguments.

This is true, but remember that the value of a variable of the reference data type is an address. In other words, "passing an object to a method" really means "passing the address of an object to a method."

When you "pass an object to a method," you are actually passing the address of an object to the method.

Figure 8.11 shows how the pass-by-value scheme works with the reference data type. We use arrows to represent that the contents of the variables are memory addresses. Notice how the value of the variable word did not change after the method myMethod was executed. It still points to the same object. However, the object itself was changed via the access from the local variable strBuf.

In many cases, we do not want the original object to change when a method is executed. In these cases, we need to create a local copy of the object inside the method and manipulate this local copy. Consider the following modified version of myMethod:

FIGURE 8.11   How the memory space for parameters are allocated and deallocated.

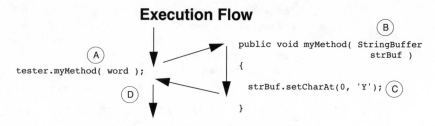

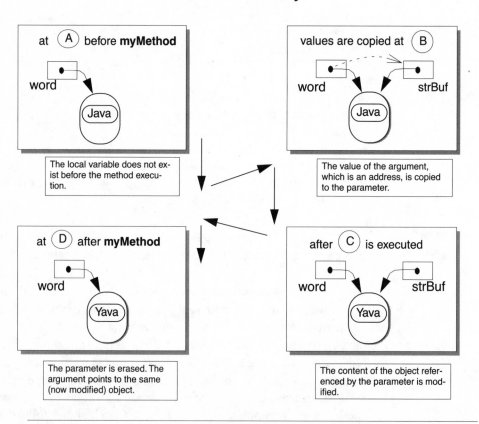

```
public void myMethod( StringBuffer strBuf)
{
    StringBuffer localCopy
        = new StringBuffer( strBuf.toString() );
    localCopy.setCharAt(0, 'Y');
}
```

Note: You need to pass a **String** object to create a new **StringBuffer** object.

Figure 8.12 shows the state-of-memory diagram for the modified **myMethod**. Notice how the local **StringBuffer** object is created. Since this is a separate copy, changing it won't affect the original **StringBuffer** object word.

Be careful not to confuse a simple assignment and an object creation. For example, if you simply assign the parameter to a local variable, such as

```
public void myMethod( StringBuffer strBuf)
{
    StringBuffer localCopy = strBuf;
    localCopy.setCharAt(0, 'Y');
}
```

This is an assignment, not an object creation.

then all you are doing is adding one more reference to the object. In the state-of-memory diagram, this is what you have:

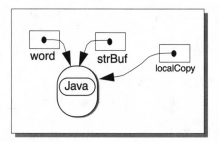

If you do not want the original object to be modified when a method is executed, make a local copy of the object inside the method. Remember that a simple assignment of the reference data type will not create a new object.

FIGURE 8.12   How a local copy of the passed object is created and manipulated. The original object will not change.

Execution Flow

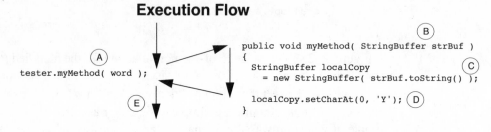

State of Memory

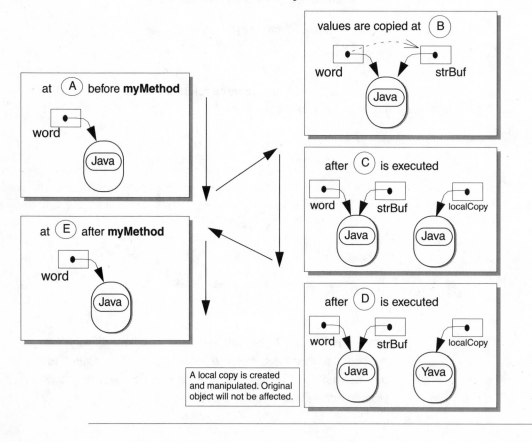

1. Draw the state-of-memory diagram for the following code:

```
String      str1 = "Daisy",
            str2 = "Iris";
Tester      tester = new Tester( );

tester.exchange( str1, str2);
...
class Tester
{
    public void exchange( String one, String two )
    {
        String temp;
        temp    = one;
        one     = two;
        two     = temp;
    }
}
```

8.6 Returning an Object from Methods

Now let's study how an object is returned from a method. In the previous section, we explained that "passing an object as an argument to a method" really means passing the address of the object to the method. The same rule applies when we "return an object from a method." In other words, we are really passing the address of the object back from the method.

To illustrate an object-returning method, let's define a method that accepts a name (String) and returns a personalized Hi greeting. For example, if the argument to the method is

```
Bill
```

then the method will return

```
Hi, Bill
```

The method is defined as

```
public String sayHi( String name )
{
    String greeting;
    greeting = "Hi, " + name;
    return greeting;
}
```

We use a local variable greeting for a new String. At the end of the method, the content of greeting, which is the address to the newly created String, is returned from the method.

Assuming the method is defined in the Tester class, we can call the sayHi method as

```
String      name,
            hiMsg;
Tester      tester;
tester      = new Tester( );

name        = inputBox.getString( );
hiMsg       = tester.sayHi( name );
```

Figure 8.13 shows how the method returns a String object. Remember that we use the expression "return an object" to mean "return the address of an object."

Dr. Caffeine

It is not necessary to create an object for every variable you declare. Many novice programmers often make this mistake. For example, if all you want is two references to the same object, you write something like this:

```
Person drCafe, profWu;
profWu = new Person();
drCafe = profWu;
```

You don't write

```
Person drCafe, profWu;
profWu = new Person();
drCafe = new Person();  //not necessary
drCafe = profWu;
```

FIGURE 8.13   How the reference data type is returned from the **sayHi** method.

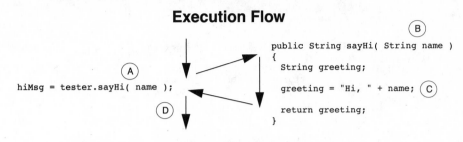

Execution Flow

```
                                              public String sayHi( String name )
                                              {
                                                  String greeting;

hiMsg = tester.sayHi( name );                     greeting = "Hi, " + name;

                                                  return greeting;
                                              }
```

State of Memory

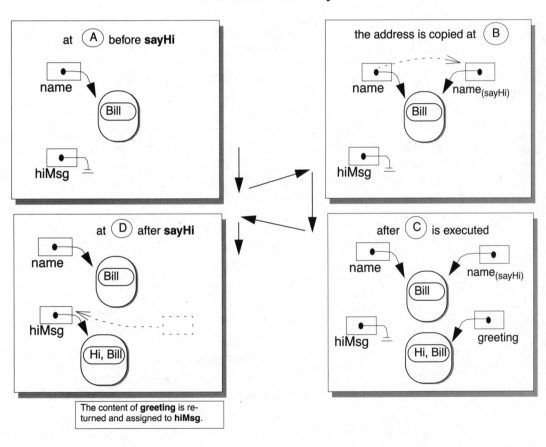

The content of **greeting** is returned and assigned to **hiMsg**.

Quick Check

1. Draw the state-of-memory diagram for the following code:

```
String      name = "Iris", str;
Tester      tester = new Tester( );
str         = tester.toUpper( name );
...
class Tester
{
    public String toUpper( String str )
    {
        String allUpper;
        allUpper = str.toUpperCase();
        return allUpper;
    }
}
```

8.7   Sample Program: Word Play

Let's review the String and StringBuffer objects by writing a sample program. We will write an application program that plays a word game called Eggy-Peggy. The program will convert a given string by placing the word **egg** in front of every vowel. For example,

```
Twinkle twinkle little star
```

becomes

```
Twegginklegge twegginklegge leggittlegge steggar
```

Problem Statement

Write an application that will play the Eggy-Peggy word play with the user. The program will convert a string given by the user to a new string by placing the word "egg" in front of all vowels in the given string.

Overall Plan

As usual, let's begin the program development by first identifying the major tasks of the program. The first task is to get an input string from the user, and the second task is to generate a new eggy-peggy string from the given string. So the user can play many times, we will add a loop to repeat these two tasks every time the user wants to play Eggy-Peggy. We can express this program logic in pseudocode as

program
tasks

```
while ( the user wants to play ) {

    Task 1: get a string from the user;

    Task 2: generate a new eggy-peggy string;

    Task 3: display the result;
}
```

Let's look at the three tasks and determine objects that will be responsible for handling the tasks. For the first task, we will use an InputBox. Although the width of an inputBox may not be wide enough to see the full string, the user can still enter a long string. We will use the getString method of InputBox to read the input string.

For the second task of generating an eggy-peggy string, we anticipate the use of a StringBuffer object. The task of placing the word egg in front of all vowels calls for a direct string manipulation, so a StringBuffer object seems to be the right object for the task. We will get into a more detailed design in a later step.

For the last task of printing out the eggy-peggy string, we will use an OutputBox. Although MessageBox is adequate if we want to show the eggy-peggy string only, we think it is more fun for the user to see both the input string and the eggy-peggy string, so we will use an OutputBox.

Finally, we will define a top-level control object that manages all other objects. We will call this class EggyPeggy. Our main class will be EggyPeggyMain, whose task is to create an instance of EggyPeggy and start the instance. We also need a way for the player to tell the program whether to play another game or not. We will use a ResponseBox object for this purpose. Here's our working design document:

program
classes

Design Document: EggyPeggy	
Class	**Purpose**
EggyPeggyMain	The main class of the program.
EggyPeggy	The top-level control object that manages other objects in the program.
InputBox	An InputBox object is used to get a string from the player. This class is from javabook.
OutputBox	An OutputBox object is used for the input string and the eggy-peggy string.
ResponseBox	A ResponseBox object is used to get the player's instruction to play another game or not.
String	String objects are used of storing strings.
StringBuffer	A StringBuffer object is used during the conversion process.
MainWindow	The main window of the application.

Figure 8.14 is the object diagram for this program.

FIGURE 8.14   The object diagram for the **EggyPeggy** program. Note: **String** and **StringBuffer** objects are not shown here.

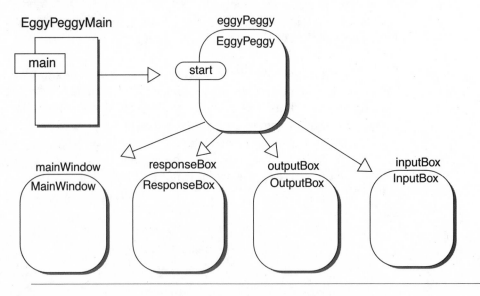

We will implement this program using the following four major steps:

development
steps

1. Start with a program skeleton. Define the EggyPeggyMain and EggyPeggy classes.

2. Add code to do the input and output routines.

3. Add code to play an Eggy-Peggy game.

4. Finalize the code by removing temporary statements and tying up loose ends.

Step 1 Development: Skeleton

Step 1 Design

The design of EggyPeggyMain is trivial. Its structure is the same as other main classes. All we need is to declare, create, and start an EggyPeggy object. In pseudocode we can express the main logic for an EggyPeggy object as

```
prompt the user to play Eggy-Peggy or not;

while ( answer is yes ) {

    get an input string;

    generate an eggy-peggy string from the input string;

    display the input and eggy-peggy strings;

    prompt the user to play another Eggy-Peggy or not;
}
```

We will use the constructor to perform necessary initialization and the method describeGame to provide a brief explanation of the Eggy-Peggy game. We will use a ResponseBox for prompting the user to play a game or not. We will define private methods for handling input and output. The object diagram for the EggyPeggy class at this point is

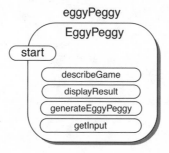

Our working design document for the EggyPeggy class is as follows:

Design Document: The EggyPeggy Class		
Method	**Visibility**	**Purpose**
`<constructor>`	`public`	Creates the objects used by an EggyPeggy object.
`start`	`public`	Starts the Eggy-Peggy game playing. The player has an option of playing a game or not.
`describeGame`	`private`	Displays the game rules in an OutputBox.
`displayResult`	`private`	Shows the input string and the eggy-peggy string in an OutputBox.
`generateEggyPeggy`	`private`	Plays one Eggy-Peggy game.
`getInput`	`private`	Gets the input string using InputBox.

Step 1 Code

For the skeleton, we include temporary output statements in the private methods to verify that they are called correctly in the right order. Here's the skeleton:

```
/*
    Program EggyPeggy

    A program to play a word game Eggy-Peggy. The program reads in a string from
    the user and generates a new converted string that contains the word "egg"
    in front of all vowels in the input string.

    Input:    A string from the user

    Output:   Display the input string and the eggy-peggy string generated
              from the input string.

*/

class EggyPeggyMain
{
    public static void main (String args[])
    {
        EggyPeggy eggyPeggy = new EggyPeggy( );
        eggyPeggy.start();
    }
}
```

```
/*
    Class EggyPeggy (Step 1: Skeleton)

    The top-level object for managing all other objects in the program.
*/

import javabook.*;
```

```
class EggyPeggy
{

/***************************
   Data Members
***************************/

   private MainWindow    mainWindow;
   private InputBox      inputBox;
   private OutputBox     outputBox;
   private ResponseBox   responseBox;

/***************************
   Constructor
***************************/

   public EggyPeggy( )
   {
       mainWindow    = new MainWindow  ("Let's Play EggyPeggy");
       outputBox     = new OutputBox   ( mainWindow );
       responseBox   = new ResponseBox ( mainWindow );
       inputBox      = new InputBox    ( mainWindow );

       mainWindow.show();
       outputBox.show();

   }

/*****************************
   Public Methods

       void start (        )

*****************************/

   public void start ( )
   {
       int answer;

       describeGame();

       answer = responseBox.prompt("Do you want to play Eggy-Peggy?);

       while ( answer = ResponseBox.YES ) {

          getInput( );
          generateEggyPeggy( );
          displayResult( );

          answer= responseBox.prompt("Do you want to play another Eggy-Peggy?");
       }
   }

/*****************************
   Private Methods

       void    describeGame            (           )
```

```
            void    displayResult         (            )
            void    generateEggyPeggy     (            )
            void    getInput              (            )

*******************************/


    /********************************************************
        Method:        describeGame

        Purpose:       Describe how the eggy-peggy strings are generated.
                       Provide description only if the user wants it.

        Parameters:    None

        Returns:       None
    */
    private void describeGame( )
    {
        outputBox.printLine("Inside describeGame");          //TEMP
    }


    /********************************************************
        Method:        displayResult

        Purpose:       Show the input string and the eggy-peggy string generated
                       from the input string.

        Parameters:    None

        Returns:       None
    */
    private void displayResult( )
    {
        outputBox.printLine("Inside displayResult");         //TEMP
    }


    /********************************************************
        Method:        generateEggyPeggy

        Purpose:       Generate a new string from the input string by putting the
                       word "egg" in front of all vowels in the input string.

        Parameters:    None

        Returns:       none
    */
    private void generateEggyPeggy( )
    {
        outputBox.printLine("Inside generateEggyPeggy");     //TEMP
    }


    /********************************************************
        Method:        getInput
```

```
        Purpose:        Read in the input string using InputBox.

        Parameters:     None

        Returns:        None
    */
    private void getInput( )
    {
        outputBox.printLine("Inside getInput");              //TEMP
    }

}
```

Step 1 Test

As before, EggyPeggyMain, the main class will not change. The class given here is the final version.We execute the main class and the skeleton EggyPeggy class to verify that the classes are coded correctly. To verify the correct execution of Step 1, we attempt to play the game

1. Zero times.

2. One time.

3. One or more times.

For the first run, we select No to the prompt Do you want to play Eggy-Peggy? and make sure the program stops without playing a game. For the second run, we select Yes to the first prompt and verify that the messages Inside get-Input and others are shown in outputBox. We next select No to the prompt Do you want to play another Eggy-Peggy? and make sure the program stops. For the third run, we verify that we can play more than one game. If everything works correctly and as expected, we move on to the next step.

Step 2 Development: Input and Output Routines

Step 2 Design

In the second development step, we add routines to handle input and output. We decided in the overall planning step that we will use an InputBox object to accept a string and an OutputBox object to display both the input string and the Eggy-Peggy string. Let's begin with the design of the input routine.

To fully design the input routine, we need to decide which strings are valid and which are not. The problem statement did not specify any condition on the input string, so let's define some validity rules ourselves. What types of strings should be considered invalid? Should we place the maximum number of characters a valid string can contain? Should a string with all spaces be considered invalid? What about a string with no characters, an empty string? For this program, we will consider any string to be valid, so the user does not have to worry about whether an input is valid or not.

Since we accept any string as a valid input, the statement using the getString method of inputBox is all that suffices for the input routine. So the getInput method will contain a single statement. We will use an instance variable inputString to store the input string. If we need to do some error checking or some form of input validation later, we can do it in this method.

The output routine in the displayResult method will print out the input string and the generated Eggy-Peggy string. We will use a second instance variable eggyPeggyString to store the Eggy-Peggy string. To verify the output routine, we will add a temporary assignment statement in the generateEggyPeggy method to assign a dummy string to eggyPeggyString.

Step 2 Code   To code the Step 2 design, we first add two new instance variables:

```
/**************************
    Data Members
*************************/

private String     inputString,
                   eggyPeggyString;
```

We then define the getInput method as

```
private void getInput( )
{
    inputString
        = inputBox.getString("Enter the original sentence:");
}
```

and temporarily define the generateEggyPeggy method as

```
private void generateEggyPeggy( )
{
    eggyPeggyString = "Dummy Eggy Peggy String";
    outputBox.printLine("Inside generateEggyPeggy");
}
```

Finally, we define the displayResult method as

```
private void displayResult( )
{
    outputBox.skipLine(3);
    outputBox.printLine("Input String:");
    outputBox.printLine("                    " + inputString);

    outputBox.skipLine(1);
    outputBox.printLine("Eggy Peggy:");
    outputBox.printLine("                    " + eggyPeggyString);
}
```

Step 2 Test

For testing, we play many games, and for each game we play, we will enter a string different from the previous strings. We will enter very long strings, very short strings, no strings, and so forth. Even though the actual processing is not yet implemented, we can still test and verify that different strings can be entered into the program. It is important to test whatever is testable at the earliest possible time.

Test a program routine at the earliest possible time.

Remember that testing an input routine will require us to enter both valid and invalid input values. For this program, we decided that all strings are valid. For the valid input values, we enter both types of values: those that are commonly expected and those that are not. For this program, we expect strings will contain several to up to 50 or so characters. We do not expect strings with less than several characters, including those with zero characters, to occur frequently. We should also test other strings that are not normally expected, such as the one with all blank spaces. The test data are as follows:

Step 1 Test Data	
Data Value	**Purpose**
`Empty string.`	Test the end case.
`String whose length is less than 3.`	Test the cases not expected to happen frequently.
`String with non letter characters, e.g., all blank spaces, all symbols, etc.`	Test the cases not expected to happen frequently.
`Strings whose length range from about 5 to 50.`	Test the normal cases.

Before proceeding to the next step, we make sure that the program accepts various types of input strings without crashing. After we verify this, we will move on to the next step.

Step 3 Development: Generate an Eggy-Peggy String

Step 3 Design   In the third development step, we add a routine that generates an Eggy-Peggy string from a given input string. The key idea is to check every character in the input string. If the character is a vowel, then we will append the word egg and the vowel to the output string. If the character is not a vowel, then we will append the character only to the output string. We will use a StringBuffer object while creating the output string. At the end of the routine, we will convert this

Alternative
Design 1   StringBuffer object to a String object. Expressing this in pseudocode, we have

```
for the first to the last character in inputString {
    if (character is a vowel) {
        append "egg" and character to output StringBuffer;
    }
    else {
        append character only to output StringBuffer;
    }
}
convert output StringBuffer to String;
```

Alternative 2
Design   An alternative approach is to use String objects only and string concatenation operations to implement the routine. Expressing this approach in pseudocode, we have

```
for the first to the last character in inputString {
    if (character is a vowel) {
        outString = outString + "egg" + character;
    }
    else {
        outString = outString + character;
    }
}
```

This alternative is less efficient than the first one, because a new String object is created for every concatenation, and the routine will perform $N + 2 * M$ concatenations, where N is the number of nonvowels and M is the number of vowels. If you do a lot of string manipulation operations, StringBuffer objects are generally preferred over String objects because no new objects are created if you use a StringBuffer object for string manipulation. We will implement the first design alternative.

Step 3 Code   The generateEggyPeggy method is defined as

```
private void generateEggyPeggy( )
{
    StringBuffer   outputStrBuf   = new StringBuffer("");
    int            length         = inputString.length();
    char           ch;

    for (int i = 0; i < length; i++ ) {
        ch = inputString.charAt(i);

        if ( isVowel(ch) ) {
            outputStrBuf.append( EGG );   //if vowel, append
        }                                 //"egg" first

        outputStrBuf.append( ch );
    }

    eggyPeggyString = outputStrBuf.toString();
}
```

Notice that we must append the character whether it is a vowel or not, so we changed the if–then–else statement in the pseudocode to an if–then statement. The word EGG is a string constant defined in the data member declaration section as

```
private final String EGG = "egg";
```

The method isVowel is a new private method that returns true if the argument character is a vowel and returns false otherwise. We are defining this method ourselves here because there is no such method in the standard library. If there was one, then we would have used it. We could have done the testing right inside the generateEggyPeggy method, but that would tend to lengthen the code,

so we decided to add a separate method. The working design document now includes this method:

Design Document: The EggyPeggy Class		
Method	**Visibility**	**Purpose**
...	...	...
isVowel	private	Returns true if the argument character is a vowel and false otherwise.

The method is defined as

```
private boolean isVowel(char letter)
{
    boolean result = false;

    if (    letter == 'a' || letter == 'A' ||
            letter == 'e' || letter == 'E' ||
            letter == 'i' || letter == 'I' ||
            letter == 'o' || letter == 'O' ||
            letter == 'u' || letter == 'U'    ) {

        result = true;
    }

    return result;
}
```

Step 3 Test

We basically repeat the testing procedures we performed in Step 2. We enter
many different types of strings including empty strings and strings with only
spaces and verify that the program works correctly.

Step 4 Development: Finalize

program
review

As always, we finalize the program in the last step. We perform a critical review
to find any inconsistency or error in the methods, any incomplete methods, places
to add more comments, and so forth.

We still have a temporary code inside the describeGame method, so we will
complete the method by adding code to describe the Eggy-Peggy game. For the
several previous sample programs also, we did not complete the method that explains the program to the user until the very last development step. We could
have implemented such method at the very first step, but there are two reasons
why we don't do that. The first one is pedagogic. The program-explaining meth-

ods follow the same pattern, and, basically, if you've seen one, you've seen them all. There is not much of pedagogic value in discussing such methods. The second one is pragmatic. If you define a program description method at the beginning, it is very likely that you have to change it in a later step. Why? Because as you go through the development steps, the program design may change, and this change would require a new description of the program.

final test

Any changes we make, no matter how trivial they may seem, could affect the program. So it is mandatory to test the program again after any changes are made. We will complete the final testing by repeating the testing procedures of the previous steps.

8.8   Exercises

1. Use boolean variables to improve the readability of the following loop statements:

    a. ```
        numberOfCharacters = sentence.length();
        index = 0;
        wLocation = 0;
        jCount = 0;
        nonJCount = 0;

        do {
            if (index < numberOfCharacters) {
                letter = sentence.charAt(index);
                if (letter == 'J' || letter == 'j')
                    jcount++;
                else if (letter == 'W')
                    wLocation = index;
                else
                    nonJCount++;
            }
            index++;

        while (index < numberOfCharacters && letter != 'W');
        ```

    b.  ```
        product = 1.0f;
        number = 0;
        while (number == 10 || !(product > 10000.0f && number < 0))
            if (number == 10)
                tenCount++;
            else if (product <= 10000.0f)
                if (number > 0)
        ```

```
              product *= number;
          else if (number == 0)
              product = 1;
```

2. What is the difference between 'a' and "a"?

3. Discuss the difference between

```
str = str + word;   //string concatenation
```

and

```
tempStringBuffer.append(word)
```

where str is a String object and tempStringBuffer is a StringBuffer object.

4. Show that if x and y are String objects and x == y is true, then x.equals(y) is also true, but the reverse is not necessarily true.

5. What will be the output from the following code?

```
StringBuffer word1, word2;
word1 = new StringBuffer("Lisa");
word2 = word1;
word2.insert(0, "Mona ");
outputBox.printLine(word1);
```

6. Show the state of memory as shown in Figure 8.10 after the execution of each statement in the following code:

```
String word1, word2;
word1 = "Hello";
word2 = word1;
word1 = "Java";
```

7. Using a state-of-memory diagram like the one shown in Figure 8.10, illustrate the difference between a null string and an empty string, a string that has no characters in it. Show the state-of-memory diagram for the following code. Variable word1 is a null string, while word2 is an empty string.

```
String word1, word2;
word1 = null;
word2 = "";
```

8. Using a state-of-memory diagram like the one shown in Figure 8.10, show how the following two groups of statements differ.

```
String word1, word2;              String word1, word2;

word1 = "French Roast";           word1 = "French Roast";
word2 = word1;                    word2 = "French Roast";
```

9. Write an applet that reads in a character and displays the character's ASCII code. The getText method of the TextField class returns a String object, so you need to use a char value as in

```
inputString    = inputField.getText();
character      = inputString.charAt(0);
```

Display an error message if more than one character is entered.

10. Write a method that returns the number of uppercase letters in a String object passed to the method as a parameter. Use the class method isUpperCase of the Character class, which returns true if the passed parameter of type char is an uppercase letter. You need to explore the Character class from the java.lang package on your own.

11. Redo exercise 10 without using the Character class. Hint: The ASCII code of any uppercase letter will fall between 65 (code for 'A') and 90 (code for 'Z').

12. Write a method that reads a sentence and prints out the sentence with all uppercase letters changed to lowercase and all lowercase letters changed to uppercase.

13. Write a method that reads a sentence and prints out the sentence in reverse order. For example, the method will display

```
?uoy era woH
```

for the input

```
How are you?
```

14. Write a method that transposes words in a given sentence. For example, given an input sentence

```
The gate to Java nirvana is near
```

the method outputs

```
ehT etag ot avaJ anavrin si raen
```

To simplify the problem, you may assume the input sentence contains no punctuation marks. You may also assume that the input sentence starts with a nonblank character and there is exactly one blank space between the words.

15. Improve the method in exercise 14 by removing the assumptions. For example, an input sentence could be

```
Hello, how are you? I    use JDK 1.1.4.    Bye-bye.
```

An input sentence may contain punctuation marks and more than one blank space between two words. Transposing the above will result in

```
olleH, woh era uoy? I esu KDJ 1.1.4. eyB-eyb.
```

Notice the position of punctuation marks does not change and only one blank space is inserted between the transposed words.

16. Write a variation of the Eggy-Peggy program. Implement the following four variations:

· Sha	Add sha to the beginning of every word.
· Na	Add na to the end of every word.
· Sha Na Na	Add sha to the beginning and na na to the end of every word.
· Ava	Move the first letter to the end of the word and add ava to it.

Use a ListBox object to list the four variations, from which the user can select one. Use InputBox for reading in a sentence. You may want to widen the InputBox object using its resize method.

17. The sample code on page 375 that counts the number of words in a given sentence has a bug. If the input sentence has one or more blank spaces at the end, the value for wordCount will be one more than the actual number of words in the sentence. Correct this bug.

18. The sample code on page 379 for counting the number of words in a given string includes the test

```
if (beginIdx != endIdx) ...
```

Describe the type of input sentences that will result in the variables beginIdx and endIdx becoming equal.

19. Write an application that reads in a sentence and displays the count of individual vowels in the sentence. Use OutputBox to display the result in the following format. Count only the lowercase vowels.

```
Vowel counts for the sentence

        Mary had a little lamb.

# of 'a' : 4
# of 'e' : 1
# of 'i' : 1
# of 'o' : 0
# of 'u' : 0
```

20. The word game Eggy-Peggy is an example of encryption. Encryption has been used since ancient times to communicate messages secretly. One of the many techniques used for encryption is called a *Caesar cipher*. With this technique, each character in the original message is shifted N positions. For example, if $N = 1$, then the message

I drink only decaf

becomes

J ! e s j o l ! p o m z ! e f d b g

The encrypted message is decrypted to the original message by shifting back every character N positions. Shifting N positions forward and backward is achieved by converting the character to ASCII code and adding or subtracting N. Write an application that reads in the original text and the value for N and displays the encrypted text. Make sure the ASCII value resulting from encryption falls between 32 and 126. For example, if you add 8 (value of N) to 122 (ASCII code for 'z'), you should "wrap around" and get 35.

21. Write an application that reads the encrypted text and the value for N and displays the original text using the Caesar cipher technique.

22. Another encryption technique is called a *Vignere cipher*. This technique is similar to a Caesar cipher in that a key is applied cyclically to the original message. For this exercise a key is composed of uppercase letters only. Encryption is done by adding the code values of the key's characters to the code values of the characters in the original message. Code values for the key characters are assigned as follows: 0 for A, 1 for B, 2 for C, . . . , and 25 for Z. Let's say the key is COFFEE and the original message is I drink only decaf. Encryption works as follows:

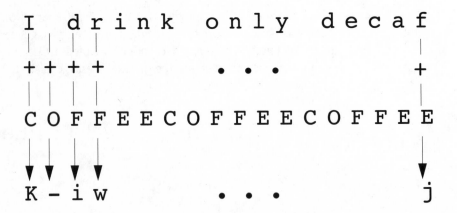

Decryption reverses the process to generate the original message. Write an application that reads in a text and displays the encrypted text. Make sure the ASCII value resulting from encryption or decryption falls between 32 and 126. You can get the code for key characters by (int) keyChar - 65.

23. Write an application that reads the encrypted text and displays the original text using the Vignere cipher technique.

24. Write an applet that determines if an input word is a palindrome. A palindrome is a string that reads the same forward and backward, for example, *noon* and *madam*. Ignore the case of the letter, so, for example, *maDaM*, *MadAm*, and *mAdaM* are all palindromes.

25. Write an applet that determines if an input sentence is a palindrome, for example, *A man, a plan, a canal, Panama!* You ignore the punctuation marks and the case of the letters.

Arrays

OBJECTIVES

After you have read and studied this chapter, you should be able to

- Manipulate a collection of data values using an array.

- Declare and use an array of primitive data types in writing a program.

- Declare and use an array of objects in writing a program.

- Describe how a two-dimensional array is implemented as an array of arrays.

- Use a MultiInputBox object from the javabook package to input an array of strings.

- Define a method that accepts an array as its parameter and a method that returns an array.

- Describe how the self-reference pointer works and use it in methods.

Introduction

Suppose you want to write a program that maintains up to 100 accounts. Would you use 100 variables without hesitation? Or would you be doubtful? If you think there must be a better way than using 100 distinct variables, you are correct. In this chapter you will learn about arrays. An *array* is a collection of data values of the same type. If your program needs to deal with a certain number of similar data values, such as 10 integers, 15 Student objects, 20 real numbers, 100 Account objects, and so forth, then you will use an array. In this chapter we will explain different types of arrays and how to use them properly in a program.

9.1   Array Basics

Suppose we want to compute the annual average rainfall from 12 monthly averages. We can use three variables and compute the annual average as

```
float sum, rainfall, annualAverage;

sum = 0;

for (int i = 0; i < 12; i++) {
    rainfall = inputBox.getFloat("Rainfall for month " + (i+1));
    sum += rainfall;
}
annualAverage = sum / 12.0f;
```

Now suppose we want to compute the difference between the annual and monthly averages for every month and display a table with three columns as shown in Figure 9.1.

To compute the difference between the annual and monthly averages, we need to remember the 12 monthly rainfall averages. Without remembering the 12 monthly averages, we won't be able to derive the monthly variations after the annual average is computed. Instead of using 12 variables januaryRainfall, februaryRainfall, and so forth to solve this problem, we use an array.

array

We mentioned that an *array* is a collection of data values of the same type. For example, we may declare an array consisting of float, but not an array consisting of both int and float. The following declares an array of float.

array declaration

```
float[] rainfall;
```

FIGURE 9.1   Monthly rainfall figures and their variation from the annual average.

Annual Average Rainfall: 15.03 mm

Month	Monthly Average	Variation from Annual Average
1	13.3	1.73
2	14.9	0.13
3	14.7	0.33
4	23.0	7.97
5	25.8	10.77
6	27.7	12.67
7	12.3	2.73
8	10.0	5.03
9	9.8	5.23
10	8.7	6.33
11	8.0	7.03
12	12.2	2.83

The square brackets indicate the array declaration. The brackets may be attached to a variable instead of the data type. For example, the declaration

```
float rainfall[];
```

is equivalent to the previous declaration. In Java, an array is an object, so we need to use the method new to actually create an array.

In Java, an array is an object.

The following statement creates an array of 12 float values and associates the identifier rainfall to the newly created array.

```
rainfall = new float[12];    //create an array of size 12
```

Figure 9.2 shows the created array.

FIGURE 9.2   An array of 12 **float** values.

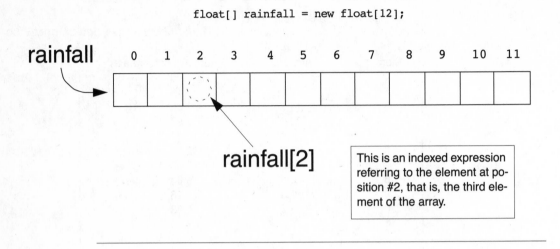

rainfall[2]

This is an indexed expression referring to the element at position #2, that is, the third element of the array.

Like any other objects, we can declare and create an array in one statement as in

```
float[] rainfall = new float[12];
```

*indexed
expression*

array element

The number 12 designates the size of the array—the number of values the array contains. We use a single identifier to refer to the whole collection and use an *indexed expression* to refer to the individual values of the collection. An individual value in an array is called an *element* of the array. Zero-based indexing is used to indicate the position of an element in the array. They are numbered 0, 1, 2, . . . , and size – 1, where size is the size of an array. For example, to refer to the third element of the rainfall array, we use the indexed expression

```
rainfall[2]
```

Instead of a literal constant like 2, we can use an expression such as

```
rainfall[i+3]
```

Notice that the index for the first position in an array is zero. Like a String object, Java uses zero-based indexing for an array.

The index of the first position in an array is 0.

Using the rainfall array, we can input 12 monthly averages and compute the annual average

> Can also declare as
> `float rainfall[] = new float[12];`

```java
float[] rainfall = new float[12];
float    annualAverage,
         sum = 0.0f;

for (int i = 0; i < 12; i++) {

    rainfall[i] = inputBox.getFloat("Rainfall for month " + (i+1));
    sum += rainfall[i];
}

annualAverage = sum / 12;
```

Figure 9.3 shows how the array would appear after all 12 values are entered.

FIGURE 9.3   An array of 12 **float** values after all 12 are assigned values.

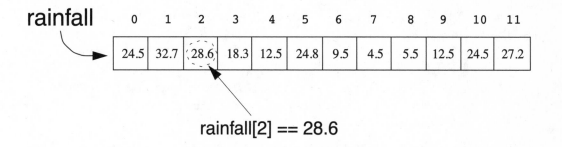

rainfall

0	1	2	3	4	5	6	7	8	9	10	11
24.5	32.7	28.6	18.3	12.5	24.8	9.5	4.5	5.5	12.5	24.5	27.2

rainfall[2] == 28.6

After the 12 monthly averages are stored in the array, we can print out the table as

```java
float difference;

for (i = 0; i < 12; i++) {
    outputBox.print( Format.rightAlign(3,i+1) ); //month #
```

```
//average rainfall for the month
outputBox.print( Format.rightAlign(17,1,rainfall[i]] );

//difference between the monthly and annual average
difference = Math.abs( rainfall[i] - annualAverage );
outputBox.printLine( Format.rightAlign(17,1,difference) );
}
```

length

An array has a public constant length for the size of an array. Using this constant, we can rewrite the for loop as

```
for (i = 0; i < rainfall.length; i++) {
    ...
}
```

This for loop is more general since we do not have to modify the loop statement when the size of an array is changed. Also, the use of length is necessary when the size of an array is not known in advance. This happens, for example, when we write a method with an array as its parameter. We need to write the method so it can handle an array of any size. We will provide an example of such a method in Section 9.3.

> It is very easy to mix up the **length** constant of an array and the **length** method of a **String** object. It is a public constant for an array, so we use it as
>
> ```
>                 int size = rainfall.length;
> ```
>
> **Dr. Caffeine**
>
> It is a method for a **String** object, so we use it as
>
> ```
>                 String str  = "This is a string";
>                 int    size = str.length();
> ```

Notice the prompts for the inputBox in the previous example are "Rainfall for month 1", "Rainfall for month 2", and so forth. A better prompt will spell out the month name, for example, "Rainfall for January", "Rainfall for February", and so forth. We can easily achieve a better prompt by using an array of strings. Here's how:

```
float[]    rainfall  = new float[12];   //an array of float
String[]   monthName = new String[12];  //an array of String
```

```
float       annualAverage,
            sum = 0.0f;

monthName[0]  = "January";
monthName[1]  = "February";
monthName[2]  = "March";
monthName[3]  = "April";
monthName[4]  = "May";
monthName[5]  = "June";
monthName[6]  = "July";
monthName[7]  = "August";
monthName[8]  = "September";
monthName[9]  = "October";
monthName[10] = "November";
monthName[11] = "December";
```

Remember these are shorthand for **String** object creation, e.g.,

```
... = new String("May");
```

```
for (int i = 0; i < rainfall.length; i++) {
    rainfall[i] = inputBox.getFloat("Rainfall for "
                                    + monthName[i]);
    sum += rainfall[i];
}

annualAverage = sum / 12.0f;
```

Instead of assigning array elements individually, we can initialize the array at the time of declaration. We can, for example, initialize the monthName array by

```
String[] monthName = {   "January", "February", "March",
                         "April", "May", "June", "July",
                         "August", "September", "October",
                         "November", "December"   };
```

No size is specified.

Notice that we do not specify the size of an array if the array elements are initialized at the time of declaration. The size of an array is determined by the number of values in the list. In the above example, there are 12 values in the list, so the size of the array monthName is set to 12.

Let's try some more examples. We assume the rainfall array is declared, and all 12 values are read in. The following code computes the average rainfall for the odd months (January, March, . . .) and the even months (February, April, . . .).

```
float   oddMonthSum, oddMonthAverage,
        evenMonthSum, evenMonthAverage;
```

```
oddMonthSum  = 0.0f;
evenMonthSum = 0.0f;

//compute the average for the odd months
for (int i = 0; i < rainfall.length; i += 2)
    oddMonthSum += rainfall[i];
oddMonthAverage = oddMonthSum / 6.0f;

//compute the average for the even months
for (int i = 1; i < rainfall.length; i += 2)
    evenMonthSum += rainfall[i];
evenMonthAverage = evenMonthSum / 6.0f;
```

We can compute the same result using one for loop as

```
for (int i = 0; i < rainfall.length; i += 2 ) {
    oddMonthSum += rainfall[i];
    evenMonthSum += rainfall[i+1];
}

oddMonthAverage  = oddMonthSum / 6;
evenMonthAverage = evenMonthSum / 6;
```

To compute the average for each quarter (Quarter 1 has January, February, and March, Quarter 2 has April, May, and June, and so forth), we can write

```
for (int i = 0; i < 3; i++ ) {
    quarter1Sum += rainfall[i];
    quarter2Sum += rainfall[i+3];
    quarter3Sum += rainfall[i+6];
    quarter4Sum += rainfall[i+9];
}

quarter1Average = quarter1Sum / 3.0f;
quarter2Average = quarter2Sum / 3.0f;
quarter3Average = quarter3Sum / 3.0f;
quarter4Average = quarter4Sum / 3.0f;
```

We can use another array to store the quarter averages instead of using four variables:

```
float[] quarterAverage = new float[4];

for (int i = 0; i < 4; i++) {
```

```
sum = 0;

for (int j = 0; j < 3; j++)        //compute the sum of
    sum += rainfall[3*i + j];      //one quarter

quarterAverage[i] = sum / 3.0f; //average for Quarter i+1
```

```
    }
```

Notice how the inner for loop is used to compute the sum of one quarter. The following table illustrates how the values for the variables i, j, and the expression 3*i + j change.

i	j	3*i + j
0	0	0
	1	1
	2	2
1	0	3
	1	4
	2	5
2	0	6
	1	7
	2	8
3	0	9
	1	10
	2	11

In the previous examples, we used a constant to specify the size of an array, such as the literal constant 12 in the following declaration:

```
float[] rainfall = new float[12];
```

Using constants to declare the array sizes does not always lead to an efficient space usage. Suppose, for example, we declare an integer array of size 100:

```
int[] number = new int[100];
```

fixed-size array declaration

We call the declaration of arrays with constants a *fixed-size array declaration*. There are two potential problems with fixed-size array declarations. The first problem is that the program can only process up to 100 numbers. What if we need to process 101 numbers? We have to modify the program and compile it again. The second problem is a possible underutilization of space. The above declaration allocates 100 spaces whether they are used or not. Suppose the program on the average processes 20 numbers. Then, the program's average space usage is only 20 percent of the allocated space. With Java, we are not limited to fixed-size array declaration. We can declare an array of different size every time we run the program. The following code prompts the user for the size of an array and declares an array of designated size:

```
int     size;
int[]   number;

size    = inputBox.getInteger("Size of an array:");
number = new int[size];
```

With this approach, every time the program is executed only the needed amount of space is allocated for the array. Any valid arithmetic expression is allowed for size specification; for example,

```
size = inputBox.getInteger();
number = new int[size*size + 2* size + 5];
```

variable-size array declaration

We call the declaration of arrays with nonconstant values a *variable-size array declaration*. You will be seeing an example of a variable-size array in the next section.

Ms. Latte:	Can I use an index other than integer?
Dr. Caffeine:	No, not with Java. You must use an integer. Also, the array index must always start with **0**.
Ms. Latte:	Why? It seems more natural to start with **1**.
Dr. Caffeine:	Java adopted this feature from the programming language C. Using the zero-based indexing, the index value of an element indicates the number of elements in front of the element. For example, an index value of zero for the first element indicates that there are zero elements in front of it; an index value of four for the fifth element indicates that there are four elements in front of it. Zero-based indexing allows a simpler formula to compute the actual memory address of array elements.

Dr. & Ms.

Quick Check

1. Which of the following statements are invalid?

    ```
    a.  float   number[23];

    b.  float   number = { 1.0f, 2.0f, 3.0f };

    c.  int     number;
        number = new Array[23];

    d.  int[]   number = [ 1, 2, 3, 4 ];
    ```

2. Given the following array, write a code fragment to compute the sum of all positive real numbers in the array.

    ```
    float[] number = new float[25];
    ```

3. Describe the difference between the following two code fragments.

    ```
    //code fragment 1
    for (int i = 0; i < number.length; i++) {
        if ( i % 2 == 0 ) {
            outputBox.printLine( number[i] );
        }
    }

    //code fragment 2
    for (int i = 0; i < number.length; i++) {
        if ( number[i] % 2 == 0 ) {
            outputBox.printLine( number[i] );
        }
    }
    ```

9.2 Arrays of Objects

Array elements are not limited to primitive data types. Indeed, since a String is an object, we have actually seen an example of an array of objects already in Section 9.1. In this section we will explore further arrays of objects. To illustrate the processing of an array of objects, we will use the Person class in the following examples. We will define this Person class later in the chapter to introduce additional object-oriented concepts. Here's the portion of the Person class definition we will use in this section:

Public Methods of the Person Class
`public    int        getAge        (                              )`
Returns the age of a person. Default age of a person is set to 0.
`public    char       getGender  (                              )`
Returns the gender of a person. The character F stands for female and M for male. Default gender of a person is set to the character U for unknown.
`public    String    getName      (                              )`
Returns the name of a person. Default name of a person is set to Not Given.
`public    void       setAge        ( int age            )`
Returns the age of a person.
`public    void       setGender  ( char gender  )`
Sets the gender of a person to the argument gender. The character F stands for female and M for male. The character U designates unknown gender.
`public    void       setName      ( String name  )`
Sets the name of a person to the argument name.

The following code creates a Person object:

```
Person latte;

latte = new Person( );
latte.setName("Ms. Latte");
latte.setAge(20);
latte.setGender('F');

outputBox.printLine( "Name: " + latte.getName()   );
outputBox.printLine( "Age : " + latte.getAge()    );
outputBox.printLine( "Sex : " + latte.getGender() );
```

Now let's study how we can create and manipulate an array of Person objects. An array of objects is declared and created just like an array of primitive data types. The following are a declaration and creation of an array of Person objects.

```
Person[]   person;        //declare the person array
person = new Person[20];   //and then create it
```

Execution of the above code will result in a state shown in Figure 9.4.

FIGURE 9.4   An array of **Person** objects after the array is created.

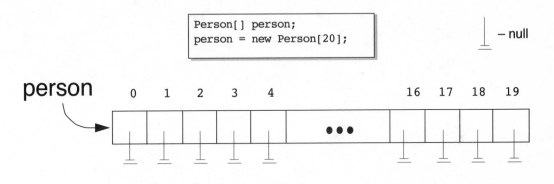

Notice that the elements, that is, Person objects, are not yet created; only the array is created. Array elements are initially null. Since each individual element is an object, it must also be created. The following code creates a Person object and sets it as the array's first element.

```
person[0] = new Person( );
```

Figure 9.5 shows the state after the first Person object is added to the array.

Notice that no data values are assigned to the object yet. The object has default values at this point. To assign data values to this object, we can execute

```
person[0].setName  ( "Ms. Latte" );
person[0].setAge    ( 20 );
person[0].setGender( 'F' );
```

The indexed expression

```
person[0]
```

FIGURE 9.5   The person array with one **Person** object added to it.

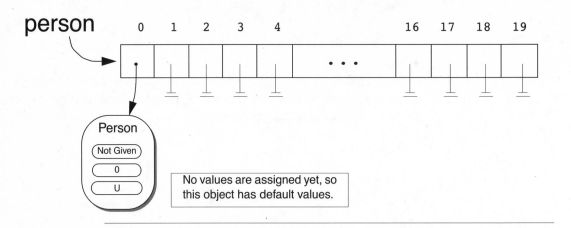

is used to refer to the first object in the person array. Since this expression refers to an object, we write

```
person[0].setAge( 20 );
```

to call this Person object's setAge method, for example. This is the syntax we use to call an object's method. We are just using an indexed expression to refer to an object instead of a simple variable.

Let's go through typical array processing to illustrate the basic operations. The first is to create Person objects and set up the person array. We assume that the person array is already declared and created.

```
String     name;
int        age;
char       gender;

for (i = 0; i < person.length; i++) {

    //read in data values
    name   = inputBox.getString("Enter name:");
    age    = inputBox.getInteger("Enter age:");
    gender = inputBox.getChar("Enter gender:");
```

```
                    //create a new Person and assign values
                    person[i] = new Person( );

                    person[i].setName  ( name   );
                    person[i].setAge   ( age    );
                    person[i].setGender( gender );
               }
```

Note: To focus on array processing, we used the most simplistic input routine. For instance, we did not perform any input error checking, but this is not to say that input error checking is unimportant. We simply want to focus on array processing.

To find the average age, we execute

find the average age

```
float sum = 0, averageAge;

for (i = 0; i < person.length; i++) {
    sum += person[i].getAge();
}
averageAge = sum / (float) person.length;
```

To print out the name and age of the youngest and the oldest persons, we can execute

find the youngest and the oldest person

```
String     nameOfYoungest, nameOfOldest;
int        min, max, age;

nameOfYoungest = nameOfOldest = person[0].getName();
min = max = person[0].getAge();

for (i = 1; i < person.length; i++) {
    age = person[i].getAge();

    if ( age < min ) {          //found a younger person
        min            = age;
        nameOfYoungest = person[i].getName();
    }
    else if ( age > max ) {   //found an older person
        max            = age;
        nameOfOldest   = person[i].getName();
    }
}
outputBox.printLine("Oldest  : " + nameOfOldest + " is "
                                  + max + "years old.");
```

```
outputBox.printLine("Youngest: " + nameOfYoungest + " is "
                                 + min + "years old.");
```

Instead of using separate String and int variables, we can use the index to the youngest and the oldest persons. Here's the code:

```
int    minIdx,        //index to the youngest person
       maxIdx;        //index to the oldest person

minIdx = maxIdx = 0;

for (i = 1; i < person.length; i++) {

    if ( person[i].getAge() < person[minIdx].getAge() ) {
        //found a younger person
        minIdx    = i;
    }
    else if (person[i].getAge() > person[maxIdx.getAge() ) {
        //found an older person
        maxIdx    = i;
    }
}

outputBox.printLine("Oldest  : " + person[maxIdx].getName()
                                 + " is "
                                 + person[maxIdx].getAge()
                                 + "years old.");

outputBox.printLine("Youngest: " + person[minIdx].getName()
                                 + " is "
                                 + person[minIdx].getAge()
                                 + "years old.");
```

Yet another approach is to use variables for Person objects. Figure 9.6 shows how the Person variables oldest and youngest point to objects in the person array. Here's the code using Person variables:

```
Person    youngest,    //points to the youngest person
          oldest;      //points to the oldest person

youngest = oldest = person[0];

for (i = 1; i < person.length; i++) {
```

FIGURE 9.6   An array of **Person** objects with two **Person** variables.

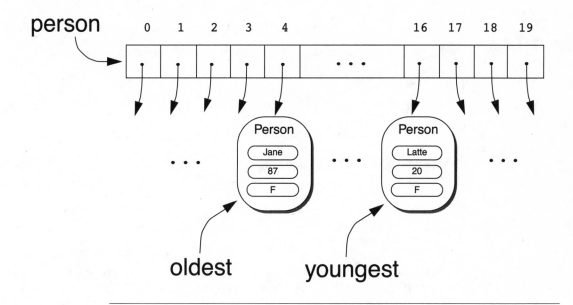

```
        if ( person[i].getAge() < youngest.getAge() ) {
            //found a younger person
            youngest  = person[i];
        }
        else if ( person[i].getAge() > oldest.getAge() ) {
            //found an older person
            oldest    = person[i];
        }
    }

    outputBox.printLine("Oldest  : " + oldest.getName() + " is "
                            + oldest.getAge() + "years old.");

    outputBox.printLine("Youngest: " + youngest.getName() + " is "
                            + youngest.getAge() + "years old.");
```

find a particular person

Our next example is to search for a particular person. We can scan through the array until the desired person is found. Suppose we want to search for a person whose name is Latte. If we assume the person is in the array, then we can write

```
int i = 0;

while ( !person[i].getName().equals("Latte") ) {
    i++;
}

outputBox.printLine("Found Ms. Latte at position" + i);
```

The expression

```
person[i].getName().equals("Latte")
```

is evaluated left to right and equivalent to

```
Person p   =  person[i];
String str =  p.getName();

str.equals("Latte");
```

In this example, we assume that the person for whom we are searching is in the array. If we cannot assume this, then we need to rewrite the terminating condition to take care of the case when the person is not in the array. Here's how:

```
int i = 0;

while ( i < person.length &&     //still more persons to search
        !person[i].getName().equals("Latte") ) {
    i++;
}

if (i == person.length) {
    //not found - unsuccessful search
    outputBox.printLine("Ms. Latte was not in the array");
}
else {
    //found - successful search
    outputBox.printLine("Found Ms. Latte at position" + i);
}
```

delete a particular person

Now let's consider the deletion operation. The deletion operation requires some kind of a search routine to locate the Person object to be removed. To concentrate on the deletion operation, we will assume there's a search method that returns the index of the Person object in the array to be removed. There are two possible ways to remove an object from the array. The first approach is to reset the array element to null. Remember that each element in an array of objects is a reference to an object, so removing an object from an array could be accomplished by setting the reference to null. Figure 9.7 illustrates how the object at position 1 is deleted using Approach 1.

FIGURE 9.7 Approach 1 Deletion: Setting a reference to **null**. The array length is 4.

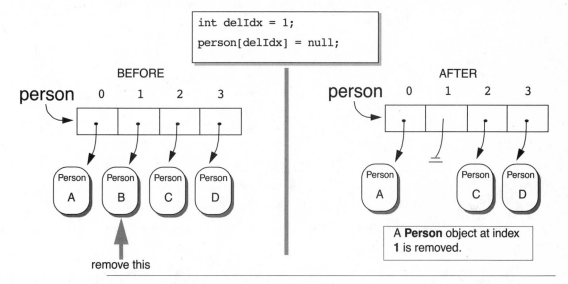

Since any index position can be set to null, there can be "holes," that is, null references, anywhere in the array. Instead of intermixing real and null references, the second approach will pack the elements so the real references occur at the beginning, and the null references at the end:

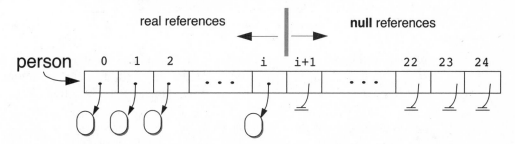

With Approach 2, we must fill the hole. There are two possible solutions. The first solution is to pack the elements. If an object at position J is removed (i.e., this position is set to null), then elements from position J+1 till the last non-null reference are shifted one position lower. And, finally, the last non-null reference is set to null. The second solution is to replace the removed element by the last element in the array. The first solution is necessary if the Person objects are arranged in some order (e.g., in ascending order of age). The second solution is a better one if the Person objects are not arranged in any order. Since we are not arranging them in any order, we will use the second solution. Figure 9.8 illustrates how the object at position 1 is replaced by the last element.

FIGURE 9.8   Approach 2 Deletion: Replace the removed element with the last element in the array. The array length is 4.

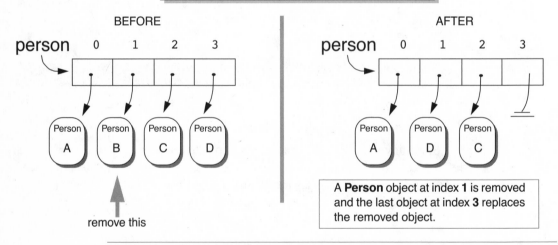

```
int delIdx   = 1;
int last     = 3;

person[delIdx]  = person[last];

person[last]    = null;
```

BEFORE

AFTER

person   0   1   2   3

person   0   1   2   3

Person A   Person B   Person C   Person D

remove this

Person A   Person D   Person C

A **Person** object at index **1** is removed and the last object at index **3** replaces the removed object.

The search routine we have presented earlier in this section assumes the full array; that is, all elements are non-null references. With the deletion routine, either Approach 1 or 2, given above, an array element could be a null. The search routine must therefore be modified to handle the null references correctly. The modified search routine is left as an exercise.

In both Figures 9.7 and 9.8, we removed the icon for Person B in the diagrams when the array element was set to null as though the object was erased from the memory. Eventually, the object will indeed get erased, but the operation of assigning null to the array element will not erase the object by itself. The operation simply initiates a chain reaction that will eventually erase the object from the memory.

As we have shown you several times already, a single object can have multiple references pointing to it. For example, the following code will result in two references pointing to a single Person object:

```
Person p1, p2;

p1 = new Person();
p2 = p1;
```

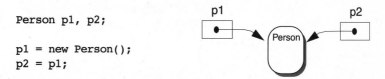

When an object has no references pointing to it, then the system will erase the object and make the memory space available for other uses. We call the erasing of an object *deallocation* of memory, and the process of deallocating memory **garbage collection** *garbage collection*. Unlike other programming languages, garbage collection is automatically done in Java, so we do not have to be conscious about it when developing Java programs.

Quick Check

1. Which of the following statements are invalid?

    a.   `Person[25] person;`

    b.   `Person[ ] person;`

    c.   `Person person[] = new Person[25];`

    d.   `Person person[25] = new Person[25];`

2. Write a code fragment to print out the name of those who are older than 20. Assume the following declaration and the array is already set up correctly.

```
Person[ ]  friend = new Person[100];
```

9.3   Passing Arrays to Methods

We discussed the passing of an object to a method using String objects as illustrations in Chapter 8. Since an array is also an object, the rules for passing an object to a method and returning an object from the method apply to arrays also. However, there are some additional rules we need to remember in passing an array to a method and returning it from a method. We will cover these topics in this section.

Let's define a method that returns the index of the smallest element in an array of real numbers. The array to search for the smallest element is passed to the method. Here's the method:

```java
public int searchMinimum(float[] number)
{
    int indexOfMinimum = 0;

    for (int i = 0; i < number.length; i++) {
        if (number[i] < number[indexOfMinimum]) { //found a
            indexOfMinimum = i;                    //smaller element
        }
    }
    return indexOfMinimum;
}
```

Notice that we use the square brackets to designate that number is an array. The square brackets may also be attached to the parameter as in

```java
public int searchMinimum(float number[])
```

To call this method (from a method of the same class), we write something like

```java
float[] arrayOne, arrayTwo;

//assign values to arrayOne and arrayTwo

//find the smallest element of arrayOne
float minOne = searchMinimum( arrayOne );

//find the smallest element of arrayTwo
float minTwo = searchMinimum( arrayTwo );
```

```
//output the result
outputBox.print("Mimimum value in Array One is ");
outputBox.print(arrayOne[minOne] + " at position " + minOne);

outputBox.skipLine(2);

outputBox.print("Mimimum value in Array Two is ");
outputBox.print(arrayTwo[minTwo] + " at position " + minTwo);
```

Just like other objects, an array is a reference data type, so we are passing the reference to an array, not the whole array, when we call the searchMinimum method. For example, when the method is called with arrayOne as its argument, the state shown in Figure 9.9 will result. There are two references to the same array object. The method does not create a separate copy of the array.

When an array is passed to a method, only its reference is passed. A copy of the array is NOT created in the method.

Now let's try another example in which we return an array (actually the reference to the array) from a method. Suppose we want to define a method that inputs float values and returns the values as an array of float. We can define the method as

```
public float[] readFloats()
{
    float[] number;
    int N = inputBox.getInteger("How many input values?");

    number = new float[N];

    for (int i = 0; i < N; i++) {
        number[i] = inputBox.getFloat("Number " + i);
    }
    return number;
}
```

The square brackets beside the method return type float indicate that the method returns an array of float. Because an array is a reference data type, when we say "returns an array of float," we are really saying "returns the reference to an array of float." We will use the shorter expression in general and use the longer expression only when we need to be precise.

FIGURE 9.9   Passing an array to a method means we are passing a reference to an array. We are not
passing the whole array.

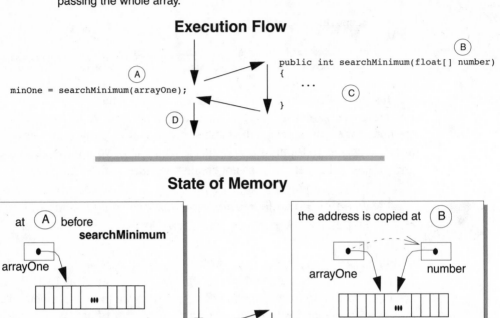

Execution Flow

State of Memory

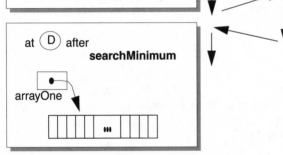

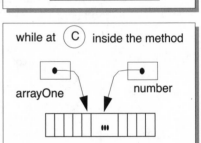

The readFloats method is called in the following manner:

```
float[] arrayOne, arrayTwo;

//assign values to arrayOne and arrayTwo
arrayOne = readFloats();

arrayTwo = readFloats();
```

Since a new array is created by the method, we do not have to create an array from the calling side. In other words, we don't have to do the following:

```
float[] arrayOne, arrayTwo;

arrayOne = new float[30]; //this statement is NOT necessary

arrayOne = readFloats();
```

It won't cause an error if you create an array from the calling side, but you are doing a very wasteful operation. First, it takes up extra memory space. And second, it slows down the whole operation because the computer must garbage collect the extra memory space that is not being used.

Let's try an alternative approach. This time, instead of creating an array inside the method and returning the array, the calling side creates an array and passes this array to the method:

```
int[] myIntArray = new int[50];

readIntegers(myIntArray);
```

The method readIntegers fills the passed array with integers. The method is defined as

```
public void readIntegers(int[] number)
{
    for (int i = 0; i < number.length; i++) {
        number[i] = inputBox.getInteger("Number " + i);
    }
}
```

Notice the return type of readIntegers is void because we are not returning an array. The method modifies the array that is passed to it.

Be careful not to mix the two alternative approaches. The following method will not work:

```
public void badMethod( float[] number )
{
    int N = inputBox.getInteger("How many input values?");

    number = new float[N];
```

```
        for (int i = 0; i < N; i++) {
            number[i] = inputbox.getFloat("Number " + i);
        }
    }
```

The code such as

```
float[] arrayOne = new float[30];

badMethod( arrayOne );
```

will leave arrayOne unchanged. Figure 9.10 shows the effect of creating a local array in badMethod and not returning it (note: the return type of badMethod is void).

Quick Check

1. What will be an output from the following code?

    ```
    int[] list = {10, 20, 30, 40 };
    myMethod( list );
    outputBox.printLine( list[1] );
    outputBox.printLine( list[3] );
    ...
    public void myMethod(int[] intArray)
    {
        for (int i = 0; i < intArray.length; i+=2) {
            intArray[i] = i;
        }
    }
    ```

2. If we replace myMethod of question 1 with the following, what will be an output?

    ```
    public void myMethod(int[] intArray)
    {
        int[] local = intArray;
        for (int i = 0; i < local.length; i+=2) {
            local[i] = i;
        }
    }
    ```

FIGURE 9.10   Effect of creating a local array and not returning it.

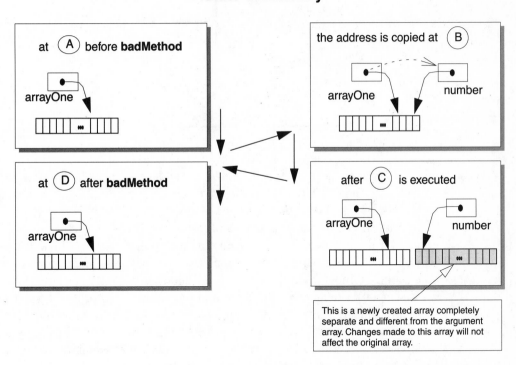

9.4   MultiInputBox

While an InputBox object is capable of accepting only a single input value, a MultiInputBox object from the javabook package can accept multiple input values. A MultiInputBox object allows the user to input *N* string values using *N* Text-Field objects. The programmer can specify *N* labels. Figure 9.11 shows a MultiInputBox with three labels and three text fields for entering bank information.

FIGURE 9.11   A **MultiInputBox** object (from the **javabook** package) to enter three values.

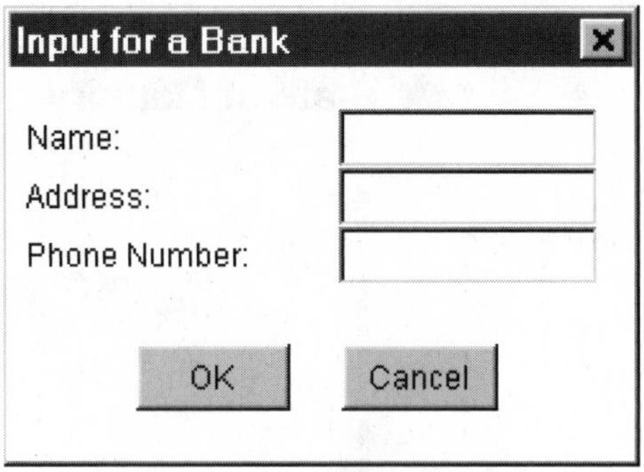

In general, designing a customized input dialog for Bank, Account, Student, and so forth is preferable, but there are times a generic dialog, such as MultiInputBox, with labels on one column and text fields on another is sufficient. Using the MultiInputBox class is a quick and easy way to handle input routines of a program if the program does not require a fancy user interface. The MultiInputBox class is useful in building prototypes also. Instead of spending time designing customized input dialogs, you can start building a program prototype by using MultiInputBox objects. When the prototype is functioning properly, you can then improve the user interface of the program with customized input dialogs.

There are two ways to create a MultiInputBox object. The first is by passing an owner frame and the integer argument that specifies the number of labels and text fields the MultiInputBox object will contain, for example:

```
MultiInputBox multiBox = new MultiInputBox(mainWindow, 3);
```

We use the setLabels method to assign the labels. The argument to the method is an array of strings. The following code creates the dialog shown in Figure 9.11.

```
String[] label = { "Name", "Address", "Phone Number"};
multiBox.setLabels(label);
```

If the setLabels method is not called, then the dialog will contain no labels.

The second way to create a MultiInputBox object is to pass an array of strings as its second parameter, for example:

```
String[] label = { "Name", "Address", "Phone Number"};
MultiInputBox multiBox = new MultiInputBox(mainWindow, label);
```

The MultiInputBox class is a descendant of Dialog, so the methods applicable to Dialog are applicable to MultiInputBox also (the title of MultiInputBox shown in Figure 9.11 is set by calling its setTitle method). We will discuss only the method unique to the MultiInputBox class.

We retrieve input values from a MultiInputBox by calling the method get-Inputs. The method returns an array of strings. For example,

```
String[] answer;

answer = multiBox.getInputs();
```

The array answer is null if either the Cancel button is clicked or no input value is entered. Notice that the getInputs method returns an array of strings. If we execute

```
MultiInputBox multiBox = new MultiInputBox(mainWindow, 3);
String[]      labels = { "Name", "Address", "Age"};
String[]      answer;

multiBox.setLabels(labels);

answer = multiBox.getInputs();
```

then the answer array like the one shown in Figure 9.12 will result.

FIGURE 9.12   The answer array returned from **multiBox**.

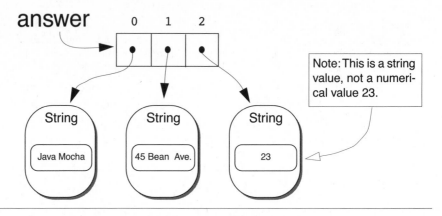

Since we want the third input as an int, we need to do a String to int conversion. You can convert using the Convert class from the javabook package as

```
int age = Convert.toInt(answers[2]);
```

or convert using the Integer class from java.lang as

```
Integer intObj = new Integer(answers[2]);
int age = intObj.intValue();
```

Table 9.1 is a list of MultiInputBox methods and class constants.

TABLE 9.1   A list of **MultiInputBox** methods.

CLASS:	MultiInputBox	
Method	**Argument**	**Description**
<constructor>	MainWindow, int	Creates a MultiInputBox object. The second argument specifies the number of labels.
<constructor>	MainWindow, array of String	Creates a MultiInputBox object. The second argument is an array of String for labels.

TABLE 9.1   A list of **MultiInputBox** methods. (Continued)

CLASS:	MultiInputBox	
Method	**Argument**	**Description**
setLabels	array of String	Sets the labels of a MultiInputBox object to the passed array of String.
getInputs	\<none>	Returns an array of String entered by the user.

9.5   Self-Referencing Pointer

In this section, we will describe an object-oriented programming concept called a *self-referencing pointer*. In Java, the reserved word this is used as a self-referencing pointer. We used the self-referencing pointer in Chapter 5, but provide only a brief explanation. We will provide a more complete explanation in this section. We will define a Person class to illustrate the use of a self-referencing pointer. The list of public methods of the Person class was given earlier in Section 9.2.

Let's begin with the data members of the Person class. For each person we maintain the name, gender, and age information. To keep track of this information, we will use instance variables. We declare the class as

```
class Person
{
/*********************
    Data Members
*********************/
    private    String    name;
    private    int       age;
    private    char      gender;

    //the rest of the class definition comes here

}
```

In the list given in Section 9.2, we see three "read" methods that return the value of instance variables—getAge, getGender, and getName—and three "write" methods that assign the values to instance variables—setAge, setGender, and setName. The "read" methods that return the values are called *accessors* or *access methods*. And the "write" methods that assign values to the object are

accessors

called *mutators* or *mutator methods* because they change the value of instance variables.

The access methods are easy. Since we have included an instance variable for each of the three items of information, all we need to do is to return the value of the respective instance variable. They are defined as

```java
public int getAge( )
{
    return age;
}

public char getGender( )
{
    return gender;
}

public String getName( )
{
    return name;
}
```

Now let's see how we can define the mutator methods. Basically, we need to do the inverse of what we did with the access methods; that is, we need to assign a value to the respective instance variable. For example, we may define the set-Age method as

```java
public void setAge( int anAge )
{
    age = anAge;
}
```

Notice how we named the parameter. We use the identifier anAge, because we cannot use the identifier age as the parameter. Doing so would conflict with the instance variable age in the method body. To avoid the naming conflict, we use the different identifier for the parameter.

A second way to avoid the naming conflict is by using the self-referencing pointer this. In order to explain the use of the self-referencing pointer, let's review how an identifier in a method is associated to a variable. If there's a matching local declaration or a matching parameter, then the identifier is associated to the local variable or the parameter. Note: The parameter is a local declaration, so you cannot have a method declaration with the local variable and the parameter sharing the same identifier, such as

```
public void bad( int local )
{
    int local;
    ...
}
```

Cannot be the same name.

Otherwise, if there's a matching instance or class variable, then the identifier is associated to the instance or class variable. Figure 9.13 illustrates these points.

FIGURE 9.13   How identifiers used in a method are associated to a local variable, parameter, or instance/class variable.

```
class Person
{
    int age;
    ...
    public void setAge( int age )
    {
        ...  age  ...

    }
}
```

There's a matching parameter, so 'age' refers to this parameter.

```
class Person
{
    int age;
    ...
    public void setAge(int pAge)
    {
        ...  age  ...

    }
}
```

There's no matching parameter or local declaration, so 'age' refers to the instance variable.

Rules for associating an identifier to a local variable, parameter, and an instance/class variable:

1. If there's a matching local variable declaration or a parameter, then the identifier refers to the local variable or the parameter.

2. Otherwise, if there's a matching instance or class variable, then the identifier refers to the instance or class variable.

3. Otherwise, it is an error because there's no matching declaration.

Using the self-referencing pointer this, we can avoid the naming conflict even if we use the same identifier for an instance variable and the parameter. We can define the setAge method as

```
public void setAge( int age )
{
    this.age = age;
}
```

Because of the matching parameter declaration, the identifier age in the method refers to this parameter. To refer to the instance variable age from this method, we use the expression this.age. Figure 9.14 shows how the associations are made. We read the expression this.age as "this object's age instance variable." By using the dot notation with the reserved word this, we are able to refer to the object's instance variable.

FIGURE 9.14   Using the self-referencing pointer to avoid the naming conflict.

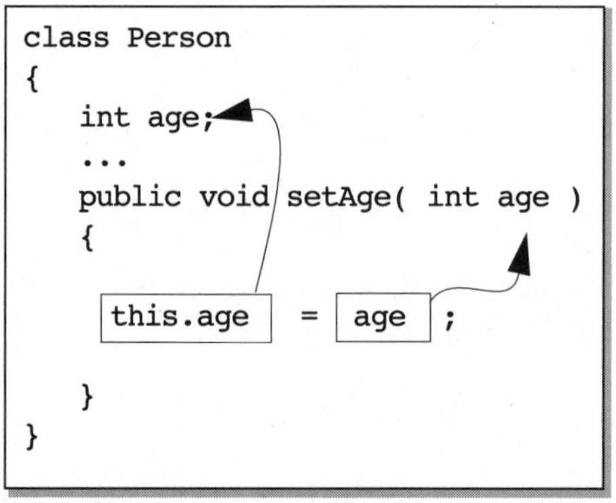

You can always use the reserved word this in referring to the object's data members and methods. In many cases, its use is optional, so we don't use it explicitly. In the case of the setAge method, because the identifier age is used as the parameter, we must use the expression this.age to avoid the naming conflict. When there are no naming conflicts, the use is optional. For example, when we write the setAge method as

```
public void setAge( int anAge )
{
    age = anAge;
}
```

then we don't have to use the self-referencing pointer, because there's no ambiguity. However, we could also write the method using the this pointer explicitly as

```
public void setAge( int age )
{
    this.age = age;
}
```

This rule applies also to calling a method that belongs to the same class. We explained earlier in Chapter 4 (see Figure 4.8 on page 177) that when we call a method from another method that belongs to the same class, no dot notation is used. Consider the following example:

```
class Tester
{
    public void methodOne( )
    {
    }

    public void methodTwo( )
    {
        methodOne();          ◄──────  You don't need dot nota-
    }                                    tion to call a method that
}                                        belongs to the same class.
```

The methodTwo method can also be written by explicitly using the dot notation with the self-referencing pointer this:

```
public void methodTwo( )
{
    this.methodOne();
}
```

The setAge method shows only one example of using the self-referencing pointer this. There are other usages that we will describe later in this section and also in the later chapters.

> The self-referencing pointer refers to an instance of a class, and therefore, the use of the this pointer is valid only inside the instance methods. The this pointer inside the class methods does not make sense, and it is not allowed.

The constructor of the Person class is defined as

```
public Person ( )
{
    age = 0;
    name = "Not Given";
    gender = 'U';
}
```

Up till now, we managed to define a class using only one constructor. However, a class is not limited to one constructor. It is possible to define multiple constructors to a class. For the Person class, we can define a second constructor that accepts three values so the three attributes of a Person object can be initialized at the time the object is created. The second constructor is defined as

```
public Person( String name, int age, char gender)
{
    this.name      = name;
    this.age       = age;
    this.gender    = gender;
}
```

and it is called as in

```
Person p = new Person( "Ms. Latte", 20, 'F' );
```

Using the self-referencing pointer this, it is possible, and preferable, to define the first constructor as

```
public Person ( )
{
    this( "Not Given", 0,'U' );
}
```

The first constructor calls the second constructor for the actual initialization, instead of performing the actual initialization. By defining the first constructor in this manner, we can guarantee consistent initialization, because the second constructor is the only method that carries out the actual initialization procedure. Since there's only one place where the initialization procedure is defined, it is also easier to manage any changes made to the initialization procedure. You may want to see how the multiple constructors for javabook classes such as InputBox and ResponseBox are defined.

Quick Check

1. What will be an output from the following code?

```
Tester testOne = new Tester();
testOne.methodOne(15);
...
class Tester
{
    private int x;

    public void methodTwo( )
    {
        System.out.println(x);
    }

    public void methodOne(int x)
    {
        this.x = x + 1;
        methodTwo();
    }
}
```

2. What's wrong with the following code?

```
public void setAge( int anAge )
{
    age = this.anAge;
}
```

9.6   Sample Development: The Address Book

In this section, we will design a class called an AddressBook to maintain a collection of Person objects. The AddressBook class is implemented by using an array. We will use the Person class defined in the previous section. Through the design of the AddressBook class, we will reiterate the key principles of object-oriented design.

Notice that we are not developing a complete program here. We are designing only one of the many classes we need for a complete address book program. For the complete program, we need a main window, objects for doing input and output, and so forth. In this section, we will concentrate on one class that is only responsible for maintaining a collection of Person objects. This class will not perform, for example, input and output of Person objects, following the Single-Task Object (STO) principle described in Chapter 6. We will discuss the importance of the STO principle while we develop the AddressBook class. One objective we have in designing the AddressBook class is to make the class reusable in many different programs. Many of the design decisions we will make during the development are based on implementing a reusable class.

Problem Statement

Write an AddressBook *class that manages a collection of* Person *objects. An* AddressBook *object will allow the programmer to add, delete, or search for a* Person *object in the address book.*

Overall Plan

Our first task is to come up with an overall design of the class. Let's begin by first identifying the core operations that an address book object must support. The problem statement indicated three major operations: add, delete, and search. These three operations are pretty much a standard in any collection of data values. For any kind of collections, you will always want to be able to add a new item, delete an old item, and search for an item or items. An address book is no exception as it is a collection of information about people for which you would want to add, delete, and search data.

Our task here is to design a class that will maintain an address book by supporting these three operations. We will define three methods for the class: add, delete, and search.

Our working design document for the AddressBook class is therefore as follows:

Design Document: The Public Methods of the AddressBook Class	
Method	**Purpose**
AddressBook	A constructor to initialize the object. We will include multiple constructors as necessary.
add	Adds a new **Person** object to the address book.
delete	Deletes a specified **Person** object from the address book.
search	Searches a specified **Person** object in the address book and returns this person if found.

The object diagram for the AddressBook class at this point is

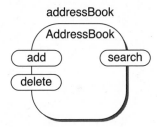

We will implement the class in the following order:

development steps

1. Implement the constructor(s).

2. Implement the add method.

3. Implement the search method.

4. Implement the delete method.

5. Finalize the class.

This order of development follows a natural sequence. To implement any instance method of a class, we need to be able to create a properly initialized object, so we will begin the class implementation by defining a constructor. As a part of defining a constructor, we will identify necessary data members. We will add more data members as we progress through the development steps. The second step is to implement the add routine, because without being able to add a new **Person** object, we won't be able to test other operations. For the third step, we will implement the search routine. And for the fourth step, we will implement the last routine. Although we could implement the delete routine before the search routine, we need some form of searching to test the correctness of the delete routine. In other words, we delete a person and attempt to search this person and verify that the search will not find the deleted person. So we will implement the search routine before the delete routine.

Step 1 Development: Skeleton with Constructors

Step 1 Design In Step 1, we will identify the data members and define a constructor(s) to initialize them. The main data member for the class is a structure we will use to keep track of a collection of **Person** objects. We will use an array, the only data structure we have learned so far for this purpose. We will create this array in the constructor. At the time we create an array, we must declare its size. Remember that the size of an array is the maximum number of elements this array can hold. The actual number of **Person** objects stored in the array will be anywhere from zero to the size of the array.

We have two possible alternatives for specifying the size of an array. First, we can let the programmer pass the size as an argument to the constructor. Second, we can set the size to a default value. Both alternatives are useful. If the programmer has a good estimate of the number of **Person** objects to manage, she can specify the size in the constructor. Otherwise, she can use the default size by not specifying the size in the constructor. We will define two constructors to support both alternatives. This will give programmers a flexibility in creating an **AddressBook** object.

If we are going to provide a constructor in which the programmer can pass the size of an array, then we need to write the constructor so it won't crash when an invalid value is passed as an argument. What would be an invalid argument value? Since we are dealing with a collection of objects, and the size of a collection cannot be negative, the argument value of less than zero is invalid. Also, even though a collection whose size is zero may make sense in theory, such a collection makes no sense in practice. Therefore, we will consider zero also as an invalid argument value. We will require an argument to a constructor to be a positive integer.

How should the constructor behave if the programmer passes an invalid argument value? The constructor does not have a return type, so we can't return a **boolean** value to report the status back (e.g., **true** for successful creation of an object, **false** otherwise). We want to define a constructor to be reliable so that an instance of the class is created and initialized to a consistent state. If there's a possibility that a constructor could fail (e.g., trying to create an array of negative size inside the constructor) and not create an instance, then we must add code to verify that an instance is indeed created every time the constructor is called. To guarantee that the constructor will create an instance, it will create an array of the default size when an invalid value is passed to it as an argument.

Increase the reliability of a class by defining a constructor that will not fail to create an instance and initialize an instance to a valid state.

Step 1 Code

At this point, we have only one data member—an array of objects. We will call it entry because a Person object is a single entry in an address book. We will set the default size of entry to 25. There is no particular reason for selecting this size. We simply picked a number that is not too small or too big. We can change this value later if we need to.

We will define two constructors. The first constructor will call the second constructor with the value 25 (default size) as its argument. The second constructor creates an array of Person objects of the size passed as its parameter. Inside the second constructor, we include a temporary test output statement. The class is defined as follows:

```
class AddressBook
{

/*************************
   Data Members
*************************/
    private static final int      DEFAULT_SIZE = 25;
    private Person[]              entry;

/*************************
   Constructors
*************************/

    public AddressBook( )
    {
        this( DEFAULT_SIZE );
    }

    public AddressBook( int size )
    {
        if (size <= 0 ) { //invalid data value, use default
            size = DEFAULT_SIZE;
        }
        entry = new Person[size];

        System.out.println("array of "+ size + " is created."); //TEMP
    }
}
```

<table>
<tr><td>Ms. Latte:</td><td>Why don't we print out an error message inside the second constructor if an invalid argument value is passed to it?</td></tr>
</table>

Ms. Latte:	Why don't we print out an error message inside the second constructor if an invalid argument value is passed to it?
Dr. Caffeine:	We don't do that because it's a bad design to include an input/output statement in a class like **AddressBook**.
Ms. Latte:	Why? There's already **System.out** used in the constructor.
Dr. Caffeine:	That **System.out** is there temporarily for testing purposes. If you include a permanent output statement such as printing of error messages, you will severely limit the usability of the class. For example, because the **AddressBook** class does not include input and output statements, you can use it in your applets or applications. You are free to use whatever input and output objects you prefer. This flexibility will be lost if the **AddressBook** does an input and output because using an **AddressBook** will dictate the use of input and output objects used in the class. Don't let a single object handle both the input/output operations and the logic of maintaining an array.
Ms. Latte:	That's the STO principle.
Dr. Caffeine:	Precisely. If there's an error, the **AddressBook** should report the status back to the programmer and let the programmer decide how to handle the error.

Dr. & Ms.

Step 1 Test

To test this class, we have included a temporary output statement inside the second constructor. We will write a test program to verify that we can create an AddressBook object correctly. The test data are as follows:

Step 1 Test Data	
Data Value	**Purpose**
Negative numbers	Test the invalid data.
0	Test the end case of invalid data.
1	Test the end case of valid data.
>= 1	Test the normal cases.

We will use a very simple test program:

```
class TestAddressBook
{
    public static void main ( String[] arg )
    {
        AddressBook myBook;

        myBook = new AddressBook( -10 ); //Error
        myBook = new AddressBook(   0 ); //Error
        myBook = new AddressBook(   4 );
    }
}
```

Run the program several times with a different set of test data and verify that you get the correct results.

Step 2 Development: Implement the add Method

Step 2 Design

In the second development step, we will implement the add method. We mentioned in the overall design step that this class will not do any input or output of person data. This decision is based on the STO principle. A single object doing both the input/output routines and maintaining the array will reduce its usability. For example, had the AddressBook class used InputBox and OutputBox to handle the input and output of person data, the use of this class would dictate or impose the style of input and output routines on the programmers. The programmer will not have an option of using the input and output objects appropriate for his or her uses.

Following the STO principle, we will let the programmer decide how she will input and output person data. The task of the add method is to accept a Person object as its parameter and add the passed Person object to the array. Since the array is limited in size, what should we do if there is no more space to add another Person object? There are two alternatives. The first alternative is to return false if a new Person object cannot be added to the array; that is, the array is full. The method will return true otherwise. The second alternative is to increase the array size. Since the size of an array object cannot be changed once the object is created, we need to create another array with a larger size than the original if we choose to implement the second alternative.

Alternative 1
Design

Alternative 2
Design

Since the second alternative is more accommodating and less restrictive to the programmer, we will implement this alternative. When the array is full, we will create a new array, copy the objects from the original array to this new array, and finally set the variable entry to point to this new array. We will set the size of the new array to one and a half times larger than the original array. This size increment is just an estimate. Any value between 125 and 200 percent of the old array is reasonable. You don't want to make it too small, say, 105 percent, since that will cause the enlarge method to be called too frequently. You don't want to make it too large either, since that will likely result in wasted space. Figure 9.15 illustrates the process of creating a larger array.

FIGURE 9.15   How a new array that is 150 percent larger than the original array is created. The size of the original array is 4.

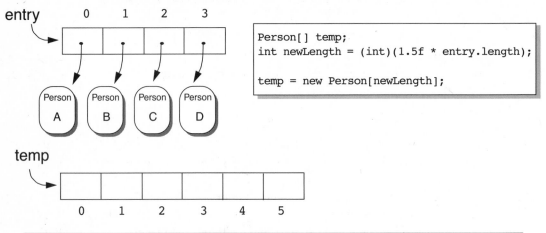

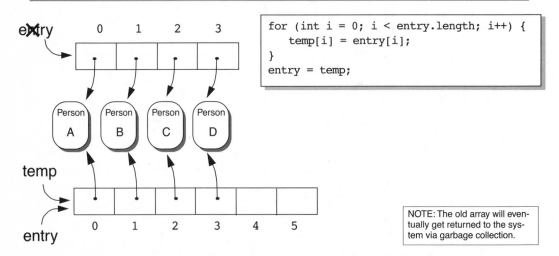

Now let's think about how to add a **Person** object to the array. To add a new object, we need to locate a position at which to insert the object. Since we are not maintaining **Person** objects in any particular order, we will add a new person at the first available position. If we fill the positions from the low to high indices (0, 1, 2, ...), we can use a variable to remember the index of the next available position. Since we are using an array, the index of the next available position is also the number of Person objects currently in the array, so we will call this variable count. Figure 9.16 illustrates the add operation.

FIGURE 9.16   Adding a new **Person** object to the next available location. The array length is 4.

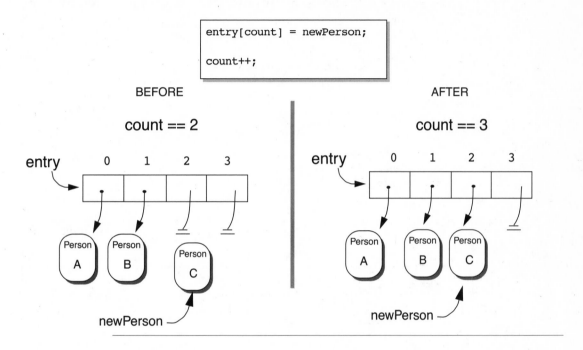

Step 2 Code

First we add a new instance variable count to the class:

```
/*************************
    Data Members
*************************/

private int        count; //number of elements in the array,
                          //it is also a position to add the
                          //next Person object
```

We modify the constructor to initialize this data member:

```
public AddressBook( int size )
{
    count = 0;

    //same as before
}
```

(Note: Because we defined the first constructor to call the second constructor, we can implement this change by rewriting only one constructor instead of two.) The add method is defined as

```
public void add( Person newPerson )
{
    if (count == entry.length) {      //no more space left,
        enlarge( );                   //create a new larger array
    }

    //at this point, entry refers to a new larger array
    entry[count] = newPerson;
    count++;
}
```

The enlarge method is a new private method that creates a new, larger array.

Design Document: The AddressBook Class		
Method	**Visibility**	**Purpose**
. . .	. . .	. . .
enlarge	private	Creates a new array that is 150 percent larger than the old array.

```
private void enlarge( )
{
    //create a new array whose size is 150% larger
    //than the current array
    int newLength = (int) (1.5f * entry.length);
    Person[] temp = new Person[newLength];

    //now copy the data to the new array
    for (int i = 0; i < entry.length; i++) {
        temp[i] = entry[i];
    }
```

```
        //finally set the variable entry to point to the new array
        entry = temp;

        System.out.println("Inside the method enlarge"); //TEMP
        System.out.println("Size of a new array: "
                                        + entry.length); //TEMP
    }
```

Step 2 Test   We will write a test program to verify that a new **Person** object is added to the array correctly. In addition, we need to test that a new array 150 percent larger than the old one is created when there are no more spaces left in the array. The test data are as follows:

Step 2 Test Data	
Test Sequence	**Purpose**
Create the array of size 4	Test that the array is created correctly.
Add four Person objects	Test that the **Person** objects are added correctly.
Add the fifth Person object	Test that the new array is created and the **Person** object is added correctly (to the new array).

The Step 2 test program is as follows:

```
class TestAddressBook
{
    public static void main ( String[] arg )
    {
        AddressBook    myBook;
        Person         person;

        myBook = new AddressBook( 4 );

        //add four Person objects
        for (int i = 0; i < 4; i++) {
            person = new Person("Ms. X"+i, 10, 'F');
            myBook.add( person );
        }

        //add the fifth person and see if a new array is created
        person = new Person("fifth one", 10, 'F');
        myBook.add( person );
    }
}
```

Run the program several times with different sizes for the address book and verify that you get the correct results.

Step 3 Development: Implement the search **Method**

Step 3 Design

In the third development step, we implement the search method. The method can return one or more Person objects that meet the search criteria. We have several options for the search criteria. Since we keep track of name, age, and gender for each person, we can use any one of them as the search criterion. In this implementation, we will use the person's name. The search routine for the other two criteria will be left as an exercise.

To implement the search method, we will make an assumption that the name is unique so that there will be at most one matching Person object. If the name is not unique, then there are two possibilities. The search method can return one Person object (among many) that matches the given name or return all Person objects that match the given name. We will leave the case when the name is not unique as an exercise. Notice that the add method we implemented in Step 2 does not check the person data. In other words, there is no mechanism to disallow the addition of a Person object with a duplicate name. We will leave the implementation of the modified add method as an exercise also.

There are two possible outcomes with the search method—a successful and an unsuccessful search. The method has to return a value by which the programmer can use to verify the result of the search. We will define the search method so that it will return a matching Person object if it is found and null otherwise. The search routine will start scanning the array from the first position until the desired Person object is found (successful search) or no more Person objects are left in the array (unsuccessful search). Expressing the search routine in pseudocode, we have

```
set loc to 0;

while ( loc < count &&
        name of Person at entry[loc] != searchName ) {
    loc++;
}

if (loc == count) {
    foundPerson = null;
}
else {
    foundPerson = entry[loc];
}
return foundPerson;
```

Step 3 Code

Translating the pseudocode into an actual code will result in the following method:

```
public Person search( String searchName )
{
    Person foundPerson;
    int    loc = 0;

    while ( loc < count &&
            !searchName.equals( entry[loc].getName() ) ) {
        loc++;
    }

    if (loc == count) {
        foundPerson = null;
    }
    else {
        foundPerson = entry[loc];
    }

    return foundPerson;
}
```

Step 3 Test

To test the search method, we will build an address book that contains five Person objects. We will give names Ms. X0, Ms. X1, . . . , and Ms. X4 to them. After the address book is set up, we test various cases of the search. We test for successful and unsuccessful searches. For the successful searches, we test for the end cases and normal cases. The end cases involve searching for persons stored at the first and last positions of the array. Off-by-one error (OBOE) is very common in processing an array, so it is very important to test these end cases.

After a successful execution, we will test the class again by changing the size of the array. One test size we should not forget to test is the end case for the array size, which is one. Also, we need to test the cases where the array is not fully filled, such as an array of size 5 containing only two Person objects.

The test data are as follows:

Step 3 Test Data	
Test Sequence	**Purpose**
Create the array of size 5 and add five **Person** objects with unique names.	Test that the array is created and set up correctly. Here, we will test the case where the array is 100 percent filled.
Search for the person in the first position of the array	Test that the successful search works correctly for the end case.
Search for the person in the last position of the array	Test another version of the end case.
Search for a person somewhere in the middle of the array.	Test the normal case.
Search for a person not in the array.	Test for the unsuccessful search.
Repeat the above steps with an array of varying sizes, especially the array of size 1.	Test that the routine works correctly for arrays of different sizes.
Repeat the testing with the cases where the array is not fully filled, say, array length is 5 and the number of objects in the array is 0 or 3.	Test that the routine works correctly for other cases.

The Step 3 test program is written as follows:

```
class Tester
{
    public static void main ( String[] arg )
    {
        TestAddressBook tester = new TestAddressBook();
        tester.setupArray( 5 );
        tester.testSearch();
    }
}

class TestAddressBook
{
    AddressBook    myBook;
    Person         person;

    private void setupArray( int N )
    {
        myBook = new AddressBook( N );
```

```
                //add N Person objects
                for (int i = 0; i < N; i++) {
                    person = new Person("Ms. X"+i, 10, 'F');
                    myBook.add( person );
                }
            }

        private void testSearch( )
        {
            //test for the end case
            person = myBook.search("Ms. X0");

            if ( person == null ) {
                System.out.println
                    ("Error: Didn't find the person it should");
            }
            else {
                System.out.println
                    (person.getName() + " is found okay.");
            }
        }
    }
```

Notice the TestAddressBook class is now an instantiable class. Since the code for testing is getting longer, it is not practical any more to do everything in a single main method. For testing, we will modify the method body of setupArray and testSearch as necessary to test all other cases described in the test data table.

Step 4 Development: Implement the delete Method

In the fourth development step, we implement the delete method. To delete a Person object, the programmer must somehow specify which Person object to remove from the address book. Similar to the search method, we will use the name of a person to specify which person to delete. Since we assume the name is unique, the delete method will remove at most one Person object. There are two possible outcomes: the specified person is removed from the address book (successful operation) and the specified person is not removed because he/she is not in the address book (unsuccessful operation). We will define the delete method so that it will return true if the operation is successful and false otherwise.

The removal of an element in an array of objects is done by setting the element to null. This will leave a "hole." We will fill this hole by replacing the removed element with the last element, as explained earlier (see Figure 9.8). This filling operation is necessary for other methods, specifically the add method, to work correctly.

To fill the hole, we need to know the location of the hole. To find this location, we write a private search method called findIndex. The method is very similar to the search method. The only difference is that the return value of findIndex is an index of an element in the array, whereas the return value of search is a Person object. Using this findIndex method, the delete method can be expressed as

```
boolean status;
int     loc;

loc = findIndex( searchName );

if ( loc is not valid) {
    status = false;
}
else { //found, pack the hole
    replace the element at index loc+1 by the last element
    at index count;

    status = true;

    count--;   //decrement count,
               //since we now have one less element
}
return status;
```

Step 4 Code   The private findIndex method will look like this:

```
private int findIndex( String searchName )
{
    int loc = 0;

    while ( loc < count &&
            !searchName.equals( entry[loc].getName() ) ) {
        loc++;
    }

    if (loc == count) {
        loc = NOT_FOUND;
    }
```

```
        return loc;
    }
```

The constant **NOT_FOUND** is set in the data member section as

```
/*************************
    Data Members
*************************/

private static final int     NOT_FOUND = -1;
```

Using this **findIndex** method the **delete** method is defined as

```
public boolean delete( String searchName )
{
    boolean     status;
    int         loc;

    loc = findIndex( searchName );

    if (loc == NOT_FOUND) {
        status = false;
    }
    else { //found, pack the hole

        entry[loc] = entry[count-1];

        status = true;
        count--;       //decrement count,
                       //since we now have one less element
    }
    return status;
}
```

Step 4 Test   To test the **delete** method, we will build an address book that contains five **Person** objects as before. Test cases are: delete the first person in the array, delete the last person in the array, delete someone in the middle (normal case), try to delete a nonexisting person.

After a successful execution, we will test the class again by changing the size of an array. One test size we should not forget to test is the end case for the array size, which is one. Also, we need to test the cases where the array is not fully filled, such as an array of size 5 containing only two **Person** objects.

The test data are as follows:

Step 4 Test Data	
Test Sequence	**Purpose**
Create the array of size 5 and add five **Person** objects with unique names.	Test the array is created and set up correctly. Here, we will test the case where the array is 100 percent filled.
Search for a person to be deleted next.	Verify that the person is in the array before deletion.
Delete the person in the array	Test the **delete** method works correctly.
Search for the deleted person.	Test the **delete** method works correctly by checking the value **null** is returned from the search.
Attempt to delete a nonexisting person.	Test that the unsuccessful operation works correctly.
Repeat the above steps by deleting persons at the first and last positions.	Test that the routine works correctly for arrays of different sizes.
Repeat the testing with the cases where the array is not fully filled, say, array length is 5 and the number of objects in the array is 0 or 3.	Test that the routine works correctly for other cases.

The Step 4 test program is written as follows:

```
class Tester
{
    public static void main ( String[] arg )
    {
        TestAddressBook tester = new TestAddressBook();
        tester.setupArray( 5 );
        tester.testDelete();
    }
}

class TestAddressBook
{
    AddressBook     myBook;
    Person          person;

    private void setupArray( int N )
    {
        myBook = new AddressBook( N );
```

```
                //add N Person objects
                for (int i = 0; i < N; i++) {
                    person = new Person("Ms. X"+i, 10, 'F');
                    myBook.add( person );
                }
        }



        private static void testDelete( )
        {
            //first make sure the person is in the array
            person = myBook.search("Ms. X2");

            if ( person == null ) {
                System.out.println
                        ("Error: Didn't find the person it should");
            }
            else {
                System.out.println
                        (person.getName() + " is found okay.");

                boolean success = myBook.delete("Ms. X2");

                if ( success ) {
                    person = myBook.search("Ms. X2");

                    if (person == null) {
                        System.out.println("Okay: Deletion works");
                    }
                    else {
                        System.out.println
                                ("Error: Person is still there");
                    }
                }
                else {
                        System.out.println
                                ("Error: Deletion has a problem");
                }
            }
        }
```

Modify the method body of **setupArray** and **testDelete** as necessary to test all other cases described in the Step 4 test data table.

Step 5 Development: Finalize

program
review

As always, we finalize the program in the last step. We perform a critical review to find any inconsistency or error in the methods, incomplete methods, places to add more comments, and so forth.

final test

Since the three operations of add, delete, and search are interrelated, it is critical to test these operations together. The test program should try out various combinations of add, delete, and search operations to verify that they work together correctly.

After we complete the class implementation and testing, we may consider improvement or extension. In addition to the several alternative designs, it is possible to add other operations. For example, we may want to add an operation to modify a Person object. Another common operation that is useful in manipu-

scanning

lating a collection of objects is scanning. *Scanning* is an operation to visit all elements in the collection. Scanning is useful in listing all Person objects in the address book. These extended operations are left as an exercise.

9.7   Two-Dimensional Arrays

A table organized in rows and columns is a very effective means for communicating many different types of information. Figure 9.17 shows sample data dis-

two-dimensional
array

played in a tabular format. In Java, we represent tables as *two-dimensional arrays*. The arrays we have discussed so far are *one-dimensional arrays* because they have only one index. In this section, we describe how two-dimensional arrays are used in Java.

Let's begin with an example. Consider the following table with four rows and five columns. The table contains the hourly rate of programmers based on their skill level. The rows represent the grade levels and the columns represent the steps within a grade level. Reading the table, we know a programmer with skill grade level 2, step 1 earns $36.50 an hour.

Step

	0	1	2	3	4
0	10.50	12.00	14.50	16.75	18.00
1	20.50	22.25	24.00	26.25	28.00
2	34.00	36.50	38.00	40.35	43.00
3	50.00	60.00	70.00	80.00	99.99

Grade

FIGURE 9.17   Examples of information represented as tables.

Distance Table (in miles)

	Los Angeles	San Francisco	San Jose	San Diego	Monterey
Los Angeles	—	600	500	150	450
San Francisco	600	—	100	750	150
San Jose	500	100	—	650	50
San Diego	150	750	650	—	600
Monterey	450	150	50	600	—

Multiplication Table

	1	2	3	4	5	6	7	8	9
1	1	2	3	4	5	6	7	8	9
2	2	4	6	8	10	12	14	16	18
3	3	6	9	12	15	18	21	24	27
4	4	8	12	16	20	24	28	32	36
5	5	10	15	20	25	30	35	40	45
6	6	12	18	24	30	36	42	48	54
7	7	14	21	28	35	42	49	56	63
8	8	16	24	32	40	48	56	64	72
9	9	18	27	36	45	54	63	72	81

Tuition Table

	Day Students	Boarding Students
Grades 1 – 6	$ 6,000.00	$ 18,000.00
Grades 7 – 8	$ 9,000.00	$ 21,000.00
Grades 9 – 12	$ 12,500.00	$ 24,500.00

We declare the pay scale table as

```
float[][] payScaleTable;
```

or

```
float payScaleTable[][];
```

and create the array as

```
payScaleTable = new float[4][5];
```

The payScaleTable array is a *two-dimensional array* because two indices—one for the row and another for the column—are used to refer to an array element. For example, to refer to the element at the second column (column #1) of the third row (row #2), we say

```
payScaleTable[2][1]
```

Figure 9.18 illustrates how the two indices are used to access an array element of a two-dimensional array.

Let's go over some examples to see how the elements of two-dimensional arrays are manipulated. The code below finds the average pay of the Grade 2 programmers.

```
float average, sum = 0;

for (int j = 0; j < 5; j++) {
    sum += payScaleTable[2][j];
}
average = sum / 5;
```

The next example prints out the pay difference between the lowest and highest steps for each grade level.

```
float difference;

for (int i = 0; i < 4; i++) {
```

FIGURE 9.18   Accessing an element of a two-dimensional array.

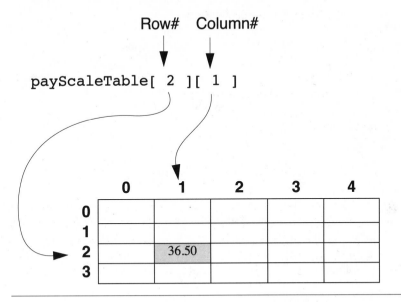

```
difference = payScaleTable[i][4] - payScaleTable[i][0];
outputBox.printLine("Pay difference at Grade Level " +
                    i + " is " + difference);
}
```

The following code adds $1.50 to every skill level.

```
for (int i = 0; i < 4; i++) {
    for (int j = 0; j < 5; j++) {
        payScaleTable[i][j] += 1.50f;
    }
}
```

In the previous examples, we used literal constants such as 5 and 4 to keep them simple. For real programs, we need to write a loop that will work for two-dimensional arrays of any size, not just with the one with four rows and five columns. We can use the length field of an array to write such a loop. Using the length field, we can rewrite the third example as

```
for (int i = 0; i < payScaleTable.length; i++) {
```

```
        for (int j = 0; j < payScaleTable[i].length; j++) {
            payScaleTable[i][j] += 1.50;
        }
    }
```

Do you notice a subtle difference in the code? Let's examine the difference between the expressions

```
    payScaleTable.length
```

and

```
    payScaleTable[i].length
```

First, there is actually no explicit structure called "two-dimensional array" in Java. We only have one-dimensional arrays in Java. However, we can have an array of arrays, and this is how the conceptual two-dimensional array is implemented in Java. The sample array creation

```
    payScaleTable = new float[4][5];
```

is really a shorthand for

```
    payScaleTable = new float[4][ ];

    payScaleTable[0] = new float[5];
    payScaleTable[1] = new float[5];
    payScaleTable[2] = new float[5];
    payScaleTable[3] = new float[5];
```

which is equivalent to

```
    payScaleTable = new float[4][ ];

    for (int i = 0; i < 4; i++) {
        payScaleTable[i] = new float[5];
    }
```

Figure 9.19 shows the effect of executing the five statements. The expression

FIGURE 9.19   Executing the statements on the left in sequence will create the array of arrays shown on the right.

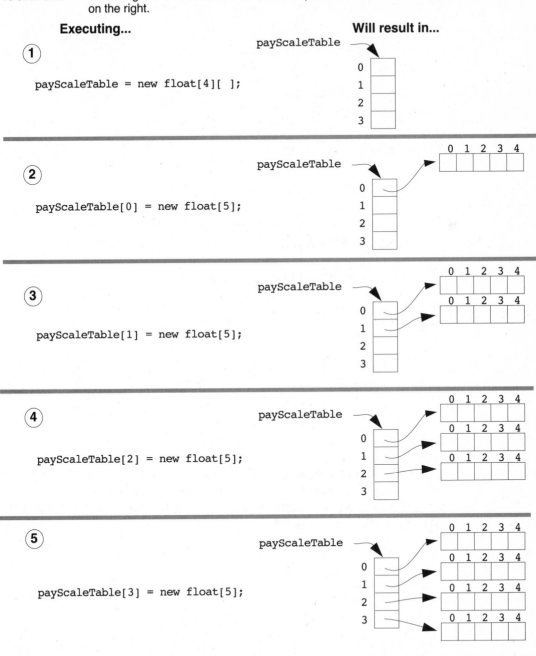

```
payScaleTable.length
```

refers to the length of the payScaleTable array itself

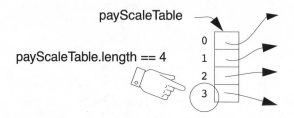

and the expression

```
payScaleTable[1].length
```

refers to the length of an array stored at row 1 of payScaleTable.

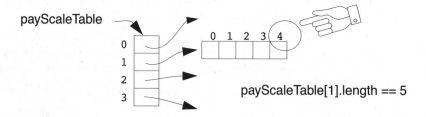

We call an array that is part of another a *subarray*. The payScaleTable has four subarrays of the same length. Since we allocate the subarrays individually, we can create subarrays of different length. The following code creates a triangular array whose subarray triangularArray[i] has length i.

```
triangularArray = new float[4][ ];

for (int i = 0; i < 4; i++)
    payScaleTable[i] = new float[i+1];
```

The resulting triangularArray looks like

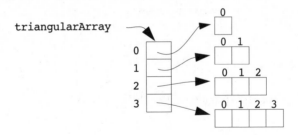

An array of arrays can be initialized at the time of declaration. The following declaration initializes the payScaleTable array:

```
float[][] payScaleTable
        = {  {10.50f, 12.00f, 14.50f, 16.75f, 18.00f},
             {20.50f, 22.25f, 24.00f, 26.25f, 28.00f},
             {34.00f, 36.50f, 38.00f, 40.35f, 43.00f},
             {50.00f, 60.00f, 70.00f, 80.00f, 99.99f}  };
```

There is no limit to the number of dimensions an array can have. We can declare three-dimensional, four-dimensional, and higher-dimensional arrays. However, arrays with dimension higher than two are not frequently used in object-oriented languages. For example, data that was represented as a three-dimensional array in a non-object-oriented language can be represented more naturally as a one-dimensional array of objects with each object containing an array or some other form of data structure (see exercise 12 on page 490).

Quick Check

1. Write a code fragment to compute the average pay of the pays stored in the payScaleTable array.

2. Write a code fragment that finds the largest integer in the following two-dimensional array.

    ```
    int[][] table = new int[10][10];
    ```

3. What is an output from the following code.

```
int[][] table = new int[10][5];

outputBox.printLine(table.length);
outputBox.printLine(table[4].length);
```

9.8   Exercises

1. Identify problems with the following code:

```
public int searchAccount( int[25] number )
{
    number = new int[15];

    for (int i = 0; i < number.length; i++)
        number[i] = number[i-1] + number[i+1];

    return number;
}
```

2. Identify problems with the following code:

```
class Q2
{
    private int alpha;
    private int beta;

    public static void classMethod()
    {
        this.beta = this.alpha * 2;
    }

    public Q2( )
    {
        Q2( 0, 0 );
    }

    public Q2( int x, int y )
    {
        alpha = this.x;
        beta = this.y;
    }
}
```

3. Declare an array of float of size 365 to store daily temperatures for one year. Using this data structure, write the code to find
   - The hottest and coldest days of the year.
   - The average temperature of each month.
   - The difference between the hottest and coldest days of every month.
   - The temperature of any given day. The day is specified by two input values: month (1 ... 12) and day (1 ... 31). Reject invalid input values (e.g., 13 for month and 32 for day).

4. Repeat exercise 3 using a two-dimensional array of float with 12 rows and each row having either 28, 30, or 31 columns.

5. Repeat exercise 3 using an array of Month objects with each Month object having an array of float of size 28, 30, or 31.

6. For exercises 3 to 5, the following three data structures are used:
   - 1-D array of float of size 365.
   - 2-D array of float with 12 rows. Each row has either 28, 30, or 31 columns.
   - An array of Month objects with each Month object having an array of float of size 28, 30, or 31.

   Discuss the pros and cons of each approach.

7. Suppose you want to maintain the highest and lowest temperatures for every day of the year. What kind of data structure would you use? Describe the alternatives and list their pros and cons.

8. In Figure 9.8 on page 444, the second statement

   ```
   person[last+1] = null;
   ```

   is significant. Show the state-of-memory diagram when the second statement is not executed.

9. Write an application that computes the standard deviation of N real numbers. The standard deviation s is computed according to the following formula:

$$s = \sqrt{\frac{(x_1 - \bar{x})^2 + (x_2 - \bar{x})^2 + \dots + (x_N - \bar{x})^2}{N}}$$

The variable $\bar{x}$ is the average of N input values x_1 through x_N. The program first prompts the user for N and then declares any array of size N.

10. Using the payScaleTable 2-D array from Section 9.5, write the code to find
    - the average pay for every grade level
    - the average pay for every step (i.e., average of every column)

11. Declare a 2-D array for the tuition table shown in Figure 9.17.

12. Suppose you want to maintain information on the location where a product is stored in a warehouse. Would you use a three-dimensional array such as location[i][j][k] where i is the warehouse number, j is the aisle number, and k is the bin number? Or would you define three classes Warehouse, Aisle, and Bin? Describe the alternatives and list their pros and cons.

13. The search method of the AddressBook class returns only one Person object. Modify the method so that it will return all Person objects that match the search criteria. You can use an array to return multiple Person objects.

14. Write new search routines for the AddressBook class. The search method given in the chapter finds a person with a given name. Add second and third search methods that find all persons given an age and a gender, respectively.

15. Modify the add method of the AddressBook class. The method given in the chapter does not check for any duplicate names. Modify the method so that no Person object with a duplicate name is added to the address book.

16. Modify the AddressBook class to allow the programmer to access all Person objects in the address book. Make this modification by adding two methods: getFirstPerson and getNextPerson. The getFirstPerson method returns the first Person object in the book. The getNextPerson method returns the next Person object if there is one. If there is no next person in the book, getNextPerson returns null. The getFirstPerson method must be called before calling the getNextPerson method.

17. Write a complete address book maintenance application. The user of the program has four options: add a new person, delete a person, modify the data of a person, and search for a person by giving the name. Use the AddressBook class, either the original one from the chapter or the modified one from the previous exercises. You have to decide how to allow the user to enter the values for a new person, display person information, and so forth.

18. Design a currency converter class whose instance will handle conversion of all currencies. In Chapter 4 we designed a currency converter class where we created one instance for each currency. A single instance of the new currency converter class you design here will handle all currencies. Instead of having specific conversion methods such as toDollar, toYen, and so forth, the new currency converter class supports one generic conversion method called exchange. The method has three arguments: fromCurrency, toCurrency, and amount. The first two arguments are String and give the names of currencies. The third argument is float. To convert 250 dollars to yen, we write

```
yen = converter.exchange( "dollar", "yen", 250.0f );
```

To set the exchange rate for a currency, we use the setRate method. This method takes two arguments: the first argument is the currency name and the second argument is the rate. For example, if the exchange rate for yen is 140 yen to a dollar, then we write

```
converter.setRate( "yen", 140.0f );
```

Use an array to keep track of exhange rates.

19. Extend the Java[2] Lo-Fat Burgers drive-through ordering system of exercise 16 on page 293 so the program can output sales figures. For each item on the menu, the program keeps track of the sales. At closing time, the program will output the sales figure in a format similar to the following:

```
   Item          Sales Count          Total
Tofu Burger         25             $   87.25
Cajun Chicken       30             $  137.70
  ...


   Today's Total Sales:   $ 2761.20
```

20. Extend the watermelon projectile computing program of exercise 22 on page 360 to output the average distance covered between each time interval. Use the formula

$$\sqrt{(x_2 - x_1)^2 + (y_2 - y_1)^2}$$

to compute the distance between two coordinate points (x_1, y_1) and (x_2, y_2).

10

File Input and Output

OBJECTIVES

After you have read and studied this chapter, you should be able to

- Include a FileDialog object in your program to let the user specify a file.

- Write bytes to a file and read them back from the file using FileOutputStream and FileInputStream.

- Write values of primitive data types to a file and read them back from the file using DataOutputStream and DataInputStream.

- Write text data to a file and read them back from the file using PrintWriter and BufferedReader.

- Write objects to a file and read them back from the file using ObjectOutputStream and ObjectInputStream.

- Write exception-handling routines using the try–catch block.

Introduction

Suppose we write a program that maintains an array of Person objects. The user can add to, delete from, or modify Person objects in the array. To make this program practical, we must save the data to a file. If we don't, then the user must re-enter the same data every time he or she runs the program because any data used by the program will be erased from the main memory at program termination. If the data were saved, then the program can read them back from the file and rebuild the array so the user can work on the data without reentering them. In this chapter you will learn how to save data to and read data from a file. We call the action of saving data to a file *file output* and the action of reading data from a file *file input*. We will introduce several classes from the java.io package for performing file input and output. We used the techniques described in this chapter to implement the saveToFile and appendToFile methods of the OutputBox class.

file output and input

10.1   File and FileDialog **Objects**

In this section we introduce two key objects for reading data from or writing data to a file. We use the term "file access" to refer to both read and write operations. If we need to be precise, we write "read access" or "write access." Let's study the read access first. Suppose we want to read the contents of a file sample.data. Before we begin the actual operation of reading data from this file, we must first create a File object (from the java.io package) and associate it to the file. We do so by calling a File constructor:

File

```
File inFile = new File("sample.data");
```

The argument to the constructor designates the name of the file to access. The system assumes the file is located in the *current directory*. For the following examples, we assume the directory structure shown in Figure 10.1, with Ch10 being the current directory. When you run a program whose source file is located in directory X, then the current directory is X. Please refer to your Java compiler manuals for other options for designating the current directory.

current directory

It is also possible to open a file that is stored in a directory other than the current directory by providing a path name and a file name. Assuming there's a file xyz.data in the Projects directory, we can open it by executing

```
File inFile = new File("C:\\Cafe\\Projects", "xyz.data");
```

FIGURE 10.1   Directory structure used for the examples in this section. We assume the Windows 95 environment.

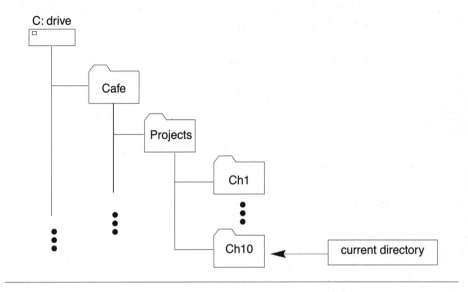

This style of designating the path name is for the Windows platform. For the UNIX platform, we use the slash for a delimiter, for example,

```
"/Cafe/Projects"
```

For the Mac platform, we use a colon. If the name of a hard disk is MacHD, then we write

```
"MacHD::Cafe:Projects"
```

We use two colons right after the hard disk name. We will assume the Windows platform for all of the examples in this chapter.

The actual path name specified by the string "C:\\Cafe\\Projects" is

```
C:\Cafe\Projects
```

because the backslash is the delimiter used in the Windows platform. However, the backslash symbol has a special purpose when used inside the double quotes.

The backslash is called an *escape character*. It is used to specify a nonprintable, control character. For example, we indicate a control character for a new line (ASCII code 10) as '\n' and a control character for a tab (ASCII code 9) as '\t'. Using a new line control character, we can express the statement such as

```
outputBox.printLine("Hello");
```

as

```
outputBox.print("Hello\n");
```

Since the backslash symbol has this special purpose, if we designate the string as

```
"C:\Cafe\Projects"
```

then the compiler will try to interpret C and P as a control character. So, to include the backslash character itself in the string, we use double slashes.

Now let's get back to the path name discussion. The path name could be absolute or relative to the current directory. The absolute path name is the full path name beginning with the disk drive name, for example,

```
"C:\\Cafe\\Projects\\Ch10"
```

The relative path name is relative to the current directory. For example, if the current directory is Ch10, then the relative path name

```
"..\\Ch1"
```

is equivalent to the full path name

```
"C:\\Cafe\\Projects\\Ch1"
```

where the two dots (..) in the string means "one directory above."

If you try to associate a File object to a nonexistent file, the File object is set to null. When the association is established, we say *the file is opened*; a file must be opened before doing any input and output to the file.

A file must be opened before performing any file access operation.

A File object also can be associated to a directory. For example, suppose we are interested in listing the content of directory Ch10. We can first create a File object and associate it to the directory. After the association is made, we can list the contents of the directory by calling the object's list method:

```
File   directory = new File("c:\\Cafe\\Projects\\Ch10");
String filename[] = directory.list();

for (int i = 0; i < filename.length; i++) {
    outputBox.printLine(filename[i]);
}
```

We check whether a File object is associated to a file or a directory by calling its boolean method isFile. The following code will print out I am a directory:

```
File file = new File("c:\\Cafe\\Projects\\Ch10");

if (file.isFile()) {
    outputBox.printLine("I am a file");
}
else {
    outputBox.printLine("I am a directory);
}
```

FileDialog   We can use a FileDialog object from the java.awt package to let the user select a file or a directory. The object has two modes: LOAD and SAVE. You open the object in the LOAD mode if you want to read data from the selected file and in the SAVE mode if you want to write data to the selected file. When the statement

```
FileDialog fileBox = new FileDialog(mainWindow, FileDialog.LOAD);
```

is executed, a FileDialog shown in Figure 10.2 appears on the screen.

The user can browse (navigate) the directories and select the desired file by clicking on the filename in the list or typing in the filename in the File name: text field. To retrieve the name of the file the user has selected, we execute the getFile method. The statement

FIGURE 10.2   A **FileDialog** object appearing on the screen in the **LOAD** mode.

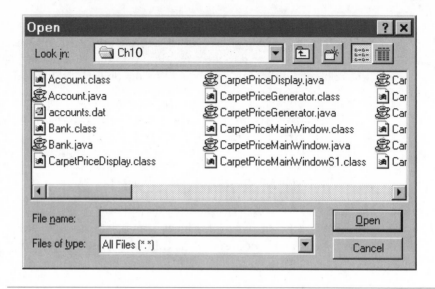

```
String filename = fileBox.getFile();
```

assigns the name of the selected file to filename. If the Cancel button of FileDialog is clicked, then the getFile method returns null. Also, if the Open button is clicked without any file being selected, then null is returned.

We can also get the path name to the directory where the selected file is located. Executing the statement

```
String directoryPath = fileBox.getDirectory();
```

will assign the path name C:\Cafe\Projects\Ch10\ to directoryPath.

To select a file for saving data, we open the FileDialog in the SAVE mode:

```
FileDialog fileBox = new FileBox(mainWindow, FileDialog.SAVE);
```

The resulting dialog is shown in Figure 10.3.

FIGURE 10.3   A **FileBox** object opened in the **SAVE** mode.

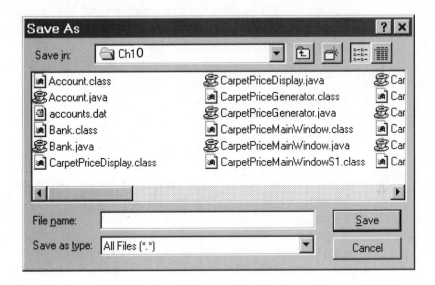

Notice that the button is now labeled Save instead of Open. When the user selects an existing file in the SAVE mode FileDialog, a warning message is displayed, as shown in Figure 10.4. This reduces the chance the user will erroneously overwrite any existing file. If the No button is clicked in the warning message box, then the FileDialog remains on the screen.

FIGURE 10.4   A message dialog warning of a file overwrite.

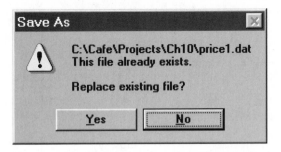

10.2 Low-Level File I/O

stream

source

destination

Once a file is opened by properly associating a File object to it, the actual file access can commence. In this section, we will introduce basic objects for file operations. In order to actually read data from or write data to a file, we must create one of the Java stream objects and attach it to the file. A *stream* is simply a sequence of data items, usually eight-bit bytes. Java has two types of streams: an input stream and an output stream. An input stream has a *source* from where the data items come, and an output stream has a *destination* to where the data items are going. To read data items from a file, we attach one of the Java input stream objects to the file. Similarly, to write data items to a file, we attach one of the Java output stream objects to the file.

Java comes with a large number of stream objects for file access operations. We will cover only those that are straightforward and easy to learn for beginners. We will study two of them in this section—FileOutputStream and FileInputStream. These two objects provide low-level file access operations. In the next section, we will study other stream objects.

FileOutput-
Stream

Let's first study how to write data values to a file using FileOutputStream. Using a FileOutputStream object, we can output only a sequence of bytes, that is, values of data type byte. In this example, we will output an array of bytes to a file named sample1.data. First, we create a File object:

```
File outFile = new File("sample1.data");
```

Then, we associate outFile to a new FileOutputStream object:

```
FileOutputStream outStream = new FileOutputStream(outFile);
```

Now we are ready for output. Consider the following byte array:

```
byte[] byteArray = {10, 20, 30, 40, 50, 60, 70, 80};
```

We write the whole byte array at once to the file by executing

```
outStream.write(byteArray);
```

Notice that we are not dealing with the File object directly, but with outStream. It is also possible to write array elements individually, for example,

```
//output the first and fifth bytes
outStream.write(byteArray[0]);
outStream.write(byteArray[4]);
```

After the values are written to the file, we must close the stream:

```
outStream.close();
```

If the stream object is not closed, then some data may get lost due to data caching. Because of the physical characteristics of secondary memory such as hard disks, the actual process of saving data to a file is a very time-consuming operation, whether you are saving one byte or 100 bytes. So instead of saving bytes individually, we save them in a block of, say, 500 bytes to reduce the overall time it takes to save the whole data. The operation of saving data as a block is called *data caching*. To carry out data caching, a part of memory is reserved as a *data buffer* or *cache,* which is used as a temporary holding place. A typical size for a data buffer is anywhere from 1K to 2K. Data are first witten to a buffer, and when the buffer becomes full, the data in the buffer are actually written to a file. If there are any remaining data in the buffer and the file is not closed, then those data will be lost. Therefore, to avoid losing any data, it is important to close the file at the end of operations.

data caching
and buffer

To ensure that all data are saved to a file, close the file at the end of file access operations.

Here's the complete program:

```
/*
    Program TestFileOutputStream

    A test program to save data to a file using FileOutputStream
*/

import java.io.*;

class TestFileOutputStream
{
    public static void main (String arg[]) throws IOException
    {
```

```
       //set up file and stream
       File             outFile    = new File("sample1.data");
       FileOutputStream  outStream = new FileOutputStream(outFile);

       //data to output
       byte[] byteArray = {10, 20, 30, 40, 50, 60, 70, 80};

       //write data to the stream
       outStream.write(byteArray);

       //output done, so close the stream
       outStream.close();
    }
}
```

Dr. & Mr.

Mr. Espresso: I don't understand why you have to create both **File** and **FileInput-Stream** objects. Why not just use one object?

Dr. Caffeine: **File** represents the physical file. **Stream** objects represent the mechanism. **Stream** objects can be associated to a serial port.

Notice the last two words in the method declaration

```
public static void main (String[] arg) throws IOException
```

exception

They indicate the method may possibly throw an I/O exception. An *exception* is an error condition that violates the semantic rules of Java programs. For example, when you try to read data from a nonexisting file or attempt to read beyond the end of the file, an I/O exception will be thrown. An I/O exception is only one of the many different types of Java exceptions. If an exception occurs while executing a method, we say that *the method raises or throws an exception*. Not all methods will throw an exception; we call those that do *exception-throwing methods*.

When we use an exception-throwing method in our program, we can do one of two things. One is to *catch* a thrown exception and provide exception-handling code to process the thrown exception. We will describe how to do this in Section 10.4. Another, which we will use here, is to propagate a thrown exception to the caller of the method. To propagate an exception, we append the words **throws IOException** (or whatever the type of the thrown exception) to the method declaration as illustrated below:

```
public static void main (String args[]) ) throws IOException
{
  ... = new FileOutputStream(outFile);
  ...
  outStream.write(byteArray);
  ...
  outStream.close();
}
```

> These statements all throw an **IOException**, and therefore, we add **throws IOException** to the method we define.

When an IOException is thrown by the method close, for example, then the method main propagates this thrown exception to its caller. The method that called our main method can either handle the exception or propagate it further. If a thrown exception is not handled by any method in the propagation chain, the Java interpreter will eventually handle it. We will discuss more on exception handling in Section 10.4. For the next two sections, we will use the propagation approach in dealing with exceptions.

FileInput-
Stream

To read the data into a program, we reverse the steps in the output routine. We use the read method of FileInputStream to read in an array of bytes. First we create a FileInputStream object:

```
File             inFile = new File("sample1.data");
FileInputStream inStream = new FileInputStream(inFile);
```

Then we read the data into an array of bytes:

```
inStream.read(byteArray);
```

Before we call the read method, we must declare and create byteArray:

```
int    filesize  = (int) inFile.length();
byte[] byteArray = new byte[filesize];
```

We use the length method of the File class to determine the size of the file, which in this case is the number of bytes in the file. We create an array of bytes whose size is the size of the file.

The following program uses **FileInputStream** to read in the byte array from the file sample1.data.

```java
/*
    Program TestFileInputStream

    A test program to read data from a file using FileInputStream
*/

import javabook.*;
import java.io.*;

class TestFileInputStream
{
    public static void main (String arg[]) throws IOException
    {
        MainWindow mainWindow   = new MainWindow();
        OutputBox outputBox     = new OutputBox(mainWindow);

        mainWindow.show();
        outputBox.show();

        //set up file and stream
        File            inFile = new File("sample1.data");
        FileInputStream inStream = new FileInputStream(inFile);

        //set up an array to read data in
        int fileSize = (int)inFile.length();
        byte[] byteArray = new byte[fileSize];

        //read data in and display them
        inStream.read(byteArray);
        for (int i = 0; i < fileSize; i++) {
            outputBox.printLine(byteArray[i]);
        }

        //input done, so close the stream
        inStream.close();
    }
}
```

It is possible to output data other than bytes if we can convert (i.e., type cast) them into bytes. For example, we can output character data by type casting them to bytes.

```java
File             outFile = new File("sample1.data");
FileOutputStream outStream = new FileOutputStream(outFile);
```

```
                   //data to output
                   byte[] byteArray = {  (byte) 'J',
                                         (byte) 'a',
                                         (byte) 'v',
                                         (byte) 'a' };
```

Type cast charac-
ters to bytes.

```
                   //write data to the stream
                   outStream.write(byteArray);

                   //output done, so close the stream
                   outStream.close();
```

To read the data back, we use the read method again. If we need to display the bytes in the original character values, we need to type cast byte to char. Without the type casting, numerical values would be displayed. The following code illustrates the type casting of byte to char for display.

```
                   MainWindow mainWindow = new MainWindow();
                   OutputBox outputBox  = new OutputBox(mainWindow);

                   File            inFile = new File("sample1.data");
                   FileInputStream inStream = new FileInputStream(inFile);

                   //set up an array to read data in
                   int    fileSize = inFile.length();
                   byte[] byteArray = new byte[fileSize];

                   //read data in and display them
                   inStream.read(byteArray);

                   for (int i = 0; i < fileSize; i++) {

                       outputBox.printLine( (char) byteArray[i] );
                   }

                   //input done, so close the stream
                   inStream.close();
```

Type cast byte
array back to
characters for
display.

Type casting char to byte or byte to char is simple because they both use eight bits. But what if we want to perform file I/O on numerical values such as integer and real numbers? It takes more than simple type casting to output these numerical values to FileOutputStream and read them back from FileInput-Stream. An integer takes four bytes, so we need to break a single integer into four bytes and perform file I/O on these four bytes. Such conversion would be too low level and tedious. Java provides stream objects that allow us to read from or write numerical values to a file without doing any conversions ourselves. We will discuss two of them in the next section.

10.3 High-Level File I/O

By using DataOutputStream, we can output Java primitive data type values. A DataOutputStream object will take care of the details of converting the primitive data type values to a sequence of bytes. Let's look at the complete program first. The following program writes out values of various Java primitive data types to a file. The names of the output methods (those preceded with write) should be self-explanatory.

```
/*
    Program TestDataOutputStream

    A test program to save data to a file using DataOutputStream for
    high-level I/O.
*/

import java.io.*;

class TestDataOutputStream
{
    public static void main (String arg[]) throws IOException
    {
        //set up the streams
        File             outFile       = new File("sample2.data");
        FileOutputStream outFileStream = new FileOutputStream(outFile);
        DataOutputStream outDataStream = new DataOutputStream(outFileStream);

        //write values of primitive data types to the stream
        outDataStream.writeInt(987654321);
        outDataStream.writeLong(11111111L);
        outDataStream.writeFloat(22222222F);
        outDataStream.writeDouble(3333333D);
        outDataStream.writeChar('A');
        outDataStream.writeBoolean(true);

        //output done, so close the stream
        outDataStream.close();
    }
}
```

> Notice the argument to the constructor for the **DataOutput-Stream**.

Notice the sequence of statements for creating a DataOutputStream object:

```
File              outFile      = new File("sample2.data");
FileOutputStream outFileStream = new FileOutputStream(outFile);
DataOutputStream outDataStream = new DataOutputStream(outFileStream);
```

DataOutput-
Stream

The argument to the DataOutputStream constructor is a FileOutputStream object. A DataOutputStream object does not get connected to a file directly. The diagram in Figure 10.5 illustrates the relationships established among the three objects. The role of the DataOutputStream object is to provide high-level access to a file by converting a primitive data value into a sequence of bytes, which are then written to a file via a FileOutputStream object.

FIGURE 10.5   A diagram showing how the three objects **outFile**, **outFileStream**, and **outDataStream** are related.

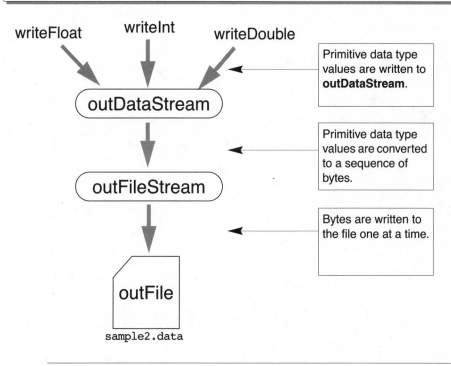

```
File              outFile      = new File("sample2.data");
FileOutputStream outFileStream = new FileOutputStream(outFile);
DataOutputStream outDataStream = new DataOutputStream(outFileStream);
```

To read the data back from the file, we reverse the operation. We use three
DataInput-
Stream
objects: File, FileInputStream and DataInputStream. The following program
reads the data saved by the program TestDataOutputStream.

```
/*
    Program TestDataInputStream

    A test program to load data from a file using DataInputStream for
    high-level I/O.
*/

import java.io.*;
import javabook.*;

class TestDataInputStream
{
    public static void main (String arg[]) throws IOException
    {
        MainWindow mainWindow = new MainWindow();
        OutputBox outputBox = new OutputBox(mainWindow);
        mainWindow.show();
        outputBox.show();

        //set up file and stream
        File inFile = new File("sample2.data");
        FileInputStream inFileStream = new FileInputStream(inFile);
        DataInputStream inDataStream = new DataInputStream(inFileStream);

        //read values back from the stream and display them
        outputBox.printLine(inDataStream.readInt());
        outputBox.printLine(inDataStream.readLong());
        outputBox.printLine(inDataStream.readFloat());
        outputBox.printLine(inDataStream.readDouble());
        outputBox.printLine(inDataStream.readChar());
        outputBox.printLine(inDataStream.readBoolean());

        //input done, so close the stream
        inDataStream.close();
    }
}
```

Figure 10.6 shows the relationship among the three objects. Notice that we
must read the data back in the precise order. In other words, if we write data in
the order of integer, float, and character, then we must read the data back in that
order, as illustrated in Figure 10.7. If we don't read them back in the correct order, the results will be unpredictable.

binary file
Both FileOutputStream and DataOutputStream objects produce a *binary file*
in which the contents are stored in the format (called *binary format*) in which
they are stored in the main memory. Instead of storing data in binary format, we

FIGURE 10.6   A diagram showing how the three objects **inFile**, **inFileStream**, and **inDataStream** are related.

```
File              inFile       = new File("sample2.data");
FileInputStream inFileStream = new FileInputStream(inFile);
DataInputStream inDataStream = new DataInputStream(inFileStream);
```

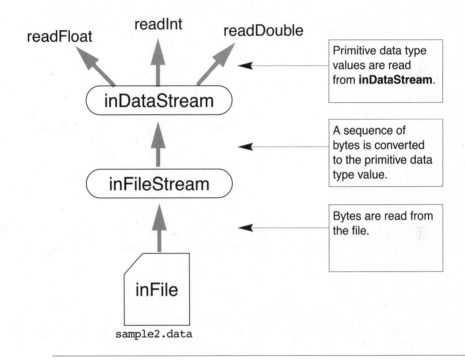

can store them in ASCII format. With the ASCII format, all data are converted to string data. A file whose contents are stored in ASCII format is called a *textfile*. One major benefit of a textfile is that we can easily read and modify the contents of a textfile using any text editor or word processor.

textfile

PrintWriter   PrintWriter is an object we use to generate a textfile. Unlike DataOutput-Stream, where we have a separate write method for each individual data type, PrintWriter supports only two output methods: print and println (for print line). An argument to the methods can be any primitive data type. The methods convert the parameter to string and output this string value. The constructor of Print-

FIGURE 10.7   The order of write and read operations must match to read the stored data back correctly.

```
outStream.writeInteger(...);
outStream.writeLong(...);
outStream.writeChar(...);
outStream.writeBoolean(...);
```

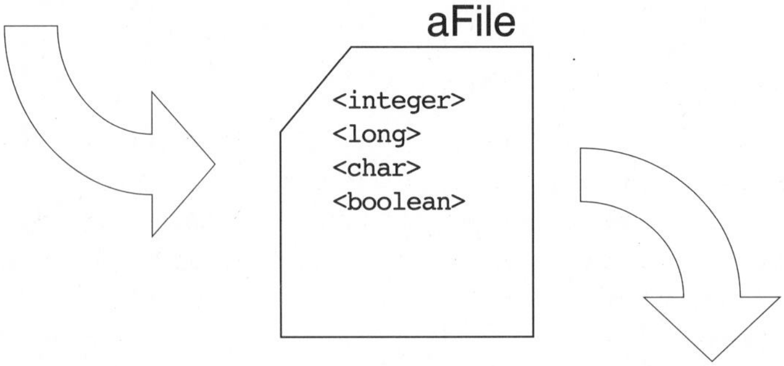

aFile

```
<integer>
<long>
<char>
<boolean>
```

```
inStream.readInteger(...);
inStream.readLong(...);
inStream.readChar(...);
inStream.readBoolean(...);
```

Writer, similar to the one for DataOutputStream, requires an output stream as its argument. In the following program, the parameter is again an instance of File-OutputStream.

```
/*
    Program TestPrintStream

    A test program to save data to a file using PrintWriter for
    high-level I/O.
*/

import java.io.*;

class TestPrintStream
{
    public static void main (String[] arg) throws IOException
    {
        //set up file and stream
        File             outFile       = new File("sample3.data");
        FileOutputStream outFileStream = new FileOutputStream(outFile);
        PrintWriter      outStream     = new PrintWriter(outFileStream);
```

```
        //write values of primitive data types to the stream
        outStream.println(987654321);
        outStream.println(11111111L);
        outStream.println(22222222F);
        outStream.println(33333333D);
        outStream.println('A');
        outStream.println(true);

        //output done, so close the stream
        outStream.close();
    }
}
```

> We use **print** and **println** with **Print-Writer**. The **print** and **println** methods convert primitive data types to strings before writing to a file.

To read the data from a textfile we use the FileReader and BufferedReader objects. The relationship between FileReader and BufferedReader is similar to the one between FileInputStream and DataInputStream. To read data back from a textfile, we first need to associate a BufferedReader object to a file. The following sequence of statements associate a BufferedReader object to a file sample3.data:

```
File           inFile    = new File( "sample3.data" );
FileReader     fileReader = new FileReader( inFile );
BufferedReader bufReader  = new BufferedReader( fileReader);
```

Then we read data using the readLine method of BufferedReader

```
String str = bufReader.readLine( );
```

and convert the String to a primitive data type as necessary.

Here's the program to read back from sample3.data, which was created by the program TestPrintWriter:

```
/*
    Program TestBufferedReader

    A test program to load data from a file using the readLine method of
    BufferedReader for high-level String input.
*/

import java.io.*;
import javabook.*; //to use the Convert class

class TestBufferedReader
{
    public static void main (String arg[]) throws IOException
```

```
{
    MainWindow mainWindow = new MainWindow();
    OutputBox outputBox = new OutputBox(mainWindow);
    mainWindow.show();
    outputBox.show();

    //set up file and stream
    File          inFile     = new File("sample3.data");
    FileReader fileReader = new FileReader(inFile);
    BufferedReader bufReader = new BufferedReader(fileReader);
    String str;

    //get integer
    str = bufReader.readLine();
    int i = Convert.toInt(str);

    //get long
    str = bufReader.readLine();
    long l = Convert.toLong(str);

    //get float
    str = bufReader.readLine();
    float f = Convert.toFloat(str);

    //get double
    str = bufReader.readLine();
    double d = Convert.toDouble(str);

    //get char
    str = bufReader.readLine();
    char c = Convert.toChar(str);

    //get boolean
    str = bufReader.readLine();
    boolean b = Convert.toBoolean(str);

    outputBox.printLine(i);
    outputBox.printLine(l);
    outputBox.printLine(f);
    outputBox.printLine(d);
    outputBox.printLine(c);
    outputBox.printLine(b);

    //input done, so close the stream
    bufReader.close();
}
}
```

Notice we are reading in strings. Numbers are stored in ASCII format, so we can't use **readInt**, **readFloat**, and so on. We need to convert strings to primitive data types.

Note: Here we only output so there's no real need to perform data conversion, but in general you need to convert String data to primitive data types before being able to use them.

Since the data stored in the file are strings, we need to convert them into primitive data types. For data conversion, the program uses the Convert class from the javabook package. If you do not use the Convert class, the code for conversion may look something like this:

```
str = inStream.readLine();
Integer intObj = Integer(str);          Could replace these with
int i = intObj.intValue();              int i = Integer.parseInt(str);

//get long
str = outStream.readLine();
Long longObj = Long(str);               Could replace these with
long l = longObj.longValue();           long l = Long.parseLong(str);

//get float
str = outStream.readLine();
Float floatObj = Float(str);
float f = floatObj.floatValue();

//get double
str = outStream.readLine();
Double doubleObj = Double(str);
double d = doubleObj.doubleValue();

//get char
str = outStream.readLine();
char c = str.charAt(0);

//get boolean
str = outStream.readLine();
Boolean booleanObj = Boolean(str);
boolean b = booleanObj.booleanValue();
```

10.4 Handling Exceptions

In Section 10.2 we mentioned that many of the file I/O methods throw exceptions. In earlier examples, we used one of the two ways to handle exceptions. We will now describe the second way of handling exceptions by catching a thrown exception and providing exception-handling code to process the thrown exception.

checked and
unchecked
exceptions

There are two types of exceptions: checked and unchecked exceptions: A *checked exception* is an exception that is checked at compile time. All other exceptions are *unchecked exceptions*, also called *runtime exceptions,* because they are unchecked at compile time and detected only at runtime. Runtime exceptions are thrown when you try to divide a number by 0 or try to access a nonexisting object, for example. Runtime exceptions are considered unrecoverable, and, therefore, we do not handle these exceptions. We only need to handle the checked exceptions. We mentioned one approach for handling checked exceptions, the IOException, in Section 10.2. We will explain another approach to handling checked exceptions in this section.

For the remainder of the section, we use the term *exception* to refer to an unchecked exception. We have two ways to take care of thrown exceptions. The first way, which we have already explained in Section 10.2, is to add a throw clause to the method header. Consider the following simplified sample object that computes the sum of three integers read from a specified file.

```
class FindSum
{
    private int sum;

    public int getSum()
    {
        return sum;
    }

    void computeSum (String fileName ) throws IOException
    {
        File inFile        = new File(fileName);

        FileInputStream inFileStream
                           = new FileInputStream(inFile);
        DataInputStream inDataStream
                           = new DataInputStream(inFileStream);

        //read three integers
        int i = inDataStream.readInt();
        int j = inDataStream.readInt();
        int k = inDataStream.readInt();

        sum = i + j + k;

        inDataStream.close();
    }
}
```

We used the propagation approach in declaring the computeSum method. The method that calls computeSum can propagate the exception thrown by computeSum. And the exception propagation can continue until the Java interpreter handles the exception. For simple programs, this may be acceptable, but in general, you should use the second approach, in which you write a response code to process a thrown exception.

Let's see how we can use the second approach in the FindSum class. To specify a response code to a thrown exception, we need to declare a catch block. Here's one way to rewrite the FindSum class:

```
class FindSum
{
    private int       sum;
    private boolean   success;

    public int getSum()
    {
        return sum;
    }

    public boolean isSuccess()
    {
        return success;
    }

    void computeSum (String fileName )
    {
        success = true;

        try {
            File inFile   = new File(fileName);
            FileInputStream inFileStream
                        = new FileInputStream(inFile);
            DataInputStream inDataStream
                        = new DataInputStream(inFileStream);

            //read three integers
            int i = inDataStream.readInt();
            int j = inDataStream.readInt();
            int k = inDataStream.readInt();

            sum = i + j + k;

            inDataStream.close();
        }
        catch (IOException e) {
            success = false;
        }
    }
}
```

The declaration of the computeSum method does not include the throw clause anymore, which means that the method will not propagate an exception. Instead, it is modified to catch a thrown IOException. The syntax for catching an exception is

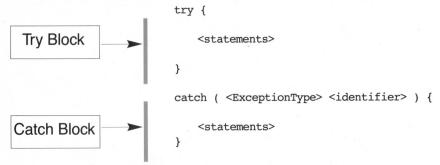

```
try {

    <statements>

}

catch ( <ExceptionType> <identifier> ) {

    <statements>
}
```

where <ExceptionType> is the class of thrown exception and <identifier> refers to an instance of the class <ExceptionType>. At the top of the exception class hierarchy is the Exception class. There are nine immediate subclasses of the Exception class, of which the IOException class is one. The IOException class is also a superclass of the classes FileNotFoundException, EOFException, InterruptedIOException, and others. When an exception occurs, an instance of the appropriate class is created and passed to a relevant catch block. An instance of Exception and its subclasses contains information regarding the thrown exception.

The idea is to place statements that call exception-throwing methods in the try block and catch a thrown exception. For the computeSum method, we placed all of the exception-throwing methods in the try block and added one catch block. Inside the catch block, we set the instance variable success to false to signal that there was an error in performing file I/O. The code for using a FindSum object can be written as

```
FindSum findSum = new FindSum();

findSum.computeSum("sampleint.dat");

if (findSum.isSuccess()) {
    int total = findSum.getSum();
    outputBox.printLine("Sum = " + total);
}
else {
    outputBox.printLine("Error in File I/O");
}
```

If an exception is thrown during the execution of the try block, then the catch block is executed and the variable success is set to false. A call to the method isSuccess returns false and the message Error in File I/O is displayed.

We can modify the catch block of the computeSum method to print out an error message to System.out, in addition to setting the instance variable success to false:

```
try {
    ...
}
catch (IOException e) {
    success = false;
    System.out.println(e);
}
```

System.out, which you may have been using already, is a PrintWriter object you use for debugging and testing purposes. Output values written to System.out are displayed in the DOS window for the Windows platform and in a similar type of window for other platforms. We can print out the sequence of method calls up to the point the exception occurs by calling the printStackTrace method of the IOException object e as

```
try {
    ...
}
catch (IOException e) {
    success = false;
    e.printStackTrack();
}
```

We can attach multiple catch blocks to a single try block, each catching a specific exception. For the computeSum method, statements that throw exceptions all throw exceptions of type IOException, but some of them are throwing more detailed exceptions. For instance, the constructor

```
new FileInputStream(inFile);
```

will throw a FileNotFoundException if the file inFile does not exist. Also, the method

```
readInt()
```

will throw an EOFException if you attempt to read beyond the end of the file. If we want to process these exceptions differently, then we can add multiple catch blocks as

```
try {
    ...
}
catch (IOException e) {
    success = false;
    System.out.println("General I/O exception is thrown");
}
catch (FileNotFoundException e) {
    success = false;
    System.out.println("File " + fileName + " does not exist.");
}
catch (EOFException e) {
    success = false;
    System.out.println("Error: Cannot read beyond end of file");
}
```

When an exception is thrown by a statement inside the try block, control is immediately passed to the matching catch block and statements following the exception-throwing statement will not get executed. If you want to include statements that will always get executed whether there is an exception or not is to place these statements in the finally block. The finally block comes at the end:

```
try {
    ...
}
catch (IOException e) {
    ...
}
finally {
    //statements placed here
    //will always get executed
}
```

You will be seeing more examples of exception handling in following chapters.

10.5 Object I/O

With Java 1.1, you can store objects just as easily as you can store primitive data values. Java 1.0 and many other object-oriented programming languages won't allow programmers to store objects directly. In those programming languages, we must write code to store individual data members of an object separately. For example, if a Person object has data members name (String), age (int), and gender (char), then we have to store the three values individually using the file I/O techniques explained earlier in the chapter. (Note: String is an object, but it can be treated much like any other primitive data types because of its immutability.) Now, if the data members of an object are all primitive data type (or a String), then storing the data members individually is a chore but not that difficult. However, if a data member is a reference to another object or to an array of objects, then storing data can become very tricky. Fortunately with Java 1.1 and 1.2, we don't have to worry about them; we can store objects directly to a file.

ObjectOutput-
Stream

ObjectInput-
Stream

In this section, we will describe various approaches for storing objects. To write objects to a file, we use ObjectOutputStream, and to read objects from a file, we use ObjectInputStream. Let's see how we write Person objects to a file. First we need to modify the definition of the Person class in order for ObjectOutputStream and ObjectInputStream to perform object I/O. We modify the definition by adding the phrase implements Serializable to it as

Serializable is
defined in **java.io**. ➤

```
import java.io.*;
class Person implements Serializable
{
    //the rest is the same
}
```

We will defer the explanation of the keyword implements until Chapter 12. For now, just remember that whenever you want to store an object to a file, modify its class definition by adding the phrase implements Serializable to it.

If you want to perform an object I/O, then the class definition must include the phrase implements Serializable.

If the class is a subclass, then the class definition will be something like

```
class Student extends Person implements Serializable
```

To write a **Person** object to a file, we first create an **ObjectOutputStream** object:

```
File            outFile
                    = new File("objects.data");
FileOutputStream  outFileStream
                    = new FileOutputStream(outFile);
ObjectOutputStream outObjectStream
                    = new ObjectOutputStream(outFileStream);
```

To save a **Person** object, we write

```
Person person = new Person("Mr. Espresso", 20, 'M');

outObjectStream.writeObject( person );
```

It is possible to save different types of objects to a single file. Assuming the **Account** and **Bank** classes are defined properly, we can save both types of objects to a single file:

```
Account    account1, account2;
Bank       bank1, bank2;

account1   = new Account();   //create objects
account2   = new Account();
bank1      = new Bank();
bank2      = new Bank();

outObjectStream.writeObject( account1 );
outObjectStream.writeObject( account2 );
outObjectStream.writeObject( bank1    );
outObjectStream.writeObject( bank2    );
```

We can even mix objects and primitive data type values, for example,

```
outObjectStream.writeInt    ( 15      );
outObjectStream.writeObject( account1 );
outObjectStream.writeChar  ( 'X'      );
```

To read objects from a file, we use **FileInputStream** and **ObjectInputStream**. We use the method **readObject** to read an object. Since we can store any types of objects to a single file, we need to type cast the object read from the file. Here's an example of reading a **Person** object we saved in the file objects.data.

```
File              inFile
                       = new File("objects.data");
FileInputStream   inFileStream
                       = new FileInputStream(inFile);
ObjectInputStream inObjectStream
                       = new ObjectInputStream(inFileStream);

Person person = (Person) inObjectStream.readObject();
```

> Need to type cast to the object type we are reading.

ClassNotFound-Exception Because there is a possibility of wrong type casting, the readObject method can throw a ClassNotFoundException, in addition to an IOException. You can catch or propagate either or both exceptions. If you propagate both exceptions, then the declaration of a method that contains the call to readObject will look like this:

```
public void myMethod( ) throws IOException, ClassNotFoundException
{
    ...
}
```

If the file contains two **Account** and two **Bank** objects, then we must read them in the correct order:

```
account1  = (Account) inObjectStream.readObject();
account2  = (Account) inObjectStream.readObject();
bank1     = (Bank)    inObjectStream.readObject();
bank2     = (Bank)    inObjectStream.readObject();
```

Consider the following array of **Person** objects where N represents some integer value:

```
Person[] people = new Person[N];
```

Assuming that all N **Person** objects are in the array, we can store them to file as

```
//save the size of an array first
outObjectStream.writeInt( people.length );

//save Person objects next
for (int i = 0; i < people.length; i++ ) {
    outObjectStream.writeObject( people[i] );
}
```

We store the size of an array at the beginning of the file so we know exactly how many Person objects to read back:

```
int N = inObjectStream.readInt();

for (int i = 0; i < N; i++) {
    people[i] = (Person) inObjectStream.readObject();
}
```

Since an array itself is an object, we can actually store the whole array at once instead of storing individual elements one at a time. The whole people array can stored at once by

```
outObjectStream.writeObject( people );
```

and the whole array is read back at once by

```
people = (Person[]) inObjectStream.readObject( );
```

Notice how the type casting is done. We are reading an array of Person objects, so the type casting is (Person[ ]).

10.6 Sample Class: Saving an AddressBook Object

As an illustration of object I/O, we will write a class that handles the storage of an AddressBook object. The class will provide methods to write an Address-Book object to a file and to read the object back from the file.

Problem Statement

Write a class that manages file I/O of an AddressBook object.

Overall Plan

Before we begin designing the class, we must modify the definition of the AddressBook class by adding the phrase implements Serializable:

```
import java.io.*;
class AddressBook implements Serializable
{
    //same as before
}
```

This modification allows us to store an AddressBook object to a file.

Since the class handles the file I/O operations, we will call the class AddressBookStorage. Following the STO (single-task object) principle, this class will be responsible solely for file I/O of an AddressBook object. The class will not perform, for instance, any operations that deal with a user interface.

What kinds of core operations should this class support? Since the class handles the file I/O, the class should support two public methods to write and read an AddressBook object. Let's call the methods write and read. The argument will be an AddressBook object we want to write or read. If fileManager is an AddressBookStorage object, then the calls should be something like

```
fileManager.write( addressBook );
```

and

```
addressBook = fileManager.read( );
```

For an AddressBookStorage to actually store an AddressBook object, it must know the file to which an address book is written or from which it is read. How should we let the programmer specify this file? One possibility is to let the programmer pass the filename to a constructor, such as

```
AddressBookStorage fileManager
            = new AddressBookStorage("book.data");
```

Another possibility is to define a method to set the file, say, setFile, which is called as

```
fileManager.setFile( "book.data" );
```

Instead of choosing one over the other, we will support both. If we don't provide the setFile method, fileManager can input and output to a single file only. By using the setFile method, the programmer can change the file if he needs to. As for the constructor, we do not want to define a constructor with no argument because we do not want the programmer to create an Address-BookStorage object without specifying a filename. Yes, he can call the setFile method later, but as the AddressBookStorage class designer, we cannot ensure he will call the setFile method. If the programmer doesn't call the method, then the subsequent calls to the write or read method will fail. You might suggest that we set a default filename in a no-argument constructor. But what will be the default filename? No matter which filename we choose, there's a possibility that a file with this filename already exists, which will result in the file being erased. To make our class reliable, we will not provide a no-argument constructor.

The object diagram for the AddressBookStorage class at this point is

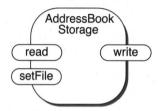

We will implement the class in the following order:

development
steps

1. Implement the constructor and the setFile method.

2. Implement the write method.

3. Implement the read method.

4. Finalize the class.

This order of development follows a natural sequence. We begin with the constructor as usual. Since the constructor and the setFile method carry out the similar operations, we will implement them together. We will identify necessary data members in this step. The second step is to implement the file output routine, because without being able to write an AddressBook object, we won't be able to test the file input routine. For the third step, we will implement the file input routine.

Step 1 Development: Constructor and setFile

Step 1 Design

In Step 1, we will identify the data members and define a constructor to initialize them. We will also implement the setFile method, which should be very similar to the constructor.

We need File, FileInputStream, FileOutputStream, ObjectInputStream, and ObjectOutputStream objects to do object I/O. Should we define a data member for each type of object? This is certainly a possibility, but we should not use any unnecessary data members. We need ObjectInputStream and ObjectOutputStream objects only at the time the actual read and write operations take place. We can create these objects in the read and write methods, only when they are needed. Had we used data members for all those objects, we would need to create and assign objects every time the setFile method is called. But calling the setFile method does not necessarily mean the actual file I/O will take place. Consider the case where the user changes the filename before actually saving an address book to a file. This will result in calling the setFile method twice before doing the actual file I/O. To avoid this type of unnecessary repetition, we will use one data member only, a String variable filename to keep the filename. The setFile method simply assigns the parameter to this variable. The constructor can do the same by calling this setFile method.

Step 1 Code

At this point, we have only one data member:

```
/*************************
    Data Members
*************************/

private  String  filename;    //name of the file to store
                              //an AddressBook object
```

The setFile method assigns the parameter to the data member as

```
public void setFile( String filename )
{
    this.filename = filename;
}
```

and the constructor will simply call this method as

```
public AddressBookStorage( String filename )
{
    setFile( filename );
}
```

The class is defined as follows:

```
class AddressBookStorage
{

/**************************
    Data Members
**************************/
    private String    filename;

/**************************
    Constructors
**************************/

    public AddressBookStorage( String filename )
    {
        setFile( filename );
    }

/**************************
    Public Methods

        void    setFile        ( String        )

**************************/

    public void setFile( String filename )
    {
        this.filename = filename;
        System.out.println("Inside setFile. Filename is " + filename ); //TEMP
    }
}
```

Step 1 Test

To test this class, we have included a temporary output statement inside the setFile method. We will write a test program to verify that we can create an AddressBookStorage object and use the setFile method correctly:

```
class TestAddressBookStorage
{
    public static void main ( String[] arg )
    {
        AddressBookStorage fileManager;

        fileManager = new AddressBookStorage( "one.data" );
        fileManager.setFile("two.data");
        fileManager.setFile("three.data");
    }
}
```

Step 2 Development: Implement the write Method

Step 2 Design   In the second development step, we will implement the write method. From the data member filename, we will create an ObjectOutputStream object and write the parameter AddressBook object to it. A sequence of method calls to create an ObjectOutputStream object can throw an IOException, so we must either propagate it or handle it. Following the STO principle, the method will propagate the thrown exception. The responsibility of an AddressBookStorage object is taking care of file I/O for others. When there's an exception, the object will inform the caller about the exception and let the caller decide what to do about it.

Step 2 Code   The write method is written as

```
public void write( AddressBook book ) throws IOException
{
    //first create an ObjectOutputStream
    File    outFile     = new File( filename );
    FileOutputStream   outFileStream
                        = new FileOutputStream(outFile);
    ObjectOutputStream outObjectStream
                        = new ObjectOutputStream(outFileStream);

    //save the data to it
    outObjectStream.writeObject( book );

    //and close it
    outObjectStream.close();
}
```

Step 2 Test   We will write a test program to verify that the data are saved to a file. Since we do not have a method to read the file contents yet, we can only verify at this point that the file is created and this file has something in it. To do so, we run the following Step 2 test program first. Then, we use whatever tool available (e.g., Windows Explorer, DOS command dir, UNIX command ls, etc.) and check that the specified file exists and the file size is greater than zero.

The Step 2 test program is as follows (TestAddressBookStorage is now an instantiable class):

```
class Tester
{
    public static void main ( String[] arg ) throws IOException
    {
        TestAddressBookWrite tester
                        = new TestAddressBookWrite( 15 );
```

```
                    tester.testWrite( "book.data" );
            }
    }


    class TestAddressBookWrite
    {
        AddressBook          myBook;
        AddressBookStorage   fileManager;

        public TestAddressBookWrite( int N )
        {
            myBook = new AddressBook( N );

            //add N Person objects
            for (int i = 0; i < N; i++) {
                person = new Person("Ms. X"+i, 10, 'F');
                myBook.add( person );
            }
        }

        public void testWrite( String filename )
        {
            fileManager = new AddressBookStorage( filename );

            try {
                fileManager.write( myBook );
            }
            catch ( IOException e ) {
                System.out.println("Error: IOException is thrown.");
            }
        }
    }
```

Run the program several times with different sizes for the address book and verify that the resulting files have different sizes.

Step 3 Development: Implement the read Method

Step 3 Design

In the third development step, we will implement the read method. The method reads the AddressBook object saved in the file and returns this object to the caller. Like the write method, if there's an exception, this method will propagate it back to the caller and let the caller decide what to do to the thrown exception.

Step 3 Code

The read method is written as

```
public AddressBook read( ) throws IOException,
                                    ClassNotFoundException
{
    AddressBook book;

    //first create an ObjectInputStream
    File     inFile     = new File( filename );
    FileInputStream  inFileStream
                        = new FileInputStream(inFile);
    ObjectInputStream inObjectStream
                        = new ObjectInputStream(inFileStream);

    //read the data from it
    book = (AddressBook) inObjectStream.readObject( );

    //close it
    inObjectStream.close();

    //and read the object
    return book;
}
```

Step 3 Test

We will write a test program to verify that the data can be read back from a file. This test program also verifies that the write method in Step 2 is saving the data correctly. Before you run this test program, don't forget to run the Step 2 test program to make sure that the file is available. The Step 3 test program is as follows:

```
class Tester
{
    public static void main ( String[] arg )
            throws IOException, ClassNotFoundException
    {
        TestAddressBookRead tester
                        = new TestAddressBookRead( );

        tester.testRead( "book.data" );
    }
}


class TestAddressBookRead
{
    AddressBook          myBook;
    AddressBookStorage   fileManager;
```

```java
public ( String filename )


public void testRead( )
{
    fileManager = new AddressBookStorage( filename );

    try {
        myBook = fileManager.read( );
        printout();
    }
    catch ( IOException e ) {
        System.out.println("Error: IOException is thrown.");
    }
    catch ( ClassNotFoundException e ) {
        System.out.println("Error: ClassNotFoundException"
                                        + " is thrown.");
    }
}

private static printout()
{
    Person person;

    person = myBook.search( "Ms. X5" );

    if (person != null) {
        System.out.println( person.getName()   );
        System.out.println( person.getAge()    );
        System.out.println( person.getGender() );
    }
    else {
        System.out.println("Error: Object not found");
    }
}
}
```

Run the program several times changing the method body of printout to access different Person objects in the address book as necessary and verify that you can read the Person object in the file correctly. If you did exercise 16 on page 490, then use the getFirstPerson and getNextPerson methods to access all Person objects in the address book.

Step 4 Development: Finalize

program
review

final test

We finalize the program in the last step. We perform a critical review for finding any inconsistency or error in the methods, incomplete methods, places to add more comments, and so forth. And, as always, we will carry out the final test. As the result of the critical review and final testing, we may identify and wish to implement any additional features.

10.7 Exercises

1. What will happen if you forget to close a file?

2. What is the difference between binary and textfiles?

3. Using the try–catch block, write code that opens a default file default.dat when trying to open a user-designated file causes an exception to be raised.

4. Using a File object, write code to display files in a user-specified directory and its subdirectories. (Note: For those who studied the optional section on recursion in Chapter 7, this problem can be implemented using recursion.)

5. Write code to store and read the contents of the payScaleTable 2-D array from Section 9.7 in the following two file formats:
    - a file of float values.
    - a file of 2-D array.

6. Write an application that reads a textfile and converts the text to an Eggy-Peggy text. Save the converted text to another textfile. Use FileDialog to let the user specify the input and output files. Create the input file using a text editor.

7. Write an application that randomly generates N integers and stores them in a binary file integers.dat. The value for N is input by the user. Open the file with a text editor and see what the contents of a binary file look like.

8. Write an application that reads the data from the file integers.dat generated in exercise 7. After the data are read, display the smallest, the largest, and the average.

9. Repeat exercise 7, but this time, store the numbers in a textfile integers.txt. Open this file with a text editor and verify that you can read the contents.

10. Repeat exercise 2 with the textfile integers.txt generated in exercise 8.

11. Write a currency converter application. Allow the user to specify the from and to currencies and the amount to exchange. Use whatever interface meth-

ods are appropriate to input these three values. When the application starts, read the exchange rates from a textfile rate.txt. Use a text editor to create this textfile. By using a textfile, you can easily update the exchange rates. The format for the textfile is as follows:

```
<name of currency> <units per dollar>
```

For example, the following shows how much a dollar is worth in five foreign currencies:

```
French franc                 5.95
Indonesian rupiah        12900.0
Japanese yen               145.91
Mexican peso                 9.18
Papua New Guinea kina        2.381
```

You can get the exchange rates from various Web sites, one of which is http://www.oanda.com.

12. Extend the AddressBookStorage class by adding import and export capabilities. Add a method export that stores the contents of AddressBook to a textfile. Add a second method import that reads the textfile back and constructs an AddressBook. This type of import/export feature is a convenient means to move data from one application to another.

13. Extend the encryption application of exercise 22 on page 422 so that the original text is read from a user-specified textfile and the encrypted text is stored to another user-specified textfile.

14. Extend the watermelon projectile computation program of exercise 22 on page 360 so the output is saved to a file. Which file format would you use for the program: a binary file or a textfile? Or would you consider using an array to keep the (x,y) coordinates and save this array using an object I/O?

15. Extend any application you have written before by adding a quote-of-the-day dialog. When the user starts the application, a quote of the day is displayed (either a MessageBox or an OutputBox). The quotes are saved in a textfile. Use a random number generator to select the quote to display.

16. Write an application that removes extra spaces from a textfile. In the days of the typewriter, it was a common practice to leave two spaces after the periods. We shouldn't be doing that anymore with the computer, but many people still do. Read an original textfile and output an edited version to another textfile. The edited version should replace two or more consecutive spaces with one space.

17. Write a mail merge application. You use two files for this program. The first is a textfile that contains a template letter in the following style:

```
Dear <<N>>,

Because you are <<A>> old and <<G>>, we have free gift for
you. You have absolutely nothing to buy; just pay the
shipping and handling charge of $9.99. To claim your gift,
call us now immediately.

Thank you,
Office of Claims Department
```

The tags <<N>>, <<A>>, and <<G>> are placeholders for the person's name, age, and gender. The second file contains the name, age, and gender information of people to whom you want to send a letter. Use whatever format you wish for the second file. Read two files and print out the letter with the placeholders replaced by the actual values from the second file. Run the program multiple times, each time using a different template file. For this program output the personalized letter to an OutputBox. You can also use saveToFile of the OutputBox class to save the personalized letters.

Reusable Classes and Packages

OBJECTIVES

After you have read and studied this chapter, you should be able to

- Describe four different object categories and use them effectively in designing classes.

- Define a package and place reusable classes in it.

- Write a method that calls the superclass's method explicitly by using the reserved word super.

- Define overloaded methods.

Introduction

reusable
classes

One of the key benefits of using object-oriented technology is reusability. We say a class is *reusable* if it can be used in different programs. For example, predefined classes in the javabook and the standard Java packages are all highly reusable. Although reusability of classes is very important, it does not mean that every class we design should be reusable. There are classes that we need to design specifically for a particular program, and these classes are not reusable at all. What is important here is to design the classes accordingly. If a class is intended to be reusable then we must design it carefully so that it is indeed reusable. In this chapter we will cover the topics related to defining reusable classes.

11.1 Object Categories

We have already mentioned on several occasions the importance of the STO principle. For a class to be reusable, we must implement it following the STO principle:

> Design a class that implements a single well-defined task. Do not overburden the class with multiple tasks.

How do we know whether a class is overburdened or not? There is no mathematical formula to answer this question, but there are guidelines we can follow. One helpful design guideline is the categorization of objects. We classify the roles objects play into four categories. We know that an object is overburdened if the object is doing two different categories of tasks, for example.

We divide object tasks into four categories: user interface, controller, application logic, and storage.

user interface
object

- A *user interface object* handles the interaction between the user and the program. InputBox, OutputBox, ResponseBox, and others from the javabook package are all user interface objects.

controller
object

- A *controller object* supervises other objects in the program. Objects such as EggyPeggy from Section 8.7 on page 404 and HiLo from Section 7.9 on page 335 are controller objects.

application logic
object

- An *application logic object* captures the logic of the real world for which the program is written. An AddressBook object from Chapter 9 that models the functionality of an address book in the real world is an example of application logic object. An application logic object does not have to model a real-world concept. It could be an intangible or imaginary object that does not have any real-world counterpart.

storage
object

- A *storage object* takes care of file input and output. An Address-
BookStorage object from Chapter 10 is a storage object.

Keep in mind that these categories are informal guidelines. It is possible to design a single object that implements more than one category of tasks. It does not necessarily imply that this object is overburdened and poorly designed. However, when you end up in an object that performs multiple categories of tasks, then you should be extra careful to make sure that the object is designed properly. If an object, for example, does both storage and user interface of the program, it is very likely that this object is not designed properly. However, just because it does two different types of tasks does not mean the object is poorly designed. Whether an object is designed properly or not depends mainly on how the object is intended to be used. For example, if an object that implements both storage and user interface tasks is very easy to reuse in many different programs, then the object meets its purpose and we can say that it is designed properly.

Normally, controller objects are specific to a particular program, so their degree of reusability is very low, almost none. Application logic objects have a good chance of being highly reusable, and to make them highly reusable, we must design them correctly. We will illustrate this point in the next section. User interface objects may be highly reusable or least reusable depending on how closely they are tied to specific application objects. For example, an Input-Box object is a generic object that can input any primitive data, so its reusability is quite high. On the other hand, a dialog object specifically designed to input three data values of a Person is less reusable. It is reusable only when the Person object is reused. A storage object's reusability depends on the degree of reusability of the application object it stores. If the storage object is designed to store any classes of objects, then its reusability is high. On the other hand, if it is designed to store one specific class of objects, then its reusability is low.

Quick Check

1. Name four categories of object roles?
2. Quickly go over the objects in the Chapters 8 and 9 sample programs, and for each object, tell its category.
3. Suppose we design an Airline Reservation System and include a Fare-Calculator class. Is an instance of this class an application logic ob-

ject? Does a FareCalculator object model a real-world counterpart? Or is it an intangible object that exists in the cyberspace of programming?

11.2 Method Overriding and Overloaded Methods

One application logic object we used earlier is the DrawingBoard class that we used in Chapter 6 to implement the DrawShape program. In this section, we will define the DrawingBoard class as promised in Chapter 6. While defining the class, we will introduce two new concepts in object-oriented programming.

The following is the table of public methods of the DrawingBoard class we used in Chapter 6. We will implement these and the second version of the drawRectangle method here.

Public Methods of DrawingBoard
`public void drawLine( int x1, int y1, int x2, int y2 )`
Draws a line from point (x1,y1) to (x2,y2)
`public void drawCircle( int centerX, int centerY, int radius)`
Draws a circle centered at (centerX,centerY) with radius radius.
`public void drawRectangle(int x, int y, int width, int height)`
Draws a rectangle whose top left corner is at (x,y) with width width and height height.
`public void setColor( Color color)`
Sets the color to color. All subsequent shapes will be drawn in the color color.

The class diagram for DrawingBoard is shown in Figure 11.1. The class has one private instance variable graphic of type Graphics. We need this Graphics object to draw lines, rectangles, and other geometric figures on a window. We have seen the Graphics class back in Chapter 2. You might want to look at the first sample applet in Chapter 2 to review the Graphics class. The variable graphic is initialized inside the show method as

```
public void show()
{
    super.show();          ◄——————  This statement calls the
    graphic = getGraphics();         ancestor's show method.
}
```

FIGURE 11.1   The diagram for the **DrawingBoard** class.

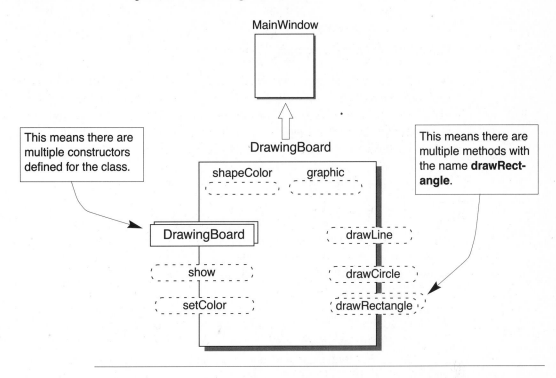

The method calls the ancestor's show method and initializes the variable graphic using the inherited method getGraphics. The syntax for calling an ancestor's method is

```
super . <method name> ( <parameters> ) ;
```

method overriding

We say the show method of the DrawingBoard class *overrides* the inherited show method of the ancestor class. The subclass's method can completely re-write the inherited method or add code to it. The show method here is the latter case. It calls the ancestor's show method and adds one line of code for initializing the variable graphic. By writing the show method this way, we made sure that the instance variable graphic refers to a valid Graphics object when the window appears on the screen.

Some of you may be wondering why we do not call the getGraphics method inside the constructor. We do not because the method is meaningful only after the window appears on the screen. In other words, if we call the method inside the constructor, before the window actually appears on the screen, then the get-Graphics method does not return a valid Graphics object. You might want to experiment with this by placing a call to the getGraphics method in the constructor instead.

The diagram in Figure 11.1 shows that the class has more than one method called drawRectangle. We used only one of them in Chapter 6. A class can have multiple methods with the same name, provided that they have different signa-

method signature

tures. The *signature* of a method is determined by the method name and the number and data types of parameters. The following three methods have different signatures:

```
public void myMethod( int one, float two)
public void myMethod( int one, double two)
public void myMethod( int one, float two, long three)
```

overloaded methods

If multiple methods have the same name but different signatures we say the method name is *overloaded* and call these methods *overloaded methods*. We have been using overloaded methods all along. For example, we can pass a numerical value or a string to the show method of MessageBox because the methods are overloaded. There are numerous overloaded methods in the javabook and the standard Java packages.

The drawRectangle methods are overloaded methods. They are defined as

```
public void drawRectangle(int x, int y, int width, int height)
{
    graphic.drawRect(x, y, width, height);
}
```

```
public void drawRectangle(Rectangle rect)
{
    graphic.drawRect(rect.x, rect.y, rect.width, rect.height);
}
```

The Rectangle class is from java.awt. A Rectangle object represents a rectangle using four public instance variables: x and y define the top left corner of the rectangle and width and height define the size of the rectangle. The class provides methods you can use to manipulate rectangles (moving, resizing, etc.). Please refer to a reference manual for more details on Rectangle.

The signature of a method does not include its modifier (public, private, static, etc.) and return type. For example, the declarations

```
public void one ( int x )
private void one ( int x )

public int two ( float y )
public float two ( float y )

public static void three ( )
public void three ( )
```

method
prototype

will result in errors because the methods with the same name do not have different signatures. We use the term *method prototype* to include the access modifier and return type with the method signature. The sample declarations above have the same signatures but different prototypes.

Method signatures do not include the access modifier and return type. Method prototypes are signatures plus the modifier and return type.

A class can have multiple constructors. In other words, we can overload constructors. There are two constructors defined for the DrawingBoard class. The first constructor is defined as

```
public DrawingBoard(String title)
{
    super(title);
    setResizable(false);
    setBackground(Color.white);      //white background
}
```

The constructor first calls the superclass's constructor and sets the window title. Then it sets the window as nonresizable and the background to white. The window title is passed to the constructor by the user as in

```
DrawingBoard doodleBoard;
doodleBoard = new DrawingBoard( "My Etch-A-Sketch" );
```

The second constructor is defined as

```
public DrawingBoard( )
{
    this( "D R A W I N G    B O A R D" );    //calls the other
                                             //constructor
}
```

When the user creates a DrawingBoard object by calling the second constructor as in

```
DrawingBoard doodleBoard;
doodleBoard = new DrawingBoard( );
```

then the window title will be DRAWING BOARD (with spaces between letters).

The second constructor simply calls the first constructor by using the reserved word this and passing a title. The reserved word this refers to "this object." So the second constructor is indicating something like "call this object's constructor." The compiler knows which constructor to invoke by matching its signature against the arguments in the call. We will discuss a further use of the reserved word this in the next chapter. We could have defined the second constructor as

```
public DrawingBoard( )
{
    super( "D R A W I N G    B O A R D" );
    setResizable(false);
    setBackground(Color.white);           //white background
}
```

but this would duplicate the code. Suppose we want to change the background color to gray. We have to change both constructors. It is not uncommon to have four or five constructors defined for a class and duplicating the code as such would make it harder to modify the code later because you have to make changes to every constructor, instead of changing just one constructor.

It is very common to find classes in the standard Java packages that support multiple constructors because they increase the usability of the class. If your class supports only one constructor, then the programmer using your class has only one way to create an instance. If, however, your class supports multiple constructors, then the programmer has an option of choosing the constructor that works best for her or him.

Try to define multiple constructors to your class to increase its usability.

The method for drawing a circle is defined as

```
public void drawCircle(int x, int y, radius)
{
    graphic.drawOval(x - radius, y - radius, radius, radius);
}
```

This method calls the drawOval method of the Graphics class. The drawCircle method is a more meaningful and intuitive function than the drawOval method to draw a circle. Instead of passing four parameters to the drawOval method, the user can draw a circle with the drawCircle method by passing three parameters—the circle's center point (x,y) and its radius.

Here's the complete class definition:

```
/*
    DrawingBoard Class

    This class provides a simple window for drawing lines,
    circles, and rectangles in color.
*/

package javabook;

import java.awt.*;

public class DrawingBoard extends MainWindow
{

/*********************
    Data Members
*********************/

    private Graphics graphic;

/*********************
    Constructors
*********************/

    public DrawingBoard( String title )
    {
        setTitle( title );
        setResizable(false);
        setBackground(Color.white);       //white background
    }

    public DrawingBoard( )
    {
        this ( "D R A W I N G   B O A R D" );
    }
```

```
/***********************
    Public Methods
            void    drawCircle      ( int, int, int        )
            void    drawLine        ( int, int, int, int   )
            void    drawRectangle   ( Rectangle            )
            void    drawRectangle   ( int, int, int, int   )

            void    setColor        ( Color                )
            void    show            (                      )

***********************/

    //Draw a circle with center point (x, y) and radius
    public void drawCircle(int x, int y, int radius)
    {
        graphic.drawOval(x - radius, y - radius, radius, radius);
    }

    //Draw a line from (x1,y1) to (x2,y2)
    public void drawLine(int x1, int x2, int y1, int y2)
    {
        graphic.drawLine(x1, x2, y1, y2);
    }

    //Draw a rectangle rect
    public void drawRectangle( Rectangle rect )
    {
        graphic.drawRect( rect.x, rect.y, rect.width, rect.height );
    }

    //Draw a rectangle at (x,y) with width and height
    public void drawRectangle(int x, int y, int width, int height)
    {
        graphic.drawRect(x, y, width, height);
    }

    //Set the color. Subsequent drawings will be in this color
    //until changed again
    public void setColor(Color color)
    {
        graphic.setColor(color);
    }

    //Make the window visible
    //and set the Graphics object
    public void show()
    {
        super.show();
        graphic = getGraphics();
    }

}
```

1. Which two of the following declarations have the same method signature?

```
public     int    quizMethod( int one, float two )
public     void   quizMethod( int one, float two )
private    void   quizMethod( int one, int two )
```

2. What is the difference between method signature and method prototype?

11.3 Sample Classes: Reusable EggyPeggy and HiLo

In Chapters 7 and 8, we wrote two sample game programs: Hi-Lo and Eggy-Peggy. In those two sample programs, we used user interface objects from the javabook package. The HiLo and EggyPeggy classes in those programs were both controller objects managing other objects. In addition, they handled the logic of the program. So they were overburdened, but this was not critical because these two classes were written specifically for those programs and never intended to be reused in other programs.

In this section, we will define them as application logic objects and show you how they can be made reusable. By defining them as application logic objects, the programmer will be able to reuse them in many different ways. Since the instances of the redesigned classes are now strictly application logic objects, the programmer must supply the code for the user interface, storage, and other tasks of the program. But this gives the programmer flexibility in building different kinds of programs. For example, it is possible for the programmer to write both application-based and applet-based Hi-Lo programs using the same HiLo application logic object. For the program's user interface and other tasks, the programmer can build the classes herself or himself or reuse existing classes.

Through the implementation of these two reusable classes, we will highlight key points of designing reusable classes. As always, we will develop the two classes incrementally. Let's begin with the EggyPeggy class.

EggyPeggy

We will design a reusable EggyPeggy class whose instance can play Eggy-Peggy games. The class implements an application logic object, and as such, an instance of the class will not handle tasks such as input/output, data storage, or control of other objects. The class is strictly geared toward playing an Eggy-Peggy game. One criterion of reusability is how general the class is. When a class is too limited in capability, then its reusability is low. For example, an EggyPeggy object that can add any user-designated word in front of every vowel is more general, and thus, more reusable, than an EggyPeggy object that can only add the fixed word egg in front of every vowel. Since our objective is to make the class reusable, we will implement a more general EggyPeggy class.

Design a class as general as possible to increase its reusability.

Problem Statement

Write a class that converts a given string to an Eggy-Peggy string by placing the programmer-specified word in front of all vowels in the given string. If the programmer does not specify the word, then the default prefix "egg" will be used.

Overall Plan

When we design a reusable class whose instance methods are called by other classes and objects, we start thinking about the public instance methods of the class. What kinds of methods should the class support so the programmer can use the class easily and effortlessly? What kinds of methods are natural and logical from the programmer's standpoint? These are the types of questions we ask ourselves in designing a reusable class.

What kinds of methods should the EggyPeggy class support? The problem statement indicated a conversion process of generating a new string from a given string. So let's define a method called convert. The programmer will use this method in the following manner:

```
String          newString, inputString;
EggyPeggy       eggyPeggyMaker;
...
eggyPeggyMaker  = new EggyPeggy();

inputString     = inputBox.getString();
newString       = eggyPeggyMaker.convert( inputString );
```

Since an EggyPeggy object is required to allow the programmer to set any word as a prefix attached in front of vowels, let's define a method to set the prefix. We will call the method setPrefixWord, and this method is used in the following manner:

```
...
eggyPggyMaker.setPrefixWord( "roll" );  //set the prefix first
...
newString  = eggyPeggyMaker.convert( inputString );
                                        //and then convert
```

Our working design document for the EggyPeggy class at this point is as follows:

Design Document: The EggyPeggy Class		
Method	**Visibility**	**Purpose**
<constructor>	public	Creates and initializes the objects used by an Eggy-Peggy object.
convert	public	Returns a new string by converting a given string passed as an argument.
setPrefixWord	public	Sets the prefix word to a String passed as an argument.

And its object diagram at this point is

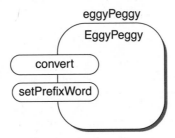

We will implement the class in the following two steps:

development steps

1. Start with a class skeleton. Define the necessary data members and constructors.

2. Implement the setPrefixWord and convert methods. Add any private methods as necessary.

Step 1 Development: Skeleton with Constructors

Let's start with data members of the class. An EggyPeggy object allows a programmer-specified prefix word, so we need a data member of type String to remember this word. If no prefix word is set by the programmer, the object will use the default prefix word egg. We can use a constant to keep this default prefix word. The declaration for the data members should look like

```
/**************************
    Data Members
**************************/
private static final String DEFAULT_PREFIX = "egg";

private String prefix;
```

What kinds of constructors should the class support? We will define one constructor with which the programmer can set the prefix word at the time an instance is created. Here's the constructor:

```
public EggyPeggy( String prefix )
{
    this.prefix = prefix;
}
```

Let's define a second constructor that will allow the programmer to create an instance with a default prefix word. Since we use a default prefix word, this constructor accepts no arguments:

```
public EggyPeggy()
{
    this( DEFAULT_PREFIX );
}
```

Here's the skeleton for the class with stub public methods:

```
/*
    EggyPeggy Class

    An EggyPeggy object plays the word game Eggy-Peggy. Pass the original string
    to the convert method, and it will return an Eggy-Peggy string, a string
    where all vowels are preceded by the word 'egg'. You can change the default
    prefix word 'egg' to any word you like by calling the setPrefixWord method.
*/
```

```
class EggyPeggy
{

/*************************
    Data Members
*************************/

    private static final String DEFAULT_PREFIX = "egg";

    private String prefix;

/*************************
    Constructors
*************************/

    public EggyPeggy()
    {
       this( DEFAULT_PREFIX );
    }

    public EggyPeggy( String prefix )
    {
       this.prefix = prefix;
    }

/*****************************
    Public Methods

       String      convert          ( String   )
       void        setPrefixWord    ( String   )

*****************************/

    /**********************************************************
       Method:        convert

       Purpose:       Converts an argument string to an Eggy-Peggy string.
                      Data member prefix is the word placed in front of
                      all vowels in the original string.

       Parameters:    String [original string]

       Returns:       String [Eggy-Peggy string]
    */
    public String convert( String originalSentence )
    {
       String newString;

       System.out.println("Inside convert; prefix is " + prefix);//TEMP

       newString = "temp new string";
       return newString;
    }


    /**********************************************************
       Method:        setPrefixWord
```

```
    Purpose:        Sets the prefix word to the passed argument.

    Parameters:     String [new prefix word]

    Returns:        None
*/
public void setPrefixWord( String prefix )
{
    System.out.println("Inside setPrefixWord");            //TEMP
}
}
```

Step 1 Test

    In order to test the skeleton EggyPeggy class, we need to write a test main class. The test main class will create an instance of the EggyPeggy class and call the convert and setPrefixWord methods several times. One possible test main class is the following:

```
class TestEggyPeggy
{
    public static void main (String args[])
    {
        EggyPeggy eggyPeggy1, eggyPeggy2;
        String     str1, str2;

        eggyPeggy1 = new EggyPeggy( );
        eggyPeggy2 = new EggyPeggy("bacon");

        eggyPeggy1.setPrefixWord("avocado");

        str1 = eggyPeggy1.convert("testing one");
        str2 = eggyPeggy2.convert("testing two");
    }
}
```

    When you execute the test main class, you should see the following printout in the standard output window System.out:

```
Inside setPrefixWord
Inside convert: prefix is egg
Inside convert: prefix is bacon
```

    Notice that the setPrefixWord method has no effect on the data member prefix at this point. We call the method in the test main class basically to verify the method is declared correctly.

Step 2 Development: Implement setPrefixWord and convert

In the second step of development, we complete the two public methods and add whatever private methods we design to support the public methods. The task of the setPrefixWord method is to set the prefix word, which can be accomplished by including the same statement we have in the second constructor:

```
this.prefix = prefix;
```

The overall idea of converting a given string to an Eggy-Peggy string was already designed in Chapter 8. Since we are now writing a method that accepts an original string as an argument and returns the converted string, we modify the pseudocode in Chapter 8 to the following:

```
for the first to the last character in argument string {

    if (character is a vowel) {
        append "egg" and character to a StringBuffer object;
    }
    else {
        append character only to a StringBuffer object;
    }

}

convert the StringBuffer to a String;

return the String;
```

We will add a private method isVowel that checks whether a given character is a vowel or not. The method returns true if the argument character is a vowel. This method was already designed and implemented in Chapter 8, and we will use it here. The EggyPeggy class document now includes one private method isVowel. The working design document now includes this method:

Design Document: The EggyPeggy Class		
Method	**Visibility**	**Purpose**
...	...	...
isVowel	private	Returns true if the argument character is a vowel and false otherwise.

The setPrefixWord method is defined as follows:

```java
public void setPrefixWord( String prefix )
{
    this.prefix = prefix;
}
```

And to avoid code duplication, we will modify the second constructor to

```java
public EggyPeggy( String prefix )
{
    setPrefixWord( prefix );
}
```

The convert method is defined as follows:

```java
public String convert( String originalSentence )
{
    int            numberOfCharacters;
    char           letter;
    StringBuffer   encryptedSentence;

    encryptedSentence    = new StringBuffer("");
    numberOfCharacters   = originalSentence.length();

    for (int index = 0; index < numberOfCharacters; index++) {
        //get the next letter
        letter = originalSentence.charAt(index);

        if ( isVowel(letter) ) {
            //add the prefix string and then the vowel
            //to encryptedSentence
            encryptedSentence.append(prefix + letter);
        }
        else {
            //add the letter to encryptedSentence
            encryptedSentence.append(letter);
        }
    }

    return encryptedSentence.toString();
}
```

The isVowel method is the same as in Chapter 8, but we will list it again here for easy reference. The method is implemented as follows:

```
private boolean isVowel(char letter)
{
    boolean result = false;

    if (   letter == 'a' || letter == 'A' ||
           letter == 'e' || letter == 'E' ||
           letter == 'i' || letter == 'I' ||
           letter == 'o' || letter == 'O' ||
           letter == 'u' || letter == 'U'      )  {

        result = true;
    }
    return result;
}
```

Step 2 Test   We modify the TestEggyPeggy main class from Step 1 to test the Step 2 program. Expressed in pseudocode, the test routine will look something like this:

```
eggyPeggy1 = new EggyPeggy( );
eggyPeggy2 = new EggyPeggy( "bacon" );

str1 = eggyPeggy1.convert( <testString1> );
output str1;

eggyPeggy1.setPrefixWord( "avocado" );
str1 = eggyPeggy1.convert( <testString1> );
output str1;

str2 = eggyPeggy2.convert( <testString2> );
output str2;

eggyPeggy2.setPrefixWord( "tomato" );
str2 = eggyPeggy2.convert( <testString2> );
output str2;
```

You should try various strings (empty string, string with one character, string with no vowels, string with only vowels, etc.) for <testString1> and <testString2>.

HiLo

Now let's move on to redesign the HiLo class so its instance becomes an application logic object. The HiLo class we developed in Chapter 7 illustrated the use of repetition control and predefined objects. A HiLo object in that program controls other objects from the javabook package. It was a controller object and not intended to be reusable. Here, we will design a new HiLo class as an application logic class that captures the functionality of game playing only. By making this class implement the logic of the Hi-Lo game, the class becomes reusable in different types of programs. For example, the programmer can use it in writing a program that supports either a GUI or a CUI (*character-based user interface*).

As we did with the application logic EggyPeggy class, we will design the new HiLo class as general as possible to increase its reusability. In the original class, the game is limited to guessing a secret number between 1 and 100. Also, the number of guesses allowed was fixed. We will remove these restrictions. Here is the new problem statement.

Problem Statement

Write an application logic class that will play Hi-Lo games. The objective of the game is for the user to guess the computer-generated secret number in the least number of tries. The programmer can set the low and high bounds of a secret number and the number of guesses the user is allowed. If the number of guesses allowed is not set by the programmer, then it is set by the HiLo object based on the designated low and high bounds. The default low and high bounds are 1 and 100. The default number of guesses for the default low and high bounds is 7.

Overall Plan

As we did with the EggyPeggy class, let's begin our design of the new HiLo class with its public instance methods. What kinds of public methods should a HiLo object support? From the given problem statement and thinking from the programmer's viewpoint, we envision our program will use a HiLo object in the following manner:

```
hiLo = new HiLo( );

while (the user wants to play game) {

    hiLo.newGame();
```

```
do {
    get next userGuess;

    answer = hiLo.nextGuess( userGuess );

    if (answer is LO)
        output LO message;

    else if (answer is HI)
        output HI message;

while ( answer != BINGO &&
        game is not over );

if ( answer == BINGO )
    output YOU WIN message;
else
    output YOU LOSE message;


}
```

The three statements surrounded by the dotted ellipse are the calls to the methods of the HiLo class. The three methods are

1. Constructor.

2. newGame to start a new game.

3. nextGuess to pass a new guess and get a result back.

Let's begin the design of the HiLo class from these methods. The constructor we included in the pseudocode passes no arguments:

```
hiLo  =  new HiLo( );
```

When this constructor is called, we will initialize a HiLo object with default values for the low and high bounds of a secret number and the number of guesses allowed. We will perform this assignment of default values so the created object is initialized properly; that is, we do not leave any attributes (data members) of an object undefined.

In addition to this constructor, we can define constructors in which the programmer can pass the values for an object's data members. The class will allow the programmer to set the low and high bounds of a secret number and the number of guesses allowed. We can define different constructors to accept any combinations of these three values, but to do so would result in far too many constructors (some of which may not be natural, e.g., passing the low bound and the number of guesses). Too many constructors would be overly complex to use the constructors. We will define two additional constructors. A second constructor will accept two arguments—the low and high bounds. The number of guesses allowed will be computed from the given low and high bounds. To create a HiLo object with 100 and 300 as the low and high bounds, for example, we call the second constructor as

```
hiLo   = new HiLo( 100, 300 );
```

A third constructor will allow the programmer to pass all three values—the low and high bounds and the number of guesses allowed. For example, the statement

```
hiLo   = new HiLo( 1, 100, 3 );
```

will create a HiLo object with low and high bounds of 1 and 100 and the number of guesses allowed of 3.

After a Hilo object is created, we will call its newGame method every time we play a new game. The newGame method will reset an object to play another game. One of the key functions of the method is to generate a new secret number. We will use a pseudorandom number generator to generate a secret number as before. The method will also initialize whatever data members that need to be initialized at the beginning of a new game.

When the programmer calls the newGame method, should we allow him or her to change the low and high bounds and the number of guesses? If we allow this option, then a single HiLo object can play different types of Hi-Lo games. If we don't allow this option, then a single instance can play many games but the values for the low and high bounds and the number of allowed guesses remain the same for every game it plays. To write a program that plays different types of Hi-Lo games, the programmer must create many instances of the HiLo class.

We will adopt the scenario that a single instance can play many games of the same type. The newGame method we define here therefore has no parameters. We will leave the alternative design of newGame as an exercise for you to think about the pros and cons of the two approaches.

Every time the user enters a new guess, we will call the nextGuess method, passing the user guess as its argument. The nextGuess method will reply back with a result. There are basically three possible results: LO, HI, or BINGO. What should be the data type for this result? One possibility is a String. The method can return a String such as "LO", "HI", and "BINGO". Although the use of a String is a very general way of passing information back, it is also error-prone. It is very easy for the programmer to make a mistake and compare the String HI against Hi, for example. When the number of values to return from a method is only a handful or less, then a simple integer is better. By declaring public class constants for each of the possible return values, we can reduce programmer errors. We will declare the constants as

```
public static final int HI = 1;
public static final int LO = 2;
//and so forth
```

Using these constants, the portion of pseudocode can be stated as

```
...
if ( answer == HiLo.LO )
    ...
else if ( answer == HiLo.HI )
    ...
```

Are there any portions in the pseudocode that we need to translate into a public method of HiLo? Notice the condition for stopping the do–while loop. The loop is continued if the secret number was not yet guessed and not all of the allowed number of guesses were used up. We use the expression

```
answer != HiLo.BINGO
```

to test that the correct guess was not yet made. How should we express that the game is not over, that is, the number of allowed guesses is not used up yet? Whose responsibility is it to check this condition? Should it be the responsibility of a programmer who is using a HiLo object? The programmer can use a counter for this purpose. Or should it be the responsibility of a HiLo object?

We indicated that the role of HiLo objects is to play Hi-Lo games. All tasks involved in playing a Hi-Lo game should be carried out by the HiLo object, including keeping track of the number of guesses made. Since this object is the one that keeps track of the number of allowed guesses, it is logical for this object to let the programmer know whether the game is over or not. In other words, the programmer should not be bothered with the task of keeping a counter for the number of guesses made. We will let a HiLo object tell the programmer when the number of allowed guesses is used up.

One way is to define a method such as isGameNotOver, which returns true if the game is not over and false otherwise. However, we usually do not include the negation in a query method, because if we indeed define such method, we have to state something like

```
!isGameNotOver()
```

to check that the game is over. Double negation is very difficult and awkward to read, so a better way is to define a method isGameOver and negate it as !hiLo.isGameOver() in the do–while loop:

```
do {

    //process one guess

} while ( answer != HiLo.BINGO &&    //guess not correct and
            !hiLo.isGameOver( ) );    //game is not yet over
```

Since a HiLo object keeps track of the number of guesses the user has made, it is possible to code the nextGuess method to return a fourth value, say, GAMEOVER in addition to LO, HI, and BINGO. With this approach, the do–while loop is expressed as

```
do {

    //process one guess

} while ( answer != HiLo.BINGO &&    //guess not correct and
            answer != HiLo.GAMEOVER ); //game is not yet over
```

We will adopt the second design because it is more consistent and logical; that is, the nextGuess method will return one of the four possible outcomes of making a guess.

Our working design document for the HiLo class at this point is as follows:

Design Document: The HiLo Class		
Method	**Visibility**	**Purpose**
`<constructors>`	`public`	Creates and initializes a HiLo object.
`newGame`	`public`	Resets an object for a new game.
`nextGuess`	`public`	Checks the next guess and returns the result. The return type int is used to indicate the result.

And its object diagram at this point is

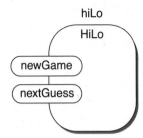

We will implement the class in the following four logical steps:

development steps

1. Start with a class skeleton. Define the necessary data members and constructors. Add any other methods necessary to implement the constructors.

2. Implement the newGame method. Add any other methods necessary to implement this method.

3. Implement the nextGuess method. Add any other methods necessary to implement this method.

4. Finalize the class implementation with final review and code modification/extension.

Step 1 Development: Skeleton with Constructors

Step 1 Design Let's start with data members of the class. Using the first constructor, a HiLo object is created with default values for the low and high bounds of a secret number and the number of guesses allowed. Let's define constants for these default values:

```
private static final int DEFAULT_MAX_GUESSES =    7;
private static final int DEFAULT_LOW         =    1;
private static final int DEFAULT_HIGH        = 100;
```

We also need to define constants for values returned by the nextGuess method:

```
public   static final int HI        = 1;
public   static final int LO        = 2;
public   static final int BINGO     = 3;
public   static final int GAMEOVER  = 4;
```

Since the low and high bounds of a secret number and the number of guesses allowed are different for each HiLo object, we need a variable for each of these values. Also, we have to keep track of number of the guesses made and the secret number for each game. The variable declarations are as follows:

```
private int numberOfGuessesAllowed;
private int guessLowBound;
private int guessHighBound;

private int guessCount;
private int secretNumber;
```

Now, let's think about the constructors. We will use the technique of defining one constructor that initializes the object and having all other constructors directly or indirectly call this constructor. We will add code to initialize the object to the constructor to accept three arguments: low bound, high bound, and number of guesses. Is the following an acceptable way to define this?

```
public HiLo( int low, int high, int numberOfGuesses )
{
    guessLowBound = low;
    guessHighBound = high;
    numberOfGuessesAllowed = numberOfGuesses;
}
```

If the programmer makes no mistakes in calling the constructor, it is acceptable, but it is not wise to assume that the programmer will make no mistakes. We must aim to design the class that is as robust as possible. What would happen if the programmer gets confused and switches the low and high by mistake?

What would happen if the programmer passes a nonpositive number as the third argument?

When an invalid value is passed to the constructor, we will initialize the data members using the following rule:

```
if ( low > high ) {
    switch the low and high;
}

if ( numberOfGuesses <= 0 ) {
    //if the given numberOfGuesses is invalid
    //derive the value from the given low and high
    numberOfGuessesAllowed = maxGuess( low, high );
}

//assign arguments to data members

//set to play a new game
newGame();
```

The maxGuess method determines the number of guesses allowed based on the low and high bounds. The idea is to derive a formula to compute the maximum number of allowed guesses based on the range of a secret number so that we allow more guesses when a range is bigger and fewer guesses when a range is smaller. What kind of formula should it be?

If you always use the middle value of low and high as the next guess, you can make a correct guess in N tries where N is derived as

$$N = \lceil \log_2(high - low + 1) \rceil$$

For example, if the low is 1 and high is 100, then N is 7. Your first guess is 50. If this guess is, say, low, then your next guess is 75. You continue in this manner, and the maximum times you need to guess the number is 7. Try it. The basic idea behind this formula is that you cannot divide 100 more than 7 times until the range of values where the secret number is located becomes empty.

Since the Math class does not support the logarithm of base 2, we need to convert the formula to the logarithm of base 10:

$$N = \left\lceil \log_2(high - low + 1) \right\rceil$$

$$= \left\lceil \frac{\log_{10}(high - low + 1)}{\log_{10}(2)} \right\rceil$$

Note: $\log_a b = \dfrac{\log_c b}{\log_c a}$

Expressing the formula in a Java statement, we have the following:

```
Math.ceil( Math.log( high - low + 1 ) / Math.log( 2 ) )
```

Now, notice the call to the method newGame at the end of the constructor. Whenever a new instance is created, it should be in a state ready to play a game, instead of relying on the programmer to always call the newGame method before starting a new game. We will work on this method in the next step.

Finally, we will define two additional constructors. These two constructors will call the three-argument constructor in the following manner. The constructor with two arguments will call the three-argument constructor as

```
this( low, high, maxGuess(low, high) );
```

In order for this call to work correctly, the maxGuess method must be a class method (i.e., with the static modifier). An instance of a class is created inside a constructor, and we can call an instance method from a constructor without a problem. However, this constructor with two arguments is calling another constructor, so no instance is actually created in this contructor. The three-argument constructor is the only constructor where an instance is actually created. For this reason, we must declare the maxGuess method as a class method.

The constructor with no argument will call the three-argument constructor as

```
this( DEFAULT_LOW, DEFAULT_HIGH, DEFAULT_MAX_GUESSES );
```

Note that it is also possible for this constructor to call the two-argument constructor instead as

```
this( DEFAULT_LOW, DEFAULT_HIGH );
```

and get rid of the constant DEFAULT_MAX_GUESS. The two-argument constructor will compute the value of 7 given DEFAULT_LOW and DEFAULT_HIGH. We will retain the constant DEFAULT_MAX_GUESS, so we can set other values for a default maximum number of guesses allowed.

Step 1 Code   Here's the Step 1 implementation of the HiLo class:

```
/* HiLo Class

   The class to play Hi-Lo games. The objective of the game is for the user to
   guess the computer-generated secret number in the least number of tries. The
   low and high bounds of a secret number and the number of guesses can be set
   by the programmer. If the number of guesses allowed is not set by the
   programmer, then the default value is determined based on the low
   and high bounds. The default low and high bounds, if not set by the
   programmer, are 1 and 100. The default number of guesses for the default low
   and high bounds is 7.
*/

class HiLo
{
/*************************
   Data Members
*************************/
   public  static final int HI        = 1;
   public  static final int LO        = 2;
   public  static final int BINGO     = 3;
   public  static final int GAMEOVER  = 4;

   private static final int DEFAULT_MAX_GUESSES =   7;
   private static final int DEFAULT_LOW         =   1;
   private static final int DEFAULT_HIGH        = 100;

   private int numberOfGuessesAllowed;
   private int guessLowBound;
   private int guessHighBound;

   private int guessCount;
   private int secretNumber;

/*************************
   Constructors
*************************/

   public HiLo( )
   {
       this(DEFAULT_LOW, DEFAULT_HIGH, DEFAULT_MAX_GUESSES);
   }

   public HiLo(int low, int high)
   {
       this( low, high, maxGuess(low,high));
   }

   public HiLo(int low, int high, int numGuess)
   {
```

```
        if (low > high) {
            int temp = low;
            low = high;
            high = temp;
        }

        if ( numGuess <=0 ) {
            numGuess = maxGuess(low, high);
        }

        guessLowBound = low;
        guessHighBound = high;
        numberOfGuessesAllowed = numGuess;

        newGame();

        System.out.println("low bound:     " + guessLowBound);           //TEMP
        System.out.println("high bound:    " + guessHighBound);          //TEMP
        System.out.println("max guesses:   " + numberOfGuessesAllowed);  //TEMP
        System.out.println("secret number: " + secretNumber);           //TEMP
        System.out.println("  ");                                        //TEMP
    }

/*****************************
    Public Methods

        void      newGame        (             )
        int       nextGuess      ( int         )

*****************************/


    /********************************************************
        Method:       newGame

        Purpose:      Sets the object for a new game.

        Parameters:   None

        Returns:      None
    */
    public void newGame()
    {
        System.out.println("Inside newGame");       //TEMP
    }

    /********************************************************
        Method:       nextGuess

        Purpose:      Determines whether or not the guess is the secret number.
                      Returns the status of guess: HI, LO, etc.

        Parameters:   int [next guess]

        Returns:      int [status of the guess]
    */
    public int nextGuess( int guess )
    {
```

```
            System.out.println("Inside nextGuess");       //TEMP

            return 0;              //Dummy return statement
        }

/*******************************
    Private Methods

        static int maxGuess          ( int, int      )

*****************************/

    /************************************************************
        Method:       maxGuess

        Purpose:      Computes the maximum number of allowed guesses.

        Parameters:   int [low bound of the secret number],
                      int [high bound of the secret number]

        Returns:      int [maximum number of guesses allowed]
    */
    private static int maxGuess( int low, int high )
    {
        return (int) Math.ceil( Math.log(high-low+1) / Math.log( 2 ) );
    }
}
```

Step 1 Test   In order to test the skeleton HiLo class, we need to write a test main class. The purpose of this test program is to verify that the constructors are executed correctly, that is, values for the data members are set correctly. To verify this, we included the temporary output statements in the third constructor. One possible test main class is the following:

```
class TestHiLo
{
    public static void main (String args[])
    {
        //create a HiLo object
        HiLo hiLo1, hiLo2, hiLo3, hiLo4;

        hiLo1 = new HiLo( );
        hiLo2 = new HiLo( 200, 500 );
        hiLo3 = new HiLo( 101, 150, 3 );
        hiLo4 = new HiLo( 500, 250 );
    }
}
```

When you execute this test program, you should see something like the following printout in the standard output window System.out. Notice the secret numbers in the actual printout would be different.

```
low bound:      1
high bound:     100
max guess:      7
secret number: 34

low bound:      200
high bound:     500
max guess:      9
secret number: 344

low bound:      101
high bound:     150
max guess:      3
secret number: 129

low bound:      250
high bound:     500
max guess:      8
secret number: 417
```

Make sure you run the test program with other argument values for the constructors, such as the following:

Test Input for the Constructors	
low	high
10	10
100	32000
−35	−150
0	1

Step 2 Development: Implement the newGame Method

Step 2 Design

In the second step of development, we complete the newGame method and add whatever methods are necessary to fully implement the newGame method. The task of the newGame method is to reset the object for a new game. To start a new game, we need to generate a new secret number. For every game, we need a counter to track the number of guesses made, so we will reset this counter in the newGame method also.

We use a pseudorandom number generator from the Math class to generate a new secret number. The code we used in the previous HiLo class in Chapter 7 is

```
double X = Math.random();
secretNumber = (int) Math.floor( X * 100 ) + 1;
```

This code is based on the fixed low and high bounds of 1 and 100. We need to generalize the code for any low and high bounds. The code is now modified to

```
double X = Math.random();
secretNumber = (int) Math.floor( X * (high-low+1) ) + low;
```

Try out different values for the low and high bounds and verify that this formula works. The value (high–low+1) gives the number of distinct values in a given range. For example, with low = 201 and high = 500, there are 300 distinct values. If you multiply this number by the pseudorandom number X, where 0 <= X < 1.0, you get a value between 0 and 299, inclusive. Finally, if you add this value to low, then you get a number anywhere between 201 and 500.

The working design document now includes the getRandomNumber method:

Design Document: The HiLo Class		
Method	**Visibility**	**Purpose**
...	...	...
getRandomNumber	private	Returns a pseudorandom number (int) between guessLowBound and guessHighBound. This number will be the secret number.

Step 2 Code   The newGame method is defined as follows:

```
public void newGame(   )
{
    guessCount = 0;
    secretNumber = getRandomNumber();
}
```

and the private getRandomNumber method is defined as follows:

```
private int getRandomNumber(   )
{
    double    X;
    int       number;

    X      = Math.random();
    number = (int) Math.floor( X * (guessHighBound -
                                    guessLowBound + 1 ) )
                       + guessLowBound;

    System.out.println("New secret number: " + number); //TEMP

    return number;
}
```

Step 2 Test

We modify the TestHiLo main class from Step 1 to verify that the correct se-cret numbers are generated. Expressed in pseudocode, the test routine will look something like this:

```
HiLo hiLo;

hiLo = new HiLo( 200, 500 );
for (int i = 0; i < 100; i++ ) {
    hiLo.newGame();
}
```

Run the program and verify that 100 correct secret numbers are generated. Once you verify this, run the program multiple times changing the values you pass in the constructor. When everything is working correctly, move on to Step 3.

Step 3 Development: Implement the nextGuess Method

Step 3 Design

In the third step of development, we complete the nextGuess method and add whatever methods necessary to fully implement this method. The basic task of this method expressed in pseudocode is as follows:

```
int status;

guessCount++;

if (userGuess == secretNumber)
    status = BINGO;

else if (guessCount == numberOfGuessesAllowed)
```

```
        status = GAMEOVER;

   else if (userGuess < secretNumber)
        status = LO;

   else  // userGuess > secretNumber
        status = HI;

   return status;
```

This pseudocode is acceptable if the passed userGuess is always valid and as long as the value for userGuess is inside the ranges of guessLowBound and guessHighBound. To make this method robust, we include code to handle the invalid userGuess. We extend the pseudocode to the following:

```
   int status;

   guessCount++;

   if (userGuess == secretNumber)
        status = BINGO;

   else if (guessCount == numberOfGuessesAllowed)
        status = GAMEOVER;

   else if ( !isValid(userGuess) )
        status = INVALID;

   else if (userGuess < secretNumber)
        status = LO;

   else  // userGuess > secretNumber
        status = HI;

   return status;
```

We add one constant to the data declaration section:

```
   public static final int INVALID = -1;
```

The isValid method is a private method that returns true if the passed argument falls between the set low and high bounds. The working design document now includes this method:

Design Document: The HiLo Class		
Method	**Visibility**	**Purpose**
...	...	...
isValid	private	Returns true if the passed argument falls between guessLowBound and guessHighBound.

Step 3 Code

The nextGuess method is defined as follows:

```
public int nextGuess( int userGuess)
{
    int status;

    guessCount++;

    if (userGuess == secretNumber) {
        status = BINGO;
    }
    else if (guessCount == numberOfGuessesAllowed) {
        status = GAMEOVER;
    }
    else if (!isValid(userGuess) ) {
        status = INVALID;
    }
    else if (userGuess < secretNumber) {
        status = LO;
    }
    else { // userGuess > secretNumber
        status = HI;
    }

    return status;
}
```

and the private isValid method is defined as follows:

```
private boolean isValid( int guess )
{
    boolean status;
```

```
        if (guessLowBound <= guess  && guess <= guessHighBound) {
            status = true;
        }
        else {
            status = false;
        }
        return status;
    }
```

Since we are returning a boolean value, we can write the method without using the if statement as

```
    private boolean isValid( int guess )
    {
        boolean status;

        status = guessLowBound <= guess && guess <= guessHighBound;

        return status;
    }
```

Step 3 Test

The testing strategy for the Step 3 HiLo class is the same as the one we employed in Chapter 7. We play multiple games testing the error cases, normal cases, and end cases. Since we still have temporary output statements in the getRandom-Number method and the third constructor, we know the secret number and other key values for each game. With this knowledge, we will be able to go through different cases to verify that the class works correctly in all cases.

Step 4 Development: Finalize

code
review

We finalize the program in the last step. We will perform a critical review of the class looking for any unfinished methods, making sure all methods work cooperatively, commenting out all temporary output statements, and confirming no necessary methods are missing. We will also review the class for any possible improvements we can make to the existing methods.

Are there any methods we might want to add to the class to increase its usability? Are there any methods we can improve? Reviewing the currently defined methods, we notice that the class does not include any access methods. When a game is over, the programmer may wish to output a message such as

```
    Sorry, you lost. You used up all 9 guesses. The secret number
    was 345, generated from the range between 100 and 500.
```

In order to output such a message, the programmer must know the values for the low and high bounds, the number of guesses allowed, and the secret number. These values are maintained by a HiLo object, so it is natural to provide access methods to get the values. We will add the following access methods to the class:

```
public int getSecretNumber( )
{
    return secretNumber;
}

public int getLowBound()
{
    return guessLowBound;
}

public int getHighBound()
{
    return guessHighBound;
}

public int getMaxGuess( )
{
    return numberOfGuessesAllowed;
}
```

11.4 Package Organization

Now that we have learned how to define reusable classes, let's study how we can manage their source files for effective reuse. The most primitive way to reuse a class is to put the source file or the bytecode file of the class in the same folder that includes the other classes of your program. This approach of reuse is, of course, unacceptable because you would end up duplicating multiple copies of the same source file in different folders. This would be a maintenance nightmare. If you have to make modifications to the class, you have to locate all copies of the source files and make changes to every copy. A proper way to reuse code is to put the source file or the bytecode file of a class in a package. We will explain how to create a package in this section.

Let's start with some basic facts about the package. First, the classes in a package must be placed in a folder whose name is the name of the package. For example, all the classes of the javabook package are placed in the javabook folder. Second, packages can be nested. For example, the standard package awt is placed in the package java. To use the classes in the package awt, we import them by using the import statement

```
import java.awt.*;
```

Third, if you want others to use the classes but not modify them, then you should place only the bytecode files in the package. If you put in the source files also, then you cannot prohibit other programmers from changing them.

To put a class in a package, we need to do a little more than just placing the bytecode (or source) file in the corresponding folder. We have to make a modification to the source file. Specifically, we need to add one declaration at the beginning of the source file and an accessibility modifier (e.g., public) to the class declaration. Let's say we want to place the HiLo and EggyPeggy classes defined in the previous section in a package called game. Here's one possible sequence of steps to achieve it:

1. Create the folder called game and put the source file of the two classes into it. You can place this new folder anywhere you want, but you should place the folder at the location where it is convenient for other programs to access. We place the javabook package under the Projects folder along with the other folders for the chapter sample code.

2. Include the declaration

    ```
    package game;
    ```

    before all other declarations and statements in the two source files and add the modifier public to the class declaration. For example, the source file for the HiLo class becomes

    ```
    /*
        HiLo Class
        ...
    */

    package game;

    public class HiLo
    {
        ...
    }
    ```

3. Compile the classes. The game folder now contains the source and bytecode files of the two classes.

To make a class in a package accessible to outside classes (classes that are not in this package), we must declare the class public. If the class has no modifier, then the class is accessible only to other classes in the same package. For example, if we declare the HiLo class as

```
public class HiLo
{
    ...
}
```

then the class is accessible to an outside class via an import statement

```
import game.*;
```

If, on the other hand, we declare the HiLo class as

```
class Hilo
{
    ...
}
```

then the class is not accessible to an outside class. In other words, the following declaration will result in an error:

```
import game.*;
...
Hilo    myHiLoGame; //Error: Class HiLo is not accessible
                    //         because it is not a public class
```

A class in a package is accessible to other classes outside of the package only if the class is declared public.

A class in a package is always accessible to other classes in the same package without using the import statement. If we declare multiple classes for the program but do not include the package statement in these classes, then the Java compiler considers these classes to be placed in a default, unnamed package. Since they are in the same package, they are accessible to each other. This is the reason why we have never put the public access modifier in the class declaration.

Once classes are placed in a package, there are several ways to make the classes in the package available to other programmers. They can get a copy of the bytecode files from you, on a floppy disk, or by downloading from a public ftp site, and then put the copy on their own machine in a folder with the same name as the package name. Or they can access the files directly from their program by specifying a full address in the import statement, such as

```
import EDU.myschool.cs/drcaffeine/Projects/javabook.*;
```

Please consult your instructor or other references for more information on direct network access. Also, please consult the reference manual or online help of the Java development environment you are using to find out specific details on how to create a package.

11.5 Exercises

1. When do you want to declare a class in a package public?

2. What is the purpose of defining multiple constructors?

3. Which of the following method declarations have the same signature?

```
public void one ( int x, int y)      /* 1 */
{
    ...
}

private void one ( int x, int y)     /* 2 */
{
    ...
}

public int one ( int x, int y)       /* 3 */
{
    ...
}

private void one ( int x, float y)   /* 4 */
{
    ...
}
```

4. Identify problems with the following class declaration. Note: The class not doing anything meaningful is not a problem here.

```
package vehicle;
package truck;

import vehicle.*;

public class OffRoad
{
    private int       weight;
    private String    vin;

    public offroad()
    {
        weight = 5000;
    }
}
```

5. Rewrite the Java^2 Lo-Fat Burgers drive-through system using instantiable classes (exercise 11 on page 357 in Chapter 7).

6. Rewrite the ComputeMonthlyPayment program of Chapter 4 using instantiable classes.

7. Define a LoanCalculator class whose instances are application logic objects. Define set methods (mutators) to assign values for loan amount, annual interest rate, and loan period. The methods computeMonthlyPayment, computeTotalPayment, and computeTotalInterest return the amounts for monthly payment, total payment, and total interest, respectively. Use this class and write an application-based or an applet-based loan calculator program.

8. Extend the LoanCalculator class of exercise 7 by adding a new method called getLoanTable that returns a loan payment schedule table as described in exercise 21 on page 359 in Chapter 7. You must decide on the data type for this table very carefully. Possible data types for the table are

　　1.　A 2-D array of float.

　　2.　A 1-D array of LoanTableEntry objects

　　3.　A LoanTable object.

A single LoanTableEntry object includes information on one row of a loan payment schedule table, that is, payment number, interest, principal, unpaid balance, and total interest paid to date. A single LoanTable object includes information on the whole table. If you choose the second or the third option, then you need to implement the LoanTableEntry or the LoanTable class yourself. Extend the loan calculator program of exercise 7 by including a new method getPaymentScheduleTable.

9. Define a Person class whose instance is used to keep track of a person's information. The Person object maintains a first and last name, address, phone number, and age. Write a test program to verify that the Person class works correctly.

10. Define a Student class as a subclass of Person. A Student object keeps the record of three midterms and one final exam. The highest possible score for the midterms is 50 and for the final is 100. The three midterms and the final exam are respectively 60 percent and 40 percent of the course score. The final course grade is computed as

Course Score	Final Course Grade
85 ≤ score ≤ 100	A
78 ≤ score < 85	B
65 ≤ score < 78	C
40 ≤ score < 65	D
0 ≤ score < 40	F

Write a test program to verify that the Student class works correctly.

11. Define a RentalCar class whose instance is used to keep track of a rental car's information, such as car model, daily rental rate, tank capacity (in gallons), number of free miles per day, the charge per mile for the miles over the mileage allowance, and the status (rented or available). Define any additional instance and class variables you think are necessary.

12. Write an application logic Encrypter class that is capable of encrypting and decrypting a given text using either Ceaser or Vignere cipher (see exercise 20 on page 421 and exercise 22 on page 422).

13. Java^2 Coffee Outlet is expanding again. This time the company is getting into the rental car business. Being a good corporate citizen keen to the need for recycling, the company started a new subsidiary, Java^2 Recycled Rentals, which specializes in renting refurbished used cars. The company maintains a fleet of five cars. You are hired as a freelance developer to write an online rental system. Using the RentalCar class from the preceding exercise, write a program that supports two operations: rental and return. When

the user selects the rental option, list the cars available for rental using a ListBox object. Display the daily rental charge, number of free miles, and the charge per mile over the mileage allowance for the car the user selected; then ask the user whether he or she wishes to rent the car. If the user says Yes, then remove the car from the available list. When a car is rented out, record the current mileage on the car. When the user selects the return option, list the cars currently rented out using a ListBox object. After the user selects a car, prompt the user for the mileage reading and the number of days rented; then display the total charge.

14. Rewrite the HiLo class so the player has an option of specifying the three levels of difficulty: Beginner, Intermediate, and Expert. The class will allow a fewer number of guesses for a higher level of difficulty. Suppose N is the number of guesses allowed that is computed automatically by the HiLo class from the given low and high bounds. If the player chooses the Beginner level, then the maximum number of guesses she is allowed to make is twice the N. If she chooses the Intermediate level, then it is N. And if she chooses the Expert level, then it is one-half of N.

15. Rewrite the HiLo class by adding a second form of newGame. The second newGame method accepts the low and high bounds of a secret number. So every time a new game is started, the programmer has the option of changing the low and high bounds. What are the advantages and disadvantages of the second newGame method?

16. Write a new class called Arithmetic that plays arithmetic games. An Arithmetic object asks N problems involving addition, subtraction, division, and multiplication, for example, 4 + 5, 5 * 3, and so forth. Each problem includes one operator, and the operands are limited to single digits. The value for N is set by the programmer. The object keeps track of the number of problems asked and the number of problems answered correctly. The programmer can prompt the Arithmetic object for the number of correct answers by calling the getCorrectCount method. Use the pseudorandom number generator from the Math class to select the operands and the operator for each problem. To select an operator, you can generate a random number between 1 and 4. If the number is 1, then use addition; if the number is 2, then use subtraction; and so forth.

17. Create a new package called game and place the EggyPeggy, HiLo, and Arithmetic classes in it. Using this package, write an application that allows the user to play three games: Eggy-Peggy, Hi-Lo, and Arithmetic. The player can choose any of them and play as many times as he or she wishes.

18. Using the game package created in exercise 17, write an applet that allows the user to play three games: Eggy-Peggy, Hi-Lo, and Arithmetic. See exercise 17.

19. Define a new class called BlackJack and add it to the game package. A BlackJack object plays the dealer for the blackjack card game. Use the pseudorandom number generator to generate numbers between 1 and 13. The numbers 11, 12, and 13 represent Jack, Queen, and King, respectively. Use an OutputBox object to display the hands of both the dealer and the player. You can use a symbol such as an asterisk to represent a card whose face is down. Use a ResponseBox object to prompt the player to hit another card or stay.

20. Extend the game-playing application from exercise 17 to include the blackjack card game created in exercise 19.

21. Write a checkbook application program. The program maintains multiple checkbooks. For each checkbook, the user can deposit, write a check, and withdraw. Since this program is for personal record-keeping use, the balance can become negative. When a new check is written, a CheckBook object will automatically assign the next available check number. The user will have the options of voiding a check and overriding the automatically assigned check number. The beginning check number is set when the object is initially created. At the beginning of the program execution, you must read in information from a file. At the end of the program execution, the data are written back to the file. Some of the classes you should include for the program are listed below:

program classes

Design Document:	CheckBook
Class	**Purpose**
CheckBookMain	The main class of the program.
CheckBookController	The top level control object that manages other objects in the program.
CheckBook	A CheckBook object contains a collection of Check objects.
Check	A Check object is used to represent a single check.
CheckBookStorage	A CheckBookStorage object is responsible for the file I/O of CheckBook objects.
<interface classes>	Standard and custom made objects for handling user interface of the program.

GUI Objects and Event-Driven Programming

Introduction

graphical
user interface

The objects from the standard java.awt packages are called *graphical user interface* (GUI) objects, and they are used to handle the user interface aspect of programs. Some of the GUI objects from the package are shown in Figure 12.1. The style of programming we use with these GUI objects is called *event-driven programming*. An *event* occurs when the user interacts with a GUI object. For example, when you move the cursor, click on a button, or select a menu choice, an event occurs. In event-driven programs, we program objects to respond to these events by defining event-handling methods. In this chapter we will introduce objects from the java.awt package and show you how to write event-handling methods. Basic event-handling topics were already discussed in Chapter 5, so for those who studied Chapter 5, some of the topics in this chapter will be a review.

event-driven
programming

FIGURE 12.1   Various GUI objects from the **java.awt** package.

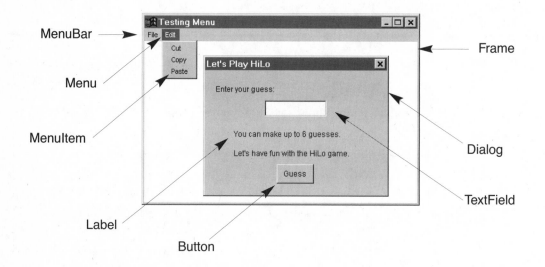

Since our objective for the chapter is to teach event-driven programming and not to teach the java.awt classes, we will cover only those that are fundamental to event-driven programming and easy to understand for beginners. We encourage you to explore other java.awt classes not covered in this chapter on your own. Since GUI objects such as ListBox in the javabook package are programmed to work in a manner similar to many of the java.awt objects, you will find many of the java.awt classes familiar. We also encourage you to study the source code of the javabook classes to see how they are implemented using the classes from java.awt.

12.1 Placing Buttons on a Frame

Let's write a simple GUI program to show how to manipulate GUI objects. The program will include one window that has two buttons labeled CANCEL and OK. When you click the CANCEL button, the window's title is changed to You clicked CANCEL. Likewise, when you click the OK button, the window's title is changed to You clicked OK. Figure 12.2 shows the window when it is first opened and after the CANCEL button is clicked.

FIGURE 12.2   A sample window when it is first opened and after the **CANCEL** button is clicked.

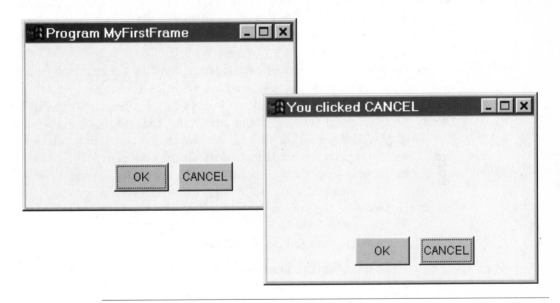

There are two types of windows in GUI programs: frame and dialog. A *frame* is a general-purpose window in which the user interacts with the application. Windows in which the user writes a document, draws a picture, sends e-mail, and so on are all frames. A Java GUI application program must have at least one frame that serves as the program's main window.

frame

A *dialog* is a limited-purpose window used primarily for displaying simple information such as error messages or getting a simple response such as yes or

dialog

no. Windows in which the user selects a file to open, confirms that he wants to print a document, and so on are all dialogs.

Two of the classes in the java.awt package are Frame and Dialog. The Frame class contains the most rudimentary functionalities to support features found in any frame window, such as minimizing the window, moving the window, resizing the window, and so forth. In writing applications, we do not create an instance of the Frame class because a Frame object is not capable of doing anything meaningful. For example, if we want to use a frame window for a word processor, we need a frame window capable of allowing the user to enter, cut, and paste text; change font; print text; and so forth. To design such a frame window, we would define a subclass of the Frame class and add methods and data members to implement the needed functionalities.The main window for our earlier sample programs is an instance of the MainWindow class from the javabook package, which is a subclass of the Frame class that adds four functionalities: set the string Sample Java Application as the default window title, terminates the program when the close box is clicked,[1] adjusts the size of the window to roughly the size of the screen, and displays the window at the center of the screen.

Similar to the Frame class, the Dialog class contains the most rudimentary functionalities to support features found in any dialog box. Again, we actually never create an instance of the Dialog class, but rather define a subclass of the Dialog class to support a dialog box in a program. The javabook classes Input-Box, ListBox, MessageBox, OutputBox, and ResponseBox are all subclasses of Dialog. We will explain how to define and use dialog classes in Section 12.6.

For our sample program, we need a frame to place two buttons, so we will first define a subclass of Frame called MyFirstFrame. Inside a constructor, we can set its properties. For this sample, we will set the following properties:

1. 300 pixels wide and 200 pixels high.

2. Not resizable (i.e., the user cannot drag the edge and change the window size).

3. Program MyFirstFrame as the frame title.

4. The top-left corner of the frame at the screen position (150, 250).

---

1. This functionality is supported by the Frame class in most platforms, but not by Windows 95.

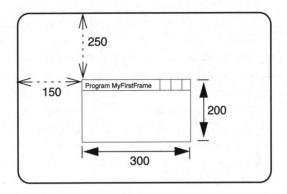

To set the frame's size, we pass its width and height to the setSize method. To designate the frame as not resizable, we pass the boolean argument false to the setResizable method. To set the frame's title, we pass the title to the setTitle method. And finally, to position the frame's top-left corner to the coordinate (x, y), we pass the values x and y to the setLocation method. The shell MyFirst-Frame class is declared as

```
import java.awt.*;

class MyFirstFrame extends Frame
{
    private static final int FRAME_WIDTH    = 300;
    private static final int FRAME_HEIGHT   = 200;
    private static final int FRAME_X_ORIGIN = 150;
    private static final int FRAME_Y_ORIGIN = 250;

    public MyFirstFrame( )
    {
        setSize      ( FRAME_WIDTH, FRAME_HEIGHT );
        setResizable ( false );
        setTitle     ( "Program MyFirstFrame" );
        setLocation  ( FRAME_X_ORIGIN, FRAME_Y_ORIGIN );
    }
}
```

To open this frame in a program, we need to define the main class, such as the following:

```
/*
    Program TestMyFirstFrame

    The main class for testing MyFirstFrame
*/
class TestMyFirstFrame
{
    public static void main (String args[] )
    {
        MyFirstFrame frame = new MyFirstFrame( );
        frame.setVisible( true );
    }
}
```

Notice that instead of using the show method, we are using the setVisible method to make the frame appear on the screen:

```
frame.setVisible( true ); //same as frame.show()
```

To hide a frame, we pass false to the setVisible method. The setVisible method is recommended for the Java 1.1 and 1.2 compilers (and may be necessary for the later compilers in the future) because the show method is now deprecated, meaning that the method may not be supported in the new versions of Java compilers. Although the show method works just fine with the Java 1.1 and 1.2 compilers, we will use the setVisible method whenever appropriate from now on.

When you run TestMyFirstFrame, an instance of MyFirstFrame appears on the screen as expected. However, when you try to close the frame, you cannot. This is because the frame does not include the code to close the window. When you click the close box of the frame, an event is generated, but there's no code in the MyFirstFrame class to process this window closing event. We will explain the event handling in the next section. But before that, let's place the buttons on this frame.

The type of button we explain here is called a *pushbutton*. Since we discuss the pushbuttons only, we will simply call them buttons. To use a button in a program, we create an instance of the Button class. We will create two buttons and place them on the frame in the constructor. Let's name the two buttons cancelButton and okButton. We add their declaration in the MyFirstFrame class as

```
class MyFirstFrame extends Frame
{
    Button cancelButton, okButton;
    ...
}
```

layout
manager

To place buttons on a frame, we can use a layout manager. We discussed the layout manager and its purpose in Chapter 5. We will repeat the discussion here for those who omitted the applet-based sample programs. The *layout manager* for a frame (and also for a dialog and an applet) controls how the GUI objects are placed on the frame. The default layout manager for a frame is a FlowLayout manager, which places GUI objects in the top-to-bottom, left-to-right order. It is also possible not to use any layout manager. If we don't use a layout manager, then we can place GUI objects precisely at the location where we want to posi-

absolute
positioning

tion them. We call this approach *absolute positioning*. We will use absolute positioning for the sample programs in the remainder of the book.

Although using a layout manager can be advantageous in some situations, knowing various layout managers does not really contribute much to the learning of object-oriented and event-driven programming. For this reason, we will not cover layout managers in this book.

> **Dr. Caffeine**
>
> A benefit of using a layout manager is the automatic adjustment of GUI objects when their container (frame, dialog, applet, etc.) is resized. For example, if you place a **Button** at the center of the container using some layout manager, then this **Button** will still be positioned at the center when the size of the container is changed. This automatic adjustment is important also when you consider running your program on different platforms, because by using a layout manager effectively you will get a more consistent look to your frames and dialogs across different platforms. With absolute positioning, a frame that looks nice on one platform may not appear as nice on another platform.

In order to use absolute positioning, we must set the layout manager of a frame to none in the constructor. We do this by passing null to the setLayout method:

```
setLayout(null);
```

After the layout manager is set to null , we place two buttons at the position and in the size we want by calling the button's setBounds method as in

```
okButton.setBounds( 100, 150, 60, 30 );
```

where the first two arguments specify the position of the button and the last two arguments specify the width and height of the button. Figure 12.3 illustrates how the four arguments are used. Notice that the positioning is relative to the frame's top-left corner.

FIGURE 12.3   The diagram illustrating how the **setBounds** method works.

```
frame = new Frame( );
frame.setSize(300,200);
frame.setLayout( null );
okButton = new Button("OK");
okButton.setBounds(100, 150, 60, 30);
```

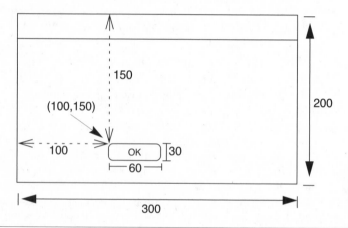

Setting the bounds of a button alone does not make it visible on the frame. To make it visible, we must attach it to the frame by calling the add method. For example, to add okButton, we call

```
add( okButton );
```

Here's the MyFirstFrame class with a modified portion that adds okButton and cancelButton:

```
class MyFirstFrame extends Frame
{
    ...
```

```
private static final int BUTTON_WIDTH   =   60;
private static final int BUTTON_HEIGHT  =   30;

Button okButton, cancelButton;

public MyFirstFrame( )
{
    ...
    okButton = new Button( "OK" );
    okButton.setBounds(100, 150,
                       BUTTON_WIDTH, BUTTON_HEIGHT);
    add( cancelButton );

    cancelButton = new Button( "CANCEL" );
    cancelButton.setBounds(170, 150,
                          BUTTON_WIDTH, BUTTON_HEIGHT);
    add( cancelButton );
}
}
```

If you run the TestMyFirstFrame program again, then you will see two buttons on the frame. When you click the buttons, of course, nothing happens because there's no code defined in the class that handles the button click event. We'll add the code to handle the button click events and the window close events in the next section.

Quick Check

1. What is a layout manager? How is it useful?
2. Using the setBounds method, position a button 50 pixels wide and 30 pixels high at the location (125, 85).
3. Give two ways to make a frame appear on the screen.

12.2 Handling Events

Let's complete the MyFirstFrame class by adding the event-handling code that processes the button click event and the window close event. We will write the code for processing the button clicks first.

delegation-based
event model

event source
and listener

action event

The event-handling model of Java is based on the concept of delegation. The *delegation-based event model*[2] classifies event-handling objects into two types: *event source objects* and *event listener objects*. An object can be an event source, event listener, or both.

An event source object sends events to event listeners. For example, when a button is clicked, the button sends an event called an *action event* to the listeners. The button where the event has originated is the event source. The button is said to "fire" or "generate" an event. For the button object to know to which listeners to send the action event, we must register listeners with the button. We do this by calling the addActionListener method of the button object. The action event is sent to all registered listeners. The listeners can then process the event.

For our sample program, cancelButton and okButton are event sources of the button click events. But which object should be an event listener? It is common to let the object that contains event sources be their event listener. In our case, this object is an instance of MyFirstFrame. To register a MyFirstFrame object as the event listener of two buttons, we add the following two statements to the constructor of MyFirstFrame:

```
cancelButton.addActionListener( this ); //add this frame as an
    okButton.addActionListener( this ); //action event listener
```

When the two buttons fire an action event, they send the fired event to their action listener by calling the listener's actionPerformed method. This means that any class that is designated as an action listener must include the actionPerformed method. To designate the MyFirstFrame class as an action listener, we must declare that the class implements the ActionListener interface as

```
import java.awt.event.*;    ◄———  Event-handling classes are in
                                  this package.

class MyFirstFrame extends Frame implements ActionListener
{
    ...
}
```

---

2. There is an old event-handling model still supported by Java 1.1 and 1.2. To distinguish the newer delegation-based event model from the old model, sometimes they are referred as JDK 1.1 event model and JDK 1.0 event model, respectively.

interface

abstract
method

ActionListener is not a class, but an interface. You have seen a sample interface Serializable in Section 10.5. An *interface* declares a new reference data type that includes only constants and abstract methods. An *abstract method* is a method that has no method body, just the method prototype. No instances can be created from an interface. To create an instance we need a class that *implements* the interface. For a class to implement an interface, the class must provide a method body to all of the abstract methods defined in the interface. The ActionListener interface includes only one abstract method, actionPerformed. An argument to the actionPerformed method is ActionEvent. An instance of ActionEvent represents an action event and supports methods we can use to find out properties of a generated event.

The actionPerformed method of MyFirstFrame is called by either cancelButton or okButton, so the logic of the method is something like this:

```
if (the event source is cancelButton) {
    set the frame title to "You clicked CANCEL"
}
else { //the event source is okButton because this listener
        //is registered with only two event sources
    set the frame title to "You clicked OK";
}
```

We can find out which object is an event source by calling the getSource method of ActionEvent. Using this method, we can define the actionPerformed method of MyFirstFrame as

```
public void actionPerformed( ActionEvent event )
{
    Button clickedButton = (Button) event.getSource();

    if (clickedButton == cancelButton) {
        setTitle( "You clicked CANCEL" );
    }
    else { //the event source is okButton
        setTitle( "You clicked OK" );
    }
}
```

Notice that we need to typecast the returned object to **Button**.

Because the getSource method can return an instance from different classes, we need to typecast the returned object to Button.

We can get the label of an event source button by calling the getActionCommand method of ActionEvent. This method returns a String object. Using this method, we can write the actionPerformed method as

```
public void actionPerformed( ActionEvent event )
{
    String label = event.getActionCommand();

    if (label.equals("CANCEL") {
        setTitle( "You clicked CANCEL" );
    }
    else { //the event source is okButton
        setTitle( "You clicked OK" );
    }
}
```

Here's the MyFirstFrame class with a modified portion that handles the button click events using the second version of actionPerformed:

```
class MyFirstFrame extends Frame implements ActionListener
{
    ...
    public MyFirstFrame( )
    {
        ...
            okButton.addActionListener( this );
        cancelButton.addActionListener( this );
    }

    public void actionPerformed( ActionEvent event )
    {
        String label = event.getActionCommand();

        if (label.equals("CANCEL")) {
            setTitle( "You clicked CANCEL" );
        }
        else { //the event source is okButton
            setTitle( "You clicked OK" );
        }
    }
}
```

Now we are ready to add the code to close the frame (i.e., make it disappear from the screen) when its close box is clicked. Since this frame is the main window of the program, we will also terminate the program when the frame's close box is clicked. If we terminate a program, all windows of the program will be closed automatically, so we do not have to call any method explicitly to close them.

window event

Actions such as resizing, moving, and clicking on the close box you perform on a frame are called *window events*, and the class that represents a window event is WindowEvent. Only frames and dialogs can be event sources of window events. The class, whose instances are window event listeners, must implement the WindowListener interface. The WindowListener interface includes seven abstract methods: windowActivated, windowClosed, windowClosing, windowDeactivated, windowDeiconified, windowIconified, and windowOpened. So any class that implements the WindowListener interface must define all seven methods. The argument to all these methods is WindowEvent. When the window is first opened, windowOpened is called. When the close box is clicked, windowClosing is called. When the window is actually closed, windowClosed is called. When the window is minimized or restored, windowIconified and windowDeiconified are called respectively. And when the window becomes active or inactive, windowActivated and windowDeactivated are called respectively.

Most of the time we are not interested in handling all seven events. If you do not want to process a certain window event, then define the corresponding event-handling method with an empty method body, that is, a method body with no statements in it. For our sample program, we want to process only the window closing event, so we will define the windowClosing method with a real method body and define all others with an empty method body.

The window event source of our program is an instance of MyFirstFrame. But which object shall we let be a window event listener? We will define a new class whose instance will be our window event listener. Let's call this class ProgramTerminator. We will define the windowClosing method to terminate the program (and consequently, close the frame). A program is terminated by calling the exit method of the System class as

```
System.exit(0);
```

Here's the complete definition of the ProgramTerminator class:

```
/*
    ProgramTerminator Class

    A ProgramTerminator object terminates the program when its main window
    generates a window closing event.
*/
import java.awt.event.*;
```

```
class ProgramTerminator implements WindowListener
{

    public void windowClosing( WindowEvent event )
    {
        System.exit(0);
    }

    public void windowActivated      ( WindowEvent event ) { }
    public void windowClosed         ( WindowEvent event ) { }
    public void windowDeactivated    ( WindowEvent event ) { }
    public void windowDeiconified    ( WindowEvent event ) { }
    public void windowIconified      ( WindowEvent event ) { }
    public void windowOpened         ( WindowEvent event ) { }
}
```

An empty method body means it contains no statement.

Need to implement all abstract methods of **WindowListener**.

Now we need to add this window event listener to the event source MyFirstFrame in the constructor:

```
public MyFirstFrame ( )
{
    ...
    addWindowListener( new ProgramTerminator( ) );
}
```

Run the TestMyFirstFrame program, and this time, when you click the frame's close box, the program will terminate. Here's the complete definition of MyFirstFrame:

```
/*
    MyFirstFrame class

    A sample frame to illustrate the placing of GUI objects and event handling.
*/

import java.awt.*;
import java.awt.event.*;

class MyFirstFrame extends Frame implements ActionListener
{
/***************************
    Data Members
***************************/
    private static final int FRAME_WIDTH     = 300;
    private static final int FRAME_HEIGHT    = 200;

    private static final int FRAME_X_ORIGIN = 150;
    private static final int FRAME_Y_ORIGIN = 250;
```

```
    private static final int BUTTON_WIDTH = 60;
    private static final int BUTTON_HEIGHT= 30;

    Button okButton, cancelButton;

/***************************
    Constructor
***************************/
    public MyFirstFrame( )
    {
        //set the frame properties
        setSize      ( FRAME_WIDTH, FRAME_HEIGHT );
        setResizable ( false );
        setTitle     ( "Program MyFirstFrame" );
        setLocation  ( FRAME_X_ORIGIN, FRAME_Y_ORIGIN );

        //create and place two buttons on the frame
        okButton = new Button( "OK" );
        okButton.setBounds(100, 150, BUTTON_WIDTH, BUTTON_HEIGHT);
        add( okButton );

        cancelButton = new Button( "CANCEL");
        cancelButton.setBounds(170, 150, BUTTON_WIDTH, BUTTON_HEIGHT);
        add( cancelButton );

        //register this frame as an action listener of two buttons
            okButton.addActionListener( this );
        cancelButton.addActionListener( this );

        //register a ProgramTerminator object as a window listener of this frame
        addWindowListener( new ProgramTerminator() );
    }

/***************************
    Action Event Handling
***************************/
    public void actionPerformed( ActionEvent event )
    {
        String label = event.getActionCommand();

        if (label.equals( "CANCEL" )) {
            setTitle( "You clicked CANCEL" );
        }
        else { //the event source is okButton
            setTitle( "You clicked OK" );
        }
    }
}
```

We mentioned earlier that a single object can be an event source and an event listener. In other words, an instance of MyFirstFrame, which is a window event source, can also be a window event listener. To make it a window event listener, the class must implement the WindowListener interface and define the abstract methods. Here's how to define MyFirstFrame as a window event listener of itself (in addition to being an action listener of two buttons):

```
class MyFirstFrame extends Frame
                        implements ActionListener, WindowListener
{
    ...
    public MyFirstFrame
    {
        ...
        addWindowListener( this );
    }


    public void windowClosing( WindowEvent event )
    {
        System.exit(0);
    }

    public void windowActivated     ( WindowEvent event ) { }
    public void windowClosed        ( WindowEvent event ) { }
    public void windowDeactivated   ( WindowEvent event ) { }
    public void windowDeiconified   ( WindowEvent event ) { }
    public void windowIconified     ( WindowEvent event ) { }
    public void windowOpened        ( WindowEvent event ) { }
}
```

12.3 Placing TextField Objects on a Frame

Another very common GUI object in the java.awt package is TextField. A Text-Field object allows the user to enter a single line of text. The input box we use to enter a value in an InputBox is a TextField object. Like the Button class, an instance of TextField generates an action event. A TextField object generates an action event when the user presses the ENTER key while the object is active (it is active when you see the vertical blinking line in it).

The way we set its size and position and register its action listener is the same as we did for the Button class. Let's modify the MyFirstFrame class by adding a TextField object. Let's call the new class MySecondFrame. The effect of clicking the buttons CANCEL and OK is the same as before. If the user presses the ENTER key while the TextField object is active, then we will change the title to whatever text is entered in this TextField object. In the data declaration part, we add

```
TextField inputLine;
```

and in the constructor we create a TextField object and register the frame as its action listener:

```
public MySecondFrame
{
    //same as the constructor of MyFirstFrame
    ...
    inputLine = new TextField( );
    inputLine.setBounds(90, 50, 130, 25);
    add( inputLine );

    inputLine.addActionListener( this );
}
```

Now we need to modify the actionPerformed method to handle the button click events and the ENTER key events. We have three event sources (two buttons and one text field), so the first thing we must do in the actionPerformed method is determine the source. We will use the instanceof operator to determine the class to which the event source belongs. Here's the general idea:

reserved word
instanceof

```
if ( event.getSource() instanceof Button ) {
    //event source is a button, either cancelButton
    //or okButton
    ...
}
else { //event source must be inputLine
    ...
}
```

We use the getText method of TextField to retrieve the text the user has entered. The complete method is written as

```
public void actionPerformed( ActionEvent event )
{
    if ( event.getSource() instanceof Button ) {
        Button clickedButton = (Button) event.getSource();
        if (clickedButton == cancelButton) {
            setTitle( "You clicked CANCEL" );
        }
        else { //the event source is okButton
```

```
                        setTitle( "You clicked OK" );
            }
        else {
            TextField textField = (TextField) event.getSource();
            setTitle("You entered '" + textField.getText() + "'");
        }
    }
```

Notice that we wrote the else part as

```
TextField textField = (TextField) event.getSource();
setTitle("You entered '" + textField.getText() + "'");
```

so style is parallel to the one used in the then part. Since we know that the event source is inputLine in the else part, we can write it more succinctly as

```
setTitle("You entered '" + inputLine.getText() + "'");
```

Quick Check

1. What is the purpose of the instanceof operator?
2. What user action will result in a TextField object generating an action event?

12.4 Menus

Nontrivial programs with a graphical user interface will almost always support menus. In this section we will describe how to display menus and process menu events using Menu, MenuItem, and Menubar from the java.awt package. Figure 12.1 shows these objects. Menubar is a bar where the menus are placed. Menu is a single menu in the Menubar. In Figure 12.1, we have two Menu objects: File and Edit. MenuItem is an individual menu choice in the Menu. When a menu selection is made (e.g., selecting the item Cut under the Edit menu), a menu action event occurs. We process the menu selections by registering an action listener to menu items. Although it is more common to register one action listener to all menu items, we could register a different listener to individual menu items.

Let's write a sample code to illustrate the display of menus and the processing of menu item selections. We will create two menus, File and Edit, with the following menu items:

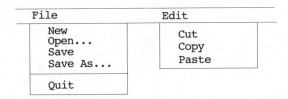

File	Edit
New	Cut
Open...	Copy
Save	Paste
Save As...	
Quit	

If the menu item Quit is selected, then we terminate the program. When a menu item other than Quit is selected, we will print a message that identifies the selected menu item, for example:

```
Menu item 'New' is selected
```

Figure 12.4 shows a MenuFrame when it is first opened and after the menu choice Save is selected.

FIGURE 12.4   **MenuFrame** window when it is first opened and after the menu item **Save** is selected.

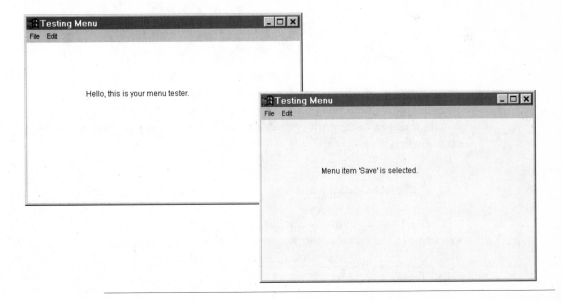

One possible sequence of steps to create and add menus is as follows:

1. Create a MenuBar object and attach it to a frame.

2. Create a Menu object.

3. Create MenuItem objects and add them to the Menu object.

4. Attach the Menu object to the MenuBar object.

Some variations to the given order are possible, but you cannot add new MenuItem objects to a Menu once it is attached to a MenuBar.

We will create two Menu objects, fileMenu and editMenu. We create a fileMenu object as

```
fileMenu = new Menu( "File" );
```

The argument to the Menu constructor is the name of the menu. After the menu is created, we add a menu item to it. A menu item is the event source of menu selection, so we need to register an action listener to every menu item we add to the menu. In this sample code, we will let a MenuFrame object be the action listener of all menu items. To create and add a menu item New to fileMenu, we execute

```
item = new MenuItem("New");          //New
item.addActionListener( this );
fileMenu.add( item );
```

We repeat this sequence for all other menu items. Menu items are placed from the top in the order they are added to the menu. We can also include a horizontal line as a separator between menu items by calling the menu's addSeparator method

```
fileMenu.addSeparator();
```

After the menus and their menu items are created, we attach them to a menubar. In the constructor, we create a MenuBar object, attach it to the frame by calling the frame's setMenuBar method, and add these two Menu objects to the menubar

```
MenuBar menuBar = new MenuBar();
setMenuBar(menuBar);                    //attach it to the frame
menuBar.add(fileMenu);
menuBar.add(editMenu);
```

To display which menu item was selected, we use a Label object response. We add response to the frame by

```
response = new Label("Hello, this is your menu tester.");
response.setBounds(100, 100, 250, 50);
add(response);
```

Finally, in the constructor, we register a ProgramTerminator object as the frame's window event listener.

When a menu item is selected, the registered action listener's actionPerformed method is called. The actionPerformed method of the MenuFrame is defined as follows: If an event source is a menu item, the getActionCommand method of ActionEvent returns the menu's text. We test if the returned text is Quit. If it is, we terminate the program. Otherwise, we set the text of response to indicate which menu item was selected. Here's the method body of Action-Performed:

```
String      menuName;

menuName = event.getActionCommand();

if ( menuName.equals("Quit") )
   System.exit(0);

else
   response.setText("Menu item '" + menuName + "' is selected");
```

Here's the complete program:

```
/*
    Class MenuFrame

    This frame includes one MenuBar, two Menu objects File and Edit,
    and eight MenuItem objects. When a menu item is selected, a string
    showing which menu choice is selected will appear on the frame.
*/

import java.awt.*;
import java.awt.event.*;
```

```
class MenuFrame extends Frame implements ActionListener
{
/***************************
    Data Members
***************************/
    private static final int FRAME_WIDTH    = 450;
    private static final int FRAME_HEIGHT   = 300;
    private static final int FRAME_X_ORIGIN = 150;
    private static final int FRAME_Y_ORIGIN = 250;

    private Label    response;
    private Menu     fileMenu;
    private Menu     editMenu;

/***************************
    Constructor
***************************/
    public MenuFrame( )
    {
        //set frame properties
        setTitle      ( "Testing Menu"  );
        setSize       ( FRAME_WIDTH, FRAME_HEIGHT );
        setResizable  ( false   );
        setLocation   ( FRAME_X_ORIGIN, FRAME_Y_ORIGIN );
        setLayout     ( null    );

        //create two menus and their menu items
        createFileMenu();
        createEditMenu();

        //add the two menus to the menubar
        MenuBar menuBar = new MenuBar();
        setMenuBar(menuBar);
        menuBar.add(fileMenu);
        menuBar.add(editMenu);

        //create and position the response label
        response = new Label("Hello, this is your menu tester.");
        response.setBounds(100, 100, 250, 50);
        add(response);

        addWindowListener( new ProgramTerminator() );
    }

/***************************
    Menu and MenuItem Creation
***************************/

    private void createFileMenu()
    {
        MenuItem    item;
```

```java
        fileMenu = new Menu( "File" );

        item = new MenuItem("New");              //New
        item.addActionListener( this );
        fileMenu.add( item );

        item = new MenuItem("Open...");          //Open...
        item.addActionListener( this );
        fileMenu.add( item );

        item = new MenuItem("Save");             //Save
        item.addActionListener( this );
        fileMenu.add( item );

        item = new MenuItem("Save As...");       //Save As...
        item.addActionListener( this );
        fileMenu.add( item );

        fileMenu.addSeparator();                 //add a horizontal separator line

        item = new MenuItem("Quit");             //Quit
        item.addActionListener( this );
        fileMenu.add( item );
    }

    private void createEditMenu()
    {
        MenuItem   item;

        editMenu = new Menu( "Edit" );

        item = new MenuItem("Cut");              //Cut
        item.addActionListener( this );
        editMenu.add( item );

        item = new MenuItem("Copy");             //Copy
        item.addActionListener( this );
        editMenu.add( item );

        item = new MenuItem("Paste");            //Paste
        item.addActionListener( this );
        editMenu.add( item );
    }


/****************************
   Action Event Handling
****************************/

    public void actionPerformed( ActionEvent event )
    {
        String menuName;
```

```
        menuName = event.getActionCommand();

        if ( menuName.equals("Quit") ) {
            System.exit(0);
        }
        else {
            response.setText("Menu item '" + menuName + "' is selected");
        }
    }

}
```

```
/*

    Program TestMenuFrame

    A main class for testing MenuFrame
*/
class TestMenuFrame
{
    public static void main (String args[])
    {
        MenuFrame frame = new MenuFrame();
        frame.setVisible( true );
    }
}
```

Dr. & Mr.

Mr. Espresso: The size of text for the response label is too small for me. Can you make it bigger?

Dr. Caffeine: Yes, do this:

```
response.setFont( new Font("Helvetica", /*font name*/
                           Font.BOLD, /*font style*/
                           16));        /*font size*/
```

The response text will be shown in 16-point size, bold Helvetica font. You should explore the **Font** class for more options.

Quick Check

1. For which object do we register as an action listener: Menu, Menu-Item, or MenuBar?

2. How do we get the text of a selected menu item in the actionPer-
    formed method?

12.5 Handling Mouse Events

In this section we describe the handling of mouse events. Mouse events include
such user interactions as moving the mouse, dragging the mouse (i.e., moving
the mouse while the mouse button is being pressed), and clicking the mouse buttons.

Let's look at an example in which we display the x and y pixel coordinates
of a location where a mouse button is pressed down. We will define a subclass of
Frame, named TrackMouseFrame, that handles the left mouse button click
events and use an OutputBox object to print out the mouse click locations. Note:
For a system with a one-button mouse, we treat this button as the left mouse button.

A TrackMouseFrame object is an event source of mouse events. We will let
this object be a mouse event listener also. For a TrackMouseFrame object to be a
mouse event listener, its class must implement MouseListener. This interface
has five abstract methods: mouseClicked, mouseEntered, mouseExited, mouse-
Pressed, and mouseReleased. The argument to all five methods is an instance
of MouseEvent.

The class declaration for TrackMouseFrame will look like this:

```
class TrackMouseFrame extends Frame implements MouseListener
{
    ...
}
```

In the constructor we set the frame properties and register this frame as a mouse
event listener of itself. We will let a ProgramTerminator be a window event listener of the frame. The constructor is defined as

```
public TrackMouseFrame
{
    //set the frame properties
    ...

    //create an outputBox for printing out
    //the mouse click points
```

```
        outputBox = new OutputBox( this );

        //register itself as its mouse event listener and
        //a ProgramTerminator as its window event listener
        addMouseListener( this );
        addWindowListener( new ProgramTerminator() );
    }
```

When the left mouse button is clicked, the mouseClicked method of its mouse event listener is called. In this method we want to find out the x and y co-ordinates of the mouse click point and print out these values in an outputBox. To find the x and y coordinate values, we use the getX and getY methods of Mouse-Event. So, the mouseClicked method of TrackMouseFrame is defined as

```
        public void mouseClicked( MouseEvent event )
        {
            int x, y;

            x = event.getX(); //return the x and y coordinates of
            y = event.getY(); //a mouse click point

            outputBox.printLine("[" + x + "," + y + "]");
        }
```

This method is called every time the left mouse button is clicked, that is, the mouse button is pressed down and released. If we want to detect the mouse button press and release separately, then we can provide a method body to the mousePressed and mouseReleased methods. For example, if we define these methods as

```
        public void mousePressed( MouseEvent event )
        {
            outputBox.printLine("Down");
        }
```

and

```
        public void mouseReleased( MouseEvent event )
        {
            outputBox.printLine("Up");
        }
```

instead of empty method bodies, then we will see something like

```
Down
Up
[200,120]
```

when we click a mouse button.
Here's the program:

```
/*
    Class TrackMouseFrame

    This frame tracks the mouse click events. When the left mouse button
    is clicked, the location where the mouse button is clicked
    will be displayed in an OutputBox.
*/

import java.awt.*;
import java.awt.event.*;
import javabook.*;

class TrackMouseFrame extends Frame implements MouseListener
{
/***************************
    Data Members
***************************/
    private static final int FRAME_WIDTH    = 450;
    private static final int FRAME_HEIGHT   = 300;
    private static final int FRAME_X_ORIGIN =  50;
    private static final int FRAME_Y_ORIGIN =  50;

    private OutputBox outputBox;

/***************************
    Constructor
***************************/
    public TrackMouseFrame()
    {
        //set the frame properties
        setTitle      ( "TrackMouseFrame" );
        setSize       ( FRAME_WIDTH, FRAME_HEIGHT );
        setResizable  ( false );
        setLocation   ( FRAME_X_ORIGIN, FRAME_Y_ORIGIN );

        outputBox = new OutputBox(this);

        addMouseListener( this );
        addWindowListener( new ProgramTerminator() );
    }
```

TrackMouseFrame is both a source and listener of mouse events.

```
    public void start()
    {
        setVisible( true );
        outputBox.setVisible( true );
    }
```

The **setVisible** method is also available for the **javabook** dialog classes.

```
/*****************************
   Mouse Event Handling
*****************************/

    public void mouseClicked( MouseEvent event )
    {
        int x, y;
        x = event.getX(); //return the x and y coordinates of
        y = event.getY(); //a mouse click point

        outputBox.printLine("[" + x + "," + y + "]");
    }

    public void mouseEntered        ( MouseEvent event ) { }
    public void mouseExited         ( MouseEvent event ) { }
    public void mousePressed        ( MouseEvent event ) { }
    public void mouseReleased       ( MouseEvent event ) { }

}
```

```
/*
    Program TestTrackMouseFrame

    A main class for testing TrackMouseFrame
*/

class TestTrackMouseFrame
{
    public static void main (String args[])
    {
        TrackMouseFrame frame = new TrackMouseFrame( );
        frame.start();
    }
}
```

Let's rewrite the mouseClicked method so that when the left mouse button is double-clicked, we will erase the contents of outputBox. We check the number of button clicks by calling the getClickCount method of MouseEvent. Here's the method that erases the contents of outputBox when a double-click occurs (a single mouse click will print out the location of a mouse click as before):

```
public void mouseClicked( MouseEvent event )
{
    if ( event.getClickCount() == 2 ) { //erase the contents
        outputBox.clear();                //of outputBox
    }
    else {                      //print out mouse click location
        int x, y;

        x = event.getX();
        y = event.getY();

        outputBox.printLine("[" + x + "," + y + "]");
    }
}
```

Because a double-click is a sequence of two single clicks, this method is called twice when you double-click. The getClickCount method returns 1 for the first call and returns 2 for the second call.

MySketchPad

Let's try another example. This time, let's implement the SketchPad class from the javabook package. To distinguish the class we define here from the original, we will call the class MySketchPad. The basic idea of MySketchPad is to keep track of three events:

1. The left mouse button is pressed down.

2. The right mouse button is pressed down.

3. The mouse is dragged.

Notice that we are processing mouse button presses, not clicks. (Note: For the Mac platform, a mouse button press is treated as the left button press and the Command-press is treated as the right button press. For a platform that supports three mouse buttons, the middle mouse button is also treated as the left mouse button.

To show you a variation, we will declare MySketchPad as a subclass of MainWindow so we don't have to worry about terminating the program when the window is closed. The code for handling the window closing event is inherited from MainWindow. MySketchPad will need to implement two interfaces: MouseListener and MouseMotionListener. Since we want a MySketchPad frame to process mouse button clicks, we must implement the MouseListener interface. In addition to this, we need to implement the MouseMotionListener interface in order to track the mouse dragging. The MouseMotionListener interface includes two abstract methods: mouseDragged and mouseMoved. The argument to both methods is an instance of MouseEvent.

When a mouse button, either the left or right button, is pressed, the event listener's mousePressed is called. Let's study how we should implement this method. If the right mouse button is pressed, then we have to erase the current drawing. If the left mouse button is pressed, then it means it is the start of a new mouse drag, so we have to remember the location where the left button is pressed. To determine which mouse button is pressed inside the mousePressed method, we call the isMetaDown method of MouseEvent as

```
if ( event.isMetaDown() ) {
    //the right button is pressed
    ...
}
```

The isMetaDown method returns true if the right button is pressed. We don't have a method such as isRightButtonPress in MouseEvent because not all platforms support the right mouse button. The Mac platform, for example, has only one mouse button, and for the Mac, the Command-press is treated as the right mouse button press.

The code to erase the contents of the window is as follows:

```
if ( event.isMetaDown() ) {
    //the right button is pressed
    //so erase the contents
    Graphics   g = getGraphics();
    Rectangle  r = getBounds();
    g.clearRect(0, 0, r.width, r.height);
    g.dispose();
}
```

We erase the contents by drawing a filled rectangle as big as the window itself with the rectangle filled in the background color. The getBounds method returns the size of a window.

If it is not a right mouse button press, then it is a left button press, so we remember the first position to draw a line as

```
if ( event.isMetaDown() ) {
    //the right button is pressed
    ...
}
```

```
          else {
              //remember the starting point of a new mouse drag
              last_x = x;
              last_y = y;
          }
```

last_x and **last_y** are instance variables.

The position (x, y) is computed at the beginning of the **mousePressed** method as

```
          int x = event.getX() + getInsets().left;
          int y = event.getY() + getInsets().top;
```

We need to add the offset values getInsets().left and getInsets().top to compute the positions x and y, because the coordinate systems for the mouse and the drawing are different. The mouse position is relative to the inset origin while the drawing position is relative to the window origin. Figure 12.5 illustrates this difference. The method getInsets returns an Insets object that contains four offset values bottom, left, right, and top. To translate the position in the mouse coordinate system to the position in the drawing coordinate system, we add getInsets().left and getInsets().top to the event.getX() and event.getY(), respectively.

WARNING:

Depending on the version of JDK 1.1, mouse coordinates may be relative to the window origin instead of the inset origin as explained in the main text. You can check this easily by running the **TrackMouseFrame** program. If it is relative to the window origin, then you don't add the inset values. The code for computing the values for x and y inside the **mouseDragged** and **mousePressed** methods will be

```
              int x = event.getX();
              int y = event.getY();
```

Dr. Caffeine

Now, to process the mouse drag event, we need to define the **mouseDragged** method. From the argument object **MouseEvent**, we get a new position (x,y) and draw a line from the previous position to this new position using the **Graphics** object g

```
          g.drawLine(last_x, last_y, x, y);
```

FIGURE 12.5   Difference between the container (window) bounds and the inset values. The inner rectangle shows the drawing area and the outer rectangle shows the window. The area between the two includes things such as the window title, scroll bars, window borders, and so forth.

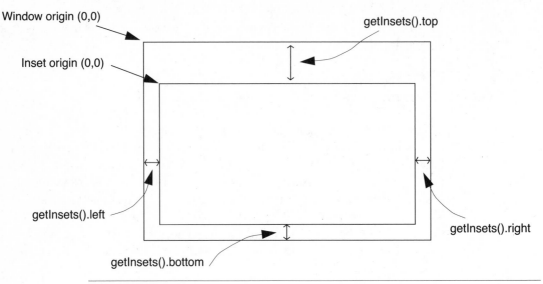

and after the drawing is done, we reset the variables as

```
last_x = x;
last_y = y;
```

Similar to the mousePressed method, the mouseDragged method is called whether the mouse was dragged with the left or right button. So we need to include the if test

```
if (!event.isMetaDown() ) {
    //it's a left mouse button drag,
    //so draw a line
    ...
}
```

inside the method so the drawing will occur only for the left mouse button drag.

Here's a complete listing of the program:

```
/*
    Class MySketchPad

    The SketchPad class from the javabook package.
*/

import java.awt.*;
import java.awt.event.*;
import javabook.*;

class MySketchPad extends MainWindow
                      implements MouseListener, MouseMotionListener
{

/***************************
    Data Members
***************************/
    private static final int FRAME_WIDTH    = 450;
    private static final int FRAME_HEIGHT   = 300;
    private static final int FRAME_X_ORIGIN = 150;
    private static final int FRAME_Y_ORIGIN = 250;

    private int last_x;
    private int last_y;

/***************************
    Constructor
***************************/
    public MySketchPad( )
    {
        //set frame properties
        setTitle      ("SketchPad for Your Doodle Art");
        setSize       ( FRAME_WIDTH, FRAME_HEIGHT );
        setResizable  ( false );
        setLocation   ( FRAME_X_ORIGIN, FRAME_Y_ORIGIN );

        last_x = last_y = 0;

        addMouseListener( this );        //add itself as mouse and
        addMouseMotionListener( this ); //mouse motion listener
    }


/***************************

    Mouse Event Handling

***************************/

    public void mousePressed( MouseEvent event )
    {
```

```
        int x = event.getX() + getInsets().left;
        int y = event.getY() + getInsets().top;

        if ( event.isMetaDown() ) {
            //the right mouse button is pressed, so erase the contents
            Graphics   g = getGraphics();
            Rectangle  r = getBounds();
            g.clearRect(0, 0, r.width, r.height);
            g.dispose();
        }
        else {
            //the left mouse button is pressed,
            //remember the starting point of a new mouse drag
            last_x = x;
            last_y = y;
        }
    }

    public void mouseClicked         ( MouseEvent event ) { }
    public void mouseEntered         ( MouseEvent event ) { }
    public void mouseExited          ( MouseEvent event ) { }
    public void mouseReleased        ( MouseEvent event ) { }


/*****************************

    Mouse Motion Event Handling

****************************/

    public void mouseDragged  ( MouseEvent event )
    {
        int x = event.getX() + getInsets().left;
        int y = event.getY() + getInsets().top;

        if ( !event.isMetaDown() ) {
            //don't process the right button drag
            Graphics   g = getGraphics();

            g.drawLine(last_x, last_y, x, y);
            g.dispose();

            last_x = x;
            last_y = y;
        }
    }

    public void mouseMoved    ( MouseEvent event ) { }
}


/*
    Program TestMySketchPad
```

```
      A main class for testing MySketchPad
*/
class TestMySketchPad
{
    public static void main (String args[])
    {
        MySketchPad frame = new MySketchPad( );
        frame.setVisible( true );
    }
}
```

Quick Check

1. Which listener object listens to mouse movements? Which listener object listens to mouse button presses and clicks?

2. What is the purpose of the isMetaDown method?

3. What is the difference between mouseClicked and mousePressed?

12.6 Other GUI Objects

Figure 12.6 shows the class hierarchy of common classes in the java.awt and java.applet packages. Notice that the Applet class is a descendant of a java.awt class called Panel. The class drawn with a parallelogram (e.g., Component and Container classes) is an abstract class. An *abstract class* contains a method called an *abstract method* that has no method body. The method body is to be defined by the descendant classes. The purpose of an abstract class is to establish the code common to all of its descendant classes for consistency and elimination of duplicate code. We will discuss further and illustrate the use of abstract classes in the next chapter.

As you can see from the hierarchy, the Frame class we have been using is a descendant of the Container class. We call an instance of the Container and any of its descendant classes a *container*. A Container object can contain other Component objects such as instances from the Button and Label classes. Because the Dialog and Applet classes are also descendant classes of the Container class, the techniques we learned to place Component objects on a frame and process the generated events apply equally to a dialog and an applet. So if you know how to place a button on a frame and process the button click event, then you already know how to do the same thing with a dialog and an applet. There are, of course,

FIGURE 12.6   The class hierarchy for some of the commonly used GUI classes. Notice how the **Applet** class is related to the **java.awt** package and all classes inherit from the **Object** class.

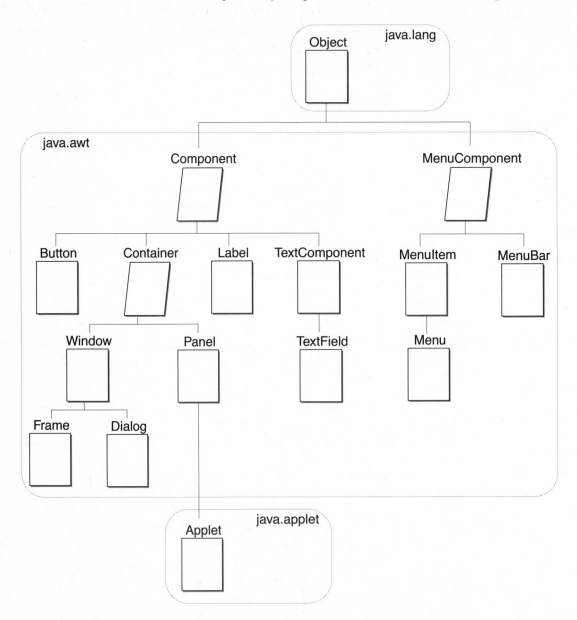

differences. Otherwise, there wouldn't be three different classes. Some of the key differences are

1. Frame can have menus; the others cannot.

2. Dialog can be modal or modeless. Frame is always modeless. Modality does not apply to Applet (see item 4). We will explain the modality in this section.

3. Dialog needs an owner Frame object, that is, a dialog cannot be the main window of a program.

4. Dialog and Frame are windows. Applet is a panel that needs to be placed on a dialog or a frame like any other Component. An applet viewer is a Frame object.

Dialogs

To illustrate how much you already know about how to program a dialog, we will create a sample dialog called MyFirstDialog that supports the same functionality of MyFirstFrame. But before we start working on MyFirstDialog, we will explain the difference between the modal and modeless dialogs.

A *modal* dialog disables all other windows once it appears on the screen. This means that once a modal dialog appears on the screen, the program execution will not continue until you close this dialog. The dialog classes such as MessageBox, InputBox, and ResponseBox from the javabook package are all modal dialogs. For example, when a MessageBox object appears on the screen, you cannot click on the main window until you close this MessageBox object. A *modeless* dialog box, on the other hand, does not disable other windows. Consider the following example. Suppose dialog1 and dialog2 are dialogs and we execute the statements

```
dialog1.show();    //or use setVisible( true );
dialog2.show();
```

If these dialogs are modal, then you will not see dialog2 until you close dialog1. If, however, these dialogs are modeless, then you will see two dialogs appearing on the screen at the same time.

Using the MyFirstDialog class as an example, we will show you how to create a modal and a modeless dialog. The class extends the Dialog class as

```
class MyFirstDialog extends Dialog
```

```
    {
        ...
    }
```

The Dialog class defines a constructor that accepts two arguments: an owner Frame object and a boolean. The boolean argument determines the modality of the created dialog: true for a modal dialog and false for a modeless dialog. A constructor we define for the MyFirstDialog will accept the same two arguments. The first statement in the constructor is a call to the constructor of Dialog:

```
public MyFirstDialog( Frame owner, boolean modal )
{
    super(owner, modal);
    ...
}
```

If a MyFirstDialog object is most frequently created as a modal dialog, then we can define a second constructor with only one argument

```
public MyFirstDialog( Frame owner )
{
    this( owner, true ); //call the first constructor
    ...
}
```

This is basically how we defined the constructors of MessageBox, InputBox, and others.

Now, to add cancelButton and okButton to MyFirstDialog and handle the button events as we did in MyFirstFrame, we just duplicate the code we used for MyFirstFrame:

```
class MyFirstDialog extends Dialog implements ActionListener
{
    //Data Members - the same as in MyFirstFrame

    public MyFirstDialog( Frame owner )
    {
        this( owner, true ); //if false, the default is modeless
    }

    public MyFirstDialog( Frame owner, boolean modal )
```

```
        {
            super( owner, modal );
            //the rest is exactly the same as
            //the MyFirstFrame constructor
        }

        //the same actionPerformed method comes here
    }
```

To use this MyFirstDialog in a program, we can use the following main class. Notice that we need a Frame object to create an instance of MyFirstDialog.

```
    class TestMyFirstDialog
    {
        public static void main( String args[] )
        {
            MainWindow frame = new MainWindow();
            MyFirstDialog dialog = new MyFirstDialog( frame, false);
            frame.setVisible( true );
            dialog.setVisible( true );
        }
    }
```

Notice that when you close a MyFirstDialog object, the program is terminated because we register a ProgramTerminator object as its window event listener. If we just want to close the dialog, we can let MyFirstDialog implement the WindowListener interface and define the windowClosing method as

```
    public void windowClosing( )
    {
        setVisible( false ); //hide it
    }
```

Applets

If you know how to program frames and dialogs, then you already know how to program applets. They are all containers, and the way to place components on them is the same. One major difference is that Applet is a panel, so it needs to be placed on a dialog or a frame like any other Component. Sample applets you have seen so far are placed on a Frame object called an applet viewer. An applet viewer is an instance of AppletViewer class, which is a subclass of Frame. An applet viewer reads information from the applet's corresponding HTML file and adjusts its size to accommodate the applet. So we can run applets without using an applet viewer; we can use any Frame object to run an applet. We will show you how in this section.

Let's say we want to run GreetingApplet from Chapter 5 without an applet viewer. We can easily do this by creating a frame and adding an instance of GreetingApplet to this frame. Here's how:

```java
import java.awt.*;

class GreetingAppletMain
{
    public static void main (String args[])
    {
        Frame myFrame = new Frame("Greeting Applet in Frame");
        myFrame.setSize(300, 270);
        myFrame.addWindowListener( new ProgramTerminator() );
        myFrame.add( new GreetingApplet() );
        myFrame.setVisible( true );
    }
}
```

Quick Check

1. Name three descendant classes of the Container class?
2. What is the difference between a modal and a modeless dialog?
3. How is an applet different from a frame and a dialog?

12.7   Sample Program: A Simple Calculator

Let's build a simple four-function calculator to summarize the concepts we covered in this chapter. Figure 12.7 shows the calculator we will develop. To implement the calculator, we will use GUI components Button and TextField, process action events generated by the buttons, and handle exceptions thrown by invalid data entry.

Problem Statement

Write a calculator that has two text fields to enter left and right operands and five operator buttons for add, subtract, divide, multiply,

FIGURE 12.7   A four-function calculator.

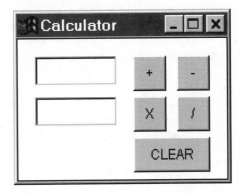

and clear. Clicking the CLEAR button clears both text fields. The result of operation is displayed in the top text field. The user can continue the calculation by entering the next number in the bottom text field and clicking the desired operator.

Overall Plan

What kind of an object is Calculator? Is it an application logic object? Is it a user interface object? Or is it a controller object? Since a Calculator object is intended to be a stand-alone program, it must be a controller object managing other objects such as instances from the TextField and Button class. Since the operations required for this calculator are very basic, we will let a Calculator be an application logic object also. We are therefore overloading the Calculator class with multiple tasks, but each task is short and not complex, so we will let the Calculator class handle the tasks of both controller and application logic. If we were to design a more realistic scientific or business calculator, then we would have to design a separate application object for handling numerical computations.

The key task of a Calculator is to perform the computation when an operator button is clicked and clear the entries if the CLEAR button is clicked. The buttons will be action event sources, and the Calculator object is an action event listener. Expressed in pseudocode, the actionPerformed method would look something like this:

```
if ( clickedButton == clearButton )
    clearEntries();

else //an operator button is clicked
    compute ( clickedButton );
```

The clearEntries method sets the text of both TextField objects to an empty string. The compute method, expressed in pseudocode, would look something like this:

```
leftOperand = get value from the top TextField;
rightOperand = get value from the bottom TextField;

switch ( operator ) {
    case addition:
                result = leftOperand + rightOperand;
                break;

    case subtraction:
                result = leftOperand - rightOperand;
                break;

    case division:
                result = leftOperand / rightOperand;
                break;

    case multiplication:
                result = leftOperand * rightOperand;
                break;
}

display result in the top TextField;
clear the bottom TextField;
```

This pseudocode assumes that the input data are valid. We need to add an input error checking code in the final version of compute. We consider any input value that cannot be converted to a float value as invalid.

Our working design document for the Calculator class at this point is as follows:

Design Document: The Calculator Class extends Frame implements ActionListener		
Method	**Visibility**	**Purpose**
`<constructor>`	`public`	Creates and initializes a Calculator object.
`setVisible`	`public`	Inherited method. Displays and starts a Calculator object.
`actionPerformed`	`public`	Determines which type of button is clicked and, depending on it, calls either the clearEntries or compute method.
`clearEntries`	`private`	Clears both TextField objects to an empty string.
`compute`	`private`	Performs the specified calculation and displays the result.

Its object diagram at this point is

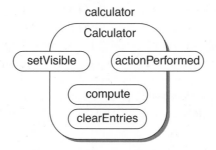

We will implement the class in the following four steps:

development steps

1. Start with a class skeleton. Define the necessary data members and constructors. Add any other methods necessary to implement the constructors.

2. Implement the actionPerformed method. Implement the private methods clearEntries and compute also. For this step, assume the input is valid.

3. Implement methods necessary to check for invalid input data.

4. Finalize the code and look for improvement.

Step 1 Development: Skeleton with Constructor

The objective of Step 1 is to identify the necessary GUI components and complete the visual appearance of the calculator. In this step, the calculator does not perform the actual computation. Let's start with data members of the class. We will use two TextField objects for the user to enter the left and right operands. We will call them leftOperand and rightOperand. We will use four Button objects for the four arithmetic operators and one Button for the CLEAR button. We declare these objects as

```
private    TextField    leftOperand,
                        rightOperand;

private    Button       plusButton,
                        minusButton,
                        multiplyButton,
                        divideButton,
                        clearButton;
```

Now, let's think about the constructors. We will support one constructor that has no parameter. We could add other constructors where the programmer can, for example, pass the window width and height as parameters. Such a constructor is meaningful if we adjust the size of buttons based on the size of the window. Since we have not covered this technique of adjusting the size of buttons using different types of layout managers, we will not support such a constructor. We will create a fix-sized calculator and use absolute positioning.

We will define the Calculator class as a subclass of Frame. We choose not to make the Calculator class the main class. The programmer must supply his own main class to derive a full calculator program. By not making the Calculator class the main class, the programmer has more flexibility in reusing a Calculator object in his program. Since the class is a subclass of Frame, we will set certain properties of Frame, such as its size and location on the screen, inside the constructor. Since it is a frame, we will include a window listener to terminate the program when the frame is closed. We will use the ProgramTerminator object defined earlier in the chapter.

To prevent the constructor from becoming too big, we will define a separate private method initGUIComponents to create and initialize the data member GUI components. We will register the Calculator object as an action listener of all five buttons in this method.

The working design document now includes this method:

Design Document: The Calculator Class		
Method	**Visibility**	**Purpose**
...	...	...
initGUICompo-nents	private	Create and initialize GUI components. Register the Calculator object as an event listener of all five buttons.

Step 1 Code   Here's the Step 1 implementation of the Calculator class:

```
/*
    Program Calculator

    This program provides a simple four function calculator with
    two input fields to enter the left and right operands of an
    arithmetic operation. The program uses the JDK 1.1 event model.
*/

import java.awt.*;
import java.awt.event.*;

class Calculator extends Frame implements ActionListener
{

/*************************

    Data Members

*************************/
    private static final int FRAME_WIDTH    = 200;
    private static final int FRAME_HEIGHT   = 150;
    private static final int FRAME_X_ORIGIN = 300;
    private static final int FRAME_Y_ORIGIN = 200;

    private TextField       leftOperand,
                            rightOperand;

    private Button          plusButton,
                            minusButton,
                            multiplyButton,
                            divideButton,
                            clearButton;

/*************************

    Constructor

*************************/
```

```
    public Calculator()
    {
        //set window properties
        super          ( "Calculator");

        setSize       ( FRAME_WIDTH, FRAME_HEIGHT      );
        setResizable ( false          );
        setLayout     ( null          );
        setLocation   ( FRAME_X_ORIGIN, FRAME_Y_ORIGIN);

        //create and lay out components
        initGUIComponents();

        addWindowListener( new ProgramTerminator() );

    }

/*************************

    Public Methods

        void    actionPerformed ( ActionEvent    )

*************************/

    /********************************************************
        Method:         actionPerformed

        Purpose:        Called when one of the five buttons is clicked.
                        Performs the specified calculation and displays
                        the result.

        Parameters:     ActionEvent

        Returns:        none
    */
    public void actionPerformed (ActionEvent event)
    {
        System.out.println("Inside actionPerformed");     //TEMP
    }


/*************************

    Private Methods

        void        initGUIComponents     (               )

*************************/

    /********************************************************
        Method:         initGUIComponents
```

```
        Purpose:        Create and initialize GUI components. Absolute positioning
                        is used.

        Parameters:     none

        Returns:        none
*/
    private void initGUIComponents( )
    {
        //create buttons
        leftOperand     = new TextField();
        rightOperand    = new TextField();

        plusButton      = new Button("+");
        minusButton     = new Button("-");
        multiplyButton  = new Button("X");
        divideButton    = new Button("/");
        clearButton     = new Button("CLEAR");


        //position buttons
        leftOperand.    setBounds ( 20,  40, 75, 25);
        rightOperand.   setBounds ( 20,  75, 75, 25);

        plusButton.     setBounds (110,  40, 30, 30);
        minusButton.    setBounds (150,  40, 30, 30);
        multiplyButton.setBounds (110,  75, 30, 30);
        divideButton.   setBounds (150,  75, 30, 30);
        clearButton.    setBounds (110, 110, 70, 30);

        //add the Calculator class as an action listener
        //to all five buttons
        plusButton.     addActionListener( this );
        minusButton.    addActionListener( this );
        multiplyButton.addActionListener( this );
        divideButton.   addActionListener( this );
        clearButton.    addActionListener( this );

         //add buttons to the calculator frame
        add( leftOperand    );
        add( rightOperand   );

        add( plusButton     );
        add( minusButton    );
        add( multiplyButton );
        add( divideButton   );

        add( clearButton    );
    }

}
```

In order to test the skeleton Calculator class, we need to write a test main class. A simple main class such as the following would suffice:

```
/*
    Program TestCalculator

    A main class for testing the Calculator class
*/
class TestCalculator
{
    public static void main (String args[])
    {
        Calculator calculator = new Calculator();
        calculator.setVisible( true );
    }
}
```

The purpose of this test program is to verify that the constructors are executed correctly and the GUI objects appear as we expected. Also, we verify that when we click a button, a temporary output message is displayed in System.out.

Step 2 Development: Implement the actionPerformed Method

In the second step of development, we will replace the temporary output statement in the actionPerformed method with the real code to carry out the computation. This method is called when any one of the five buttons is clicked. If the clicked button is CLEAR, then we call clearEntries. Otherwise, one of the four operator buttons is clicked, so we call compute. The compute method will actually carry out the computation. Since the compute method needs to know which button is clicked, we will pass the clicked button to the compute method as an argument. To determine which button is clicked, we use the getSource method of ActionEvent. The method body of actionPerformed looks like this:

```
Button clickedButton = (Button) event.getSource();

if (clickedButton == clearButton) {
    clearEntries();
}
else {
    compute( clickedButton );
}
```

The clearEntries method sets the contents of both TextField objects to the empty string

```
leftOperand.setText( "" );
rightOperand.setText( "" );
```

In this step, we assume the input is valid and do not worry about input error checking. We first want to make sure that we can compute correctly, given a valid input. The compute method first retrieves data from the leftOperand and right-Operand objects. We will use a private method called getNumberFrom for this purpose. This method assumes the entry in the TextField object can be converted correctly to a float. Its method body is as follows:

```
return Convert.toFloat( operand.getText() );
```

where operand is a method parameter of type TextField. After the numbers are fetched from the TextField objects, the compute method determines which button is clicked and carries out the computation. To display the result, we will use another private method called displayResult. The displayResult method displays the result to the leftOperand object, the TextField object at the top.

The working design document now includes four new private methods:

Design Document: The Calculator Class		
Method	**Visibility**	**Purpose**
...	...	...
getNumberFrom	private	Returns a float value converted from the text in the argument TextField object.
compute	private	Computes the result.
clearEntries	private	Clears the entries in leftOperand and rightOperand.
displayResult	private	Displays the argument float value in the top TextField object.

Step 2 Code

We add a new import statement

```
import javabook.*;
```

so we can use the Convert class in the program.

The actionPerformed method is defined as follows:

```
public void actionPerformed( ActionEvent event )
{
    Button clickedButton = (Button) event.getSource();

    if (clickedButton == clearButton) {
        clearEntries();
    }
    else {
        compute( clickedButton );
    }
}
```

The clearEntries method clears both TextField objects:

```
private void clearEntries( )
{
    leftOperand.setText( "" );
    rightOperand.setText( "" );
}
```

The compute method is defined as

```
private void compute (Button operatorButton)
{
    float    leftOperandValue,
             rightOperandValue,
             result = 0f;

    //get the two operands
    leftOperandValue  = getNumberFrom(leftOperand);
    rightOperandValue = getNumberFrom(rightOperand);

    //compute the result
    if      ( operatorButton == plusButton ) {
        result = leftOperandValue + rightOperandValue;
    }
    else if ( operatorButton == minusButton ) {
        result = leftOperandValue - rightOperandValue;
    }
    else if ( operatorButton == divideButton ) {
        result = leftOperandValue / rightOperandValue;
```

```
    }
    else if ( operatorButton == multiplyButton ) {
        result = leftOperandValue * rightOperandValue;
    }

    displayResult(result);
}
```

Finally, the displayResult method is defined as

```
private void displayResult( float value )
{
    leftOperand.setText( Convert.toString( value ) );
    rightOperand.setText( "" );
}
```

Step 2 Test   We run the TestCalculator class from Step 1 and verify that the calculator works correctly. Since we did not include any input error checking, we only input correct values. We test all four operations and verify that the correct results are computed. We also test the CLEAR button works as intended.

Step 3 Development: Implement the Input Error Checking Routine

Step 3 Design   In the third step of development, we complete the class by adding an input error checking routine. We will modify the compute method so that the method first verifies the correctness of entries inside leftOperand and rightOperand. For input error checking, we will define a separate method isOperandValid. The argument to this method is TextField and the method returns true if the content of the passed TextField can be converted to a float. Using this method, the compute method becomes

```
if ( isOperandValid( leftOperand ) &&
        isOperandValid( rightOperand ) )
    //input okay
    //compute and display the result
    //this part is the code of compute from Step 2

else
    display the error message "Invalid entry";
```

The isOperandValid method attempts to convert the String data in the Text-Field using the Convert class from the javabook package. If no exception is thrown, then the entry is valid and the method returns true. Otherwise, there's some error in the entry, so the method returns false.

The working design document now includes this method:

Design Document: The Calculator Class		
Method	**Visibility**	**Purpose**
...	...	...
isOperandValid	private	Returns true if the argument TextField object contains a text that can be converted to a float.

Step 3 Code

The compute method is modified to the following:

```
private void compute (Button operatorButton)
{
    float   leftOperandValue, rightOperandValue,
            result = 0f;

    if (isOperandValid(leftOperand) &&
            isOperandValid(rightOperand) {
        //both operands okay, so
        //get the two operands
        leftOperandValue  = getNumberFrom(leftOperand);
        rightOperandValue = getNumberFrom(rightOperand);

        //compute the result
        if      ( operatorButton == plusButton )
            result = leftOperandValue + rightOperandValue;

        else if ( operatorButton == minusButton )
            result = leftOperandValue - rightOperandValue;

        else if ( operatorButton == divideButton )
            result = leftOperandValue / rightOperandValue;

        else if ( operatorButton == multiplyButton )
            result = leftOperandValue * rightOperandValue;

        displayResult(result);
    }
    else { //Error: display the message in leftOperand
        leftOperand.setText("Error: Invalid data");
    }
}
```

and the private isOperandValid method is defined as follows:

```
private boolean isOperandValid( TextField operand )
{
    boolean status;

    try {
        float number = Convert.toFloat(operand.getText());
        status = true;
    }
    catch ( NumberFormatException e ) {
        status = false;
    }

    return status;
}
```

Step 3 Test

For the Step 3 Calculator class, we test end cases, normal cases, and error cases. Try entering very large numbers, zeroes, very small numbers, invalid data, and so forth, and verify the correctness of the program.

Step 4 Development: Finalize

code review

improving code

As always, we will perform a critical review of the class looking for any unfinished methods. We will also review the class for any possible improvements. In fact, there are several possible improvements. First, we should display a better error message. The current calculator displays the same message Invalid Data for all types of input errors. The error message should provide more meaningful information. Second, the calculator allows a divide-by-zero operation. If you try to divide a number by zero, the calculator will display the result Infinity, because Java sets the result of divide-by-zero operation to infinity. Instead, the calculator should display an error message. Third, the ENTER key press should be processed for quick operation. For example, when the user enters the right operand and presses the ENTER key, the calculator can compute the sum of two numbers. With this feature, the user can compute the sum of N numbers very quickly without his or her hands leaving the keyboard. These improvements are left as exercises.

12.8 Exercises

1. Discuss the major difference between a frame and a dialog.

2. If you want your program to run both as an applet and an application, how would you design your classes?

3. One of the GUI objects in the java.awt package that we did not cover in this chapter is List. Look up this class in a Java reference manual and review the ListBox class from the javabook package. Do you see the similarities between the two? Identify the GUI components used in the ListBox. Read the definition of ListBox. Do you understand the code?

4. One of the GUI objects in the java.awt package that we did not cover in this chapter is TextArea. Look up this class in a Java reference manual and review the OutputBox class from the javabook package. Identify the GUI components used in the OutputBox. Read the definition of OutputBox. Do you understand the code?

5. Rewrite the Arithmetic class in the game package from Chapter 9 as a dialog. The ArithmeticDialog class uses a Label for a problem and a TextField for the user answer. When the user presses the ENTER key (while the TextField object is active) or clicks the OK button, the dialog displays a message stating whether the user's answer is correct or not. Use another Label for the message. Consider using a larger font for the Label and TextField text.

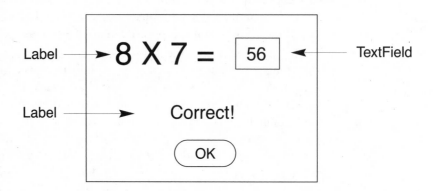

6. Rewrite the EggyPeggy class in the game package from Chapter 9 as a dialog. The EggyPeggyDialog class uses two TextField objects for entering the original text and displaying the encrypted text. When the user presses the

ENTER key (while the original text TextField object is active) or clicks the OK button, the dialog displays the encrypted text in the second TextField.

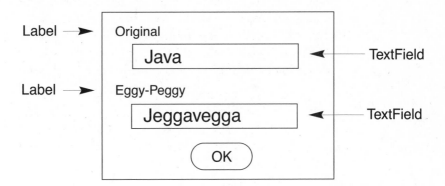

Consider using TextArea objects instead of TextField objects so the user can enter multiple lines of original text. TextArea is a GUI object not covered in this chapter. See exercise 4.

7. Extend the HiLoDialog class so the user has the option of quitting the game. Add a button Give Up to the dialog. When the user clicks on the Give Up button, the dialog displays the secret number and the number of guesses the user has made. The dialog then resets itself for a new game.

8. Extend the HiLoDialog class to include the listing of guesses made by the user. Use a List object to list the user's guesses; see exercise 3.

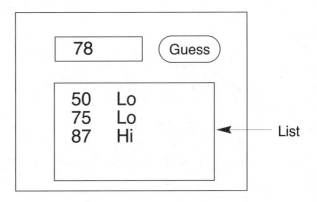

9. Modify the EggyPeggyDialog class of exercise 6 so now the dialog has three choices for encryption: Sha, Na, and Ava. The encryption methods are explained in exercise 16 on page 420.

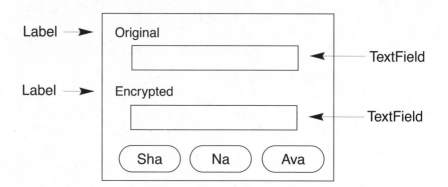

You should design one class to handle the user interaction and another class for encrypting the original text instead of doing everything in a single class.

10. Extend the MySketchPad class to allow the user to sketch in color. Add the following menu choices.

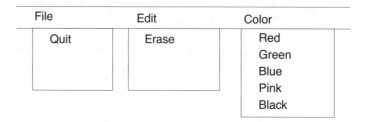

When the user selects a color, set the color of a Graphics object so the subsequent sketching is made in the selected color. Selecting the menu item Erase will erase the drawing.

11. In the Calculator program from Section 12.7, an error message was displayed in the leftOperand text field. This could potentially overwrite good data (e.g., when the invalid input occurs in the rightOperand text field). Modify the class to eliminate this problem.

12. (Challenge) Write a class that implements a more realistic calculator than the one defined in this chapter.

The user enters a number using digit buttons only (see exercise 13). Some of the issues you need to consider:

- How to determine whether the user is entering a left operand or a right operand.

- How to handle the entering of multiple decimal points. A typical calculator accepts the first decimal point and ignores the rest. For example, if you press 1 . 4 . 3 . . the number entered is 1.43.

- When the display is 0 and the user enters 0, the display will not change. However, if the display is nonzero and the user enters 0, the 0 is appended to the number currently displayed.

- How to handle the operator precedence. For example, what will be the result if the user enters 4 + 3 X 2? Will it be 14 or 10? It is easier to treat all operators as having equal precedence and process them from left to right.

Study any real four-function calculator and try to implement a software calculator that simulates the real calculator as faithfully as possible, but feel free to make any reasonable changes.

13. Extend the calculator of exercise 12 to allow the user to enter a number using the keyboard. The class needs to implement the **KeyListener** interface and define the **keyTyped** method. You have to find information on **KeyListener** and **KeyEvent** from a Java API reference manual.

14. Modify the mortgage table program of exercise 21 on page 359. Add the following menu

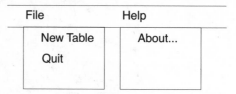

to the program. When the user selects the menu choice **New Table**, the program opens a dialog in which the user can enter three input values. The input dialog should look something like this:

| Loan Amount: |
| Interest Rate: |
| Loan Period: |
| Cancel   Compute |

If the user clicks on the **Compute** button and the three input values are valid, generate a mortgage table. If the input values are invalid, then print out an appropriate error message. Decide the range of valid values for the loan amount, interest rate, and loan period. When the user selects the menu choice **About...**, describe the purpose of the program using an **OutputBox**. You may want to use a dedicated **OutputBox** for this purpose instead of using the same **OutputBox** for displaying both the mortgage table and the program description.

15. Modify exercise 12 on page 357 using any GUI objects and techniques you learned in this chapter.

13

Inheritance and Polymorphism

Introduction

polymorphism

In this chapter, we will describe two important and powerful features in object-oriented programming—inheritance and polymorphism. The inheritance feature of object-oriented programming was introduced in Chapter 1, and we have been using inheritance in defining classes since Chapter 2. We will provide a more detailed explanation of inheritance in this chapter. Another indispensable feature in object-oriented programming is *polymorphism*, which allows programmers to send the same message to objects from different classes. Consider the statement

```
account.computeMonthlyFee();
```

polymorphic
message

where account could refer to either a SavingsAccount or CheckingAccount object. If account is a SavingsAccount object, then the method computeMonthlyFee defined for the SavingsAccount class is executed. Likewise, if account is a CheckingAccount object, then the method computeMonthlyFee defined for the CheckingAccount class is executed. Sending the same message therefore could result in executing different methods. The message computeMonthlyFee is called a *polymorphic message* because depending on the receiver object, different methods are executed. Polymorphism helps us write code that is easy to modify and extend. We will explain polymorphism in this chapter.

13.1 Defining Classes with Inheritance

Suppose we want to maintain a class roster for a class whose enrolled students include both undergraduate and graduate students. For each student, we record his/her name, three test scores, and the final course grade. The final course grade, either pass or no pass, is determined by the following formula:

Type of Student	Grading Scheme
Undergraduate	Pass if (test1+test2+test3)/3 >= 70
Graduate	Pass if (test1+test2+test3)/3 >= 80

unrelated
classes

What kind of objects should we use to model undergraduate and graduate students? There are basically two broad ways to design the classes to model them. The first way is to define two unrelated classes, one for undergraduate students and another for graduate students. We calle the two classes *unrelated* if they are not connected in an inheritance relationship; that is, neither one is an ancestor or descendant class of the other nor do they share a common ancestor.[1] The second way is to model undergraduate and graduate students using classes that are related in an inheritance hierarchy.

Defining two unrelated classes for entities that share common data or behavior would make class definition ineffective because we would end up duplicating code common to both classes. Although different, graduate and undergraduate students do share many common data and behaviors, so we will design these two classes using inheritance.

We will actually define three classes. The first is the Student class to incorporate behavior and data common to both graduate and undergraduate students. The second and third classes are the GraduateStudent class to incorporate behavior specific to graduate students and the UndergraduateStudent class to incorporate behavior specific to undergraduate students. The Student class is defined as

```
class Student
{

/*********************************
    Data Members
*********************************/

    public final static int     NUM_OF_TESTS = 3;

    protected String            name;
    protected int[]             test;
    protected String            courseGrade;

/*********************************
    Constructor
*********************************/

    public Student(String studentName)
    {
        name        = studentName;
        test        = new int[NUM_OF_TESTS];
        courseGrade = "****";
    }

/*********************************
    Public Methods
```

> Protected fields are visible to the descendant objects.

---

1. In Java, the class Object is automatically set to be the superclass of a class if the class definition does not include the keyword extends. To be technically precise, we must say that two classes are unrelated if they do not share a common ancestor besides Object.

```
        String  getCourseGrade     (          )
        String  getName            (          )
        int     getTestScore       ( int      )

        void    setName            ( String   )
        void    setTestScore       ( int, int )
**********************************/

    public String getCourseGrade( )
    {
        return courseGrade;
    }

    public String getName( )
    {
        return name;
    }

    public int getTestScore(int testNumber)
    {
        return test[testNumber-1];
    }

    public void setName(String newName)
    {
        name = newName;
    }

    public void setTestScore(int testNumber, int testScore)
    {
        test[testNumber-1] = testScore;
    }
}
```

Notice the modifier for the instance variables is protected, making them visible and accessible to the instances of the class and the descendant classes. If you declare a data member of a class private, then this data member is accessible only to the instances of the class. If you declare a data member public, this data member is accessible to everybody. We declare them protected so they become accessible only to the instances of the class and the descendant classes. We will explore further the protected modifier later in the chapter.

extends

We define the classes UndergraduateStudent and GraduateStudent as subclasses of the Student class. In Java, we say a subclass *extends* its superclass. The difference between the classes GraduateStudent and UndergraduateStudent lies in the way their final course grades are computed. The two subclasses are defined as follows:

```
class GraduateStudent extends Student
{
    public void computeCourseGrade()
    {
        int total = 0;
        for (int i = 0; i < NUM_OF_TESTS; i++) {
            total += test[i];
        }

        if (total/NUM_OF_TESTS >= 80) {
            courseGrade = "Pass";
        }
        else {
            courseGrade = "No Pass";
        }
    }
}
```

```
class UndergraduateStudent extends Student
{
    public void computeCourseGrade()
    {
        int total = 0;
        for (int i = 0; i < NUM_OF_TESTS; i++) {
            total += test[i];
        }

        if (total/NUM_OF_TESTS >= 70) {
            courseGrade = "Pass";
        }
        else {
            courseGrade = "No Pass";
        }
    }
}
```

Figure 13.1 shows the class diagram relating the three classes. Notice that we do not show inherited data fields and methods in the subclasses. To do so would clutter the diagram. By seeing an inheritance arrow connecting a subclass to its superclass, we know that data members and methods indicated on the superclass are applicable to the subclass also. We attach methods and data members to the subclasses only if they are defined in the subclasses or if they are overridden in the subclasses (we will discuss more on overriding later in the chapter). In Figure 13.1, both subclasses have the method computeCourse-Grade attached to them because the method is defined in the subclasses.

FIGURE 13.1   A superclass **Student** and its subclasses **GraduateStudent** and **UndergraduateStudent**.

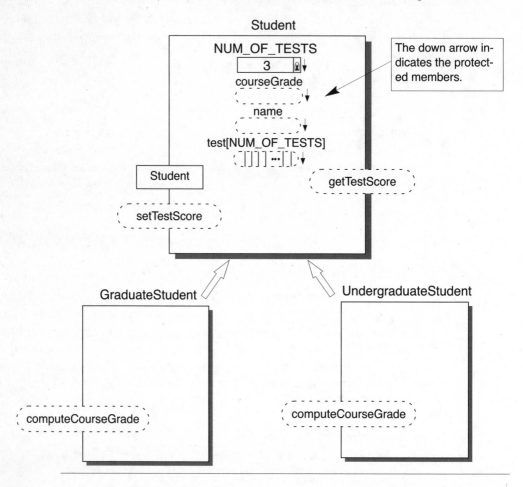

 Quick Check

1. Which is the subclass and which is the superclass in the following declaration?

```
class X extends Y { ... }
```

2. Which visibility modifier allows the data members of a superclass to be accessible to the instances of subclasses?

13.2 Using Classes Effectively with Polymorphism

Now let's see how the Student class and its subclasses can be used effectively in the class roster program. Since both undergraduate and graduate students are enrolled in a class, should we declare two arrays shown below to maintain the class roster?

```
GraduateStudent          gradRoster[20];
UndergraduateStudent     undergradRoster[20];
```

We mentioned in Chapter 11 that an array must contain elements of the same data type. For example, we cannot store integers and real numbers in the same array. Following this rule, it seems necessary for us to declare two separate arrays, one for graduate students and another for undergraduate students. This rule, however, does not apply when the array elements are objects. We only need to declare a single array, for example,

```
Student roster[40];
```

Elements of the roster array can be instances of either the Student class or any of its descendant GraduateStudent or UndergraduateStudent classes. Figure 13.2 illustrates the array with both types of students as array elements.

Before showing how this array is used in the program, we will explain the concept of polymorphism. In its simplest form, *polymorphism* allows a single variable to refer to objects from different classes. Consider, for example, the following declaration:

```
Student student;
```

With this declaration, not only can we say

```
student = new Student( );
```

but also

```
student = new GraduateStudent( );
```

or

```
student = new UndergraduateStudent( );
```

FIGURE 13.2   The **roster** array with elements referring to instances of **GraduateStudent** or **UndergraduateStudent** classes.

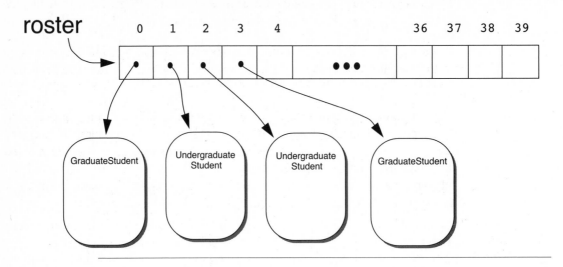

In other words, the single variable student is not limited to referring to an object from the Student class but can refer to any object from the descendant classes of Student. In a similar manner we can say something like

```
roster[0] = new GraduateStudent( );
roster[1] = new UndergraduateStudent( );
roster[2] = new UndergraduateStudent( );
roster[3] = new GraduateStudent( );
...
```

sibling classes

However, you cannot make a variable of class X refer to an object from the superclass or sibling classes of X. *Sibling* classes are those that share the common ancestor class. For example, the following assignment statements are both invalid.

```
GraduateStudent grad1, grad2;
```

✗ NOT VALID
```
grad1 = new Student( );
grad2 = new UndergraduateStudent( );
```

Now, to compute the course grade using the roster array, we execute

```
for (int i = 0; i < numberOfStudents; i++) {
    roster[i].computeCourseGrade();
}
```

If roster[i] refers to a GraduateStudent then the computeCourseGrade method of the GraduateStudent class is executed and if it refers to an Undergraduate-Student then the computeCourseGrade method of the UndergraduateStudent is executed. We call the message computeCourseGrade *polymorphic* because the message refers to methods from different classes depending on the object referenced by roster[i]. Polymorphism allows us to maintain the class roster with one array instead of maintaining a separate array for each type of student, and this simplifies the processing tremendously.

benefits of
polymorphism

Polymorphism makes possible smooth and easy extension and modification of a program. Suppose, for example, we have to add a third type of student, say, audit student, to the class roster program. If we have to define a separate array for each type of student, this extension forces us to define a new class and a third array for audit students. But with polymorphism, we only have to define a new subclass of Student. And as long as this new subclass includes the correct computeCourseGrade method, the for loop to compute the course grade for students remains the same. Without polymorphism, not only do we have to add the new code, we have to rewrite existing code to accommodate the change. With polymorphism, on the other hand, we don't have to touch the existing code. Modifying existing code is a tedious and error-prone activity. A slight change to existing code could cause a program to stop working correctly. To be certain that a change in one portion of existing code won't affect other portions of existing code adversely, we must understand the existing code completely. And understanding code, especially the one that is long and/or written by somebody else, is a very time-consuming task.

An element of the roster array is a reference to an instance of either the GraduateStudent or UndergraduateStudent class. Most of the time, we do not have to know which is which. There are times, however, when we need to know the class of a referenced object. For example, we may want to find out the number of undergraduate students who passed the course. To determine the class of an object, we use the instanceof operator. We used this operator in Chapter 12 to determine whether an event source is a Button or a TextField object. We can use this operator here; for example,

```
Student x = new UndergraduateStudent( );

if ( x instanceof UndergraduateStudent ) {
    System.out.println("Mr. X is an undergraduate student");
}
else {
    System.out.println("Mr. X is a graduate student");
}
```

will print out Mr. X is an undergraduate student. The following code counts the number of undergraduate students in the roster array.

```
int underGradCount = 0;
for (int i = 0; i < numberOfStudents; i++) {
    if ( roster[i] instanceOf UndergraduateStudent ) {
        underGradCount++;
    }
}
```

Quick Check

1. Suppose Truck and Motorcycle are subclasses of Vehicle. Which of the following declarations are invalid?

```
Truck      t = new Vehicle();
Vehicle    v = new Truck();
Motorcycle m1 = new Vehicle();
Motorcycle m2 = new Truck();
```

2. What is the purpose of the instanceof operator?

13.3 Inheritance and Member Accessibility

We will describe the rules of inheritance in this and the next two sections. In this section, we will explain which members (variables and methods) of a superclass are inherited by a subclass and how these members are accessed. In addition to declaring members private and public, we can declare them protected. The protected modifier is meaningful only if used with inheritance. Consider the following declarations:

```
class Super
{
    public    int      public_Super_Field;
    protected int      protected_Super_Field;
    private   int      private_Super_Field;

    public Super()
    {
        public_Super_Field     = 10;
        protected_Super_Field  = 20;
        private_Super_Field    = 30;
    }
    ...
}

class Sub extends Super
{
    public    int      public_Sub_Field;
    protected int      protected_Sub_Field;
    private   int      private_Sub_Field;

    public Sub()
    {
        public_Sub_Field       = 100;
        protected_Sub_Field    = 200;
        private_Sub_Field      = 300;
    }
    ...
}
```

We use instance variables for illustration, but the rules we describe here are equally applicable to other types of members (class variables, class methods, and instance methods). We use the graphical representation shown in Figure 13.3 for the three modifiers.

You already know the difference between the public and private modifiers. A public member is accessible to any methods, but a private member is accessible only to the methods that belong to the same class. Let's illustrate this point. Consider a class that is unrelated to the classes Super and Sub:

```
class Client
{
    public void test()
    {
        Super  mySuper = new Super();
        Sub    mySub   = new Sub();
```

FIGURE 13.3   A graphical representation of super and subclasses with **public**, **private**, and **protected** members.

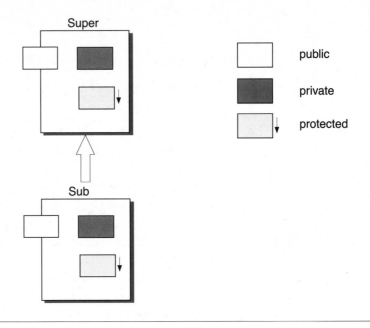

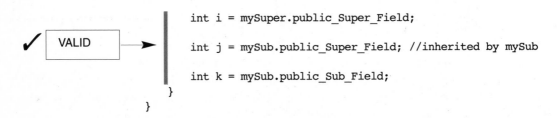

```
                        int i = mySuper.public_Super_Field;

   ✓  VALID   ──────►   int j = mySub.public_Super_Field; //inherited by mySub

                        int k = mySub.public_Sub_Field;
                    }
                }
```

Public members of a class, whether they are inherited or not, are accessible from any object or class. Private members of a class, on the other hand, are never accessible from any outside object or class. The following statements, if placed in the test method of the Client class, are therefore all invalid.

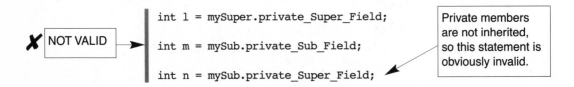

```
            int l = mySuper.private_Super_Field;

  ✗ NOT VALID ──────►  int m = mySub.private_Sub_Field;

            int n = mySub.private_Super_Field;
```

Private members are not inherited, so this statement is obviously invalid.

A protected member is accessible only to the methods that belong to the same class or to the descendant classes. It is inaccessible to the methods of an unrelated class. The following statements, if placed in the test method of the Client class, are all invalid.

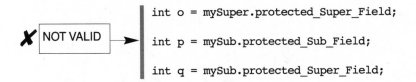

```
int o = mySuper.protected_Super_Field;

int p = mySub.protected_Sub_Field;

int q = mySub.protected_Super_Field;
```

Figure 13.4 summarizes the accessibility of class members from a method of an unrelated class.

Now let's study the accessibility of class members from the methods of a Sub object. A method in the Sub object can access both the protected and public

FIGURE 13.4   The difference between **public**, **private**, and **protected** modifiers. Only public members are visible from outside.

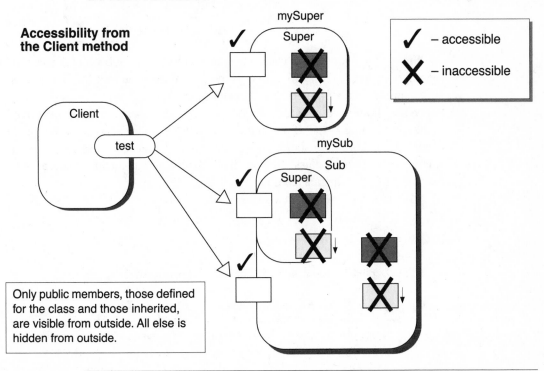

members of Super, but not the private members of Super. Figure 13.5 summarizes the accessibility of members from a method of a Sub object.

FIGURE 13.5   The difference between **public, private,** and **protected** modifiers. Everything except the **private** members of the **Super** class is visible from a method of the **Sub** class.

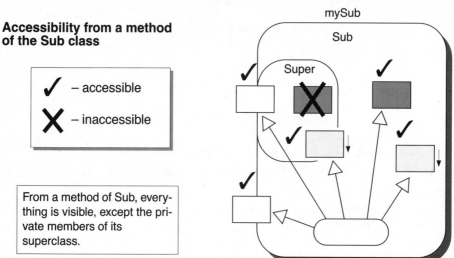

Accessibility from a method of the Sub class

✔ – accessible

✘ – inaccessible

From a method of Sub, everything is visible, except the private members of its superclass.

Figure 13.5 shows the case where a method of a Sub object is accessing members of itself. Everything except the private members of the Super class is accessible from a method of the Sub class.

What about accessing the members of an object from another object that belongs to the same class? If a member X, whether inherited or defined in a class, is accessible from an instance of the class, then X is also accessible from all instances of the same class. Figure 13.6 illustrates that an instance can access members of other instances of the same class.

Consider the following two classes:

```
class Super
{
    ...
    public void superToSuper( Super anotherSuper)
    {
        int i = anotherSuper.public_Super_Field;
        int j = anotherSuper.protected_Super_Field;
        int l = anotherSuper.private_Super_Field;
    }
    ...
}
```

✔ VALID →

FIGURE 13.6   Data members accessible from an instance are also accessible from other instances of the same class.

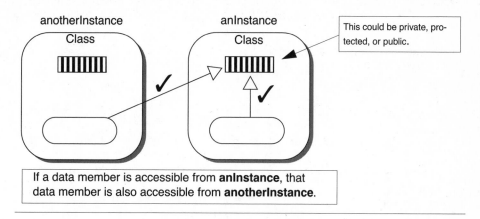

class Sub
{
    ...
    public void subToSub(Sub anotherSub)
    {
        int i = anotherSub.public_Sub_Field;
        int j = anotherSub.protected_Sub_Field;
        int k = anotherSub.private_Sub_Field;

        int l = anotherSub.public_Super_Field;   //inherited
        int m = anotherSub.protected_Super_Field; //members

        int n = anotherSub.private_Super_Field;
    }
    ...
}

✓ VALID
✓ VALID
✗ NOT VALID

All statements in the two methods, except the last one in subToSub, are valid because members accessible to an object are also accessible from other objects of the same class. Now, consider the following two classes:

class Super
{
    ...
    public void superToSub(Sub sub)

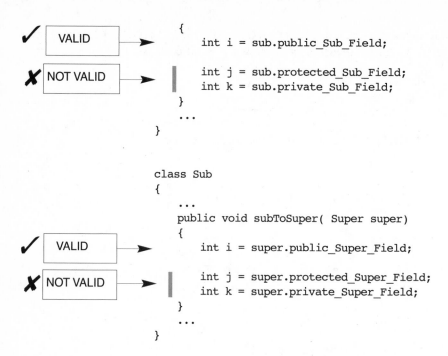

The two methods show that only the public members of an object are accessible from another object if the two objects belong to different classes. Whether one class is a subclass of the other class is irrelevant here.

 Quick Check

1. If X is a private member of the Super class, is X accessible from a subclass of Super?
2. If X is a protected member of the Super class, is an instance's X accessible from another instance of Super? What about from the instances of a subclass of Super?

13.4 Inheritance and Constructor

In this section, we explain how the constructors of a class are affected by inheritance. Unlike other members of a superclass, constructors of a superclass are not inherited by its subclasses. This means that you must define a constructor for a class or use the default constructor added by the compiler. As we mentioned in Chapter 4, a default constructor is added to a class if you do not declare any constructor for the class. A class definition such as

```
class Person
{
    public void sayHello( )
    {
        System.out.println("Well, hello.");
    }
}
```

is equivalent to

```
class Person
{

    public Person( )
    {
        super();
    }

    public void sayHello( )
    {
        System.out.println("Well, hello.");
    }

}
```

Automatically added to the class by the compiler.

This statement calls the super-class's constructor.

The statement

```
super();
```

calls the superclass's constructor. Every class has a superclass. If the class declaration does not explicitly designate the superclass with the **extends** clause, then the class's superclass is the **Object** class.

If you declare a constructor, then no default constructor is added to the class. For example, if you define a class as

```
class MyClass
{
    public MyClass( int x )
    {
        ...
    }
}
```

then a statement such as

```
MyClass test = new MyClass();
```

is invalid because **MyClass** has no matching constructor.

If the constructor you define does not contain an explicit call to a superclass constructor, then the compiler adds the statement

```
super();
```

as the first statement of the constructor. For example, if you define a constructor as

```
class MyClass
{
    private int myInt;

    public MyClass( )
    (
        myInt = 10;
    }

}
```

then the compiler will rewrite the constructor to

```
public MyClass( )
{
    super();
    myInt = 10;
}
```

Let's look at another example. Consider the following class definitions:

```
class Vehicle
{
    private String vin;

    public Vehicle(String vehicleIdNumber)
        {
```

```
            vin = vehicleIdNumber;
        }

        public void getVIN( )
        {
            return vin;
        }
    }
```

Since the class has a constructor, no default constructor is added to the class. This means a statement such as

```
Vehicle myCar = new Vehicle();
```

causes a compilation error because the class does not have a matching constructor. This is actually what we want because we do not want to create an instance of Vehicle without a vehicle identification number. Now let's consider a subclass definition for trucks. A Truck object has one additional instance variable called cargoWeightLimit that refers to a maximum weight of cargo the truck can carry. We assume the truck's weight limit for cargo can vary (say, depending on how much the owner pays in fees). Here's our first attempt:

```
class Truck extends Vehicle
{
    private int cargoWeightLimit;

    public void setWeightLimit( int newLimit)
    {
        cargoWeightLimit = newLimit;
    }

    public int getWeightLimit( )
    {
        return cargoWeightLimit;
    }
}
```

If you compile this definition, you will get a compiler error. Since no constructor is defined for the class, the compiler adds a default constructor

```
public void Truck()
{
    super();
}
```

This constructor calls the superclass's constructor with no arguments, but there's no matching constructor in the superclass. Thus, the compilation error results. Here's a correct definition:

```
class Truck extends Vehicle
{
    private int cargoWeightLimit;

    public Truck(int weightLimit, String vin)
    {
        super(vin);
        cargoWeightLimit = weightLimit;
    }

    public void setWeightLimit( int newLimit)
    {
        cargoWeightLimit = newLimit;
    }

    public int getWeightLimit( )
    {
        return cargoWeightLimit;
    }
}
```

You need to make this call. Otherwise, the compiler will add **super()**, which will result in an error because there is no matching constructor in **Vehicle**.

Now let's apply this knowledge to the design of the UndergraduateStudent and GraduateStudent classes. If we want a constructor that accepts the name, then we need to define such a constructor in both classes, because the constructor defined for the Student class is not inherited by these classes. Notice that we can create instances of these classes by

```
student1 = new UndergraduateStudent( );
student2 = new GraduateStudent( );
```

because the default constructor is added by the compiler, not because the one defined in the Student class is inherited by the subclasses. Remember that constructors of a superclass are not inherited by its subclasses.

Here are a rule and guideline to remember for a subclass constructor:

If a class has a superclass that is not the Object class, then a constructor of the class should make an explicit call to a constructor of the superclass.

Always provide a constructor for every class you define.
Don't rely on default constructors.

Quick Check

1. How do you call the super class's constructor from its subclass?

2. What statement will be added to a constructor of a subclass if it is not included in the constructor explicitly by the programmer?

3. Modify the definition of GraduateStudent and UndergraduateStudent in Section 13.1 so we can create their instances in the following way:

```
student1 = new UndergraduateStudent();
student2 = new UndergraduateStudent("Mr. Espresso");
student3 = new GraduateStudent();
student4 = new GraduateStudent("Ms. Latte");
```

13.5 Abstract Superclasses and Abstract Methods

When we define a superclass we often do not need to create any instances of the superclass. In the previous section, we defined the Student superclass and its two subclasses GraduateStudent and UndergraduateStudent. We gave examples of creating instances of GraduateStudent and UndergraduateStudent, but not of creating instances of Student. Does it make sense to create an instance of the Student class? Depending on whether or not we need to create instances of Student, we must define the class differently. We will describe different ways of defining a superclass in this section.

Even though we can create an instance of Student if we wanted to (because of the way the class is currently defined), is there a need to create an instance of Student? If a student can only be a graduate or undergraduate student, then there is no need to create an instance of Student. In fact, because of the way the class is defined, had we created an instance of Student and stored it in the roster array, the program would crash. Why? Because the Student class does not have a computeCourseGrade method.

In the following discussion, we will consider two cases. In the first case, we assume that a student must be either a graduate or an undergraduate student. In the second case, we assume that a student does not have to be a graduate or an undergraduate student (e.g., he could be a nonmatriculated auditing student, etc.).

Case 1: Student Must Be Undergraduate or Graduate

abstract
class

For the case where a student must be a graduate or an undergraduate student, we only need instances of GraduateStudent and UndergraduateStudent. So we must define the Student class in such a way that no instances of it can be created. One way is to define Student as an abstract class. An *abstract class* is a class defined with the modifier abstract, and no instances can be created from an abstract class. Let's see how the abstract Student class is defined.

> The keyword **abstract** here denotes an abstract class.

```
abstract class Student
{
     protected final static int   NUM_OF_TESTS = 3;
     protected String             name;
     protected int[]              test;
     protected String             courseGrade;

     public Student( )
     {
         this("No name");
     }

     public Student(String studentName)
     {
         name        = studentName;
         test        = new int[NUM_OF_TESTS];
         courseGrade = "****";
     }

     abstract public void computeCourseGrade();

     public String getCourseGrade( )
     {
         return courseGrade;
     }

     public String getName( )
     {
         return name;
     }
```

> Abstract method has no method body, just a semicolon.

> The keyword **abstract** here denotes an abstract method.

```
public int getTestScore(int testNumber)
{
    return test[testNumber-1];
}

public void setName(String newName)
{
    name = newName;
}

public void setTestScore(int testNumber, int testScore)
{
    test[testNumber-1] = testScore;
}
}
```

abstract method

An *abstract method* is a method with the keyword abstract, and it ends with a semicolon instead of a method body. A class is *abstract* if the class contains an abstract method or does not provide an implementation of an inherited abstract method. We say a method is *implemented* if it has a method body. If a subclass has no abstract methods and no unimplemented inherited abstract methods, then the subclass is no longer abstract, and thus, its instances can be created.

implementing a method

An abstract class must include the keyword abstract in its definition. Notice that the abstract class Student has an incomplete definition because the class includes the abstract method computeCourseGrade that does not have a method body. The intent is to let its subclasses provide the implementation of the computeCourseGrade method. If a subclass does not provide an implementation of the inherited abstract method, the subclass is also an abstract class, and therefore, no instances of the subclass can be created. Since an abstract class can only make sense when it is a superclass, we frequently use the term *abstract superclass*.

abstract superclass

In an object diagram, we represent an abstract class using a parallelogram. The Student abstract superclass is drawn as

Student

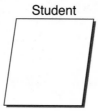

Ms. Latte:	Is the **Math** class an abstract class?
Dr. Caffeine:	It is true that we cannot create an instance of the **Math** class, but it is not an abstract class. If a class is abstract, then you cannot create an instance of the class, but not being able to create an instance does not necessarily imply that the class is abstract.
Ms. Latte:	What do you mean?
Dr. Caffeine:	The intent of an abstract class is to define common aspects of all of its subclasses and leave some portions, that is, abstract methods, to be completed by the individual subclasses.
Ms. Latte:	Then how would you classify the **Math** class?
Dr. Caffeine:	It is a noninstantiable class, a class for which we cannot create an instance. Notice that an abstract class is a noninstantiable class by definition, but the reverse is not always true. There are noninstantiable classes, for example, the **Math** class, that are not abstract.
Ms. Latte:	How do I define a noninstantiable class?
Dr. Caffeine:	Very easy. Declare a private constructor with no arguments and declare no other constructors for the class.

Dr. & Ms.

Case 2: Student Does Not Have to Be Undergraduate or Graduate

For the second case, where a student does not have to be a graduate or an undergraduate student, we can design classes in two different ways. The first approach is to make the Student class instantiable. The second approach is to leave the Student class abstract and add a third subclass, say OtherStudent, to handle a student who is neither a graduate nor an undergraduate student. Let's call students who are neither graduate nor undergraduate students *nonregular students*. Let's assume further that the nonregular students will receive a pass grade if their average test score is greater than or equal to 50. With the first approach, we define the Student class as

```
class Student
{
    protected final static int    NUM_OF_TESTS = 3;
    protected String              name;
```

Not an abstract class anymore.

```
protected int[]              test;
protected String             courseGrade;

public Student(String studentName)
{
    name        = studentName;
    test        = new int[NUM_OF_TESTS];
    courseGrade = "****";
}

public void computeCourseGrade()
{
    int total = 0;
    for (int i = 0; i < NUM_OF_TESTS; i++) {
        total += test[i];
    }

    if (total/NUM_OF_TESTS >= 50) {
        courseGrade = "Pass";
    }
    else {
        courseGrade = "No Pass";
    }
}

public String getCourseGrade( )
{
    return courseGrade;
}

public String getName( )
{
    return name;
}

public int getTestScore(int testNumber)
{
    return test[testNumber-1];
}

public void setName(String newName)
{
    name = newName;
}

public void setTestScore(int testNumber, int testScore)
{
```

Not an abstract method anymore.

```
                    test[testNumber-1] = testScore;
            }
    }
```

The class is no longer abstract, and we can create an instance of **Student** to represent a nonregular student.

With the second approach, we leave the **Student** class abstract. To represent nonregular students, we define a third subclass called **OtherStudent** as follows:

```
class OtherStudent extends Student
{
    public void computeCourseGrade()
    {
        int total = 0;
        for (int i = 0; i < NUM_OF_TESTS; i++) {
            total += test[i];
        }

        if (total/NUM_OF_TESTS >= 50) {
            courseGrade = "Pass";
        }
        else {
            courseGrade = "No Pass";
        }
    }
}
```

Figure 13.7 is an object diagram that includes the third subclass.

Which approach is better? There's no easy answer. It all depends on a given situation. To determine which approach is better for a given situation, we can ask ourselves which approach allows us easier modification and extension. Consider, for example, which approach will facilitate easier modification if we have to add a new type of student, say, scholarship students. Or consider the case where the rule for assigning a course grade for the undergraduate and graduate students is modified, say, they become the same.

Finally, not all methods can be declared abstract.

The following types of methods cannot be declared as abstract:

- Private methods.
- Static methods.

FIGURE 13.7   An object diagram of the abstract superclass **Student** and its three subclasses.

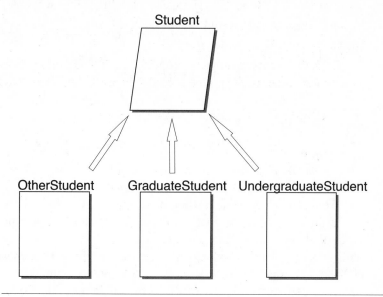

Quick Check

1. Can you create an instance of an abstract class?
2. Must an abstract class include an abstract method?
3. What is wrong with the following declaration?

```
class Vehicle
{
    abstract public getVIN();
    ...
}
```

13.6 When and When Not to Use Inheritance

The inheritance mechanism is a very powerful feature of object-oriented programming, and because of its power, it is open to misuse. You should keep in
mind that inheritance is only one of the techniques available for code reuse. In-

heritance is a technique we use if we want to design a more specialized class from an existing class. For example, suppose you want a dialog to display the text in different colors. The OutputBox class from the javabook package is capable of displaying the text in black only. So one way to create your desired object is by defining a subclass of OutputBox. Let's call this subclass ColorTextDisplay. The ColorTextDisplay will add public methods that will allow programmers to display the text in different colors. For example,

```
public void setTextColor( Color textColor )
```

Once the color is set, subsequent printing will be done in the set color. Because ColorTextDisplay is a subclass of OutputBox, the programmer can print out the text using the inherited method printLine or print.

We use inheritance also when we want to model the related entities we use in the program. This is what we did earlier in the chapter modeling different types of students. We designed the Student class and its two subclasses GraduateStudent and UndergraduateStudent. Here again, we are encapsulating a specialized functionality in the subclasses. We place common, generic information in the Student class and a specialized functionality in the GraduateStudent and UndergraduateStudent classes. The example of Vehicle and Truck in Section 13.4 also shows this relationship.

In all of these examples where we used inheritance, the classes are related in

IS-A relationship

an *IS-A* relationship. We can characterize them as Truck IS-A Vehicle, ColorTextDisplay IS-A(n) OutputBox, and so forth. So when you declare a class A as a subclass of B, you should ask yourself, is A a B? This is not the only way to use inheritance, but for beginners, thinking in terms of an IS-A relationship is helpful.

If an entity A is a specialized form of another entity B, that is, A is a B, then model them by using inheritance. Declare A as a subclass of B.

Now, let's consider another case of code reuse. This time you want to design a class for other programmers to use. You want to design an object that allows programmers to display the name of the students who either pass or do not pass the course. Let's call this class StudentList. The programmer will send the roster array to a StudentList object as

```
StudentList lister = new StudentList( );
lister.showPass( roster );
```

or

```
lister.showNoPass( roster );
```

How would you implement the StudentList class? One possibility is to use a ListBox object from the javabook package. We can make StudentList a subclass of ListBox and add needed methods to StudentList. However, this is a misuse of inheritance. Why? If we make StudentList as a subclass of ListBox, then we cannot prohibit programmers from using the ListBox methods, which in this case does not make sense. We do not want the programmers to call the methods of ListBox in using an instance of StudentList. As a designer of StudentList, we want to reuse the ListBox class, but we do not want to relate them in an IS-A relationship.

code reuse
by composition

Instead of using inheritance, we design the StudentList class by including a ListBox object as its data member. We call this type of code reuse *code reuse by composition*. In other words, a StudentList object is composed of a ListBox object (and others). The relationship here is a *HAS-A* relationship; that is, StudentList HAS-A ListBox. We will give an example of code reuse by composition in the next chapter.

13.7 Sample Program: Computing Course Grades

Let's develop a program that illustrates the use of Student and its subclasses GraduateStudent and UndergraduateStudent. The program will input student data from a user-designated textfile, compute the course grades, and display the results. We assume the input textfile is created by using a text editor or another application. For example, a teacher may have kept his student grades in a notebook. Instead of manually computing the grades with a pencil and calculator, he enters data into a textfile and uses this program to compute the course grades. Another possible scenario is that the teacher uses some kind of application software that allows him to maintain student records. However, this application will not allow the teacher to use different formulas for computing the course grades of undergraduate and graduate students. If this application is capable, then the teacher can export data to a textfile and use our program to compute the course grades for undergraduate and graduate students using the different formulas.

Using textfiles to transfer data from one application to another application is a very common technique used in software applications.

To focus on the data processing aspect of the program, we will keep its user interface very simple and leave it as an exercise to design a better user interface. We will also leave the task of saving the results back to a textfile in a different format (e.g., saving only the last name and the final course grade) or to an object-based file as an exercise.

Problem Statement

Write an application that reads in a textfile organized in the manner shown below and displays the final course grades. The course grades are computed differently for the undergraduate and graduate students based on the formulas listed on page 640. The input textfile format is as follows:

- *A single line is used for information on one student.*
- *Each line uses the format*

    <Type> <Name> <Test 1> <Test 2> <Test 3>

    where <Type> designates either a graduate or undergraduate student, <Name> designates the student's first and last name, and <Test i> designates the ith test score.

- *End of input is designated by the word END. The case of the letters is insignificant.*

Figure 13.8 shows a sample input textfile.

FIGURE 13.8   A sample textfile containing student names and test scores. **U** at the beginning of a line designates an undergraduate student and **G** designates a graduate student.

<Type>	<Name>		<Test 1>	<Test 2>	<Test 3>
U	John	Doe	87	78	90
G	Jill	Jones	90	95	87
G	Jack	Smith	67	77	68
U	Mary	Hines	80	85	80
U	Mick	Taylor	76	69	79
END					

Overall Plan

We will implement a class that will

1. Read an input textfile.

2. Compute the course grades.

3. Print out the result.

To read a textfile, we will use the standard file I/O objects File, FileReader, and BufferedReader. To compute the course grades, we will use the Student, Undergraduate, and Graduate classes as defined earlier in the chapter. The formulas for calculating the course grades are defined in their respective compute-CourseGrades methods. Since the input file is a textfile, we must create either a Graduate and Undergraduate object for each line of input, so we will be able to call its computeCourseGrades method. To store the created student objects (instances of either Graduate or Undergraduate), we will use an array of Student.

To display the computed course grades, we will use an OutputBox from the javabook package. Since the OutputBox class supports the saveToFile method, it is an easy task to save the input data and the course grades back to a textfile. You just have to call the saveToFile method after all the results are displayed on an OutputBox. The task we leave as an exercise is a little more difficult than this. Often we need the capability to save the results in different format. For example, assuming the student information includes the student ID number, the teacher may want to save only the last four digits of the ID numbers and the final course grades so the results can be posted. Also, if the input data are sorted in alphabetical order by the students' last name, it would be better to save the results in a random order so the students cannot guess the other students' grades by their position in the posted listing.

Let's name the class ComputeGrades and make it a subclass of the Main-Window class from the javabook package. By making ComputeGrades a subclass of MainWindow, we can add menus to it (adding menus will be left as an exercise) and let it be an owner frame of an OutputBox and possibly other dialogs. Also, MainWindow already includes the necessary code to terminate the program when the window is closed, so we don't have to worry about it. We will supply a minimal main class whose main method will create and start a ComputeGrades object.

Here's our working design document:

Design Document:	ComputeGrades
Class	**Purpose**
ComputeGradesMain	The main class of the program.
ComputeGrades	The top-level control object that manages other objects in the program. The class is a subclass of MainWindow from java-book.
OutputBox	An OutputBox object is used to display the input data and computed course grades.
Student, Under-GraduateStudent, GraduateStudent	Application logic objects for students. The Student class is an abstract superclass.
File, FileReader, BufferedReader	Objects necessary for reading data from a textfile.

Figure 13.9 is an object diagram of the program at this point.

Now let's think about the methods of ComputeGrades. What kinds of public methods should the class support? Since a ComputeGrades object is a top-level controller object, we need a single public method to initiate the operations. Let's define a method called processData that will carry out the three main tasks. The main method of ComputeGradesMain will call this method

```
ComputeGrades gradeComputer = new ComputeGrades();
gradeComputer.processData();
```

The processData method, expressed in pseudocode, will look something like this:

```
this.show();          //display itself, a main window
outputBox.show();     //and outputBox

boolean success = readData();

if (success) {
    computeGrade();
    printResult();
}
else
    print error message "File Input Error";
```

FIGURE 13.9   An object diagram of the **ComputeGrades** program. **javabook** and **FileDialog** objects are not shown.

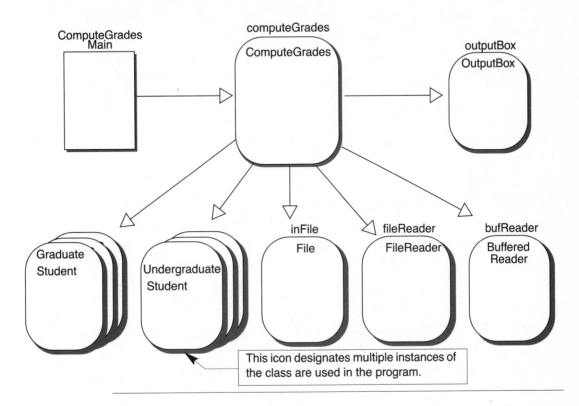

The readData method returns true if the input data are read in correctly from a textfile and the array of Student objects is properly created. The object diagram for the ComputeGrades class at this point is

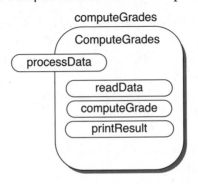

Our working design document for the ComputeGrades class is as follows:

Design Document: The ComputeGrades Class		
Method	**Visibility**	**Purpose**
`<constructor>`	`public`	Creates and initializes the objects used by a Compute-Grades object.
`processData`	`public`	Displays itself and carries out three main tasks.
`readData`	`private`	Opens and reads data from a textfile and creates an array of Student objects from the input data. If the operation is successful, returns true.
`computeGrade`	`private`	Scans through the array of Student objects and compute the course grades.
`printResult`	`private`	Prints out the student information along with the computed grades to an OutputBox.

We will develop the program in five incremental steps:

1. Start with the program skeleton. Define the ComputeGradesMain and skeleton ComputeGrades classes.

2. Implement the printResult method. Define any other methods necessary to implement printResult.

3. Implement the computeGrade method. Define any other methods necessary to implement computeGrade.

4. Implement the readData method. Define any other methods necessary to implement readData.

5. Finalize and look for improvements.

We defer the implementation of the hardest method, readData, till the last. Some programmers prefer to deal with the hardest aspect of the program first, and there's no strict rule for ordering the implementation steps. You should order the steps in a way with which you are most comfortable. However, this does not mean you can implement the methods at random. You must always plan the implementation steps carefully so the steps follow a logical sequence. For this program, we start with the output routine so we can use the final output routine for testing other methods, instead of defining a temporary output routine for testing purposes.

Step 1 Development: Program Skeleton

Step 1 Design   Let's begin with the data members and the constructors for the ComputeGrades class. We will start with the following data members:

```
private    OutputBox        outputBox;     //for output

private    File             inFile;        //for input
private    FileReader       fileReader;
private    BufferedReader   bufReader;

private    Student[ ]       roster;        //for maintaining
                                           //student info
```

It is a straightforward operation to create the first four objects, but we need to think a little about the roster array. How big should the array be? There are several possibilities:

1. Create an array of an arbitrary size, say, 25.

2. Let the programmer pass the size in the constructor.

3. Do not create it in the constructor. Modify the input textfile to include the size of an array in the first line.

Option 3 is not attractive because it will require a change in the problem specification. Moreover, requiring the size information in the input file will put a lot of burden on the user because he must go over the textfile and count the number of lines the file contains. Such a burdensome task should be left to a computer. So, we will implement Options 1 and 2. If the data cannot fit into an array of a pre-designated size, then we will use the technique discussed in Chapter 9 to expand the array.

We declare a constant

```
private static final int    DEFAULT_SIZE = 25;
```

and declare the two constructors as

```
public ComputeGrades( )
{
    this( DEFAULT_SIZE );
}
```

```
public ComputeGrades( int arraySize )
{
    super();    //an explicit call to the superclass constructor

    outputBox = new OutputBox( this );
    roster = new Student[arraySize];
}
```

Notice that we can't create inFile, fileReader, and bufReader until we know the actual file to open. We will create these objects in one of the methods we define later.

Step 1 Code   For the skeleton program, we include temporary output statements in the private methods to verify that they are called correctly in the right order. Here's the skeleton:

```
/*
    Program ComputeGrades

    A program that inputs a textfile containing student names and test scores,
    computes the course grades, and displays the result.

*/

class ComputeGradesMain
{
    public static void main (String args[])
    {
        ComputeGrades gradeComputer = new ComputeGrades();
        gradeComputer.processData();
    }
}
```

```
/*
    Class ComputeGrades

    The top-level object for managing all other objects in the program.
*/

import javabook.*;
import java.io.*;

class ComputeGrades extends MainWindow
{

/***************************
    Data Members
***************************/

private static final int     DEFAULT_SIZE = 25;
```

```
private    OutputBox         outputBox;     //for output

private    File              inFile;        //for input
private    FileReader        fileReader;
private    BufferedReader    bufReader;

private    Student[ ]        roster;        //for maintaining student info

/***************************
   Constructors
***************************/

public ComputeGrades( )
{
   this( DEFAULT_SIZE );
}

public ComputeGrades( int arraySize )
{
   super();   //an explicit call to the superclass constructor

   outputBox  = new OutputBox( this );
   roster     = new Student[arraySize];
}


/******************************
   Public Methods

      void    processData        (      )

*****************************/

   /********************************************************
      Method:        processData

      Purpose:       Read in data from a textfile, compute grades,
                     and display the result in an outputBox.

      Parameters:    None

      Returns:       None
   */
   public void processData ( )
   {
      setVisible( true ); //display the main window
      outputBox.setVisible( true );

      boolean success = readData();

      if (success) {
         computeGrade();
```

```
            printResult();
        }
        else
            outputBox.printLine( "File Input Error") ;
    }

/*****************************
    Private Methods

        void        computeGrade        (           )
        void        printResult         (           )
        boolean     readData            (           )

******************************/

    /*********************************************************
        Method:        computeGrade

        Purpose:       Scan through the roster array and compute
                       the course grades.

        Parameters:    None

        Returns:       None
    */
    private void computeGrade( )
    {
        outputBox.printLine("Inside computeGrade");           //TEMP
    }


    /*********************************************************
        Method:        printResult

        Purpose:       Display the result in an outputBox.

        Parameters:    None

        Returns:       None
    */
    private void printResult( )
    {
        outputBox.printLine("Inside printResult");            //TEMP
    }


    /*********************************************************
        Method:        readData

        Purpose:       Open a textfile, read in data, and
                       construct the roster array.

        Parameters:    None
```

```
     Returns:        boolean [true if successful]
*/
private boolean readData( )
{
    outputBox.printLine("Inside readData");            //TEMP
    return true;                                        //TEMP
}

}
```

Step 1 Test

We execute the main class and the skeleton ComputeGrades class to verify that the classes are coded correctly. When executed, we will see the main window (ComputeGrades) and an OutputBox appearing on the screen and the following messages in the OutputBox:

```
Inside readData
Inside computeGrade
Inside printResult
```

Step 2 Development: Implement the printResult Method

Step 2 Design

In the second development step, we add a routine that places the result in an outputBox. To implement and test this method, we need to create the roster array. We will include temporary code inside the readData method to build a test roster array. We can use for loops such as

```
for (int i = 0; i < 15; i++) {
    roster[i] = new UndergraduateStudent( );
    roster[i].setName( "Undergrad # " + i );

    roster[i].setTestScore(1, 70+ i);
    roster[i].setTestScore(2, 75+ i);
    roster[i].setTestScore(3, 80+ i);
}
```

The first half of the array is undergraduate students.

```
for (int i = 15; i < DEFAULT_SIZE; i++) {
    roster[i] = new GraduateStudent( );
    roster[i].setName( "Grad # " + i );

    roster[i].setTestScore(1, 80+ i);
    roster[i].setTestScore(2, 85+ i);
    roster[i].setTestScore(3, 90+ i);
}
```

The second half of the array is graduate students.

to create a temporary roster for testing purposes.

Now, let's design the printResult method. When this method is called, we have the roster array built. The method scans through the array and retrieves the student data using the getName, getCourseGrade, and getTestScore methods. Expressed in pseudocode, we have the following:

```
for each element i in the roster array {

    output the name of roster[i];

    output the test scores of roster[i];

    output the course grade of roster[i];

    skip to the next line;
}
```

How should we terminate the loop? We should realize first that the roster array may or may not be full. For example, its default size is 25, but the actual number of elements may be less than 25, so using the value of roster.length will not work. Since roster is an array of objects, one possible way to express the loop is as follows:

```
while ( roster[i] != null ) {

    //output roster[i] information

}
```

One problem with this while loop is that we must have at least one empty slot in the array for the loop to terminate correctly. We can improve it by using the length value as

```
while ( i < roster.length && roster[i] != null ) {
    ...
}
```

Another possibility is to keep the count, which we set in the readData method. This count will be a data member of type int. Let's call this count variable studentCount. Then the processing loop becomes

```
for (int i = 0; i < studentCount; i++) {

    //output roster[i] information
}
```

We will adopt this approach because having this count information is useful for other purposes. For example, if we want to compute the percentage of the students passing the course, we can use studentCount to compute it. If we don't have this variable, then every time we need to compute the percentage, we have to find out the number of students in the roster array.

Finally, to print out student information so the data will align properly, we will use the Format class from javabook.

Step 2 Code   We first add the declaration for a new data member studentCount:

```
/***************************
    Data Members
***************************/
private int            studentCount;
```

This data member is initialized to 0 in the constructor as

```
public ComputeGrades( int arraySize )
{
    ...
    studentCount = 0;
}
```

and incremented by one every time new student information is read inside the readData method. In this step, the readData method is temporary, so student-Count is set to the number of student objects created, which is DEFAULT_SIZE.

The printResult method is defined as follows:

```
private void printResult()
{
    for (int i = 0; i < studentCount; i++)  {

        //print one student
        outputBox.print( Format.leftAlign ( 15,
                              roster[i].getName() ));

        for (int testNum = 1; testNum <= Student.NUM_OF_TESTS;
                              testNum++) {
```

Name ⟶

Test scores ⟶

```
                              outputBox.print( Format.centerAlign ( 8,
                                       roster[i].getTestScore(testNum) ));
                          }
                          outputBox.printLine( Format.rightAlign ( 8,
                                       roster[i].getCourseGrade() ));
                      }
                  }
```

Course grade ⟶ (points to the `outputBox.printLine( Format.rightAlign ( 8, roster[i].getCourseGrade() ));` line)

Step 2 Test   We verify two items in this step. First, the temporary readData method includes creating student objects and calling their methods. Correct execution will verify that we are including the correct student classes and using their methods properly. Second, the printResult method should display the output as intended. Since we have not implemented the computeGrade method, we will see four asterisks for the course grades. We have to run the program several times and adjust the values for the alignment methods of Format before deciding on the final values. Also, it is important to try different values for names and test scores before moving to the next step.

Step 3 Development: Implement the computeGrade Method

Step 3 Design   The functionality of computing the course grades is embedded inside the student classes, specifically, inside the respective computeCourseGrade methods of the GraduateStudent and UndergraduateStudent classes. Therefore, all we need to do in the computeGrade method is to scan through the roster array and call the element's computeCourseGrade method. This simplicity is a direct result of polymorphism.

Step 3 Code   The computeGrade method is defined as

```
private void computeGrade( )
{
    for (int i = 0; i < studentCount; i++ ) {
        roster[i].computeCourseGrade();
    }
}
```

Step 3 Test   We repeat the same testing routines of Step 2. Instead of seeing four asterisks for the course grades, we should be seeing correct values. To make the verification easy, we can set the fixed test scores for all students. Make sure you assign test scores that will result in students both passing and not passing. Don't forget to try out end cases such as zero for all three test scores. What about negative test scores? Will the student classes handle them correctly? If we identify serious problems with the Student classes at this point, we may have to suspend our development until we correct the Student class.

Step 4 Development: Implement the readData **Method**

Step 4 Design   We will now design the core function of the class, the readData method. We can express the overall logic of the method in pseudocode as

```
get the filename from the user;

if (the filename is provided)
    read in data and build the roster array;
else
    output an error message;
```

We will use a FileDialog object from the standard java.awt package to let the user specify the file. If the user cancels this dialog, then null is returned. In this case, we print out an error message and stop. If the user specifies a file, then we pass this information to a private method buildRoster, which will read data from the designated file and build the roster array.

The buildRoster method will read one line of data from the designated file at a time, and for each line of data, it creates an appropriate student object (an instance of GraduateStudent if the type is G and an instance of Undergraduate–Student if the type is U). The counter studentCount is incremented by one after each line is processed. When the line contains the terminator END, the method completes its execution. If the data in a line do not conform to the designated format, then the line is ignored. The method, expressed in pseudocode, is as follows:

```
try {
    set bufReader for input;

    while ( !done ) {
        line = get next line;

        if (line is END) {
            done = true;
        }
        else {
            student = createStudent( line );

            if (student != null) {
```

> **createStudent** will return **null** if the **line** does not conform to the designated format.

```
                              roster[studentCount] = student; //add to roster
                              studentCount++;
                          }
                      }
                  }
              }
              catch (IOException e) {
                  output an error message;
              }
```

We use the try–catch block because the creation of the BufferedReader object bufReader from a given filename could result in an exception. The create-Student method accepts a String argument, which is one line of the input file, and returns either an instance of GraduateStudent or UndergraduateStudent depending on the type specified in the line. If there's an error in the input line, then createStudent returns null. Instead of terminating the whole program, we will simply ignore the lines that do not conform to the specified format.

In a very simplied form, the createStudent method looks like this:

newStudentWith-Data will return **null** if the **inputLine** contains invalid data.

```
type    = first element of inputLine;

if (type.equals("U") || type.equals("G")) {
    student = newStudentWithData( inputLine );
}
else { //invalid type is encountered
    student = null;
}

return student;
```

The top statement requires us to extract the first item in the input line (String). How should we do it? The newStudentWithData method, which creates an instance of GraduateStudent or UndergraduateStudent and assigns data to it, also requires an operation to extract individual elements of data from a single line. We can write our own string processing routine to parse a given line and extract data on type, name, and test scores, but there's a better solution. We can use a standard class called StringTokenizer from the java.util package. We will take a quick detour to explain this class.

StringTokenizer   A StringTokenizer object is used to extract tokens from a given string. A *token* is a string of characters separated by *delimiter characters*, or simply *delimiters*. Any character can be designated as a delimiter, but space is the most commonly used delimiter. By default, a StringTokenizer object uses a white space (blank, tab, newline, or return) as its delimiter. Here's an example. The following code

```
String inputString
            = "I drink   100 cups of coffee every morning.";

StringTokenizer parser = new StringTokenizer( inputString );

while ( parser.hasMoreTokens() )  {
    System.out.println( parser.nextToken() );
}
```

will print out

```
I
drink
100
cups
of
coffee
every
morning.
```

The hasMoreTokens method returns true if there are more tokens remaining in parser, and the nextToken method returns the next token in parser. The next-Token method throws a NoSuchElementException if there is no token to return. Please refer to a java.util reference manual for more information on StringToken-izer.

Now let's get back to the design. Using a SringTokenizer object, we can express the createStudent method as

```
StringTokenizer    parser = new StringTokenizer( line );
String             type

try {
    type    = parser.nextToken();

    if (type.equals("U") || type.equals("G")) {
        student = newStudentWithData(type, parser);
    }
    else  { //invalid type is encountered
        student = null;
```

Ms. Latte:	It's great if you already know about **StringTokenizer**, but if you don't, you're out of luck. You would end up programming the functionality of **StringTokenizer** yourself, redoing something that has been done already.
Dr. Caffeine:	That's a challenge for all programmers, not just for beginners. My suggestion is that whenever you encounter a situation that seems to call for a common programming task, first look up the Java API reference manuals. You can also ask your fellow classmates, T.A., or instructor for guidance. They may know something. You should also make a habit of browsing the Java API reference manuals so you will have general knowledge about the standard classes. The key is always to look for the existing classes to reuse.
Ms. Latte:	In other words, you should avoid reinventing the wheel.
Dr. Caffeine:	Precisely.

```
        }
    }
    catch (NoSuchElementException e) { //no token
        student = null;
    }

    return student;
```

A private **newStudentWithData** method accepts a String that specifies the type of student and a StringTokenizer object. The method creates an instance of **UndergraduateStudent** or **GraduateStudent** and assigns data to the object by calling the StringTokenizer object's nextToken method repeatedly:

```
//type and parser are the parameter
try {
    if ( type.equals("U") ) {
        student = new UndergraduateStudent();
    }
    else {
        student = new GraduateStudent();
    }

    set the student name //use parser.nextToken() to extract
                         //data from a line
```

```
        set the student test scores //use Convert.toInt() to convert

    }
    catch (Exception e) { //thrown by parser.nextToken() or
        student = null;    //Convert.toInt(...)
    }

    return student;
```

Our design document for the ComputeGrades class now includes three more private methods:

Design Document: The ComputeGrades Class		
Method	**Visibility**	**Purpose**
...	...	...
buildRoster	private	Reads one line of data from the designated file at a time, and for each line of data, it creates an appropriate student object. If the data in a line do not conform to the designated format, then the line is ignored.
createStudent	private	Creates a student object by calling newStudentWith-Data if the type in the input line is U or G. If successful, returns the created student. Otherwise returns null.
newStudentWithData	private	Creates an instance of UndergraduateStudent or GraduateStudent and assigns data to the object by calling the StringTokenizer object's nextToken method repeatly.

Step 4 Code

Let's implement the methods. First, we add new import statements

```
import java.util.*;   //for StringTokenizer
import java.awt.*;    //for FileDialog
```

to the ComputeGrades class.

The readData method is defined as

```
private boolean readData()
{
    //get the file to open
    FileDialog fileBox
        = new FileDialog(this, "Open file", FileDialog.LOAD);
```

<table>
<tr><td>

You need get the
full pathname. →

</td><td>

```
fileBox.setVisible( true );
String filename = fileBox.getDirectory()
                           + fileBox.getFile();

if (filename != null) {
    return buildRoster(filename);
}
else {
    return false;
}
}
```

</td></tr>
</table>

The buildRoster method, the workhorse method of the class, is defined as

```
private boolean buildRoster(String filename)
{
    String  inputLine;
    Student student;

    boolean status   = true;
    boolean done     = false;

    try {
        inFile     = new File(filename);
        fileReader = new FileReader(inFile);
        bufReader  = new BufferedReader(fileReader);

        while ( !done ) {

            inputLine = bufReader.readLine();//read one line

            if (inputLine.equalsIgnoreCase ("END")) {
                done = true;                //end of file, so stop
            }
            else {
                student = createStudent(inputLine);

                if (student != null) { //okay, add it to roster
                    roster[studentCount] = student;
                    studentCount++;
                }
            }
        } //while

        bufReader.close();
    }
```

Set up the file
for input. →

Create a new
student and
add it to **roster**. →

```
        catch (IOException e) {
            status = false;
        }

        return status;
    }
```

The createStudent method is defined as

```
    private Student createStudent(String line )
    {
        Student            student;
        StringTokenizer    parser = new StringTokenizer( line );
        String             type

        try {
            type    = parser.nextToken();

            if (type.equals("U") || type.equals("G")) {
                student = newStudentWithData(type, parser);
            }
            else { //invalid type is encountered
                student = null;
            }
        }
        catch (NoSuchElementException e) { //no token
            student = null;
        }

        return student;
    }
```

And, finally, the newStudentWithData method is defined as

```
    private Student newStudentWithData(String            type,
                                       StringTokenizer parser)
    {
        Student student;

        try {
            if ( type.equals("U") ) {
                student = new UndergraduateStudent();
            }
            else {
                student = new GraduateStudent();
            }
```

Create a graduate
or undergraduate
student.

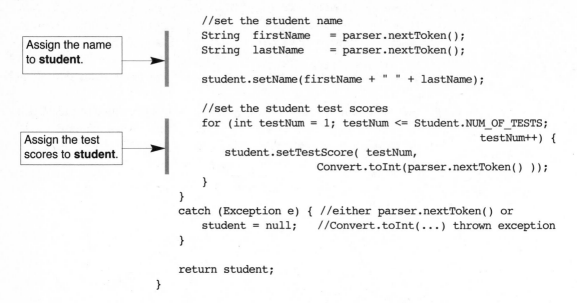

```
                                //set the student name
  ┌─────────────────┐           String  firstName  = parser.nextToken();
  │ Assign the name │           String  lastName   = parser.nextToken();
  │ to student.     │──────▶
  └─────────────────┘           student.setName(firstName + " " + lastName);

                                //set the student test scores
  ┌─────────────────┐           for (int testNum = 1; testNum <= Student.NUM_OF_TESTS;
  │ Assign the test │                                                testNum++) {
  │ scores to student.│────▶        student.setTestScore( testNum,
  └─────────────────┘                          Convert.toInt(parser.nextToken() ));
                                    }
                                }
                                catch (Exception e) { //either parser.nextToken() or
                                    student = null;   //Convert.toInt(...) thrown exception
                                }

                                return student;
                            }
```

Step 4 Test   We run through a more complete testing routine in this step. We need to run the program for various types of input files. Some of the possible file contents are as follows:

Step 4 Test Data	
Test File	**Purpose**
File with 5 to 20 entries of student information with all lines in correct format.	Test the normal case.
File with 5 to 20 entries of student information with some lines in incorrect format.	Test that **readData** and supporting methods handle the error case properly.
File with no entries.	Test that **buildRoster** method handles the error case properly.
File with more than 25 entries.	Test that **readData** and supporting methods handle the case where the number of entries is larger than the default size for the **roster** array.

Step 5 Development: Finalize and Improve

program review   As always, we will finalize the program by correcting any remaining errors, inconsistency, or unfinished methods. We also look for improvement in the last step. One improvement we can always look for is the length of the methods. Although there are no hard rules for the length, a method should not be any longer than a single page. The buildRoster and newStudentWithData methods are close to the maximum. If we notice the method is getting longer in the coding stage, we may want to rethink our design. For example, if the buildRoster method becomes too big, then we can define a new method that takes care of a portion of the method, such as moving the if–then–else statement in the method to a new method.

One problem that remains (which would have been identified in Step 4 testing) is the missing method for expanding the roster array when the input file includes more student entries than the set default size of 25. We leave this method as an exercise. We also leave some of the possible improvements as exercises.

13.8 Exercises

1. Consider the following class definitions. Identify invalid statements.

```
class Car
{
    public      String     make;
    protected   int        weight;
    private     String     color;


    ...
}

class ElectricCar extends Car
{
    private     int     rechargeHour;

    public ElectricCar( )
    {
        ...
    }

    //copy constructor
    public ElectricCar ( ElectricCar car )
    {
        this.make         = car.make;
        this.weight       = car.weight;
        this.color        = new String( car.color );
        this.rechargeHour = car.rechargeHour;
    }
    ...
}
```

```
class TestMain
{
    public static void main ( String args[] )
    {
        Car          myCar;
        ElectricCar  myElecCar;

        myCar = new Car();
        myCar.make = "Chevy";
        myCar.weight = 1000;
        myCar.color = "Red";

        myElecCar = new ElectricCar();
        myCar.make = "Chevy";
        myCar.weight = 500;
        myCar.color = "Silver";
    }
}
```

2. Consider the following class definitions. Identify which calls to the constructor are invalid.

```
class Car
{
    public     String    make;
    protected  int       weight;
    private    String    color;

    private Car ( String make, int weight, String color )
    {
        this.make   = make;
        this.weight = weight;
        this.color  = color;
    }

    public Car ( )
    {
        this( "unknown", -1, "white" );
    }

class ElectricCar extends Car
{
    private    int       rechargeHour;

    public ElectricCar( )
    {
```

```
        this( 10 );
    }

    private ElectricCar(int charge )
    {
        super( );
        rechargeHour = charge;
    }
}

class TestMain
{
    public static void main ( String args[] )
    {
        Car           myCar1, myCar2;
        ElectricCar   myElec1, myElec2;

        myCar1  = new Car();
        myCar2  = new Car("Ford", 1200, "Green");

        myElec1 = new ElectricCar( );
        myElec2 = new ElectricCar( 15 );
    }
}
```

3. In the ComputeGrades sample program, we set the default size of the roster array to 25. Modify the program so the size of the array will be increased if the input file contains more than 25 students. You need to add a method that expands the array, say, by 50 percent.

4. Extend the ComputeGrades sample program by storing the roster array using ObjectOutputStream. To allow the user to create and read the data using any text editor, add the menu choices Import and Export, which will read in a textfile (this is how the original ComputeGrades works) and write out data in ASCII format to a textfile.

5. Extend the ComputeGrades sample program to include menu choices Save, Open, and Quit. With the current program, you can open one file for each execution of the program. Extend the program so the user can open more than one file by selecting the menu choice Open repeatedly. Selecting the menu choice Save will allow the user to save the computed results to a file he or she specifies.

6. How would you modify the ComputeGrades sample program, if the formula for computing the course grade is different for freshmen, sophomore, jun-

ior, and senior undergraduate students? Would you design four subclasses of UndergraduateStudent? Or would you modify the body of the compute-CourseGrade method of UndergraduateStudent? Discuss the pros and cons of each approach.

7. Write a personal finance manager program that maintains information on your bank accounts. Incorporate the following rules:

    · For the savings accounts, you can make a maximum of three withdrawals in a month without incurring a fee. The bank charges $1.00 for every withdrawal after the third.

    · For the checking accounts, the bank charges $0.50 for every check you write for the first 20 checks (i.e., withdrawals) in a month. After that, there will be no charge.

    You should be able to open and save account information to a file. You should be able to list all transactions of a given account or of all accounts. Include appropriate menus to select the options supported by the program. Consider using the Date class to record the date of transactions. The Date class is from the java.util package. Please refer to a java.util reference manual for information on this class.

8. Extend the address book sample program from Chapter 9. Instead of managing a single type of Person, incorporate additional types of persons such as PersonalFriend, BusinessAssociate, etc. Define these classes as a subclass of Person. Design carefully to decide whether the Person class will be an abstract class or not.

9. Consider an asset tracking program that will track four types of assets: electronic appliances, automobiles, furniture, and compact discs. What classes would you design for the program? Would you define four unrelated classes or one superclass and four subclasses? If you design a superclass, will it be an abstract superclass?

10. Implement the asset tracking program of exercise 9. Allow the user to add, modify, and delete electronic appliances, automobiles, furniture, and compact discs. Allow the user to list the assets by category and search for an asset by its serial number.

11. Extend the asset tracking program of exercise 10 by adding an object I/O capability.

12. Write an application that reads daily temperatures for 12 months and allows the user to get statistics. Support at least three options: monthly average of a

given month, yearly average, and lowest and highest temperatures of a given month. Use a textfile to store temperatures. A line in the textfile contains daily temperatures for one month. The first line in the textfile contains temperatures for January, the second line for February, and so forth. Use String-Tokenizer to parse a line into temperatures of type float. For a data structure, consider using either an array of Month or a 2-D array of float. Month is a class you define yourself.

Class Roster
Maintenance Program

OBJECTIVES

After you have read and studied this chapter, you should be able to

- Develop large programs incrementally using multiple objects from object categories controller, storage, application logic, and user interface.

- Develop large programs that are extensible and modifiable by applying polymorphism and inheritance effectively in program design.

- Document how the methods in the classes are related by using method call sequence diagrams.

Introduction

In this chapter, as a culmination of what we have studied in this book, we will develop a program that is substantially larger than any of the previous sample programs. Traditionally, this program would be considered quite large and complex for an introductory programming book. We believe, however, that after studying this book, you are now conversant with object-oriented thinking and would not find this program too difficult to understand or beyond your reach. We are confident that you will be able to develop equally large programs on your own, too.

We will develop a class roster maintenance program, which requires a careful design and development plan because of its complexity. We will present the design and discuss design alternatives wherever appropriate and walk through the carefully planned incremental development steps.

14.1 Method Call Sequence Diagram

Before we start our development, we will introduce another diagramming technique called a method call sequence diagram. A *method call sequence* diagram shows the sequence of method calls starting from a given method. The object diagram is useful in showing the overall structure of a program, but it does not provide a detailed picture of how the methods are interrelated. In describing complex programs, method call sequence diagrams are very useful. We will use them extensively in this chapter.

As an example, let's draw a method sequence diagram for the processData method of the ComputeGradesMainWindow class from Chapter 13. This method reads student information from a user-designated textfile, computes the course grades, and prints out the results. The method is defined as

```
public void processData ( )
{
    this.show();        //display the main window
    outputBox.show();

    boolean success = readData();

    if (success) {
        computeGrade();
        printResult();
    }
    else
        outputBox.printLine( "File Input Error") ;
}
```

The readData method calls the buildRoster method, which in turn calls the createStudent and addStudentWithData methods repeatedly. Figure 14.1 is the method call sequence of the processData method.

FIGURE 14.1   Method call sequence of the **processData** method. Only the methods of **ComputeGradesMainWindow** are shown in the diagram.

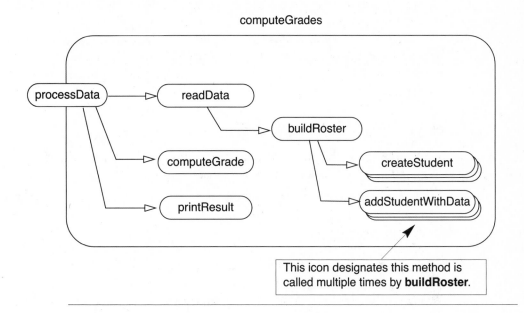

14.2 Problem Statement

Now let's start the development of the class roster maintenance program. We begin with its problem statement.

Write a class roster maintenance program that will allow the user to

- *Create a new roster.*
- *Open an existing roster (can open one roster at a time).*
- *Save the current roster to a file.*
- *Add and delete students from a roster.*
- *Change the name of students.*

> · *Edit the test scores of students.*
>
> · *Display the name, test scores, and course grade of a single student or all students in the roster.*

The program maintains both graduate and undergraduate students. For each student, we maintain his or her name, test scores, and final course grade. The final course grade is computed by using the following formula (from Chapter 13):

Type of Student	Grading Scheme
Undergraduate	*Pass if (test1+test2+test3)/3 >= 70*
Graduate	*Pass if (test1+test2+test3)/3 >= 80*

14.3 Overall Planning

What kinds of objects do we need for this program? Summarizing the tasks listed in the problem statement, we see that the program is capable of

1. Maintaining (i.e., adding, deleting, and modifying) student information.

2. Reading and writing student information to a file.

3. Displaying student information individually or as a group.

We mentioned the usefulness of classifying objects into the categories of controller, user interface, storage, and application logic. Thinking in terms of object categories, we notice that the first task calls for a storage object, the second task calls for a user interface object, and the third task calls for an application logic object. Beyond these objects, we need some kind of user interface object to accept student information from the user. We also need one or more controller objects to control these objects.

In earlier sample programs, we managed to identify almost all objects used in the programs in the overall planning stage. As this program is more complex, we will start our development by identifying only key classes and define additional classes as we progress through the development steps. Let's start thinking from the top-level controller object.

We will need a top-level window for this program. Instead of defining a subclass of Frame, we will make this class a subclass of MainWindow from java-book so we can reuse the functionality of MainWindow. We will call the class GradeRosterMainWindow. We use the prefix GradeRoster for naming classes

GradeRoster
MainWindow

instead of ClassRoster or Roster because the main purpose of this program is to maintain student grades, and it is kind of awkward to repeat the same word in a declaration, like class ClassRoster.

The role of GradeRosterMainWindow, as the top-level controller object of the program, is to display and process menu choices. For each menu selection, the actual processing is done by other objects. The task of GradeRosterMain-Window object is to delegate the work to subordinate objects instead of doing the work itself.

What will be the menu choices supported by the program? We want to organize the capabilities of the program into logically grouped menu choices. One possible grouping is as follows:

menu
structure

File	Edit	Show
New Open... Save Save As... Quit	Test Scores... Compute Grades Student Name... Add New Student... Delete Student...	All Students One Student...

The first menu is named File, and it includes operations related to opening and saving data files. It also includes the menu choice Quit. The second menu is named Edit, and it includes operations related to maintaining the student information. The third menu is named Show, and it includes operations related to displaying student information.

There are many other ways to organize menu choices, but we should try to adhere to the standard as closely as possible so the user will not get confused with an idiosyncratic menu structure. The structure of File, for example, follows the standard way of organizing the file operations.

GradeRoster

To maintain student information, we need an application logic object. We will call the class GradeRoster. An instance of the GradeRoster class will maintain information on students in one course. The role of GradeRoster is to add, delete, and modify student information. Individual student information is kept in an instance of GraduateStudent or UndergraduateStudent. These two classes are subclasses of the abstract superclass Student. These three classes were discussed in the previous chapter.

A GradeRoster object is an application logic object for maintaining a grade roster. In the program, we need some object to control it; for example, to create a new GradeRoster object when the New menu choice is selected. Should the responsibility of controlling a GradeRoster object be given to GradeRoster-

MainWindow? That is one possibility, but to do so we will have to overload the GradeRosterMainWindow class. It is a much cleaner design to let GradeRoster-MainWindow manage the menu handling only. In other words, when a menu choice is selected, it will let other objects carry out the selected operation. We will define a class called GradeRosterControl that will manage GradeRoster objects. A GradeRosterControl object works under the control of GradeRoster-MainWindow.

GradeRoster Control

Next, we need a storage object that is capable of saving GradeRoster to a file and reading it back from a file. We will call this class GradeRosterStorage. A GradeRosterStorage object works under the control of GradeRosterMain-Window.

GradeRoster Storage

For the display of student information, we will define a class GradeRoster-Display. This object will be capable of displaying information of a single student or of all students. A GradeRosterDisplay object also works under the control of GradeRosterMainWindow.

GradeRoster Display

Finally, we will use various javabook objects as needed in the program. For example, we will use MessageBox to output error messages and messages from temporary output statements.

Here's our working design document:

program classes

Design Document:	GradeRoster Program
Class	**Purpose**
GradeRosterMain	The main class of the program.
GradeRosterMain-Window	The top level control object that manages other objects in the program. The class is a subclass of MainWindow from java-book.
GradeRosterControl	An object that controls a GradeRoster object. The object works under the control of GradeRosterMainWindow. The object manages StudentNameDialog and TestScoreDialog objects.
GradeRosterDisplay	An object responsible for displaying class rosters. The object works under the control of GradeRosterMainWindow.
GradeRosterStorage	An object for handling the file input and output operations. The object works under the control of GradeRosterMain-Window.
GradeRoster	An object that actually maintains the roster. The object works under the control of GradeRosterControl.
Student	An abstract class that captures common behavior and data of both undergraduate and graduate students.

program
classes

Design Document:	GradeRoster Program
Class	**Purpose**
`GraduateStudent`	An object to model a graduate student.
`UndergraduateStudent`	An object to model an undergraduate student.
`MessageBox`	A javabook object to print out error messages and messages from temporary output statements.

Figure 14.2 is the object diagram of the program at this point.

We will develop the program in eight incremental steps:

1. Start with the program skeleton. Define the GradeRosterMain and skeleton GradeRosterMainWindow classes.

2. Implement the methods to create a new roster.

3. Implement the methods to add students to a roster.

4. Implement the methods to delete students from a roster.

5. Implement the methods to edit student information.

6. Implement the methods to edit test scores and compute the final course grades.

7. Implement the methods to display the student information of a single student or all students.

8. Implement the methods to save a roster to a file and read a roster from a file.

9. Finalize and look for improvements.

There are other possible sequences of steps. For example, we could implement Step 7 or 8 after Step 3. We will develop the program in the order as presented to work on more difficult tasks early in the development. Steps 7 and 8 are pretty straightforward operations compared to others, so we will work on them at the end.

14.4 Step 1 Development: Program Shell with Menus

Step 1 Design

We start with GradeRosterMain and the shell GradeRosterMainWindow. The shell class contains all menu choices. We will include a complete actionPer-

FIGURE 14.2   A simplified object diagram for the grade roster program. Primary objects are shown here. Secondary objects such as MessageBox, InputBox, and others are not shown.

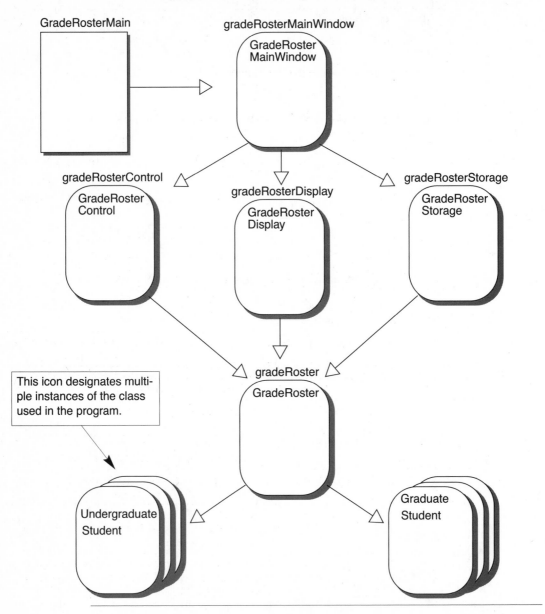

formed method in the class to filter the menu choice selection. For each menu choice, we will define a corresponding method that will include the code to process the selected menu choice. The task of actionPerformed is to call a method that corresponds to the selected menu choice. The flow of the method looks like this:

```
if (menu selected is "New") {
    newRoster();
}
else if (menu selected is "Open...") {
    openRoster();
}
else if (menu selected is "Save") {
    saveRoster();
}
//and so forth
```

Our working design document for the GradeRosterMainWindow class is as follows:

Design Document: The GradeRosterMainWindow Class		
Method	**Visibility**	**Purpose**
`<constructor>`	`public`	Creates and initializes the objects used by a GradeRosterMainWindow object.
`setVisible`	`public`	Displays itself. The GradeRosterMain class main method calls this method.
`actionPerformed`	`public`	Calls a method corresponding to the selected menu choice.
`createMenu`	`private`	Creates necessary objects for attaching the menu choices. This method is called from the constructor.
`newRoster`	`private`	Creates a new GradeRoster object. This method corresponds to menu choice File/New.
`openRoster`	`private`	Opens a GradeRoster object (i.e., reads the data in from a user-specified file). This method corresponds to menu choice File/Open.
`saveRoster`	`private`	Saves the currently opened GradeRoster object to the file from which it is read. This method corresponds to menu choice File/Save.

Design Document: The GradeRosterMainWindow Class		
Method	**Visibility**	**Purpose**
saveAsRoster	private	Saves the currently opened GradeRoster object to a file designated by the user. This method corresponds to menu choice File/Save As.
quitProgram	private	Quits the program. This method corresponds to menu choice File/Quit.
editTestScores	private	Edits the test scores of a designated student. This method corresponds to menu choice Edit/Test Scores.
computeGrades	private	Computes the course grades of all students in the grade roster. This method corresponds to menu choice Edit/ Compute Grades.
editStudentName	private	Edits the name of a designated student. This method corresponds to menu choice Edit/Student Name.
addNewStudent	private	Adds a new student to the grade roster. This method corresponds to menu choice Edit/Add New Student.
deleteStudent	private	Deletes a student from the grade roster. This method corresponds to menu choice Edit/Delete Student.
showAllStudents	private	Displays information of all students in the grade roster. This method corresponds to menu choice Show/All Students.
showOneStudent	private	Displays information of a designated student in the grade roster. This method corresponds to menu choice Show/ One Student.

For each step, we will summarize the work to be done in the following format:

	Objects	**To Do**
Step 1	GradeRoster Main	Implement the full class. The **main** method creates an instance of GradeRosterMain-Window and calls its setVisible method.
	GradeRoster MainWindow	Implement the shell of the main class that includes menu choices and corresponding methods for processing menu choices.

Step 1 Code

The GradeRosterMain class includes the main method only. The method opens an instance of GradeRosterMainWindow:

```
class GradeRosterMain
{
    public static void main (String args[])
    {
        GradeRosterMainWindow mainWindow
                = new GradeRosterMainWindow();
        mainWindow.setVisible( true );
    }
}
```

The constructor for GradeRosterMainWindow creates and initializes the objects used in this step:

```
public GradeRosterMainWindow()
{
    createMenu( );

    messageBox  = new MessageBox(this);
}
```

The private method createMenu constructs the menu choices and attaches the GradeRosterMainWindow object as their action event listener:

```
private void createMenu()
{
    MenuItem    item;
    Menu        menu;
    MenuBar     menuBar;

    menuBar = new MenuBar();

    menu    = new Menu("File");      //File Menu
    menuBar.add(menu);

        item = new MenuItem("New");             //New
        item.addActionListener( this );
        menu.add(item);

        item = new MenuItem("Open...");         //Open...
        item.addActionListener( this );
        menu.add(item);

        item = new MenuItem("Save");            //Save
        item.addActionListener( this );
```

| File menu |

| We intentionally indent here to reflect the **Menu/MenuItem** structure. |

```
                            menu.add(item);

                            item = new MenuItem("Save As...");        //Save As...
                            item.addActionListener( this );
                            menu.add(item);

                            item = new MenuItem("Quit");            //Quit
                            item.addActionListener( this );
                            menu.add(item);
```

Edit menu

```
          menu    = new Menu("Edit");        //Edit Menu
          menuBar.add(menu);

                            item = new MenuItem("Test Scores...");  //Test Scores...
                            item.addActionListener( this );
                            menu.add(item);

                            item = new MenuItem("Compute Grades");  //Compute Grades
                            item.addActionListener( this );
                            menu.add(item);

                            item = new MenuItem("Student Name..."); //Student
                            item.addActionListener( this );         //Name...
                            menu.add(item);

                            item = new MenuItem("Add New Student..."); //Add New
                            item.addActionListener( this );            //Student...
                            menu.add(item);

                            item = new MenuItem("Delete Student..."); //Delete
                            item.addActionListener( this );           //Student...
                            menu.add(item);
```

Show menu

```
          menu   = new Menu("Show");        //Show Menu
          menuBar.add(menu);

                            item = new MenuItem("All Students");      //All Students
                            item.addActionListener( this );
                            menu.add(item);

                            item = new MenuItem("One Student..."); //One Student...
                            item.addActionListener( this );
                            menu.add(item);

          setMenuBar(menuBar); //attach the menubar to the window
     }
```

The actionPerformed method of GradeRosterMainWindow will filter the selected menu choice and call the corresponding private method for processing:

```java
public void actionPerformed(ActionEvent event)
{
    String menuName;

    menuName = event.getActionCommand();

    if (menuName.equals("New")) {
        newRoster();
    }
    else if (menuName.equals("Open...")) {
        openRoster();
    }
    else if (menuName.equals("Save")) {
        saveRoster();
    }
    else if (menuName.equals("Save As...")) {
        saveAsRoster();
    }
    else if (menuName.equals("Quit")) {
        quitProgram();
    }
    else if (menuName.equals("Test Scores...")) {
        editTestScores();
    }
    else if (menuName.equals("Compute Grades")) {
        computeGrades();
    }
    else if (menuName.equals("Student Name...")) {
        editStudentName();
    }
    else if (menuName.equals("Add New Student...")) {
        addNewStudent();
    }
    else if (menuName.equals("Delete Student...")) {
        deleteStudent();
    }
    else if (menuName.equals("All Students")) {
        showAllStudents();
    }
    else if (menuName.equals("One Student...")) {
        showOneStudent();
    }
}
```

The private methods for processing the selected menu choices at this step include only temporary output statements, except the quitProgram method. All of these methods are written in the following style:

```
private void newRoster( )
{
    messageBox.show("Inside newRoster");
}
```

The quitProgram method is defined as

```
private void quitProgram( )
{
    System.exit(0);
}
```

Step 1 Test   We execute the main class and the skeleton GradeRosterMainWindow class to verify that the classes are coded correctly. When we run the program, we select every menu choice and verify that the correct message for the menu choice is displayed by the temporary output statements. We select the menu choice **Quit** and make sure the program terminates. Once this is verified, we move on to implement one by one the private methods of GradeRosterMainWindow that correspond to the menu choices. To implement these methods fully, we may have to modify or extend existing classes or design additional new classes.

14.5 Step 2 Development: Create a New Roster

Step 2 Design   The very first operation we need to implement is the capability to create a new grade roster. Without this capability, we will not be able to work on other operations. We decided that the program can open one grade roster at a time. When the user selects the menu choice **New**, we will create a new GradeRoster object. However, we cannot simply create a new grade roster. What will happen when there is a currently open grade roster?

Consider the behavior of a common text editor. Let's say that after you open and edit a document, you try to create a new document. What should happen to the currently open document? The text editor will ask you whether you want to save the document before creating a new one. We will make our program behave in a similar manner. When there's a currently open grade roster, we will give the user an option of saving it before creating a new grade roster.

Another behavior we model after a text editor is the labeling of the window title. When you open a document in a text editor, the window title will include the filename of the document. We will change the title of the main window to include the name of a newly created grade roster.

Since the responsibility of managing GradeRoster belongs to GradeRoster-Control, the newRoster method asks GradeRosterControl whether there is currently an open grade roster. If there is no current grade roster, then we will create a new roster. Otherwise, we prompt the user and give him or her the option of saving the current roster. Here's the pseudocode:

```
if (gradeRosterControl does not have an open roster) {
    createNewRoster();
}
else {
    int answer = saveBox.prompt("Save the current roster?");

    switch (answer ) {
        case SAVE:
            saveRoster();           //save the current roster first
            createNewRoster();
            break;
        case NO_SAVE:
            createNewRoster();      //discard the current roster
            break;
        case CANCEL:                //cancel creating a new roster
            //do nothing
            break;
    }
}
```

We use saveBox, a ResponseBox object with three buttons labeled Save, Don't Save, and Cancel, to get the user's direction.

The createNewRoster method creates a new grade roster by calling the newGradeRoster method of GradeRosterControl and resets its window title by calling the private method setNewTitle. Since GradeRosterControl is the one that directly manages a grade roster, its newGradeRoster is the method that actually creates a GradeRoster object. This is the pattern we have for this program. The task of gradeRosterMainWindow is to delegate the actual work to one of the subordinate objects gradeRosterControl, gradeRosterDisplay, and grade-RosterStorage.

Inside the newGradeRoster method, we will create an instance of Grade-Roster, so we need to think about a constructor for GradeRoster. What information should we pass to a constructor when creating an instance of GradeRoster? We could associate many different types of information to a grade roster; let's decide that we will maintain the title and instructor information for each course. We will pass these two pieces of information to a GradeRoster constructor. To add flexibility to the class, we will also define a second constructor that will allow the programmer to specify the enrollment size of the course. The newGradeRoster method uses the first constructor of GradeRoster and looks like this:

```
String title    = inputBox.getString("title");
String instructor = inputBox.getString("instructor");

//use the first constructor
gradeRoster = new GradeRoster(title, instructor);
```

The setNewTitle method resets the window title to reflect the course title of a newly created grade roster. To get the course title, it calls the getCourseTitle of GradeRosterControl. The course title is actually kept by a GradeRoster object, so why not call a method of GradeRoster directly from setNewTitle? We certainly could, but doing so would complicate the connection links among objects in the program. We want to maintain the connection links simple and clean, as shown in the object diagram of Figure 14.2. Increasing the number of links from a single object makes program maintenance more difficult. The method body of setNewTitle will be

```
String title = gradeRosterControl.getCourseTitle();
setTitle("C L A S S   R O S T E R  for:  " + title);
```

The getCourseTitle method returns the title by

```
return gradeRoster.getTitle();
```

where getTitle of GradeRoster returns the value of its data member courseTitle:

```
return courseTitle;
```

Figure 14.3 is the method call sequence diagram.

FIGURE 14.3   Method call sequence for the **newRoster** method. Calls to standard **javabook** objects are not shown.

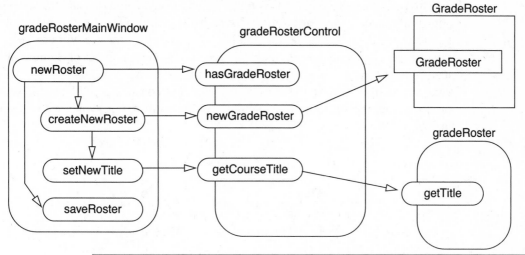

From this step, we start using an instance of GradeRosterControl, so we need to implement its constructor. In the constructor, we will create the data member objects, which include GradeRoster and InputBox at this point. We already designed an instance of GradeRoster that will be created in the newGradeRoster method, so we won't be creating it in the constructor. As for an InputBox object, we will create it in the constructor. Since InputBox is a dialog, we need a Frame object to create an InputBox object. If we create it inside a method of the MainWindow or Frame descendant class, we call the InputBox constructor

```
inputBox = new InputBox( this );
```

We cannot make such a call from the constructor of GradeRosterControl because it is not a subclass of MainWindow or Frame. We will solve this problem by passing the GradeRosterMainWindow object to the constructor of Grade-RosterControl. The constructor will look like this:

```
public GradeRosterControl( Frame mainWindow )
{
    owner = mainWindow;
    ...
    inputBox = new InputBox( owner );
}
```

We also need to implement a GradeRoster constructor. What will be the data members we need to create and initialize in the constructor? We already have decided that we will include two constructors in the GradeRoster class. The first constructor accepts the course title and instructor name, and the second constructor accepts the enrollment size as its third parameter. We will use data members to store the course title and instructor. For a roster, we will use an array of Student objects named roster. To keep track of the number of Student objects in the array, we use an int variable rosterSize. These four data members are created and initialized in the constructor. The first constructor will call the second constructor by passing the default array length of roster, which we will set to 25.

Here's the summary of work to be done in Step 2:

	Objects	To Do

Step 2	GradeRoster MainWindow	Implement the methods
		    newRoster
		    createNewRoster
		    setNewTitle
		
		Modify the constructor as necessary.
		
		Add a ResponseBox called saveBox as a new data member.
		
		Define constants SAVE, NO_SAVE, and CANCEL.

	GradeRoster Control	Implement the methods
		    <constructor>
		    getCourseTitle
		    hasGradeRoster
		    newGradeRoster
		
		Add InputBox as a new data member.

	GradeRoster	Implement the methods <constructor> getTitle

Step 2 Code   We will list the code modification for each class in order.

GradeRosterMainWindow
Add the following data member declarations:

```
private static final int SAVE    = ResponseBox.BUTTON1;
private static final int NO_SAVE = ResponseBox.BUTTON2;
private static final int CANCEL  = ResponseBox.BUTTON3;

private    ResponseBox           saveBox;

private    GradeRosterControl    gradeRosterControl;
```

Modify the constructor to

```
public GradeRosterMainWindow()
{
    //as before

        saveBox = new ResponseBox(this,3);
        saveBox.setLabel(SAVE,"Save");
        saveBox.setLabel(NO_SAVE,"Don't Save");
        saveBox.setLabel(CANCEL,"Cancel");

        gradeRosterControl = new GradeRosterControl(this);

}
```

Define the following private methods:

```
private void newRoster()
{
    if (!gradeRosterControl.hasGradeRoster()) {
        createNewRoster();
    }
    else {
        //save current gradeRoster?
        int answer
            = saveBox.prompt("Save the current grade roster?");

        switch (answer) {
            case SAVE:
                saveRoster();
                createNewRoster();
                break;
            case NO_SAVE:
                createNewRoster();
                break;
```

```
                case CANCEL:
                    //do nothing
                    break;
            }
        }
    }


    private void createNewRoster()
    {
        gradeRosterControl.newGradeRoster();

        setNewTitle();
    }


    private void setNewTitle()
    {
        String title = gradeRosterControl.getCourseTitle();

        setTitle("C L A S S    R O S T E R    f o r:  " + title);
    }
```

GradeRosterControl

Add the following data member declarations:

```
    private    Frame          owner;
    private    InputBox       inputBox;
    private    GradeRoster    gradeRoster;
```

Define the constructor and methods:

```
    public GradeRosterControl(Frame mainWindow)
    {
        owner         = mainWindow;
        gradeRoster   = null;

        inputBox      = new InputBox(owner);
    }


    public void newGradeRoster( )
    {
```

```
        String title, instructor;

        title  = inputBox.getString("Enter Course Title:");

        instructor
             = inputBox.getString("Enter Course Instructor:");

        gradeRoster = new GradeRoster(title, instructor);
    }


    public String getCourseTitle()
    {
        return gradeRoster.getTitle();
    }
```

GradeRoster

Add the data member declarations:

```
    private static final int DEFAULT_LENGTH = 25;

    private String    courseTitle;
    private String    courseInstructor;
    private Student[] roster;
    private int       rosterSize; //number of students in roster
```

Define the constructor and methods:

```
    public GradeRoster(String title, String instructor)
    {
        this( title, instructor, DEFAULT_LENGTH );
    }


    public GradeRoster(String title, String instructor, int length)
    {
        courseTitle       = title;
        courseInstructor  = instructor;
        roster            = new Student[length];
        rosterSize        = 0;

        System.out.println("Inside GradeRoster constructor");//TEMP
        System.out.println(courseTitle);                     //TEMP
        System.out.println(courseInstructor);                //TEMP
```

```
                         System.out.println("roster length: " +roster.length);//TEMP
                  }


                  public String getTitle( )
                  {
                      return courseTitle;
                  }
```

Step 2 Test   We run the program and verify that a new grade roster object is created properly. We select the menu choice File/New and verify that correct Grade-RosterControl and GradeRoster objects are created. We included temporary output statements in the constructor of GradeRoster for testing purposes.

14.6 Step 3 Development: Add Students

Step 3 Design   Once we have methods to create a new roster, we're ready to define methods to add students to and delete students from a roster. The methods corresponding to the menu choices Edit/Add Student and Edit/Delete Student are addNewStudent and deleteStudent. We will work on the addNewStudent method in this step and on the deleteStudent method in the next step.

     The main task of addNewStudent is to tell gradeRosterControl to add a new student if there's an open grade roster. If no grade roster is currently open, then we will display an error message. The logic of the method is as follows:

```
            if (gradeRosterControl.hasGradeRoster()) {
                gradeRosterControl.addStudent();
            }
            else {
                messageBox.show("No grade roster is currently open");
            }
```

     The method addStudent of gradeRosterControl first asks the user which type of student does he or she wish to add to a roster. Depending on the response, the method calls the private addGraduateStudent or addUndergraduate-Student. We use a ResponseBox object named selectionBox, which has two buttons labeled Undergraduate and Graduate, to prompt the user. The addStudent method in pseudocode is as follows:

```
            //input student information
            answer = selectionBox.prompt("Select the student type");
```

```
if (answer == GRAD_STUDENT)
   addGraduateStudent();

else if (answer == UNDERGRAD_STUDENT)
   addUndergraduateStudent();

//else dialog is canceled, so do nothing
```

The two methods to add a student, addGraduateStudent and addUndergraduateStudent, are almost identical except for the creation of an instance of GraduateStudent or UndergraduateStudent. In this program, we make an assumption that the names of students in the roster are unique. To maintain this assumption, we will not add a student if there's a student with the same name already in the roster. We check for a duplicate name by calling the getStudent method of GradeRoster. The method returns a Student object whose name matches the passed String parameter. The method returns null if no Student object with the given name is found. Since we want to add a new student, we expect null to be returned by the method. If the value returned is null, then we create either a GraduateStudent or an UndergraduateStudent object and add it to the roster by calling the method addStudent. Here are the two methods expressed in pseudocode:

```
//add a graduate student
studentName
        = inputBox.getString("Enter Graduate Student Name:");

student = gradeRoster.getStudent(studentName);

if (student == null) {
   newGradStudent = new GraduateStudent(studentName);
   gradeRoster.addStudent(newGradStudent);
}
else {
   messageBox.show("Duplicate name exists." +
                     " No new student is added.");
}

//add an undergraduate student
studentName
     = inputBox.getString("Enter Undergraduate Student Name:");

student = gradeRoster.getStudent(studentName);
```

```
    if (student == null) {
        newUndergradStudent
                  = new UndergraduateStudent(studentName);
        gradeRoster.addStudent(newUndergradStudent);
    }
    else {
        messageBox.show("Duplicate name exists." +
                            " No new student is added.");
    }
```

The getStudent method of GradeRoster searches the roster for a student whose name matches the passed String value. If the matching student is found, then this object is returned. Otherwise, null is returned. The search routine is implemented as follows:

```
//search for student with studentName
//return null if not found

int    loc    = 0;

while (loc < rosterSize //still more elements to search
        &&
        !studentName.equals(roster[loc].getName())
                        //not a duplicate name
{
    loc++;
}

if (loc < rosterSize) {
    return roster[loc];   //return the student if found
}
else {
    return null;          //return null otherwise
}
```

To add a new student in the addStudent method, we first check to see if there is a space left in the roster array. If there is a space, we add this student to the roster array at position rosterSize. If there is no more space left in the roster array, we expand the roster array by calling the private method expandRoster before adding a new student. The logic of the addStudent method of GradeRoster is as follows:

```
//if there's no more space to add the student
//make the roster larger
```

```
if (rosterSize == roster.length) {
    expandRoster();
}
roster[rosterSize] = student;
rosterSize++;
```

The private method expandRoster expands the roster array by 50 percent:

```
//expand the roster by 50%
```

The value is set to 1.5f.

```
int newSize = (int) (roster.length * EXPAND_FACTOR);

Student newArray[] = new Student[newSize];

for (int i = 0; i < roster.length; i++) {
    newArray[i] = roster[i];
}
roster = newArray;
```

The method call sequence diagram is shown in Figure 14.4.
Here's the summary of work to do in Step 3:

	Objects	To Do
Step 3	GradeRoster MainWindow	Implement the method addNewStudent

	GradeRoster
	Control
		Implement the methods
		    addStudent
		    addGraduateStudent
		    addUndergraduateStudent
		
		Modify the constructor as necessary.

	GradeRoster	Implement the methods
		    addStudent
		    getStudent
		    expandRoster

Step 3 Code

We will list the code modification for each class in order.

GradeRosterMainWindow

Define the addNewStudent method:

```
private void addNewStudent( )
{
    if (gradeRosterControl.hasGradeRoster()) {
```

FIGURE 14.4   Method call sequence for the **addNewStudent** method. Calls to standard **javabook** objects are not shown.

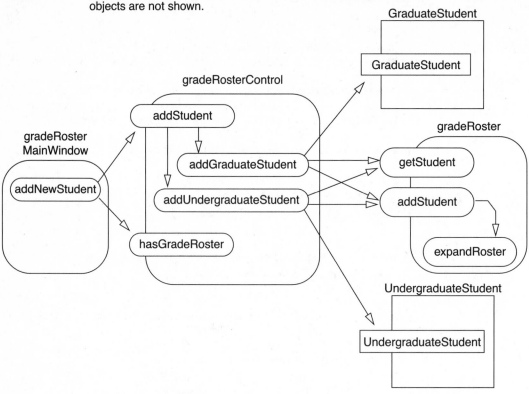

```
                    gradeRosterControl.addStudent();
    }
    else {
        messageBox.show("No grade roster is currently open.");
    }
}
```

GradeRosterControl

Add the data member declarations:

```
private static final int   GRAD_STUDENT   = ResponseBox.BUTTON1;
private static final int   UNDERGRAD_STUDENT
                                          = ResponseBox.BUTTON2;

private ResponseBox        selectionBox;
```

```
        private MessageBox            messageBox;
```

Modify the constructor to

```
public GradeRosterControl(Frame mainWindow)
{
    ...
    selectionBox    = new ResponseBox(owner);
    selectionBox.setLabel(GRAD_STUDENT,      "Undergraduate");
    selectionBox.setLabel(UNDERGRAD_STUDENT," Graduate    ");

    messageBox      = new MessageBox(owner);

}
```

Define the following public and private methods:

```
public void addStudent( )
{
    //input student information
    int answer
          = selectionBox.prompt("Select the student type.");

    if (answer == GRAD_STUDENT) {
        addGraduateStudent();
    }
    else if (answer == UNDERGRAD_STUDENT) {
        addUndergraduateStudent();
    }
    //else canceled, so do nothing
}

private void addGraduateStudent( )
{
    String studentName
          = inputBox.getString("Enter Graduate Student Name:");

    Student student = gradeRoster.getStudent(studentName);

    if (student == null) {
        GraduateStudent newGradStudent =
                          new GraduateStudent(studentName);
        gradeRoster.addStudent(newGradStudent);
    }
```

```
        else {
            messageBox.show("Duplicate name exists." +
                        " No new student is added.");
        }
    }

    private void addUndergraduateStudent( )
    {
        String studentName
          = inputBox.getString("Enter Undergraduate Student Name:");
        Student student = gradeRoster.getStudent(studentName);

        if (student == null) {
            UndergraduateStudent newUndergradStudent =
                            new UndergraduateStudent(studentName);
            gradeRoster.addStudent(newUndergradStudent);
        }
        else {
            messageBox.show("Duplicate name exists." +
                        " No new student is added.");
        }
    }
```

GradeRoster

Add the data member declaration:

```
    private static final float EXPAND_FACTOR = 1.5f;
```

Add the following public and private methods:

```
    public Student getStudent(String studentName)
    {
        //search for student with studentName
        //return null if not found

        int    loc    = 0;

        while (loc < rosterSize //still more elements to search
              &&
              !studentName.equals(roster[loc].getName())
                            //not a duplicate name
        {
            loc++;
        }
```

```
            if ( loc < rosterSize ) {
                return roster[loc];
            }
            else {
                return null;
            }
        }


    public void addStudent( Student student)
    {
        //if there's no more space to add the student
        //make the roster larger
        if (rosterSize == roster.length) {
            expandRoster();
        }
        roster[rosterSize] = student;
        rosterSize++;

        System.out.println("Inside addStudent");            //TEMP
        System.out.println("Position added:" + rosterSize-1);//TEMP
    }


    private void expandRoster( )
    {
        //expand the roster by 50%

        int newSize = (int) (roster.length * EXPAND_FACTOR);

        Student newArray[] = new Student[newSize];

        for (int i = 0; i < roster.length; i++) {
            newArray[i] = roster[i];
        }

        roster = newArray;

        System.out.println("Inside expandRoster");           //TEMP
        System.out.println("New length: " + roster.length);//TEMP
    }
```

Step 3 Test   We run the program and verify that a new student can be added correctly to the roster. One possible sequence of testing operations is as follows:

1. Run the program and select **Edit/Add Student**. Verify that we get an error message.

2. Select **File/New** and create a new roster.

3. Select **Edit/Add Student** three or four times and add students. Verify that students are added correctly to the roster. Make sure to create both undergraduate and graduate students.

4. Select **Edit/Add Student** and enter a duplicate name. Verify that we get an error message.

Also, to test the **expandRoster** method, we change the value for DEFAULT_LENGTH to something like 4, run the program, and verify that the roster is expanded when a fifth student is added to the roster.

14.7 Step 4 Development: Delete Students

Step 4 Design   We will implement the delete operation in this step. The **deleteStudent** method is structurally similar to the **addNewStudent** method: the main task of the method is to tell **gradeRosterControl** to delete a student if there's an open grade roster. If no grade roster is currently open, then we will display an error message. The logic of the method is as follows:

```
if (gradeRosterControl.hasGradeRoster()) {
    gradeRosterControl.deleteStudent();
}
else {
    messageBox.show("No grade roster is open.");
}
```

The **deleteStudent** method of **gradeRosterControl** gets the name of a student to delete and checks to see if there's a student with the matching name. If there is, then it calls the **deleteStudent** method of **gradeRoster**. The method in pseudocode is as follows:

```
get studentName;

student = gradeRoster.getStudent(studentName);

if (student == null) {
    messageBox.show("Cannot delete: Student not found.");
```

```
}
else {
    gradeRoster.deleteStudent(student);
}
```

The deleteStudent method of gradeRoster locates the position of a student to be deleted in the roster array. Here's the logic of the method:

```
//search for student
int loc = 0;

while (loc < rosterSize && roster[loc] != student) {
    loc++;
}
if (roster[loc] == student) { //student was found, so
    compactRoster(loc);        //compact the array
}
```

Once the position loc is found, we call the private method compactRoster to fill the gap left by the deletion and decrement rosterSize by one. Its logic is as follows:

```
roster[loc] = roster[rosterSize-1];
roster[rosterSize-1] = null;

rosterSize--;
```

Figure 14.5 is the method call sequence diagram for the deleteStudent method.

Here's the summary of work to do in Step 4:

	Objects	To Do
Step 4	GradeRoster MainWindow	Implement the method deleteStudent
	GradeRoster Control	Implement the method deleteStudent
	GradeRoster	Implement the methods deleteStudent compactRoster

---

FIGURE 14.5   Method call sequence for the **deleteStudent** method. Calls to standard **javabook** objects are not shown.

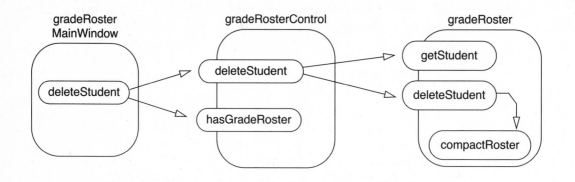

Step 3 Code   We will list the code modification for each class in order.

GradeRosterMainWindow
Define the deleteStudent method:

```
private void deleteStudent( )
{
    if (gradeRosterControl.hasGradeRoster()) {
        gradeRosterControl.deleteStudent();
    }
    else {
        messageBox.show("No grade roster is open.");
    }
}
```

GradeRosterControl
Define the deleteStudent method:

```
public void deleteStudent(   )
{

    String studentName = inputBox.getString
                        ("Enter the name of student to delete:");

    Student student = gradeRoster.getStudent(studentName);
```

```
                      if (student == null) {
                          messageBox.show("Cannot delete: Student not found.");
                      }
                      else {
                          gradeRoster.deleteStudent(student);
                      }
                  }
```

GradeRoster

Define the following methods:

```
        public void deleteStudent( Student student )
        {
            int loc = 0;

            while (loc < rosterSize && roster[loc] != student) {
                loc++;
            }
            if (roster[loc] == student) { //student was found, so
                compactRoster(loc);          //compact the array
            }
        }

        private void compactRoster(int loc)
        {
            //remove the student at position loc from the roster
            //and replace it by the element at position rosterSize-1

            roster[loc] = roster[rosterSize-1];
            roster[rosterSize-1] = null;

            rosterSize--;
        }
```

Step 4 Test

We run the program and verify that a student can be deleted correctly from the roster. One possible sequence of testing operations is as follows:

1. Run the program and select Edit/Delete Student. Verify that we get an error message.

2. Select File/New and create a new roster.

3. Select Edit/Add Student three or four times and add students. Make sure to create both undergraduate and graduate students.

4. Select Edit/Delete Student and enter a name that does not match the name of any student in the roster. Verify that we get an error message.

5. Select Edit/Delete Student and enter the name of a student in the roster. Verify that the student is deleted by trying to delete the same student again. We will get an error message if the deletion operation was executed successfully.

14.8 Step 5 Development: Edit Student Names

Step 5 Design

In the fifth step, we implement the methods that allow the user to edit student names. In what ways should we allow the user to edit student names? To change a student's name, we must have two values: the current and the new one. We use the current name to locate the student object in the roster array, and if found, we change the name to a new one, provided that the given new name is distinct from all other names in the roster. To input two names, we can use an InputBox object, as in

```
currentName    = inputBox.getString("Current Name:");
newName        = inputBox.getString("New Name:");
```

This approach works but does not support a good user interface. For instance, the user cannot go back and correct the value of currentName once it is entered. Also, the user cannot cancel the operation. Both names must be entered to continue with the program. We will support a better user interface by creating a special dialog for inputting these two values. We will call this dialog StudentNameDialog; a sample dialog is shown in Figure 14.6.

Who should manage this StudentNameDialog object? Two possible candidates are GradeRosterMainWindow and GradeRosterControl. The responsibility of GradeRosterMainWindow is the top-level interaction with the user via menu processing and the management of GradeRosterControl, GradeRosterDisplay, and GradeRosterStorage. Giving an additional object to manage to GradeRosterMainWindow will overload it and degrade the clarity of the overall program structure. Since managing a GradeRoster object is the responsibility of GradeRosterControl, we will let it manage a StudentNameDialog. The modified object

FIGURE 14.6   A **StudentNameDialog** dialog for inputting the current and new names of a student.

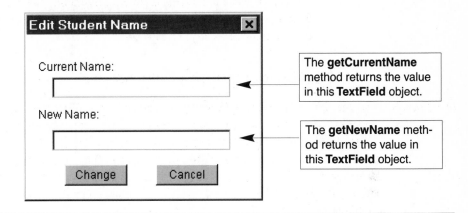

diagram shown in Figure 14.7 now includes StudentNameDialog and the class is added to the program design document:

program
classes

Design Document:	GradeRoster Program
Class	**Purpose**
...	...
StudentNameDialog	A dialog used to enter the new and current names of a student. This dialog is managed by GradeRosterControl.

Some of you may wonder why we don't let GradeRoster control StudentNameDialog, since the GradeRoster object is the one that maintains a grade roster. Remember, GradeRoster is an application logic object, and as a guideline, we do not let application logic objects handle input and output. This will increase the reusability of application logic objects.

Now let's develop the StudentNameDialog class. Developing a completely new class calls for another incremental development cycle. There are two ways to handle the development of StudentNameDialog. The first approach is to integrate the StudentNameDialog development into our current development. The second approach is to develop the class completely separate from our current development effort.

If we adopt the first approach, then we will initiate a sort of minidevelopment cycle, starting from a shell and gradually building up the StudentNameDi-

FIGURE 14.7   An extended object diagram for the grade roster program now includes **StudentNameDialog**.

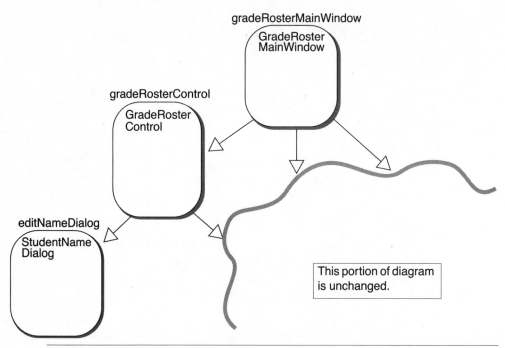

alog class. We incorporate the partially completed class into the program we are developing and test the class at each step of minidevelopment.

If we adopt the second approach, then we will either suspend the current development until we finish implementing the StudentNameDialog class or continue the development with a placeholder StudentNameDialog class. If we develop the StudentNameDialog class ourselves, then we need to suspend the current development until we complete its implementation. However, if we delegate the task of StudentNameDialog development to other programmers, we can proceed with our current development simultaneously. As long as we agree on the public methods of the StudentNameDialog class, we can continue our development by using a placeholder StudentNameDialog class.

We will use the second approach here. In order to streamline the presentation, we will develop the class in Section 14.13. We will present the design document of the class here and continue the development using the public methods listed in the design document. If you wish, you can read Section 14.13 before continuing this section. Here's the design document for the StudentNameDialog:

Design Document: The StudentNameDialog Class		
Method	**Visibility**	**Purpose**
`<constructor>`	`public`	Creates an instance. The constructor accepts a Frame object as its argument.
`getCurrentName`	`public`	Returns the text value in the CurrentName text field.
`getNewName`	`public`	Returns the text value in the NewName text field.
`isCanceled`	`public`	Returns true if the dialog's CANCEL button was clicked.
`show`	`public`	Displays the dialog.

The role of the editStudentName method of gradeRosterMainWindow is to delegate the task to gradeRosterControl as

```
gradeRosterControl.editStudentName();
```

The editStudentName method of gradeRosterControl uses a StudentNameDialog box called editNameBox to get the current and new names. If the dialog is not canceled, then we retrieve the current and new names using getCurrentName and getNewName methods. If a student with the name matching the input current name is found, then the student's name is changed to the given new name. The logic of the method is expressed as follows:

```
editNameBox.setVisible( true );

if ( editNameBox is not canceled ) {
    currentName = editNameBox.getCurrentName();
    newName     = editNameBox.getNewName();

    student    = gradeRoster.getStudent(currentName);
    duplicate  = gradeRoster.getStudent(newName);

    if (student == null) {
        messageBox.show("Cannot locate " + currentName);
    }
    else if (duplicate != null) {
        messageBox.show("There's already a person called "
                            + newName + "in the roster");
    }
}
```

Search the student with **currentName** and **newName**.

```
else {
    student.setName(newName);
}
```

Figure 14.8 is the method call sequence diagram.

FIGURE 14.8 A method call sequence diagram for the **deleteStudent** method. Calls to standard **javabook** objects are not shown.

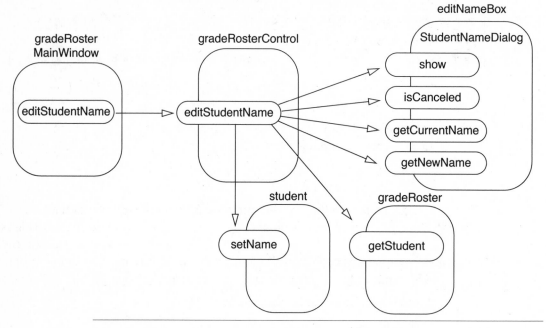

Here's the table that summarizes the work to be done in Step 5.

	Objects	To Do
Step 5	GradeRoster MainWindow	Implement the method editStudentName
	GradeRoster Control	Implement the method editStudentName Modify the constructor and data member declaration as necessary.
	StudentName Dialog	Define this class fully.

Step 5 Code

We will list the code modification for each class in order.

GradeRosterMainWindow

Define the editStudentName method:

```
private void editStudentName()
{
    gradeRosterControl.editStudentName();
}
```

GradeRosterControl

Add the data member declaration

```
private StudentNameDialog    editNameBox;
```

And modify the constructor to

```
public GradeRosterControl(Frame mainWindow)
{
    ...
    editNameBox      = new StudentNameDialog(owner);
}
```

Define the editStudentName method:

```
public void editStudentName()
{
    String currentName, newName;
    Student student, duplicate;

    editNameBox.show();

    if (!editNameBox.isCanceled()) {
        currentName = editNameBox.getCurrentName();
        newName      = editNameBox.getNewName();

        student = gradeRoster.getStudent(currentName);
        duplicate = gradeRoster.getStudent(newName);

        if (student == null) {
            messageBox.show("Cannot locate " + currentName);
        }
        else if (duplicate != null) {
```

```
                    messageBox.show("There's already a person called "
                                        + newName + "in the roster");
            }
            else {
                student.setName(newName);
            }
        }
    }
```

We run the program and verify that the student names can be changed. One possible sequence of testing operations is as follows:

1. Select Edit/Add Student three or four times and add students. Make sure to create both undergraduate and graduate students.

2. Select Edit/Student Name and enter a current name that does not match the name of any other student in the roster. Verify that we get an error message.

3. Select Edit/Student Name and enter a new name that matches the name of a student in the roster. Verify that we get an error message.

4. Select Edit/Student Name and enter a current name that does match and a new name that does not match the name in the roster. Verify the name of this student is changed correctly.

14.9 Step 6 Development: Edit Test Scores and Compute Grades

In the sixth step, we add the methods for editing the test scores and computing the final course grades. We will design the methods for editing the test scores first. Although possible, using an InputBox object for this purpose reduces the quality of the user interface. Therefore, as we did in the previous section, we will come up with a custom-made dialog. We will call the dialog TestScoreDialog. This dialog will display the test scores of a student, and the user can add new test scores or overwrite the existing test scores. A sample dialog is shown in Figure 14.9.

FIGURE 14.9   A sample **TestScoreDialog** object for editing test scores.

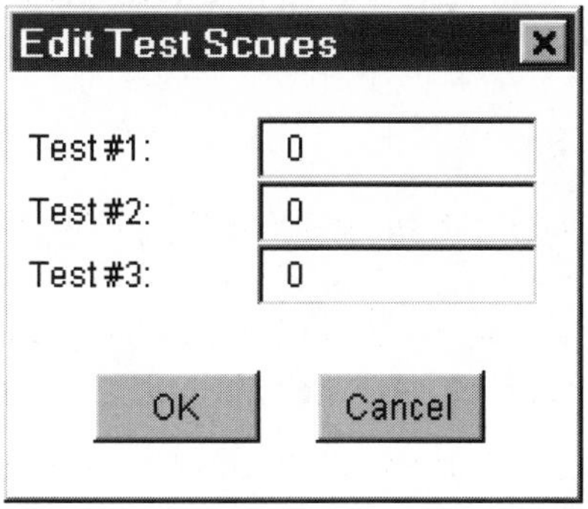

The modified object diagram shown in Figure 14.10 now includes TestScoreDialog, and the class is added to the program design document:

program
classes

Design Document:	**GradeRoster Program**
Class	**Purpose**
. . .	. . .
TestScoreDialog	A dialog used to enter and edit the test scores of a student. This dialog is managed by GradeRosterControl.

As we did with the StudentNameDialog, we will develop this class separate from the current development in Section 14.14. We will present the design document of the class here and continue the development using the public methods listed in the design document. If you wish, you can read Section 14.14 before continuing this section. Here's the design document of the TestScoreDialog:

Design Document: The TestScoreDialog Class		
Method	**Visibility**	**Purpose**
<constructor>	public	Creates an instance. The constructor accepts a Frame object as its argument.
getTestScores	public	Returns the test scores as an array of int.
isCanceled	public	Returns true if the dialog's CANCEL button was clicked.
show	public	Displays the dialog.

FIGURE 14.10   An extended object diagram for the grade roster program now includes **TestScoreDialog**.

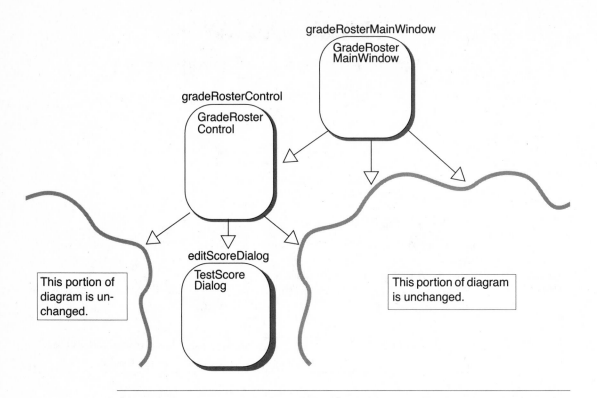

The editTestScores method of gradeRosterMainWindow delegates the task to gradeRosterControl as

```
gradeRosterControl.editTestScores();
```

The editTestScores method of gradeRosterControl uses a TestScoreDialog box called editScoreBox shown in Figure 14.9 to get the test scores. First we get the name of a student whose test scores we want to edit. We search for this student, and, if found, we use editScoreBox to let the user edit the student's test scores. If the dialog is not canceled, then we retrieve the test scores using the getTestScores method. Here's the method:

```
name = inputBox.getString("Enter Student Name:");

student = gradeRoster.getStudent(name);

if (student == null) {
    messageBox.show("Cannot locate " + name);
}
else { //student found, so edit the test scores

    editScoreBox.show(student);

    if (!editScoreBox.isCanceled()) {

        int score[] = editScoreBox.getTestScores();

        student.setTestScores(score);
    }
}
```

Figure 14.11 is the method call sequence diagram for the editTestScores method.

FIGURE 14.11   Method call sequence for the **editTestScores** method. Calls to standard **javabook** objects are not shown.

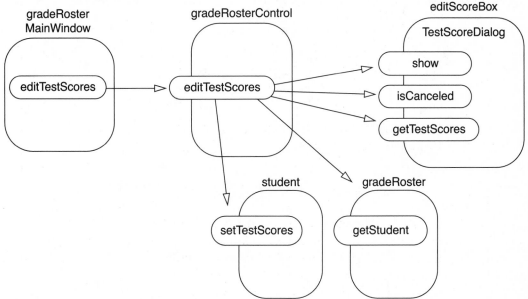

Now, let's design the methods to compute the course grades. The compute-Grades method of gradeRosterMainWindow calls the computeGrades method of gradeRosterControl as

```
gradeRosterControl.computeGrades();
```

The computeGrades method of gradeRosterControl in turn calls the com-puteGrades method of gradeRoster as

```
gradeRoster.computeGrades();
```

Finally, the computeGrades method GradeRoster goes through its roster ar-ray and calls the computeCourseGrade method of either a GraduateStudent or an UndergraduateStudent object in the array:

```
for (int i = 0; i < rosterSize; i++) {
    roster[i].computeCourseGrade();
}
```

Figure 14.12 is the method call sequence diagram of the computeGrades method.

Here's the summary of the tasks to be done in Step 6:

	Objects	To Do
Step 6	GradeRoster MainWindow	Implement the methods editTestScores computeGrades
	GradeRoster Control	Implement the methods editTestScores computeGrades Modify the constructor and data member declaration as necessary.
	GradeRoster	Implement the method computeGrades
	TestScore Dialog	Implement the class fully.

Step 6 Code

We will list the code modification for each class in order.

FIGURE 14.12   Method call sequence for the **computeGrades** method. Calls to standard **javabook** objects are not shown.

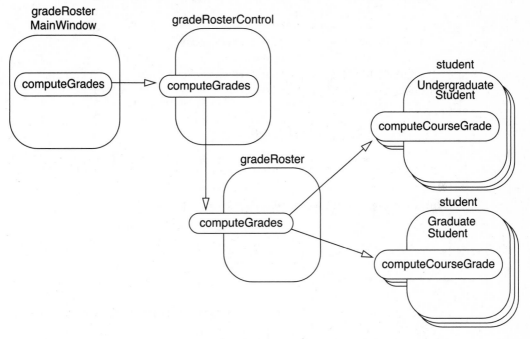

GradeRosterMainWindow
Define the following method:

```
public void editTestScores()
{
    gradeRosterControl.editTestScores();
}


public void computeGrades()
{
    gradeRosterControl.computeGrades();
}
```

GradeRosterControl

Add the data member declaration

```
        private TestScoreDialog    editScoreBox;
```

And modify the constructor to

```java
    public GradeRosterControl(Frame mainWindow)
    {
        owner = mainWindow;
        ...
        editScoreBox      = new TestScoreDialog(owner);
    }
```

Define the following methods:

```java
    public void editTestScores()
    {
        String name = inputBox.getString("Enter Student Name:");

        Student student = gradeRoster.getStudent(name);

        if (student == null) {
            messageBox.show("Cannot locate " + name);
        }
        else {

            editScoreBox.show(student);

            if (!editScoreBox.isCanceled()) {

                int score[] = editScoreBox.getTestScores();

                student.setTestScores(score);
            }
        }
    }


    public void computeGrades( )
    {
        gradeRoster.computeGrades();
    }
```

GradeRoster

Define the computeGrades method:

```
public void computeGrades( )
{
    for (int i = 0; i < rosterSize; i++) {
        roster[i].computeCourseGrade();

        System.out.print(roster[i].getName() + "  ");      //TEMP
        System.out.print(roster[i].getTestScore(1) + " ");//TEMP
        System.out.print(roster[i].getTestScore(2) + " ");//TEMP
        System.out.print(roster[i].getTestScore(3) + " ");//TEMP
        System.out.println(roster[i].getCourseGrade());   //TEMP
    }
}
```

Step 6 Test

We run the program and verify that the test scores can be edited and the final course grades are computed correctly. One possible sequence of testing operations is as follows:

1. Select Edit/Add Student three or four times and add students. Make sure to create both undergraduate and graduate students.

2. Select Edit/Test Scores and enter test scores. Repeat this step to enter test scores for all students.

3. Select Edit/Compute Grades and verify that course grades are computed correctly.

4. Select Edit/Test Scores and change the test scores of a student so the student's course grade will be different. Select Edit/Compute Grades and verify that a new course grade is computed correctly. Repeat this step using different values for test scores.

14.10 Step 7 Development: Display Student Information

Step 7 Design

In the seventh step, we implement the methods that display information of all students or a selected student. The GradeRosterDisplay class is the one responsible for displaying student information. How should we display student information? For each type of display, we can create a custom-made dialog or reuse some generic user interface object. As most of us prefer a custom-tailored outfit over off-the-rack clothing, we prefer custom-made dialogs over generic dialogs in most cases. However, designing custom-made dialogs takes time and effort. If the program can be made usable without any custom-made dialogs, we may opt for generic dialogs. Later, if the demand calls for an improvement, we may replace the generic dialogs with custom-made dialogs.

The advantage of using an object-oriented technique is the ease of replacing one implementation of a class with another implementation. For instance, we can start with one implementation of GradeRosterDisplay using a generic user interface object. Later, if the demand and budget warrant it, we can replace the first implementation of GradeRosterDisplay with a new version that includes custom-made dialogs. If the public components (constructors, constants, and methods) of GradeRosterDisplay remain the same, then the rest of the program will continue to work without modification.

We will take this approach of first using an implementation with generic objects and leaving an implementation with custom-made objects as a possible future improvement. We will implement GradeRosterDisplay using a generic OutputBox object and leave the implementation of GradeRosterDisplay that uses custom-made dialogs as an exercise.

Now let's begin our design of GradeRosterDisplay. A GradeRoster object is a controller object that manages an OutputBox object to display student information. There are two menu choices related to the display of student information: Show/All Students and Show/One Student. The showAllStudents method of GradeRosterMainWindow is executed when the first menu choice is selected, and the showOneStudent is executed when the second menu choice is selected. We will design the showAllStudents method first.

Since a grade roster is managed by gradeRosterControl and the actual task of displaying student information is done by gradeRosterDisplay, the showAllStudents method asks gradeRosterControl for a list of students and then passes this list to gradeRosterDisplay. The method expressed in pseudocode will look like this:

```
list = gradeRosterControl.getAllStudents();
gradeRosterDisplay.displayAll( list );
```

In what form should we return this list of students? One possibility is to return a GradeRoster object. Another possibility is to return an array of Student objects. Passing a GradeRoster object is more general because gradeRosterDisplay will have access to additional information beyond the list of students. For example, gradeRosterDisplay will have access to the course title and instructor information also. If a GradeRoster object is modified to keep an average for each of the three test scores, this information will also become available to gradeRosterDisplay. In contrast, if we pass an array of Student objects, then other information kept by a gradeRoster is not available to gradeRosterDisplay.

A possible disadvantage of passing a GradeRoster object is the cost of modifying the program. Suppose we pass an array of Student objects to grade-RosterDisplay, and gradeRosterDisplay does not make any call to a GradeRoster object. Since there is no direct connection link from gradeRoster-Display to a GradeRoster object, any changes made to GradeRoster will not affect the implementation of GradeRosterDisplay. In general, we should reduce the number of connection links among program classes as much as possible. Although the larger the number of links you establish among classes, the more expensive the modification cost is potentially going to be, we can minimize it by carefully designing the classes.

Weighing the pros and cons, we choose to pass a GradeRoster object. The pseudocode for showAllStudents of GradeRosterMainWindow will then be

```
if ( gradeRosterControl.hasGradeRoster() ) {
    GradeRoster roster = gradeRosterControl.getRoster();
    gradeRosterDisplay.displayAll( roster );
}
else
    print out an error message;
```

Since a GradeRoster object is a data member of GradeRosterControl, the getRoster method simply returns this data member as

```
return gradeRoster; //return its GradeRoster data member
```

Receiving this GradeRoster object as an argument, the displayAll method of gradeRosterDisplay will display the information of all students. What kind of display would be appropriate for listing student information? A common style for listing information on multiple objects, which we adopt here, is a tabular format such as the following:

Name	Test1	Test2	Test 3	Grade
Mr. Expresso	76.3	88.4	92.2	Pass
Ms. Latte	76.3	88.4	92.2	Pass
Mr. Bancha	56.3	68.4	52.2	No Pass

The displayAll method labels each column with a heading and uses one row of OutputBox for a single student's information. We will display the column headings first and then go through the students in a roster displaying one student at a time:

```
displayHeading();

for each student in a roster {
    display this student using one line of outputBox;
}

outputBox.show();   // make outputBox visible;
```

We can get a student's name, test scores, and course grade by calling the corresponding public methods of the Student class. To access all students in a grade roster, we will define a method in the GradeRoster class called getAllStudents that returns an array of Student objects. The loop to access all students then becomes

```
Student[ ] studentList = gradeRoster.getAllStudents();

for (int i = 0; i < studentList.length; i++) {
    displayOneRow( studentList[i] );
}
```

We now have two private methods—displayHeading and displayOneRow—to add to the GradeRosterDisplay class. The displayHeading method outputs the column headings. To display information in an easy-to-read style, we need to set a field width for each column and align the values in it. How shall we set the field widths? We should not set some fixed sizes for field widths because that will limit the usability. We want the GradeRosterDisplay class to work with student names that contain a maximum of 10 characters or 20 characters. Likewise, we want the class to work with a list of students having three, seven, or any number of tests. To enable such flexibility, we will require the programmer to specify the field widths and the label for each column when a GradeRosterDisplay object is created.

We will define two data members: an integer array widthForColumn to store field widths and a String array headingForColumn to store column headings. These two arrays are set in a constructor that accepts four parameters: a Frame object owner, an integer columnCnt, a String array heading, and a int array width. Here's the body of the constructor:

```
outputBox          = new OutputBox( owner );
headingForColumn   = new String[columnCnt];
widthForColumn     = new int[columnCnt];

for (int i = 0; i < columnCnt; i++ ) {
    headingForColumn[i]   = heading[i];
    widthForColumn[i]     = width[i];
}
```

Notice the for loop to assign elements of heading and width individually to headingForColumn and widthForColumn. We do not simply assign the two array arguments to the data members as

```
headingForColumn   = heading;
widthForColumn     = width;
```

Do you know why? Remember that an array is an object, and only its reference is passed as a parameter. If we only assign a reference and do not create a separate local copy, any changes made to the original arrays would damage the operation of the class.

For example, to create a GradeRosterDisplay for showing student information with a name, three test scores, and a course grade, we can do the following:

```
String heading = { "Name, "Test1", "Test2", "Test3", "Grade" };
int fieldWidth = { 15, 8, 8, 8, 10 };

gradeRosterDisplay
    = new GradeRosterDisplay( this,  5, heading, fieldWidth );
```

With the data members widthForColumn and headingForColumn properly set, the logic of displayHeading can be expressed as

```
for (int i = 0; i < headingForColumn.length; i++) {
    outputBox.print(Format.centerAlign
                        ( widthForColumn[i],
                          headingForColumn[i] ) );
}
outputBox.skipLine(2); //leave a blank space after the heading
```

The displayOneRow method uses one line of OutputBox to display information of one student. The number of values to display on one line varies, depending on the number of test scores kept for students. To accommodate this variation, we will define a new method named getValues to the Student class that returns student information as an array of String values. Figure 14.13 shows how the getValues method works.

FIGURE 14.13   The **getValues** method returns an array of **String** that contains student information.

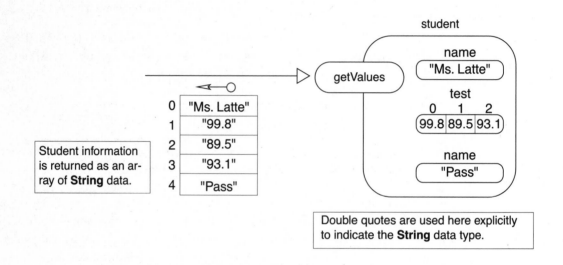

Using the getValues method, the logic of displayOneRow can be expressed as follows:

```
String oneRow[] = student.getValues(); //student is one element
                                       //in the studentList
                                       //array

for (int i = 0; i < oneRow.length; i++) {
    outputBox.print( Format.centerAlign
                        ( widthForColumn[i], oneRow[i] ) );
}

outputBox.skipLine(1); //move to the next line
```

Figure 14.14 is the method call sequence diagram for displaying student information for all students.

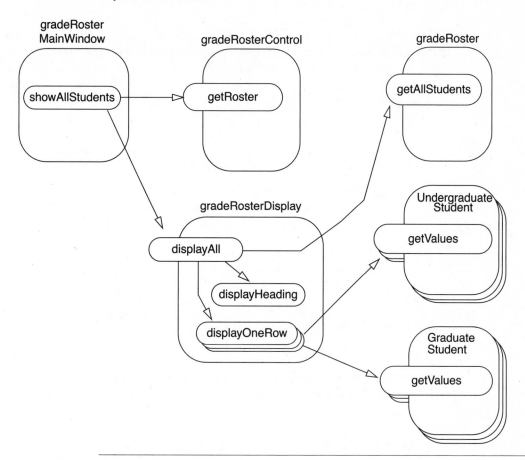

FIGURE 14.14   Method call sequence for the **showAllStudents** method. Calls to standard **javabook** objects are not shown.

The showOneStudent method of gradeRosterMainWindow displays information of a selected student. A student to be displayed will be selected by specifying the student's name. We will share most of the methods used to implement the showAllStudents method here.

The showOneStudent method of GradeRosterMainWindow calls the getRoster method of gradeRosterControl to get a grade roster and passes this roster to gradeRosterDisplay. The logic of this method is

```
      if (gradeRosterControl.hasGradeRoster() ) {
          roster = gradeRosterControl.getRoster();
          gradeRosterDisplay.displayOne( roster );
      }
      else {
          print out an error message;
      }
```

The displayOne method of GradeRosterDisplay first prompts the user for the name of a student to display. It then passes the name to the getStudent method of GradeRoster. The getStudent method was defined already in Step 3. If the getStudent returns null, then we print out an error message. Otherwise, we display the column headings and the information of the student returned by getStudent. Here's the logic of the method:

```
      String  name      = inputBox.getString("Enter Student Name:");
      Student student    = roster.getStudent(name);

      if (student == null) {
          outputBox.printLine( "No student with a given name" +
                                      " is in the roster" );
      }
      else {
          displayHeading( );
          displayOneRow( student );
      }

      outputBox.show();
```

Since the method uses an InputBox object, we will add it as a new data member of the GradeRosterDisplay class and initialize it in the constructor.

Figure 14.15 is the method call sequence of the showOneStudent method.

FIGURE 14.15   Method call sequence for the **showOneStudent** method. Calls to standard **javabook** objects are not shown.

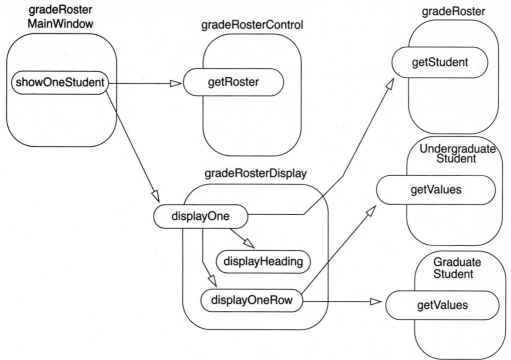

The following table summarizes the work done in Step 7:

	Objects	**To Do**
Step 7	GradeRoster MainWindow	Implement the methods showAllStudents showOneStudent Modify the constructor to create and initialize an instance of GradeRosterDisplay.
	GradeRoster Control	Implement the method getRoster
	GradeRoster Display	Implement the methods displayAll displayOne Declare the data members and the constructor.

	Objects	To Do
	Student	Implement the method getValues
	GradeRoster	Implement the method getAllStudents

Step 7 Code   We will list the code modification for each class in order.

GradeRosterMainWindow
We add a new data member

```
GradeRosterDisplay    gradeRosterDisplay;
```

and initialize it in the constructor:

```
public GradeRosterMainWindow( )
{
   ...
   String heading
            = { "Name, "Test1", "Test2", "Test3", "Grade" };
   int fieldWidth = { 15, 8, 8, 8, 10 };

   gradeRosterDisplay = new GradeRosterDisplay( this,  5,
                                      heading, fieldWidth );
}
```

Define the following methods:

```
private void showAllStudents()
{
   GradeRoster roster;

   if ( gradeRosterControl.hasGradeRoster() ) {
      roster = gradeRosterControl.getRoster();
      gradeRosterDisplay.displayAll( roster );
   }
   else {
      messageBox.show("No roster is open.");
   }
}
```

```
        private void showOneStudent()
        {
            GradeRoster roster;

            if ( gradeRosterControl.hasGradeRoster() ) {
                roster = gradeRosterControl.getRoster();
                gradeRosterDisplay.displayOne( roster );
            }
            else {
                messageBox.show("No roster is open.");
            }
        }
```

GradeRosterControl
We add a method that returns a grade roster:

```
        public GradeRoster getRoster( )
        {
            return gradeRoster; //return its GradeRoster data member
        }
```

GradeRosterDisplay
We define the data members and the constructor for the class:

```
        private int         widthForColumn[];
        private String      headingForColumn[];
        private OutputBox   outputBox;
        private InputBox    inputBox;

        public GradeRosterDisplay(  Frame      owner,
                                    int        columnCnt,
                                    String[]   heading,
                                    int[]      width       )
        {
            outputBox          = new OutputBox( owner );
            inputBox           = new InputBox( owner );
            headingForColumn   = new String[columnCnt];
            widthForColumn     = new int[columnCnt];

            for (int i = 0; i < columnCnt; i++ ) {
                headingForColumn[i]   = heading[i];
                widthForColumn[i]     = width[i];
            }
        }
```

Define the following public and private methods:

```
public void displayAll( GradeRoster roster )
{
    Student[] student = roster.getAllStudents();

    displayHeading();

    for (int i = 0; i < student.length; i++) {
        displayOneRow(student[i]);
    }

    outputBox.show();
}


public void displayOne( GradeRoster roster )
{
    String    name;
    Student   student;

    name     = inputBox.getString("Enter Student Name:");
    student  = roster.getStudent(name);

    if (student == null) {
        outputBox.printLine( "No student with a given name" +
                             " is in the roster" );
    }
    else {
        displayHeading( );
        displayOneRow( student );
    }

    outputBox.show();
}


private void displayHeading()
{
    for (int i = 0; i < headingForColumn.length; i++) {
        outputBox.print(Format.centerAlign(widthForColumn[i],
                                    headingForColumn[i]));
    }

    outputBox.skipLine(1);
}
```

```
private void displayOneRow( Student student )
{
    String oneRow[] = student.getValues();

    for (int i = 0; i < oneRow.length; i++) {
        outputBox.print(Format.centerAlign
                                (widthForColumn[i],oneRow[i]));
    }

    outputBox.skipLine(1);
}
```

Student

We add a method that returns student information as an array of String to the Student class (and inherited by its subclasses GraduateStudent and Under–graduateStudent):

```
public String[] getValues( )
{
    String value[] = new String[NUM_OF_TESTS + 2];
    value[0] = name;

    for (int i = 0; i < value.length; i++) {
        value[i+1] = Convert.toString(test[i]);
    }

    value[value.length-1] = courseGrade;

    return value;
}
```

GradeRoster

We add a method that returns student all Student objects:

```
public Student[] getAllStudents( )
{
    return roster;
}
```

Step 7 Test

We run the program and verify that student information is displayed correctly. One possible sequence for testing operations is as follows:

1. Select Show/All Students and verify that the display works correctly when no roster is open.

2. Select Edit/Add Student three or four times and add students. Make sure to create both undergraduate and graduate students.

3. Select Show/All Students and verify the display is valid. Since no test scores are entered, the display should correctly reflect this fact.

4. Select Show/One Student and enter the name of a student in the roster. Verify that the display of this student's information is correct.

5. Select Show/One Student and enter the name of a nonexisting student. Verify the program works correctly in this case also.

6. Select Edit/Test Scores and enter test scores. Repeat this step to enter test scores for all the students.

7. Select Edit/Compute Grades and verify that course grades are computed correctly.

8. Select Show/All Students and verify that the updated student information is displayed.

14.11 Step 8 Development: Storing Grade Rosters

Step 8 Design   In the eighth step, we will complete the program by implementing the methods that handle file input and output of grade rosters. A GradeRosterStorage object is the one responsible for storing GradeRoster objects using the object file I/O technique. The methods corresponding to the menu choices File/Open, File/Save, and File/Save As are openRoster, saveRoster, and saveAsRoster. We will implement the file output operations first.

The saveAsRoster and saveRoster methods of GradeRosterMainWindow are similarly defined. The methods get a GradeRoster object to save from grade-RosterControl and call either the save or saveAs method of gradeRosterStorage. If the save or saveAs method returns false, then there was an error in saving a roster, so an error message is displayed. The logic of the saveRoster and saveAsRoster methods is

```
//saveRoster of GradeRosterMainWindow
roster  = gradeRosterControl.getRoster();
success = gradeRosterStorage.save( roster );

if (!success) {
```

```
        messageBox.show("ERROR in saving data.");
    }

    //saveAsRoster of GradeRosterMainWindow
    roster  = gradeRosterControl.getRoster();
    success = gradeRosterStorage.saveAs( roster );

    if (!success) {
        messageBox.show("ERROR in saving data.");
    }
```

The **save** method of **GradeRosterStorage** saves a **GradeRoster** object to a current file. When the data are read from or written to a file, this file becomes the *current file* of the program. If there's no current file (that is, the user is working on a newly created grade roster that has not been saved yet), then **save** calls the **saveAs** method. We define an instance variable **filename** to **Grade-RosterStorage** to keep track of the current file. The **save** method first checks the instance variable **filename**. If it is a **null**, there is no current file, so the **save** method simply calls the **saveAs** method. If it is not **null**, then there is a current file, so the method calls the private **saveData** method instead. The method is defined as

current file

```
        //save of GradeRosterStorage
        boolean status;

        if (filename == null) {
            status = saveAs(roster);
        }
        else  { //save the data
            status = saveData(roster);
        }
        return status;
```

The **saveAs** method of **GradeRosterStorage** writes the data to a user designated file. If a valid file is specified, then a **GradeRoster** object is written to the file using **saveData**. The **saveAs** is defined as

```
        //saveAs of GradeRosterStorage
        boolean status;

        get filename using a FileDialog;
```

```
                if (filename == null) { //file dialog is canceled, so do nothing
                    status = false;
                }
                else {
                    status = saveData(roster);
                }
                return status;
```

When the saveData method is called from the save or saveAs methods, we know the data member filename is not a null. The saveData method sets up an object output stream for filename, and if no exception is thrown, the method writes roster to the file. The saveData method is defined as

```
        //saveData of GradeRosterStorage
        boolean status = true;

        try {
            set up an ObjectOutputStream for filename;
            outObjectStream.writeObject( roster );
            outObjectStream.close();
        }
        catch (IOException e) {
            status = false;
        }

        return status;
```

Figures 14.16 and 14.17 are the method call sequence diagrams of the saveAsRoster and saveRoster methods.

The openRoster method of GradeRosterMainWindow calls the open method of gradeRosterStorage to read a grade roster object from a file. If the open method returns a null, then there was some kind of error reading a roster object. If the method returns a GradeRoster object, then we pass the object to the setGradeRoster method of gradeRosterControl. The openRoster method is defined as

```
        roster = gradeRosterStorage.open();

        if (roster == null) {

            messageBox.show("ERROR: No file is opened.");
        }
```

FIGURE 14.16   Method call sequence for the **saveAsRoster** method. Calls to the **javabook** objects are not shown.

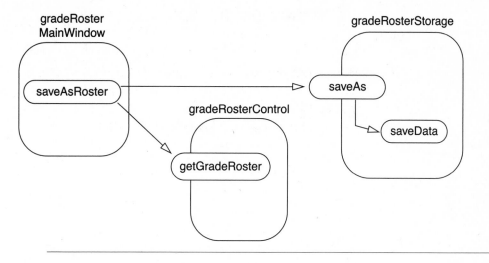

FIGURE 14.17   Method call sequence for the **saveRoster** method. Calls to the **javabook** objects are not shown.

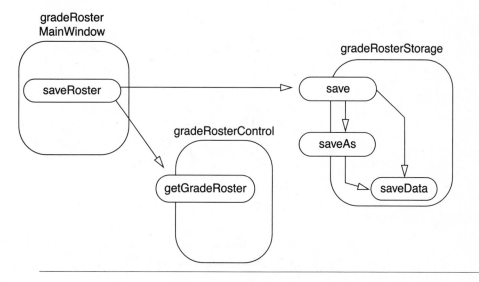

```
else {
    gradeRosterControl.setGradeRoster( roster );
}
```

The open method of gradeRosterStorage uses a FileDialog object to get the filename of a file to open from the user. If a valid filename is given, then we call the method loadData to read a GradeRoster object from the specified file. The two methods are defined as

```
//open of GradeRosterStorage
get the filename of a file to open using FileDialog

if (filename == null) { //FileDialog is canceled
    roster = null;
}
else {
    roster = loadData();
}

return roster;
```

```
//loadData of GradeRosterStorage
GradeRoster roster;

try {

    set up an ObjectInputStream for filename
    roster = (GradeRoster) inObjectStream.readObject();
    inObjectStream.close();

}
catch (IOException e) {
    roster = null;
}
catch (ClassNotFoundException e) {
    roster = null;
}

return roster;
```

Figure 14.18 is the method call sequence diagram for reading a grade roster object from a file and assigning it to gradeRosterControl.

FIGURE 14.18   Method call sequence for the **openRoster** method. Calls to standard **javabook** objects are not shown.

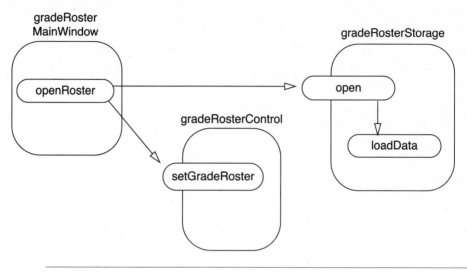

The following table summarizes the work to be done in Step 8:

	Objects	To Do

Step 8	GradeRoster MainWindow	Implement the methods
		    openRoster
		    saveRoster
		    saveAsRoster
		Modify the constructor to create and initialize an instance of GradeRosterStorage.

	GradeRoster Control	Implement the method setGradeRoster

	GradeRoster Storage	Implement the methods
		    save
		    saveAs
		    saveData
		    open
		    loadData
		Define the constructor to create and initialize data members.

We will list the code modification for each class in order.

GradeRosterMainWindow
We add a new data member

```
GradeRosterStorage    gradeRosterStorage;
```

and initialize it in the constructor:

```
public GradeRosterMainWindow( )
{
    ...

    gradeRosterStorage = new GradeRosterStorage( this );
}
```

We add three methods to the class:

```
private void openRoster()
{
    GradeRoster roster = gradeRosterStorage.open();

    if (roster == null) {
        messageBox.show("Error: Open failed.");
    }
    else {
        gradeRosterControl.setRoster(roster);
    }
}

private void saveRoster()
{
    GradeRoster roster  = gradeRosterControl.getRoster();
    boolean     success = gradeRosterStorage.save( roster );

    if (!success) {
        messageBox.show("Error: No data was saved to a file");
    }
}

private void saveAsRoster()
{
    GradeRoster roster  = gradeRosterControl.getRoster();
```

```
        boolean      success = gradeRosterStorage.saveAs( roster );

        if (!success) {
            messageBox.show("Error: No data was saved to a file");
        }
    }
```

GradeRosterControl

We define the public method setGradeRoster:

```
    public void setGradeRoster( GradeRoster roster )
    {
        gradeRoster = roster;
    }
```

GradeRosterStorage

We define the data members and the constructor for the class:

```
    private Frame        owner;
    private String       filename;


    public GradeRosterStorage(    Frame       mainWindow )
    {
        owner = mainWindow;
    )
```

Define the following public and private methods:

```
    public GradeRoster open( )
    {
        GradeRoster roster;

        FileDialog fileDialog = new FileDialog(owner,
                                    "Load Grade Roster...",
                                    FileDialog.LOAD);

        fileDialog.show();

        filename = fileDialog.getFile();

        if (filename == null) {
            roster = null;
```

```
        }
        else {
           roster = loadData( );
        }

        return roster;
    }


    private GradeRoster loadData( )
    {
        GradeRoster roster;

        try {

            //set up file and stream
            File inFile = new File(filename);
            FileInputStream inFileStream
                                = new FileInputStream(inFile);
            ObjectInputStream inObjectStream
                        = new ObjectInputStream(inFileStream);

            roster = (GradeRoster) inObjectStream.readObject( );

            inObjectStream.close( );
        }
        catch (IOException e) {
            roster = null;
            System.out.println(e);
        }
        catch (ClassNotFoundException e) {
            roster = null;
            System.out.println(e);
        }

        return roster;
    }


    public boolean saveAs( GradeRoster roster )
    {
        boolean status;

        FileDialog fileDialog = new FileDialog(owner,
                                        "Save Grade Roster...",
                                        FileDialog.SAVE);
        fileDialog.show( );
```

```
        filename = fileDialog.getFile();
        if (filename == null) {
            status = false;
        }
        else {
            status = saveData(roster);
        }

        return status;
    }


    private boolean saveData( GradeRoster roster )
    {
        boolean status = true;

        try {
            //set up the streams
            File outFile = new File(filename);
            FileOutputStream outFileStream
                            = new FileOutputStream(outFile);
            ObjectOutputStream outObjectStream
                        = new ObjectOutputStream(outFileStream);

            outObjectStream.writeObject(roster);

            outObjectStream.close();
        }
        catch (IOException e) {
            status = false;
            System.out.println(e);
        }

        return status;
    }

    public boolean save( GradeRoster roster)
    {
        boolean status;

        if (filename == null) {
            status = saveAs(roster);
        }
        else { //save the data
            status = saveData(roster);
        }
```

```
        return status;

    }
```

Step 8 Test   We run the program and verify that student information is displayed correctly. One possible sequence of testing operations is as follows:

1. Select Show/All Students and verify that the display works correctly when no roster is open.

2. Select Edit/Add Student three or four times and add students. Make sure to create both undergraduate and graduate students.

3. Select Edit/Test Scores and enter test scores. Repeat this step to enter test scores for all students.

4. Select Edit/Compute Grades and verify that course grades are computed correctly.

5. Select File/Save As and save the roster to a file, say, rosterOne.dat. You can use any name you wish for the filename. Verify that the file is created and the file size is not zero.

6. Add one or two more students to the roster and save this roster to another file, say, rosterTwo.dat.

7. Select File/Open and open rosterOne.dat. List all students in the roster and verify the information is correct.

8. Select File/Open and open rosterTwo.dat. List all students in the roster and verify the information is correct.

9. Modify the grade roster contents by editing test scores and deleting a couple of students. Save the data to a file by selecting File/Save. Open the file and list the contents. Verify that changes are made correctly.

14.12 Step 9 Development: Finalize and Improve

We are almost done with the development. Our task in the last step is to finalize and look for any improvements. With so many classes in the program, it is very important to perform a thorough and critical review of the program. We review all classes for consistency and completeness. Some of the questions we ask ourselves while reviewing the classes are

1. Are the methods named logically and consistently over the classes?

2. Are there any overburdened classes that handle too many tasks?

3. Are the links between the classes clear and logical? Are there too many links between the classes?

4. Have we considered all possible operations? Are there any other operations we should support?

5. Is the program's user interface logical and easy to use?

To identify any remaining problem spots, we run the program through another round of testing. We basically repeat the testing procedures we performed in the earlier development steps. For a program of this size, it is also beneficial to perform a beta testing. We create a simple user manual and ask others to test the program. Beta testing is a very common way for commercial software companies to do a final testing before releasing their software to the general public.

14.13 The StudentNameDialog Class

In this section, we will implement the StudentNameDialog class identified in Step 5. We will implement this class using a separate development cycle. The design document was already created in Step 5 and, therefore, our job here is to implement it. Of course, if the given design contains any inconsistency or error, we may have to modify the design.

Problem Statement

Write a dialog that allows the user to enter two string values, one for the current name and another for a new name. The dialog will include CANCEL *and* CHANGE *buttons. Its visual appearance will be as shown in Figure 14.6. The class must support the four public methods listed in the design document from Section 14.8.*

Overall Plan

What kind of behavior does the programmer who uses a StudentNameDialog expect from the class? One common behavior among the javabook dialog objects such as MessageBox, InputBox, and others is the displaying of a dialog at the center of the screen. We will incorporate this behavior into StudentNameDialog. This common behavior is programmed in the JavaBookDialog abstract class in the javabook package. MessageBox, InputBox, ResponseBox, and all other dialogs in javabook are subclasses of the JavaBookDialog class. We will make StudentNameDialog a subclass of JavaBookDialog and inherit the centering behavior from its superclass.

One condition to make a class a subclass of JavaBookDialog is to implement the abstract method adjustSize. A subclass must implement this method by including code to set the size of the dialog and the size and position of the components in the dialog. The superclass JavaBookDialog is programmed in such a way that the adjustSize method is called when an instance of its subclass is created.

In addition to implementing the required adjustSize method, we need to implement three public methods: getCurrentName, getNewName, and isCanceled. Furthermore, because we have to process the button click event, we need to implement the action-handling method actionPerformed. The object diagram at this point is

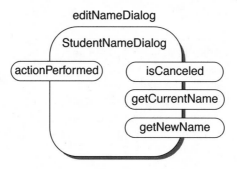

We will implement the class in the following three steps:

development
steps

1. Start with a class skeleton with the necessary data member declarations and constructors. Implement the superclass abstract method adjustSize.

2. Implement the actionPerformed method.

3. Implement the public methods getCurrentName, getNewName, and isCanceled.

Step 1 Development: Skeleton with Constructor and adjustSize

Step 1 Design   The objective of Step 1 is to identify the necessary GUI components and complete the visual appearance of the dialog. We will also implement the adjustSize method in this step. We will use two TextField objects for the user to enter the new and current names. We will call them newNameTextField and currentNameTextField. We will use two Label objects currentNameLabel and newNameLabel to label the two TextField objects. And finally, we will have two Button objects for CANCEL and OK. These two buttons will be the only action event sources for this dialog. We declare these objects as

```
private TextField      currentNameTextField,
                       newNameTextField;

private Label          currentNameLabel,
                       newNameLabel;

private Button         changeButton,
                       cancelButton;
```

We will initialize these objects in the constructor and set their size and position in the adjustSize method. The constructor for this dialog is pretty standard:

```
//set the properties of the dialog
call the super's constructor;
set title to "Edit Student Name";
set layout to null;
set resizable to false;

//create GUI objects
...

//add the created GUI objects to the dialog
add( currentNameLabel );
add( newNameLabel );
...

//set the dialog as an action listener of two buttons
cancelButton.addActionListener( this );
changeButton.addActionListener( this );
```

The adjustSize method will set the size and location of the GUI objects as

```
addNotify(); //must call this method at the beginning
Insets inset = getInsets();

//Adjust the size of the dialog
setSize(inset.left + inset.right + 250,
        inset.top + inset.bottom + 170);

//Adjust the size of components in the dialog
```

```
currentNameLabel.setBounds
                (inset.left +  13, inset.top +  25,  81,  17);
newNameLabel.setBounds
                (inset.left +  13, inset.top +  75,  81,  17);

...
```

We need to call addNotify before calling the insets method so the correct inset values are computed. Remember that the inset values provide the boundary width on the four sides of a window. The purpose of inset values was explained in Chapter 12 (see Figure 12.5 on page 612). The addNotify method actually creates a platform-dependent data structure for managing a window, and without having this platform-dependent data structure created, the insets method does not return the correct values.

Step 1 Code   We will list the key portions of the StudentNameDialog class source code. The import statements and class declaration will be

```
import java.awt.event.*;
import java.awt.*;
import javabook.*;

class StudentNameDialog extends JavaBookDialog
                        implements ActionListener {
...
```

The constructor is defined as

```
public StudentNameDialog(Frame owner)
{
    //set the properties of the dialog
    super(owner);
    setTitle("Edit Student Name");
    setResizable(false);
    setLayout(null);

    //create GUI objects
    currentNameLabel = new Label("Current Name:");
    newNameLabel = new Label("New Name:");

    currentNameTextField = new TextField("");
    newNameTextField = new TextField("");

    changeButton = new Button("Change");
    cancelButton = new Button("Cancel");
```

```
            //add the created GUI objects to the dialog
            add(currentNameLabel);
            add(newNameLabel);
            add(currentNameTextField);
            add(newNameTextField);
            add(changeButton);
            add(cancelButton);

            //set the dialog as an action listener of the two buttons
            cancelButton.addActionListener( this );
            changeButton.addActionListener( this );
    }
```

and the adjustSize method is defined as

```
    protected void adjustSize()
    {
        addNotify();
        Insets inset = getInsets();

        setSize(inset.left + inset.right + 250,
                inset.top + inset.bottom + 170);

        currentNameLabel.setBounds
                    (inset.left +  13, inset.top +  25,  81, 17);
        newNameLabel.setBounds
                    (inset.left +  13, inset.top +  75,  81, 17);
        currentNameTextField.setBounds
                    (inset.left +  28, inset.top +  45, 192, 22);
        newNameTextField.setBounds
                    (inset.left +  28, inset.top + 100, 192, 22);
        changeButton.setBounds
                    (inset.left +  41, inset.top + 136,  67, 22);
        cancelButton.setBounds
                    (inset.left + 139, inset.top + 136,  67, 22);
    }
```

Step 1 Test   In order to test the skeleton StudentNameDialog class, we need to write a test main class because we are developing this class separate from the main development. A simple main class such as the following would suffice:

```
    /*
        Program TestStudentNameDialog

        A main class to test the StudentNameDialog class
```

```
*/
import javabook.*;

class TestStudentNameDialog
{
    public static void main (String args[])
    {
        MainWindow        topWindow = new MainWindow();
        StudentNameDialog testDialog
                            = StudentNameDialog( topWindow );
        topWindow.setVisible( true );
        testDialog.setVisible( true );
    }
}
```

The purpose of this test program is to verify that the constructor is executed correctly and the placement and size of GUI objects are as we expected.

Step 2 Development: Implement the actionPerformed Method

Step 2 Design

In the second step of development, we will implement the actionPerformed method. This method is called when the CANCEL or CHANGE button is clicked. If the clicked button is CANCEL, then we close the dialog and clear any entry in currentNameTextField and newNameTextField. If we don't clear them, the entry values will still be visible when we display the dialog the next time. We will define a private method clearEntries to clear the contents of two TextField objects. In addition, we need to remember the fact that the dialog is canceled, so the object can reply correctly when the programmer calls the boolean method isCanceled. For this purpose, we will declare a boolean instance variable canceled and set this variable to true when the CANCEL button is clicked.

If the CHANGE button is clicked, then we need to remember the two String values entered in the two TextField objects and set canceled to false. To remember the two input values, we declare two String instance variables currentName and newName. We will define a private method setNames to set these String variables.

The method body of actionPerformed looks like this:

```
Button clickedButton = (Button) event.getSource();

if (clickedButton == cancelButton) {
    canceled = true;
}
else { //changeButton is clicked
```

```
            setNames();
        }

    setVisible( false ); //make the dialog disappear
    clearEntries( );
```

The clearEntries method sets the contents of both TextField objects to empty strings

```
    currentNameTextField.setText( "" );
        newNameTextField.setText( "" );
```

We will use a stub method for setNames in this step. What we need to achieve in this step is only the framework to process the action events. We will include temporary output statements in the stub setNames method.The working design document now includes this method:

Design Document: The StudentNameDialog Class		
Method	**Visibility**	**Purpose**
...	...	...
clearEntries	private	Sets the contents of the two TextField objects to an empty string.
setNames	private	Assigns the contents of the two TextField objects to currentName and newName.

Step 2 Code

The actionPerformed method is defined as follows:

```
    public void actionPerformed( ActionEvent event )
    {
        Button clickedButton = (Button) event.getSource();

        if (clickedButton == cancelButton) {
            canceled = true;
        }
        else { //changeButton is clicked
            setNames();
        }

        setVisible( false ); //make the dialog disappear
        clearEntries( );
    }
```

The clearEntries method clears both TextField objects:

```
private void clearEntries( )
{
    currentNameTextField.setText( "" );
        newNameTextField.setText( "" );
}
```

The setNames method is temporarily defined as

```
private void setNames()
{
    //get data from two TextField objects
    currentName = currentNameTextField.getText();
    newName     = newNameTextField.getText();

    System.out.println("current:" + currentName);   //TEMP
    System.out.println("new:     " + newName);       //TEMP
    canceled = false;                                //TEMP
}
```

Step 2 Test   We run the same TestStudentNameDialog main class from Step 1 and verify that the action events generated by the two buttons are processed correctly.

Step 3 Development: Implement the Public Methods

Step 3 Design   In the last step of development, we complete the class by finalizing the setNames method and defining three public methods isCanceled, getCurrentName, and getNewName. The three public methods only need to return the value of the corresponding instance variable—canceled, currentName, or newName:

```
//isCanceled
return canceled;

//getCurrentName
return currentName;

//getNewName
return newName;
```

In the final setNames method, we need to incorporate some error-checking routine. What should happen when the user clicks on the CHANGE button without entering any value for the current and new names? If we do nothing, then the two instance variables remain empty strings. We could require the programmer to check the value returned by getCurrentName and getNewName, but this will put unnecessary burden on the programmer. The task of this dialog is to input two names, current and new. If the user fails to provide either value, then it is really the same as canceling the dialog. So if either entry is an empty string, then we will set the variable canceled to true. Here's the logic of the method:

```
currentName = currentNameTextField.getText( );
newName     =     newNameTextField.getText( );

//make sure both are nonempty strings
if ( currentName.equals("") || newName.equals("") ) {

    canceled = true;
}
else {
    //input okay, so close
    canceled = false;
}
```

Step 3 Code   The three public methods are defined as

```
public boolean isCanceled()
{
    return canceled;
}

public String getCurrentName()
{
    return currentName;
}

public String getNewName()
{
    return newName;
}
```

and the setNames method is defined as

```
private void setName( )
{
```

```
        currentName = currentNameTextField.getText();
        newName     =      newNameTextField.getText();

        //make sure both are nonempty strings
        if ( currentName.equals("") || newName.equals("") ) {

            canceled = true;
        }
        else {
            //input okay, so close
            canceled = false;
        }
    }
```

Step 3 Test

We will modify the test program to verify the correctness of the Step 3 StudentNameDialog class. Here's the modified test program:

```
class TestStudentNameDialog
{
    public static void main (String args[])
    {
        MainWindow     topWindow = new MainWindow();
        MessageBox     messageBox = new MessageBox(topWindow);

        StudentNameDialog testDialog
                        = StudentNameDialog( topWindow );
        topWindow.setVisible( true );
        testDialog.setVisible( true );

        if ( testDialog.isCanceled () )
            messageBox.show("Canceled");

        else {
            messageBox.show( testDialog.getCurrentName() );
            messageBox.show( testDialog.getNewName() );
        }
    }
}
```

We run the test program and do the following:

1. Click the CANCEL button without entering any value and verify that the message Canceled is displayed.

2. Enter values into TextField objects and click CANCEL. Verify that the message Canceled is displayed.

3. Enter values into one TextField object and click CHANGE. Verify that the entered values are displayed.

4. Click the CHANGE button without entering any value and verify that the message Canceled is displayed.

5. Enter values for both TextField objects and verify that the entered names are displayed correctly.

14.14 The TestScoreDialog Class

In this section, we will implement the TestScoreDialog class identified in Step 6. To implement this class, we repeat the process we employed in developing the StudentNameDialog class. Namely, we will implement this class using a separate development cycle with the design document already created in Step 6.

Problem Statement

Write a dialog that allows the user to enter test scores. Its visual appearance will be as shown in Figure 14.9. The class must support the three public methods listed in the design document from Section 14.9.

Overall Plan

What will be the capabilities of the TestScoreDialog class? In Figure 14.9 we see a dialog for entering three test scores. Should the class we design here be capable of entering just three test scores or any number of test scores? Since the Student class can be modified to include any number of test scores, we will design the class to allow the editing of N test scores.

The StudentNameDialog class was designed as a subclass of JavaBookDialog. Should we do the same for TestScoreDialog? It is a possibility, but if we make it a subclass of JavaBookDialog, we need to add code to create a varying number of TextField objects, for instance. It is not difficult but time-consuming to work out all the details. Instead of doing that ourselves, is there any class for which we can make TestScoreDialog its subclass? How about the MultiInputBox class? Yes, this class from javabook has all the capabilities we need for TestScoreDialog.

code reuse by composition

We will reuse MultiInputBox to implement TestScoreDialog, but not with inheritance. We will use a technique called *code reuse by composition*. Instead of making TestScoreDialog a subclass of MultiInputBox, we will declare an instance variable that is a MultiInputBox object:

```
class TestScoreDialog
{
    ...
    private MultiInputBox     scoreBox;
    ...
```

Why do we do it this way? If we make TestScoreDialog a subclass of MultiInputBox, then all methods of MultiInputBox will become available to the programmer who uses TestScoreDialog. If the programmer uses inherited methods in the wrong way, TestScoreDialog will not work correctly. What we want to do is to reuse the functionality of MultiInputBox but also protect the class from misuse by hiding the methods of MultiInputBox. We can do this by making MultiInputBox a part of the TestScoreDialog class.

Based on the design document from Section 14.9, the object diagram at this point is

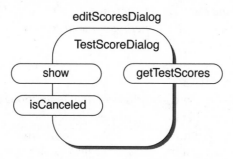

We will implement the class in the following two steps:

development steps

1. Start with a class skeleton with the necessary data member declarations and constructors.

2. Implement the show and getTestScores methods.

Step 1 Development: Skeleton with Constructor

Step 1 Design   In Step 1 we identify the necessary data members and define a constructor. One data member will be a MultiInputBox object. We need another data member to keep track of input test scores. We will use an array of int for this purpose. We declare these objects as

```
private    MultiInputBox      scoreBox;

private    int[]              score;
```

The constructor will initialize these objects. What will be the size for the **score** array? This size is also the number we pass to **scoreBox** so the correct number of **TextField** objects appear on **scoreBox**. We will make the size an argument to the constructor. To create an instance of **MultiInputBox**, we need a **Frame** object; we will make it a second argument to the constructor. The constructor will look like this:

```
scoreBox = new MultiInputBox(owner, size); //owner is a Frame
score    = new int[size];

//set the labels of scoreBox
//to Test 1, Test 2, and so forth
```

In order to make a dialog appear on the screen, we will write a temporary **show** method. It contains only one statement

```
scoreBox.getInputs();
```

Step 1 Code   The constructor of the **TestScoreDialog** class is defined as

```
public TestScoreDialog(Frame owner, int size)
{
    scoreBox = new MultiInputBox(owner, size);
    score    = new int[size];

    //set the labels of scoreBox
    String label[] = new String[size];

    for (int i = 0; i < size; i++) {
        label[i] = "Test  #" + (i+1);
    }
    scoreBox.setLabels(label);
}
```

and the temporary **show** method is defined as

```
public show( )
{
    scoreBox.getInputs();
}
```

Step 1 Test   As always, in order to test the skeleton TestScoreDialog class, we need to write a test main class. A simple main class such as the following would suffice:

```
/*
        Program CheckTestScoreDialog

        A main class to test the StudentNameDialog class
*/
import javabook.*;

class CheckTestScoreDialog
{
    public static void main (String args[])
    {
        MainWindow        topWindow = new MainWindow();
        TestScoreDialog    testDialog
                                = TestScoreDialog( topWindow, 3 );
        topWindow.setVisible( true );
        testDialog.setVisible( true );
    }
}
```

We run the program and verify that the constructor is executed correctly, and the dialog has the correct number of GUI objects. We run the program again with different values of the size argument of the constructor.

Step 2 Development: **Implement** show **and** getTestScores

Step 2 Design   We will complete the development by finalizing the show method and defining the getTestScores method. A TestScoreDialog will allow the user to edit the current test scores of a student. This means the dialog must be able to accept the current test scores and display them. We will add one parameter to the show method to accept the test scores. This parameter will be a Student object. The values in this array will be passed to scoreBox using its setValue method. Then the show method calls the getInputs method of scoreBox. Finally, the elements in the array of String returned by getInputs are converted to float and assigned to the data member array score. Here's the logic of the method:

```
int value;
for (int i = 0; i < Student.NUM_OF_TESTS; i++ ) {
    value = student.getTestScore(i);        //student is a
    scoreBox.setValue( i, value );          //parameter
}
```

```
inputString = scoreBox.getInputs();

for (int i = 0; i < inputString.length; i++ ) {
    score[i] = Convert.toInt(inputString[i]);
}
```

The score array is set in the show method, so the getTestScores method only needs to return this score array

```
return score;
```

Step 2 Code   The final show method is defined as follows:

```
public void show( Student student )
{
    String inputString;
    int     value;

    for (int i = 0; i < Student.NUM_OF_TESTS; i++ ) {
        value = student.getTestScore(i);
        scoreBox.setValue( i, value );
    }

    inputString = scoreBox.getInputs();

    for (int i = 0; i < inputString.length; i++ ) {
        score[i] = Convert.toFloat(inputString[i]);
    }
}
```

The getTestScores method is defined as

```
public int[] getTestScores( )
{
    return score;
}
```

Step 2 Test   We run the following modified CheckTestScoreDialog main class and verify that the values entered in the dialog are correctly displayed.

```
class CheckTestScoreDialog
{
    public static void main (String args[])
    {
        MainWindow        topWindow = new MainWindow();
        OutputBox         outputBox = new OutputBox(topWindow);
        TestScoreDialog   testDialog
                              = TestScoreDialog( topWindow, 3 );
        topWindow.setVisible( true );
        outputBox.setVisible( true );

        Student student = new Student( "Decaf Latte");
        student.setTestScore(1, 70);
        student.setTestScore(2, 80);
        student.setTestScore(3, 90);

        testDialog.show( student );

        score = testDialog.getTestScores( );

        for (int i = 0; i < score.length; i++ ) {
            outputBox.println("Test # " + i + ":   " + score[i] );
        }
    }
}
```

We run the program again with different sizes and verify that the program works for all cases.

14.15 Exercises

1. Improve the routine to get course information in the grade roster program. Instead of using an InputBox to input a course title and instructor name, define a new custom dialog class for this purpose.

2. Add import and export features to the grade roster program. Add the menu choices Import and Export to the program. Import data from and export data to a user-designated textfile. To simplify the process, use the same data format for both the import and export files.

3. Design a custom dialog for displaying information of a single student. The following is a suggested layout:

```
┌─────────────────────────────────────────────┐
│                                             │
│                                             │
│   Name:          ┌──────────────────┐       │
│                  └──────────────────┘       │
│                                             │
│                  ┌──────┬──────┬──────┐     │
│   Test Scores:   │      │      │      │     │
│                  └──────┴──────┴──────┘     │
│                                             │
│   Final Grade:   ┌──────────────────┐       │
│                  └──────────────────┘       │
│                                             │
│                 ╭──────────────╮            │
│                 │     OK       │            │
│                 ╰──────────────╯            │
└─────────────────────────────────────────────┘
```

4. Latte Gallery in Carmel, California, is a small gallery that specializes in selling contemporary fine art, especially lithographs and photographs. All items sold in the gallery are signed and numbered. Write an application that keeps track of:

 · Customers and their art purchases.

 · Artists and their works that have appeared in the gallery.

 · Current inventory.

Allow the user to add, delete, or modify customer, artist, and artwork information. An inventory will include the purchase prices of the artworks and the selling price when sold. Give the user an option to list all customers or one customer. The user will specify the customer to display by entering the customer's last name and phone number.

Define at least four data members for each type of information. For customers, include the name, phone number, address, and artwork and artist preferences. For artists, include the name, speciality, whether alive or deceased, and price ranges of artworks. For artworks, include the title, date purchased, date sold, and artist. Feel free to add more data members as you see fit.

Design custom dialogs for entering and editing customers, artists, and artworks.

5. Improve the Latte Gallery Information Manager application by adding the following capabilities:

 · List all customers who bought an artwork by a given artist.

- List all artists who are still alive (so you can buy their artworks while the price is still reasonable).
- List all artworks in the inventory that did not sell for over three months. (This requires the use of Date class from the java.util package.)

6. Improve the Latte Gallery Information Manager application by adding a feature that allows the user to select a customer from the list of all customers by clicking on the customer he or she wants to see. The listing of all customers will include their names. When the user clicks on a name, a dialog displaying the full information of the selected customer will appear on the screen. Consider using a ListBox from javabook to list the names of all customers. For an improved user interface, consider defining a custom dialog using the List class from java.awt.

7. Write a program that plays the game of Fermi. The program generates three distinct random digits between 0 and 9. These digits are assigned to Positions 1, 2, and 3. The goal of the game is for the player to guess the digits in three positions correctly in the least number of tries. For each guess, the player provides three digits for Positions 1, 2, and 3. The program replies with a hint consisting of Fermi, Pico, or Nano. If the digit guessed for a given position is correct, then the reply is Fermi. If the digits guessed for a given position is in a different position, the reply is Pico. If the digit guessed for a given position does not match any of the three digits, then the reply is Nano. Here are sample replies for the three secret digits 6, 5, and 8 at Positions 1, 2, and 3, respectively:

Guess	Hint	Explanation
1 2 5	Nano Nano Pico	5 matches but at the wrong position.
8 5 3	Pico Fermi Nano	5 matches at the correct position. 8 matches but at the wrong position.
5 8 6	Pico Pico Pico	All match at the wrong positions.

Notice that if the hints like the above are given, the player can tell which number did not match. For example, given the hint for the second guess, we can tell that 3 is not one of the secret numbers. To avoid this, provide hints in a random order or in alphabetical order (e.g., it will be Fermi Nano Pico instead of Pico Fermi Nano for the second reply). Design the program so that it can easily be run as an applet or an application.

8. Extend the Fermi playing program by allowing the player to
   - Select the number of secret digits.
   - Select alphabets instead of digits.
   - Include duplicate secret digits.

9. Write a personal scheduler application. Each entry in the scheduler is either an appointment, a to-do item, or a memo. Each entry has the date and the time it is entered. An entry can be locked, and if locked, the user cannot modify it. For an appointment entry, include the person and the place of meeting. For a to-do entry, include a short description of a task and the due date. For a memo, include a text. Design a custom dialog for each type of entry. Consider using GUI components, such as Checkbox, Choice, and TextArea from java.awt.Use the Date class to record the date and the time of an entry.

10. Write a rental point tracking system for an up-and-coming Espresso's Dynamo Mopeds in Monterey, California. To compete against Ms. Latte's Moped R Us, Espresso's Dynamo Mopeds decided to install an automated points tracking system. When a customer first rents a moped, his or her information is entered into a database. For each rental, a customer receives points, and when the total points reaches 100, the customer can rent a moped free for three hours or redeem a free movie rental coupon from Espresso's Majestic Movies. The points are earned in the following scheme:

Renter	Type	Points
College Student	50cc Moppi	15
	150cc Magnum	20
Adult	50cc Moppi	10
	150cc Magnum	15
Senior	50cc Moppi	20
	150cc Magnum	30

In addition to the basic operations of updating the points information for every rental, include an operation to list all customers who earned over 100 points. Also, support an operation to edit the customer information.

11. Update the rental point tracking system to support a new rental system and point awarding rules for Espresso's Dynamo Mopeds. Now the customers

can rent only on an hourly basis and the points are awarded accordingly. Upon rental, the customer will state the number of hours he or she will rent in increments of one hour with the maximum of 10 hours. The rental fee is based on the following formula:

Renter	Type	Total Rental ≤ 5 hours	Total Rental > 5 hours
College Student	50cc Moppi	$3.50 per hour	$2.50 per hour
	150cc Magnum	$4.50 per hour	$3.50 per hour
Adult	50cc Moppi	$5.00 per hour	$4.00 per hour
	150cc Magnum	$6.50 per hour	$5.00 per hour
Senior	50cc Moppi	$4.00 per hour	$3.00 per hour
	150cc Magnum	$5.25 per hour	$4.00 per hour

The point awarding rule is as follows:

Renter	Type	Points
College Student	50cc Moppi	5 points for each hour
	150cc Magnum	7 points for each hour
Adult	50cc Moppi	3 points for each hour
	150cc Magnum	5 points for each hour
Senior	50cc Moppi	4 points for each hour
	150cc Magnum	6 points for each hour

At the time of rental, record the time it is rented out and the number of hours to be rented. Upon the return, record the time, and if it is overdue, double the charge and give no award points. Keep track of the late returns, and if the customer fails to return on time for three times, he or she will not be allowed to rent.

15

Searching, Sorting, and Recursive Algorithms

OBJECTIVES

After you have read and studied this chapter, you should be able to

- Write recursive algorithms for mathematical functions and non-numerical operations.

- Perform linear and binary search algorithms on small arrays.

- Determine whether linear or binary search is more effective for a given situation.

- Perform selection and bubble sort algorithms.

- Describe the recursive quicksort algorithm and explain how its performance is better than the other two sorting algorithms.

Introduction

In this chapter, we cover two major topics in computer science. The first topic is searching and sorting, and the second topic is recursion. In the previous chapter, we presented a case study of maintaining a class roster and described a basic searching method to locate a student given his/her name. In this chapter, we will present a better searching algorithm called *binary search*. Another fundamental operation we study in computer science is sorting—a technique to arrange elements in some order. We will explain basic sorting algorithms in this chapter. To keep our examples simple, we will use an array of integers to illustrate searching and sorting algorithms, but all the techniques we present here are equally applicable to any array of objects as well as primitive data types.

We introduced recursion in Chapter 7 and showed how to write recursive methods to implement mathematical functions. We used mathematical functions in Chapter 7 because it is easier to see how the recursion works with mathematical functions. However, recursive methods are not limited to implementing mathematical functions, and we will present several nonnumerical recursive algorithms in this chapter. We will also discuss some criteria for deciding when to use recursion and when not to. All recursive algorithms we provide in this chapter, other than those we use for explanation, are algorithms that should be written recursively.

15.1 Searching

We begin our study of fundamental algorithms with searching. Let's start with the problem statement for searching:

> *Given a value* X, *return the index of* X *in the array, if such* X *exists. Otherwise, return* NOT_FOUND *(-1). We assume there are no duplicate entries in the array.*

successful and
unsuccessful
search

There are two possible outcomes in searching: either we locate an *X* or we don't. We will call the first a *successful search* and the latter an *unsuccessful search*. Figure 15.1 illustrates the successful and unsuccessful searches. As obvious as this may sound, it is critical to differentiate the two because it is possible for one searching algorithm to perform superbly for successful searches, but very poorly for unsuccessful searches. When we analyze the performance of a searching algorithm, we normally derive two separate performances, one for a successful search and another for an unsuccessful search.

FIGURE 15.1   Successful and unsuccessful searches.

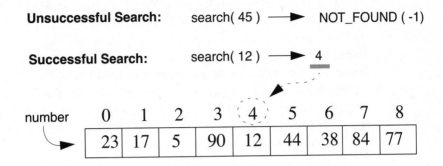

Linear Search

linear search

The search technique we used earlier in the book is called a *linear search* because we search the array from the first to the last position in a linear progression. The linear search is also called a *sequential search*. The linear search algorithm can be expressed as

```
public int linearSearch ( int[] number, int searchValue )
{
    int         loc    = 0;

    while ( loc < number.length &&
            number[loc] != searchValue ) {

        loc++;
    }

    if ( loc == number.length) { //Not found
        return NOT_FOUND;
    }
    else {
        return loc;              //Found, return the position
    }
}
```

There are still more elements to search.

*And **searchValue** is not found yet.*

If the number of entries in the array is N, then there will be N comparisons for an unsuccessful search (i.e., you search for a value not in the array). In the case of a successful search, there will be a minimum of one comparison and a maximum of N comparisons. On the average, there will be approximately $N / 2$ comparisons.

Is there a way to improve the linear search? If the array is sorted, then we can improve the search routine using the binary search technique.

Binary Search

binary search

If the values in the array are arranged in ascending or descending order, then we call the array *sorted*. In the following explanation of the binary search, we assume the array is sorted in ascending order. The crux of binary search is the winning strategy you apply for the Hi-Lo game. When you try to guess a secret number, say, between 1 and 100, your first guess would be 50. If your guess is HI, then you know the secret number is between 1 and 49. If your guess is LO, then you know the secret number is between 51 and 100. By guessing once, you eliminated half of the possible range of values from further consideration. This is the core idea of binary search.

Consider the following sorted array:

number	0	1	2	3	4	5	6	7	8
	5	12	17	23	38	44	77	84	90

Let's suppose we are searching for 77. We first search the middle position of the array. Since this array has 9 elements, the index of the middle position is 4, so we search number[4]. The value 77 is not in this position. Since 77 is larger than 38 and because the array is sorted, we know that if 77 is in the array, it must be in the right half of the array. So next, we search the middle position of the right half of the array, which is position 6. Figure 15.2 illustrates the effect of making one comparison in the binary search.

The search value 77 was found after two comparisons. In contrast, the linear search would take seven comparisons to locate 77. So there is a net reduction of five comparisons. How good is the binary search in general? Let's study the worst-case situation. In the binary search, after we make one comparison, we can eliminate one-half of the array from further consideration. So the number of comparisons in the worst case is the number of times you can divide the array into halves. Suppose the original size of an array is N and the value we search is not in the array. Then after one comparison, we have to search the remaining $N/2$ elements. After two comparisons, we have to search $N/4$ elements, and so on. The following table shows this relationship. The left column is the number of

FIGURE 15.2   Effect of one comparison in binary search.

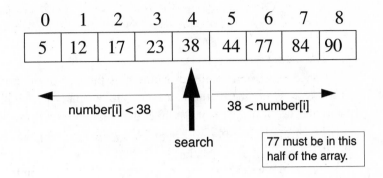

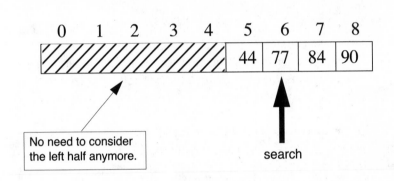

comparisons and the right column is the number of elements we still need to
search after making K comparisons.

Number of Comparisons	Number of Elements
0	N
1	$N/2 = N/2^1$
2	$N/4 = N/2^2$
. . .	. . .
K	$N/2^K$

The maximum number of comparisons K is derived by solving the following equation:

$$N = 2^K$$

$$\log_2 N = K$$

This is a remarkable improvement. If the size of the original array is 2048, for example, then the unsuccessful binary search takes at most $\log_2 2048 = 10$ comparisons, while the unsuccessful linear search takes 2048 comparisons. The difference between the two algorithms gets larger and larger as the size of an array gets larger.

Now let's write a binary search method. The key point in the method is how to stop the search. If the search value is in the array, we will eventually locate it, so the stopping condition for the successful search is easy. What about the case for an unsuccessful search? How can we detect that there are no more elements in the array to search for? Should we use some kind of a counter? We certainly can use a counter, but we can implement the method without using any counter. To compute the middle location for the next comparison, we need two index— low and high. The low and high indexes are initialized to 0 and $N-1$. The middle location is computed as

```
mid = (low + high) / 2; //the result is truncated
```

If number[mid] is less than the search value, then low is reset to mid+1. If number[mid] is greater than the search value, then high is reset to mid-1. And the search continues. Eventually, we will locate the search value or we will run out of elements to compare. We know that there are no more elements to compare when low becomes larger than high. Figure 15.3 shows how this works.

Here's the binarySearch method:

```
public int binarySearch ( int[] number, int searchValue )
{
    int        low    = 0,
               high   = number.length - 1,
               mid    = (low + high) / 2;

    while ( low <= high && number[mid] != searchValue ) {

        if (number[mid] < searchValue) {
```

```
        low = mid + 1;
    }
    else  { //number[mid] > searchValue
        high = mid - 1;
    }

    mid    = (low + high) / 2;
}
```

FIGURE 15.3   How the unsuccessful search is terminated in the binary search routine.

Suppose we search for **45**

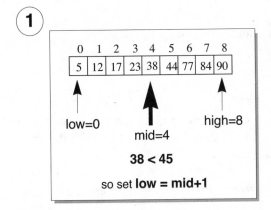

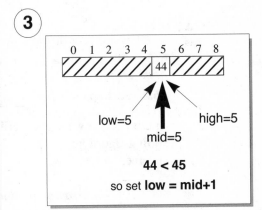

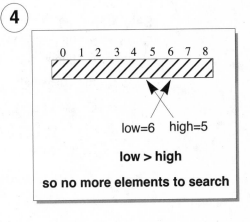

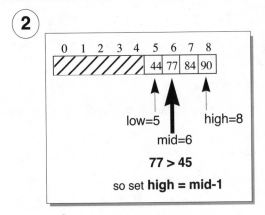

```
                    if ( low > high) {
                        mid = NOT_FOUND;
                    }

                    return mid;
                }
```

Quick Check

1. Suppose an array contains 2048 elements. What are the least and the most numbers of comparisons for a successful search using linear search?

2. Repeat the previous question with binary search.

15.2 Sorting

In this section we will describe two basic sorting algorithms. A more advanced sorting algorithm will be presented in Section 15.3. Let's start with the problem statement for sorting:

Given an array of N values, arrange the values into ascending order.

Selection Sort

Given a list of integers, how would you sort them? The most natural sorting algorithm for a human looks something like this:

1. Find the smallest integer in the list.

2. Cross out the number from further consideration and copy it to a new (sorted) list.

3. Repeat Steps 1 and 2 until all numbers are crossed out in the list.

Figure 15.4 shows this human sorting algorithm with the first three numbers being copied to the new list.

FIGURE 15.4   Human sorting algorithm after three numbers are moved to the sorted list.

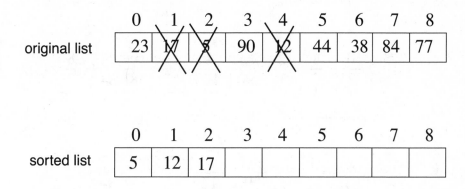

We can write a real computer program based on this sorting algorithm, but the resulting program will not be a good one. There are two problems. First, we need an extra array to keep the sorted list. This may not sound like much, but when you consider an array of, say, 10,000 elements, using a second array is very wasteful. Second, crossing out numbers is effective for humans only. We humans can see the cross marks and will not consider the numbers once they are crossed out, but in computer programs, we still have to write code to check every element whether it is crossed out or not.[1] So crossing out the numbers does not reduce the number of comparisons in the program.

Although we do not want to implement this human sorting algorithm as is, we can derive an algorithm based on the idea of finding the smallest number in a given list and moving it to the correct position in the list. This sorting algorithm is called *selection sort*.

selection sort

sorting passes

The selection sort is comprised of *passes*. Figure 15.5 shows the effect of the first pass on a sample array of N (= 9) elements. First we locate the smallest element in the array and set the index min to point to this element. Then we exchange number[start] and number[min]. After the first pass, the smallest element is moved to the correct position. We increment the value of start by one and then execute the second pass. We start the first pass with start = 0 and end the

---

1. We can "cross out" an element by replacing it with a negative number, say, –1, if the numbers are all positive. If not, then we have to use other means to "cross out" an element.

last pass with start = N-2. Figure 15.6 shows the sequence of eight passes made to the sample array.

FIGURE 15.5   Effect of executing the first pass in the selection sort.

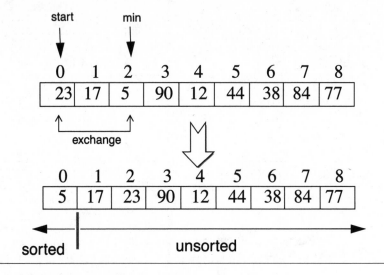

Here's the selectionSort method:

```
public void selectionSort( int[] number )
{
    int startIndex, minIndex, length, temp;
    length = number.length;

    for (startIndex = 0; startIndex <= length-2; startIndex++){
        //each iteration of the for loop is one pass

        minIndex = startIndex;

        //find the smallest in this pass at position minIndex
        for (i = startIndex+1; i <= length-1; i++) {
            if (element[i] < element[minIndex]) minIndex = i;
        }
        //exchange number[startIndex] and number[minIndex]
        temp             = number[startIndex];
        number[startIndex] = number[minIndex];
        number[minIndex]  = temp;
    }
}
```

FIGURE 15.6   Eight passes to sort the sample array of nine elements.

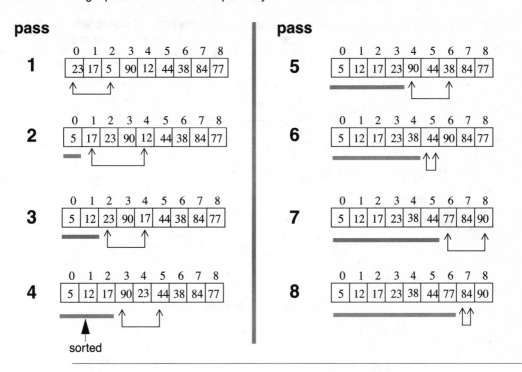

Let's analyze the selection sort algorithm. In analyzing different sorting algorithms, we normally count two things: the number of comparisons and the number of data movements (exchanges). We will show you how to count the number of comparisons here. Counting the number of data movements is left as an exercise. Keep in mind that the analysis we provide in this chapter is an informal one. A detailed analysis is beyond the scope of this book, so we will give only a taste of formal analysis.

The selection sort has one comparison (the if statement inside the nested for loop), so we can easily count the total number of comparisons by counting the number of times the inner loop is executed. For each execution of the outer loop, the inner loop is executed length – start times. The variable start ranges from 0 to length-2. So the total number of comparisons is computed by finding the sum of the right column in the following table:

Start	Number of Comparisons (Length – Start)
0	length
1	length – 1
2	length – 2
. . .	. . .
length – 2	2

The variable length is the size of the array. Replacing length with N, the size of the array, the sum of the right column is

$$N + (N-1) + (N-2) + \ldots + 2$$

$$= \sum_{t=2}^{N}(i) = \sum_{i=1}^{N} i - 1 = \frac{N(N+1)}{2} - 1$$

$$= \frac{N^2 + N - 2}{2} \cong N^2$$

The total number of comparisons is approximately the square of the size of an array. This is a quadratic function, so the number of comparisons grows very fast as the size of an array gets larger. Is there a better sorting algorithm? The answer is yes.

Bubble Sort

The effect of one pass of the selection sort is the movement of the smallest element to its correct position. Since an array gets sorted only by moving the elements to their correct position, the whole sorting routine will complete sooner if we increase the number of data movements. In the selection sort, we make one exchange per pass. If we could move more elements toward their correct positions in one pass, we would be able to complete the sorting sooner than with the selection sort. The bubble sort is one such algorithm that increases the number of data movements for the same number of comparisons as the selection sort makes.

The key point of the bubble sort is to make pairwise comparisons and exchange the positions of the pair if they are out of order. Figure 15.7 shows the effect of pairwise comparisons in the first past of the bubble sort. After the first pass, the largest element 90 has moved to its correct position in the array. This is the guaranteed effect of one pass. In addition, we notice that many other elements also have moved toward their correction position, like bubbles move toward the water's surface.

In the worst case, the bubble sort will make $N-1$ passes, so the worst case performance is the same as for the selection sort. However, in the average case, we can expect a better performance from the bubble sort. The bubble sort exhibits the following two properties:

· After one pass through the array, the largest element will be at the end of the array.

· During one pass, if no pair of consecutive entries is out of order, then the array is sorted.

Using these properties, we can express the bubbleSort method in pseudocode as

```
bottom = number.length - 2;
exchanged = true;

while ( exchanged ) { //continue if the exchange is made

    //do one pass of sorting
    exchanged = false; //reset the variable

    for (i = 0; i < bottom; i++) {
        if ( number[i] > number[i+1] ) { //pairwise comparison
            //the pair is out of order
            exchange them;

            exchanged = true; //remember that an exchange
                              //is made
        }
    }

    //one pass is done, decrement the bottom index by one
    bottom--;
}
```

This **while** loop performs at most N–1 passes for an array with N elements. The loop will terminate when there are no exchanges in one pass.

One pass of bubble sort.

Translating the pseudocode into an actual method, we have

FIGURE 15.7   Effect of executing the first pass in the bubble sort.

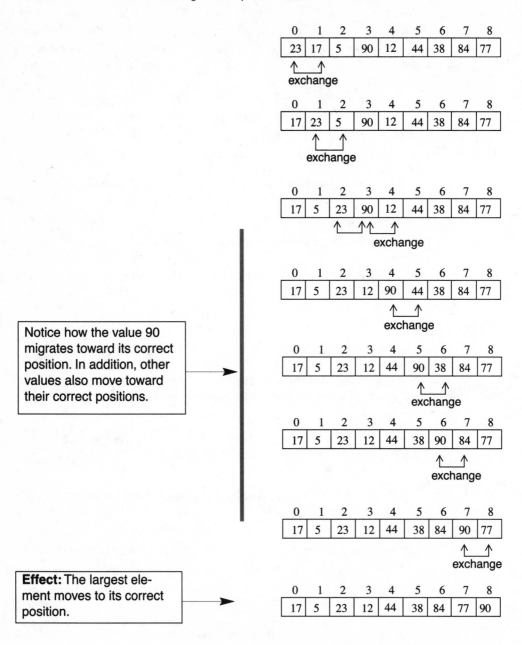

Notice how the value 90 migrates toward its correct position. In addition, other values also move toward their correct positions.

Effect: The largest element moves to its correct position.

```
public void bubbleSort( int[] number )
{
    int        temp, bottom, i;
    boolean    exchanged = true;

    bottom = number.length - 2;

    while ( exchanged )  {

        exchanged = false;

        for (i = 0; i < bottom; i++) {
            if (number[i] > number[i+1]) {

                temp        = number[i];       //exchange
                number[i]   = number[i+1];
                number[i+1] = temp;

                exchanged   = true; //exchange is made
            }
        }

        bottom--;
    }
}
```

On the average, we expect the bubble sort to finish sorting sooner than the selection sort, because there will be more data movements for the same number of comparisons and there is a test to exit the method when the array gets sorted. The worst case of the bubble sort happens when the original array is in descending order. Notice that if the original array is already sorted, the bubble sort will perform only one pass whereas the selection sort will perform $N - 1$ passes.

Quick Check

1. Show the result of the second pass of bubble sort applied to the array at the bottom of Figure 15.7.

2. For an array with N elements, what is the least number of comparisons the bubble sort will execute?

15.3 Recursion

A *recursive method* is a method that contains a statement (or statements) that makes a call to itself. In Chapter 7, we implemented three mathematical functions using recursion. In this chapter, we will present recursive algorithms for nonnumerical operations. But before we introduce new examples, let's review one of the recursive algorithms we presented in Chapter 7. The *factorial* of *N* is the product of the first *N* positive integers, denoted mathematically as

```
N! = N * (N-1) * (N-2) * ... * 2 * 1
```

We define the factorial of N recursively as

$$factorial(N) = \begin{cases} 1 & \text{if N = 1} \\ N * factorial(N-1) & \text{otherwise} \end{cases}$$

and implement a recursive factorial method as

```
public int factorial(int N)
{
    if (N == 1) {          ◀—— Test to stop or continue.

        return 1;          ◀—— End case: recursion stops.
    }
    else {                      Recursive case: recursion
                                continues with a recursive
                                call.
        return N * factorial(N-1);
    }
}
```

Three necessary components in any recursive methods are

1. A test to stop or continue the recursion.

2. An end case that terminates the recursion.

3. A recursive call(s) that continues recursion.

Directory Listing

Let's try some recursive algorithms for nonnumerical applications. A first non-numerical recursive algorithm will list the filename of all files in a given directory (or folder) of a hard disk and its subdirectories. We will use a File object from the java.io package to implement the method. Assuming a Windows 9x platform, we create a File object by passing the name of a file or a directory as in

```
File file = new File("D:\\Java\\Projects");
```

Notice that we pass the full pathname. If a File object represents a directory, then the boolean method isDirectory returns true. To get an array of names of files and subdirectories in a directory, we use the list method

```
String[] fileList = file.list();
```

Let's call the method directoryListing. The argument to the method will be a File object that represents a directory. The basic idea can be expressed as follows:

```
public void directoryListing( File dir )
{
    //assumption: dir represents a directory

    fileList = an array of names of files and
               subdirectories in the directory dir;

    for (each element in fileList) {

        if (an element is a file) {
            output the element's filename;   //end case: its
                                             //a file.
        }
        else { //recursive case: it's a directory
            call directoryListing with element as an argument;
        }
    }
}
```

The complete method is as follows:

```
public void directoryListing( File dir )
{
    //assumption: dir represents a directory

    String[] fileList = dir.list();  //get the contents
    String   dirPath = dir.getAbsolutePath();

    for (int i = 0; i < fileList.length; i++) {

        File file = new File( dirPath + "\\" + fileList[i] );

        if ( file.isFile() ) {     //its a file

            System.out.println( file.getName() );
        }
        else {

            directoryListing( file ); //its a directory
        }                                  //so recurse
    }
}
```

| Test |
| End case |
| Recursive case |

Notice the argument we pass to create a new File object inside the for loop is

```
File file = new File( dirPath + "\\" + fileList[i] );
```

where dirPath is set as

```
String dirPath    = dir.getAbsolutePath();
```

The getAbsolutePath method returns the full pathname for the directory and we need to prepend it to the name (fileList[i]) of a file or a subdirectory in this directory in order to make the testing

```
if ( file.isFile() ) ...
```

work correctly.

To give you more practice in reading recursive methods, we will remove the assumption that the argument File represents a directory and rewrite the method. If the argument File object to directoryListing can be either a file or a directory, then we need to check this first. If the argument object is a file, then we list its filename and stop the recursion. If the argument object is a directory, then we get the list of contents in the directory and make recursive calls. Here's the second version:

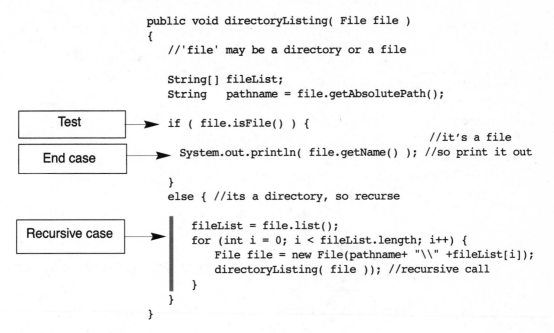

```java
public void directoryListing( File file )
{
    //'file' may be a directory or a file

    String[] fileList;
    String   pathname = file.getAbsolutePath();

    if ( file.isFile() ) {
                                              //it's a file
        System.out.println( file.getName() ); //so print it out

    }
    else { //its a directory, so recurse

        fileList = file.list();
        for (int i = 0; i < fileList.length; i++) {
            File file = new File(pathname+ "\\" +fileList[i]);
            directoryListing( file )); //recursive call
        }
    }
}
```

Labels: Test → `if ( file.isFile() ) {`; End case → `System.out.println( file.getName() );`; Recursive case → the for loop block.

Anagram

Our second example of a nonnumerical recursive method is deriving all anagrams of a given word. An *anagram* is a word or phrase formed by reordering the letters of another word or phrase. If a word is CAT, for example, then its anagrams are:

anagram

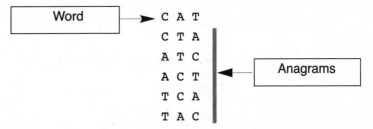

```
Word →   C A T
         C T A
         A T C
         A C T
         T C A
         T A C
```

← Anagrams

Figure 15.8 illustrates the basic idea of using recursion to list all anagrams of a word.

FIGURE 15.8   How to generate all anagrams of a word using recursion.

Find all anagrams of a word

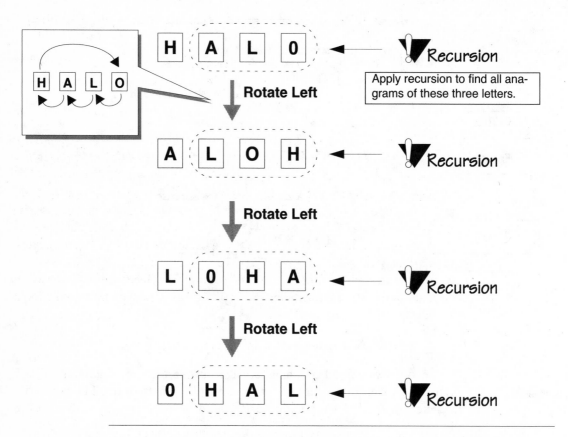

Expressing the basic idea in pseudocode, we have something like this:

```
public void anagram( String word )
{
    int numOfChars = word.length();

    if (numOfChars == 1) {
        //End case: there's only one character left,
```

```
        //              so we can't recurse anymore
    }
    else {
        for (int i = 1; i <= numOfChars; i++ ) {

            char firstLetter = word.charAt(0);

            suffix = word.substring(1, numOfChars);

            anagram( suffix );      //recurse with the remaining
                                    //letters in the word
            //rotate left
            word = suffix + firstLetter;
        }
    }
}
```

> This **for** loop is illustrated in Figure 15.8.

To derive the real method that executes correctly, we must finalize a number of things. First, what will we do when the recursion stops? Hitting upon the end case means that we have found one anagram, so we will print it out. Now, this is the tricky part. When we call the method recursively, we are passing a word that has the first letter chopped off. This means the words being passed to successive recursive calls are getting shorter and shorter. But we need to access all letters in a word to print it out. We can resolve this problem by passing two parameters: the prefix and the suffix of a word. In each successive call, the prefix becomes one letter more and the suffix becomes one letter less. When the suffix becomes one letter only, then the recursion stops. Using this idea, the method now looks like this:

```
public void anagram( String prefix, String suffix )
{
    int numOfChars = suffix.length();

    if (numOfChars == 1) {
        //End case: print out one anagram
        outputBox.printLine( prefix + suffix );
    }
    else {
        ...
    }
}
```

and this method is initially set with an empty prefix and the word being the suffix, as in

```
anagram( "", "HALO" );
```

Now, using the two parameters prefix and suffix, the for loop is written as

```
for (int i = 1; i <=numOfChars; i++ ) {

    newSuffix = suffix.substring(1, numOfChars);
    newPrefix = prefix + suffix.charAt(0);

    anagram( newPrefix, newSuffix ); //recursive case

    //rotate left to create a rearranged suffix
    suffix = newSuffix + suffix.charAt(0);
}
```

Putting everything together, we have the final anagram method:

```
public void anagram( String prefix, String suffix )
{
    String newPrefix, newSuffix;
    int numOfChars = suffix.length();

    if (numOfChars == 1) {
        //End case: print out one anagram
        outputBox.printLine( prefix + suffix );
    }
    else {
        for (int i = 1; i <= numOfChars; i++ ) {
            newSuffix = suffix.substring(1, numOfChars);
            newPrefix = prefix + suffix.charAt(0);

            anagram( newPrefix, newSuffix ); //recursive call

            //rotate left to create a rearranged suffix
            suffix = newSuffix + suffix.charAt(0);
        }
    }
}
```

| Test |
| End case |
| Recursive case |

Because the ending condition for recursion is tricky, let's study carefully the test to stop the recursion. We set the test to

```
if (numOfChars == 1 ) ...
```

Is there any assumption we must make to the parameters to make this method work correctly? We mentioned earlier that the initial call to the recursive method is something like

```
anagram( "", "HALO" );
```

What would happen if we make the call initially like

```
String str = inputBox.getString();
anagram( "", str );
```

and the user enters an empty string? This is left as an exercise.

Tower of Hanoi

The objective of a puzzle called *Tower of Hanoi* is deceptively simple, but finding a solution is another matter. The goal of the puzzle is to move *N* disks from Peg 1 to Peg 3 by moving one disk at a time and never placing a larger disk on top of a smaller disk. See Figure 15.9.

FIGURE 15.9   Tower of Hanoi with N = 4 disks.

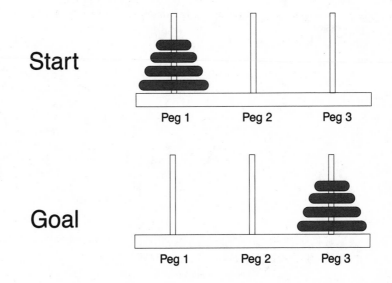

The Tower of Hanoi puzzle can be solved very nicely using recursion. The Aha! moment to this puzzle is when you realize that you can solve the puzzle if somehow you can move the top *N*–1 disks to Peg 2. After the top *N*–1 disks are moved to Peg 2 temporarily, you move the largest disk from Peg 1 to Peg 3, and finally move the *N*–1 disks from Peg 2 to Peg 3. Figure 15.10 illustrates these three steps. The first and the third steps are of course the same puzzle with one fewer disk and the destination peg changed. So you apply the same logic recursively to the first and third steps. When the number of disks becomes one, then the recursion stops. Applying this recursive thinking, we can write the method as

FIGURE 15.10   Recursive solution to the Tower of Hanoi puzzle.

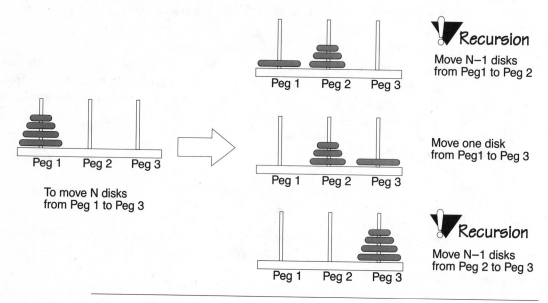

```
public void towerOfHanoi( int N,        //number of disks
                          int from,     //origin peg
                          int to,       //destination peg
                          int spare )   //"middle" peg
        {
        if ( N == 1 )
            moveOne( from, to );
        else {
            towerOfHanoi( N-1, from, spare, to );

            moveOne( from, to );
```

```
            towerOfHanoi( N-1, spare, to, from );
        }
    }
```

The moveOne disk is the method that actually moves the disk. Here we will define the method to print out the move using an outputBox:

```
private void moveOne( int from, int to )
{
    outputBox.printLine( from + " ---> " + to );
}
```

When we run this method with $N = 4$, we get the following output:

```
1 ---> 2
1 ---> 3
2 ---> 3
1 ---> 2
3 ---> 1
3 ---> 2
1 ---> 2
1 ---> 3
2 ---> 3
2 ---> 1
3 ---> 1
2 ---> 3
1 ---> 2
1 ---> 3
2 ---> 3
```

The output is very difficult to read. We can improve the output considerably by padding a varying number of blank spaces to show the level of recursion. We can change the output to

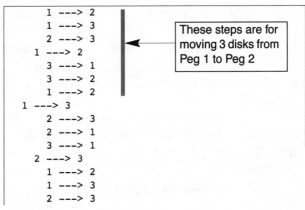

These steps are for moving 3 disks from Peg 1 to Peg 2

```
        1 ---> 2
        1 ---> 3
        2 ---> 3
      1 ---> 2
        3 ---> 1
        3 ---> 2
        1 ---> 2
    1 ---> 3
        2 ---> 3
        2 ---> 1
        3 ---> 1
      2 ---> 3
        1 ---> 2
        1 ---> 3
        2 ---> 3
```

by rewriting the methods as

```
public void towerOfHanoi( int N,        //number of disks
                          int from,     //origin peg
                          int to,       //destination peg
                          int spare,    //"middle" peg
                          int indent )  //# of leading spaces
{
    if ( N == 1 )
        moveOne( from, to, indent );

    else {
        towerOfHanoi( N-1, from, spare, to, indent+2 );

        moveOne( from, to, indent+2 );

        towerOfHanoi( N-1, spare, to, from, indent+2 );
    }
}

private void moveOne( int from, int to, int indent )
{
    outputBox.printLine( Format.rightAlign(indent," ") +
                         from + " ---> " + to );
}
```

Quicksort

We will present a third sorting algorithm that uses recursion in this section. This sorting algorithm is called *quicksort*, and we will compare the performance of quicksort against the previous two sorting algorithms at the end of this section to verify that quicksort deserves its name.

Figure 15.11 illustrates the core thinking of quicksort. To sort an array from index low to high, we first select a pivot element p. We can select any element in the array as a pivot, but for simplicity, we choose number[low] as the pivot. Using p as the pivot, we scan through the array and move all elements smaller than p to the lower half (left half in the figure) and all elements larger than p to the upper half. Then we sort the lower and upper halves recursively using quicksort. The variable mid points to the position where the pivot is placed. So the lower half of the array is from index low to mid-1 and the upper half of the array is from index mid+1 to high. The recursion stops when the condition low >= high becomes true.

Here's the quicksort algorithm:

FIGURE 15.11   The core idea of the quicksort algorithm.

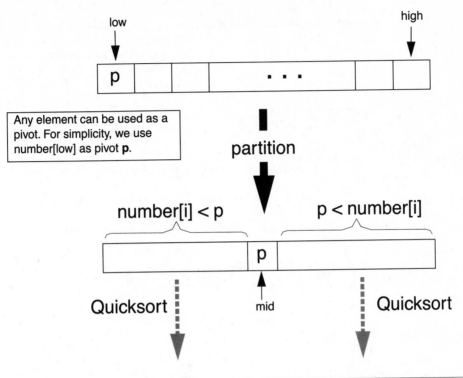

```
public void quickSort( int[] number, int low, int high )
{
    if ( low < high ) {

        int mid = partition( number, low, high );

        quickSort( number,   low, mid-1 );
        quickSort( number, mid+1, high  );
    }
}
```

The partition method splits the array elements number[low] to number[high] into two halves as shown in Figure 15.11. We use number[low] as the pivot element. The method returns the position where the pivot element is placed.

Figure 15.12 shows the result of partitioning the array using the element 23 as a pivot.

FIGURE 15.12   Result of partitioning using 23 as a pivot.

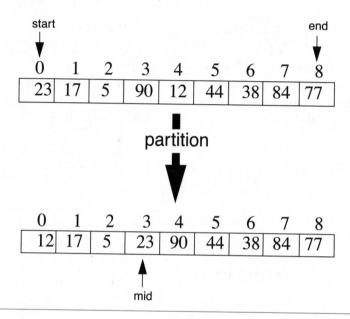

We first set pivot to number[low]. Then we start looking for a number smaller than pivot from position high, high-1, and so forth. Let's say the number is found at position J. Since this number is smaller than pivot, we move it to position low. Now we start looking for a number larger than pivot from low+1, low+2, and so forth. Let's say the number is found at position I. We move it to position J. We then repeat the process, this time looking for a number smaller than pivot from J-1, J-2, and so forth. Figure 15.13 shows the details the partitioning process.

Here's the partition method:

```
private void partition( int[] number, int start, int end )
{
    //set the pivot
    int pivot = number[start];

    do {
        //look for a number smaller than pivot from the end
```

FIGURE 15.13   Details of one partitioning.

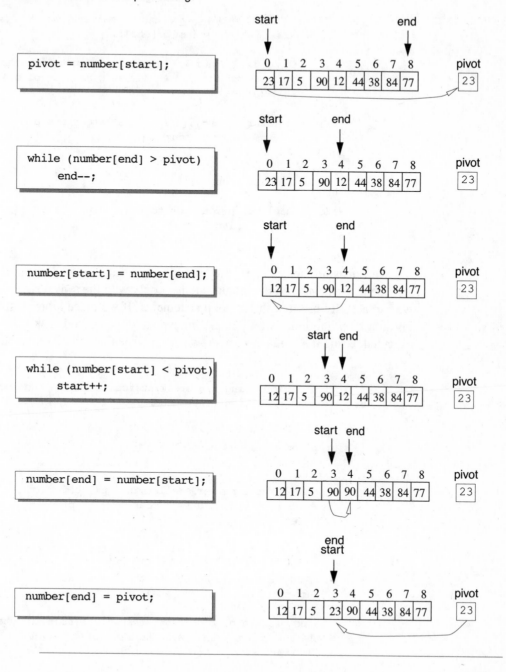

```
            while ( start < end && number[end] >= pivot)
                end--;

            if ( start < end ) { //found a smaller number
                number[start] = number[end];

                //now find a number larger than pivot from the start
                while ( start < end && number[start] <= pivot)
                    start++;

                if (start < end) { //found a larger number
                    number[end] = number[start];
            }

        } while ( start < end );

        //done, move the pivot back to the array
        number[start] = pivot;
    }
```

We can avoid the nested if statement in the partition method using the break statement. We have used the break statement only with the switch statement, but we can actually use it with any loop statements. If we place a break statement inside a loop, the loop is terminated immediately when the break statement is executed. Using the break statement, we can rewrite the partition method as

```
//Second version using the break statement inside the loop
private void partition( int[] number, int start, int end )
{
    //set the pivot
    int pivot = number[start];

    do {
        //look for a number smaller than pivot from the end
        while ( start < end && number[end] >= pivot)
            end--;

        if ( start = end ) break; //stop the repetition

        //move a smaller number to the lower half
        number[start] = number[end];

        //now find a number larger than pivot from the start
        while ( start < end && number[start] <= pivot)
            start++;
```

```
            if (start = end) break; //stop the repetition

            //move a larger number to the upper half
            number[end] = number[start];
        }

    } while ( start < end );

    //done, move the pivot back to the array
    number[start] = pivot;
}
```

How good is quicksort? Does the algorithm execute a fewer number of comparisons than the selection or bubble sort? The answer is no in the worst case. Quicksort executes roughly the same number of comparisons as the selection sort and bubble sort in the worst case. When the original list is either already sorted or in descending order, then after a partition process, either the lower half or the upper half has $N-1$ elements. The effect is the same as the previous two sorting algorithms, that is, either the smallest or the largest number moves to its correct position. The worst situation can be improved somewhat if we select the median of three numbers, say, number[low], number[high], and number[(low+high)/2], as the pivot element. Even with this improvement, the number of comparisons in the worst case is still approximately the square of the size of the array.

Is the name quicksort a kind of false advertisement? Not really. On the average, we can expect a partition process to split the array into two subarrays of roughly equal size. Figure 15.14 shows how the original array is partitioned into smaller subarrays. When the size of all subarrays becomes 1, then the array becomes sorted. At level i, there are 2^i subarrays of size $N/2^i$. So there will be $N/2^i$ partition processes at level i. The total number of comparisons of all those partition processes at level i is therefore $2^i * N/2^i = N$. Since there are K levels, the total number of comparisons for sorting the whole array is

$$K \cdot N$$

but

$$N = 2^K$$

$$\log_2 N = K$$

so

$$K \cdot N = N\log_2 N$$

The total number of comparisons is proportional to $N\log_2 N$ which is a great improvement over N^2. A more rigorous mathematical analysis will show that the quicksort on the average requires approximately $2N\log_2 N$ comparisons.

FIGURE 15.14 A hierarchy of partitioning an array into smaller and smaller arrays in the quicksort.

Level No.		Number of subarrays at Level i	Size of each subarray at Level i
0		$1 = 2^0$	$N = N / 2^0$
1		$2 = 2^1$	$N/2 = N / 2^1$
2		$4 = 2^4$	$N/4 = N / 2^2$
K	$\cdots$	N	$1 = N / 2^K$

Quick Check

1. Partition the following arrays using the partition method:

   a.

0	1	2	3	4	5	6	7	8
18	19	5	77	12	14	13	84	45

   b.

0	1	2	3	4	5	6	7	8
98	19	15	86	12	44	13	24	45

2. Determine the output of the following calls without actually running the method:

   ```
   a. anagram( "", "DOG" );
   b. anagram( "", "CAFE");
   ```

15.4 When Not to Use Recursion

Recursion is a powerful tool to express complex algorithms succinctly. For example, writing a nonrecursive algorithm for the Tower of Hanoi is unexpectedly difficult. Likewise, a recursive quicksort algorithm is easier to understand than its nonrecursive counterpart. For both problems, we prefer recursive algorithms because recursion is the most natural way to express their solution. However, just being natural is not the criterion for selecting a recursive solution over a nonrecursive one.

Consider a solution for computing the Nth Fibonacci number. A Fibonacci number is defined recursively as

$$\text{fibonacci(N)} = \begin{cases} 1 & \text{if N = 0} \\ & \text{or N = 1} \\ \\ \text{fibonacci(N-1)} \\ \quad + \text{factorial(N-2)} & \text{otherwise} \end{cases}$$

Because the function is defined recursively, it is natural to implement the function using a recursive method as the following:

```
public int fibonacci( int N )
{
    if (N == 0 || N == 1) {
        return 1;               //end case
    }
    else { //recursive case
        return fibonacci(N-1) + fibonacci(N-2);
    }
}
```

This recursive method is succinct, easy to understand, and elegant. But is this the way to implement it? The answer is no, because the recursive method is grossly inefficient and a nonrecursive version is just as easy to understand. The method is inefficient because the same value is computed over and over. Figure 15.15 shows the recursive calls for computing the fifth Fibonacci num-

ber. Notice that the same value, for example, fibonacci(2) is computed repeatedly.

FIGURE 15.15   Recursive calls to compute **fibonacci(5)**.

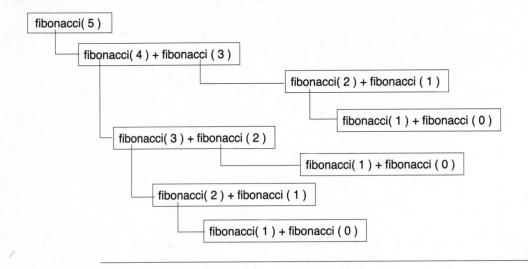

The *N*th Fibonacci number can be computed using a nonrecursive method
as

```
public int fibonacci( int N )
{
    int fibN, fibN1, fibN2, cnt;

    if (N == 0 or N == 1 ) {
        return 1;
    }
    else {

        fibN1 = fibN2 = 1;
        cnt = 2;

        while ( cnt <= N ) {
            fibN = fibN1 + fibN2; //get the next Fib no.

            fibN1 = fibN2;
            fibN2 = fibN;
```

```
            cnt ++;
        }
        return fibN;
    }
}
```

The nonrecursive method is not as succinct as the recursive version, but at the same time, it is not that much difficult to understand either. The nonrecursive version is much more efficient, and it is the one that should be used.

There is no clear cut rule to determine whether a routine should be implemented recursively or nonrecursively. In general, we should always search for a nonrecursive solution first. We should use recursion only when a recursive solution is more natural and easier to understand and the resulting method is not too inefficient. We repeat the guideline for using recursive methods we mentioned in Section 7.10.

Use recursion if

1. A recursive solution is natural and easy to understand.
2. A recursive solution does not result in excessive duplicate computation.
3. The equivalent iterative solution is too complex.

15.5 Exercises

1. Write a recursive method to find the smallest element in an array. Note: This is strictly for exercise. You should not write the real method recursively.

2. Write a recursive method to compute the average of the elements in an array. Note: This is strictly for exercise. You should not write the real method recursively.

3. Write a recursive method to determine whether a given string is a palindrome or not. A string is a palindrome if it reads the same forward and backward. Ignore the case of the letters and punctuation marks.

4. Write a recursive binary search method. Should this method be written recursively or nonrecursively in practice?

5. Write a recursive method to compute the greatest common divisor of two integer values. The greatest common divisor (GCD) of two integers is derived by using the following rules:

$$
GCD(i, j) = \begin{cases} i & \text{if } j = 0 \\ GCD(j, i \bmod j) & \text{if } j \mathrel{!}= 0 \end{cases}
$$

6. Write a nonrecursive version of GCD in exercise 5 and compare the two solutions. Which version is the one you should use in practice?

7. In this chapter we analyze sorting algorithms by counting the number of comparisons. Another possible analysis is counting the number of data exchanges. How many data exchanges do the selection and bubble sort make?

8. Consider the following property about the bubble sort:

   • *If the last exchange made in some pass occurs at the Jth and (J+1)st positions, then all elements from the (J+1)st to the Nth are in their correct position.*

   Rewrite the bubble sort algorithm using this property.

9. The partition method of the quicksort selects the first element as its pivot. Improve the method by using the median of the values in the first, the middle, and the last element of an array. If an array number to partition has 8 elements indexed from 0 to 7, then the first element is number[0], the middle element is number[4], and the last element is number[7]. If these elements are 55, 34, and 89, for example, then the median is 55.

10. Another recursive sorting algorithm is called *merge sort*. The merge sort divides the array into two halves, sorts the two halves recursively using

mergesort, and finally merges the two sorted halves into a sorted list. In diagram, the process of merge sort looks like this:

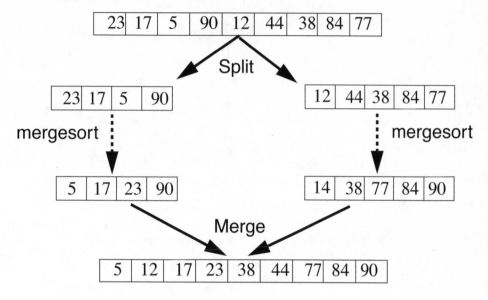

Write the mergesort method.

11. What would happen if the anagram method is called initially by passing an empty string as the second parameter:

```
anagram( "", "" );
```

Will the method work? Why or why not? If not, correct the problem. If yes, then would it be logical to leave it as is or should the method be corrected to make it more logical?

The javabook Package

We document the javabook classes in this appendix. You can get information on the standard Java packages from a number of sources. If you use commercial Java compilers from Borland, Microsoft, Symantec, and others, you can access desired information from their help menu. You can also access the online documentation from the Web site at http://java.sun.com/products/jdk/1.1/docs/api/packages.html. Reference books on the standard Java packages such as P. Chan and R. Lee, *The Java Class Libraries, Vol. 1* and *2*, 2nd ed. [Reading, MA: Addison-Wesley, 1998] and D. Flanagan, *Java in a Nutshell*, 2nd ed. [Sebastapol, CA: O'Reilly & Associates, Inc., 1997] are good sources of information. If you are interested in the official language specification of Java, you should get a copy of J. Gosling, B. Joy, and G. Steele, *The Java Language Specification,* [Reading, MA: Addison-Wesley, 1996].

Documentation provided in this appendix is intended for the users of the package. As such, only the public methods and constants are included (in case of JavaBookDialog, the protected method is included also). We direct those who are interested in learning how the classes are implemented to our Web site at http://www.mhhe.com/engcs. The Web site includes the most up-to-date online documentation on the javabook package that you can download. We plan to update the javabook package periodically, so please visit our Web site regularly. Also, if you notice any discrepancy between the information provided in this appendix and the software, please visit our Web site to get the most up-to-date information.

PACKAGE:	javabook
Class	**Description**
Convert	The class provides methods for converting a value of one data type to another data type.
DrawingBoard	A frame window that is capable of drawing lines, circles, and rectangles.
Format	The class provides methods for formatting integers, real numbers, and strings.
InputBox	A dialog for getting an input value from the user. An InputBox object can be used to accept integers, real numbers, and strings.
JavaBookDialog	An abstract superclass that encapsulates behavior common to all dialogs in this package: InputBox, ListBox, MessageBox, MultiInputBox, OutputBox, and ResponseBox.
ListBox	A dialog for displaying a list of choices and allowing the user to select a choice in the list.
MainWindow	A frame window that serves as the main window of an application. A MainWindow object is almost as big as the screen and is displayed at the center of the screen.
MessageBox	A dialog for displaying a single line of text. A MessageBox object is intended for displaying a short warning or error message.
MultiInputBox	A dialog for getting multiple input values from the user. A MultiInputBox object can be used to accept *N* string values.
OutputBox	A dialog for displaying multiple lines of text.
ResponseBox	A dialog for getting a yes or no answer from the user.
SketchPad	A frame window that allows the user to draw freeform lines using a mouse.

For each class description, we include

- The purpose of the class.
- The page and section number where the class is introduced.
- The ancestors of the class. If the superclass is also in the javabook package, then only this superclass is shown.
- The public constants of the class.
- The public methods of the class.

Class:	javabook.Convert

Purpose: This class provides methods for converting a data value of one data type to another data type. This class is noninstantiable; all methods are class methods.

Introduced in: Section 9.4 page 454.

Hierarchy:

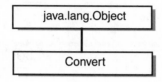

Public constants: None

Public methods:
```
toBoolean
toChar
toDouble
toFloat
toInt
toLong
toString
```

`public static boolean    toBoolean  ( String str )`

Converts the argument str to a boolean.

`public static char       toChar     ( String str )`

Converts the argument str to a char.

`public static double     toDouble   ( String str )`

Converts the argument str to a double.

`public static float      toFloat    ( String str )`

Converts the argument str to a float.

`public static int        toInt      ( String str )`

Converts the argument str to an int.

```
public static long        toLong      ( String str        )
```

Converts the argument str to a long.

```
public static String      toString    ( boolean bool   )
public static String      toString    ( char    ch     )
public static String      toString    ( double  number )
public static String      toString    ( float   number )
public static String      toString    ( int     number )
public static String      toString    ( long    number )
```

Converts the argument to a String.

Class: javabook.DrawingBoard

Purpose: This class is used in the sample program from Chapter 6. A DrawingBoard
                        object supports methods for drawing circles, lines, and rectangles.

Introduced in: Section 6.6 page 267.

Hierarchy:

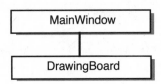

Public constants: None

Public methods: DrawingBoard
                        drawCircle
                        drawLine
                        drawRectangle
                        setColor
                        show

```
public DrawingBoard ( )
public DrawingBoard ( String  title )
```

A DrawingBoard object with the default title DRAWING BOARD is created. The window is not resizable and the background color is set to white.

| `public void` | `drawCircle` | `( int x, int y, int r )` |

Draws a circle with radius r and whose center point is (x, y).

| `public void` | `drawLine` | `( int x1, int y1, int x2, int y2 )` |

Draws a line from point (x1, y1) to (x2, y2).

| `public void` | `drawRectangle ( int x, int y, int w, int h )` |

| `public void` | `drawRectangle ( Rectangle rect )` |

The first version draws a rectangle with width w and height h and its top-left corner at position (x, y). The second version draws a rectangle with the dimension set by the Rectangle object rect.

| `public void` | `show ( )` |

Overrides the superclass's show to initialize the data member Graphics object so the drawing works correctly.

See also:

java.awt.Rectangle
Explanation of the coordinate system for the drawing is given in Section 2.6 and Section 12.1.

| **Class:** | javabook.Format |

Purpose:

This class provides methods for formatting a value in a field of a given length. Three possible alignments are left, center, and right. The alignment is done by converting a value to a String with a given length and placing the value at the beginning, middle, or end of the String. This class is noninstantiable; all methods are class methods.

Introduced in: Section 7.7 page 325.

Hierarchy:

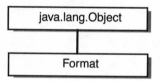

Public constants: None

Public methods: centerAlign
leftAlign
rightAlign

```
public String centerAlign ( int width, int decimalPlaces, double num )
public String centerAlign ( int width, long     num    )
public String centerAlign ( int width, String str       )
```

Returns a String that has width characters in it. The value num or str is positioned at the center of the resulting String. For the first version, the resulting String will have a decimal point and the designated number of decimal places. If the given value cannot fit into the width characters, the value converted to a String without any alignment is returned.

```
public String leftAlign ( int width, int decimalPlaces, double num )
public String leftAlign ( int width, long     num    )
public String leftAlign ( int width, String   str    )
```

The same functionality as centerAlign, but with the left alignment.

```
public String rightAlign ( int width, int decimalPlaces, double num )
public String rightAlign ( int width, long     num    )
public String rightAlign ( int width, String   str    )
```

The same functionality as centerAlign, but with the right alignment.

Class: javabook.InputBox

Purpose: A dialog that allows the user to enter a value. An InputBox object can accept both numerical and textual values. The user cannot close the dialog until he/she enters a valid value of the designated data type.

Introduced in: Section 3.5 page 103.

Hierarchy:

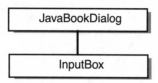

Public constants: None

Public methods:
```
InputBox
getInteger
getFloat
getString
```

```
public InputBox ( Frame owner )
public InputBox ( Frame owner, String title)
```
Creates an **InputBox** object with **owner** as its controlling **Frame** object. In the second version, the title of a dialog is set to the **String** passed as the second argument.

```
public int     getInteger (                    )
public int     getInteger ( String prompt   )
```
The method returns the integer value entered by the user. This method does not complete until the user enters a valid integer. For the first version, the prompt is set to a default word **Enter an integer:**. In the second version, the prompt is set to the passed **String** argument.

```
public float   getFloat   (                    )
public float   getFloat   ( String prompt   )
```
The same behavior as the **getInteger** methods. The **getFloat** methods return a **float** instead of an **int**.

```
public String getString  (                    )
public String getString  ( String prompt   )
```
The same behavior as the **getInteger** methods. The **getString** methods return a **String** instead of an **int**.

Class:	javabook.JavaBookDialog

Purpose: An abstract class that encapsulates behavior common to the other dialogs in this package. Create a subclass of JavaBookDialog if you want your dialog to include the common behavior of placing the dialog at the center of the screen. A subclass of JavaBookDialog must implement the abstract method adjustSize.

Introduced in: Section 14.13 page 765

Hierarchy:

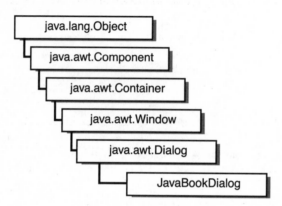

Public constants: None

Public methods: show

---

public void show ( )

Overrides the superclass's show. This method calls the protected adjustSize method before making the dialog visible. If you create a subclass of JavaBookDialog, then you must define the adjustSize method in your subclass.

Protected Methods: adjustSize

---

abstract protected void adjustSize ( )

Define this method in your subclass. You use this method to adjust the size of a dialog based on the components placed on the dialog.

See also: For a sample of defining a subclass of JavaBookDialog, please read the StudentNameDialog class in Section 14.13.

Class: javabook.ListBox

Purpose: A dialog that allows the user to select an entry from a list of selections.

Introduced in: Section 6.4 page 256.

Hierarchy:

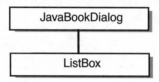

Public constants: CANCEL
NO_SELECTION

Public methods: ListBox
addItem
deleteItem
getSelectedIndex
getSelectedItem
isCanceled

```
public ListBox ( Frame owner )
public ListBox ( Frame owner, String  title )
public ListBox ( Frame owner, boolean modal )
public ListBox ( Frame owner, String  title, boolean modal )
```

Creates a ListBox object with owner as its controlling Frame object. The default title of the dialog is Select One: and the default mode is modal. Pass a String value and/or a boolean value to change the default. You pass true for modal and false for modeless dialogs.

```
public void   deleteItem        ( int  index      )
```

Deletes the entry at position index. The topmost entry is index 0, the next is index 1, and so forth.

```
public void    addItem              ( String entry    )
```

Adds an entry to the list. The newly added entry is placed at the bottom of the list, that is, the newly added entry has the highest index value.

```
public int     getSelectedIndex  (                        )
```

Returns the index of the entry selected by the user. If the user clicks the CANCEL button or closes the dialog, then the public constant CANCEL is returned. If the user clicks the OK button without selecting an entry, then the public constant NO_SELECTION is returned.

```
public String getItemFromIndex  ( int index        )
```

Returns the value (String) of the entry at position index.

```
public boolean isCanceled (                    )
```

Returns true if the dialog was canceled or closed without an entry being selected. Returns false otherwise.

Class: javabook.MainWindow

Purpose: A frame that serves as the main window of an application. By default, the frame size is almost as large as the screen, and it is displayed at the center of the screen.

Introduced in: Section 2.1 page 42.

Hierarchy:

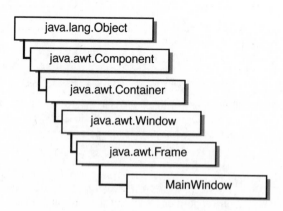

Public constants: None

Public methods: `MainWindow`
                       `show`

```
public MainWindow (                )
public MainWindow ( String title   )
```
    Creates a **MainWindow** object with the text **Sample Java Appliation** as its default title.
    Use the second constructor to change the default title.

```
public void    show    (        )
```
    Displays the **MainWindow** object.

Class:	javabook.MessageBox

Purpose: A dialog that displays a single line of text. This dialog is suitable for display-
                    ing error or warning messages.

Introduced in: Section 2.5 page 65.

Hierarchy:

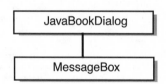

Public constants: None

Public methods: `MessageBox`
                       `show`

```
public MessageBox ( Frame owner )
public MessageBox ( Frame owner, boolean modal )
```
    Creates a **MessageBox** object with **owner** as its controlling **Frame** object. The default
    mode is modal. The second argument determines the modality: pass **true** for modal and
    false for modeless.

```
public void   show   ( long           number )
public void   show   ( double         number )
public void   show   ( String         str    )
public void   show   ( StringBuffer   strBuf )
```

Displays the passed argument. Non-String values are converted to a String value before the display. The dialog appears at the center of the screen.

```
public void   show   ( long           number,   int x, int y )
public void   show   ( double         number,   int x, int y )
public void   show   ( String         str,      int x, int y )
public void   show   ( StringBuffer   strBuf,   int x, int y )
```

Displays the passed argument. Non-String values are converted to a String value before the display. The top left corner of the dialog is set to position (x, y).

Class: javabook.MultiInputBox

Purpose: A dialog that allows the user to enter *N* input String values. TextField objects are used for accepting input values.

Introduced in: Section 9.4 page 452.

Hierarchy:

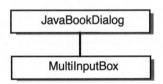

Public constants: None

Public methods:
```
MultiInputBox
getInputs
isCanceled
setLabels
setValue
```

```
public MultiInputBox ( Frame owner, int      size   )
public MultiInputBox ( Frame owner, String[] labels )
```

Creates a MultiInputBox object with owner as its controlling Frame object. The second argument can be either an integer or an array of String objects. The integer value determines N—the number of input values the user can enter. If an array of String values is passed, then the value for N is determined by the length of the array. In addition, the String values will become the labels for the N TextField objects.

```
public String[] getInputs (              )
```

Returns the N input text values entered by the user. An empty String is returned for a TextField that has no entry.

```
public boolean isCanceled (              )
```

Returns true if the dialog was canceled or closed. Returns false otherwise.

```
public void    setLabels ( String[] labels )
```

Sets the labels for N TextField objects.

```
public void    setValue ( int index, String value )
```

The text of the TextField object at position index is set to value. The N TextField objects are indexed by using zero-based indexing, that is, the topmost object has index 0. This method is useful for showing the user a typically expected input value.

See also: java.awt.TextField

Class: javabook.OutputBox

Purpose: A dialog for displaying multiple lines of text. This dialog is intended for displaying program output.

Introduced in: Section 3.6 page 106.

Hierarchy:

```
JavaBookDialog
     |
  OutputBox
```

Public constants: None

Public methods: OutputBox
                      appendToFile
                      print
                      printLine
                      saveToFile
                      setFont
                      skipLine
                      waitUntilClose

```
public OutputBox ( Frame owner )
public OutputBox ( Frame owner, String title )
public OutputBox ( Frame owner, int width, int height )
public OutputBox ( Frame owner, int width, int height, String title )
```

Creates an OutputBox object with owner as its controlling Frame object.

```
public void    appendToFile ( String    filename )
```

Appends the contents of an OutputBox to the file whose name is filename. If no such file exists, then the method creates a new file and saves the contents of an OutputBox.

```
public void    print    ( boolean      bool    )
public void    print    ( char         ch      )
public void    print    ( double       num     )
public void    print    ( long         num     )
public void    print    ( String       str     )
public void    print    ( StringBuffer strBuf  )
```

Prints out the argument.

```
public void    printLine ( boolean      bool    )
public void    printLine ( char         ch      )
public void    printLine ( double       num     )
public void    printLine ( long         num     )
public void    printLine ( String       str     )
public void    printLine ( StringBuffer strBuf  )
```

Prints out the argument and moves the cursor to the next line.

```
public void    saveToFile ( String      filename )
```

Saves the contents of an OutputBox to the file whose name is filename. If the file already exists, then the original contents of the file will be replaced by the contents of an OutputBox.

`public void    setFont    (   Font newFont    )`

Sets the font to **newFont**. The default is size 12, plain Courier font.

`public void    skipLine    ( int numLines        )`

Skip **numLines** lines. The effect is the same as if you press the **ENTER** key **numLines** times.

`public void    waitUntilClose (                    )`

An **OutputBox** dialog is always modeless. There are times, however, you want to close the dialog before continuing the execution of a program, that is, you want it to behave like a modal dialog. When this method is called, the program execution will not continue until the user closes the **OutputBox** object.

See also: java.awt.Font

Class: javabook.ResponseBox

Purpose: A dialog for displaying multiple lines of text. This dialog is intended for displaying program output.

Introduced in: Section 7.4 page 312.

Hierarchy:

```
┌─────────────────────┐
│   JavaBookDialog    │
└─────────────────────┘
          │
┌─────────────────────┐
│    ResponseBox      │
└─────────────────────┘
```

Public constants: YES
NO
CANCEL
BUTTON1 (== YES)
BUTTON2 (== NO)
BUTTON3

Public methods: ResponseBox
prompt
setLabel

```
public ResponseBox ( Frame owner )
public ResponseBox ( Frame owner, int buttonCount )
```

Creates a ResponseBox object with owner as its controlling Frame object. The default ResponseBox object has two buttons labeled Yes and No. These buttons are identified by the class constants YES and NO. You can create a ResponseBox object with N, $1 \leq N \leq 3$, buttons by passing N as the second argument. The buttons are identified from left to right by the class constants BUTTON1, BUTTON2, and BUTTON3.

```
public int     prompt    ( String str)
```

Prompts the user for a response. The argument str is the query you pose to the user. The user responds to the query by clicking one of the buttons.

```
public void    setLabel   ( int id, String label)
```

Set the label of button id to label.

Class: javabook.SketchPad

Purpose: A frame window that allows the user to draw freeform lines using a mouse. You draw lines by dragging the mouse and erase them by clicking the right mouse button (Command-click on the Mac).

Introduced in: Section 1.6 page 33.

Hierarchy:

Public constants: None

Public methods: SketchPad

```
public SketchPad (   )
```

Creates a SketchPad object.

Index

B

J

Object Diagram Summary

Frame

MainWindow

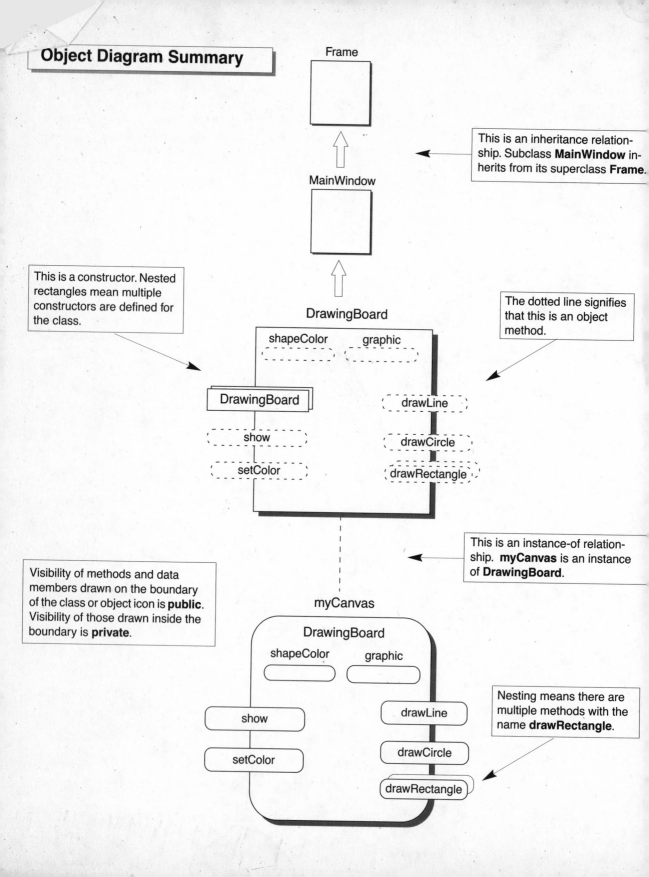

This is an inheritance relationship. Subclass **MainWindow** inherits from its superclass **Frame**.

This is a constructor. Nested rectangles mean multiple constructors are defined for the class.

DrawingBoard

shapeColor   graphic

The dotted line signifies that this is an object method.

DrawingBoard

show   drawLine

setColor   drawCircle

drawRectangle

This is an instance-of relationship. **myCanvas** is an instance of **DrawingBoard**.

Visibility of methods and data members drawn on the boundary of the class or object icon is **public**. Visibility of those drawn inside the boundary is **private**.

myCanvas

DrawingBoard

shapeColor   graphic

show   drawLine

setColor   drawCircle

drawRectangle

Nesting means there are multiple methods with the name **drawRectangle**.